WP

IDEAS
AND INSTITUTIONS
IN EUROPEAN HISTORY
800≈1715

Select Problems in Historical Interpretation

THOMAS C. MENDENHALL
BASIL D. HENNING
A. S. FOORD
Department of History, Yale University

Henry Holt and Company, New York

Printed in the United States of America

PREFACE

"Reading history ready-made," wrote A. F. Pollard, "is to making it out oneself from documents what looking on at a football match is to playing the game oneself, or what reading a detective story is to tracking out a criminal; and to teach the intelligent use of documents is the first of the neglected duties of our schools of history." It was the desire to perform this neglected duty—to make, in Carl Becker's phrase, "every man his own historian"—which led to the publication of this volume.

The editors do not claim to be the first to have experienced this desire. "Selections from the Sources," "Readings in European History" crowd the shelves of most libraries, and organized problems in the sources long ago made possible the systematic study of historical documents by undergraduates. But this book differs in purpose, method, and content both from volumes of supplementary readings and from the earlier attempts to arrange these materials in problem form.

The purpose of these Problems is, first of all, to make the student aware of the complexity of history. Every survey course in European history must, of course, impart a knowledge of events, of what happened in the long European past. And no student can pretend to an understanding of European history without a grasp of its narrative. But in addition a comprehension of the interdependence of the many forces operating in society is essential; if the student learns only the narrative of events his knowledge of history will be painfully superficial. It is believed that the study of these Problems, combined with the use of a textbook and the interpretation derived from lectures, will allow the student to obtain a fuller understanding of the complicated pattern of European civilization. Only a genuine awareness of the sweep and the complexity of this civilization will enable the undergraduate to partake of the philosophical insight, of the serenity which comes with the long view and the deep comprehension, and of the intellectual and moral inspiration that is the ultimate reason for studying history.

In the realm of method, the Problems are designed to demonstrate to the undergraduate the principles upon which historical reasoning is based and to allow him to test them out. The student has been doing this very thing in the laboratory work accompanying courses in the natural sciences, but too often the historian has acted as if his techniques were a trade secret and has preferred to guard loyally his fellow guildsman's book from student attack. Often the undergraduate critic has had only common sense or principles drawn from another discipline with which to challenge the dogmatism of the textbook and the prejudices of the pedagogue. This is particularly to be regretted since the historian by his training is especially qualified to teach the student to seek and to find, to evaluate, and to interpret man-made evidence. These lessons are what the Problems are designed to teach, and it is here that they differ most from collections of supplementary readings whose principal and laudable purpose is to enliven and enrich a text.

In this volume the materials have been carefully selected and organized into a series of Problems which combine to illustrate the main ideas and institutions in European history from 800 to 1715. Each Problem possesses an internal unity which serves not only to make the student acquire for himself an understanding of and judgment on a specific aspect of European history, but also, in the process, to teach him to appraise varied and often controversial evidence. Sometimes this may be the meticulous determination of a historical fact or again it may consist of the thoughtful evaluation of the final interpretation. In any case the student is made to feel that a healthy scepticism for the written word and a historical awareness of what lies behind the printed page are not the monopoly of the professional historian but rather the birthright of any educated man.

To assist the student in his task the editors have provided a certain amount of consistency in arrangement. Each Problem has been divided into two Parts, each Part representing one assignment, though the instructor will find quickly that this division is sufficiently flexible to permit a different emphasis if desired. Each Problem is preceded by an introduction which sets the scene by indicating the reason for studying this specific subject and furnishing the necessary background. Included in each Problem are questions for study, designed to guide the student in handling and evaluating the very disparate material which he is called upon to study. At the rate of one Problem per week there are actually more Problems in the volume than can be covered in most college terms or semesters. These extra Problems have been deliberately provided to give additional freedom to the instructor.

In teaching these Problems for the last three years at Yale University, it has been the experience of the authors that college students actually enjoy working at the stuff of history for themselves, that these readings in original materials, if properly organized, can be made the central, rather than a supplementary part of a course, and that the techniques of the historian need not be taught at the level of unimportant details or unsolvable enigmas but can contribute much to the intellectual powers of every undergraduate.

In a volume of this sort the authors' indebtedness to others has of necessity been very great. We would first like to thank our fellow members in the History Department at Yale who have patiently endured our questions during the last three years; in particular its Chairman, Leonard W. Labaree, whose encouragement and understanding have made the whole project possible; William H. Dunham, who helped to father the problem approach; Robert S. Lopez, for his suggestions in the field of medieval economic history; Harry R. Rudin, whose work on the earlier versions of the material was most helpful; and especially Franklin L. Baumer and John H. Kennedy, who have shared with us the teaching of these materials during the last two years.

Special mention should be made of our colleagues in the Department of History of Art, Professors Sumner McK. Crosby, George H. Hamilton, George A. Kubler, and Carroll L. V. Meeks, who were responsible for Problems VI and XIV. Their counsel and labors have been essential to this extension of the problem approach into the field of the fine arts. The Carnegie Corporation of New York has, by a generous grant, made it possible to furnish, at a reasonable cost, the pictorial materials necessary for the study of these problems. The materials may be obtained from the publishers of this volume. Among our fellow historians throughout the country we would particularly like to thank Gordon A. Craig, T. E. Mommsen, Herbert Heaton, Robert L. Reynolds, George E. Woodbine, and Chester McA. Destler for advice cheerfully given.

Anyone who is familiar with earlier collections of sources and readings will immediately recognize how much we owe to our predecessors in this field; the works of Fling, Robinson, Ogg, Henderson, Laffan, Duncalf and Krey, White and Notestein, the *Pennsylvania Translations and Reprints,* and the *Columbia Readings in Contemporary Civilization* have all been an inspiration and an example in our common task of making the student learn his history at first hand.

William Emerson and Thurman Philoon labored manfully on translations and references. And a noble band of typists and bursary students, including Marjorie Barbour, Julie Champlin, Eleanor Hutchins, Mary Pye, and Charmian Perry, made it possible to experiment for three years with these materials in mimeograph form. And finally, we are profoundly grateful to the students in History 10 at Yale, past, present, and future, who are ultimately responsible for the writing of this book.

For permission to reprint translations and documents either verbatim or in adapted form, the authors wish to acknowledge their obligations to the following publishers. In each case the publisher has been listed with the volumes in the notes: Allen & Unwin, Ltd.; American Book Co.; George Bell; Ernest Benn, Ltd.; Basil Blackwell & Mott, Ltd.; Bruce Publishing Co.; Cambridge University Press; Clarendon Press; Columbia University Press; F. S. Crofts & Co.; J. M. Dent & Sons, Ltd.; E. P. Dutton & Co., Inc.; Ginn & Co.; Hakluyt Society; Harper & Brothers; Harvard University Press; Houghton Mifflin Co.; Jackson, Son & Co.; John Lane, The Bodley Head, Ltd.; Longmans, Green & Co.; John W. Luce & Co.; The Macmillan Co.; Methuen & Co., Ltd.; Muhlenberg Press; Oxford University Press; Packard & Co.; G. P. Putnam's Sons; George Routledge & Sons; Charles Scribner's Sons; Society for Promoting Christian Knowledge; University of Minnesota Press; University of Pennsylvania Press; University Press of Liverpool; Viking Press Inc.; Yale University Press.

T. C. M.
Yale University   A. S. F.
January 26, 1948.   B. D. H.

CONTENTS

[vii]

I
Feudalism

WILLIAM [the Conqueror] next invented a system according to which everybody had to belong to somebody else, and everybody else to the King. This was called the Feutile System. . . .

Simon de Montfort, though only a Frenchman, was thus a Good Thing, and is very notable as being the only good Baron in history. The other Barons were, of course, all wicked Barons. They had, however, many important duties under the Banorial system. These were:

1. To be armed to the teeth.
2. To extract from the Villain Saccage and Soccage, tollage and tallage, pillage and ullage, and, in extreme cases, all other banorial amenities such as umbrage and porrage. (These may be collectively defined as the banorial rites of carnage and wreckage.)
3. To hasten the King's death, deposition, insanity, etc., and make quite sure that there were always at least three false claimants to the throne.
4. To resent the Attitude of the Church. (The Barons were secretly jealous of the Church, which they accused of encroaching on their rites.)
5. To keep up the Middle Ages.

1066 and All That

CONTENTS

[1]

QUESTIONS FOR STUDY

PART I

1. How do the conditions described in the *Annals of Xanten* explain the development of feudal government?

2. What evils might result from the practice described in the Capitulary of Kiersy (p. 11)?

3. Why is the *type* of document found on pp. 8–9 regarded as particularly valuable by the historian?

4. Why should a man wish to commend himself to a lord? What obligations did man and lord assume?

5. Why should a landowner wish to turn his lands into a *precarium?*

6. What motives might lead a ruler to grant an immunity?

7. "The Agreement among Lothaire, Louis the German, and Charles the Bald (p. 9) is a royal admission of failure." Is this true?

PART II

8. What services did a vassal owe his lord in return for his fief? How are those services performed today?

9. What do the documents reproduced on pp. 15–16 indicate concerning the nature of the vassal's title to his fief?

10. Why was a lord anxious to enforce his rights of wardship and marriage?

11. "The case of John of Toul (p. 11) demonstrates the fundamental weakness of the feudal system." Explain.

12. What institutions and practices illustrated in Part II of this problem are derived from institutions and practices illustrated in Part I?

13. From the point of view of a commanding general, what was the unsatisfactory feature of feudal military service?

14. "In the Middle Ages an ambitious king usually had to undo the work of his predecessors." Explain.

15. How did the positions of King Louis the Fat and King Henry I differ from that of King Charles the Simple?

16. What does the behavior of Burchard of Montmorency (p. 17) indicate about the nature of the feudal judicial process?

17. What important conclusions might the historian draw from his reading of the Peace of God (pp. 18–19)?

18. What motive inspired the treaty between the earls of Gloucester and Hereford (p. 19)? What machinery was employed to guarantee the observance of the treaty by both parties?

19. Estimate the difference between ideal and reality in feudal government.

INTRODUCTION TO THE PROBLEM

The disintegration of the Carolingian Empire after 814 left Western Europe without strong central government. In the ensuing chaos men were forced to seek a new form of rule to supply the needs of the individual—particularly the need for protection—which are normally provided by central government. The form eventually evolved was the Feudal System.

The Feudal System did not suddenly spring into existence as the Carolingian Empire fell apart. This new form of government grew slowly from old institutions which had existed in late Roman and Merovingian times. It did not appear as a clear-cut system of rule until after many years of evolution, nor did it appear everywhere in Europe at the same time. But Feudalism gradually became prevalent throughout Western Europe.

This new institution was characterized by a ruling caste of warriors who exercised governmental functions by virtue of land tenure. That is to say, public duties and obligations, formerly performed by the individual as a citizen of the state, now became private and personal services performed by members of a small military class in their capacity as land-holders. Public office became inseparable from the soil, and the inheritance of real property insured the inheritance of public office.

The nominal head of a feudal state was the king. His realm was divided into *fiefs* or offices for the government of a parcel of territory. The size of a *fief* varied from a small farm to a large province. But regardless of its size, the *fief* was normally held as an hereditary office by a noble warrior. This fief-holder was legally known as a *vassal,* who owed service to the king as his *lord* in return for the right to hold his fief. This relationship between lord and vassal was called the *feudal contract.* Under it the lord was obligated to protect his vassal, and the vassal was required to pay service, usually of a governmental nature, to his lord. In this manner the government of a kingdom was "farmed out" to a group of vassals holding the right to rule fiefs and to pass that right on to their heirs, providing the heirs assumed the obligations of the feudal contract.

The process of "farming out" government to vassals was known as *infeudation.* It was a process that could be repeated indefinitely under this form of government. For example, the Duke of *A* holds a fief from the king. He may divide that fief into a group of smaller fiefs, which he grants to vassals of his own under the feudal contract. The Duke of *A* thereby becomes the lord of these vassals, though he remains a vassal of the king. A man could thus be a lord and a vassal at the same time. Moreover, the vassals of the Duke of *A* could in turn subdivide their fiefs and become lords of vassals of their own. It was therefore common in feudal society for a member of the warrior caste to be both a lord and a vassal.

Whether lord or vassal or both, every man who held a fief was a member of the ruling class. Vassalage was an honorable status, and the government of the feudal state was entirely in the hands of this ruling group, who exercised their functions as private services to their lords.

The documents printed in Part I are designed to show the origins of the feudal system, the institutions out of which this form of government evolved. The documents in Part II are representative of the different aspects of the feudal contract, by which the rulers of the Middle Ages exercised the functions of government. The student should endeavor to understand the nature of the feudal relationship and should form conclusions as to the strength and weakness of feudal government.

Part I. THE ORIGINS OF FEUDALISM

"It is necessary . . . in all institutional history to distinguish very carefully between two sets of causes or antecedents. First, there is the general cause, or the prevailing condition of things in the society of the time, which renders a new institution necessary; and, second, there is the old institution, on which the prevailing cause seizes, and which it transforms into a new one." [1] In the selections which follow an attempt has been made to provide evidence of the general causes of feudalism and evidence of certain prefeudal institutions and practices which may have been transformed into feudal institutions and practices.

A. CONDITIONS CONDUCIVE TO THE RISE OF FEUDALISM

1. *The Melancholy Ninth Century.* The following account of conditions in the ninth century is taken from the *Annals of Xanten,* a contemporary chronicle probably drawn up in the archbishopric of Cologne. [2]

(842) . . . And Lothaire after he had laid waste Gaul returned to Aachen. Later on during the summer Louis and Charles raided the district of Vangiona and attacked Coblenz along the narrow steep route through the Hunsrueck. There Lothaire advanced against them under arms. But when he saw that he had been taken in by them, he fled to Lingones and took up a position, having recovered his strength. The above-mentioned kings ravaged the whole region of the Ripuarians and pursued Lothaire to Lingones. There some powerful men intervened, and once more the kingdom of the Franks was divided into three portions. The three kings withdrew in peace, but the peace was very insecure. Lothaire went to Aachen, Charles to Gaul, and Louis to Saxony. . . .

(843) The above-mentioned kings sent their chief retainers as ambassadors, one for each king, to redivide the royal domain of the Franks into three equal portions on the basis of the estate divisions, which had already been marked out. When the ambassadors failed to agree, the kings themselves came together into one place and settled the dispute and separated from each other. In the same year in the city of Tours the Empress Judith, who had been robbed of all her property by her son, departed this world.

(844) Pope Gregory departed this world, and Sergius succeeded him as Pope. Count Bernhard was killed by Charles. Pippin, the king of Aquitaine, the son of Pippin, together with the son of Bernhard, routed the army of Charles. There the Abbot Hugo was killed. At the same time King Louis advanced against the Wends with his army. There Gestimus, who was one of the kings of the Wends, met his end, and the remaining kings came to Louis with a pledge of loyalty which they broke when Louis left. After these events Lothaire, Louis, and Charles met in Diedenhofen, and after they had held a conference, they departed from one another in peace.

(845) Twice in the canton of Worms there was an earthquake; the first in the night following Palm Sunday, the second in the holy night of Christ's Resurrection. In the same year the heathen broke in upon the Christians at many points, but more than twelve thousand of them were killed by the Frisians. Another party of invaders devastated Gaul; of these more than six hundred men perished. Yet owing to his indolence Charles agreed to give them many thousand pounds of gold and silver if they would leave Gaul, and this they did. Nevertheless the cloisters of most of the saints were destroyed and many of the Christians were led away captive. After all this had taken place, king Louis collected an army and advanced against the Wends. When the heathen learned of this, they sent ambassadors into Saxony and sent gifts and hostages to Louis and asked for peace. He granted peace and returned home from Saxony.

(846) According to their custom the Northmen plundered Eastern and Western Frisia and burned the town of Dordrecht, with two other villages, before the eyes of Lothaire, who was then in the castle of Nimwegen, but could not punish the crime. The Northmen, with their boats filled with immense booty, including both men and goods, returned to their own country.

In the same year Louis sent an expedition from Saxony against the Wends across the Elbe. He personally, however, went with his army against the Bohemians, whom we call Beuwinitha, but with great risk. Charles advanced against the Britons, but accomplished nothing.

At this time, as no one can mention or hear

without great sadness, the mother of all the churches, the basilica of the apostle Peter, was taken and plundered by the Moors, or Saracens, who had already occupied the region of Beneventum. The Saracens, moreover, slaughtered all the Christians whom they found outside the walls of Rome, either within or without this church. They also carried men and women away prisoners. They tore down, among many others, the altar of the blessed Peter, and their crimes from day to day bring sorrow to Christians. Pope Sergius departed life this year.

(847) After the death of Sergius no mention of the Apostolic See has come in any way to our ears. Rabanus, master and abbot of Fulda, was solemnly chosen archbishop as the successor of Bishop Otger, who had died. Moreover the Northmen here and there plundered the Christians and engaged in a battle with the counts Sigir and Liuthar. They continued up the Rhine as far as Dordrecht, and nine miles farther to Meginhard, when they turned back, having taken their booty.

(848) On 4 February lightning flashed and thunder was heard as evening came on. The heathen, as was their custom, inflicted injury on the Christians. In the same year King Louis held an assembly of the people near Mainz. At this synod a heresy was brought forward by a few monks in regard to predestination. These were convicted and beaten, to their shame, before all the people. They were sent back to Gaul whence they had come, and, thanks be to God, the condition of the Church remained uninjured.

(849) While King Louis was ill his army of Bavaria took its way against the Bohemians. Many of these were killed and the remainder withdrew, much humiliated, into their own country. The heathen from the North wrought havoc in Christendom as usual and grew greater in strength; but it is revolting to say any more of this matter.

(850) On January 1st, that is in the Octave of the Lord . . . Toward evening on that same day there was heard a great deal of thunder and a mighty flash of lightning was seen; and an overflow of water afflicted the human race during this winter. In the following summer an all too great heat of the sun burned the earth. Leo, Pope of the Apostolic See, an extraordinary man, built a fortification round the church of St. Peter the Apostle. The Moors, however, devastated here and there the coastal towns in Italy. The Norman Rorik, brother of the above-mentioned younger Heriold, who earlier had fled dishonored from Lothaire, again took Dordrecht and did much evil treacherously to the Christians. In the same year so great a peace

existed between the two brothers—Emperor Lothaire and King Louis—that together with a few companions they spent many days hunting in Westphalia. A great many people were amazed at this. Then they went their own way in peace.

(851) The bodies of certain saints were sent from Rome to Saxony,—that of Alexander, one of seven brethren, and those of Romanus and Emerentiana. In the same year Emperor Lothaire's wife, the very noble empress, Irmingard by name, departed this world. The Normans inflicted much harm in Frisia and about the Rhine. A mighty army of them collected by the river Elbe against the Saxons, and some of the Saxon towns were besieged, others burned, and most terribly did they oppress the Christians. A meeting of our kings took place on the Maas River.

(852) The steel of the heathen glistened; excessive heat; a famine followed. There was not fodder enough for the animals. The pasturage for the swine was more than sufficient.

(853) A great famine in Saxony so that many were forced to live on horse meat.

(857) A great plague of swelling blisters went through the people and consumed them with a loathsome rottenness so that their limbs fell off before they died.

2. *The Treaty of St. Clair-sur-Epte, 911/ 912.* Writing some fifty years after the event, the monkish chronicler, Dudo of St. Quentin, gives his version of an agreement made between a heathen Norse invader and King Charles the Simple of France.[3]

King Charles quickly sent Franco, the archbishop of Rouen, to Rollo, the chief of the Normans, and when he came to him, he spoke to him as follows, ". . . If you are willing to become a Christian, you can enjoy peace both now and for the future, and you can settle on this land and be a very rich man, for the long suffering King Charles, influenced by the advice of his followers, is willing to grant to you this whole coast . . . which you have devastated too much already. But that there may be peace, harmony and a stable, lasting, and firm friendship for all time between you and him, he will give you his daughter Gisela for a wife. . . ."

At the appointed time, Charles and Rollo came together at the place which had been decided upon, namely St. Clair. . . .

[Everything went smoothly until the time came for Rollo to seal the bargain. Then trouble arose.] The bishops said to Rollo, who was unwilling to kiss the king's foot, "Whoever receives such a gift should salute the king's foot with a kiss."

Rollo replied, "I will never bend my knee to

anyone's knee, and I will never kiss anyone's foot."

But moved by the entreaties of the Franks, he ordered one of his warriors to kiss the king's foot. The warrior immediately lifted up the king's foot, threw the king on his back, and kissed the foot, while he was standing up and the king was flat on his back. At that there was a great roar of laughter and great excitement among those present.

Nevertheless King Charles, duke Robert, the counts and leading men, the bishops and abbots, swore on oath of the Catholic faith to the patrician Rollo on their lives, limbs, and the honor of the whole kingdom, that he should hold and possess the territory in question and pass it on to his heirs. . . . When these things had been done as we have mentioned, King Charles returned to his country, and Robert and Franco remained with Rollo. . . .

Thus in the year of the incarnation of our Lord Jesus Christ 912, Franco the archbishop baptized Rollo in the name of the Catholic faith and the most Holy Trinity. And Robert, duke of the Franks, received him at the font and gave him his own name and enriched him with great honors and gifts. Not only Rollo but his counts and whole army had themselves baptized and instructed in the faith of the Christian religion by the clerics who were present. . . .

Then after great preparations were carried out, the duke of the Normans took as his wife Gisela, the daughter of the king, for whose sake he reconciled himself with the Franks and made peace with them. He gave security to all people who wished to stay in his territory, made a survey of his lands, and divided them among his faithful followers. He restored the country which had been everywhere desolate for so long.

B.   PREFEUDAL INSTITUTIONS AND PRACTICES

1. *The Growth of Personal Dependence: the Comitatus.* The Teutonic institution of the Comitatus, meaning "retinue" or "following," is here described by the Roman historian Tacitus, whose work *Germania* was written about 98 A.D.[4]

They undertake no business whatever either of a public or a private character save they be armed. But it is not customary for any one to assume arms until the tribe has recognized his competence to use them. Then in a full assembly some one of the chiefs or the father or relatives of the youth invest him with the shield and spear. This has the same meaning as the assumption of the toga by Roman boys; it is their first honor. Before this he was only a member of a household, hereafter he is a member of the tribe. Distinguished rank or the great services of their parents secure even for mere striplings the claim to be ranked as chiefs. They attach themselves to certain more experienced chiefs of approved merit; nor are they ashamed to be looked upon as belonging to their followings. There are grades even within the train of followers assigned by the judgment of its leader. There is great rivalry among these companions as to who shall rank first with the chief, and among the chiefs as to who shall have the most and the bravest followers. It is an honor and a source of strength always to be surrounded by a great band of chosen youths, for they are an ornament in peace, a defence in war. It brings reputation and glory to a leader not only in his own tribe but also among the neighboring peoples if his following is superior in numbers and courage; for he is

courted by embassies and honored by gifts, and often his very fame decides the issue of wars.

When they go into battle it is a disgrace for the chief to be outdone in deeds of valor and for the following not to match the courage of their chief; furthermore for any of the followers to have survived his chief and come unharmed out of a battle is life-long infamy and reproach. It is in accordance with their most sacred oath of allegiance to defend and protect him and to ascribe their bravest deeds to his renown. The chief fights for victory; the men of his following, for their chief. If the tribe to which they belong sinks into the lethargy of long peace and quiet, many of the noble youths voluntarily seek other tribes that are still carrying on war, because a quiet life is irksome to the Germans, and they gain renown more readily in the midst of perils, while a large following is not to be provided for except by violence and war. For they look to the liberality of their chief for their war-horse and their deadly and victorious spear; the feasts and entertainments, however, furnished them on a homely but liberal scale, fall to their lot as mere pay. The means for this bounty are acquired through war and plunder. Nor could you persuade them to till the soil and await the yearly produce so easily as you could induce them to stir up an enemy and earn glorious wounds. Nay even they think it tame and stupid to acquire by their sweat what they can purchase by their blood.

2. *The Growth of Personal Dependence: Commendation.* The two blank forms which follow illustrate the Frankish practice of

Commendation in the seventh century. The relationship established by Commendation was strikingly similar to the Roman institution of patronage (*patrocinium*) which had come into existence at least three centuries earlier.[5]

(*Application*) To that magnificent Lord ———, I ———. Since it is very well known to everyone how very little I have wherewith to feed and clothe myself, I have therefore sought your piety, and your good will has allowed me to hand myself over or commend myself to your guardianship. This I have done in the following manner: that you are to aid and succor me with both food and clothing insofar as I shall be able to be of service to you and shall deserve it.

As long as I live, I am to provide service and honor to you in accordance with my status as a free man.

During my lifetime I shall not have the power to withdraw from your guardianship and power, but all the days of my life I am to remain under your power and your defense. Hence it is agreed that if either one of us wishes to make any changes in this agreement, he shall pay ——— shillings to his companion and this agreement shall remain in force.

Wherefore it is agreed that they should make up or confirm between them two documents with the same meaning from this form. This have they done.

(*Acceptance*) It is right that those who promise unimpaired loyalty to us should be protected by our help. And because ———, one of our faithful men, by the grace of God, has come here into our palace with his arms and has seen fit to swear faith and loyalty to us in our hands, We, therefore, by this present decree, do ordain and command that from now on the aforesaid ——— shall be enrolled in the number of our followers. And if any one should by chance presume to slay him, let that man know that he shall be held liable for his *wergeld* [fine paid to the relatives of murdered man] of 600 shillings.

3. *The Growth of Dependent Land Tenure: the Precarium.* The two blank forms which follow are the instruments for effecting a *precarium* or "benefice" in the seventh century. This form of land grant, which is made to the church in the documents below, might also be made to lay lords.[6]

(*Grant*) I, ———, in the name of God. The pleasant thought has come to my mind that I should give some of my possessions for the benefit of my soul, which I have therefore done. This now is what I hand over in the district called ———, in the place called ———, all of the property

which my father left me there when he died and which legally fell as my portion in the division of the property among my brothers and the other heirs and also whatever I was able to add to these possessions afterwards by dint of honest labor. All this I hand over complete and undivided, i.e. the manor, buildings, slaves, peasants' huts, fields cultivated and uncultivated, meadow land, woods, waters, mills etc.

These, as I have said before, together with all things adjacent and appurtenant, I hand over to the church built in honor of St. ———, or to the monastery called ——— where ———, as abbot, is recognized to rule over God's flock in accordance with the regulations; on condition that as long as there is life in my body, the above-mentioned property I shall receive from you [the abbot] as a benefice for my use. The due payment which I shall make to you and your successors each year is ———. My son shall retain the same property for his lifetime only and shall make the above-mentioned payment. . . . After his death, this property together with all improvements shall revert to your control to be kept forever. . . . If my son does not survive me, however, these same possessions shall after my death without any subterfuge of any kind, by right of your authority, revert to you to be retained forever.

But if anyone—which I do not believe will ever be the case—if I myself or anyone else at all should wish to question the validity of this grant, contrary to the truth, may this deceit in no way succeed, and for his reckless daring let him pay to the above-mentioned monastery double the sum which he was prevented from obtaining through his evil greed. And furthermore let him be liable to the royal authority for a payment of ——— in gold. Moreover, may this present charter with all it contains remain inviolate, with the witnesses listed below.

Done at ———, publicly. Those who were present are listed below together with the remaining countless crowd of people.

(*Acceptance*) In the name of God, I Abbot ——— together with our commissioned brothers. Since it is well known how you ——— by the suggestion of divine exhortation did hand over to the monastery ——— and to the church which has been built there in honor of Saint ——— all of the property in ——— which your father left you there when he died and which legally fell as your portion in the division of the property between your brother and ———, a co-heir, and also whatever you were able to add to these possessions afterwards by dint of honest labor: the manor, buildings, gardens, orchards, the slaves herein named ———, ———, ———, the peasants' huts, meadow land, forests, cultivated and uncultivated fields with all things adjacent and appurtenant thereunto which it would be too long a task to mention. All this have you handed over in complete good faith to the above-mentioned monastery where we, under the guidance of God, carry on the pastoral office.

But after you had done this, it seemed fitting to us—since you requested it—that we return all this property to you to be held by you for your use, and you shall not neglect to pay the annual payment due upon it which is ———. . . . Likewise the sons which we see that you now have shall have this same property and make the same payment for their lifetime. After they die, the above-mentioned property shall revert to us and our successors forever. . . .

Nor may any one at all, either ourselves or our successors, have any success in a rash attempt to render this agreement invalid, but inasmuch as the present situation calls for the *precarium* in question, may the agreement, which we with the consent of our brothers have decided to ratify, remain in force without alteration.

Done at ———, in the presence of ——— and the others whom there is no need to mention. The seal of Abbot ——— who has caused this *precarium* to be made.

4. *The Feudalization of Governmental Functions: Military Service.* The following document is a portion of the Capitulary of Lestinnes, which was issued by a Carolingian mayor of the palace in 743. Though it has been established that church lands were appropriated for military purposes at an earlier date, this is the first known document in which the state so acted formally.[7]

With the consent of the servants of God and our Christian people, we have decided, because of threats of war and because of the raids of certain tribes located on our borders, with the indulgence of God, to appropriate some portion of church property for the time being to support our army. This property is to be held as a *precarium* and a fixed rent is to be paid each year to church or monastery in the amount of 1 shilling or 12 pennies for each peasant's hut. When the holder dies the church will regain possession.

If, however, the circumstances of the times require it, the prince may order that the *precarium* be renewed and reassigned. Let great care be taken that no church or monastery suffer want or poverty because of the granting of *precaria*. If poverty compels it, let the whole property be restored to the Church and the house of God.

5. *The Feudalization of Governmental Functions: Military Service.* Below is an agreement made in 847 among Lothaire, Louis the German, and Charles the Bald. These are the princes who figure so prominently in the *Annals of Xanten* as the rulers of western Europe in the middle of the ninth century.[8]

We decree that every freeman shall accept whatever lord he wishes in our kingdom, from among us and our faithful subjects.

We command that no man shall leave his lord without good cause, and that no lord shall receive a man who has left his own lord, unless it be in accordance with the customs of our predecessors.

Every subject of each one of us shall go to war or other necessary expedition with his lord unless the kingdom is invaded and all the subjects are called out in mass to repel it, which [mass army] is called Landwehr.

6. *The Feudalization of Governmental Functions: Immunities.* Below is a seventh-century formula for the grant of an immunity by a king to a bishop. The immunity was one of the most important developments among prefeudal practices.[9]

We believe that we shall make our reign more memorable if we grant fitting benefits to churches —or ——— (fill in the blank)—with pious intent, and if with God's protection we put them in writing so that they shall continue steadfast. Therefore, let it be known to you that at the request of that apostolic man, the bishop of ———, and for the salvation of our soul, we have ordained as follows: into the villas of the said bishop's church, which he is now seen to hold as gifts either from us or any one else, or which may afterwards be granted to said church, no public official may enter either to try cases or to collect taxes. But the said bishop and his successors shall rule the said lands in the name of God and with full and complete immunity.

We therefore ordain that neither you nor your subordinates nor your successors nor any public official is to presume to enter into the estates of the said church, wheresoever in our kingdom they may be located, to try cases, collect taxes and revenues, or to receive entertainment or to seize supplies or securities. All of the taxes and other revenue which should come to the royal treasury by law from the people living on said estates, whether they be slave or free, Roman or barbarian, we grant out of our generosity and for the future salvation of our soul to be used by the officials of said church forever in the best interests of said church. . . .

7. *The Feudalization of Governmental Functions: Immunities.* Following is the grant of an immunity to a layman by the Emperor, Louis the Pious, in 815.[10]

In the name of our Lord and Savior Jesus Christ, Louis, by divine providence, emperor augustus. Be it known to all the faithful clergy of the Holy Church and to all our subjects both present and future that a certain faithful subject, whose name is John, has come into our presence and commended himself to us and has asked us to confirm him in the possession of the lands which we and our father granted to him and also those which he and his sons and their men have cleared and occupied, and has shown to us by way of precedent what our father did for him. . . . We therefore grant to this our faithful man, John, the following lands and estates . . . to be held in peace and security by him, his sons, and their descendants. No count, vicar, or any other public official shall presume to judge or constrain any person living on said lands, but John, his sons, and their descendants shall judge and constrain them. In order that this grant may remain more firmly in force as long as John, his sons, and their descendants shall remain faithful to us, our sons, and their descendants, we have ordered this charter to be sealed with our ring so that it may have full credence. . . .

8. *The Feudalization of Governmental Functions: Inheritance of Offices.* The Capitulary of Kiersy, portions of which are reproduced below, was issued by Charles the Bald shortly before he left his kingdom of France to go to Italy. It was designed to regulate the affairs of the kingdom, which he intrusted to his son (later Louis II) during his absence. It is dated 877.[11]

If a count of this kingdom should die when his son is away with us, our son with the advice of our loyal subjects shall designate one of the closest relatives of said count to rule the county in conjunction with the public officials of said county and the bishop in whose diocese said county is located, until the matter shall come to our notice and we have time to bestow the honors of the late count upon his son who is away with us. But if the deceased count shall leave a minor son, that son shall govern the county with the aid of the officials and the bishop in whose diocese it is, until the death of the said count has been brought to our notice and we endow the son with his father's honors. But if the count shall not leave a son, our son with the advice of our faithful subjects shall appoint someone to govern the county with the aid of the officials of the county and the bishop, until our commands in respect to it are made known. And no one shall feel aggrieved, if we give the county to another than the one who governed it up to the time of our appointment. The same procedure shall be observed in regard to our vassals; and the bishops, abbots, and counts of our kingdom, and our other faithful subjects, shall do the same toward their men.

Part II.   FEUDAL PRACTICES

Despite the infinite variety within the feudal "system" a general pattern can be discerned. The selections printed below describe feudal practices and institutions fairly typical of France and England in the Middle Ages.

A.   THE FEUDAL RELATIONSHIP

1. *Homage: A Norman Definition.* The following is an excerpt from the records of feudal customs in Normandy, written in the late thirteenth or early fourteenth century.[12]

Now we must speak about homage. Homage is a promise to keep faith in matters just and necessary and to give aid and counsel. He who does homage should place his hands between those of him who is to receive it and say these words: "I become your man and I shall keep faith with you against all others except for my allegiance to the duke of Normandy."

2. *Fealty: An English Definition.* The following statement is taken from a fifteenth-century treatise on feudal tenures by the English jurist, Sir Thomas Littleton.[13]

Fealty is the same that *fidelitas* is in Latin. And when a freeholder doth fealty to his lord, he shall hold his right hand upon a book and shall say thus: "Know ye this, my lord, that I shall be faithful and true unto you, and faith to you shall bear for the lands which I claim to hold of you, and that I shall lawfully do to you the customs and services which I ought to do, at the terms assigned, so help me God and His saints"; and he shall kiss the book. But he shall not kneel when he maketh his fealty nor shall make such humble reverence as is aforesaid in homage.

And there is great diversity between the doing

of fealty and of homage; for homage cannot be done to any but to the lord himself, but the steward of the lord's court, or bailiff, may take fealty for the lord.

3. *Performance of Homage, Fealty, and Investiture.* Below is a Flemish chronicler's account of the ceremonies which took place in 1127 at the court of William, count of Flanders, upon the death of his father, Charles.[14]

Through the whole remaining part of the day those who had been previously enfeoffed by the most pious count Charles, did homage to the new count, taking up now again their fiefs and offices and whatever they had before rightfully and legitimately obtained. On Thursday, the seventh of April, homages were again made to the count, being completed in the following order of faith and security:

First they did their homage thus. The count asked if he was willing to become completely his man, and the other replied, "I am willing"; and with clasped hands, between the hands of the count, they were bound together by a kiss. Secondly, he who had done homage gave his fealty to the representative of the count in these words, "I promise on my faith that I will in future be faithful to Count William, and will observe my homage to him completely, against all persons, in good faith, and without deceit." Thirdly, he took his oath to this upon the relics of the saints. Afterwards, with a little rod which the count held in his hand, he gave investitures to all who by this agreement had given their security and homage and accompanying oath.

4. *An Oath of Homage.* The following passage illustrates the obligations often associated with homage. This oath was taken by Theobald, count of Troyes, to the King of France in 1198.[15]

Philip, by the grace of God king of France. Be it known to all men, present and future, that we have received our beloved nephew, Theobald, count of Troyes, as our liege man, against every creature, living or dead, for all the lands which his father, count Henry, our uncle, held from our father, and which count Henry, the brother of Theobald, held from us. Count Theobald has sworn to us on the most holy body of the Lord and on the holy gospel that he will aid us in good faith, as his liege lord, against every creature, living or dead; at his command the following persons have sworn to us that they approve of this and will support and aid him in keeping this oath: Guy of Dampierre, Gualcher of Châtillon, Geoffroy, marshal of Champagne, etc. [vassals of the count of Champagne]. If count Theobald fails in his duty to us and does not make amends within a month from the time when they learn of it, they will surrender themselves to us at Paris, to be held as prisoners until he makes amends; and this shall be done every time that he fails in his duty to us. We have sworn with our own hand that we will aid count Theobald against every creature, living or dead; at our command the following men have sworn that they approve of this and will support and aid us in keeping this oath: Peter, count of Nevers, Drogo of Mello, William of Galande, etc. [vassals of the king]. If we fail in our duty to count Theobald, and do not make amends within a month from the time when they learn of it, they will surrender themselves to him at Troyes to be held as prisoners there until we make amends; and they shall do this every time that we fail in our duty to him. . . . During the daytime they can leave the manor where they are being held as prisoners provided they give their oath to return that very night. . . . We have also agreed that our beloved uncle, William, archbishop of Rheims, and the bishops of Châlons and Meaux, may place those of our lands that are in their dioceses under interdict, as often as we fail in our duty to count Theobald, unless we make amends within a month from the time when they learn of it; and count Theobald has agreed that the same archbishop and bishops may place his lands under an interdict as often as he fails in his duty to us, unless he makes amends within a month from the time when they learn of it.

5. *An Oath of Homage.* Below is the oath of homage of a French noble, John of Toul, to Beatrice, countess of Troyes, in the early thirteenth century.[16]

I, John of Toul, make it known that I am the liege man of the lady Beatrice, Countess of Troyes, and of my most dear lord, Theobald, count of Champagne, her son, against all persons living or dead, except for my allegiance to lord Enjorand of Coucy, lord John of Arcis and the count of Grandpré. If it should happen that the count of Grandpré should be at war with the countess and count of Champagne on his own quarrel, I will aid the count of Grandpré in my own person, and will send to the count and the countess of Champagne the knights whose service I owe them for the fief which I hold of them. But if the count of Grandpré shall make war on the countess and the count of Champagne on behalf of his friends and not in his own quarrel, I will aid in my own person the countess and count of Champagne, and will send one knight to the count of Grandpré for the service which I owe him for the fief which I hold of him, but I will not go myself into the territory of the count of Grandpré to make war on him.

6. *An Act of Investiture.* In the following document the French king bears witness to a lay lord's investiture of a bishop with certain lands.[17]

In the name of the Holy and undivided Trinity, Amen. I, Louis, by the grace of God king of the French, make known to all present as well as to come, that at Mantes in our presence, count Henry of Champagne conceded the fief of Savigny to Bartholomew, bishop of Beauvais, and his successors. And for that fief the said bishop has made promise and engagement for one knight and justice and service to count Henry; and he also agreed that the bishops who shall come after him will do likewise. In order that this may be understood and known to posterity we have caused the present charter to be attested by our seal. Done at Mantes, in the year of the Incarnate Word, 1167; present in our palace those whose names and seals are appended: seal of Theobald, our steward; seal of Guy, the butler; seal of Matthew, the chamberlain; seal of Ralph, the constable. Given by the hand of Hugh, the chancellor.

B. THE MUTUAL OBLIGATIONS OF LORD AND VASSAL

1. *General Obligations.* The following letter was written by Bishop Fulbert of Chartres in 1020.[18]

To William, most glorious duke of the Aquitanians, Bishop Fulbert, the favor of his prayers:

Asked to write something concerning the form of fealty, I have noted briefly for you, on the authority of the books, the things which follow. He who swears fealty to his lord ought always to have these six things in memory: What is harmless, safe, honorable, useful, easy, practicable. *Harmless,* that is to say, that he should not injure his lord in his body; *safe,* that he should not injure him in betraying his secrets or the defenses upon which he relies for safety; *honorable,* that he should not injure him in his justice or in other cases that pertain to his honor; *useful,* that he should not injure him in his possessions; *easy* and *practicable,* that that good which his lord is able to do easily he make not difficult, nor that which is practicable he make not impossible to him.

It is right that the faithful vassal should avoid giving these injuries, but he does not deserve his holding merely on the ground that he abstains from evil, unless he also does good too. It remains, therefore, that in the same six matters above-mentioned, he should faithfully offer aid and counsel to his lord if he is to be considered worthy of his benefice and to be secure in the fealty he has sworn.

The lord ought also to act toward his faithful vassal reciprocally in all these things. And if he does not do this, he will be justly considered guilty of bad faith; just as the former, if he should be detected in avoiding or consenting to the avoidance of his duties, he would be perfidious and perjured.

I would have written to you at greater length, if I had not been occupied with many other things, including the rebuilding of our city and church, which was lately entirely consumed in a terrible fire. We could not help for a while being very much disturbed by this loss, yet now we breathe again supported by the hope of God's comfort and yours.

2. *Military Service: Knight Service.* The following is drawn from the ordinances of King Louis IX, who reigned in France from 1226 to 1270.[19]

The barons and the vassals of the king ought to appear in his army when they shall be summoned, and ought to serve at their own expense for forty days and forty nights, with whatever number of knights they owe. And he possesses the right to exact from them these services when he wishes and when he has need of them. If, however, the king shall wish to keep them more than forty days and forty nights at their own expense, they need not remain unless they desire. But if he shall wish to retain them at his cost for the defense of the kingdom, they ought lawfully to remain. But if he shall propose to lead them outside of the kingdom, they need not go unless they are willing, for they have already served their forty days and forty nights.

3. *Military Service: Knight Service.* The contemporary record reproduced below shows how Philip III of France secured knights for military service in 1272.[20]

These are the men who appeared at Tours on the 15th day after Easter for the army of the lord king of France:

In the year 1272 the bishop of Paris came to Tours at the citation of the lord king and presented himself in the king's house on the second Sunday after Easter, before Ferrario of Verneuil, knight, marshal of France, saying that he had come at the citation of the lord king prepared to fulfill his duty; Ferrario told him that he should either come himself or send some one the next day at the first hour in the morning, since he was not able to tell him anything or make a reply, because Gregory of St. Martin of Tours was not present on account of his weakness, and besides he was expecting new orders from the king.

On the next day, and on Tuesday, the aforesaid bishop presented himself before the said marshal, saying that he had come ready for the service of the king with three knights, whose names were John of Marcey, John of Julliaco, and Adam of Blois. He said that if he was held to send more, he was ready to do what he ought; and if he had furnished more than he owed, that this should not bind either him or the church of Paris for the future.

The bishop of Troyes appeared for his see, saying that he owed two knights, whose names were Ralph and Drogo of Préaux.

The bishop of Noyon was represented by Theobald of Boesseria, a knight who acknowledged that the said bishop owed five knights and sent three knights beyond what he owed. The names of the knights are as follows: Ansold of Rancorolis, Nevelon of Rancorolis, his brother, etc. . . . They went forth to the service of the king.

The bishop of Bayeux was represented by Thomas of Semilly, his procurator, who acknowledged that the said bishop owed ten knights for the service of the king in the army. These he sent, namely, John of Bellengreville, John of Caenchy, Richard of Rovancestre, William of Surrain, and others. . . .

The bishop of Beauvais admitted that he owed five knights and sent them.

John of Rouvray, a knight, lord of Yneto, appeared for himself, confessing that he owed, by reason of his holding of Rouvray, one knight, whom he brought with him, namely, John of Caim.

Fulk of Bauquenzay, a knight, appeared for the abbot of St. Ebrulf, and went forth for the said abbot, as he should, and was held to do.

The archdeacon of Cheuteville did not appear, but sent one knight, namely, Peter of Maucomble.

Reginald Trihan, a knight, appeared and went forth for himself.

John of Rouvray, a knight, appeared for himself, saying that he owed one knight for his fief of Corbon and its appurtenances. He offered for himself John of Meler, a knight. What service he owed on his wife's part he did not know.

Robert Bertran, a squire, appeared and said that he owed the lord king two knights and a half.

John of Saucey appeared for himself and said that he owed 40 days service in the army and sent John of Fontibus, a knight, to serve for him.

The abbot St. Columba at Sens appeared in person, and said he had never known his monastery to do military service by furnishing knights. The service was rendered in money, namely, eight score pounds for the army and the sum of seventeen Parisian pounds.

Hugh of Conflent, knight, marshal of Champagne, appeared for the king of Navarre, and brought with him sixty knights, to do the service owed to the king.

Stephanus Mener and Adam Allutarius appeared for the city of Villeneuve-le-Roi, near Sens, and said they owed no military service to the king, unless they chose to render it out of sheer courtesy. And they would do the bidding of the lord king only on condition that they go only as far from Villeneuve as they can return thither in one day, during the sunlight or daylight.

The representative chosen by the abbot of Ferrières appeared in person, and said that he owed no military service with horses and arms, but only the sum of seventeen pounds Parisian and his followers six score pounds, namely, sixty pounds for Ferrières and sixty for Beausse.

John of Alleman, an old and weak knight, sent his son, a squire, in his place, and the son went.

Philip of Lisserville, a squire, appeared for himself, but he was poor and was therefore sent back home.

4. *Military Service: Serjeanty.* Although the most common form of military service was knight service, as illustrated above, a vassal might owe other forms of military service, such as the furnishing of castle-guards. In return for such service—described in the following twelfth-century document—land was held in "serjeanty tenure," of which there were also numerous non-military forms.[21]

Be it known to all faithful men, present and future, that I, Geoffrey de Turville, have given to John of Lee one hide of my demesne in Weston, with all its appurtenances, as was settled before me and my men, and with the hide I have given him the mill which William held with all its appurtenance in land and in meadow. All this I have granted to him in fee and inheritance, free and quit of all service and exaction, except that John and his heirs shall keep post for me in the castle of Weston for forty days in time of war with a destrier and a rouncey, and for three weeks in time of peace. Be it known also that I have done this because John has given up to me his inheritance, namely the land of Lee which I have given to the canons of Missenden in alms, and the aforesaid John has quitclaimed it to the aforesaid canons and pledged his faith to acquit it to them according to his power against all men so far as he is concerned, and has released it and abjured it.

5. *Court Service.* The following selection is taken from the Laws of Henry I of England (1100–35) to illustrate another important

type of service owed by a vassal to his lord.[22]

Chapter LV, The rights of a lord in respect to his vassal:

To every lord it is allowed to summon his man that he may be at right to him in his court; and even if he is resident at the most distant manor of that honor from which he holds, he shall go to the plea if his lord summons him. If his lord holds different fiefs, the man of one honor is not compelled by law to go to another plea, unless the cause belongs to the other to which his lord has summoned him.

If a man holds fiefs from several lords, however much he holds from others, he owes most and will be subject for justice to him of whom he is the liege man.

Every vassal owes to his lord fidelity concerning his life and members and earthly honor and keeping of his counsel in what is honorable and useful saving the faith of God and of the prince of the land. However, theft and treason and murder and whatever things are against God and the catholic faith are not to be required of or performed by any one; but faith shall be held to all lords, saving the faith of the earlier ones, and the more to the one of which he is the liege. And let permission be given him, if any of his men seek another lord for himself.

C.   FEUDAL AIDS AND INCIDENTS

1. *The Three Customary Aids: A Norman Definition.* The following selection is taken from the records of feudal customs in Normandy, written in the late thirteenth or early fourteenth century.[23]

In Normandy there are three chief aids. The first is, of course, aid in making of the lord's eldest son a knight; the second is aid at the time of the marriage of the lord's eldest daughter; the third is to ransom the body of the lord from prison when he shall be taken captive during a war for the duke of Normandy. By this it appears that the knighthood-aid is due when the eldest son of the lord is made a knight. The eldest son is he who has the dignity of primogeniture. The marriage-aid is due when the eldest daughter is married. The ransom-aid is due when it is necessary to deliver the lord from the prisons of the enemies of the duke of Normandy. These aids are paid in some fiefs at the rate of half a relief, and in some at the rate of a third.

2. *Feudal Incidents: Wardship and Marriage.* Below is a description from the same Norman customal, or book of custom, of the "incidental" rights and obligations of lords with regard to the wives and children of deceased vassals.[24]

Heirs should be placed under guardians until they reach the age of twenty years; and those who hold them as wards should give over to them all the fiefs which came under their control by reason of wardship, provided they have not lost anything by judicial process. . . . When the heirs pass out of the condition of wardship, their lords shall not impose upon them any reliefs for their fiefs, for the profits of wardship shall be reckoned in place of the relief.

When the female ward reaches the proper age to marry, she should be married by the advice and consent of her relatives and friends, according as the nobility of her ancestry and the value of her fief may require; and upon the marriage the fief which has been held in guardianship should be given over to her. A woman cannot be freed from wardship except by marriage; and let it not be said that she is of age until she is twenty years old. But if she be married at the age at which it is allowable for a woman to marry, the fact of her marriage makes her of age and delivers her fief from wardship. . . . A woman has the status and legal position of her husband.

The fiefs of those who are under wardship should be cared for attentively by their lords, who are entitled to receive the produce and profits. And in this connection let it be known that the lord ought to preserve in their former condition the buildings, the manor-houses, the forests and meadows, the gardens, the ponds, the mills, the fisheries, and the other things of which he has the profits. And he should not sell, destroy, or remove the woods, the houses, or the trees. . . .

3. *Feudal Incidents: Relief.* The payment made by an heir before entering upon possession of his fief was termed "relief." The following definition of relief is taken from the "Laws of William I" of England, a twelfth-century document.[25]

The relief of an earl which the king receives is eight horses, of which four are to have saddles and bridles. There are to be also four breastplates, four helmets, four lances, four shields, and four swords. The other horses are to be either riding or hunting horses and to be equipped with bridles and coverings.

The relief of a baron is four horses, of which two are to have saddles and bridles, and with them two breastplates, two shields, two helmets, two lances, and two swords; and of the other two horses, one shall be a riding horse, the other a hunter, with bridles and coverings.

The relief of a lesser vassal which the liege lord receives is the horse the vassal's father had when he died, together with a breastplate, helmet, shield, lance, and sword. If by chance he should not have these, he may discharge the debt by paying 100 shillings.

4. *Feudal Incidents: Relief.* Below are excerpts from English treasury records of the twelfth and thirteenth centuries, which show the reliefs paid by the king's vassals.[26]

Walter Hait renders an account of 5 marks of silver for the relief of the land of his father.

William Fitz William paid 25 marks for the relief of his land.

Walter Brito renders an account of £66, 13s. and 4d. for the relief of his land.

Richard of Estre renders an account of £15 for the relief of 3 knights' fees which he holds from the honor of Mortain.

Walter Fitz Thomas, of Newington, owes 28s. 4d. for having a fourth part of one knight's fee which had been seized into the hand of the king for default of relief.

John of Venetia renders an account of 300 marks for the fine of his land and for the relief of the land which was his father's which he held from the king *in capite.*

John of Balliol owes £150 for the relief of 30 knights' fees which Hugh of Balliol, his father, held from the king *in capite,* that is 100s. for each fee.

Peter of Bruce renders an account of £100 for his relief for the barony which was of Peter his father.

Henry of Bloio gave 70 marks to have a fee of seven knights, in Cornwall, which was his father Alan's. . . .

Robert of Satebroi gave 100 shillings relief for one knight's fee.

5. *Feudal Incidents: Escheat.* The following definition of escheat is taken from an English law book written about 1178. It describes only the relationship between the king and his vassals, though in fact escheat applied equally to all lords and their vassals.[27]

Escheat is the common name for what falls to the exchequer when those who are tenants in chief of the king die, and there does not remain an heir by blood. . . . But when the father of the family, be he knight or serjeant, who is a tenant in chief of the king shall have paid his debt to fate, leaving children, of which the eldest however is a minor, his revenues, indeed, revert to the exchequer; but in this case it is not simply called escheat but escheat with heir. [wardship] And thus neither is the heir taken from the inheritance nor the inheritance from the heir; but, being placed, together with his inheritance, under the guardianship of the king for the time of his minority, both he and the other children shall receive from that inheritance, through the officials of the king, what is necessary. The rest of the income of the estate falls to the king to use.

6. *Feudal Incidents: Forfeiture.* The following document, a record of the court of the Count of Toulouse in 1249, indicates the rights of a lord if a vassal failed to fulfill his obligations.[28]

Raymond, by the grace of God count of Toulouse, marquis of Provence, to the nobleman Arnold Atton, viscount of Lomagne, greeting:

Let it be known to your nobility by the tenor of these presents what has been done in the matter of the complaints which we have made about you before the court of Agen [the feudal court of the count of Toulouse]; that you have not taken the trouble to keep or fulfill the agreements sworn by you to us, as is more fully contained in the instrument drawn up there, sealed with our seal by the public notary; and that you have refused contemptuously to appear before the said court for the purpose of doing justice, and you have been frequently and grossly delinquent toward us in other matters. As your faults have required, the aforesaid court of Agen has unanimously and concordantly pronounced sentence against you, and for these matters have condemned you to hand over and restore to us the chateau of Auvillars and all that land which you hold from us in feudal tenure to be had and held by us by right of the obligation by which you have bound it to us for fulfilling and keeping the said agreements.

Likewise it has declared that we are to be put into possession of the said land and that it is to be handed over to us, on account of your insolence, because you have not been willing to appear before the same court on the days which were assigned to you. Moreover, it has declared that you shall be held and required to restore the said land in whatsoever way we wish to receive it, with few or many, in peace or in anger, in our own person, by right of lordship. Likewise it has declared that you shall restore to us all the expenses which we have incurred, or the court itself has incurred, on those days which were assigned to you, or because of those days, and has condemned you to repay these to us. Likewise it has been declared that you shall set free that noble man Gerald of Armanhow whom you hold captive and send him a free man, to us. We demand that you free him by virtue of our right of lordship. . . .

7. *Feudal Incidents: Forfeiture.* Below is a court record from the reign of King John of England (1199–1216).[29]

It is presented by the jurors above named that the manor of Chinnore along with the hamlet of Sydenham was held of old, from the time of the Conquest, from the lord king of England, by a certain man who was named Walter de Vernon, as one knight's fee; and because the said Walter de Vernon refused to perform his due service from the said manor to the lord king John, in the time of the war which sprang up between the lord king John and the king of France, the lord

king John with the advice of his council seized that same manor with the appurtenances, and removed the said Walter de Vernon, on account of his ingratitude, from the possession of the aforesaid manor forever. And the lord king John granted that same manor with its appurtenances, for the services that to the same lord king were from it, to Saer de Quincy, formerly earl of Winchester, to hold for himself and his heirs as tenants in chief from the lord king as one knight's fee; and the heirs of the said Saer held the aforesaid manor in succession, and still hold it, except the hamlet Sydenham, which the abbot of Thame holds as a gift from Roger de Quincy.

D.   THE POSITION OF THE KING IN FEUDAL SOCIETY

1. *The English King, 1100.* The coronation oath of Henry I, printed below, illustrates certain problems confronting a monarch under feudalism.[30]

In the year of the incarnation of our Lord 1101, Henry, son of King William, who after the death of his brother William is by God's Grace king of the English, greetings to all his faithful subjects.

1. Know that by the mercy of God, and by the common counsel of the barons of the whole kingdom of England, I have been crowned king of the same kingdom; and because the kingdom has been oppressed by unjust exactions, I, from regard to God, and from the love which I have toward you, in the first place make the holy church of God free, so that I will neither sell nor place at rent, nor, when archbishop, or bishop, or abbot is dead, will I take anything from the domain of the church, or from its men, until a successor is installed into it. And all the evil customs by which the realm of England was unjustly oppressed will I take away, which evil customs I partly set down here.

2. If any of my barons, or earls, or others who hold from me shall have died, his heir shall not redeem his land as he did in the time of my brother, but shall relieve it by a just and legitimate relief. Similarly also the men of my barons shall relieve their lands from their lords by a just and legitimate relief.

3. And if any of the barons or other men of mine wishes to give his daughter in marriage, or his sister or niece or relation, he must speak with me about it, but I will neither take anything from him for this permission, nor forbid him to give her in marriage, unless he should wish to join her to my enemy. And if when a baron or other man of mine is dead, a daughter remains as his heir, I will give her in marriage according to the judgment of my barons, along with her land. And if when a man is dead his wife remains, and is with-

out children, she shall have her dowry and right of marriage, and I will not give her to a husband except according to her will.

4. And if a wife has survived with children, she shall have her dowry and right of marriage, so long as she shall have kept her body legitimately, and I will not give her in marriage, except according to her will. And the guardian of the land and children shall be either the wife or another one of the relatives as shall seem to be most just. And I require that my barons should deal similarly with the sons and daughters or wives of their men.

6. I remit all fines and debts which were owed by my brother, except my lawful rents and those revenues which had been agreed upon in behalf of the heirs of others or in behalf of those things which more justly affected others. And if any one has pledged any thing in behalf of his own inheritance, this I remit and all reliefs which had been agreed upon for lawful inheritances.

8. If any of my barons or men shall have committed an offense he shall not give security to the extent of forfeiture of his money, as he did in the time of my father, or of my brother, but according to the measure of the offense so shall he pay, as he would have paid from the time of my father backward, in the time of my other predecessors; so that if he shall have been convicted of treachery or of crime, he shall pay as is just.

10. The forests, by the common agreement of my barons, I have retained in my own hand, as my father held them.

12. A firm peace in my whole kingdom I establish and require to be kept from henceforth.

13. The law of King Edward I give to you again with those changes with which my father changed it by the counsel of his barons.

14. If any one has taken anything from my possessions since the death of King William, my brother, or from the possessions of any one, let the whole be immediately returned without alter-

ation, and if any one shall have retained anything thence, he upon whom it is found will pay it heavily to me. Witnesses Maurice, bishop of London, and Gundulf, bishop, and William, bishop-elect, and Henry, earl, and Simon, earl, and Walter Giffard, and Robert de Montfort, and Roger Bigod, and Henry de Port, at London, when I was crowned.

2. *The French King, c. 1100.* The following account is taken from the biography of Louis VI of France, written by his chief adviser, Abbot Suger.[31]

As a young man Louis was so well known for being jovial, friendly, and well-intentioned, that he got a reputation of lacking force of character; but he had scarcely become a man when he showed himself a conspicuous and zealous defender of his father's kingdom. He took care of the needs of the church and strove to obtain peace for those who pray, those who work, and those who are poor. No one had been in the habit of doing these things for a long time.

Now it came to pass at this time that certain disputes arose between Adam, the venerable abbot of St. Denis, and a nobleman, Burchard, lord of Montmorency [his vassal], concerning certain customs. The controversy waxed so hot and reached such extremes of irritation that all ties of homage were broken between vassal and lord, and the two disputants betook themselves to arms, war, and fire.

When the affair came to the ears of Lord Louis he was very much disturbed. He did not hesitate, but ordered the aforesaid Burchard, duly summoned, to appear before his father in the castle of Poissy for judgment. Burchard lost his case, but refused to submit to the judgment. He was not taken prisoner, for that is not the custom of the French, but having withdrawn to his estates, he straightway learned what manner of injury and calamity the king's majesty can inflict on his disobedient subjects. For this famous youth [Prince Louis] advanced with the army against him and his criminal allies, Matthew, count of Beaumont, and Drogo of Mouchy-le-Châtel, vigorous and warlike men. He laid waste the land of Burchard with fire, famine, and the sword; and overthrew all the defenses and buildings, except the castle itself, and razed them to the ground. When his enemies undertook to defend themselves in the castle, he besieged them with the French and the Flemish troops of his uncle Robert, as well as with his own. By these and other blows he brought the humiliated Burchard to repentance, bent him to his will and pleasure, and satisfactorily adjusted the dispute which had given rise to the trouble. . . .

Meanwhile Matthew, count of Beaumont, who had a long standing quarrel with Hugh of Clermont, a noble man but simple and easy to influence, whose daughter Matthew had married, seized the whole of the castle of Luzarches—he had a half-interest in it by right of marriage—and did all that he could to fortify the tower with soldiers and weapons.

What could Hugh do but hurry to the defender of the kingdom, throw himself at his feet, and beg him with tears in his eyes to have compassion on an old man and help him, for he was grievously oppressed. "I would rather, O dearest Lord," he said, "that thou shouldst have all my land, because I hold it of thee, than that my son-in-law unworthy of the name should have it. If he robs me of it, I wish to die." Deeply moved in his heart by the sad misfortune of the man, the prince gave him his hand in friendly fashion and promised help. Thus he sent Hugh away cheered by hope, and this hope was not in vain.

Swiftly, messengers went forth from the court, who sought the count and commanded him by authority of Hugh's defender, to restore to Hugh the estate of which he had been illegally despoiled; and they summoned him to appear at the court, upon a day appointed, to defend his cause.

The count did not obey this summons, so the defender made haste to execute vengeance. He gathered a large army and went forth against the rebel. He fell upon the castle and attacked it with arms and fire. By hard fighting he stormed and took it; he then placed a strong guard in the keep, and after he had fortified it he restored it to Hugh just as he had promised to do. . . .

By these acts and others the future king advanced in virtue and actively and wisely carried on the administration of the realm as the opportunity presented itself, conquering those who rebelled and capturing or bringing under control the castles of those who revolted.

For example, Guy Troussel, son of that violent man and troubler of the kingdom, Milo of Montlhéry, came back home from an expedition to the Holy Sepulcher, weakened by the hardships of the long journey and by many trials. He had been moved by exceeding great fear of Corbaran, and had descended from the wall of Antioch and left the Army of God beleaguered within, and so he was forsaken by all. Fearing that his only daughter might in consequence be deprived of her heritage, he yielded to the desire and persuasions of Philip, the king, and of Louis, his son, who ardently longed for his castle, and gave his daughter in marriage to Philip, the king's younger son by his mistress, the countess of Anjou.

When the castle of Montlhéry fell in this manner into their hands, the King and his son rejoiced as if they had plucked a straw from their eyes or had torn down bars by which they had been confined. And, indeed, we have heard the father say to his son Louis, "Go, son Louis, keep that tower with all vigilance, whose ravages have well-nigh made us grow old, and whose wiles and criminal frauds have never let me rest in good peace and quiet."

Indeed, its unfaithfulness made the faithful faithless, the faithless most faithless. It brought together the treacherous from far and near, and no ill was done in the whole kingdom without its support. And since the territory of Paris was commanded on the river Seine by Corbeil, midway by Montlhéry, on the right by Châteaufort, there resulted such confusion and chaos in the communications between the men of Paris and of Orléans that neither could go to visit the others without the consent of these faithless men, unless they traveled with a strong guard. But the marriage of which we have spoken tore down the barrier and made travel easy between the two cities.

E. FEUDALISM AND PUBLIC ORDER

1. *The Peace and Truce of God, c. 1050.* The frequency of warfare under feudal government occasionally led men to seek some extra-governmental method of limiting hostilities or securing peace. Typical of medieval church efforts to that end is the following decree issued in the middle of the eleventh century by the clergy of Toulanges, France.[32]

I. This peace has been ratified by the bishops, abbots, counts, viscounts, and the other important God-fearing nobles in this diocese; to wit, that from this day forward no one shall do violence in a church nor in the surrounding area nor in the houses which are or may be within 30 paces of the church, nor in the church burial ground.

II. We do not include in this act the churches which are or shall be fortified as castles, those churches in which thieves or robbers have stored their booty and plunder or which offer to them a place of refuge or a place from which they set out to do wrong. Nevertheless we desire that such churches be under this protection until complaint of them shall be made to the bishop, or to the chapter. If the bishop or chapter act upon such information and lay hold of the malefactors, and if the latter refuse to give themselves up to the justice of the bishop or chapter, the malefactors and all their possessions shall not be immune, even within the church. A man who breaks into a church, or into the space within thirty paces around it except the above-mentioned evil doers, but pay a fine for sacrilege, and double this amount to the person wronged.

III. Furthermore, it is forbidden that any one attack the clergy who do not bear arms or the monks and religious persons, or do them any wrong; likewise it is forbidden to despoil or pillage the communities of canons, monks, and religious persons, the ecclesiastical lands which are under the protection of the Church, or the clergy who do not bear arms; and if any shall do such a thing, let him pay double fine. . . .

V. Let no one burn or destroy the dwellings of the peasants or the clergy who do not bear arms, the dove-cotes and the granaries. Let no man dare to kill, to beat, or to wound a serf or his wife or any of the clergy, monks or other religious persons who do not bear arms. Nor shall he seize any of these or carry them off except for misdemeanors which they may have committed; but it is not forbidden to lay hold of them in order to bring them to justice, and it is allowable to do this even before they shall have been summoned to appear. Let not the raiment of the peasants be stolen; let not their ploughs, or their hoes, or their olive-fields be burned.

VI. . . . Let any one who has broken the peace, and has not paid his fines within a fortnight, make amends to him whom he has injured by paying a double amount, which shall go to the bishop and to the count who shall have charge of the case.

VII. The bishops of whom we have spoken have solemnly confirmed the Truce of God, which has been enjoined upon all Christians, from the setting of the sun of the fourth day of the week, that is to say, Wednesday, until the rising of the sun on Monday, the second day. . . . If any one during the Truce shall violate it, let him pay a double composition and subsequently undergo the ordeal of cold water. When any one during the Truce shall kill a man, it has been ordained, with the approval of all Christians, that if the crime was committed intentionally the murderer shall be condemned to perpetual exile, but if it occurred by accident the slayer shall be banished for a period of time to be fixed by the bishops and the canons. If any one during the Truce shall attempt to seize a man or to carry him off from his castle, and does not succeed in his purpose, let him pay a fine to the bishop and to the chapter, just as if he had succeeded. It is likewise forbidden during the Truce, Advent and Lent, to build any castle or fortification, unless it was begun a fortnight before the time of the Truce. It has been ordained also that at all times disputes and suits on the subject of the Peace and Truce of God shall be settled before the bishop and his chapter, and likewise for the peace of the churches which have before been enumerated. When the bishop and the chapter have pronounced sentences to recall men to the observance of the Peace and the Truce of God, the sureties and hostages who show themselves hostile to the bishop and the chapter shall be excommunicated by the chapter and the bishop, with their protectors and partisans, as guilty of violating the Peace and the Truce of the Lord; they and their possessions shall be excluded from the Peace and the Truce of the Lord.

2. *The Treaty between the Earls of Gloucester and Hereford, 1142.* That attempts to limit hostilities were not confined to the clergy is shown by the following treaty between two powerful nobles in a period when England was distracted by dynastic war and feudal vendettas.[33]

Let all men know that this is a treaty of love between Robert, earl of Gloucester, and Miles, earl of Hereford. Robert, earl of Gloucester, has assured Miles, earl of Hereford, in good faith and by an oath that he will guard him to the full extent of his ability and without any trickery in his life, his limbs, and his earthly honor, and that he will aid him to guard his castles, his legal rights, his inheritances, and the acquisitions which he now has or afterwards will get, and also his customary rights, his legal rights, and his privileges in pasture land, fields, water, and he will aid him as well to obtain the inheritances which he does not now have. If any person wishes to harm the earl of Hereford or to take anything from him, or if the earl of Hereford wishes to go to war, Robert, earl of Gloucester, shall side with him and aid him, so far as he is able, without trickery and with loyalty. And he shall not make any peace or treaty with anyone who is injuring the earl of Hereford except with the consent and permission of the earl of Hereford; and particularly in this present war which is going on between the Empress and King Stephen, he will hold himself to the alliance with the earl of Hereford and be of one purpose with him. This same condition is to obtain in all other wars as well.

And in this treaty of love, the countess of Gloucester has asserted that she, insofar as she is able, will keep her lord well disposed toward Miles, earl of Hereford. If he should try to break the treaty, she shall hold him to it insofar as she is able. Should she not be able to, she shall have, if there be need, a legal record made of the treaty to the best of her knowledge.

To keep this treaty firmly in force, these hostages are given on the part of the earl of Gloucester because of his loyalty and oath to the earl of Hereford: on this condition, that if the earl of Gloucester should wish to get out of this treaty, they shall require their lord, the earl of Gloucester to stand up for the earl of Hereford. But if,

within forty days, he should be unwilling to stand up for the earl of Hereford, they shall deliver themselves to the earl of Hereford to do with them as he pleases, either to retain them in his service until he shall declare that they are free, or to hold them for legal ransom so that they shall not lose their lands. And should there be need, they shall make a legal record of this treaty. The hostages are Godfrey of Waltervill, Richard of Grenville, Osbern Ottdevers, Reynold of Cahagnis, Hubert Dapfer, Odo Sorus, Gilbert of Umfravil, Richard of Saint Quentin.

To confirm this treaty on the part of Miles, earl of Hereford, he has granted to Robert, earl of Gloucester, his son Mathew to be held as an hostage until the war between the Empress, King Stephen, and the Empress's son Henry shall come to an end.

Meanwhile if Miles, earl of Hereford, should wish to place any other of his sons in the place of Mathew, that son shall be accepted, provided that he is in good health.

And after the war shall be over and both Robert, earl of Gloucester, and Miles, earl of Hereford, shall have regained their lands and their legal rights, Robert, earl of Gloucester, shall restore the son of Miles, earl of Hereford, to him. Hostages and securities shall be discussed and taken from the good men of each earl for the purpose of keeping the earls themselves on good terms forever.

And in regard to this treaty of love, Roger, the son of the earl of Hereford has affirmed and sworn to the earl of Gloucester that he, insofar as he shall be able, will hold his father to it. But if the earl of Hereford should wish to get out of the treaty, Roger, his son, shall hold him to it and correct him. And if the earl of Hereford should be unwilling to stand up for the earl of Gloucester, he shall lose the service of his son until such time as he shall stand up for the earl of Gloucester.

And in regard to this treaty, these hostages are given on the part of the earl of Hereford to the earl of Gloucester because of his oath: on this condition, that if the earl of Hereford should get out of this treaty, they shall require their lord, the earl of Hereford, to stand up for the Earl of Gloucester. But if within forty days he should be unwilling to stand up for the earl of Gloucester, they shall deliver themselves to the earl of Gloucester to do with them as he pleases, either to retain them in his service until he shall declare that they are free, or to hold them for legal ransom so that they shall not lose their lands. And should there be need they shall make a legal record of this treaty in the Curia. The hostages are Robert Corbet, William Mansel, and Hugh of the Hese.

II

The Medieval Church

THERE were two spirits, two parties, or as Saint Augustine called them, two cities in the world. The City of Satan, whatever its artifices in art, war, or philosophy, was essentially corrupt and impious. . . . Lost, as it seemed, within this Babylon, or visible only in its obscure and forgotten purlieus, lived on at the same time the City of God, the society of all the souls God predestined to salvation; a city which, however humble and inconspicuous it might seem on earth, counted its myriad transfigured citizens in heaven, and had its destinies, like its foundations, in eternity. To this City of God belonged, in the first place, the patriarchs and the prophets who, throughout their plaintive and ardent lives, were faithful to what echoes still remained of a primeval revelation, and waited patiently for the greater revelation to come. . . . To the same city belonged finally all those who, believing in the reality and efficacy of Christ's mission, relied on his merits and followed his commandment of unearthly love. All history was henceforth essentially nothing but the conflict between these two cities; two moralities, one natural, the other supernatural; two philosophies, one rational, the other revealed; two beauties, one corporeal, the other spiritual; two glories, one temporal, the other eternal; two institutions, one the world, the other the Church. These, whatever their momentary alliances or compromises, were radically opposed and fundamentally alien to one another.

George Santayana

CONTENTS

[21]

QUESTIONS FOR STUDY

PART I

1. What reasons did Cyprian give for the necessity for unity in the Church?

2. Why were the sacraments "the spiritual basis of the Church's monopoly"?

3. "By means of the sacramental system the Church met the major crises in the life of the individual." Explain.

4. What disabilities, spiritual and temporal, were suffered by an excommunicated person?

5. Why was the interdict such a powerful weapon? Why might this power be resented by secular rulers?

6. What was the *primary* interest of the Church in a heretic?

7. Why was a heretic considered dangerous?

8. What modern crime does heresy most resemble?

9. To what fundamental human instinct did the veneration of the saints and the worship of relics appeal?

PART II

10. What motives impelled an individual to lead an ascetic life?

11. "St. Benedict, with true Roman practicality, converted useless hermits into useful citizens of the city of God." Explain.

12. What universal threat to a truly spiritual life for both the individual Christian and the Church were the monastic foundations attempting to meet?

13. "The founding of a monastery at Clairvaux by St. Bernard was in itself a monastic reform." Explain.

14. Why was St. Francis insistent that his followers possess no permanent abode?

15. Over what aspects of the life of medieval man did the Church exert its authority? What possibilities exist for conflicts in authority between the Church and the secular power?

In the first problem the student examined the political organization of medieval society, wherein public authority was uniquely localized into private hands. As a system of authority feudal government differed greatly from the customary modern concept of the state, and the relation of the individual to authority amid the complicated web of status and tenure was likewise unusual by modern standards.

Medieval man, moreover, was intimately tied to yet another source of authority, the medieval church. "The medieval period is chiefly characterized by the fact that thirty generations of human beings recognized, with a remarkable approach to unanimity, that the conduct of life according to the laws of God was the whole duty of man." [1] This preoccupation with religion is what earned for the Middle Ages the title, "The Age of Faith." In the Age of Faith the Roman Catholic Church was preëminent. It is difficult for most modern students to realize the importance of the Church and the extent of its influence on men's lives, but the fact is that hardly a day passed in which the Church did not in some way affect the life of the individual.

As is the case with most institutions, the Church had very simple beginnings. Its visible origin can be found in the small company of the disciples of Jesus in Palestine. Though small, this group was enthusiastically evangelical; converts were made fairly rapidly and Christian communities were established throughout the Roman Empire. At first these communities were bound only by personal connections and common enthusiasms. As the movement spread, however, the need for organization became apparent so that the purity of Christian teaching and ritual might be preserved. Leaders, later to be known as "bishops," began to assume increased authority, and doctrines and ritual became more complex and also more standardized. This institutional development took place under intermittent and ineffective persecution by the Roman government, but by the beginning of the fourth century Christianity had become too popular and too powerful for the State to suppress, and by the end of the century it had become the official religion of the Empire.

Lifted to partnership with the Roman State, the Church, during the disintegration of that state, in some respects supplanted it as the unifying force in western Europe. This process was undertaken under the leadership of the Popes—the Bishops of Rome—who, by the seventh century, had been pretty generally recognized as superior to other bishops. Under them the Church was so organized as to resemble a state itself, possessing the tangible characteristics of statehood such as administrative officials, law courts, and armed forces, and demanding allegiance from its members.

At the head of this great administrative machine was the Pope, surrounded by his court or curia, the most important members being the cardinals. Next in rank were the archbishops, who controlled a number of bishops, each one of whom governed a diocese. Each diocese was usually divided into deaneries, each presided over by an archdeacon, and each deanery was divided into parishes, whose members were under the care of the parish priest, the clergyman who came most in contact with laymen.

The clergy in this hierarchy were known as "secular" clergy, since their work was in the world (*saeculum*). Another great body of clergy were the monks, friars, and nuns, called "regular" clergy, since they lived under monastic rules (*regula*).

To support these hierarchies and to perform the multifarious functions of the Church, revenue was necessary. Perhaps the greatest source of Church wealth was its enormous land holdings, derived from the gifts of the faithful over many centuries. Another main source was "Peter's Pence," a penny paid annually by each household in Christendom. In addition to these revenues, the Church derived considerable income from fees charged for marriage, confirmation and other rites, and for cases tried in ecclesiastical courts. It has been estimated that during the 13th century the income from all these sources was greater than the incomes of all the secular rulers in Europe put together.

This extensive and wealthy organization was regarded as necessary for the spiritual mission of the Church. The documents in this problem are intended to indicate the nature of the Church as a spiritual agency and to illustrate certain prominent aspects of medieval religion as well as the relationship of the individual to this great institution.

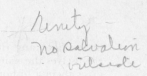

Part I.   THE CHURCH IN THE WORLD

A.   THE MONOPOLY OF SALVATION

From the very earliest times there existed the idea that there was only one true Church, and that only within that Church could the individual attain salvation. In the first selection printed below this concept is enunciated by St. Cyprian, Bishop of Carthage, who was martyred in 258. The second and third selections indicate what support the Church had in implementing this concept.

1. *Cyprian on the Unity of the Church, 251.*[2] What is more clever and crafty than that the enemy, . . . beholding his idols abandoned and his seats and temples deserted through the exceeding number of believers, should have devised a novel deceit, in order to delude the unwary by claiming the title "Christian"? He has invented heresies and schisms to subvert faith, corrupt truth, break up unity. Those whom he cannot keep in the blindness of the old way, he cheats and deceives by leading them astray on a new road. He snatches men from the Church itself, and, while they appear to themselves to have drawn near the light and to have escaped the night of the world, he plunges them anew into darkness—though they know it not—so that, standing neither with the Gospel of Christ nor with his laws and ordinances, and walking in darkness, they imagine themselves to have the light, while their adversary flatters and cajoles them; for, according to the word of the Apostle, he transforms himself "into an angel of light," and adorns his servants like servants of righteousness, declaring night for day, death for salvation, despair for a garb of hope, anti-Christ under the name of Christ, in order that, uttering plausible lies, they may by their cunning wiles make truth of none effect. . . .

. . . The Lord speaks to Peter: "I say unto thee that thou art Peter, and upon this rock I will build my church, and the gates of hell shall not prevail against it. And I will give unto thee the keys of the kingdom of heaven; and whatsoever things thou shalt bind on earth, shall be bound also in heaven; and whatsoever things thou shalt loose on earth, shall be loosed also in heaven." And a second time, after His resurrection, He says unto him: "Feed my sheep." And although to all the Apostles, after His resurrection, He gives equal power, saying: "As the Father hath sent me, even so send I you. Receive ye the Holy Spirit. Whosoever sins ye remit, they shall be remitted to him; whosoever sins ye retain, they shall be retained:" yet, in order that he might manifest unity, by his own authority he placed the origin of the same unity, as beginning from one. Certainly the rest of the Apostles were what Peter was, endued with an equal fellowship of dignity and power; but the beginning starts from unity, that the Church of Christ may be shown forth as one. . . .

This unity we ought to hold and to maintain, especially we, the Bishops, who preside over the Church, that we may prove the episcopate itself one and indivisible. Let no man deceive the brotherhood with a lie; let no man corrupt the truth of the faith by faithlessness and treachery. The episcopate is one—a joint property in which we all severally share. The Church is one, though it spreads abroad into a multitude of churches, with a fruitfulness that goes on increasing; even as the sun has many rays but one light, and a tree many branches yet one strength, deep-seated in the clinging root. And while from one source flows down many a stream, albeit innumerable waters seem diffused by the bounty of its overflow, yet is unity preserved in the source itself. Pluck a ray from the body of the sun, and its unity admits no division of the light; break a branch from a tree; broken, it will bud no more; cut a rill from the fountain-head, and the rill, cut off, dries up. So too the Church, flooded by the light of the Lord, puts forth rays through the whole world. Yet is it one light which is diffused everywhere. . . .

. . . Whoever, separating himself from the Church, is joined to an adulteress, is cut off from the promises of the Church; nor will he who leaves the Church of Christ attain to Christ's promises. He is an alien, a castaway, a foe. No longer can he have God for his father who has not the Church for his mother. If anyone was able to escape who was outside the ark of Noah, then will he escape who is outside the pale of the Church. . . .

. . . These are they who, without divine dispensation, of their own initiative set themselves over their rash comrades, appoint themselves rulers without any rite of ordination, who take to themselves the name of "bishop," though no man gives them a bishopric. These the Holy Spirit describes, in the Psalms, as "sitting in the chair of pestilence," plagues and blights of faith, deceiving with the serpent's mouth, spueing out deadly poisons from plague-bearing tongues, whose words "spread like an ulcer," whose writings pour a deadly venom into the hearts and breasts of men.

. . . Though such men be slain in confessing the Name, not even by blood is that stain washed away; inexpiable and grievous is the guilt of discord, nor is it purged by suffering. No martyr can he be who is not in the Church; never can he come to the kingdom who abandons her who is destined to reign. . . .

. . . Though they burn in flames, and lay down their lives, a prey to flames or to wild beasts, not theirs shall be the crown of faith, but the punishment of unfaithfulness; not the glorious end of religion and virtue, but the death of despair. Such a man may be slain; crowned he cannot be.

2. *An Edict of the Emperor Theodosius, 380.*[3] We desire that all those who are under the sway of our clemency shall adhere to that religion which, according to his own testimony, coming down even to our own day, the blessed apostle Peter delivered to the Romans, namely, the doctrine which the pontiff Damasus [bishop of Rome] and Peter, bishop of Alexandria, a man of apostolic sanctity, accept. According to the teachings of the Apostles and of the Gospel, we believe in one Godhead of the Father, Son, and Holy Ghost, the blessed Trinity, alike in majesty.

We ordain that the name of Catholic Christians shall apply to all those who obey this present law. All others we judge to be mad and demented; we declare them guilty of the infamy of holding heretical doctrine; their assemblies shall not receive the name of churches. They shall first suffer the wrath of God, then the punishment which in accordance with divine judgment we shall inflict.

3. *Charlemagne's Capitulary Concerning the Saxon Territory, c. 780.*[4] . . . 6. If any one deceived by the devil shall have believed, after the manner of the pagans, that any man or woman is a witch and eats men, and on this account shall have burned the person, or shall have given the person's flesh to others to eat, or shall have eaten it himself, let him be punished by a capital sentence.

7. If any one, in accordance with pagan rites, shall have caused the body of a dead man to be burned and shall have reduced his bones to ashes, let him be punished capitally.

8. If any one of the race of the Saxons hereafter concealed among them shall have wished to hide himself unbaptized, and shall have scorned to come to baptism and shall have wished to remain a pagan, let him be punished by death.

9. If any one shall have sacrificed a man to the devil, and after the manner of the pagans shall have presented him as a victim of the demons, let him be punished by death.

B. THE BASIS OF THE MONOPOLY

The principal basis of the Church's monopoly of salvation was its administration of the sacraments. According to Catholic doctrine an individual was saved or, to use the technical term, "justified" by God's grace through faith and good works. Among good works the sacraments were of the utmost importance since they were the channels through which the individual received divine grace.

1. *The Doctrine of the Sacraments.* In early times there had been considerable discussion as to the number of the sacraments but by the twelfth century it was generally agreed that there were seven. The doctrine of the sacramental system is expounded in the following selections from the bull *Exultate Deo,* issued by Pope Eugene IV in 1439.[5]

. . . There are seven sacraments under the new law: that is to say, baptism, confirmation, the eucharist, penance, extreme unction, ordination, and matrimony. These differ essentially from the sacraments of the old law; for the latter do not confer grace, but only typify that grace which can be given by the passion of Christ alone. But these our sacraments both contain grace and confer it upon all who receive them worthily.

The first five sacraments are intended to secure the spiritual perfection of every man individually; the two last are ordained for the governance and increase of the Church. For through baptism we are born again of the spirit; through confirmation we grow in grace and are strengthened in the faith; and when we have been born again and strengthened we are fed by the divine food of the mass; but if, through sin, we bring sickness upon our souls, we are made spiritually whole by penance; and by extreme unction we are healed, both spiritually and corporeally, according as our souls have need; by ordination the Church is governed and multiplied spiritually; by matrimony it is materially increased.

To effect these sacraments three things are necessary: the things (or symbols), that is, the "material"; the words, that is, the "form"; and the person of the ministrant, who administers the sacrament with the intention of carrying out what the Church effects through him. If any of these things be lacking, the sacrament is not accomplished.

Three of these sacraments—baptism, confirmation, and ordination—impress indelibly upon the soul a character, a certain spiritual sign, distinct from all others; so they are not repeated for the same person. The other four do not imprint a character upon the soul, and admit of repetition.

Holy baptism holds the first place among all the sacraments because it is the gate of spiritual life; for by it we are made members of Christ and of the body of the Church. Since through the first man death entered into the world, unless we are born again of water, and of the spirit, we cannot, so saith Truth, enter into the kingdom of heaven. The material of this sacrament is water, real and natural—it matters nothing whether it be cold or warm. Now the form is: "I baptize thee in the name of the Father, and of the Son, and of the Holy Ghost . . ."

The ministrant of this sacrament is the priest, for baptism belongs to his office. But in the case of necessity not only a priest or deacon may baptize, but a layman or a woman—nay, even a pagan or a heretic, provided he use the form of the Church and intend to do what the Church effects. The efficacy of this sacrament is the remission of all sin, original sin and actual, and of all penalties incurred through this guilt. Therefore no satisfaction for past sin should be imposed on those who are baptized; but if they die before they commit any sin, they shall straightway attain the kingdom of heaven and the sight of God.

The second sacrament is confirmation. The material is the chrism made from oil, which signifies purity of conscience, and from balsam, which signifies the odor of fair fame; and it must be blessed by the bishop. The form is: "I sign thee with the sign of the cross and confirm thee with the chrism of salvation, in the name of the Father, and of the Son, and of the Holy Ghost." The proper ministrant of this sacrament is the bishop. While a simple priest avails to perform the anointings, this one none can confer save the bishop only; for it is written of the apostles alone that by the laying on of hands they gave the Holy Ghost, and the bishops hold the office of the apostles. . . . Yet we read that sometimes, for reasonable

and urgent cause, by dispensation from the Holy See, a simple priest has been permitted to administer confirmation with a chrism prepared by a bishop.

In this sacrament the Holy Ghost is given to strengthen us, as it was given to the apostles on the day of Pentecost, that the Christian may confess boldly the name of Christ. And therefore he is confirmed upon the brow, the seat of shame, that he may never blush to confess the name of Christ and especially his cross, which is a stumbling-block to the Jews and foolishness to the Gentiles, according to the apostle. Therefore he is signed with the sign of the cross.

The third sacrament is the eucharist. The material is wheaten bread and wine of the grape, which before consecration should be mixed very sparingly with water; because, according to the testimony of the holy fathers and doctors of the Church set forth in former times in disputation, it is believed that the Lord Himself instituted this sacrament with wine mixed with water, and also because this corresponds with the accounts of our Lord's passion. . . .

Moreover the mixing of water with the wine fitly signifies the efficacy of this sacrament, namely, the union of Christian people with Christ, for water signifies "people," according to the passage in the Apocalypse which says, "many waters, many people." And Julius, second pope after the blessed Sylvester, says: "According to the provisions of the canons the cup of the Lord should be offered filled with wine mixed with water, because a people is signified by the water, and in the wine is manifested the blood of Christ. Therefore when the wine and water are mixed in the cup the people are joined to Christ, and the host of the faithful is united with him in whom they believe." . . .

The form of this sacrament is furnished by the words of the Savior when he instituted it, and the priest, speaking in the person of Christ, consummates this sacrament. By virtue of these words, the substance of the bread is turned into the body of Christ and the substance of the wine into His blood. This is accomplished in such wise that the whole Christ is altogether present under the semblance of the wine. Moreover, after the consecrated host and the consecrated wine have been divided, the whole Christ is present in any part of them. The benefit effected by this sacrament in the souls who receive it worthily is the union of man with Christ. And since through grace man is made one body with Christ and united in His members, it follows that through this sacrament grace is increased for those who partake of it worthily. Every effect of material food and drink upon the physical life, in nourishment, growth, and pleasure, is wrought by this sacrament for the spiritual life. By it we recall the beloved memory of our Savior; by it we are withheld from evil, and strengthened in good, and go forward to renewed growth in virtues and graces.

The fourth sacrament is penance. The material, as we may say, consists in the acts of penitence, which are divided into three parts. The first of these is contrition of the heart, wherein the sinner must grieve for the sins he has committed, with the resolve to commit no further sins. Second comes confession with the mouth, to which it pertains that the sinner should make confession to his priest of all the sins he holds in his memory. The third is satisfaction for sins according to the judgment of the priest, and this is made chiefly by prayer, fasting, and almsgiving. The form of this sacrament consists in the words of absolution which the priest speaks when he says, "I absolve thee," etc.; and the minister of this sacrament is the priest, who has authority to absolve either regularly or by the commission of a superior. The benefit of this sacrament is absolution from sins.

The fifth sacrament is extreme unction, and the material is oil of the olive, blessed by a bishop. This sacrament shall not be given to any except the sick who are in fear of death. They shall be anointed in the following places: the eyes on account of the sight, the ears on account of the hearing, the nostrils on account of smell, the mouth on account of taste and speech, the hands on account of touch, the feet on account of walking, and the loins as the seat of pleasure. The form of this sacrament is as follows: "Through this holy unction and His most tender compassion, the Lord grants thee forgiveness for whatever sins thou has committed by the sight,"—

and in the same way for the other members. The minister of this sacrament is a priest. The benefit is even the healing of the mind, and, so far as is expedient, of the body also. . . .

The sixth sacrament is ordination. The material for the priesthood is the cup with the wine and the paten with the bread; for the deaconate, the books of the Gospel; for the subdeaconate, an empty cup placed upon an empty paten; and in like manner, other offices are conferred by giving to the candidates those things which pertain to their secular ministrations. The form for priests is this: "Receive the power to offer sacrifice in the Church for the living and the dead, in the name of the Father, and of the Son, and of the Holy Ghost." And so for each order the proper form shall be used, as fully stated in the Roman pontifical. The regular minister of this sacrament is a bishop; the benefit, growth in grace, to the end that whosoever is ordained may be a worthy minister.

The seventh sacrament is matrimony, the type of the union of Christ and the Church, according to the apostle, who saith, "This is a great mystery; but I speak concerning Christ and the Church." The efficient cause of marriage is regularly the mutual consent uttered aloud on the spot. These advantages are to be ascribed of marriage: first, the begetting of children and their bringing up in the worship of the Lord; secondly, the fidelity that husband and wife should each maintain toward each other; thirdly, the indissoluble character of marriage, for this typifies the indissoluble union of Christ and the Church. Although for the cause of adultery separation is permissible, for no other cause may marriage be infringed, since the bond of marriage once legitimately contracted is perpetual.

C. THE EXERCISE OF THE MONOPOLY

The Church's possession of the monopoly of salvation made effective certain weapons against those who resisted its authority or broke its laws. The principal weapons were excommunication and interdict. Excommunication applied to an individual; interdict, to the whole population of a town, province, or kingdom.

1. *A Formula for the Excommunication of Petty Thieves and Similar Malefactors, 10th Century.*[6] By the authority of God the omnipotent Father, and of the Son, and of the Holy Ghost, and of the sacred canons, and of the holy and unsullied Virgin Mary the Mother of God, and of all the heavenly Virtues, Angels, Archangels, Thrones, Dominations, Powers, Cherubim and Seraphim, and of the holy Patriarchs, Prophets, and all the Apostles and Evangelists, and of the holy Innocents who alone are worthy in the sight of the Lamb to sing the new song, and of the

holy martyrs, and the holy confessors and the holy virgins and of all the saints and elect of God, we excommunicate and anathematize this thief, or this malefactor, and we expel him from the holy church of God, that he may be delivered over to eternal torment with Dathan and Abiram and with those who cried to the Lord God, "Away from us, we wish not to know Thy Ways." And as fire is quenched with water, so may his light be quenched for ever and ever, unless he repent and render full satisfaction. Amen. Be he accursed of God the Father, who created man;

accursed of God the Son, who suffered for man; accursed of the Holy Ghost which cometh in baptism; accursed of the Holy Cross which the triumphant Christ ascended for our salvation; accursed of the Holy Virgin Mary, the mother of God; accursed of St. Michael, the receiver of blessed souls; accursed of the angels and archangels, the princes and powers, and all the hosts of heaven; accursed of the worthy legion of Prophets and Patriarchs; accursed of St. John, the forerunner and baptizer of Christ; accursed of St. Peter and St. Paul and St. Andrew, and all the apostles of Christ, and the other disciples, and the Four Evangelists who converted the world; accursed of the wonder-working band of martyrs and confessors whose good works have been pleasing to God; accursed of all the holy virgins who have shunned the world for the love of Christ; accursed of all the Saints, beloved of God, from the beginning even unto the end of the world; accursed of heaven and of earth and of all that is holy therein. Let him be accursed wherever he be, whether at home or abroad, in the road or in the path, or in the wood, or in the water, or in the church. Let him be accursed living and dying, eating, drinking, lying, working, idling . . . and bleeding. Let him be accursed in all the forces of his body. Let him be accursed outside and inside; accursed in his hair and accursed in his brain; accursed in the crown of his head, in his temples, in his forehead, in his ears, in his brows, in his eyes, in his cheeks, in his jaws, in his nostrils, in his front teeth, in his back teeth, in his lips, in his throat, in his shoulders, in his upper arms, in his lower arms, in his hands, in his fingers, in his breast, in his heart, in his stomach and liver, in his kidneys, in his loins, in his hips . . . in his thighs, in his knees, in his shins, in his feet, in his toes, and in his nails. Let him be accursed in every joint of his body. Let there be no health in him, from the crown of his head to the sole of his foot. May Christ, the Son of the Living God, curse him throughout His Kingdom, and may Heaven with all its Virtues rise up against him to his damnation, unless he repents and renders due satisfaction. Amen. So be it. So be it. Amen.

2. Civil Disabilities Incurred by Excommunication.

The following legal opinions are taken from two thirteenth-century English lawbooks: [7]

(*Of Plaintiffs*) . . . Plaintiffs are those who seek their own right or another's by plaints. All save those forbidden by law can bring accusations and plaints. The following cannot accuse: lepers, idiots without guardians, children under age without guardians, criminals, outlaws, exiles, banished men . . . serfs without their owners . . . excommunicated persons . . .

(*Of Contracts*) . . . Anyone may make a contract who is not forbidden to do so by law. Law forbids one to make a contract with an enemy of the heavenly or the earthly king, or with those who are in mortal sin, or with those who are not of the Christian faith, or with outlaws . . . or with confessed felons or excommunicates . . . or with the deaf or the dumb, or with born fools, or with lunatics. . . .

(*Of Exceptions*) . . . The tenant may still aid himself by exceptions against the person of the plaintiff as that he is excommunicated. For a person excommunicate is one that is out of communion on account of a leprosy of the soul, as a leper is for disease of the body; and so long as a person is excommunicated, he ought not to commune with anyone nor anyone with him, neither is he entitled to be answered in any action as shall be noticed in the plea of right.

3. An Interdict on France, 1200.

Pope Innocent III imposed this interdict when Philip Augustus, king of France, refused to submit his case for the annulment of his marriage to the judgment of the Church. The interdict was in force from January until September, when the king was forced to abandon his plan for the annulment.[8]

Let all the churches be closed; let no one be admitted to them except to baptize infants; let them not be otherwise opened except for the purpose of lighting the lamps, or when the priest shall come for the Eucharist and holy water for the use of the sick. We permit mass to be celebrated once a week on Friday early in the morning to consecrate the Host for the use of the sick, but only one clerk is to be admitted to assist the priest. Let the clergy preach on Sunday in the vestibules of the churches, and in place of the mass let them disseminate the word of God. Let them recite the canonical hours outside the churches, where the people do not hear them; if they recite an epistle or a gospel let them beware lest the laity hear them; and let them not permit the dead to be interred, nor their bodies to be placed unburied in the cemeteries. Let them, moreover, say to the laity that they sin and transgress grievously by burying bodies in the earth, even in unconsecrated ground, for in so doing they arrogate to themselves an office pertaining to others. Let them forbid their parishioners to enter churches that may be open in the king's territory and let them not bless the wallets of pilgrims except outside the churches. Let them not celebrate the offices in Passion week, but refrain even till Easter day, and then let them celebrate in private, no one being admitted except the assisting priest, as above directed; let no one communicate even at Easter, except he be sick and in danger of death. During the same week, or on Palm Sunday, let them announce to their parishioners that they may assemble on Easter morning before the church and there have permission to eat flesh and consecrated bread. Women are expressly forbidden to be admitted into the churches for purification, but are to be warned to gather their neighbors together on the day of purification and pray outside the church, nor may the women who are to be purified enter even to raise their children to the sacred font of baptism until they are admitted by the priest after the expiration of the interdict. Let the priest confess all who desire it in the portico of the church;

if the church have no portico we direct that in bad or rainy weather, and not otherwise, the nearest door of the church may be opened and confessions heard on its threshold (all being excluded except the one who is to confess) so that the priest and the penitent can be heard by those who are outside the church. If, however, the weather be fair, let the confession be heard in front of the closed doors. Let no vessels of holy water be placed outside of the church, nor shall the priests carry them anywhere, for all the sacraments of the church beyond these two which were reserved are absolutely prohibited. Extreme unction, which is a holy sacrament, may not be given.

D. THE OPPOSITION TO THE MONOPOLY: HERESY

There were always those who ventured to deny the monopoly of the Church and questioned certain of its teachings. It must be remembered that criticism of the clergy or of the administration of the Church was not heresy, although it might lead an individual into heresy. Only if one refused to accept an established doctrine of the Church was one technically guilty of heresy.

1. *The Albigensian Heretics.* This description of the Albigenses is taken from the *Inquisitor's Guide,* written by a Dominican, Bernard Gui, in 1323. The Albigenses (so styled because their heresy originated in the town of Albi, in southern France) were often called *Cathari,* a word meaning "the Pure" or "the Puritans." [9]

It would take too long to describe in detail the manner in which these . . . heretics preach, and teach their followers, but it must be briefly considered here.

In the first place they usually say of themselves that they are good Christians, who do not swear, or lie, or speak evil of others; that they do not kill any man or animal nor any thing having the breath of life, and that they hold the faith of the Lord Jesus Christ and His Gospel, as Christ and His apostles taught. They assert that they occupy the place of the apostles, and that on account of the above mentioned things those of the Roman Church, namely, the prelates, clerks and monks, persecute them, especially the Inquisitors of Heresy, and call them heretics, although they are good men and good Christians, and that they are persecuted just as Christ and His apostles were by the Pharisees.

They moreover talk to the laity of the evil lives of clerks and prelates of the Roman Church, pointing out, and setting forth their pride, cupidity, avarice and uncleanness of life and such other evils as they know. They invoke with their own interpretation, and according to their abilities, the authority of the Gospels and the Epistles

against the condition of the prelates, churchmen and monks, whom they call Pharisees and false prophets, who say, but do not.

Then they attack and vituperate, one after the other, all the sacraments of the Church, especially the sacrament of the Eucharist, saying that it cannot contain the body of Christ, for had this been as great as the largest mountain, Christians would have consumed it entirely before this. They assert that the host comes from straw, that it passes through the tails of horses, to wit, when the flour is cleaned by a sieve [of horse hair]. That moreover it passes through the body and comes to a vile end which, they say, could not happen if God were in it. Of baptism, they assert that water is material and corruptible, and is therefore the creation of the Evil Power and cannot sanctify the soul, but that the churchmen sell this water out of avarice, just as they sell earth for the burial of the dead, and oil to the sick when they anoint them, and as they sell the confession of sins as made to the priests. Hence, they claim that confession made to the priests of the Roman Church is useless, and that since the priests may be sinners, they cannot loose nor bind, and being unclean themselves, cannot make another clean.

They assert, moreover, that the Cross of Christ should not be adored or venerated, because, as they urge, no one would venerate or adore the gallows upon which a father, relative or friend had been hung. They urge farther that they who adore the cross ought for similar reasons to worship all thorns and lances because, as Christ's body was on the cross during the passion, so was the crown of thorns on His head, and the soldier's lance in His side. They proclaim many other scandalous things in regard to the sacraments. They, moreover, read from the Gospels and the Epistles in the vulgar tongue, applying and expounding them in their favor and against the condition of the Roman Church in a manner which it would take too long to describe in detail, but all that relates to this subject may be read more fully in the books they have written and infected, and may be learned from the confessions of such of their followers as have been converted.

2. *The Popular Attitude towards Heresy.* The following account is taken from *The Other Life,* written by Luke of Tuy, a thirteenth-century Spanish bishop.[10]

From the lips of the same brother Elias, a venerable man, I learned that when certain heretics were scattering the virulent seeds of error in parts of Burgundy, both the Preaching Friars and the Minorites drew the two-edged sword of God's word against these same heretics, opposing them valiantly until they were finally taken by the magistrate of the district. He sent them to the fiery stake as they merited, in order that these workers of iniquity should perish with their wickedness as a wholesome lesson to others. Quantities of wood having been supplied in plenty to feed the flames, suddenly a toad of wonderful size which is sometimes called *crapaldus,* appeared, and without being driven betook itself of its own accord into the midst of the flames. One of the heretics, who was reported to be their bishop, had fallen on his back in the fire. The toad took his place on this man's face and in the sight of all, ate out the heretic's tongue. By the next day his whole body except his bones, had been turned into disgusting toads, which could not be counted for their great number.

The inhabitants, seeing the miracle, glorified God and praised Him in His servants, the preaching monks, because the Lord had, in His mercy, delivered them from the horror of such pollution. God omnipotent surely wished to show through the most unseemly and filthiest of animals, how foul and infamous are the teachings of heretics, so that all might thereafter carefully shun the heretic, as they would the poisonous toad. Just as among four-footed creatures the toad is held the foulest, so the teachings of the heretic are more debased and filthy than those of any other religious sect. The blindness of heresy justifies the perfidy of the Jews. Its pollution makes the madness of the Mohammedans a pure thing in contrast. The licentiousness of the heretics would leave Sodom and Gomorrah stainless. What is held most enormous in crime, becomes most holy, when compared with the shame and ignominy of

heresy. Thus, Dear Christian, flee this unspeakable evil, in comparison with which all other crimes are as trifles.

3. *The Church's Attitude towards Heresy.* An authoritative statement of the Church's attitude towards heresy is found in the *Summa Theologica* written between 1265 and 1272 by St. Thomas Aquinas.[11]

With regard to heretics two points must be observed: one, on their own side, the other, on the side of the Church. On their own side there is the sin, whereby they deserve not only to be separated from the Church by excommunication, but also to be severed from the world by death. For it is a much graver matter to corrupt the faith which quickens the soul, than to forge money, which supports temporal life. Wherefore if forgers of money and other evil-doers are forthwith condemned to death by the secular authorities, much more reason is there for heretics, as soon as they are convicted of heresy, to be not only excommunicated but even put to death.

On the part of the Church, however, there is mercy which looks to the conversion of the wanderer, wherefore she condemns not at once, but "after the first and second admonition," as the Apostle directs: after that, if he is yet stubborn, the Church no longer hoping for his conversion, looks to the salvation of others, by excommunicating him and separating him from the Church, and furthermore delivers him to the secular tribunal to be exterminated thereby from the world by death. For Jerome commenting on Gal. v. 9, "A little leaven," says: "Cut off the decayed flesh, expel the mangy sheep from the fold, lest the whole house, the whole paste, and the whole body, the whole flock, burn, perish, rot, die. Arius was but one spark in Alexandria, but as that spark was not at once put out, the whole earth was laid waste by its flame." [Here St. Thomas refers to a Christian heresy prevalent in the fourth century.]

I answer that, In obedience to Our Lord's institution, the Church extends her charity to all, not only to friends, but also to foes who persecute her, according to Matth. v. 44: "Love your enemies; do good to them that hate you." Now it is part of charity that we should both wish and work our neighbor's good. Again, good is twofold; one is spiritual, namely the health of the soul, which good is chiefly the object of charity, since it is this chiefly that we should wish for one another. Consequently, from this point of view, heretics who return after falling no matter how often, are admitted by the Church to Penance whereby the way of salvation is opened to them.

The other good is that which charity considers secondarily, viz. temporal good, such as the life of the body, worldly possessions, good repute, ecclesiastical or secular dignity, for we are not bound by charity to wish others this good, except in relation to the eternal salvation of them and of others. Hence if the presence of one of these goods in one individual might be an obstacle to eternal salvation in many, we are not bound out of charity to wish such a good to that person, rather should we desire him to be without it, both because eternal salvation takes precedence of temporal good, and because the good of the many is to be preferred to the good of one. Now if heretics were always received on their return, in order to save their lives and other temporal goods, this might be prejudicial to the salvation of others, both because they would infect others if they relapsed again, and because, if they escaped without punishment, others would feel more assured in lapsing into heresy. For it is written (Eccles. viii, 11) : "For because sentence is not speedily pronounced against the evil, the children of men commit evils without any fear."

For this reason the Church not only admits to Penance those who return from heresy for the first time, but also safeguards their lives, and sometimes by dispensation, restores them to the ecclesiastical dignities which they may have had before, should their conversion appear to be sincere: we read of this as having frequently been done for the good of peace. But when they fall again, after having been received, this seems to prove them to be inconstant in faith, wherefore when they return again, they are admitted to Penance, but are not delivered from the pain of death.

4. *The State's Attitude towards Heresy.* The following selections are taken from the Constitution of the Kingdom of Sicily, promulgated in 1231 by the Emperor Frederick II.[12]

The heretics endeavor to rend the seamless garment of our Lord, and in accordance with their vicious name, which means division, they would destroy the unity of that same indivisible faith. They would withdraw the sheep from Peter's guardianship, to which they were entrusted by the Good Shepherd. They are ravening wolves within, but feign a love for the flock, until they shall have crept into the Lord's fold. They are bad angels, sons of perversity, appointed by the father of lies and deception to mislead the simple minded. They are serpents who deceive the doves. Like serpents they creep stealthily abroad; with honeyed sweetness they vomit forth their virus. While they pretend to offer life-giving food, they strike with their tail, and prepare a deadly draught, as with some dire poison. These sects do not assume the old names, lest they should be recognized, but, what is perhaps more heinous, not content like the Arians, who took their name from Arius, or

the Nestorians from Nestorius, and others of the same class, they must imitate the example of the martyrs, who suffered death for the catholic faith. They call themselves Patarins, as if they, too, were sufferers. These same wretched Patarins, who refuse to accept the holy belief in the eternal Trinity, under a single combination of wickedness offer a triple offense. They offend God, their neighbor and themselves,—God, since they refuse to place their faith in Him or recognize His Son; their fellow-men they deceive, for they offer them the seductions of a perverse heresy under the form of spiritual nurture. They rage even more fiercely against themselves for, prodigal of life and careless of death, in addition to the sacrifice of their souls, they involve their bodies in the toils of a horrible end, which they might avoid by acknowledging the truth and adhering to the true faith. What is worst of all, the survivors are not terrified by such examples.

Against these who offend alike against God, themselves and their fellow-men, we cannot restrain ourselves and must draw forth the sword of merited retribution. We pursue them the more closely, inasmuch as they are known, to the obvious prejudice of the Christian faith, to extend the crimes of their superstition toward the Roman Church, which is regarded as the head of all other churches. Thus from the confines of Italy, especially from parts of Lombardy, where we are convinced that their wickedness is widespread, we now find rivulets of their perfidy reaching even to our kingdom of Sicily. Feeling this most acutely, we decree, in the first place, that the crime of heresy and of reprehensible teaching of whatever kind, by whatever name its adherents may be known, shall, as provided by the older laws, be included among the recognized crimes. (For, should not what is recognized to be an offense against the Divine Majesty, be judged more terrible than the crime of lese-majesty directed against ourself, although in the eyes of the law one is not graver than the other?)

As the crime of treason deprives the guilty of life and property, and even blackens the memory of the dead, so in the aforesaid crimes of which the Patarins are guilty, we wish the same rules to be observed in all respects. And in order that the wickedness of those who walk in darkness, since they do not follow God, should be thoroughly exterminated, we wish those who practice this class of crimes should, like other malefactors, be diligently sought for and hunted out by our officers. If such be discovered, even if there be only the slightest suspicion of their guilt, we command that they shall be examined by churchmen and prelates. If they shall be discovered by these to have deviated from the Catholic faith, even in a single respect, and if, when admonished by such churchmen, in their function of pastors, they refuse, by leaving the wiles of the Devil, to recognize the God of light, and stubbornly adhere to their error, we command, by this our present edict, that such condemned Patarins shall suffer the death they court; that, condemned to the sentence of the flames, they shall be burned alive in the sight of the people. Nor are we loath to satisfy their cravings in this respect, for they only suffer the penalty of their crime and reap no farther gain. No one shall dare to intercede with us for any such, and should any one presume to do this, we shall properly direct the darts of our indignation against him, too . . .

All who shall receive, trust, aid or abet the Patarins, in any way, seeking to shield others from a penalty which they rashly do not fear for themselves, shall be deprived of all their goods and banished forever. Their sons shall thereafter be excluded from all honors whatsoever and shall be branded with perpetual disgrace. They shall not be permitted to act as witnesses in any case, but shall be rejected as infamous. But if any one of the sons of such harborers or favour shall point out a Patarin, whose guilt shall be thus proven, he shall, by the imperial clemency, be freed from the opprobrium and restored to his full rights in view of the good faith which he has shown.

E.   Popular Religion: the Age of Miracles

To the people of the Middle Ages their world was a world filled with supernatural forces, and one in which divine or satanic intervention was to be expected. Divine intervention might be induced and satanic intervention frustrated by an appeal to a saint or by the use of sacred relics. The selections which follow illustrate this aspect of medieval religion.

1. *The Power of the Virgin Mary.* The following selection is taken from a *Liber Exemplorum,* or book of illustrations for sermons, written about 1275.[13]

One more instance of the loving kindness of the glorious Virgin I found in an ancient sermon, and certainly it should not be despised. A certain poor woman loved the Blessed Virgin, decking her image with roses and lilies and such ornaments as she could find. It befell that her son was taken and hanged. The woman, in the bitterness of her soul, went to the image of the Blessed Virgin and besought her to restore her son; and, seeing that she recovered not her son as soon as she wished, she said: "Is this then the price of service to thee, that thou succorest me not in my need?" Then, as though maddened by the excess of her grief, she said: "If thou restore me not my son, I will take away thy Son." And, as she reached out her hand impetuously to bear away the image of the little Babe, behold! her son stood by her and seized her cloak and cried, "What dost thou, Mother? Hast thou lost thy senses? Behold, the Mother of God hath restored me to thee." So the mother rejoiced to recover her son.

2. *The Choice of a Patron Saint.* The following selection is taken from the *Dialogus Miraculorum,* written between 1220 and 1235 by Caesarius, Prior of the monastery of Heisterbach.[14]

It is a very common custom among the matrons of our province to choose an Apostle for their very own by the following lottery: the names of the twelve Apostles are written each on twelve tapers,

which are blessed by the priest and laid on the altar at the same moment. Then the woman comes and draws a taper; and whatever name that taper shall chance to bear, to that Apostle she renders special honor and service. A certain matron, having thus drawn St. Andrew, and being displeased to have drawn him, laid the taper back on the altar and would have drawn another; but the same came to her hand again. Why should I make a long story? At length she drew one that pleased her, to whom she paid faithful devotion all the days of her life; nevertheless, when she came to her last end and was at the point of death, she saw not him but the Blessed Andrew standing at her bedside. "Lo!" he said, "I am that despised Andrew!" from which we can gather that sometimes saints thrust themselves even of their own accord into men's devotion. . . . Another matron, desiring to have a special Apostle, proceeded after the same fashion; but, having drawn the Blessed Jude (as I think), she cast that taper, apostolic name and all, behind the altar-chest; for she would have had one of the more famous Apostles, such as St. John the Evangelist or the Blessed James. The other, therefore, came to her in a dream by night and rebuked her sternly, complaining that she had displeased him and cast him shamefully behind the chest; nor was he appeased even so until he had added stripes to words, for she lay palsy-stricken on her bed for a whole year long. . . .

3. *A Busy Saint.* The following account is taken from an English monastic chronicle written at the end of the fourteenth century.[15]

For few can be found in this age of ours who deserve to taste of the sweetness of divine revelation; not that God is niggardly, but that our spiritual palate is infected: howbeit a certain holy virgin, long consecrated to the life of a recluse, had in this year a revelation which I must not pass over in silence. . . . [She was caught up to heaven on the Feast of St. Francis] . . . and when she inquired the names [of the saints whom she saw there], and asked wherefore St. Francis was nowhere to be seen, then St. John the Baptist made answer, "He, on this his own holy-day, must needs intercede before God for many that call on him as a new-made saint; wherefore he could not come on this occasion."

4. *An Inventory of Relics.* There follows a list of relics owned by a church in France in 1346.[16]

A piece of the Lord's sign of the Cross, of His lance, and His column. Of the manna which rained from Heaven. Of the stone whereon Christ's blood was spilt. Item, another little cross of silvered wood, containing pieces of the Lord's sepulcher and of St. Margaret's veil. Of the Lord's cradle in a certain copper reliquary.

Given by the Lord Dean [Bocheux]. In a certain crystal vessel, portions of the stone tables whereon God wrote the law for Moses with His finger. Item, in the same vessel, of the stone whereupon St. James crossed the sea. Item, of the Lord's winding-sheet. Item, of Aaron's rod, of the altar whereupon St. Peter sang mass, of St. Boniface; and all this in a glass tube.

Of St. Mary. Of the hairs of St. Mary; item, of her robe; item, a shallow ivory box without any ornament save only a knob of copper, which box containeth some of the flower which the Blessed Virgin held before her Son, and of the window through which the Angel Gabriel entered when he saluted her. Item, of the Blessed Mary's oil from Sardinia. Item, in the same place, of the Blessed Mary's sepulcher in [the vale of] Jehoshaphat, in a certain leaden case enclosed in a little ivory casket. Item, of the wax which was miraculously given to the play-actors, in a certain box with a glass cover.

Of the Martyrs. Of the tunic of St. Thomas of Canterbury, Archbishop and Martyr; of his hair shirt, of his dust, of his hairs, of his cowl, of his seat; again of his hairs. Again of his cowl and of the shavings of his crown. Again of his hairs, of the blanket that covered him, of his woolen shirt; again of the aforesaid St. Thomas's hairshirt, in a certain pouch contained in an ivory box. Item, of the blood of the same St. Thomas of Canterbury. Item, the staff of the aforesaid St. Thomas the Martyr, Archbishop of Canterbury.

5. *A Precious Windfall.* The following selection is taken from the contemporary *Life of St. William.* St. William (d. 1203) was a canon of Ste. Geneviève in Paris, and later Abbot of Eskilsoe in Sweden.[17]

While Abbot William was yet in this corruptible body, weighed down with old age, two teeth were torn from his head, which he committed to Brother Saxo, saying: "Keep these two teeth in thy charge, and see that thou lose them not." He said as the Abbot had required him, pondering in his own mind wherefore this command had been laid upon him. When however the Lord had taken him away from before our face, then his surviving disciples, in memory of so holy a Father, besought that somewhat might be given to them of his possessions or of his garments; among whom one Brice, the Sacrist, complained that naught had fallen to his share saving a fur cap which the Saint had been wont to wear on his head. To which complaints this Brother made answer to whom these teeth had been entrusted: "I will give thee no small gift—nay, a mighty one, a pearl of price, no less than a tooth of our Father who in his lifetime loved thee not only with a special love, but thee above all others." With these words he delivered to him the tooth; and the Sacrist, rendering manifold thanks for this grace conferred upon him, took the tooth and held it in that dear veneration which it deserved. Oh what gifts did God afterwards confer upon mortal men through that tooth!—gifts which, if they were written down, man's weak intellect would never be content to believe!

Part II.

MONASTICISM

A.

THE ASCETIC IMPULSE

Asceticism has been a part of many religions, and the asceticism preached and practiced by Christians in the Middle Ages was an especially important element in medieval civilization. One of the most eloquent ascetics was St. Peter Damian (1007–1072), prior of the Hermits of Fonte-Avellana, an Italian order renowned for the austerity of its discipline. Against his will Damian became a Prince of the Church when, in 1058, the Pope made him Cardinal-Bishop of Ostia, and as such he was deeply involved in the ecclesiastical and imperial politics of the time. His true vocation, however, was not "in the world," and the following passages from his *Perfection of the Monastic Life* illustrate his devotion to the ascetic ideal.[18]

St. Peter Damian on the Ascetic Ideal. The wise man, bent on safeguarding his salvation, watches always to destroy his vices; he girds his loins— and his belly—with the girdle of perfect mortification. Truly that takes place when the itching palate is suppressed, when the pert tongue is held in silence, the ear is shut off from evil-speaking and the eye from unpermitted sights; when the hand is held from cruel striking, and the foot from vainly roving; when the heart is withstood, that it may not envy another's felicity, nor through avarice covet what is not its own, nor through anger sever itself from fraternal love, nor vaunt itself arrogantly above its fellows, nor yield to the ticklings of lust, nor immoderately sink itself in grief or abandon itself wantonly to joy. Since, then, the human mind has not the power to remain entirely empty, and unoccupied with the love of something, it is girt around with a wall of the virtues.

In this way, then, our mind begins to be at rest in its Author and to taste the sweetness of that intimacy. At once it rejects whatever it deems contrary to the divine law, shrinks from what does not agree with the rule of supernal rightcousness.

Hence true mortification is born; hence it comes that man bearing the Cross of his Redeemer seems dead to the world. No longer he delights in silly fables, nor is content to waste his time with idle talk. But he is free for psalms and hymns and spiritual songs; he seeks seclusion, he longs for a hiding-place; he regards the cloister as a shop for talkers, a public forum, and rejoices in nooks and pries out corners; and that he may the more freely attend to the contemplation of his Creator, so far as he may he declines colloquy with men. . . .

It further behooves each brother who with his whole heart has abandoned the world, to unlearn and forget forever whatever is injurious. He should not be disputatious as to cookery, nor clever in the petty matters of the town; nor an adept in rhetoric's jinglings, or in jokes or word play. He should love fasts and cherish penury; he should flee the sight of man, restrain himself under the censorship of silence, withdraw from affairs, keep his mouth from idle talk, and seek the hiding-place of his soul, and in such hiding be on fire to see the face of his Creator. Let him pant for tears, and implore God for them by daily prayer.

B. THE BENEDICTINE REFORMATION

Early Christian asceticism was essentially unorganized and a matter for the individuals concerned. Soon, however, individual ascetics, or hermits, tended to gather together in communities. Thus the hermits became monks and their communities monasteries. These ascetic societies, like all societies, needed rules to govern their communal lives, and perhaps the most famous rule or code was that of St. Benedict. In 529 St. Benedict founded and became the first abbot of the celebrated monastery of Monte Cassino in Italy. Here he worked out his Rule, which was adopted by hundreds of other monasteries and had the effect of reforming the monastic institution in the western Church.[19]

The Rule of St. Benedict

What the Abbot should be like. An abbot who is worthy to preside over a monastery ought always to remember what he is called, and carry out with his deeds the name of a Superior. For he is believed to be Christ's representative, since he is called by His name, the apostle saying: "Ye have received the spirit of adoption of sons, whereby we call Abba, Father." And so the abbot should not—grant that he may not—teach, or decree, or order, any thing apart from the precept of the Lord; but his order or teaching should be sprinkled with the ferment of divine justice in the

minds of his disciples. . . . The abbot ought always to remember what he is, to remember what he is called, and to know that from him to whom more is committed, the more is demanded. And let him know what a difficult and arduous thing he has undertaken,—to rule the souls and aid the morals of many. And in one case indeed with blandishments, in another with rebukes, in another with persuasion—according to the quality or intelligence of each one,—he shall so conform and adapt himself to all, that not only shall he not suffer detriment to come to the flock committed to him, but shall rejoice in the increase of a good flock. Above all things, let him not, dissimulating or undervaluing the safety of the souls committed to him, give more heed to transitory and earthly and passing things: but let him always reflect that he has undertaken to rule souls for which he is to render account . . .

About calling in the brethren to take council. As often as anything especial is to be done in the monastery, the abbot shall call together the whole congregation, and shall himself explain the question at issue. And, having heard the advice of the brethren, he shall think it over by himself, and shall do what he considers most advantageous. And for this reason, moreover, we have said that all ought to be called to take counsel: because often it is to a younger person that God reveals what is best. The brethren, moreover, with all subjection of humility, ought so to give their advice, that they do not presume boldly to defend what seems good to them; but it should rather depend on the judgment of the abbot; so that whatever he decides to be the more salutary, they should all agree to it. But even as it behooves the disciples to obey the master, so it is fitting that he should providently and justly arrange all matters. In all things, indeed, let all follow the Rule as their guide; and let no one rashly deviate from it. Let no one in the monastery follow the inclination of his own heart; and let no one boldly presume to dispute with his abbot, within or without the monastery. But, if he should so presume, let him be subject to the discipline of the Rule. The abbot, on the other hand, shall do all things fearing the Lord and observing the Rule; knowing that he, without a doubt, shall have to render account to God as to a most impartial judge, for all his decisions. But if any lesser matters for the good of the monastery are to be decided upon, he shall employ the counsel of the elder members alone, since it is written: "Do all things with counsel, and after it is done thou wilt not repent." . . .

Concerning obedience. The first grade of humility is obedience without delay. This becomes those who, on account of the holy service which they have professed, or on account of the fear of hell or the glory of eternal life consider nothing dearer to them than Christ: so that, so soon as anything is commanded by their superior, they may not know how to suffer delay in doing it, even as if it were a divine command. . . . Therefore let all such, straightway leaving their own affairs and giving up their own will, with unoccupied hands and leaving incomplete what they were doing—the foot of obedience being foremost—follow with their deeds the voice of him who orders. . . . Thus, not living according to their own judgment nor obeying their own desires and pleasures, but walking under another's judgment and command, passing their time in

monasteries, let them desire an abbot to rule over them. Without doubt all such live up to that precept of the Lord in which he says: "I am not come to do my own will but the will of Him that sent me. . . ."

Concerning silence. Let us do as the prophet says: "I said, I will take heed to my ways that I sin not with my tongue, I have kept my mouth with a bridle; I was dumb with silence, I held my peace even from good; and my sorrow was stirred." Here the prophet shows that if one ought at times, for the sake of silence, to refrain from good sayings; how much more, as a punishment for sin, ought one to cease from evil words. . . . And therefore, if anything is to be asked of the prior, let it be asked with all humility and subjection of reverence; lest one seem to speak more than is fitting. Scurrilities, however, or idle words and those exciting laughter, we condemn in all places with a lasting prohibition: nor do we permit a disciple to open his mouth for such sayings.

Concerning humility . . . The sixth grade of humility is that a monk be contented with all lowliness or extremity, and consider himself, with regard to everything which is enjoined on him, as a poor and unworthy workman; saying to himself with the prophet: "I was reduced to nothing and was ignorant; I was made as the cattle before thee, and I am always with thee." The seventh grade of humility is, not only that he, with his tongue, pronounce himself viler and more worthless than all; but that he also believe it in the innermost workings of his heart; humbling himself and saying with the prophet, etc. . . . The eighth degree of humility is that a monk do nothing except what the common rule of the monastery, or the example of his elders, urges him to do. The ninth degree of humility is that a monk restrain his tongue from speaking; and, keeping silence, do not speak until he is spoken to. The tenth grade of humility is that he be not ready, and easily inclined, to laugh . . . The eleventh grade of humility is that a monk, when he speaks, speak slowly and without laughter, humbly with gravity, using few and reasonable words; and that he be not loud of voice . . . The twelfth grade of humility is that a monk, shall not only with his heart but also with his body, always show humility to all who see him: that is, when at work, in the oratory, in the monastery, in the garden, on the road, in the fields, and everywhere, sitting or walking or standing, let him always be with head inclined, his looks fixed upon the ground; remembering every hour that he is guilty of his sins. Let him think that he is already being presented before the tremendous judgment of God, saying always to himself in his heart what that publican of the Gospel, fixing his eyes on the earth, said: "Lord I am not worthy,

I a sinner, so much as to lift up mine eyes unto heaven." . . .

Whether the monks should have anything of their own. More than any thing else is this special vice to be cut off root and branch from the monastery, that one should presume to give or receive anything without the order of the abbot, or should have anything of his own. He should have absolutely not anything: neither a book, nor tablets, nor a pen—nothing at all. For indeed it is not allowed to the monks to have their own bodies or wills in their own power. But all things necessary they must expect from the Father of the monastery; nor is it allowable to have anything which the abbot did not give or permit. All things shall be common to all, as it is written: "Let not any man presume or call anything his own." But if any one shall have been discovered delighting in this most evil vice: being warned once and again, if he do not amend, let him be subjected to punishment . . .

We believe, moreover, that for the daily refection of the sixth as well as of the ninth hour, two cooked dishes, on account of the infirmities of the different ones, are enough for all tables: so that whoever, perchance, can not eat of one may partake of the other. Therefore let two cooked dishes suffice for all the brothers: and, if it is possible to obtain apples or growing vegetables, a third may be added. One full pound of bread shall suffice for a day, whether there be one refection, or a breakfast and a supper. But if they are going to have supper, the third part of that same pound shall be reserved by the cellarer, to be given back to those who are about to sup. But if, perchance, some greater labor shall have been performed, it shall be in the will and the power of the abbot, if it is expedient, to increase anything; surfeiting above all things being guarded against, so that indigestion may never seize a monk: for nothing is so contrary to every Christian as surfeiting, as our Lord says: "Take heed to yourselves, lest your hearts be overcharged with surfeiting." But to younger boys the same quantity shall not be served, but less than that to the older ones; moderation being observed in all things. But the eating of the flesh of quadrupeds shall be abstained from altogether by every one, excepting alone the weak and the sick.

Concerning the amount of drink. Each one has his own gift from God, the one in this way, the other in that. Therefore it is with some hesitation that the amount of daily sustenance for others is fixed by us. Nevertheless, in view of the weakness of the infirm we believe that a hemina [not quite half a liter] of wine a day is enough for each one. Those moreover to whom God gives the ability of bearing abstinence shall know that they will have their own reward. But the prior shall judge if either the needs of the place, or labor or the heat of summer, requires more; considering in all things lest satiety or drunkenness creep in . . .

Concerning the daily manual labor. Idleness is the enemy of the soul. And therefore, at fixed times, the brothers ought to be occupied in manual labor; and again, at fixed times, in sacred reading. Therefore we believe that according to this disposition, both seasons ought to be arranged; so that, from Easter until the Calends of October, going out early, from the first until the fourth hour they shall do what labor may be necessary. Moreover, from the fourth hour until about the sixth, they shall be free for reading. After the meal of the sixth hour, moreover, rising from table, they shall rest in their beds with all silence; or, perchance, he that wishes to read may so read to himself that he do not disturb another. And the nona (the second meal) shall be gone through with more moderately about the middle of the eighth hour; and again they shall work at what is to be done until Vespers. But, if the exigency or poverty of the place demands that they be occupied by themselves in picking fruits, they shall not be dismayed: for then they are truly monks if they live by the labors of their hands; as did also our fathers and the apostles. Let all things be done with moderation, however, on account of the faint hearted. From the Calends of October, moreover, until the beginning of Lent they shall be free for reading until the second full hour. At the second hour the tertia (morning service) shall be held, and all shall labor at the task which is enjoined upon them until the ninth. The first signal, moreover, of the ninth hour having been given, they shall each one leave off his work; and be ready when the second signal strikes. Moreover after the refection they shall be free for their readings or for psalms. But in the days of Lent, from dawn until the third full hour, they shall be free for their readings; and, until the tenth full hour, they shall do the labor that is enjoined on them. In which days of Lent they shall all receive separate books from the library; which they shall read entirely through in order. These books are to be given out on the first day of Lent. Above all there shall certainly be appointed one or two elders, who shall go round the monastery at the hours in which the brothers are engaged in reading, and see to it that no troublesome brother chance to be found who is open to idleness and trifling, and is not intent upon his reading; being not only of no use to himself, but also stirring up others. If such a one—may it not happen—be found, he shall be admonished once and a second time. If he do not amend, he shall be subject, under the Rule, to such punishment that the others may have fear. Nor shall brother join brother at unsuitable hours. Moreover on Sunday all shall engage in reading: excepting those who are deputed to various duties. But if anyone be so negligent and lazy that he will not or can not read, some task shall be imposed upon him which he can do; so that he be not idle. On feeble or delicate brothers such a labor or art is to be imposed, that they shall neither be idle, nor shall they be so oppressed by the violence of labor as to be driven to take flight. Their weakness is to be taken into consideration by the abbot. . . .

Concerning the reception of guests. All guests who come shall be received as though they were Christ: for He Himself said: "I was a stranger and ye took me in." And to all, fitting honor shall be shown; but, most of all, to servants of the faith and to pilgrims. When, therefore, a guest is announced, the prior or the brothers shall run to meet him, with every office of love. And first they shall pray together; and thus they shall be joined together in peace. . . . Chiefly in the reception of the poor and of pilgrims shall care be most anxiously exhibited: for in them Christ is received the more. For the very fear of the rich exacts honor for them. The kitchen of the abbot and the guests shall be by itself; so that guests coming at uncertain hours, as is always happening in a monastery, may not disturb the brothers. . . .

C.   The Cluniac Reformation

Constant effort was required to maintain monastic discipline. All during the Middle Ages devout churchmen and laymen, deploring the evils which had crept into monastic life, sought to reform it. One explanation for the relaxation of monastic discipline was the feudalization of the monasteries. Monastic properties were regarded as ordinary fiefs, and usually feudal lords had power to appoint the abbots, a practice which led to the selection of laymen or of clerics lacking the true monastic spirit. The "Cluniac Reformation" was an attempt to overcome this evil. The monastery of Cluny was founded in 910 by William, duke of Aquitaine, and the terms of its charter, reproduced below, indicate the method of reformation. The idea took hold and many daughter monasteries were founded all over Europe.[20]

The Foundation Charter of Cluny, 910. To all right thinkers it is clear that the providence of God has so provided for certain rich men that, by means of their transitory possessions, if they use them well, they may be able to merit everlasting rewards. As to which thing, indeed, the divine word, showing it to be possible and altogether advising it, says: "The riches of a man are the redemption of his soul." (Prov. xiii.) I, William, count and duke by the grace of God, diligently pondering this, and desiring to provide for my own safety while I am still able, have considered it advisable—nay, most necessary, that from the temporal goods which have been conferred upon me I should give some little portion for the gain of my soul. . . .

Therefore be it known to all who live in the unity of the faith and who await the mercy of Christ, and to those who shall succeed them and who shall continue to exist until the end of the world, that, for the love of God and of our Savior Jesus Christ, I hand over from my own rule to the holy apostles, Peter, namely, and Paul, the possessions over which I hold sway, the town of Cluny, namely, with the court and demesne manor, and the church in honor of St. Mary the mother of God and of St. Peter the prince of the apostles, together with all the things pertaining to it, the vills [villages], indeed, the chapels, the serfs of both sexes, the vines, the fields, the meadows, the woods, the waters and their outlets, the mills, the incomes and revenues, what is cultivated and what is not, all in their entirety. . . . I give these things, moreover, with this understanding, that in Cluny a regular monastery shall be constructed in honor of the holy apostles Peter and Paul, and that there the monks shall congregate and live according to the rule of St. Benedict, and that they shall possess, hold, have and order these same things unto all time. . . .

And let the monks themselves, together with all the aforesaid possessions, be under the power and dominion of the abbot Borno, who, as long as he shall live, shall preside over them regularly according to his knowledge and ability. But after his death, those same monks shall have power and permission to elect any one of their order whom they please as abbot and rector, following the will of God and the rule promulgated by St. Benedict, —in such wise that neither by the intervention of our own or of any other power may they be impeded from making a purely canonical election. Every five years, moreover, the aforesaid monks shall pay to the church of the apostles in Rome ten shillings to supply them with lights; and they shall have the protection of those same apostles and the defense of the Roman pontiff; and those monks may, with their whole heart and soul, according to their ability and knowledge, build up the aforesaid place. We will, further, that in our times and in those of our successors, according as the opportunities and possibilities of that place shall allow, there shall daily, with the greatest zeal be performed there works of mercy towards the poor, the needy, strangers and pilgrims.

It has pleased us also to insert in this document that, from this day, those same monks there congregated shall be subject neither to our yoke, nor to that of our relatives, nor to the sway of the royal might, nor to that of any earthly power. And, through God and all his saints, and by the awful day of judgment, I warn and objure that no one of the secular princes, no count, no bishop whatever, nor the pontiff of the aforesaid Roman see, shall invade the property of these servants of God, or alienate it, or diminish it, or exchange it, or give it as a benefice to any one, or constitute any prelate over them against their will. And that such unhallowed act may be more strictly prohibited to all rash and wicked men, I subjoin the following, giving force to the warning. I adjure ye, oh holy apostles and glorious princes of the world, Peter and Paul, and thee, oh supreme pontiff of the apostolic see, that, through the canonical and apostolic authority which ye have received from God, ye do remove from participation in the holy church and in eternal life, the robbers and invaders and alienators of these possessions which I do give to ye with joyful heart and ready will; and be ye protectors and defenders of the aforementioned place of Cluny and of the servants of God abiding there, and of all these possessions—on account of the clemency and mercy of the most holy Redeemer.

If any one—which Heaven forbid, and which, through the mercy of God and the protection of the apostles I do not think will happen,—whether he be a neighbor or a stranger, no matter what his condition or power, should, through any kind of wile, attempt to do any act of violence contrary

to this deed of gift which we have ordered to be drawn up for love of almighty God and for reverence of the chief apostles Peter and Paul; first, indeed, let him incur the wrath of almighty God and let God remove him from the land of the living and wipe out his name from the book of life, and let his portion be with those who said to the Lord God: Depart from us; and, with Dathan and Abiron whom the earth, opening its jaws, swallowed up, and hell absorbed while still alive, let him incur everlasting damnation. And being made a companion of Judas let him be kept thrust down there with eternal tortures, and, lest it seem to human eyes that he pass through the present world with impunity, let him experience in his own body, indeed, the torments of future damnation, sharing the double disaster with Heliodorus and Antiochus, of whom one being coerced with sharp blows scarcely escaped alive; and the other, struck down by the divine will, his members putrefying and swarming with vermin, perished most miserably. And let him be a partaker with other sacrilegious persons and presume to plunder the treasure of the house of God; and let him, unless he come to his senses, have as enemy and as the one who will refuse him entrance into the blessed paradise, the key-bearer of the whole hierarchy of the church, and, joined with the latter, St. Paul; both of whom, if he had wished, he might have had as most holy mediators for him. But as far as the worldly law is concerned, he shall be required, the judicial power compelling him, to pay a hundred pounds of gold to those whom he has harmed; and his attempted attack, being frustrated, shall have no effect at all. But the validity of this deed of gift, endowed with all authority, shall always remain inviolate and unshaken, together with the stipulation subjoined. Done publicly in the city of Bourges. I, William, commanded this act to be made and drawn up, and confirmed it with my own hand.

D.   THE CISTERCIAN REFORMATION

One of the most famous of monastic reformers was St. Bernard of Clairvaux (1091–1153). Repelled by the worldliness of many monks and the slackness of the discipline in many monasteries, he sought to restore the strictness of early monasticism. St. Bernard's followers were known as "Cistercians," the name being taken from the monastery at Cîteaux, of which St. Bernard was a member. The following selections are from lives of the Saint written soon after his death.[21]

The Life of St. Bernard. Determined that it would be best for him to abandon the world, he began to inquire where his soul, under the yoke of Christ, would be able to find the most complete and sure repose. The recent establishment of the order of Cîteaux suggested itself to his thought.

The harvest was abundant, but the laborers were few, for hardly any one had sought happiness by taking up residence there, because of the excessive austerity of life and the poverty which there prevailed, but which had no terrors for the soul truly seeking God. Without hesitation or misgivings, he turned his steps to that place, thinking that there he would be able to find seclusion and, in the secret of the presence of God, escape the importunities of men; wishing particularly there to gain a refuge from the vain glory of the noble's life, and to win purity of soul, and perhaps the name of saint. . . .

At that time, the young and feeble establishment at Cîteaux, under the venerable abbot Stephen, began to be seriously weakened by its paucity of numbers and to lose all hope of having successors to perpetuate the heritage of holy poverty, for everybody revered the life of these monks for its sanctity but held aloof from it because of its austerity. But the monastery was suddenly visited and made glad by the Lord in a happy and unhoped-for manner. In 1113, fifteen years after the foundation of the monastery, the servant of God, Bernard, then about twenty-three years of age, entered the establishment under the abbot Stephen, with his companions to the number of more than thirty, and submitted himself to the blessed yoke of Christ. From that day God prospered the house, and that vine of the Lord bore fruit, putting forth its branches from sea to sea.

Such were the holy beginnings of the monastic life of that man of God. It is impossible to any one who has not been imbued as he with the spirit of God to recount the illustrious deeds of his career, and his angelic conduct, during his life on earth. He entered the monastery poor in spirit, still obscure and of no fame, with the intention of there perishing in the heart and memory of men, and hoping to be forgotten and ignored like a lost vessel. But God ordered it otherwise, and prepared him as a chosen vessel, not only to strengthen and extend the monastic order, but also to bear His name before kings and peoples to the ends of the earth. . . .

Twelve monks and their abbot, representing our Lord and His apostles, were assembled in the church. Stephen placed a cross in Bernard's hands, who solemnly, at the head of his small band, walked forth from Cîteaux. . . . Bernard struck away to the northward. For a distance of nearly ninety miles he kept this course, passing up by the source of the Seine, by Châtillon, of schoolday memories, until he arrived at La Ferté, about equally distant between Troyes and Chaumont, in the diocese of Langres, and situated on the river Aube. About four miles beyond La Ferté was a deep valley opening to the east. Thick umbrageous forests gave it a character of gloom and wildness; but a gushing stream of limpid water which ran through it was sufficient to redeem every disadvantage.

In June, 1115, Bernard took up his abode in the "Valley of Wormwood," as it was called, and began to look for means of shelter and sustenance against the approaching winter. The rude fabric which he and his monks raised with their own hands was long preserved by the pious veneration of the Cistercians. It consisted of a building covered by a single roof, under which chapel, dormitory, and refectory were all included. Neither stone nor wood hid the bare earth, which served for a floor. Windows scarcely wider than a man's head admitted a feeble light. In this room the monks took their frugal meals of herbs and water. Immediately above the refectory was the sleeping apartment. It was reached by a ladder, and was, in truth, a sort of loft. Here were the monks' beds, which were peculiar. They were made in the form of boxes, or bins, of wooden planks, long and wide enough for a man to lie down in. A small space, hewn out with an axe, allowed room for the sleeper to get in or out. The inside was strewn with chaff, or dried leaves, which with the woodwork, seem to have been the only covering permitted. . . .

The monks had thus got a house over their heads; but they had very little else. They had left Cîteaux in June. Their journey had probably occupied them a fortnight; their clearing, preparations, and building, perhaps two months; and thus they were near September when this portion of their labor was accomplished. Autumn and winter were approaching, and they had no store laid by. Their food during the summer had been a compound of leaves intermixed with coarse grain. Beechnuts and roots were to be their main support during the winter. And now to the privations of insufficient food was added the wearing out of their shoes and clothes. Their necessities grew with the severity of the season, until at last even salt failed them; and presently Bernard heard murmurs. He argued and exhorted; he spoke to them of the fear and love of God, and strove to rouse their drooping spirits by dwelling on the hopes of eternal life and Divine recompense. Their sufferings made them deaf and indifferent to their abbot's words. They would not remain in this valley of bitterness; they would return to Cîteaux. Bernard, seeing they had lost their trust in God, reproved them no more; but himself sought in earnest prayer for release from their difficulties. Presently a voice from heaven said, "Arise, Bernard, thy prayer is granted thee." Upon which the monks said, "What didst thou ask of the Lord?" "Wait, and ye shall see, ye of little faith," was the reply; and presently came a stranger who gave the abbot ten livres. . . .

At the first glance as you entered Clairvaux by descending the hill you could see that it was a temple of God; and the still, silent valley bespoke, in the modest simplicity of its buildings, the unfeigned humility of Christ's poor. Moreover, in this valley full of men, where no one was permitted to be idle, where one and all were occupied with their allotted tasks, a silence deep as that of night prevailed. The sounds of labor, or the chants of the brethren in the choral service, were the only exceptions. The orderliness of this silence, and the report that went forth concerning it, struck such a reverence even into secular persons that they dreaded breaking it,—I will not say by idle or wicked conversation, but even by proper remarks. The solitude, also, of the place— between dense forests in a narrow gorge of neighboring hills—in a certain sense recalled the cave of our father St. Benedict, so that while they strove to imitate his life, they also had some similarity to him in their habitation and loneliness. . . .

For my part, the more attentively I watch them day by day, the more do I believe that they are perfect followers of Christ in all things. When they pray and speak to God in spirit and in truth, by their friendly and quiet speech to Him, as well as by their humbleness of demeanor, they are plainly seen to be God's companions and friends. When, on the other hand, they openly praise God with psalms, how pure and fervent are their minds, is shown by their posture of body in holy fear and reverence, while by their careful pronunciation and modulation of the psalms is shown how sweet to their lips are the words of God— sweeter than honey to their mouths. As I watch them, therefore, singing without fatigue from before midnight to the dawn of day, with only a brief interval, they appear a little less than the angels, but much more than men. . . .

As regards their manual labor, so patiently and placidly, with such quiet countenances, in such sweet and holy order, do they perform all things, that although they exercise themselves at many works, they never seem moved or burdened in anything, whatever the labor may be. Whence it is manifest that that Holy Spirit worketh in them who disposeth of all things with sweetness, in whom they are refreshed, so that they rest even in their toil. Many of them, I hear, are bishops and earls, and many illustrious through their birth or knowledge; but now, by God's grace, all distinction of persons being dead among them, the greater any one thought himself in the world, the more in this flock does he regard himself as less than the least. I see them in the garden with hoes, in the meadows with forks or rakes, in the fields with scythes, in the forest with axes. To judge from their outward appearance, their tools, their bad and disordered clothes, they appear a race of fools, without speech or sense. But a true thought in my mind tells me that their life in Christ is hidden in the heavens. Among them I see Godfrey of Peronne, Raynald of Picardy, William of St. Omer, Walter of Lisle, all of whom I knew formerly in the old man, whereof I now see no trace, by God's favor. I knew them proud and puffed up; I see them walking humbly under the merciful hand of God.

E. THE FRANCISCAN REFORMATION

A new expression of the ascetic impulse is seen in the various orders of Friars which appeared at the beginning of the 13th century. Unlike the monks, they were not required to be continually cloistered, but moved about in the world, particularly in the towns which were springing up at this time. Famous among the new orders was the Franciscan, founded by St. Francis about 1208. The aim of St. Francis was a return to primitive and literal Christianity, and the movement was not only an attempt to reform monasticism, but served also as an answer to those who criticized the worldliness of the clergy.

1. *The Rule of St. Francis, 1223.*[22] This is the rule and way of living of the minorite brothers: namely to observe the holy Gospel of our Lord Jesus Christ, living in obedience, without personal possessions, and in chastity. Brother Francis promises obedience and reverence to our lord Pope Honorius, and to his successors who canonically enter upon their office, and to the Roman Church. And the other brothers shall be bound to obey Brother Francis and his successors. . . .

And those who have now promised obedience shall have one gown with a cowl, and another, if they wish it, without a cowl. And those who are compelled by necessity, may wear shoes. And all the brothers shall wear humble garments, and may repair them with sack cloth and other remnants, with the benediction of God. And I warn and exhort them lest they despise or judge men whom they shall see clad in soft garments and in colors, using delicate food and drink; but each one shall the rather judge and despise himself. . . .

I advise, warn and exhort my brothers in the Lord Jesus Christ, that, when they go into the world, they shall not quarrel, nor contend with words, nor judge others. But they shall be gentle, peaceable, and modest, merciful and humble, honestly speaking with all, as is becoming. And they ought not to ride unless they are compelled by manifest necessity or by infirmity. Into whatever house they enter they shall first say: peace be to this house. And according to the holy Gospel it is lawful for them to eat of all the dishes which are placed before them.

I firmly command all the brothers by no means to receive coin or money, of themselves or through an intervening person. But for the needs of the sick and for clothing the other brothers, the ministers alone and the guardians shall provide through spiritual friends, as it may seem to them that necessity demands, according to time, place and cold temperature. This one thing being always regarded, that, as has been said, they receive neither coin nor money.

Those brothers to whom God has given the ability to labor, shall labor faithfully and devoutly; in such way that idleness, the enemy of the soul, being excluded, they may not extinguish the spirit of holy prayer and devotion; to which other temporal things should be subservient. As a reward, moreover, for their labor, they may receive for themselves and their brothers the necessaries of life, but not coin or money; and this humbly, as becomes the servants of God and the followers of most holy poverty.

The brothers shall appropriate nothing to themselves, neither a house, nor a place, nor anything; but as pilgrims and strangers in this world, in poverty and humility serving God, they shall confidently go seeking for alms. Nor need they be ashamed, for the Lord made Himself poor for us in this world. This is that height of most lofty poverty, which has constituted you my most beloved brothers heirs and kings of the kingdom of Heaven, has made you poor in possessions, has exalted you in virtues. This be your portion, which leads on to the land of the living.

2. *The Will of St. Francis, 1226.*[23] God gave it to me, Brother Francis, to begin to do penance in the following manner: when I was yet in my sins it seemed to me too painful to look upon the lepers, but the Lord Himself led me among them, and I had compassion upon them. When I left them, that which had seemed to me bitter had become sweet and easy. A little while after, I left the world, and God gave me such faith that I would kneel down with simplicity in any of his churches, and I would say, "We adore Thee, Lord Jesus Christ, here and in all Thy churches which are in the world, and we bless Thee that by Thy holy cross Thou hast ransomed the world."

Afterward the Lord gave me, and still gives me,

so great a faith in priests who live according to the form of the holy Roman Church, because of their sacerdotal character, that even if they persecuted me I would have recourse to them, and even though I had all the wisdom of Solomon, if I should find poor secular priests, I would not preach in their parishes against their will. I desire to respect them like all the others, to love them and honor them as my lords, I will not consider their sins, for in them I see the Son of God, and they are my lords. I do this because here below I see nothing, I perceive nothing physically of the most high Son of God, except His most holy body and blood, which the priests receive and alone distribute to others.

Those who volunteered to follow this kind of life distributed all they had to the poor. They contented themselves with one tunic, patched within and without, with the cord and breeches, and we desired to have nothing more. . . . We loved to live in poor and abandoned churches, and we were ignorant and were submissive to all. I worked with my hands and would still do so, and I firmly desire also that all the other brothers work, for this makes for goodness. Let those who know no trade learn one, not for the purpose of receiving wages for their toil, but for their good example and to escape idleness. And when we are not given the price of our work, let us resort to the table of the Lord, begging our bread from door to door. The Lord revealed to me the salutation which we ought to give: "God give you peace!"

Let the brothers take great care not to accept churches, dwellings, or any buildings erected for them, except as all is in accordance with the holy poverty which we have vowed in the Rule; and let them not live in them except as strangers and pilgrims. I absolutely forbid all the brothers, in whatsoever place they may be found, to ask any bull from the court of Rome, whether directly or indirectly, in the interest of church or convent, or under pretext of preaching, or even for the protection of their bodies. If they are not received anywhere, let them go of themselves elsewhere, thus doing penance with the benediction of God. . . .

And let the brothers not say, "This is a new Rule"; for this is only a reminder, a warning, an exhortation. It is my last will and testament, that I, little Brother Francis, make for you, my blessed brothers, in order that we may observe in a more Catholic way the Rule which we promised the Lord to keep.

III

Canossa, 1077

THE creative spirits of the Roman Church who set themselves in the eleventh century to rescue our Western Society
from a feudal anarchy by establishing a Christian Republic
found themselves in the same dilemma as their spiritual
heirs who are attempting in our own day to replace an international anarchy by a world order. The essence of their aim
was to substitute authority for physical force, and the spiritual sword was the weapon with which their supreme victories
were won. But there were occasions on which it seemed as
though the established regime of physical force was in a
position to defy the spiritual sword with impunity; and it
was in such situations that the Roman Church Militant was
challenged to give its answer to the riddle of the Sphinx.
Was the soldier of God to deny himself the use of any but
his own spiritual arms at the risk of seeing his advance
brought to a standstill? Or was he to fight God's battle
against the Devil with the adversary's own weapons?

Arnold Toynbee

CONTENTS

[43]

QUESTIONS FOR STUDY

PART I

1. How had the position of the Papacy changed between 1046 and 1073? What were some of the stages in this change?

2. What reforms was Gregory attempting to effect? Why?

3. What were some of the difficulties facing the young Henry IV?

4. Describe the relations between Gregory and Henry from 1073 to 1076.

5. Why did Henry call the Synod of Worms?

6. How did Gregory justify his deposition of Henry?

7. What were the political implications of Gregory's action?

8. During the years 1046 to 1076 what correlation can be made between conditions in Germany and the papal policy of the German kings?

PART II

9. What were the provisions of the agreement at Oppenheim? Why did Henry agree to them?

10. Why did he decide to go to the pope in Italy?

11. Describe his journey. Why did he take the route he did?

12. How was he received in Italy?

13. How did the pope happen to be at Canossa?

14. Describe the meeting.

15. Compare and evaluate the accounts of the different chroniclers about Canossa.

16. What conditions did Henry have to meet before seeing the pope? On what conditions was he reconciled?

17. In your estimation, who triumphed at Canossa, pope or emperor?

18. What were the basic matters at issue?

19. In your estimation, how much importance should be attached to the personalities of the two protagonists in determining the cause of the conflict? In determining the result?

20. *To be handed in at class.* Write a 200-word narrative of one of the following, giving in the form of footnotes references for every statement of fact or opinion you make:
   a. Why Henry went to Canossa, or
   b. What happened at Canossa.

One of the most momentous themes in medieval history is the conflict between two standards of value—the temporal and the spiritual—for place and power in the world. King and prelate, merchant and priest, monastery and jousting place, or cathedral choir and peasant's close, the protagonists change and the locale is shifted, but the basic issue remains the same. This Problem is concerned with one crisis in this historic struggle: the young German king, Henry IV (1056–1106), and the mighty maker of Popes, now Pope himself, Gregory VII (1073–1085), are the main actors in the drama; Italy and Germany in the third quarter of the eleventh century provide the stage.

Although this conflict between the two cities, as St. Augustine defined it, pervades medieval civilization, it was possibly most apparent in the realm of politics. There the champions carried the most prestige, the stakes were highest, and the issues, in the end at least, best defined. Since the mid-fifth century under the headship of the Bishop of Rome or Pope, the Church, as it gradually supplanted the decaying Roman Empire, had asserted papal supremacy over religion and ultimate supremacy over the secular power. On the other hand, in the form of the emergent monarchies of the west, the state, as it struggled to reassert or recover its former authority, laid claim to a residuum of ultimate power which the Church would not let go unchallenged. Both parties had claims, rooted in history and theory, which if pressed would inevitably clash. Both had innumerable points of contact with each other, at all levels of local government and daily living where skirmishes, preliminary to the main battle, were constantly being fought.

Furthermore, their relationship during the troubled period between the disappearance of the Roman Empire in the west and the establishment of the feudal monarchies had been intimate and often cooperative. In their struggle against feudal anarchy the secular rulers had found in the Church a model and ally, while the latter had always preferred the wider authority of the growing monarchy to the particularism of the local warlords. At the top, the Papacy, as the spiritual reincarnation of Rome and successor to much of her power, was the transmitter of the greater part of the governmental heritage of the Middle Ages. For their part, the secular rulers, in the persons of the Frankish kings of the eighth century and the German kings two centuries later, had come to the rescue of the beleaguered Papacy, whose efforts to maintain its territorial independence amid the frequent turbulence of Italy had often necessitated non-Italian assistance.

The relationship between Church and state had been particularly close in tenth-century Germany. Both were firmly united against the ambitions of the dukes, the German church because the crown was a lesser threat to the local independence of the Church and a greater source of lands and power, the German kings because the bishops represented the finest source of administrative talent then available and the Church was for the moment more ally than threat to the monarchy. The results of this alliance were the establishment of powerful ecclesiastical principalities and the corresponding secularization of the Church through the evolution of a veritable "ecclesiastical feudalism" wherein the churchmen functioned in a way more befitting lay vassals of the crown than men of God. Finally, in 962, Otto I revived the ideal of imperial unity by having himself crowned emperor at Rome. The immediate result was the establishment of German sovereignty over central Italy and the reduction of the Papacy to a position comparable to that of a German bishop, both steps of immense significance for the future.

The stage was thus almost set for the great drama of the next century and only two further developments need be mentioned. The first is the adoption by the Papacy, in the second quarter of the eleventh century, of a reform program, largely Cluniac in inspiration. Founded in 910 in protest against the growing feudalization of the Church, the Burgundian monastery of Cluny found a ripe audience in many a prelate, with its insistence on a return to the earlier canons—on the celibacy of the clergy, methods of clerical election, and lay interference with church property. With the growing authority of the reformer, Hildebrand, in the councils of the Papacy after 1050, the implications of the movement for the position of the Papacy within the Church as well as its relations to temporal authority became momentous. At the same time the Empire was experiencing one of its fateful reversals of fortune, and the inheritance of the six-year-old Henry IV who succeeded his father in 1056 was hardly to be envied: "A Germany seething with discontent, a nobility on the point of rebellion, and in Italy the Papacy under the thumb of the reforming Hildebrand and his allies." [1]

THE PROBLEM

Part I. PAPACY AND EMPIRE

The roots of the controversy between Papacy and Empire lay deep in the past of both institutions. But the immediate background of the eleventh century furnishes many a clue as to the causes of the actual outbreak and even some indications prophetic of its outcome. In the first Part of the Problem the student is to examine the condition of the Papacy and the nature of the reform movement, the state of Germany during the early years of the young Henry, and finally the break between Pope and king. It is already clear that this was to be no passing quarrel; the intimate, historic relationship between the two parties and their central positions on the contemporary scene would combine to underline the significance of even the most trifling act. Mindful that the outcome of the rivalry was of vital importance to all who commented on it, the student must attempt to dissect the forces involved and judiciously assess their comparative importance.

A. THE PAPACY IN THE ELEVENTH CENTURY

1. *The Papal Election of 1046.* In the following selection a contemporary chronicler describes the visit of Henry III (1017–1056) to Italy in 1046.[2]

The first and great synod was held at Pavia in the presence of the lord Henry, then king. The second at Sutri, at which in the presence of the king and according to the provisions of the canons two popes, the second and the third, were deposed. The third synod was held at Rome on the Tuesday and Wednesday before the Nativity of our Lord. At it Pope Benedict was canonically and synodically deposed; and by the unanimous election of the clergy and people Suidger, Bishop of Bamberg, was substituted for him. Suidger was consecrated pope with name of Clement [II] on the next day [December 25]; and, by the will and with the overwhelming approval of the Roman people, he crowned the lord Henry emperor.

2. *The Decree on Papal Elections, 1059.* At the Lateran Council, or synod, of 1059, the Pope, Nicholas II, promulgated a set of regulations redefining the organization of Papal elections. The first selection which follows is from a pro-papal version of the decree; the second, by a follower of the Emperor.[3]

[*Papal Version*] . . . we [Pope Nicholas II] decide and establish that, on the death of the pontiff of this Roman universal church, first of all the cardinal bishops shall discuss with most diligent consideration and then shall summon the cardinal clergy to join them; and afterwards the rest of the clergy and people shall give their assent to the new election. That, lest the disease of venality

creep in by any means godly men shall take the chief part in the election of the pontiff, and the others shall follow their lead. [This method of election is then declared regular and in conformity with precedent, especially with the words of St. Leo.] "No argument," he says, "will permit them to be considered bishops who have not been elected by the clergy, nor demanded by the people, nor consecrated by the bishops of the province with the approval of the metropolitan." But since the apostolic see is raised above all churches in the world and therefore can have no metropolitan over it, the cardinal bishops without doubt perform the function of a metropolitan, when they raise the pontiff elect to the apostolic eminence. They shall elect someone from amongst this church [the Roman church] if a suitable candidate be found; if not, he shall be chosen from another church. Saving the honor and reverence due to our beloved son Henry, who at present is acknowledged King and, it is hoped, will be Emperor, if God permit; as we have granted to him and to such of his successors as obtain this right in person from the apostolic see. But, if the perversity of evil and wicked men shall make it impossible to hold a pure, sincere and uncorrupt election in the city, the cardinal bishops with the godly clergy and catholic laymen, even though few, shall have the lawful power to elect the pontiff of the apostolic see in any place which they shall consider more convenient. After an election has been clearly made, if the fierceness of war or the malignant endeavors of any man shall prevent him who is elected from being enthroned on the apostolic seat according to custom, the elect shall nevertheless have authority as Pope to rule the holy Roman church and to dispose of its resources, as we know that blessed Gregory did before his consecration. . . .

[*Imperial Version*] I, Nicholas, bishop of the holy, Catholic and apostolic Roman church, have signed this decree promulgated by us, as is set out above. I, Boniface, by God's grace bishop of Albano, have signed. I, Humbert, bishop of the holy church of Silva Candida, have signed. I, Peter, bishop of the church of Ostia, have signed. And 76 other bishops with priests and deacons have signed.

1. That, when the pontiff of this Roman church universal dies, the cardinals, after first conferring together with most diligent consideration—saving the honor and reverence due to our beloved son Henry, who is at present called king, and will be in the future, as it is hoped, emperor by God's grace, according as we now, by the mediation of his envoy W. the chancellor of Lombardy, have granted to him and to those of his successors who shall obtain this right personally from this apostolic see,—shall approach and consent to the new election.

2. That—lest the disease of venality creep in through any excuse whatever—the men of the church, together with our most serene son king Henry, shall be the leaders in carrying on the election of a pope, the others merely followers.

3. They shall make their choice, moreover, from the lap of this [Roman] church itself, if a suitable man is to be found there. But if not, one shall be chosen from another church.

4. But, if the perversity of depraved and wicked men shall so prevail that a pure, sincere and free election can not be held in Rome, they may have the right and power, even though few in numbers, of electing a pontiff for the apostolic see wherever it may seem to them, together with the most unconquerable king, Henry, to be most suitable.

3. *The Election of Gregory VII, 1073.* The conjunction of a man and a movement will always remain one of the most inflammatory forces in history. Hildebrand (1023–1085), the future Gregory VII, was born in Tuscany, entered a reformed (Cluniac) monastery and then began his more political career as chaplain to the exiled Gregory VI at Cologne, where he learned much of German politics. Returning to Rome in 1049 with Leo IX, he was employed by a succession of Popes on missions and negotiations of ever-increasing importance. In 1073 his turn came, as is described in the selection which follows.[4]

On the same day, after the body of the aforesaid pontiff [Alexander II, 1061–73] had been buried in the church of the Holy Savior [St. John Lateran], while the venerable Hildebrand was at-

tending to his burial, there rushed in all of a sudden a crowd of clerics, men and women: and a cry was raised, "Let Hildebrand be bishop!" On hearing this, the venerable archdeacon took alarm, and, desiring to quiet the people hurried to the pulpit. But Hugh the White anticipated him, and addressed the multitude thus: "Men and brethren, you know how from the days of Pope Leo [IX, 1048–54], Hildebrand has exalted the holy Roman church, and delivered our city. As it is impossible to find a better man, or his equal, whom we may elect, we elect him who has been ordained in our church, is well known to you as to us, and thoroughly approved." The Cardinal-bishops, priests and deacons, with the inferior clergy, after the accustomed manner, shouted "Blessed Peter has elected Gregory as Pope!" And forthwith, he was seized and carried off by the people to the church of St. Peter [ad Vincula]: where, though against his will, he was enthroned.

4. *The Church and Temporal Power, 1073.* Something of the extent of Gregory's claims can be realized from the following letter to the princes who were bent on conquering Spain. The letters of eminent men afford the historian a happy combination of personality and information. In the case of Gregory VII, a complete collection of his letters has been preserved. In using these letters the student must attempt to evaluate them both as official records and as personal documents.[5]

We suppose you know that the kingdom of Spain belonged of old to St. Peter, and that this right has never been lost, although the land has long been occupied by pagans. Therefore the ownership of this land inheres in the apostolic see alone, for whatever has come into the possession of the churches by the will of God, while it may be alienated from their use, may not by any lapse of time be separated from their ownership except by lawful grant. Count Evolus of Roceio, whose fame you must know, wishes to attack that land and rescue it from the heathen. Therefore we have granted him the possession of such territory as he may win from the pagans by his own efforts or with the aid of allies, on conditions agreed upon by us as the representative of St. Peter. You who join him in this undertaking should do so to the honor of St. Peter, that St. Peter may protect you from danger and reward your fidelity to him. But if any of you plan to attack that land independently with your own forces, you should do so in a spirit of devotion and with righteous motives. Beware lest after you have conquered the land you wrong St. Peter in the same way as the infidels do who now hold it. Unless you are prepared to recognize the rights

Magdeburg

Harzburg

Hersfeld

Mayence

Oppenheim
Worms
Spires

Toul

Bamberg
Forcheim

Regina

Augsburg

Besancon

Geneva

Vercelli   Milan

Mt. Cenis   Pavia

Turin

Canossa

Sutri

STATES
OF THE
CHURCH

Rome

NORMAN

PRINCIPALITIES

Rhine R.

T H E

E M P I R E

PAPACY AND EMPIRE, 1077

[49]

of St. Peter by making an equitable agreement with us, we will forbid you by our apostolic authority to go thither, that your holy and universal mother, the church, may not suffer from her sons the same injuries which she now suffers from her enemies, to the loss not only of her property, but also of the devotion of her children. To this end we have sent to Spain our beloved son, Hugo, cardinal priest of the holy Roman church, and he will inform you more fully of our terms and conditions.

5. *Gregory on the State of Christendom, 1075.* To ascertain more completely the motives behind Gregory's actions remains vital to any understanding of the matters at issue. Thus, his writings must always be scrutinized for all possible clues. The selections which follow are from a letter of Gregory's to Hugh, Abbot of Cluny, one of the inspirations for reform.[6]

If it were possible, I should like you fully to appreciate what great tribulation presses upon me, and what great labor, daily renewed tires me out and increases, to my deep distress. . . . For grievous sorrow and utter sadness surround me, because the Eastern Church, by suggestion of the devil, has abandoned the Catholic Faith; and the ancient foe by his members puts Christians to death on all sides: so that, by spiritually killing the head, he causes the members carnally to perish, lest at any time by divine grace they should repent.

Then again, if I take a mental survey, and look round upon the regions of west, south or north, I scarcely find any bishops lawfully appointed and of regular life who rule the people of God for the love of Christ and not for worldly ambition. And among all the secular princes there is hardly one who prefers the honor of God and righteousness to his own advantage. Those among whom I live—Romans, Lombards and Normans, as I often tell them, I count as worse somehow than Jews or pagans.

Returning to myself, I find myself so overburdened by the weight of my own doings, that no hope of salvation remains for me except in the sole mercy of Christ. For if I did not hope for a better life and to be of more profit to holy Church, I would not in any wise remain in Rome where, as God is witness, I have been obliged to live these five and twenty years. . . .

B. THE PAPACY AND REFORM

Although the reform movement of the eleventh-century church was to a considerable extent monastic in its origins and its early manifestations, it nevertheless came inevitably to involve the Papacy itself.

1. *Gregory VII to the Adherents of the Papacy in Lombardy, 1073.* In the selection which follows, the new Pope warns the Lombards of one of the evils besetting the Church.[7]

I desire you to know, beloved brethren, as many of you do know already, that we are so placed that, whether we will or no, we are bound to proclaim truth and righteousness to all peoples, especially to Christians, according to the word of the Lord: "Cry aloud; spare not, lift up thy voice like a trumpet and declare unto my people their transgressions!" And elsewhere: "If thou shalt not declare his wickedness unto the wicked, I will require his soul at thy hand." Also saith the prophet: "Cursed be he that keepeth back his sword from blood!" that is, he that keepeth back the word of preaching from reproving the carnally minded. We make this prelude because, among the many ills which afflict the whole world, certain ministers of Satan and heralds of Antichrist in Lombardy are striving to overturn even the Christian faith and thus are bringing down the wrath of God upon themselves.

As you well know, during the life of Guido, called archbishop of Milan, Godfrey had the audacity to purchase, like any vile wench, that church which once through the merits of Mary, most glorious Virgin and Mother of God, and through the fame of that most noted doctor, St. Ambrose, shone forth among the churches of Lombardy by its piety, its freedom and its own peculiar glory—that is to say, he prostituted the bride of Christ to the Devil and befouled her with the criminal heresy of Simony by trying to separate her from the catholic faith.

Hearing of this the Roman Church, mother of you and, as you know, mistress of all Christendom, called together a council from several countries and, supported by the approval of many priests and members of divers orders, through the authority of St. Peter, prince of the Apostles, pierced him with the lance of anathema as an enemy of the catholic faith and of the canon law, together with all those who took his part. This right of excommunication, as even the enemies of the Church cannot deny, was approved of old by holy fathers and has been confirmed and is still confirmed by Catholics through all the holy churches.

Wherefore, beloved brethren, in the name of

Almighty God, Father, Son and Holy Spirit, and of the blessed Peter and Paul, chiefs of the Apostles, we warn, exhort and command you to have no dealings whatever with the aforesaid heretic Godfrey, seeing that to side with him in this crime is to deny the faith of Christ. Resist him by whatever means you can as sons of God and defend the Christian faith whereby you are to be saved. And let no pride of men deter you; for he who is with us is greater than all, is ever unconquered, and it is his will that we labor for him, and he will give the crown to those who fight fairly, as the Apostle promises. For our captain [dux] is wont to crush the many and the proud by means of the few and the humble, and to confound the things that are strong by the things that are weak. Such is the will and pleasure of our invincible prince.

May Almighty God, who especially entrusted his sheep to St. Peter and gave him rule over all the Church, strengthen you in your devotion to him so that, delivered from your sins by his authority, you may have grace to withstand the enemies of God and win their hearts to repentance.

2. *Gregory VII and the Monk of Toul, 1074.* The reforming zeal of the Pope is seen in this order to the archbishop of Trier in October, 1074.[8]

We urge you, our brother, to give as prompt and careful attention to the matters we are entrusting to you as the nature of the case and the circumstances will permit. We hope that you will so consider both in the affair described below, that we may find you, as we believe you to be, our faithful and devoted fellow worker.

This monk of Toul, said to be a clerk, came to us and complained that his lord, said to be bishop of Toul, was enraged against him and that he had been driven into exile and deprived of all his goods, and he prayed to be relieved from his distress by apostolic charity. We inquired carefully how this had happened to him, and he replied that he had demanded of the bishop a certain benefice which he claimed as lawfully belonging to the office of *custos* which he held. The bishop, angered by this demand, not only refused him the benefice but forbade him upon his obedience to perform any duties of his office. To this he replied that he owed the bishop no duty of obedience because he [the bishop] had sold archdeaconates, consecrations of churches, and even churches themselves, and had thus made himself guilty of the heresy of Simony. Further, he charged that the bishop had lived in open relations with a certain woman, by whom he had had a child, and report had it that he had joined himself to her by a solemn promise and by a marriage after the man-

ner of laymen. Some said also that he had bought his way into the episcopal office.

When the bishop heard all this he spoke with this monk and also with others of the brethren about making amends as if he repented of the sins that had been brought to light, but finally broke out into a public display of anger against this man.

Shortly afterward in the absence of the bishop some of his men-at-arms, knowing his wishes, endangered the peace of this man and threatened him to his face within the cloister. When he learned that his life and honor were being plotted against he went away secretly, hoping that his absence would moderate the violence of this excitement. But the bishop straightway ordered that all his goods should be seized and sold, and he made his complaint that he had long been living in poverty and exile.

This seems to me against due order and very unjust. If the charges are true the bishop—nay the ex-bishop—hated, not this man, but his own conscience and ought to be brought to trial. But if they are false—as I hope they are—still it was not right that the man should be seized and flogged by soldiers but rather that he should be disciplined according to the law of the Church. Wherefore it is our will that you, my brother, being advised and supported by apostolic authority, invite our beloved colleague, Herman, the venerable bishop of Metz, to join with you in summoning the bishop of Toul to your presence. You are to order him to receive this clerk back into his cloister free from all danger to his life and safe from every form of insult. He shall restore to him the office of *custos* together with the benefice which he demanded, if he has a lawful claim to it, also all the other rights which lawfully belong to him, together with his provostship and his mastership of the scholars, and all the goods which were taken from him, and shall make good all the damage so unjustly inflicted upon him.

Then call the clergy of Toul together and give them strict orders upon their obedience and under penalty of anathema to disclose to you whatever they may know as to the life of the bishop and his accession to office, and after you have probed the truth from every side, fail not to inform us in writing at or before the synod which we are to hold during the first week of Lent what we ought to think of the matter. But if the bishop shall be proved innocent—as we hope he may be—of these many and grave charges we shall see to it with God's help that the rash offense of the clerk in seeking a hearing from us shall be duly corrected. If, however, the bishop shall not be able to clear himself of the charges brought against him, then in no wise is it to be endured that the wolf shall hold the shepherd's place.

3. *The Papal Decrees of 1074–75*. In the synods of 1074 and 1075 Gregory VII formally promulgated the principles of the reform movement. Earlier popes had denounced both simony and lay investiture and since the seventh century the Church in the west had been increasingly opposed to marriage for the clergy, for reasons of a theological as well as an economic nature. It is worth noting that the first three paragraphs quoted below are from Gregory's letters while the last decree survives only in the indirect reference by a Milanese historian.[9]

(1074) Those who have been advanced to any grade of holy orders, or to any office, through simony, that is, by the payment of money, shall hereafter have no right to officiate in the holy church. Those also who have secured churches by giving money shall certainly be deprived of them. And in the future it shall be illegal for anyone to buy or to sell [any ecclesiastical office, position, etc.].

Nor shall clergymen who are married say mass or serve the altar in any way. We decree also that if they refuse to obey our orders, or rather those of the holy fathers, the people shall refuse to receive their ministrations, in order that those who disregard the love of God and the dignity of their office may be brought to their senses through feeling the shame of the world and the reproof of the people. . . .

(1074) If there are any priests, deacons, or sub-deacons who are married, by the power of omnipotent God and the authority of St. Peter we forbid them to enter a church until they repent and mend their ways. But if any remain with their wives, no one shall dare hear them [when they officiate in the church], because their benediction is turned into a curse, and their prayer into a sin. For the Lord says through the prophet, "I will curse your blessings" [Mal. 2:2]. Whoever shall refuse to obey this most salutary command shall be guilty of the sin of idolatry. For Samuel says: "For rebellion is as the sin of witchcraft, and stubbornness is as iniquity and idolatry" [1 Sam. 15:23]. Whoever therefore asserts that he is a Christian but refuses to obey the apostolic see, is guilty of paganism.

(1075) The Pope held a council at Rome and publicly forbade the King thenceforth to have any rights in the conferring of bishoprics, and he withdrew the investiture of churches from all lay persons.

C. Conditions in Germany

The rise and fall of royal fortunes in Germany represents one of the more dramatic aspects of medieval history. The Saxon dynasty had died out in 1024; though elected according to the old practise, the first Franconian king, Conrad II (1024–39) proved to be unusually able. Carefully controlling the church he attempted to develop a loyal, secular administrative corps. He played off the lesser nobles against the all-powerful dukes and concentrated vacant dukedoms in his own family. Henry III (1039–46) appeared to touch new heights of royal power, but both his German policy of regranting the duchies out of his family and his papal policy of introducing the reformers to Rome boded ill for the future.

1. *The Early Years of Henry IV*. In the selection which follows a contemporary German chronicler describes the early years of Henry IV. Succeeding his father at the age of six, the young king was a minor in the custody of his mother from 1056 to 1065. Although his dates are occasionally confused, Ekkehard of Aurach is most informative on Henry's difficulties.[10]

In the year 1057 of the Incarnation of our Lord, and the year 1808 since the founding of the city, Henry IV, son of Emperor Henry, while still a boy, began to reign in the place of his father. At the time that this book is being written, he is reigning, in his forty-second year, as the eighty-seventh emperor since Augustus. . . .

In the year of our Lord 1058, Frederick. who as pope was called Stephen, died, and Alexander, bishop of Lucca, followed him. At that time Hildebrand, who later became pope, administered the office of archdeacon in Rome.

In the year of our Lord 1059, Pope Stephen died, and Gerhard followed him under the name of Nicholas [II]. Henry, king of France, died, and Philip, his son, reigned in his stead.

In the year of our Lord 1060, Luitpold, archbishop of Mayence, died and Siegfried, abbot of Fulda, followed him, who later allied himself with others in a conspiracy against his lord the king.

In the year of our Lord 1062, Archbishop Anno of Cologne, with the consent of the leaders of the empire, brought the prince [Henry IV], of whose person he had taken violent possession, under his control, and withdrew from the prince's mother the government of the empire, as if he felt it to be unworthy that the state should be ruled by the empress, who, though a woman, was enabled to exercise power after the manner of a man. After he had given an account before all of what he had done, he again gained the favor of his lord the king, and was again reconciled to the mother through the son. . . .

In the year of our Lord 1063, Pope Nicholas died and was followed by Bishop Alexander of Lucca. . . .

In the year of our Lord 1066, a comet glowed long over the whole earth. In the same year England was terribly desolated by the Norman William and finally subjugated, and he had himself made king. He then drove almost all the bishops of the said kingdom into banishment and had the nobles killed. The commons he gave over in bondage to his knights, and he compelled the wives of the natives to marry the invaders.

In the year of our Lord 1067, King Henry took to wife Bertha, daughter of a certain Otto, an Italian, and of Adelheid; and he celebrated the wedding at Tribur. Conrad, councilor of the church at Cologne, whom King Henry had designated as bishop of Trier, was taken prisoner by Theodoric, count of that city, and was carried into the forest by his followers and thrown down three times from the top of a mountain, but since he still remained unhurt, they dispatched him with a sword.

In the year of our Lord 1068, King Henry, with youthful recklessness, began to reside in Saxony alone of all the Roman Empire, to despise the princes, oppress the nobles, exalt the lowborn, and to devote himself (as was said) to the chase, to gaming and other occupations of this kind, more than to the administration of justice. He married the daughters of the nobles to his favorites of low origin, and, full of distrust against the powerful of the empire, he began to build certain castles. By thus recklessly sowing the seeds of discord it fell out that the number of those who proposed to deprive the king not only of his kingdom but even of his life grew rapidly. However, as he had not yet fully reached the years of maturity, many judged that the responsibility did not fall so much upon him as upon Archbishop Adelbert of Bremen, since everything was done on his advice.

In the year of our Lord 1069, the Empress Agnes, mother of King Henry, through vexation, or better, through divine inspiration, surrendered the duchy of Bavaria, and, discarding the reins of government in her devotion to Christ, betook herself to Rome, where, with marvelous humility, she brought forth the fruits of repentance and after a few years closed this earthly life in the Lord.

In the year of our Lord 1070, Margrave Teti,

not without the connivance of the Saxon princes, established a tyranny directed against the king's followers. This was, however, suppressed through the intervention of the heavenly as well as the earthly majesty, for his castles of Beichlingen and Burgsheidungen were destroyed by the king; his son, likewise a warrior, was killed by some of his servants, and he himself soon died a natural death.

In the year of our Lord 1071, Duke Otto lost the duchy of Bavaria. He was a Saxon by origin, a man of excellent rank, to whom few could be compared in insight and military power. He enjoyed such respect among all the princes that the king, who was already an object of suspicion and hate to the Saxons, was fearful lest this Otto might, should the king's influence decline, attempt to win the royal throne itself.

A certain Egino, of mean origin and insignificant resources, took advantage of the situation for his evil ends. Although well known for his impudence and shameless conduct, he managed to slip into the court under the protection of certain of the king's adherents. He lied to the king, saying that that great hero, Otto, who in reality had never known him, had conspired with him to murder the king. He offered himself, as was the custom, as a hostage until the truth of what he had said should be settled by a duel between him and the duke. What more need be said? After royal councils had been announced, one at Mayence and the other at Goslar, Otto disdained to fight with Egino,—the duke with the rogue, the prince with the common man,—nevertheless his innocence and Egino's shamelessness remained by no means concealed.

So Otto, guilty of lese-majesty, lost the duchy of Bavaria, which a certain Welf received, a distinguished, brave, warlike person, a Swabian by birth. From this seed, alas, did great dissension spring, which grew into the wretched fruit of continuous battles, of rebelliousness, robbery, and destruction, division in the Church, heresy, and many deaths.

In the year of our Lord 1072, the king followed Otto everywhere, destroyed as many of his fortresses as he could, wasted his lands, and strove completely to annihilate him, as an enemy of the state. Nevertheless, Otto, with a select following, and with his own stout arm and his heart full of bitter hate, since he might not fight directly with the royal troops, sought to avenge the injury which he had suffered, now by plundering, now by fire, now by the sword, wherever opportunity offered.

At his inspiration the Saxon people—of a very violent disposition as they are—ceased not, with one accord, to organize a conspiracy against the king; sent letters full of insulting and unheard-of accusations against the king to the apostolic see, and sought allies by letter and messenger throughout the whole German empire.

In the first place they made friends with Siegfried, the archbishop of Mayence, Adelbert of Worms, Adelberon of Würzburg, Gebhardt of Salzburg, and other bishops, as many as they could, and then through these they gained Pope Alexander. Many assert too that, last and greatest, Anno, archbishop of Cologne, was one of those privy to this conspiracy. Frightened at last by these intrigues, the king left Saxony and conducted the business of the empire in other regions.

In the year of our Lord 1073, the archbishop of Cologne and Herman of Babenberg were sent to Rome in order to get together the money which was owing the king there. They brought back, on their return, a letter from Pope Alexander, in which the king was ordered to give an account of his heresy, simony, and many other similar matters which called for improvement, rumors of which had reached him in Rome.

Thereupon the Saxons built many strongholds, for up to this time that country had had but few of them. Moreover they completely destroyed the castles which the king had built some time before. Among these they tore down the castle which was called Harzburg, the cathedral and the abbey which stood there, destroying all these in their rage and perversity, down to the very ground. Horrible to say, they took up the bones of the innocent son of the king, who had been buried there, and scattered them about as an insult to the father.

In the year of our Lord 1074, after Pope Alexander of blessed memory had died, Hildebrand, later called Gregory, followed him; by profession and rank he was a monk and archdeacon. Under him the Roman Empire and the whole Church began to be threatened by new and unheard-of divisions and turmoil. Since Gregory had reached this height of power without the king's permission, simply through the favor of the Romans, some asserted that he was not rightfully chosen, but had seized the papal dignity with his own hand. Therefore he was not recognized by some of the bishops. Gregory repeatedly summoned King Henry through messengers and letters to answer for his deeds before a synod.

In the year of our Lord 1074, Pope Gregory, after holding a synod, condemned the simonists, namely those who bought and sold the gift of the Holy Ghost, and provided that the Nicolaitae, that is to say, the priests who had married, should be removed from the service of the altar, and forbade the laity to attend masses performed by them.

In the year of the Lord 1075, King Henry moved against the Saxons, after he had collected a strong army from Alemannia, Bavaria, and Germania, and from Bohemia. He fought with the Saxons on the river Unstrut and after much blood had been shed on both sides, he finally returned home victorious.

Rudolph, duke of Alemannia and Burgundy, who later usurped the imperial crown, fought bravely there with his followers for the king. Bishop Herman of Babenberg was deposed, on account of his simoniacal practices, by command of Pope Hildebrand, and Ruotpert was put in his place by the king. In this year died Anno, archbishop of Cologne, rich in merits of piety, and was buried in the cloister of Siegburg, which he himself had built. He was followed by Hildolf.

2. *Gregory VII and the German Church, September 1075.* During the early years of his pontificate Gregory vigorously attempted to impose his reforming decrees on the German clergy. Three bishops were suspended for failing to appear at the Roman synod of February, 1075. The decrees of this synod were communicated to Archbishop Siegfried of Mainz who objected to enforcing them and to the calling of a synod of the German clergy. In the following letter the Pope replied to the reluctant archbishop.[11]

In your letter, my brother, you have brought forward many excuses [for not calling a German Council], plausible and from a human point of view valid, nor would they seem to me without force if such reasoning could excuse us before the judgment seat of God. It does indeed seem a reasonable explanation that the kingdom is in confusion, with wars, rebellions, hostile invasion, ruin of your property and the fear of death which seems to threaten our brethren from the hatred of the king, and also the dread lest men from different and mutually hostile sections coming together in one place might break out into violent conflict. All these seem to be amply sufficient excuses.

But, if we consider the wide difference between divine and human judgments, we find scarcely any pretext that we could safely offer in that last day for drawing back from the rescue of souls—not the loss of property, nor the assaults of the wicked, nor the wrath of the mighty, nor the sacrifice of our safety or of life itself. This is the difference between hirelings and shepherds: that when the wolf comes the hireling fears for himself, not for the sheep, abandons his flock and flees, leaving them to destruction; but the shepherd who truly loves his sheep does not desert them when danger approaches, and does not hesitate to sacrifice even his life for them. . . .

And now let us come to a matter which is at present weighing upon our mind and which is, as it were, the reason of this our discourse, namely, how we can bear with patience the reports we have received as to the conduct of our brother, the bishop of Strasbourg, not a few of which we know by trustworthy information to be true. We desire and command you, therefore, to investigate carefully one of them about which we are still in doubt, that is, the infection with the heresy of Simony. Whatever you discover with certainty upon this point, fail not to inform us at once, so that if the report be true the Church of Christ may be cleansed of this foulness and his soul may be rescued from destruction. But if, as we rather pray, it be false, then may this great calumny be turned away from him with the help of divine grace.

And now let those who say that the council which we have proclaimed ought to be postponed answer this question: What would the soldiers of a king do when they had been summoned to prepare for war and the enemy was already in the king's court with fire and sword? Let them say whether they ought to rush to arms and crush the enemy or idly watch what he is about? For what are those evil spirits doing but striving unceasingly to lay waste the Church of Christ with the flames of their vicious lives? And what ought those royal soldiers, the holy priests, to do, but to rise up against their fury, armed with the shield of priestly charity and girded with the sword of the divine word? As for what you say, that certain brethren cannot come to the council on account of the enmity of their prince, we say that it is enough for them if they send some of their clerks to answer for them.

But, since we are aware that you are being dissuaded by many carnally minded persons from working diligently and faithfully in the Lord's vineyard for the welfare of souls lest you suffer loss of fortune and incur the enmity of the powerful, we exhort and command you, in the name of Almighty God and by authority of St. Peter, that you venture not to turn aside from the straight way through fear or favor of anyone or through any loss of earthly goods, but that, so far as the Holy Spirit may grant, you shall diligently inquire into everything and report to us immediately whatever you ascertain. We ought to regard it as a shameful thing that the soldiers of this world daily stand up to fight for their earthly prince and shrink not from deadly conflict, while we, who are called priests of God, will not fight for our king who created all things out of nothing, and who did not hesitate to suffer death for us and has promised us an eternal reward.

This also we enjoin upon you, my brother, that you make diligent inquiry into the simoniac heresy and fornication of your clergy, as you have been instructed by the Apostolic See, and that whatever you find has been committed in the past you punish according to law and thoroughly root it out, and give strictest orders that it shall not occur in future.

D.   POPE AND KING

Henry IV was twenty-six years old in 1076 and Gregory VII was over fifty when at long last he came out from behind the scenes and became Pope himself. The contrast in their ages and characters was obviously to be one of the determining factors in the course and outcome of their encounter.

1. *The Young King Addresses the New Pope, 1073.* A few months after the election of Gregory VII in April 1073, the young king wrote to the Pope as follows.[12]

To the most watchful and best beloved lord, Pope Gregory, by divine will invested with the apostolic dignity, Henry, by the grace of God King of the Romans, presents his due and faithful service.

Kingdom and priesthood, if they are to be duly administered in Christ, need his continual support, and therefore, my beloved lord and father, they must never be in dissension but must inseparably cleave to each other in the bonds of Christ. For in this way and no other can the harmony of Christian unity and the institution of the Church be held in the bond of perfect love and peace.

But we, who by God's will have now for some time held the kingly office, have not in all respects shown toward the priesthood such reverence and honor as was due to it. Not without reason have we borne the sword of justice entrusted to us by God; but we have not always unsheathed it as we should have done against the guilty. Now, however, somewhat repentant and remorseful, we turn to your fatherly indulgence, accusing ourselves and trusting to you in the Lord that we may be found worthy of absolution by your apostolic authority.

Alas for me, guilty and unhappy that I am! Partly through the impulses of my deceitful youth, partly through the seductive counsels of my advisers, I have sinned against heaven and before you with fraudulent disloyalty and am no more worthy to be called your son. Not only have I encroached upon the property of the

Church, but I have sold churches themselves to unworthy persons, men poisoned with the gall of Simony, men who entered not by the gate but by other ways, and I have not defended the churches as I ought to have done.

But now, since I cannot regulate the churches alone, without authority from you, I most earnestly beg your advice and help in this and in all my affairs. Your directions shall be scrupulously followed in all respects. And first, in regard to the church of Milan, which has fallen into error through my fault, I beg that it may be restored according to law by your apostolic sentence and that then you will proceed to the regulation of other churches by your authority. I shall not fail you, so God will, and I humbly beseech your fatherly support in all my interests.

You will soon receive letters from me by the hands of most trustworthy messengers and from these you will, please God, learn more fully what remains to be said.

2. *The Pope Defines His Policy, 1073.* In the following letters Gregory announces his German policy to two of the German Dukes.[13]

(*To Duke Godfrey of Lorraine, May 1073.*) As regards the king, you may fully understand our purpose and our wishes. So far as God gives us to know, we believe there is no one more anxious or more desirous for his present and future glory than ourself. It is our wish at the first available opportunity to come to an understanding with him through our legates upon the matters which we think important for the welfare of the Church and the honor of his kingly office—with fatherly affection and admonition. If he will then listen to us we shall rejoice for his sake as well as for our own. Of a certainty he will find his profit in maintaining justice in accordance with our advice and warnings.

But if—which God forbid!—he shall repay our love with hate and show contempt toward Almighty God for the high office conferred upon him, then may the judgment which declares, "Cursed be he that keepeth back his sword from blood!" not fall upon us in the providence of God. For we are not free to set aside the law of God for the sake of any person, neither to draw back from the path of rectitude for any favor of men, according to the word of the Apostle, "If I were still pleasing men I should not be a servant of Christ."

(*To Duke Rudolph of Swabia, September 1073.*) Although your zeal in the past has made it clear that you are devoted to the honor of the Holy Roman Church, your recent letter shows your fervent affection for it and proves how greatly you surpass all the other princes of those parts in this respect. Among other welcome ex-pressions therein, this seemed especially calculated to advance the glory of the imperial government and also to strengthen the power of Holy Church, namely, that the empire and the priesthood should be bound together in harmonious union. For, as the human body is guided by two eyes for its physical illumination, so the body of the Church is guided and enlightened with spiritual light when these two offices work together in the cause of pure religion.

Wherefore we desire Your Excellency to know that we have no ill will toward King Henry, to whom we are under obligation because he was our choice as king, and because his father of honored memory, the Emperor Henry, treated me with especial honor among all the Italians at his court, and at his death commended his son to the Roman Church in the person of Pope Victor [II] of reverend memory. Nor, so God help us, would we willingly hate any Christian man, according to the word of the Apostle: "If I give my body to be burned, and if I bestow all my goods to feed the poor and have not love, I am nothing." But, since the harmony of Empire and Priesthood ought to be pure and free from all deceit, it seems to us highly important first to take counsel with you and the empress Agnes, the countess Beatrice, and Rainald, bishop of Como, and other God-fearing men. Then, after you have thoroughly understood our wishes, if our reasons seem sound to you, you may come to an agreement with us; but, if you find that anything should be added to our arguments or stricken from them, we shall be ready, with God's approval, to accept your advice.

3. *The New Pope Addresses the Young King, 1075–1076.* Five letters survive from Gregory to Henry in the three years 1073–76, before the outbreak of trouble. Selections from two of them follow. In the second letter (winter 1075–76) Gregory refers to Henry's investing of Tedold, rather than Gregory's candidate, with the archbishopric of Milan in the fall of 1075.[14]

Gregory . . . to King Henry, greeting . . . [July 20, 1075].

Among other praiseworthy actions, my beloved son, to which you are reported to have risen in your efforts at self-improvement, there are two that have specially commended you to your holy mother, the Roman Church: first, that you have valiantly withstood those guilty of Simony; and second, that you freely approve, and strenuously desire to enforce, the chastity of the clergy as servants of God. For these reasons you have given us cause to expect of you still higher and better things with God's help. Wherefore we earnestly pray that you may hold fast by these, and we beseech our Lord God that he may deign to increase your zeal more and more.

But now, as regards the church of Bamberg, which according to the ordinance of its founder [King Henry II] belongs to the Holy and Apostolic See as the shoulder to the head, that is, as a most intimate member, by a certain special bond of duty, we are greatly disturbed and we are forced by the obligation of our office to come to the rescue of its distress with all our powers. That simoniac so-called bishop Herman, summoned to a Roman synod this present year, failed to appear. He came within a short distance of Rome, but there halted and sent forward messengers with ample gifts, trying, with his well-known trickery, to impose upon our innocence and, if possible, to corrupt the integrity of our colleagues by a pecuniary bargain. But when this turned out contrary to his hopes, convinced of his own damnation he hastily retreated and, soothing the minds of the clergy who were with him by smooth and deceitful promises, declared that if he were able to regain his own country he would resign his bishopric and enter the monastic life.

How he kept these promises Your Highness, beloved son, well knows. With increasing audacity he plundered the clergy who were upholding the welfare and the honor of their church, and had not your royal power restrained him, as we are informed, he would have completely ruined them. After careful consideration of these outrages we removed him from his episcopal and priestly office. Further, as he dared to oppress the church of Bamberg, under the apostolic patronage of St. Peter, more cruelly and more harshly than before, we placed him in the bonds of anathema until he should lay down his usurped dignity and, nevertheless, present himself for trial before the Apostolic See.

Now, therefore, most excellent son, we ask Your Highness and urge you by our dutiful obligation to take counsel with men of piety and so to regulate the affairs of that church according to God's order, that you may be worthy of divine protection through the intercession of St. Peter, in whose name and under whose patronage the church was founded.

(*Gregory to Henry, December 8, 1075, or January 8, 1076.*) Considering and weighing carefully to how strict a judge we must render an account of the stewardship committed to us by St. Peter, prince of the Apostles, we have hesitated to send you the apostolic benediction, since you are reported to be in voluntary communication with men who are under the censure of the Apostolic See and of a synod. If this is true, you yourself know that you cannot receive the favor of God nor the apostolic blessing unless you shall first put away those excommunicated persons and

force them to do penance and shall yourself obtain absolution and forgiveness for your sin by due repentance and satisfaction. Wherefore we counsel Your Excellency, if you feel yourself guilty in this matter, to make your confession at once to some pious bishop who, with our sanction, may impose upon you a penance suited to the offense, may absolve you and with your consent in writing may be free to send us a true report of the manner of your penance.

We marvel exceedingly that you have sent us so many devoted letters and displayed such humility by the spoken words of your legates, calling yourself a son of our Holy Mother Church and subject to us in faith, singular in affection, a leader in devotion, commending yourself with every expression of gentleness and reverence, and yet in action showing yourself most bitterly hostile to the canons and apostolic decrees in those duties especially required by loyalty to the Church. Not to mention other cases, the way you have observed your promises in the Milan affair, made through your mother and through bishops, our colleagues, whom we sent to you, and what your intentions were in making them is evident to all. And now, heaping wounds upon wounds, you have handed over the sees of Fermo and Spoleto—if indeed a church may be given over by any human power—to persons entirely unknown to us, whereas it is not lawful to consecrate anyone except after probation and with due knowledge.

It would have been becoming to you, since you confess yourself to be a son of the Church, to give more respectful attention to the master of the Church, that is, to Peter, prince of the Apostles. To him, if you are of the Lord's flock, you have been committed for your pasture, since Christ said to him: "Peter, feed my sheep," and again: "To thee are given the keys of Heaven, and whatsoever thou shalt bind on earth shall be bound in Heaven, and whatsoever thou shalt loose on earth shall be loosed in Heaven." Now, while we, unworthy sinner that we are, stand in his place of power, still whatever you send to us, whether in writing or by word of mouth, he himself receives, and while we read what is written or hear the voice of those who speak, he discerns with subtle insight from what spirit the message comes. . . .

At a synod held at Rome during the current year, and over which Divine Providence willed us to preside, several of your subjects being present, we saw that the order of the Christian religion had long been greatly disturbed and its chief and proper function, the redemption of souls, had fallen low and through the wiles of the Devil had been trodden under foot. Startled by this danger and by the manifest ruin of the

Lord's flock we returned to the teaching of the holy fathers, declaring no novelties nor any inventions of our own, but holding that the primary and only rule of discipline and the well-trodden way of the saints should again be sought and followed, all wandering paths to be abandoned. For we know that there is no other way of salvation and eternal life for the flock of Christ and their shepherds except that shown by him who said: "I am the door and he who enters by me shall be saved and shall find pasture." This was taught by the Apostles and observed by the holy fathers and we have learned it from the Gospels and from every page of Holy Writ.

This edict [against lay investiture], which some who place the honor of men above that of God call an intolerable burden, we, using the right word, call rather a truth and a light necessary for salvation, and we have given judgment that it is to be heartily accepted and obeyed, not only by you and your subjects but by all princes and peoples who confess and worship Christ—though it is our especial wish and would be especially fitting for you, that you should excel others in devotion to Christ as you are their superior in fame, in station and in valor.

Nevertheless, in order that these demands may not seem to you too burdensome or unfair we have sent you word by your own liegemen not to be troubled by this reform of an evil practice but to send us prudent and pious legates from your own people. If these can show in any reasonable way how we can moderate the decision of the holy fathers [at the Council] saving the honor of the eternal king and without peril to our own soul, we will condescend to hear their counsel. It would in fact have been the fair thing for you, even if you had not been so graciously admonished, to make reasonable inquiry of us in what respect we had offended you or assailed

your honor, before you proceeded to violate the apostolic decrees. But how little you cared for our warnings or for doing right was shown by your later actions.

However, since the long-enduring patience of God summons you to improvement, we hope that with increase of understanding your heart and mind may be turned to obey the commands of God. We warn you with a father's love that you accept the rule of Christ, that you consider the peril of preferring your own honor to his, that you do not hamper by your actions the freedom of that Church which he deigned to bind to himself as a bride by a divine union, but, that she may increase as greatly as possible, you will begin to lend to Almighty God and to St. Peter, by whom also your own glory may merit increase, the aid of your valor by faithful devotion.

Now you ought to recognize your special obligation to them for the triumph over your enemies which they have granted you, and while they are making you happy and singularly prosperous, they ought to find your devotion increased by their favor to you. That the fear of God, in whose hand is all the might of kings and emperors, may impress this upon you more than any admonitions of mine, bear in mind what happened to Saul after he had won a victory by command of the prophet, how he boasted of his triumph, scorning the prophet's admonitions, and how he was rebuked by the Lord, and also what favor followed David the king as a reward for his humility in the midst of the tokens of his bravery.

Finally, as to what we have read in your letters and do not mention here we will give you no decided answer until your legates, Radbod, Adalbert and Odescalcus, to whom we entrust this, have returned to us and have more fully reported your decision upon the matters which we commissioned them to discuss with you.

E.   THE COUNCIL OF WORMS, JANUARY 1076

Gregory's last letter to Henry (December 1075–January 1076) was reinforced verbally by his envoys who delivered a virtual ultimatum to the king: compliance or else. Henry's reply was to summon the bishops of Germany to a council at Worms for January 24, 1076.

1. *The Council to the Pope, January 24, 1076.* With apparently little persuasion and less deliberation, the Council sent the following letter to the Pope.[15]

Siegfried, Archbishop of Mainz, Udo of Trier, William of Utrecht, Herman of Metz, Henry of Liège, Ricbert of Verden, Bibo of Toul, Hozemann of Speyer, Burckhard of Halberstadt, Werner of Strassburg, Burchard of Basel, Otto of Constance, Adalbero of Würzburg, Rodbert of Bamberg, Otto of Regensburg, Ellinard of Freising,

Udalric of Eichstädt, Frederick of Münster, Eilbert of Minden, Hezil of Hildesheim, Benno of Osnabrück, Eppo of Naumburg, Imadus of Paderborn, Tiedo of Brandenburg, Burchard of Lausanne, Bruno of Verona—to brother Hildebrand.

Although, when thou didst first seize the control of the church, it was clear to us how unlawful and wicked a thing thou hadst presumed to do contrary to right and justice with thine usual arrogance; nevertheless we thought fit to cover the evil beginnings of thine inauguration with an indulgent silence, hoping that these iniquitous preliminaries would be emended and outweighed by the integrity and diligence of thy subsequent administration. But now, as the lamentable condition of the whole church sadly proclaims, thou art consistently and pertinaciously faithful to thine evil beginnings, in the increasing iniquity of thine actions and decrees. . . . The flame of discord, which thou didst arouse with bitter disputes in the Roman church, thou hast scattered with senseless fury throughout all the churches of Italy, Germany, Gaul and Spain. For to the utmost of thy power thou hast deprived the bishops of all the power, known to have been divinely given to them by the grace of the Holy Spirit, Who operates above all in ordinations. Thou hast given all oversight over ecclesiastical matters to the unstable mob. None is now acknowledged a bishop or a priest, unless by unworthy subservience he has obtained his office from thy magnificence. Thou hast thrown into wretched confusion all the life of the apostolic institution and that perfect interrelation of the members of Christ, which the teacher of the gentiles so often commends and inculcates.

Thus, because of thine ambitious decrees—with tears it must be said—the name of Christ has all but perished. Who is not outraged by thine unworthy conduct in arrogating to thyself a new and improper power in order to destroy the lawful rights of the whole brotherhood? For thou dost assert that, if the mere news of a sin committed by a member of our flocks reaches thee, none of us has thenceforth any power to bind or loose him, but thou only or he whom thou shalt specially delegate for the purpose. Who, that is learned in the sacred scriptures, does not see that this decree exceeds all madness? Wherefore . . . we have decided, by common consent of us all, to make known to thee that on which we have hitherto kept silence, namely why thou canst not now, nor ever could, preside over the apostolic see. Thou didst bind thyself with a corporal oath in the time of the Emperor Henry of blessed memory that never in the Emperor's lifetime, nor in that of his son, our present reigning and glorious King, wouldst thou thyself accept the papacy, or, as far as in thee lay, wouldst thou suffer another to accept it, without the consent and approval of the father, while he was alive, or of the son, while he lived. And there are today many bishops who witnessed that oath; who saw it with their eyes and heard it with their ears. Remember too how, when ambition to be pope moved several of the cardinals, to remove all rivalry on that occasion, thou didst bind thyself with an oath, on condition that they did the same, never to hold the papacy. See how faithfully thou hast kept both these oaths.

Further, when a synod was held in the time of Pope Nicholas, whereat 125 bishops assisted, it was established and decreed under pain of anathema that none should ever be made Pope except by the election of the cardinals, the approbation of the people and the consent and authorization of the king. And of that decision and decree thou thyself wast the author, promoter and signatory.

Also thou hast, as it were, filled the whole church with the stench of a grave scandal by associating more intimately than is necessary with a woman not of thy kin. This is a matter of propriety rather than of morality; and yet this general complaint is everywhere made, that at the apostolic see all judgments and all decrees are the work of women, and that the whole church is governed by this new senate of women. . . . And finally, no amount of complaint is adequate to express the insults and outrages you have heaped upon the bishops, calling them sons of harlots and other vile names. Therefore, since your pontificate was begun in perjury and crime, since your innovations have placed the church of God in the gravest peril, since your life and conduct are stained with infamy; we now renounce our obedience, which indeed was never legally promised to you. You have declared publicly that you do not consider us to be bishops; we reply that no one of us shall ever hold you to be the pope.

2. *The King to the Pope, January 24, 1076.* The King also wrote to the Pope describing the decision of the council.[16]

Henry, king not by usurpation, but by the holy ordination of God, to Hildebrand, not pope, but false monk.

This is the salutation which you deserve, for you have never held any office in the church without making it a source of confusion and a curse to Christian men instead of an honor and a blessing. To mention only the most obvious cases out of many, you have not only dared to touch the Lord's anointed, the archbishops, bishops, and priests; but you have scorned them and abused them, as if they were ignorant servants not fit to know what their master was doing. This you have done to gain favor with the vulgar crowd. You have declared that the bishops know nothing and that you know everything; but if you have such great wisdom you have used it not to build but to destroy. Therefore we believe that St. Gregory, whose name you have presumed to take, had you in mind when he said: "The heart of the prelate is puffed up by the abundance of subjects, and he thinks himself more powerful than all others." All this we have endured because of our respect for the papal office, but you have mistaken our humility for fear, and have dared to make an attack upon the royal and imperial authority which we received from God. You have even threatened to take it away, as if we had received it from you, and as if the empire and kingdom were in your disposal and not in the disposal of God. Our Lord Jesus Christ has called us to the government of the empire, but he never called you to the rule of the church. This is the way you have gained advancement in the church; through craft you have obtained wealth; through wealth you have obtained favor; through favor, the power of the sword; and through the power of the sword, the papal seat, which is the seat of peace; and then from the seat of peace you have expelled peace. For you have incited subjects to rebel against their prelates by teaching them to despise the bishops, their rightful rulers. You have given to laymen the authority over priests, whereby they condemn and depose those whom the bishops have put over them to teach them. You have attacked me, who, unworthy as I am, have yet been anointed to rule among the anointed of God, and who, according to the teaching of the fathers, can be judged by no one save God alone, and can be deposed for no crime except infidelity. For the holy fathers in the time of the apostate Julian did not presume to

pronounce sentence of deposition against him, but left him to be judged and condemned by God. St. Peter himself said: "Fear God, honor the king" [1 Pet. 2:17]. But you, who fear not God, have dishonored me, whom He hath established. St. Paul, who said that even an angel from heaven should be accursed who taught any other than the true doctrine, did not make an exception in your favor, to permit you to teach false doctrines. For he says: "But though we, or an angel from heaven, preach any other gospel unto you than that which we have preached unto you, let him be accursed" [Gal. 1:8]. Come down, then, from that apostolic seat which you have obtained by violence; for you have been declared accursed by St. Paul for your false doctrines and have been condemned by us and our bishops for your evil rule. Let another ascend the throne of St. Peter, one who will not use religion as a cloak of violence, but will teach the life-giving doctrine of that prince of the apostles. I, Henry, king by the grace of God, with all my bishops, say unto you: "Come down, come down, and be accursed through all the ages."

F. THE PAPAL REPLY, FEBRUARY 1076

The year 1075 had been a busy one for the Pope, culminating in December in the violent capture and imprisonment of Gregory by a Roman noble. An outraged Roman populace rescued him, and it was amid this outburst of enthusiasm that the news of Worms reached Rome. Henry and his German bishops had persuaded the Italian bishops to concur with the actions taken at Worms. An Italian bishop was then sent to convey the sentence of deposition to Rome. He arrived just as the Lenten Synod was commencing. Something of the effect produced by his message can be gathered from the documents which follow.

1. *The Lenten Synod of 1076.* The following excerpt from the Papal records should be compared with the decisions of the Council of Worms both as to tone and as to argument.[17]

In the year of the Incarnation 1075, our lord Pope Gregory held a synod at Rome in the church of Our Savior which is called the Constantiniana. A great number of bishops and abbots and clergy and laymen of various orders were present.

At this synod, among the decrees promulgated was the excommunication of Siegfried, archbishop of Mainz, in the following form:

In accordance with the judgment of the Holy Spirit and by authority of the blessed Apostles Peter and Paul, we suspend from every espiscopal function, and exclude from the communion of the body and blood of the Lord, Siegfried, archbishop of Mainz, who has attempted to cut off the bishops and abbots of Germany from the Holy Roman Church, their spiritual mother—unless perchance in the hour of death, and then

only if he shall come to himself and truly repent. Those who voluntarily joined his schism and still persist in their evil deeds, we also suspend from all episcopal functions. Those, however, who consented against their will we allow time until the feast of St. Peter [August 1]; but if within that term they shall not have given due satisfaction in person or by messengers in our presence, they shall thenceforth be deprived of their episcopal office.

(*Excommunication of the bishops of Lombardy.*) The bishops of Lombardy who, in contempt of canonical and apostolic authority, have joined in a sworn conspiracy against St. Peter, prince of the Apostles, we suspend from their episcopal functions and exclude them from the communion of the Holy Church.

[Here follows a list of excommunications of prelates and laymen beyond the Alps, ending with the proclamation against King Henry IV.]

O blessed Peter, prince of the Apostles, mercifully incline thine ear, we [sic] pray, and hear me, thy servant, whom thou hast cherished from infancy and hast delivered until now from the hand of the wicked who have hated and still hate me for my loyalty to thee. Thou art my witness, as are also my Lady, the Mother of God, and the blessed Paul, thy brother among all the saints, that thy Holy Roman Church forced me against my will to be its ruler. I had no thought of ascending thy throne as a robber, nay, rather would I have chosen to end my life as a pilgrim than to seize upon thy place for earthly glory and by devices of this world. Therefore, by thy favor, not by any works of mine, I believe that it is and has been thy will, that the Christian people especially committed to thee should render obedience to me, thy especially constituted representative. To me is given by thy grace the power of binding and loosing in Heaven and upon earth.

Wherefore, relying upon this commission, and for the honor and defense of thy Church, in the name of Almighty God, Father, Son and Holy Spirit, through thy power and authority, I deprive King Henry, son of the emperor Henry, who has rebelled against thy Church with unheard-of audacity, of the government over the whole kingdom of Germany and Italy, and I release all Christian men from the allegiance which they have sworn or may swear to him, and I forbid anyone to serve him as king. For it is fitting that he who seeks to diminish the glory of thy Church should lose the glory which he seems to have.

And, since he has refused to obey as a Christian should or to return to the God whom he has abandoned by taking part with excommunicated persons, has spurned my warnings which I gave him for his soul's welfare, as thou knowest, and has separated himself from thy Church and tried to rend it asunder, I bind him in the bonds of anathema in thy stead and I bind him thus as commissioned by thee, that the nations may know and be convinced that thou art Peter and that upon thy rock the son of the living God has built his Church and the gates of hell shall not prevail against it.

2. *Gregory Explains His Action.* In the following circular letter, sent out shortly after the Lenten Synod, Gregory gave a more detailed description of his action.[18]

Gregory, Bishop, slave of the slaves of God, to all bishops, dukes, counts and others of the faithful, defenders of the Christian faith in the kingdom of Germans, greeting and apostolic benediction.

We have heard that some of you are in doubt and perplexity about the excommunication which we have inflicted on the king. . . . Wherefore we have carefully set forth before the eyes and minds of all, as accurately as possible (our conscience is our witness), how we were led to excommunicate him; not so much, as it were with uplifted voice, publicly to proclaim the various causes (which alas! are but too well known), as to satisfy the minds of those, who think that we have drawn the spiritual sword rashly and more on the promptings of our own mind than through fear of God or zeal for righteousness.

Formerly, when we were occupying the post of deacon, there reached us an evil and very discreditable account of the king's actions. But from consideration for the imperial dignity and reverence for his father and mother, as also from the hope and desire for his correction, we frequently admonished him by letters and envoys to desist from his wickedness, and, mindful of his noble birth and dignity, to order his life with behavior fitting a king, and, if God permit, future Emperor. But since we in our unworthiness have been raised to the supreme pontificate, while his wickedness has increased with his advancing age, we have much more earnestly exhorted him in every way, arguing, entreating, rebuking, to amend his life—knowing that Almighty God would the more strictly require his soul at our hands, for that permission and authority to rebuke him had been given to us before all other men. He often sent us loyal salutations and letters . . . and in words has promised from day to day that he would most readily accept our warnings; but in fact and by the increase of his sins he has spurned them.

Meanwhile we summoned to repentance certain members of his court, through whose counsels and schemings he had defiled bishoprics and many monasteries with the simoniacal heresy, intruding, for money, wolves in place of shepherds; in order that, while amendment was possible, they should restore the property of the churches, which with sacrilegious hand they had obtained by this criminal commerce, to the venerable places to which it appertained, and that they themselves by heartfelt penitence should make satisfaction to God for the iniquity committed. But when we knew that they disregarded the grace afforded to them for fulfilling these duties and obstinately continued in their former wickedness, then, as was right, we separated them, as sacrilegious persons and as servants and members of the devil, from the communion and body of the whole church; and we admonished the king to dismiss them as excommunicates, from his house, his councils and all communion with himself.

Meanwhile the revolt of the Saxons against the king increased; and when he saw that the forces and defenders of the kingdom were for the more part prepared to abandon him, he again sent us a supplicatory letter, full of all humility. . . . And in this [i.e. ecclesiastical law] he promised us his entire obedience, consent and faithful support. And again later, when he was admitted to penance by our brothers and legates, Humbert, Bishop of Preneste, and Gerald, Bishop of Ostia, whom we sent to him, he repeated to them his promise and confirmed it on the sacred stoles which they wore upon their necks.

Some time later, after a battle with the Saxons, the king, in return for the victory gained, gave thanks and offerings to God thus—he continued to break the oaths which he had made about the amendment of his life; ignoring his promises, he admitted the excommunicates to the intimacy of his court; and he kept the churches in the same confusion as before. . . . [Gregory then dwells on his exhortation to Henry to amend his morals and to dismiss the excommunicates.]

He could not tolerate being reproved or criticized by anyone, and not only could not be induced to make amends for his offenses, but, overcome by yet greater madness of moral judgment, did not cease till he caused nearly all of the bishops in Italy and as many as he could in the German lands to make shipwreck concerning the faith of Christ, in that he forced them to deny to blessed Peter and the Apostolic See the obedience and honor due to them and granted by our Lord Jesus Christ.

Therefore, when we perceived that his wickedness had reached its climax, for the following causes—first because he refused to withdraw himself from intercourse with those who for sacrilege and conviction of simoniacal heresy had been excommunicated; further because he was unwilling—I do not say to undergo—but even to promise penance for the wickednesses of his life, thus giving the lie to the penitence which he had professed before our legates; and also because he did not shrink from dismembering the body of Christ, that is the unity of holy Church—for these offences, I say, we excommunicated him by sentence of a synod; in order that we may, with God's help, by severity recall to the way of salvation him, whom we could not move by gentleness, or, if he be unmoved—which God forbid—by the sentence of segregation. Our own soul at any rate may not incur the risk of negligence or cowardice.

If, therefore, anyone shall hold that this sentence has been unjustly or unreasonably pronounced, and if he be willing to apply his intellect to the sacred canons, let him communicate with us and, patiently hearing not what we, but what the divine authority teaches and commands, what the unanimous voice of the holy fathers decides, let him acquiesce. We do not think that any one of the faithful who knows the laws of the church is so mastered by this error as not to believe in his heart, even if he dare not publicly affirm his faith, that justice has been done.

Nevertheless, even if—which God forbid—we have thus bound him for insufficiently weighty cause or out of due order, the sentence, as the holy fathers assert, should not on that account be defied, but absolution should be sought with all humility. . . .

But if, inspired by God, he be willing to come to his senses, whatever he may attempt against us, he will always find us prepared to receive him into the holy communion, as your charity shall counsel us.

3. *The Royal Summons to a Diet at Worms, April–May, 1076.* Something of the effect of Gregory's actions on the leaders of the church in Germany can be gained from the following document, the summons of Henry to the bishops and princes of Germany to meet in a diet at Worms. Henry's efforts to convene this diet, as well as one at Mainz, were apparently unsuccessful.[19]

Henry, king by the grace of God, sends favor, greeting, love—not to all, but to a few.

In very important matters the wisest counsels of the greatest men are needed—men who shall both outwardly have the ability and inwardly shall not be without the will to give their best advice in a matter in which they are interested. For there is nothing whatever in the carrying out of which either ability without will or will without ability avails. Both of which thou, most faithful one, dost possess, as we think, in equal measure; or to speak more truly, although thou who art very great are not lacking in very great ability, —nevertheless, if we know thee rightly and have noted thy fidelity with proper care, thou dost abound with a good will greater even than this very great ability; to our own and to the country's advantage. For from the faithful services of the past we are led to hope for still more faithful services in the future. We rely moreover on thy love not to let thy faithfulness disappoint our expectations; for from the loyalty of none of the princes or bishops of the land do we hope for greater things than from thine, rejoicing, as we have done, not only in the showing of the past but also in what thou hast led us to expect from thee in the future. Let, therefore, thy timely good will be present now with thy ability; for it is called for not only by our own straits but also by those of all thy fellow-bishops and brothers— nay, of the whole oppressed church. Thou art not ignorant, indeed, of this oppression; only see to it that thou do not withdraw thy aid from the oppressed church, but that thou do give thy sympathy to the kingdom and the priesthood. For in both of these, even as the church has hitherto been exalted, so now, alas, in both it is humiliated and bereaved. Inasmuch as one man has claimed for himself both; nor has he helped the one, seeing that he neither would nor could help either. But, lest we keep from thee any longer the name of one who is known to thee, learn of whom we are speaking—Hildebrand, namely, outwardly, indeed, a monk; called pope, but presiding over the apostolic see rather with the violence of an invader than with the care of a pastor, and, from the seat of universal peace, sundering the chains of peace and unity—as thou thyself dost clearly know. For, to mention a few cases out of many, he usurped for himself the kingdom and the priesthood without God's sanction, despising God's holy ordination which willed essentially that they—namely the kingdom and the priesthood—should remain not in the hands of one, but, as two, in the hands of two. For the Saviour Himself, during His Passion, intimated that this was the meaning of the typical sufficiency of the two swords. For when it was said to Him: "Behold, Lord, here are two swords"—He answered: "It is enough," signifying by this sufficing duality that a spiritual and a carnal sword were to be wielded in the church, and that by them every thing evil was about to be cut off—by the sacerdotal sword, namely, to the end that the king, for God's sake, should be obeyed; but by the royal one to the end that the enemies of Christ without should be expelled, and that the priesthood within should be obeyed. And He taught that every man should be constrained so to extend his love from one to the other that the kingdom should neither lack the honor due to the priesthood, nor the priesthood the honor due to the kingdom. In what way the madness of Hildebrand confounded this ordinance of God thou thyself dost know, if thou

hast been ready or willing to know. For in his judgment no one is rightfully priest save him who has bought permission from his own capricious self. Me also whom God called to the kingdom—not, however, having called him to the priesthood—he strove to deprive of my royal power, threatening to take away my kingdom and my soul, neither of which he had granted, because he saw me wishing to hold my rule from God and not from him—because he himself had not constituted me king. Although he had often, as thou dost know, thrown out these and similar things to shame us, he was not as yet satisfied with that but needs must inflict upon us from day to day new and ingenious kinds of confusion—as he recently proved in the case of our envoys. For a page will not suffice to tell how he treated those same envoys of ours, how cruelly he imprisoned them and afflicted them, when captive, with nakedness, cold, hunger and thirst and blows; and how at length he ordered them to be led like martyrs through the midst of the city, furnishing a spectacle for all; so that one would call him and believe him as mad as Decius the tyrant, and a burner of saints. Wherefore, beloved, be not tardy—may all in common not be tardy—to give ear to my request, and to that of thy fellow-bishops, that thou do come to Worms at Pentecost; and that thou there, with the other princes, do listen to many things a few of which are mentioned in this letter; and that thou do show what is to be done. Thou art asked to do this for love of thy fellow-bishops, warned to for the good of the church, bound to for the honor of our life and of the whole land.

Part II.   THE ROAD TO CANOSSA

The first Part of this Problem concentrated on the broad issues, the main lines of development which contributed to the controversy between Papacy and Empire. Now the focus changes. The particular question of lay investiture was to be settled in different ways all over Europe during the fifty years after 1075, and the general issue of spiritual versus temporal power was perhaps never to be definitively resolved. Nevertheless, the rest of this Problem is concerned primarily with the details of the immediate outcome of the dispute between Gregory VII and Henry IV which culminated in Henry's dramatic journey to Canossa. Canossa has something more than dramatic but passing importance; the student, aware of the larger matters at stake, can make of the most minute details a microcosm of a greater whole.

A.   THE PAPAL POSITION REAFFIRMED, AUGUST–SEPTEMBER 1076

1. *Gregory on the Excommunication of a King, August 1076.* Bishop Herman of Metz had apparently been forced to sign the decree of the bishops at Worms. In the following let-ter Gregory elaborates on the original papal position, in reply to some questions from the worried Herman who was desirous of strengthening his spirits for the battle ahead.[20]

You have asked a great many questions of me, a very busy man, and have sent me an extremely urgent messenger. Wherefore I beg you to bear with me patiently if my reply is not sufficiently ample.

There is no need to ask me who are the excommunicated bishops, priests, or laymen; since beyond a doubt they are those who are known to be in communication with the excommunicated King Henry—if, indeed, he may properly be called king. They do not hesitate to place the fear and favor of man before the commands of the eternal King nor to expose their king to the wrath of Almighty God by giving him their support.

He too feared not to incur the penalty of excommunication by dealing with followers who had been excommunicated for the heresy of Simony nor to draw others into excommunication through their dealings with him. How can we think of such things but in the words of the Psalmist: "The fool hath said in his heart there is no God," or again: "They are all gone astray in their wills."

Now to those who say: "A king may not be excommunicated," although we are not bound to reply to such a fatuous notion, yet, lest we seem to pass over their foolishness impatiently we will recall them to sound doctrine by directing their attention to the words and acts of the holy fathers. Let them read what instructions St. Peter gave to the Christian community in his ordination of St. Clement in regard to one who had not the approval of the pontiff. Let them learn why the Apostle said, "Being prompt to punish every disobedience"; and of whom he said, "Do not even take food with such people." Let them consider why Pope Zachary deposed a king of the Franks and released all his subjects from their oaths of allegiance. Let them read in the records [*registra*] of St. Gregory how in his grants to certain churches he not merely excommunicated kings and dukes who opposed him but declared them deprived of their royal dignity. And let them not forget that St. Ambrose not only excommunicated the emperor Theodosius but forbade him to stand in the room of the priests within the church.

But perhaps those people would imagine that when God commended his Church to Peter three times saying, "Feed my sheep," he made an exception of kings! Why do they not see, or rather confess with shame that, when God gave to Peter as leader the power of binding and loosing in heaven and on earth he excepted no one, withheld no one from his power? For if a man says that he cannot be bound by the ban of the Church, it is evident that he could not be loosed by its authority, and he who shamelessly denies this cuts himself off absolutely from Christ. If the

Holy Apostolic See, through the princely power divinely bestowed upon it, has jurisdiction over spiritual things, why not also over temporal things? When kings and princes of this world set their own dignity and profit higher than God's righteousness and seek their own honor, neglecting the glory of God, you know whose members they are, to whom they give their allegiance. Just as those who place God above their own wills and obey his commands rather than those of men are members of Christ, so those of whom we spoke are members of Antichrist. If then spiritual men are to be judged, as is fitting, why should not men of the world be held to account still more strictly for their evil deeds?

Perchance they imagine that royal dignity is higher than that of bishops, but how great the difference between them is, they may learn from the difference in their origins. The former came from human lust of power; the latter was instituted by divine grace. The former constantly strives after empty glory; the latter aspires ever toward the heavenly life. Let them learn what Anastasius the pope said to Anastasius the emperor regarding these two dignities, and how St. Ambrose in his pastoral letter distinguished between them. He said: "If you compare the episcopal dignity with the splendor of kings and the crowns of princes, these are far more inferior to it than lead is to glistening gold." And, knowing this, the emperor Constantine chose, not the highest, but the lowest seat among the bishops; for he knew that God resists the haughty, but confers his grace upon the humble.

Meantime, be it known to you, my brother, that, upon receipt of letters from certain of our clerical brethren and political leaders we have given apostolic authority to those bishops to absolve such persons excommunicated by us as have dared to cut themselves loose from the king. But as to the king himself, we have absolutely forbidden anyone to dare to absolve him until we shall have been made certain by competent witnesses of his sincere repentance and reparation; so that at the same time we may determine, if divine grace shall have visited him, in what form we may grant him absolution, to God's glory and his own salvation. For it has not escaped our knowledge that there are some of you who, pretending to be authorized by us, but really led astray by fear or the favor of men, would presume to absolve him if I [*sic*] did not forbid them, thus widening the wound instead of healing it. And if others, bishops in very truth, should oppose them, they would say that these were actuated, not by a sense of justice, but by personal hostility.

Moreover ordination and consecration by those bishops who dare to communicate with an excommunicated king become in the sight of God an execration, according to St. Gregory. For since they in their pride refuse to obey the Apostolic See, they incur the charge of idolatry, according to Samuel. If he is said to be of God who is stirred by divine love to punish crime, certainly he is not of God who refuses to rebuke the lives of carnal men so far as in him lies. And if he is accursed who withholds his sword from blood— that is to say, the word of preaching from destroying the life of the flesh—how much more is he accursed who through fear or favor drives his brother's soul into everlasting perdition! Furthermore you cannot find in the teaching of any of the holy fathers that men accursed and excommunicated can convey to others that blessing and that divine grace which they do not fear to deny by their actions.

2. *Gregory to the Faithful of Germany, September 1076.* In the following letter to his German supporters, the Pope suggests a policy for them to pursue in relation to King Henry.[21]

Gregory . . . to all the beloved brethren in Christ, fellow bishops, dukes, counts and all defenders of the Christian faith dwelling in the kingdom of Germany, greeting and absolution from all their sins through the apostolic benediction.

If you weigh carefully the decree in which Henry, king so-called, was excommunicated in a holy synod by judgment of the Holy Spirit, you will see beyond a doubt what action ought to be taken in his case. It will there be seen why he was bound in the bondage of anathema and deposed from his royal dignity, and that every people formerly subject to him is released from its oath of allegiance.

But because, as God knows, we are not moved against him by any pride or empty desire for the things of this world, but only by zeal for the Holy See and our common mother, the Church, we admonish you in the Lord Jesus and beg you as beloved brethren to receive him kindly if with his whole heart he shall turn to God, and to show toward him not merely justice which would prohibit him from ruling, but mercy which wipes out many crimes. Be mindful, I beg you, of the frailty of our common human nature and do not forget the pious and noble memory of his father and his mother, rulers the like of whom cannot be found in this our day.

Apply, however, the oil of kindness to his wounds in such a way that the scars may not grow foul by neglect of the wine of discipline and thus the honor of Holy Church and of the Roman Empire fall in widespread ruin through our indifference. Let those evil counselors be far removed

from him, who excommunicated for the heresy of Simony, have not scrupled to infect their master with their own disease and by diverse crimes have seduced him into splitting our Holy Church in twain and have brought upon him the wrath of God and of Saint Peter. Let other advisors be given him who care more for his advantage than their own and who place God above all earthly profit. Let him no longer imagine that Holy Church is his subject or his handmaid but rather let him recognize her as his superior and his mistress. Let him not be puffed up with the spirit of pride and defend practices invented to check the liberty of Holy Church, but let him observe the teaching of the holy fathers which divine power taught them for our salvation.

But if he shall have given you reliable information as to these and other demands which may properly be made upon him, we desire that you give us immediate notice by competent messengers so that, taking counsel together, we may with God's help decide upon the right course of action. Above all, we forbid, in the name of St. Peter, that any one of you should venture to absolve him from excommunication until the above-mentioned information shall have been given to us and you shall have received the consent of the Apostolic See and our renewed answer. We are distrustful of the conflicting counsels of different persons and have our suspicions of the fear and favor of men.

But now, if through the crimes of many [others] —which God forbid!—he shall not with whole heart turn to God, let another ruler of the kingdom be found by divine favor, such an one as shall bind himself by unquestionable obligations to carry out the measures we have indicated and any others that may be necessary for the safety of the Christian religion and of the whole empire. Further, in order that we may confirm your choice —if it shall be necessary to make a choice—and support the new order in our time, as we know was done by the holy fathers before us, inform us at the earliest possible moment as to the person, the character and the occupation of the candidate. Proceeding thus with pious and practical method you will deserve well of us in the present case and will merit the favor of the Apostolic See by divine grace and the blessing of St. Peter, prince of the Apostles.

As to the oath which you have taken to our best beloved daughter, the empress Agnes, in case her son should die before her, you need have no scruples, because, if she should be led by overfondness for her son to resist the course of justice or, on the other hand, should defend justice and consent to his deposition, you will know how to do the rest. This, however, would seem to be advisable: that when you have come to a firm

decision among yourselves that he shall be removed, you should take counsel with her and
with us as to the person to be entrusted with
the government of the kingdom. Then either she

will give her assent to the common judgment of
us all, or the authority of the Apostolic See will
release all bonds which stand in the way of justice.

B. THE AGREEMENT AT OPPENHEIM, OCTOBER 1076

Which was to prevail, Pope or King? Each had ordered the other to descend from his lofty
position. Part of the answer is to be found in the events leading up to Oppenheim on the
Rhine in October 1076. At this point the student starts to make increasing use of the
evidence of chroniclers, whose relative value, prejudice, and credibility must always be
carefully appraised.

1. *Oppenheim: The Evidence of the
Chroniclers.* Of the many chroniclers available for this momentous period in German
history, two are of particular value. The first
selection is from *The Annals of Berthold*
which were compiled by a monk from the
South German monastery of Reichenau,
Baden. The *Annals,* rather voluminous in
character and comparatively literary in flavor,
were written shortly after the events described, to which the writer had not been an
eyewitness. The second selection is from a
work by a Saxon churchman, Bruno, *Concerning the Saxon War.* Bruno, who wrote
his account about the year 1082, eventually
received office from Rudolph Duke of
Swabia, the leader of the Saxon opposition
to Henry.[22]

(*Annals of Berthold*) In the anathema itself
the lord pope had, on the part and in the name
of the omnipotent Father, Son, and Holy Ghost,
and by the authority of St. Peter, commanded all
Christians not to obey the excommunicated king
thenceforth as king in any way or serve him or
keep an oath which they had made or were to
make with him. This not the smallest part of
the princes of the realm observed, and, though
they were very often called to come to the king,
they refused, striving diligently to have zeal for
the Lord as they knew it. Even if they had
known him to have been unjustly and uncanon-
ically excommunicated, yet, according to the decree of the council of Sardica, they must not communicate with him in any way until they knew
that he had been reconciled. Wherefore, fearing
to associate with the king as yet unreconciled,
since they could neither persuade him nor punish
nor correct him, and since they shuddered to
agree with him, they strove, as was fitting, to
avoid him. Therefore the lords of the kingdom
agreed, in the fall, to have a conference with
him at Magdeburg, where they could by general
council define what ought to be done about the
matter of such great importance, and where they

might be allowed to serve their king and lord,
when he had been admonished, turned to penance, and reconciled.

When they assembled there with no small force
of soldiers, the king and his advisors were en-
camped on the other side of the Rhine at the
town of Oppenheim with a considerable gathering of loyal men, threateningly and angrily
wrought up. The princes of the realm, however,
remained on this side of the Rhine; they questioned among themselves and, with God's assent,
conferred more intimately one with another as
to what conclusion they should reach in such an
unusual matter. Thither had come the legates
of the Apostolic See with letters pertaining to this
matter, by which the pope had intrusted the
bishop of Patavia, already long accepted as apostolic representative, to reconcile all canonically,
the king excepted, who fittingly came to render
satisfaction and do worthy penance, those namely
who wished to stand on the side of St. Peter. Of
these, the archbishop of Mainz with his knights,
the bishops of Trier, of Strasburg, of Verdun, of
Luttich, of Münster, the elect of Utrecht, of
Spires, of Basel, of Constance, the one at Ulm,
and several abbots, as well as a considerable host
of more or less important personages who had
been excommunicated because of the crime of
associating with the king for disobedience or because they had received masses and offices from
priests condemned for incontinence or the heresy
of simony, were there reconciled and received into
communion.

Finally, after they had spent ten days in such
matters, the king, when he saw and heard that
so many and such great men had yielded to the
apostolic see, and that they were considering making another king in his place, pretended to yield,
though unwilling and reluctant and no longer
with any spirit beyond his grief, not only to the
pope, but also to the princes of the realm, in all
that they wished to impose on him or wanted him
to observe. To them it then seemed, in addition
to other things, that in the first place the see
and city should be freely returned to the bishop

of Worms, that the queen should leave it with all her following, that their hostages should be returned to the Saxons, and that the king should entirely separate himself from his excommunicated followers, and that he should also, without delay, send letters to pope Gregory, strongly intimating that he would perform due obedience, satisfaction, and fitting penance, and that he himself should await the apostolic answer and reconciliation, meanwhile abiding by their advice.

These and all the other matters the king performed there, though not with entire candor. From thence he despatched the letters, composed as they had agreed between themselves and sealed in their presence—he, nevertheless, later secretly altered and changed these to suit his will—to be presented to the pope at Rome by the archbishop of Trier. But the princes of the kingdom, fearing the tricks and the usual folly of the king's counselors, which they had so often experienced, likewise directed to Rome, in haste, trustworthy legates, who had been present at everything there enacted, so that the pope might not be deceived by their tricks, and to implore him, humbly supplicated through the mercy of God, to deign to come to these parts to settle this dissension. Furthermore, in order to constrain the king more perfectly to obedience to the Apostolic See, they took oath before they separated that if the king by his own fault remained excommunicated longer than a year they would no longer hold him as their king. Then, for fear of the king's future wrath and vengeance upon them, since many of them had left him, without visiting and greeting him, so that he was greatly angered with them, they pledged each other aid if anything should be done against them on this account, and returned, joyfully, each to his own home.

(*Bruno, Concerning the Saxon War*) And when they had already begun to confer about choosing a new king the Saxons wanted to choose one of the Swabians; the Swabians wanted one of the Saxons. Over on the other bank of the Rhine the town of Mainz held Henry, all hope of holding his kingdom gone. Nevertheless, he sent messengers to arouse their pity that they might accord him the privilege of making reparation, for he had been punished enough. Our party, however, absolutely refused to deal with them until he had been absolved from the anathema by the papal legate. To hasten the account, they agreed to endure the humility of penance on the conditions which our party held out. When he had agreed to this our men proposed first that he reinstate in full authority the bishop of Worms, who had been long expelled from his city; secondly, that he should have letters written in which he admitted that he had unjustly afflicted the Saxons. These letters were to be looked over

by our men, were to be signed with the royal seal in their presence, and, thus sealed, were to be given to them and carried by their messengers throughout Germany and Italy. Then he himself was to go to Rome and, by making fitting amendment, free himself from the bonds of the anathema.

Accordingly, the bishop was installed in the city with great honor. The letters were written and signed in the presence of our men and sent by our messengers throughout Germany and Italy, while the king prepared in all haste to free himself from the bonds of the anathema through the indulgence of the pope. But every one of our men took oath that unless Henry IV, son of the emperor Henry, was absolved from the ban by the pope at the beginning of February, never would he be, or be called, their king. This oath the patriarch was the first to take, and when it was set down on parchment he placed it among the letters in his wallet. Nevertheless, he kept it better in writing than he did in deed, and, as was said shortly before, he suffered a cruel punishment.

Then the bishop of Patavia, legate of the Roman see, did likewise. After them all the bishops, dukes, counts, and all the other greater and lesser dignitaries who were present took the oath. But the bishops accomplished more than the others, for they kept it among their letters. Then they despatched a legate to the pope to have him come to Augsburg early in February in order to have the case considered carefully in the presence of all. There the pope might either absolve him from the ban or constrain him more closely than before. In the latter event they might then, with the pope's counsel, select another king who knew how to rule. When these matters had been accomplished the two armies separated with great friendship and marched home, rejoicing and singing the praise of the Lord.

2. *The Agreement at Oppenheim, October 1076.* The decisions of the diet at Oppenheim were formally recorded in two decrees, the promise of the king to the pope, and a general edict. Both decrees are printed below.[23]

(*Promise of the King to Offer Obedience to the Pope.*) Being admonished to do so by the counsel of our faithful ones, I promise to observe in all things the obedience due to the Apostolic See and to thee, Pope Gregory, and will take care devoutly to correct and to render satisfaction for anything whereby a derogation to the honor of that same see, or to thine, has arisen through us. Since, moreover, certain very grave charges are brought against us concerning attempts which I am supposed to have made against that same see and against thy reverence: these, at a suitable time, I will either refute by the help of innocence and by the favor of God, or, failing this, I will at length willingly undergo a suitable penance for them. It behooves thy holiness also, moreover, not to veil those things which, spread abroad concerning thee, cause scandal to the church—but rather, by removing this scruple too from the public conscience, to establish through thy wisdom the universal tranquillity of the church as well as of the kingdom.

(*Edict Cancelling the Sentence against Gregory VII, October, 1076.*) Henry, king by the grace of God, sends to the archbishops, bishops, margraves, counts and dignitaries of every rank the honorable distinction of his goodwill. Inasmuch as we have been brought to recognize, through the rep-

resentations of our faithful ones, that we have been wanting in clemency, in some regards, towards the Apostolic See and its venerable bishop, Pope Gregory: it has pleased us, in accordance with healthful counsel, to change our former sentence and to observe, after the manner of our predecessors and progenitors, due obedience in all things to the holy see and to him who is known to preside over it, our master Gregory the Pope. And if we have presumed to act too severely against him we will atone for it by rendering fitting satisfaction. We will, moreover, that ye also, warned by our Highness's example, do not hesitate to render solemn satisfaction to St. Peter and to his vicar; and that those of you who understand themselves to be bound by his ban do strive to be solemnly absolved by him—by our master, namely, Gregory the Pope.

C. WHAT HAPPENED AT CANOSSA

His obvious plight seemed to Henry to warrant desperate measures. A variety of chroniclers described this famous series of events, and selections have been reprinted from several who contribute in an important way to the reconstruction of the actual narrative. In this task the student will find it necessary to compare the stories of two or more chroniclers and, sometimes, to reconcile conflicts in this evidence as best he can. The last selection contains Gregory's own version of the incident.

1. *The Annals of Augsburg.* These *Annals* are the record by the clerk of the town of the events of the year which seemed noteworthy. This determined their nature—terse, often crude or very local in character—and to a considerable extent their value. Such town annals were quite common in the Middle Ages and these of Augsburg may be taken as typical of their kind.[24]

A most disgraceful discord between pope and king, between bishops and dukes, between clergy and laymen. The pope, on account of his zeal for the house of God, is repudiated. At Rome the legates of the king are ill treated by the partisans of the pope. Priests are wretchedly thrown out by laymen for being married, or for buying their offices; everything, sacred and profane, is mingled in confusion. The pope, repudiated, retires to strongly fortified castles and other safe places. A conference between king and dukes at Oppenheim. The winter continuously severe, and an excess of snow from the Calends of November to the Calends of April so that the trees wither. So barren of fruits is the soil that even the seed fails. A council of the pope and dukes against the emperor.

King Henry, going into Italy, is received with all honor by the pope at Canossa, though before repudiated by a council of the dukes. After he is

absolved from the ban he is honorably treated. While the king is staying in Italy Rudolph is made king at Foresheim, in an unhallowed spot on the estate of Pontius Pilate, in the middle of the Quadragesima. He, cursed with maledictions rather than consecrated, is anointed on the same day, contrary to the laws of the church. To add to his damnation, on that very day and in the same place—i.e., Mainz—a great many people are killed. King Henry, returning from Pavia, is received with all loyalty. Rudolph is driven into Saxony, his partisans in arms are visited with plunder, fires, and destruction of various kinds; his unhappy and sacrilegious followers suffer devastation and death. Laymen seize the possessions of churches and churchmen; both sides plunder and burn; many are deprived of their inheritance and benefices, many also of their lives. . . . King Henry spent the birthday of Mary in Augsburg [September 8].

2. *The Annals of Lambert.* In sharp contrast to the records of the town clerk are the *Annals* of Lambert, a monk of Hersfeld in Westphalia in northern Germany. Though not an eyewitness, his dramatic and readable description has always been popular. The monastery had had considerable contact with King Henry, once sheltering him in his youth, and was a frequent stopping-place for

travellers of distinction. Lambert began his story with Adam and ended just before the election of the anti-king, Rudolph, in 1077.[25]

When Worms had been surrendered and the bishop was assured a most peaceful position the Saxons and Swabians returned home proudly happy. They had sent legates to the pope to insure his presence on the day set for calming the storms of civil war throughout Gaul [i.e., Germany]. The king, for his part, realized that his safety depended upon his obtaining absolution from the anathema before the year was up. Furthermore, for reasons of his own, he did not regard it as very safe to air his case before the pope in the presence of such hostile accusers. Under the circumstances, therefore, he came to the conclusion that it would be best to meet the pope in Italy just as he was setting out for Gaul. There he would try to gain absolution from the anathema in any way that he could. Once this was obtained, his other difficulties must be easily dispelled. No religious scruples would then interfere with his holding a meeting with the princes and obtaining the counsel and loyalty of his friends against his enemies.

Leaving Spires accordingly a few days before Christmas, he began the journey with his wife and young son. No German of any prominence, only one man of inferior rank, accompanied him on this journey out of the kingdom. In need of provisions for so long a journey he besought aid of many whom he had helped in his happier days. Only a few, grateful either for past favors or compassionate for his present condition, afforded him any assistance. To this state of calamity and misfortune had he suddenly fallen from the very height of rank and affluence. There were at the same time other excommunicates who were hurrying to Rome with a most ardent desire to obtain absolution; but either from fear of the princes or, even more, of the pope, they would not let the king join them.

The winter this year was consistently violent and inclement. The Rhine, ice-bound, remained passable for pedestrians from the Festival of St. Martin [November 11] almost to the Calends of April. The vines in most places withered up, their roots snapped off by the cold. King Henry, on his way to Italy, celebrated Christmas in Burgundy at a place called Besançon. He was received here magnificently enough, considering his condition at the time, and was entertained by his maternal uncle, count William, who had very large and prosperous holdings there. His reason for veering from the right road off into Burgundy was that he ascertained that all the roads and approaches into Italy, commonly called passes, had been closed with guards by the dukes Rudolph, Welf,

and Berthold for the very purpose of preventing his passage.

After a proper observance of Christmas he set out from there and came to a place called Cinis [Mt. Cenis]. Here he met his mother-in-law and her son, Amadeus, a man of eminent authority, extensive possessions, and very honorable reputation in these parts. At his approach they received him with honor. Nevertheless, they refused to grant him an escort through their territory unless he paid them the five adjacent Italian bishoprics as the price of the journey. This the counselors of the king regarded as excessive and intolerable. But, since it was absolutely necessary for him to procure passage in any way that he could, and since they were unaffected by any ties of relationship or compassion for his misfortune, it was reluctantly arranged, after much negotiation, that they were to receive a certain province of Burgundy that was rich in all things as the price of his passage. Thus did the indignation of the Lord turn from him persons bound to him not only by oath and many benefices, but actual friends and relatives. . . .

His trouble in getting permission to cross was followed by another difficulty. The winter was very bitter and the mountains through which the passage lay, stretching far and wide with peaks reared up almost to the clouds, were encumbered with masses of snow and ice. Passage by horse or footman over that slippery and precipitous descent was impossible without great danger. But the anniversary of the day on which the king had been excommunicated was threateningly near and would permit no delay in the journey. He knew that, unless he were absolved from the anathema by this day, it was decreed by a general sentence of the princes that his cause be forever lost and his kingdom gone without hope of restitution.

Accordingly he procured some of the natives, who were familiar with the country and accustomed to the rugged summit of the Alps, to go ahead and in every way possible mitigate the difficulties of the trip for his party. Under their guidance they reached the crest of the range with some difficulty, but the descent, precipitous and, as has been said, slippery with glacial ice, defied any farther advance. The men, however, were ready to brave all danger by strength. Now crawling on hands and feet, now leaning on the shoulders of their guides, staggering over the slippery places, falling sometimes, sliding more, and at a serious risk of their lives, they managed at last to reach the level land. The queen and the women in attendance on her were placed on the skins of oxen and dragged along by the guides in charge of the party. Of the horses, some were placed on certain contrivances, while the others were dragged along with their feet tied together. Many of them died while they were being dragged along, more sickened, while but few passed through the danger whole and unaffected.

When the rumor spread through Italy that the king was coming, that he had overcome the dangers of the mountains and was established within the confines of Italy, all the bishops and counts of the region crowded to him and received him with the greatest honor and magnificence as befitted a king. Within a few days he was surrounded by an innumerable host. For there were those who from the very beginning of his reign had desired this advent. Italy was constantly infested with wars, party strife, robberies, and assaults of various kinds on individuals. This and every other invasion upon the law and the rights of the many by the presumptuous few they expected him to correct with the royal censure. Then, too, it had been noised about that he was hastening in great anger to depose the pope. This also pleased many, for it would afford them the opportunity of obtaining fitting vengeance upon him who had so long suspended them from ecclesiastical communion.

Meantime, the pope was on his way to Germany. The princes who had met at Oppenheim had sent letters to him urging him to meet them at Augsburg on the day of the Purification of Saint Mary (February 2) to discuss the case of the king. Accordingly, in spite of the dissuasion of the Roman nobles who feared the uncertain outcome of the affair, he hastened his departure as much as he could in order to be there on the appointed day. His escort was furnished by the countess Matilda. . . . When he had started he learned unexpectedly that the king was already in Italy. At the urgence of Matilda, therefore, he retired into a certain highly fortified place called Canossa, to wait there until he had more carefully ascertained the purpose of the king's coming. He wished to know whether the king came to ask for pardon, or whether he was wrathfully seeking to avenge the excommunication by force.

King Henry, however, had a conference with the countess Matilda, and sent her to the pope, laden with prayers and promises. With her he sent also his mother-in-law, his son, likewise the margrave Azzo, the abbot of Cluny, as well as some of the princes of Italy who need not be mentioned. They begged the pope to absolve him from the excommunication and not rashly to place faith in the accusations of the German princes who were moved rather by the passion of spite than by the love of justice. When the pope heard this message he said that it was unfitting and quite contrary to ecclesiastical law to air the case of a defendant in the absence of the accusers. Nay, more, he told them that if the king were confident of his innocence he should lay aside

every scruple of fear and trustfully present himself at Augsburg on the day on which the princes had decided to come together. There, when the charges of both sides had been heard, he would receive most righteous justice on every point, without prejudice or favor, according to ecclesiastical law.

To this they answered that the king would never in the world evade a trial which he knew would be a most unassailable vindication and recommendation of his equity and innocence. But, they urged, the anniversary of the day on which the king had been excommunicated was drawing near, and the princes of the kingdom who had held aloof thus far pending the outcome of this affair were growing impatient. If he were not absolved before that day, according to Palatine law, he would be held unworthy of royal dignity and undeserving of any further hearing to prove his innocence. For this reason, they said, he seeks absolution so resolutely, and is ready to offer any form of satisfaction which the pope may demand in order only to be absolved from the anathema and to receive the grace of ecclesiastical communion. As for the charges which his accusers bring against him, he will be ready to make full answer, as if nothing had been done by this agreement, when and wherever the pope may ordain. Then, according to the pope's sentence, he will be ready to receive his kingdom again if he refute the charges, or resign with equanimity if his case is lost.

For a long time the pope refused to consider it, for he feared that the king was inconstant and of a disposition easily influenced by his immediate attendants. Overcome at last by the importunities of these zealous advocates as well as by the weight of their opinions, he said, "If he is truly penitent, let him give to our power his crown and other insignia of his kingdom as an evidence of truth and as an act of penance; and, after being so obstinate, let him profess himself unworthy of the kingdom." The envoys considered this too harsh, and they urged him strongly to temper his sentence and not utterly destroy a reed, already shattered, by the severity of his decision. Upon this exhortation he very reluctantly agreed that the king might come in person and, if he performed true penance for his admitted errors, the sin which he had committed by inflicting contumely upon the apostolic chair he might now expiate by obedience to it.

He came as he was ordered; the castle being inclosed by a triple wall, he himself was admitted within the inclosure of the second wall, while his attendants were left outside. There, his royal regalia laid aside and without any evidence of royalty or display of pomp, he stood as a humble penitent with bare feet from morning to night seeking the sentence of the pope. This he did on the next day, and again on the third. On the fourth he was finally admitted to the papal presence, and after much discussion on both sides he was at last absolved from excommunication on the following conditions.

First, that at the time and place which the pope should designate, he should appear before the German princes assembled in general council and should answer the charges preferred against him. There, with the pope as judge, if so it seemed to expedite matters, he should accept his decision, retain his kingdom if he refuted the charges, or give it up with equanimity if the charges were proven and he was held unworthy of the throne according to ecclesiastical law.

Second, that whether he retained or lost his kingdom, he should seek vengeance on no one for this trouble.

Third, that up to the day when, after proper discussion, his case had been ended, he should wear no ornaments of royal elegance, no insignia of royal dignity; he should not by his own right do anything in the administration as he was wont to do; decide nothing which ought rightly to be considered; and, finally, he should levy no royal or public taxes except for the sustenance of himself and his immediate servants.

Fourth, that all who had pledged loyalty to him by oath should meantime in the presence of God and men remain free and unhindered by the bonds of this oath and the obligations of loyalty.

Fifth, that he should forever dismiss from intimacy with himself Robert, bishop of Babenberg, Oudalric of Cosheim, and others by whose counsel he had betrayed himself and his state.

Sixth, that if the charges were refuted and he retained his kingdom, he should always be obedient to the Roman pontiff and comply with his decrees, and in accord with him stand forth as the worldly powerful co-operator in the correction of the abuses against the laws of the church which had by a pernicious custom grown up in the kingdom.

Last, that if he falsely agreed to any of these conditions the absolution which he had so earnestly sought would be endangered; nay, more, he would be considered as already convicted and confessed. He should then seek no further audience to prove his innocence, and the princes of the kingdom, thereby freed from all religious scruples in regard to their oath, would create another king upon whom they could agree.

These conditions the king accepted gratefully and promised with the most sacred assertions possible that he would observe all of them. And it was not a case of an acceptance of faith by one making rash promises, for the abbot of Cluny, though his monastic religion kept him from taking oath, interposed his faith before the eyes of the All-seeing God, while the bishop of Zeitz, the bishop of Vercelli, the margrave Azzo, and the other princes at the gathering confirmed by oath, over sacred relics, that the king would do as he had promised and would be led from his word neither by any temporary straits nor by a change in succeeding events.

When the excommunication was thus absolved the pope celebrated the solemn mass. When the sacred offering was ready he called the king and the rest of the people to the altar. Extending the body of the Lord with his hand, he said, "I have for some time received letters from you and your adherents in which you claim that I occupy the papal chair through the heresy of simony and that my life is spotted with various other crimes before as well as after I had received the episcopate, which, according to the canons, would have prevented all access to the sacred orders. This I could refute by the testimony of many suitable witnesses, both of those who are intimately acquainted with my career from the very beginning, as well as of those who are responsible for my elevation to the episcopacy. Yet, lest I seem to rely too much on human rather than on divine witness and in order to bring the whole scandal to short account before all, behold this body of the Lord which I am about to take. May it be for me this day the test of my innocence. May the Omnipotent God by His judgment either clear me of the crime charged against me if I am innocent or strike me with a sudden death if I am guilty."

With these and other terrible words he prayed the Lord to be most just judge of his case and asserter of his innocence, and then he took part of the sacred wafer and consumed it. This he did freely while the people acclaimed aloud their praises to God and offered thanks for his innocence. Then, commanding silence, he turned to the king and said: "Do therefore, my son, if it pleases you, what you have just seen me do. The princes of Germany have for days confused our ears with their accusations. They heap a great multitude of crimes upon you for which they think that you should not only be suspended from all administration of public affairs, but from ecclesiastical communion also, and even from any intercourse in secular life whatever for all time. They are especially anxious to fix a day and place and have an audience accorded them for the discussion of the charges which they bring against you. And you know best that human judgments often vacillate, and that falsity is sometimes more persuasive than truth. An untruth adorned with ornaments of words, with suavity, and by the genius and fluency of eloquent men, receives a more welcome hearing than the truth ungraced with eloquence which is often despised. Since, therefore, I wish you good counsel, all the more since you have in your calamities sought the patronage of the apostolic chair as a suppliant, so do as I admonish. If you know that you are innocent and that your reputation has been assailed with false charges by your enemies in a spirit of calumny, take the remainder of this sacred wafer and thus free, in a moment, the Church from the scandal of God and yourself from the uncertainty of a long dispute. Then your innocence will be proved by God's witness, every mouth turned against you in scandal will be stopped, and, with me as your advocate and the most vehement maintainor of your innocence, the princes will be reconciled to you, the kingdom restored, and the storms of civil war, with which it has been so long harassed, allayed."

The king, astonished at this unexpected situation, became very much embarrassed, looked around for excuses, and, drawing away from the multitude, he discussed with his friends how he might evade such an awful test, which was a matter of difficulty. When he had recovered his spirits he talked to the pope of the absence of the princes who had kept faith with him in his trouble; that without the accord of the accusers the effect of such a test would be destroyed, and that the incredulous would question a satisfaction rendered in the presence of the few here assembled. Therefore, he earnestly besought the pope to defer the whole matter to a general council where, while the accusers were gathered together and the accusations and the persons of the accusers were discussed according to the ecclesiastical law as the princes of the realm had proposed, he might refute the charges.

With great dignity the pope granted his petition, and when the solemn mass was ended he invited the king to dinner. And when this was ended and he had instructed him carefully as to what he must observe, the pope dismissed him with kindness and in peace to the men who had so long remained outside the walls. Furthermore, he sent out the bishop of Zeitz, Eppo, before him to absolve from their excommunication those who had incurred it by indifferently associating with the excommunicate before his absolution, kindly warning them not to occasion any stain upon the communion just newly received.

3. *The Annals of Berthold.* Berthold of Reichenau, to whom the student has already been introduced, furnishes an interesting comparison with Lambert; neither was an eyewitness and both wrote very shortly after the events they describe.[26]

When this colloquy had come to an end, about the Calends of November, a heavy snow, far greater than usual, began to cover the lands everywhere. This, an omen and sign of evil to come, greatly astounded not only the regions on this side of the Alps, but, which is more amazing, all Lombardy with its unheard-of amount. In fact, the Rhine and the Po alike, to say nothing of other streams, were so hardened by the excessive freezing cold that for a long time they afforded in themselves an icy road for all wanderers as though over land. Thus did the bitter and snow-laden winter continue with constant cold even to the Ides of March—that is, from the conference at Oppenheim to the colloquy which was held by the princes at Foresheim. Finally, on that very day, the snow began little by little to grow less, until after some time had elapsed it fairly flowed.

The king, however, when the said conference at Oppenheim had come to an end, remained for some time at Spires with the supporters and overseers whom the princes of the realm had assigned to him, and lived like a penitent. Then, suspecting on account of the aforesaid oath that their [the princes'] treachery and cunning would be turned against himself, he collected his counselors again from all sides and rashly disregarded the pleasure of the princes, and, to the end that he might not be deprived of his kingdom, he fortified himself most diligently with all the industry and attention of his own genius, with all the various investigations of his counselors, and by conferring on plans together.

The bishop of Toul, and also the one of Spires, with many others upon whom this had been imposed as a mark of obedience by the bishop of Patavia, soon hastened to Rome and gave themselves up to the pope as guilty, with due satisfaction and obedience. When these had been canonically reconciled he had them imprisoned in the jails of certain monasteries in order to test their obedience for some time, until by the intervention of the empress they were released therefrom and were permitted to return home with the grant of communion, but without having their rank restored.

Upon their footsteps the archbishop of Trier followed in great haste with the letters of the royal embassy, saluted the pope, and presented to him the falsified letters. These the pope was unwilling to have read except in the presence of the legates of the princes, so that they, who had also been present at the writing, might be witnesses at the reading. Accordingly, after these had been read, the legates recognizing the material as far other than that which had been composed and sealed in the presence of the princes of the realm, protested most freely by the Lord God that it was not the same, but that it had been altered and changed in places. So the archbishop of Trier, though at first he began to defend the letters, yet at length when he had been caught and reminded by these men confessed publicly that the fraud in these letters was not his, but the work of some one else whom he did not know. Thus the lord pope, together with the empress, watchfully discovered that all which this lying letter said of the obedience of the king was not a truth from the heart but was feigned statement full of deception. Thus what the king most anxiously entreated—namely, that he be permitted to come to Rome to be reconciled with the pope, the pope was unwilling to grant at all, but with apostolic authority commanded him to meet him at Augsburg in the presence of the princes of the realm, to be heard and reconciled by him, and he sent back word emphatically enough by the legates of both parties that he would come there to them about the feast of the Purification of St. Mary if God willed it. When they had received the letters of apostolic benediction in which, as is fitting, he admonished them very carefully, especially about his escort, about other necessaries, and about the peace, they returned joyfully to their fatherland to announce the coming of so great a guest.

Accordingly, when the princes had gratefully heard what these letters conveyed, they strove with every effort to make every preparation, not a little exhilarated by the great hope of restoring the ecclesiastical religion and observance. The heart of the king, stirred with far different intention, when he found out the proposition of the pope, strove industriously, with many consultations, to meet him before he entered our territory. For he proposed either to force the pope into flight in terror of the very great force of soldiers which he had gathered together at any price or, with the help of the Romans and his other counselors whom he had corrupted with such great gifts and thus made them each his supporter, to force the pope to his wish. If that failed, however, they, as warlike and angry as himself, should together fight to drive the pope unhurt from the church and substitute another after the heart of the king; and, thus elected and ordained as emperor by that pope, he would, with his wife, return to his fatherland in glory; that if, he however foolishly enough planned, by all these measures he succeeded in making the pope, overcome by the threats and blandishments of the Romans, compliant to himself, he would then be pious toward him, but very severe toward his adversaries.

Advised and encouraged by these and, as rumor has it, not a few other senseless proposals of his counselors, he obstinately set himself against the correction arranged by the princes and against the restoration of the church and did not cease to oppress their [the princes'] magistrates in every way and to free himself entirely from them as he wished. To this purpose a certain margrave, Opertus by name, who came at this time from Lombardy, encouraged him more than the others. This man, magnificently loaded by him with gifts and honors, was seized with sudden death near Augsburg as he was on his way to his own country. He had fallen from his horse, and thus as he died a wretch condemned, he discovered how great a load the apostolic anathema was, although he had formerly regarded it as nothing.

The king celebrated the birth of the Lord at Besançon in Burgundy as best he could, for he remained there scarcely a day. Then after he had taken up his wife and son and also a whole host of followers, as had already been previously arranged, crossing the Rhone at Geneva, climbing and crawling over the Alps by the most difficult way, he entered Lombardy through the bishopric of Turin. There, collecting to himself also the host of excommunicated bishops, and as if to fortify their case by a sort of defensive majesty, he told them craftily that he would speak to the pope not only about the sentence of anathema on himself, but rather to have the harmful sentence over them investigated by him.

They, however, on the contrary, tried to dissuade the king from calling him pope, whom they had at his command cast forth from the church abjured, and whom they had forever separated from the body of the church as condemned by an anathema. Nevertheless, they thought it fitting to yield to time and comply, since he was constrained by the bond of such unavoidable necessity lest he, as false king, should rashly annul the pleasure of the princes entirely, and thus most justly incur their opposition; but then, that is to say, after this dispensation and the address to the pope, so necessary to him, he should, together with them, labor with every effort to free himself and the whole kingdom from so sacrilegious a man; but if he did not do this he should not ignore the fact that he himself would, by the most crafty spite and arrogance of him who bore the apostolic name, be deprived not only of his kingdom and honor but probably of his life, and he should not in the least doubt that they, who had always been undaunted and prepared to go with him to death and destruction, would perish and be condemned likewise.

When, however, the legates of the king and of the princes had been dismissed by the pope and had begun their journey home, the pope, ever most ready to devote himself to his flock, at the appointed time went to the place which they had agreed upon; and there, as they had arranged, he awaited the escort for his march with impatience. But in vain; for when the princes found out about the stealthy and unexpected flight of the king over the Alps, they feared the wiles and assaults of the king; and though they were reluctant and unwilling, they ceased trying to send the agreed escort to meet the pope. So the pope waited for them some time at the castle of Canossa.

But when they, with difficulty, sent word to the pope that they could not come to him in the face of such dangers, then he was very much vexed that he had come there in vain, but not giving up hope of being later able to reach the Teutonic lands for the needs of the church, he was disposed to stop there for some time to wait for such an event. Then, reflecting that the journey of the king and his counselors was not of much advantage to the church and himself—nay, that it would render the Lombards, whom he had found rebellious to God and himself, much more rebellious; that it had troubled the people of Germany, distracted by no mean schism, and greatly worried them as to what they should do about so senseless a man; and that it had greatly disturbed the whole kingdom on all sides—he placed all his cares on the Lord, as befits an apostolic man, and prayed with tears day and night that the Divinity inspire him how he might rightly arrange to settle such a great matter synodically.

Then the king, accepting the wholesome advice of his men, laid aside the plan which he had with mad anger and malice conceived against the pope, and decided, with the intervention and aid of the countess lady Matilda, of his mother-in-law, marchioness Adelaide, of the abbot of Cluny, who had himself come there after he had just recently been reconciled at Rome for having associated with the king, and of all the others whom he could attract to his side, to meet the pope and submit, yield, obey, and agree with him in everything. With this intention, though he concealed it somewhat from the Lombards, he sent messengers to bring the aforesaid mediators to himself, and he himself followed them shortly to the aforesaid castle. These, meeting the king at the appointed place, aired the matter for which they had come together at great length, and considered it in every way with the usual consultations, but I know not what tricky and deceitful promises they gave in their most careful consideration, which they were quite afraid to bear as straightforward and true to the pope, who was, in truth, most experienced, for he had long been and was almost daily dealing with such cases. Nevertheless, since necessity so demanded it, they soon came back and related to the pope truthfully, and in order, everything which they thought colored and false.

The king, following hurriedly in their footsteps, came precipitately to the door of the castle with his excommunicated friends, though as yet unexpected and without the answer of the pope or a word of invitation, and, knocking sufficiently, he begged with all his strength to be allowed to enter. There, dressed in coarse woolen garments, with bare feet and freezing, he stayed outside the castle, even to the third day, with his friends, and thus, most strictly tested by many trials and temptations and found obedient as far as human judgment extends, he demanded with tears, as is the custom of penitents, the favor of Christian communion and the apostolic reconciliation.

The lord pope, however, who was most cautious and as unwilling to be deceived as to deceive, and who had so frequently been deluded by so many promises of the king, did not very easily credit his words. After much exchange of opinion he was at last persuaded that if the king would come most promptly to confirm by oath in person, or through others whom he might name as witnesses for himself, these conditions which he would now impose for the welfare of the holy church, and should in addition consent to give pledges into the hands of those intermediaries who were present for the observance of this oath and also of the empress, who was not yet there; if he should thus bind the compact he would not refuse to receive him again to the favor of Christian communion. The king with his followers, however, when he heard this answer of the pope, regarded the proposal as too harsh; but since he could not otherwise be reconciled, willing or unwilling, he agreed to it most sadly.

At length they intervened with the pope, who agreed that the king need not take the oath; two bishops, however, of Naumburg and Vercelli, besides other friends of his who would take oath, were chosen to take the oath for him. Who, that we may commemorate this most important oath, swore in this fashion—namely, that their lord Henry, whenever within the year pope Gregory should decide, would come into peace and concord with the princes of the realm either according to the judgment or the compassion of the pope, and that neither he nor any of his men would inflict any harm upon the pope or his legates into whatever parts of the kingdom they should come for the welfare of the church, nor should he capture or kill them; and if they were harmed by any other person, he should aid them in good faith as soon as he could; and if there were any obstacle in his way so that he could not meet the engagement which the pope had fixed, then as soon as possible he should meet it without further delay.

When this agreement had been made as before said, the king, weeping copiously, and the other excommunicates also in tears, were allowed access to the pope. What tears were shed by either party no one can easily say. When the pope, not a little moved for these lost sheep who were again seeking God with their pitiable lament, had delivered a suitable address on canonical reconciliation and apostolic consolation to them, after they had prostrated themselves with fitting humility and had confessed their rash presumption, and thus with apostolic indulgence and benediction, reconciled and restored to Christian communion, he took them into the church. Then, when he had made the customary oration and had greeted the king and the five bishops of Strasburg, Bremen, Lausanne, Basel, and Naumburg, and many others with the holy kiss, he called the king to the place of communion and extended to him the Eucharist which he had before forbidden him. The king, protesting that he was unworthy of participation in it, departed without the communion. Wherefore the pope not unwisely took it as an indication of impurity and an evidence of some hypocrisy latent in him, which the Spirit revealed, and after that he never presumed to place full faith in his words. But then when the dinner was quite ready they ate together at the same table and satisfied their wants with sober food; then, rising with the act of grace, they talked together about the most necessary matters of the promise of obedience, the pledges given, that the oath should not be violated, about the perfection of penance, as well as about avoiding contact with the excommunicated Lombards.

Then the king, after he had received the apostolic freedom and benediction, departed with all of his followers except the bishops, whom the pope ordered to be imprisoned as suited his good pleasure. Furthermore, the binding of this oath, which remained still to be done by the friends of the king, he insisted should be performed by them. This they tried to change from its agreed form, in fear that they would soon be taken by the pope as guilty of perjury; and in order not to swear they fled in every direction. One of them, the bishop of Augsburg, fled clandestinely at night without the permission of the pope and without being reconciled to him. Thus in the first compact which they had agreed upon these mendacious men left the pope craftily deluded and deceived.

About the same time that Roman Quintius, who to the addition of his damnation now held the bishop of Como captive, near the church of St. Peter at Rome, thought to visit the king at Pavia, and expected the king to treat him magnificently; nay, he didn't doubt at all that he deserved to have great gifts given to himself, not only for the capture of the bishop, but also for the sacrilegious seizure of the pope. When he came to the court the king did not dare to receive him with the kiss as he was wont to greet his friends, since Quintius was excommunicated, but feigned that on account of the many important affairs which now occupied him he could not receive him as was fitting and as he so much de-

served, and thus he put off meeting his friend for some days. Quintius, however, somewhat angered, proclaimed that he was being disdained and deceived until he at length extorted from the king the promise of favors and most certain evidences of a fitting reception. But on the night before the appointed day he was suffocated by a sudden deadly tumor in his neck, and without seeing or greeting the king he most quickly descended to the infernal regions, condemned to eternal death.

4. *Bruno, Concerning the Saxon War.* This Saxon churchman and author is already familiar to the student.[27]

The pope had, in accordance with the wishes of the princes, started toward Augsburg in order to reach there at the beginning of February in the year of our Lord 1077. Our men, too, were hastening there to receive him with due veneration when, lo! it was announced to the pope that Henry had entered Italy with a large army. It was furthermore reported that if he had come across the mountains with his original intention it was to set up another pope. Accordingly, he [the pope] sent an envoy to meet our men while he himself turned back with many fears to save Italy from fire and sword.

Henry, however, wandered through Italy, geographically, but even more was he uncertain in thought as to what he should do, for he feared that whatever he did he would lose his kingdom. If he did not come as a suppliant to the pope and receive absolution from the ban, he knew certainly that he was lost; if he did come as a suppliant to render satisfaction, he feared that the pope would deprive him of the kingdom on account of the enormity of his crimes; or, if he were disobedient to the pope the chains of papal restraint over him would be doubled. By such worries was he torn. Yet, though he felt that he was lost and would lose anyway, he selected that course as an alternative which offered most hope. Dressed in woolen garments and with bare feet he went to the pope and told him that he cared much more for the celestial than for the earthly kingdom, and offered to accept humbly whatever penance he would inflict. The pope was pleased at the extreme humility of so great a man. He bade him, therefore, not to wear the insignia of royalty until he himself permitted it, so that the contrition of his heart might be more acceptable to omnipotent God if his vile garments bore external evidence of it. He admonished him further to keep away from his court and counsel those who were excommunicated, lest the cleanliness gained by a proper conversion with the grace of God should become uncleanly by contagion with others. Both of these conditions he promised to observe, and was legally absolved. Then he was dismissed by the pope, though not without further admonitions not to lie to God, and that if he did not fulfil his promises not only would the former bonds not be taken off, but others even more stringent would be added.

So he went back to his people and began to dismiss the objectionable from his court. Thereupon they began to cause trouble, saying that if he now dismissed from his presence those by whose wisdom and courage he had thus far held his throne the pope could neither give him back that kingdom nor provide him with another. By such arguments his mind was changed. He returned to his former habits and bad counsel. He placed the golden crown upon his head and thus bound the anathema upon his heart with a grip stronger than that of iron. He held intercourse with the excommunicated, and from communion with the pious he was an outcast. It was therefore, manifest to all that his statement that he loved the celestial kingdom more than the earthly was not true. If he had but a moment remained in obedience he would not be holding his earthly kingdom in peace and when the time came would gain the celestial to hold without end. Now, however, that he is disobedient, he will now obtain this which he loves without great labor, and will not gain the other unless he greatly changes his whole life.

Meanwhile the Saxons and Swabians met at Foresheim, but there were present also legates from other regions who indicated that their people approved whatever these should suitably accomplish in regard to the republic. There was present likewise a legate of the pope who strengthened with the authority of the apostolic sublimity all the measures which our men took for the effective arrangement of the kingdom. From the many whom they brought forth in the election as of proven worth, nevertheless, the Saxons and Swabians with one accord chose Rudolph of the Swabians as their king.

But when they had to approve him as king one by one some of them wanted to impose some conditions, to elevate him as king over themselves according to this law, when he had made an especial promise to them of justification of their injuries. For Duke Otto was unwilling to make him his king until he should promise to restore the honor unjustly taken from him. In the same manner also many others interposed individual conditions which they wanted him to promise to correct. The apostolic legate, learning of this, kept it from being done, and pointing out that the king would be king not of single states, but of all, he regarded it sufficient if the king promised to be just to all. He said likewise, that if the king were elected in the manner in which they had begun, each exacting promises in advance, the election would not

be sincere, but would seem to be polluted with the poison of the heresy of simony. Nevertheless, certain cases were especially excepted which, because they had unjustly flourished, he ought to correct—namely, that he should not grant bishoprics for money or friendship, but to allow to each church the election by its members as the canons command.

This was likewise approved there by general assent and confirmed by the authority of the Roman pontiff, that the royal power should fall to no one by heredity, as the custom had been before, but that the son of a king, even if he were very worthy, should become king through a free election, rather than by lineal descent; on the other hand, if the son of a king were unworthy, or if the people didn't wish him, the people should have him in power whom they wished to make king.

After all these matters had been legally settled they conducted Rudolph, the king-elect, to Mainz with great honor, and supported him while he was receiving the royal consecration with veneration and with might, as was soon apparent. He was, however, consecrated by Siegfried, archbishop of the city of Mainz, in the presence and with the assistance of very many others in the year of the Lord 1077 on the 7th day from the Calends of April (26th of March).

5. *The Anonymous Life of the Emperor Henry IV.* This *Life* was probably written by a churchman and companion of the king shortly after the latter's death in 1106.[28]

Their [the Saxons'] conspiracy was further strengthened by the addition of some of the Lombards, Franks, Bavarians, and Swabians. Exchanging mutual pledges of faith, they combined to wage war on the king from all sides. They saw, however, that while they might wage war on him they could not dislodge or overcome him; nay, his strength was as yet unassailable. In order to weaken his power, therefore, they drew up a lot of fictitious charges against him. These charges were the foulest and worst that spite and malice could conceive, charges so foul that, should I set them down, they would nauseate me to write them, you to read them. Mingling truth with falsehood, they sent the indictment to Pope Gregory. It held that so disgraceful a person, better known for his crimes than by his name, was unfit to rule, especially since he had not obtained his royal dignity at Rome, that its rights in constituting kings ought to be returned to it, and that the pope and Rome should, with the counsel of the princes, select a king whose wisdom and conduct accorded with so great an honor.

The pope was both misled by this fraudulent representation and lured on by the honor of creating a king, which they so falsely held out to him. He placed the king under a ban and commanded the bishops and princes to abstain from all intercourse with the excommunicated sovereign. Furthermore, he announced that he would speedily come to the Teutonic lands to deal with the affairs of the church, and especially with those of the kingdom. Nay, he even went further. He absolved from their oath of fidelity all who were so bound to the king in order that this absolution might turn against him all whom that bond still held.

This displeased many—if, indeed, any one may be displeased at what the pope does—and they asserted that this deed was as ineffectively as it was illegally done. But I dare not set forth their assertions lest I seem with them to disapprove the deed of the pope. Soon most of the bishops who sided with the king either from affection or from fear withdrew from his side for fear of their positions. So, also, did most of their followers.

When the king saw his affairs in such a plight he secretly made a shrewd resolve. Suddenly and unexpectedly he set out to meet the pope. And thereby he accomplished two things—he received absolution from the ban and intercepted the suspicious conference of his enemies and the pope. As to the crimes charged against him he made no particular reply, for, he asserted, it was not for him to answer the accusation of his enemies, even if it were true. What advantage has it been to you to have had him put under the ban when, now released of that ban, he enjoys his power fully? What has it profited you to have accused him of fictitious charges when, with his easy answer, he has scattered your accusation like a puff of wind? Nay, what madness put you in arms against your king, the ruler of the world? Your malicious conspiracy has accomplished nothing, has profited nothing. Whom the hand of God has confirmed in his rule you cannot dethrone. Where is that loyalty which you swore to him? Wherefore have you been unmindful of the benefices which he conferred on you with royal favor? Henceforth employ wise counsel, not rage. Be penitent for your venture and thankful that he did not rise up in his might and conquer you; that he did not grind you in the dust under his feet and inflict that vengeance on you which would show to future ages what the hand of a king could do. At all events, O bishop, see that you do not wander from the paths of justice; see that you become not transgressors of your plighted faith. Nay, you know what the consequences will be to you.

6. *The Book of Bonizo to a Friend.* The author was bishop of Sutri and an intimate friend and partisan of Gregory. His *Book,*

in reality a church history, was written soon after Gregory's death in 1085.[29]

Meanwhile the venerable Gregory started with the grace of peace on his journey to Augsburg with the greatest difficulty on the march, for a most severe winter was then raging. The king, in truth, holding his oath of little account, very suddenly entered Italy. And there are those who say that he wished to capture the pope unaware. Which seems sufficiently like the truth, for Gregory, bishop of Vercelli, his chancellor in fact—he whom the princes had commanded to conduct the pope over the mountains—after he had crossed the yoke of the Apennines, heard that he had secretly come within the town of Vercelli. When he announced this to the pope the pope straightway went into Canossa, a most safely fortified camp of the most excellent Matilda.

The king, in the meantime, seeing that his schemes had been divulged, as was evident to every one, laid aside his ferocity, and approached Canossa clothed in dove-like simplicity. And, by suffering for several days with bare feet on the snow and ice, he deceived all the less wise, and from the venerable Gregory, who, nevertheless, was not ignorant of his tricks, he obtained the absolution which he sought, the Lord's sacrament taking a part in the celebration of the mass in this manner. For he made him a participant in the divine supper in the presence of the bishops, abbots, religious clerks, and laymen in this way, so that if the king had humiliated himself in mind as in body and believed him to be rightful pope, that he himself had been excommunicated after the example of Photius and Diocurus, and that he could be absolved through this sacrament, the supper would be to his salvation, but otherwise Satan would enter him after the host. What more? When the mass had been celebrated they had dinner together. Then he and all those absolved from the excommunication were commanded to avoid all association with the excommunicate. But there are some who say that he swore to the pope his life and his limb and his honor. But I do not at all affirm what I do not know.

7. *Donizo's Life of Matilda.* Matilda, countess of Tuscany, was heiress to lands of extreme strategic importance to Pope and German king alike. Her mother, Beatrice, had married Godfrey, Duke of Lorraine, as her second husband, whose opposition to the royal house was indefatigable. Matilda and Beatrice were friends and confidants of Gregory and Canossa was one of the countess' castles. Donizo was actually a monk in a monastery at Canossa, but his *Life* was not

completed until 1115 and remained essentially a paean in verse of the pious Matilda's virtues.[30]

Shortly after the death of her [Matilda's] mother the rumor spread through the world that the king had been condemned by the renowned pope. The brave and the powerful throughout the kingdom were indeed much wrought up, and said it was rash and arrogance not to yield sincerely and graciously to the Roman see, which holds the keys of heaven. Wherefore they rightly decided to shun him until he should yield; until he should strive to regain the peace of the pope. When the king realized that he could not otherwise recover his rule he sent word to his relation, Matilda. He begged her without fail to devise some plan to get the pope to come to Lombardy from the city that he himself might seek fitting indulgence.

And the pope, when he heard the prayers of Matilda, granted her request. The worthy shepherd left Rome, came to Canossa, and tarried there. Here she fittingly received him as the vicar of St. Peter, and was greeted by him. There, too, was the queen, wife of King Henry, accompanied by Matilda, and there was a great throng besides. Beyond me [i.e. at Canossa] there became a new Rome while these things were going on. O city, to your honor, behold! With me are king and pope alike, as well as the lords of Italy, and also of Gaul, Ultramontane, and Rome, effulgent with the pontifical garland. Many wise men, too, are here. Among them stands Hugh, abbot of Cluny, who was godfather of the baptism of the king.

These lords held discussions of peace, and, though they remained in discussion for three days, there was no peace. And the king, wishing to withdraw, went to the chapel of St. Nicholas and tearfully implored the pastor Hugh to become surety for his peace. To the king's entreaty the abbot replied, "This may not be." Then he asked it of Matilda, but she also replied, "This no one may do but you, I believe." Then on bended knees he said to her: "Unless you aid me greatly nevermore will I shatter a shield, for the pope has punished me severely. Go, powerful cousin, do me this favor." She raised him and pledged him her word. Then she left him and went up to the pope while the king remained below. She spoke to the pope, crying out against the end of the king, and in the earnestly spoken words of the venerable lady he put faith. Nevertheless, the recalled king was to swear to be faithful to the holy see and to do whatever the patron Gregory willed.

January this year was very cold, and there was a great deal of snow. Seven days before the end of the month the king, his naked feet nipped by the cold, was admitted to the presence of the pope. He threw himself on the cross, shouting again and again: "Spare me, blessed father! Holy father, spare me, I beseech thee." And the pope, gazing upon him crying, pitied him very much, and after having blessed him accorded him peace. Then he conducted mass himself and gave him the body of the Lord. They ate together in the castle of Canossa, and after he had taken his oath the pope dismissed him. He went to the city of Regina, where there was a great throng hostile to the pope and fearful that this peace would be made.

8. *Gregory to the German Princes, January 28, 1077.* Immediately after the events described by the chroniclers, the pope issued a circular letter to the princes of Germany, giving his version of the incident at Canossa. The text of his letter follows.[31]

Whereas, for love of justice you have made common cause with us and taken the same risks in the warfare of Christian service, we have taken special care to send you this accurate account of the king's penitential humiliation, his absolution, and the course of the whole affair from his entrance into Italy to the present time.

According to the arrangement made with the legates sent to us by you we came to Lombardy about twenty days before the date at which some of your leaders were to meet us at the pass and waited for their arrival to enable us to cross over into that region. But when the time had elapsed and we were told that on account of the troublous times—as indeed we well believe—no escort could be sent to us, having no other way of coming to you we were in no little anxiety as to what was our best course to take.

Meanwhile we received certain information that the king was on the way to us. Before he entered Italy he sent us word that he would make satisfaction to God and St. Peter and offered to amend his way of life and to continue obedient to us, provided only that he should obtain from us absolution and the apostolic blessing. For a long time we delayed our reply and held long consultations, reproaching him bitterly through messengers back and forth for his outrageous conduct, until finally, of his own accord and without any show of hostility or defiance, he came with a few followers to the fortress of Canossa where we were staying. There, on three successive days, standing before the castle gate, laying aside all royal insignia, barefooted and in coarse attire, he ceased not with many tears to beseech the apostolic help and comfort until all who were present or who had heard the story were so moved by pity and compassion that they pleaded his cause with prayers and tears. All marveled at our unwonted severity, and some even cried out that we were showing, not the seriousness of apostolic authority, but rather the cruelty of a savage tyrant.

At last, overcome by his persistent show of penitence and the urgency of all present, we released him from the bonds of anathema and received him into the grace of Holy Mother Church, accepting from him the guarantees described below, confirmed by the signatures of the abbot of Cluny, of our daughters, the countess Matilda and the Countess Adelaide, and other princes, bishops and laymen who seemed to be of service to us.

And now that these matters have been arranged, we desire to come over into your country at the first opportunity, that with God's help we may more fully establish all matters pertaining to the peace of the Church and the good order of the land. For we wish you clearly to understand that, as you may see in the written guarantees, the whole negotiation is held in suspense, so that our coming and your unanimous consent are in the highest degree necessary. Strive, therefore, all of you, as you love justice, to hold in good faith, the obligations into which you have entered. Remember that we have not bound ourselves to the king in any way except by frank statement—as our custom is—that he may expect our aid for his safety and his honor, whether through justice or through mercy, and without peril to his soul or to our own. . . .

The Oath of Henry, king of the Germans:

I, Henry, king, within the term which our lord Pope Gregory shall fix, will either give satisfaction according to his decision, in regard to the discontent and discord for which the archbishops, bishops, dukes, counts and other princes of the kingdom of Germany are accusing me, or I will make an agreement according to his advice—unless some positive hindrance shall prevent him or myself—and when this is done I will be prepared to carry it out.

Item: If the same lord Pope Gregory shall desire to go beyond the mountains or elsewhere he shall be safe, so far as I and all whom I can constrain are concerned, from all injury to life or limb and from capture—both he himself and all who are in his company or who are sent out by him or who may come to him from any place whatsoever—in coming, remaining, or returning. Nor shall he with my consent suffer any hindrance contrary to his honor; and if anyone shall offer such hindrance, I will come to his assistance with all my power.

IV
Manor, Town, and Industry

ECONOMIC history traces through the past the matters with which economics is concerned. These are the thoughts and acts of men and women in those relations which have to do with their work and livelihood, such relations as those of buyers and sellers, producers and consumers, town-dwellers and countrymen, rich and poor, borrowers and lenders, masters and men or, as we say nowadays, employers and employees, and unemployed too. In economic history there is never a definite starting point. However far back we go into the past, we have to do with men who worked along with their fathers, in an economic world which was already a going concern when they were born, until the older generation dropped out and their own sons were working beside them. If we were to go back to paleolithic times, we should be dealing with a very experienced world in which there had been many changes and in which new practices were growing up while others were obsolescent.

G. N. Clark

CONTENTS

QUESTIONS FOR STUDY

PART I

1. How large was Alwalton? Who lived at Alwalton? What different kinds of income did the abbey derive from the manor?

2. What differences of tenure and status are to be noted between Thomas le Boteler and Hugh Miller? How independent of the outside world does Alwalton appear to have been in 1279?

3. Over what different types of offenses did the manorial courts of the priory of Durham have jurisdiction? Were these offenses against persons or against the public?

4. To what extent is the court an administrative as well as a judicial body?

5. What differences in tenure can be noted between the tenants of Warkington (p. 88) and the tenants of Alwalton (pp. 85–6)?

6. Describe the industrial organization represented by the craft guilds. What seems to have been the internal organization of these guilds? Their relations to each other? To the town?

7. Is any sort of hierarchy distinguishable among the guilds within the textile industry?

8. What are some of the sources of friction, internal and external, discernible?

9. Compare a craft guild with a modern trade union.

PART II

10. What is the difference between a loan and a *Commenda?* Between the *Commenda* and the partnership on p. 94? Between that partnership and the articles of partnership for the Barcelona Bank?

11. What is the difference between a loan and a bill of exchange?

12. "The story of the development of instruments of credit is essentially the problem of the allocation of risk." Discuss.

13. What were some of the risks surrounding medieval commerce?

14. From the documents available compare the attitude of the guild, the town, the state, and the Church towards economic activity. Which had the public interest most at heart? Which was the most modern in its outlook?

15. What would St. Thomas probably have said about the loan on p. 93?

INTRODUCTION TO THE PROBLEM

Mankind has always been concerned with making a living and realizing its material desires. Medieval man was no exception. He had to make this living out of a certain environment, which, either through inherited techniques or through his own inventiveness, he was able to adapt at least partially to his purposes. He did not come at the task alone, for he and his fellows were constantly cooperating to attack this common problem. In fact the collective institutions and practices so developed constitute one of the more significant parts of the medieval economic story. Finally, this economic activity did not take place in a world apart. It was not only inseparably connected with many other aspects of medieval life, but also subject to a complex of controls, some imposed from within, some originating in an external authority, local or national, and others deriving from the general mores and ethics that pervaded the society as a whole.

The continent of Europe afforded medieval man a peculiarly happy environment for his labors. Its three main zones—the southern lands of the Mediterranean basin, the mountain mass which bordered this area to the north, and the cooler northern plain arching from the Bay of Biscay to the Urals and beyond—were all productive in their own different fashions. Furthermore, geography tended to encourage intercourse among them. The Mediterranean had already provided a focal point for many of the ancient civilizations. The mountain barrier was breached at convenient intervals leading into the northern plain and the latter was interlaced with a network of great river systems which facilitated communication between north and south. For the most part the configuration of the European coastline was one to encourage coastwise commerce. It was this high degree of accessibility which underlay the gradual rise of northern and western Europe to economic importance by early modern times. Finally, although the great explorations of the fifteenth and sixteenth centuries would be required to circumvent the desert barrier separating Europe from the tropics and the east, it faced its neighbor Africa across the Mediterranean and possessed a geographic relationship to the vast Asiatic continent which was continuously to influence the course of European history.

As was the case with the political institutions of feudalism, the economy of the Middle Ages can never be completely separated from the economy of the ancient world. Although there were newcomers in the fourth century and later—the Germans or the Northmen, for instance—"the prevailing condition of things" which made necessary medieval economy, and "the old institutions" to be transformed into the new, were both to be found in the Mediterranean center of the ancient world. As the fabric of the Roman empire disintegrated, the parts were forced to rely on their own efforts and products for survival. The result was the growth amid the confusion of the fourth and fifth centuries of a predominantly local agrarian economy. Yet much of the old survived. Constantinople, the Eastern empire, and the trading cities of Italy kept alive something more than a regional economy. The Church functioned as a rallying point for urban activity, a pillar of order in the troubled times and the ultimate authority for the business ethics as well as the general morality of medieval society. Finally, the Moslems and their eruption into the Mediterranean world between the seventh and ninth centuries may well stand for the epitome of the change from ancient to medieval economy. If the Saracen invaders dealt yet another blow to the already-disintegrating Roman empire, one which furthered if it did not compel the return to agrarianism, they also were instrumental in the economic recovery of the Middle Ages.

Spoiled by the wealth of statistics available for the economic analysis of modern society, the student may be puzzled as to how to study the economy of the Middle Ages. Neither the technique of assembling such statistics, nor, in many cases, the curiosity to obtain the information they represent, was present. Thus, in the documents which follow the student must work by indirection, argue from fragments, or seek to read between the lines information which the writer did not particularly care to reveal. The language too may be obscure or even archaic, and a glossary has been provided to explain the more technical expressions encountered in the texts.

GLOSSARY

Assize: Statutory price; or periodical sessions of a court in England.

Bedel: A parish constable.

Burgess: Inhabitant of a borough or incorporated town, with full municipal rights.

Croft: Enclosed piece of land; a small holding.

Curtilage: Area attached to dwelling house.

Demesne: That section of the lord's holding which has not been let out to tenants.

Fine: Payment made to a lord by anyone who acquired land in a manor in any way other than by inheritance.

Heriot: A payment made to a lord, consisting of the best beast, on taking possession of a holding acquired by inheritance.

Hide: A measure of land, usually about 120 acres; as much as would support one family and dependents.

Livres: Throughout the selection the symbol £, has been used for pounds or *livres*. The pound was always identified with a particular place (*i.e.,* pound of Genoa) and until sometime after 1250 the pound was only a unit for accounting, not an actual coin.

Mercet or *Merchet:* Fine paid by a tenant or bondsman to his overlord for liberty to give his daughter in marriage.

Messuage: Dwelling house, with outbuildings and lands assigned to its use.

Put himself upon the country: Submit to trial by a jury made up of neighbors or fellow countrymen.

Reeve: A bailiff, steward, or overseer, appointed by the lord.

Perch: One square rod.

Relief: A payment made to a lord by one who acquired land in the manor by inheritance.

Rood: Forty square rods.

Tallage: A manorial tax levied by the lord upon his tenants.

Terrar and Bursar: Official of a religious house who received rents and made disbursements.

View of frank pledge: A court held periodically for the production of the mutually responsible members of the neighborhood.

Villein: Tenant holding his land by menial services.

Virgate: An early English land measure, varying greatly in extent, from twenty to forty acres.

Works: A single day's worth of the customary labor owed by a tenant.

Part I.   MANOR, TOWN, AND INDUSTRY

The economic environment of the Middle Ages was predominantly rural and agrarian in sharp contrast to the increasingly urban and industrial society of modern times. For any sustained or extensive exploitation of this environment medieval man had to develop methods of cooperation with his fellows. In the first section which follows this process is seen in agriculture, on the manor. The second section concerns the efforts of the towns-men to work together, the beginnings of a modern industrial organization.

A.   ECONOMIC ORGANIZATION: THE MANOR

The most characteristic and fundamental institution of medieval agrarian society was the manor. In the first place it was a *territorial* unit (roughly equivalent to a villa, vil, or township). As such it represented "a stretch of country occupied by a rural population, grouped in a single village, or perhaps in several hamlets, surrounded by agricultural lands." [1] In another sense a manor was a unit of *agriculture,* with an organization based upon a unique form of land distribution, certain methods of farming in common, and certain complex relationships involving the lord's land and the rest of the lands on the manor. Finally the manor was a *political* or *legal* body, for under the leadership of the lord or his representatives the members of the manorial community were united in a governmental system. Though typical, the manor was by no means a universal or a uniform phenomenon in the Middle Ages, but occurred in different forms at different places and at different times. And in some areas the free village community or the scattered holdings of free tenants persisted throughout the period.

1. *A Thirteenth-century Manor* (1279). A medieval English landlord who was desirous of discovering the value of his holdings might call upon his steward or some other representative for a survey or description of his manors. Here is a survey of the manor of Alwalton, in Huntingdonshire, one of the manors of the Abbey of Peterborough.[2]

The abbot of Peterborough holds the manor of Alwalton and vill from the lord king directly; which manor and vill with its appurtenances the lord Edward, formerly king of England gave to the said abbot and convent of that place in free, pure, and perpetual alms. And the court of the said manor with its garden contains one-half an acre. And to the whole of the said vill of Alwalton belongs 5 hides and a half and 1 virgate of land and a half; of which each hide contains 5 virgates of land and each virgate contains 25 acres. Of these hides the said abbot has in demesne 1 hide and a half of land and half a virgate, which contain as above. Likewise he has there 8 acres of meadow. Also he has there separable pasture which contains 1 acre. Likewise he has there a common fish pond with a fish-weir on the bank of the Nene, which begins at Wildlake and extends to the mill of Newton

and contains in length 2 leagues. Likewise he has there a ferry with a boat.

Free Tenants. Thomas le Boteler holds a messuage with a court yard which contains 1 rood, and 3 acres of land, by charter, paying thence yearly to the said abbot 14s.

Likewise the rector of the church of Alwalton holds 1 virgate of land with its appurtenances, with which the said church was anciently endowed. Likewise the said rector has a holding the tenant of which holds 1 rood of ground by paying to the said rector yearly 1d.

And the abbot of Peterborough is patron of the church.

Villeins. Hugh Miller holds 1 virgate of land in villenage by paying thence to the said abbot 3s 1d. Likewise the same Hugh works through the whole year except 1 week at Christmas, 1 week at Easter, and 1 at Whitsuntide, that is in each week 3 days, each day with 1 man, and in autumn each day with 2 men, performing the said works at the will of the said abbot as in plowing and other work. Likewise he gives 1 bushel of wheat for benseed and 18 sheaves of oats for fodder-corn. Likewise he gives 3 hens and 1 cock yearly and 5 eggs at Easter. Likewise he does carrying to Peterborough and to Jakele and nowhere else, at the will of the said abbot. Likewise if he sells a brood mare in his court yard for 10s or more, he shall give to the said abbot 4d, and if for less he shall give nothing to the aforesaid. He gives also merchet and heriot, and is tallaged at the feast of St. Michael, at the will of the said abbot. There are also there 17 other villeins, viz. John of Ganesoupe, Robert son of Walter, Ralph son of the reeve, Emma at Pertre, William son of Reginald, Thomas son of Gunnilda, Eda widow of Ralph, Ralph Reeve, William Reeve, William son of William Reeve, Thomas Flegg, Henry Abbot, William Hereward, Serle son of William Reeve, Walter Palmer, William Abbot, Henry Serle; each of whom holds 1 virgate of land in villenage, paying and doing in all things, each for himself, to the said abbot yearly just as the said Hugh Miller. There are also 5 other villeins, viz. Simon Mariot, Robert of Hastone, Thomas Smith, John Mustard, and William Carter, each of whom holds half a virgate of land by paying and doing in all things half of the whole service which Hugh Miller pays and does.

Cotters. Henry, son of the miller, holds a cottage with a croft which contains 1 rood, paying thence yearly to the said abbot 2s. Likewise he works for 3 days in carrying hay and in other works at the will of the said abbot, each day with 1 man and in autumn 1 day in cutting grain with 1 man.

Likewise Ralph Miller holds a cottage with a croft which contains a rood, paying to the said abbot 2s.; and he works just as the said Henry.

Likewise William Arnold holds a cottage with a croft which contains half a rood, paying to the abbot 2d; and he works just as the said Henry.

Likewise Hugh Day holds a cottage with a croft which contains 1 rood, paying to the abbot 8d; and he works just as the said Henry.

Likewise Sara, widow of Matthew Miller, holds a cottage and a croft which contains half a rood, paying to the said abbot 4d; and she works just as the said Henry.

Likewise Sara, widow of William Miller, holds a cottage and a croft which contains half a rood, paying to the abbot 4d; and she works just as the said Henry.

Likewise William Kendale holds a cottage and a croft which contains 1 rood, paying to the abbot 8d; and he works just as the said Henry.

Likewise William Drake holds a cottage with a croft which contains half a rood, paying to the abbot 6d; and he works just as the said Henry.

There are there also 6 other cotters, viz. William Drake, Jr., Amycia the widow, Alice the widow, Robert son of Eda, William Pepper, William Coleman, each of whom holds a cottage with a croft which contains half a rood, paying and doing in all things, each for himself, just as the said William Drake.

Likewise William Russel holds a cottage with a croft which contains half a rood, paying to the abbot 8d; and he works in all things just as the said Henry Miller.

There are moreover there 5 other cotters, viz. Walter Pestel, Ralph Shepherd, Henry Abbot, Matilda Tut, Jordan Mustard, each of whom holds a cottage with a croft which contains half a rood, paying thence and doing in all things to the said abbot just as the said William Russel.

Likewise Beatrice of Hampton holds a cottage and a croft which contains 1 rood, paying to the abbot 12d; and she works in all things just as the said Henry.

Likewise Hugh Miller holds 3 acres of land, paying to the abbot 42d.

Likewise Thomas, son of Richard, holds a cottage with a croft which contains half a rood, and 3 acres of land, paying to the abbot 4s; and he works just as the said Henry.

Likewise Ralph Reeve holds a cottage with a croft which contains 1 rood, and 1 acre of land, paying to the abbot 2s; and he works just as the said Henry.

Likewise each of the said cottagers, except the widows, gives yearly after Christmas a penny which is called head-penny.

2. *Records of a Manor Court, 1345–1370.* The lord of the manor usually possessed rights of jurisdiction over its inhabitants. In England after the middle of the thirteenth century the records of the proceedings of these manorial courts were put down on rolls which were kept by the lord's steward as he passed from manor to manor holding court. The selections which follow are from the rolls of the halmotes, or manorial courts, of the priory of Durham, which were held three times a year on each of the priory's fifteen manors.[3]

First Tourn of the Halmotes of the Priory of Durham, beginning at Fery, July 6th A.D. 1345, before lords William of Chareton and Robert of Benton, Terrar and Bursar, and Simon Esshe, Steward.

Spen, 1345. Agnes widow of Adam of Mora has taken a house and 50 acres of land which her husband Adam formerly held, paying annually for her life 33s 4d. And there is remitted to her 16s 8d a year from the old rent on account of her age and weakness of mind.

Billingham, 1345. Agnes daughter of William Nouthird has taken a cottage with the curtilage, which the said William her father formerly held, to be held on payment of 6d a year and 20 autumn works in the manor of Billingham, provided she has food. Fine, 2s; pledges J. of Stokton and Alexander son of Gilbert.

The reeve and jurors complain and present that certain persons named below do not hold land by reason of which they have any right to have part in the common pasture, and yet they feed their cattle on the pasture of the vill to the injury of those who hold land. It is therefore required that they remove their animals from the pasture so that for the future they shall not thus overstock the pasture; under penalty of half a mark.

North Pittington, 1358. Bonageus Moneyer came here into court and took a messuage and 28 acres of land which had been Christiana Ponchoun's, because no one of the blood of the said Christiana was willing to fine for them, to have and hold for the term of his life, on payment for the first 3 years of 13s. 4d. a year, and afterward 20s. a year. And the same Bonageus will repair within a year, at his own cost, the building of the foresaid messuage. And he gives for a fine 20s. of which 13s. 4d. is remitted for the repairs of the foresaid buildings. Pledges for the rent and for all other things which are required Robert Thomson and John Ponchoun.

Bonageus Moneyer came here and took a messuage and 20 acres of land formerly in the tenure of Richard of Aucland vicar of Pittington, which were seized into the hand of the lord because he left them and rented them without license of the lord; to have and hold for the term of his life, paying the ancient rent and doing for the lord and his neighbors what is required; on the pledge of John Ponchoun and Robert Thomson. And he gives as fine 13s. 4d.

West Raynton, 1364. It is reported by the inquisition upon which Hugh Urkyll has placed himself, viz. on the oath of etc. [8 names] that the said Hugh is a nativus [that is, a bondman of the lord born on the manor] of the lord prior and that his father and grandfather were considered as nativi of the said lord prior. And moreover this same Hugh made his fealty here in court just as pertains to a nativus. It is reported by the same inquisition that John Wydowson is a nativus of the lord and of like condition, etc.; and besides this, etc. has made his fealty, etc. It is ordained and enjoined on all who were on the foresaid inquisition that each of them hold what was said among them as a secret, under penalty of payment of 40d. by the one who is found guilty. It is enjoined on all the tenants of that vill and the vill of East Raynton that no one of them call any one of those vills "nativus" of the lord, under penalty of payment of 20s. by the one who is found guilty.

Billingham, 1364. It is enjoined upon all the tenants of the vill that none of them grind his grain outside of the domain so long as the mill of the lord prior is able to grind, under penalty of 20s.

Coupon, 1365. It is reported by the jury that Thomas son of Richard of Billingham staying at Melsonby and acting as common herdman there, is a nativus of the lord.

Newton Bewley, 1365. From John of Baumburg for his transgression against Adam of Marton, in calling him false, perjured, and a rustic; to the loss of the same Adam of Marton 40d., penalty 13d.

Mid-Merrington, 1365. From Richard, son of Thomas, because he has not recalled his son from school [schools for priests were forbidden to villein's sons] before the feast of St. Michael as enjoined upon him at the last Halmote, penalty 40d. It is enjoined upon all the tenants of the vill that none of them insult the pounder while fulfilling his duty, nor swear at him.

West Raynton, 1365. A day is given to all the tenants of the vill to make a law that neither they nor their wives nor their servants shall cut down anything within the woods, nor carry anything green away from the woods; each of them at the next court six-handed [i.e., taking an oath of his innocence supported by the oath of five other men].

Coupon, 1365. From Agnes Postell and Alice of Belasis, for breaking the assize of ale, 12d. From Alice of Belasis, for bad ale, and moreover because the ale which she sent to the Terrar was of no strength, as was proved in court, 2s.

Ackley, 1365. It is ordained by common consent that no one permit colts, calves, young steers or any other animals within the field in which grain is sowed until the grain is cut and carried off, under penalty of half a mark.

Fery, 1365. It is ordained by common consent that Robert Todd should keep his sheep from feeding on the grain of his neighbors and on the cowpasture, under penalty of 40d.; and moreover that each tenant keep his pigs, cows, horses, and other animals from feeding on the grain or treading it, and that the cottagers should keep their cattle within the common pasture, under the penalty foresaid.

Ackley, 1366. It is required of John, son of Thomas of Chilton, living at Coites that he recall his son from the schools before the feast of the Purification of the Virgin next.

West Merrington, 1367. It is enjoined on all the tenants of the vill that each of them cause to be plowed the outer parts of the field and then the inner parts, so that none of them . . . lose on account of lack of plowing.

Coupon, 1368. John Pulter and Robert Fauks were elected aletasters, and were sworn.

Newton Bewley, 1368. From Alice, servant of Adam of Marton, for leyr [leyr was a fine imposed upon women who had been guilty of incontinence] 6d. From Thomas, servant of the same for drawing his knife to strike John Smith, penalty 40d, by grace 12d.

Wallsend, 1368. It is enjoined upon all the tenants of the vill that each of them come on the summons of the reeve to discuss the common business touching the profit of the vill.

Hesylden, 1368. From Robert, son and heir of John son of Matilda, as a heriot for 1 messuage and 20 acres of land which he holds freely, for homage, and fealty and service of 40d and a heriot, viz. the best beast; 15s and nothing for relief.

Monkton, 1369. Robert Jackson, nativus of the lord, made his fealty to the lord at Jarrow, Thursday next after the feast of St. Luke the Evangelist, in the 69th year.

Heworths, 1370. It is enjoined upon all the tenants of the vill that they have the common forge and the common oven repaired.

East Raynton, 1370. From Margaret daughter of Robert Wright for merchet, pledge, Alice, her mother, 2s.

Fery, 1370. From Margaret Ferywoman for leyr, 6d. From Adam Graundorge for his transgression made against Robert Latany by killing his cow to the loss of 7s, 3d. A day is given to the same Adam to make his law against Richard, son of Peter, that he has not broken the leg of his cow. At the next court, with six hands. He has not found a pledge. Therefore let the said Richard recover against him. From Adam Graundorge for 1 cow of Richard, son of Peter, killed, to the loss of 10s, penalty 3d.

Wallsend, 1370. It is ordained by common consent that each tenant should come to the making of the hay of the common meadow when they shall be warned, under penalty of losing their part and even under penalty of heavy fine.

3. *Forces Working for Change: Manorialism in the Fourteenth Century.* The manor as an institution was no more static than it was uniform. Change can be discerned in the following selection, an agreement drawn up in 1386 between an English landlord, the Abbot of Bury St. Edmunds, and his tenants on the manor of Warkington.[4]

At the view of frankpledge held there on 20 October, 10 Richard II, it was granted to all the lord's tenants in the presence of John Mulso, Nicholas Lovet, Edmund Bifeld, Stephen Walker of Keteryng, and others there present, that if it pleased the lord they might hold certain bond lands and tenements at a certain rent and service, as follows, during a term of six years next after the date above-written, the term beginning at Michaelmas last past; to wit, that each tenant of a messuage and a virgate of bond land shall render to the lord 18s. yearly at four terms, to wit, at the feasts of St. Edmund the King and Martyr, Palm Sunday, the Nativity of St. John the Baptist, and Michaelmas, by equal portions, and shall do two ploughings a year at what times of the year he shall be forewarned by the bailiff of the manor for the time being, and shall work in "le Keormede" as he used before, save that the lord shall find him food and drink for the ancient customs, that is, for half a sheep and for each scythe 1/2d., and so he shall reap in autumn for two days, to wit, one day with two men and another day with one man, at the lord's dinner; he shall give 4d. for a colt if he sell it, he shall pay heriot if he die within the term, and he shall make fine for marrying his daughters and for his sons attending school, and for "leyrewite" [fine for having an illegitimate child] as he used before.

B.   ECONOMIC ORGANIZATION: TOWNS AND MERCHANTS

A general decline of urban activity had been one of the symptoms of the decline of the ancient world. Although certain towns (the trading towns of Italy or towns of an administrative or religious importance) had survived the troubled times, the early Middle Ages marked a low point in town life. Thus the revival of towns from the ninth century onwards represented one of the dynamic elements in medieval life. Their founding and survival were both determined by a combination of geographic, administrative, and economic factors: site, location, defense, commerce, and industry. Few of these towns had as many as 10,000 inhabitants, but their influence far outweighed either their size or their numbers. Of particular importance was the economic activity they sheltered and fostered. It did much to undermine the self-sufficiency of the countryside, to engender that new social phenomenon—the bourgeois or townsman, and to create a far-reaching interdependence among areas. The materials in the section which follows illustrate the nature, extent, and purpose of this cooperative economic activity in the medieval town.

1. *Business Organizes: The Shearers of Arras, 1236.* In the Middle Ages the organization of production displayed almost as much

variety as it does now. The householder producing for his own use, the small handicraftsman and his little shop, and the large-scale craftsman dependent on distant areas for both raw materials and markets were all to be found. In certain trades, notably textiles, an even more complicated system of production developed. The document which follows contains the regulations of the shearer's guild of Arras in northern France, which, like neighboring Flanders and the towns of northern Italy, was a center of the textile industry. Merchants purchased the raw wool and then put it out successively to the spinners, weavers, and finishers to be manufactured into cloth. The shearers, who received the cloth from the weavers and trimmed it down to the nap, plied one of the finishing trades.[5]

Here is the Shearers' Charter, on which they were first founded.

This is the first ordinance of the shearers, who were founded in the name of the Fraternity of God and St. Julien, with the agreement and consent of those who were at the time mayor and aldermen [*officers of the guild*].

1. Whoever would engage in the trade of a shearer shall be in the Confraternity of St. Julien, and shall pay all the dues, and observe the decrees made by the brethren.

2. That is to say: first, that whoever is a master shearer shall pay 14 solidi to the Fraternity. And there may not be more than one master shearer working in a house. And he shall be a master shearer all the year, and have arms for the need of the town.

3. And a journeyman shall pay 5 solidi to the Fraternity.

4. And whoever wishes to learn the trade shall be the son of a burgess or he shall live in the town for a year and a day; and he shall serve three years to learn this trade.

5. And he shall give to his master 3 muids [approx. 52 liters of grain] for his bed and board; and he ought to bring the first muid to his master at the beginning of his apprenticeship, and another muid a year from that day, and a third muid at the beginning of the third year.

6. And no one may be a master of this trade of shearer if he has not lived a year and a day in the town, in order that it may be known whether or not he comes from a good place. . . .

8. And if masters, or journeymen, or apprentices, stay in the town to do their work they owe 40 solidi, if they have done this without the permission of the aldermen of Arras.

9. And whoever does work on Saturday afternoon, or on the Eve of the Feast of Our Lady, or after Vespers on the Eve of the Feast of St. Julien, and completes the day by working, shall pay, if he be a master, 12 denarii, and if he be a journeyman, 6 denarii. And whoever works in

the four days of Christmas, or in the eight days of Easter, or in the eight days of Pentecost, owes 5 solidi. . . .

11. And an apprentice owes to the Fraternity for his apprenticeship 5 solidi.

12. And whoever puts the cloth of another in pledge shall pay 10 solidi to the Fraternity, and he shall not work at the trade for a year and a day.

13. And whoever does work in defiance of the mayor and aldermen shall pay 5 solidi.

14. And if a master flee outside the town with another's cloth and a journeyman aids him to flee, if he does not tell the mayor and aldermen, the master shall pay 20 solidi to the Fraternity and the journeyman 10 solidi: and they shall not work at the trade for a year and a day. . . .

16. And those who are fed at the expense of the city shall be put to work first. And he who slights them for strangers owes 5 solidi: but if the stranger be put to work he cannot be removed as long as the master wishes to keep him. . . . And when a master does not work hard he pays 5 solidi, and a journeyman 2 solidi. . . .

18. And after the half year the mayor and aldermen shall fix such wages as he ought to have.

19. And whatever journeyman shall carry off from his master, or from his fellow man, or from a burgess of the town, anything for which complaint is made, shall pay 5 solidi.

20. And whoever maligns the mayor and aldermen, that is while on the business of the Fraternity, shall pay 5 solidi. . . .

22. And no one who is not a shearer may be a master, in order that the work may be done in the best way, and no draper may cut cloth in his house, if it be not his own work, except he be a shearer, because drapers cannot be masters.

23. And if a draper or a merchant has work to do in his house, he may take such workmen as he wishes into his house, so long as the work be done in his house. And he who infringes this shall give 5 solidi to the Fraternity. . . .

25. And each master ought to have his arms when he is summoned. And if he has not he should pay 20 solidi.

26–30. [Other regulations concerning defense.]

31. And whatever brother has finished cloth in his house and does not inform the mayor and aldermen, and it be found in his house, whatever he may say, shall forfeit 10 solidi to the Fraternity.

32. And if a master does not give a journeyman such wage as is his due, then he shall pay 5 solidi.

33. And he who overlooks the forfeits of this Fraternity, if he does not wish to pay them when the mayor and aldermen summon him either for

the army or the district, then he owes 10 solidi, and he shall not work at the trade until he has paid. Every forfeit of 5 solidi, and the fines which the mayor and aldermen command, shall be written down. All the fines of the Fraternity ought to go for the purchase of arms and for the needs of the Fraternity.

34. And whatever brother of this Fraternity shall betray his confrère for others shall not work at the trade for a year and a day.

35. And whatever brother of this Fraternity perjures himself shall not work at the trade for forty days. And if he does so he shall pay 10 solidi if he be a master, but if he be a journeyman let him pay 5 solidi.

36. And should a master of this Fraternity die and leave a male heir he may learn the trade anywhere where there is no apprentice.

37. And no apprentice shall cut to the selvage for half a year, and this is to obtain good work. And no master or journeyman may cut by himself because no one can measure cloth well alone. And whoever infringes this rule shall pay 5 solidi to the Fraternity for each offense.

38. Any brother whatsoever who lays hands on, or does wrong to, the mayor and aldermen of this Fraternity, as long as they work for the city and the Fraternity, shall not work at his trade in the city for a year and a day. And if he should do so, let him be banished from the town for a year and a day, saving the appeal to Monseigneur the King and his Castellan.

39. And the brethren of this Fraternity, and the mayor and aldermen shall not forbid any brother to give law and do right and justice to all when it is demanded of them, or when some one claims from them. And he who infringes this shall not have the help of the aldermen at all.

2. *Organization Multiplies: The Crafts of Florence, 1316.* The following list of the crafts of Florence, most of which had been in existence for a long time, was drawn up early in the fourteenth century on the occasion of the levying of a tax by the town.[6]

1. Importers and finishers of cloth.
2. Cloth manufacturers.
3. St. Mary's Gate [silk].
4. Spicers.
5. Physicians.
6. Furriers.
7. Butchers.
8. Cobblers.
9. Smiths.
10. Dealers in used and new locks.
11. Stonemasons and woodcutters.
12. Old clothes and linen dealers.
13. Armor smiths and sword smiths.
14. Tanners, wholesale and retail.
15. Bakers [for bakeovens].
16. Goldsmiths and flaskmakers.
17. Innkeepers.
18. Harness and beltmakers.
19. Manufacturers of iron and wooden shields.
20. Saddlers.
21. Combmakers.
22. Rough carpenters and manufacturers of saddles for asses and mules.
23. Manufacturers of pack-saddles.
24. Retail winemerchants, as tax, 2 denarii per pound received from the sale of wine.
25. Linen and yarn merchants.
26. Dealers in bedfeathers and mattress makers.
27. Oil, cheese, and grain merchants; chaff [?] and fodder makers [?].
28. Helmetsmiths and brass workers.
29. Purse makers.
30. Chest and trunk makers.
31. Coopers, barrel makers, coffin makers, kneading trough makers.
32. Cloth-folders and finishers of French cloth.
33. Cloth-folders and finishers of Florentine cloth.
34. Greengrocers.
35. Hat and cap makers.
36. Dyers of all kinds.
37. Painters.
38. Bowlmakers, dart makers, turners, spinning-wheel finishers.
39. Barbers.
40. Makers and sellers of glass vessels.
41. Spiked helmets, buckle, and clasp makers.
42. Parchment merchants and bookbinders.
43. Tailors, seamstresses, and menders.
44. Fletchers and arrow makers.
45. Public weighers.
46. Packers.
47. Dicemakers.
48. City river fishermen.
49. Brick and lime burners, and makers of earthen vessels.
50. Manufacturers of glass vessels in the district.
51. Lenders of draught mules.
52. Brokers of all kinds.
53. Crossbow and bow makers.
54. Basket makers.
55. Cooks, sellers of tripe, cooked beans, and bean meal, vegetables, vermicelli, stews, etc.
56. Tallow merchants and catgut makers.
57. Wagon or carriage makers.
58. Ass drivers, haulers of sand, lime, mortar, paving stone, tiles, slates, stones, and hewn stones.
59. Proprietors of bath rooms.
60. Hand porters.
61. Teachers of grammar, arithmetic, reading, and writing.
62. Town criers.

63. Judges and notaries.
64. Money changers or bankers.
65. Sewer cleaners and garbage removers.
66. Weavers of all kinds.
67. Journeymen and apprentices to dealers in merchandise.
68. Smelters and workers at furnaces, coin makers; as well as those who put the gold and silver in the furnaces; also the assayers in all money operations.
69. Bell founders.
70. Wheel makers.
71. Millstone makers.
72. Workers in the quarry, and sellers of quarry products.
73. Workers in the marble and sandstone quarries.

3. *Organizational Disputes: The Master Saddlers and Their Journeymen, London, 1396.* Something of the hierarchy of guild organization has already been seen. Although the road from apprentice to independent master was nominally straight and clear, often an indefinite "post-graduate" period as a journeyman was exacted from the candidate. The following selection from the records of the city of London describes a dispute between the master saddlers and their journeymen.[8]

Whereas there had arisen no small dissension and strife between the masters of the trade of Saddlers, of London, and the serving-men, called yeomen, in that trade; because that the serving-men aforesaid, against the consent, and without leave, of their masters, were wont to array themselves all in a new and like suit once in the year, and oftentimes held divers meetings, at Stratford and elsewhere without the liberty of the said city, as well as in divers places within the City; whereby many inconveniences and perils ensued to the trade aforesaid; and also, very many losses might happen thereto in future times, unless some quick and speedy remedy should by the rulers of the said city be found for the same:—therefore the masters of the said trade, on the 10th day of the month of July, in the 20th year etc., made grievous complaint thereon to the excellent men, William More, Mayor, and the Aldermen of the City aforesaid, urgently entreating that, for the reasons before mentioned, they would deign to send for Gilbert Dustone, William Gylowe, John Clay, John Hiltone, William Berigge, and Nicholas Mason, the then governors of the serving-men aforesaid; to appear before them on the 12th day of July then next ensuing.

And thereupon, on the same 10th day of July, precept was given to John Parker, sergeant of the Chamber, to give notice to the same persons to be here on the said 12th day of July etc.

Which governors of the serving-men appeared, and, being interrogated as to the matters aforesaid, they said that time out of mind the serving-men of the said trade had had a certain Fraternity among themselves, and had been wont to array themselves all in like suit once in the year, and, after meeting together at Stratford, on the Feast of the Assumption of the Blessed Virgin Mary [15 August], to come from thence to the Church of St. Vedast, in London, there to hear Mass on the same day, in honor of the said glorious Virgin.

But the said masters of the trade asserted to the contrary of all this, and said that the fraternity, and the being so arrayed in like suit, among the serving-men, dated from only thirteen years back, and even then had been discontinued of late years; and that under a certain feigned color of sanctity, many of the serving-men in the trade had influenced the journeymen among them, and had formed covins [a collusive agreement] thereon, with the object of raising their wages greatly in excess; to such an extent, namely, that whereas a master in the said trade could before have had a serving-man or journeyman for 40 shillings or 5 marks yearly, and his board, now such a man would not agree with his master for less than 10 or 12 marks, or even 10 pounds, yearly; to the great deterioration of the trade.

And further, that the serving-men aforesaid, according to an ordinance made among themselves, would oftentimes cause the journeymen of the said masters to be summoned by a bedel, thereunto appointed, to attend at Vigils of the dead, who were members of the said fraternity, and at making offering for them on the morrow, under a certain penalty to be levied; whereby the said masters were very greatly aggrieved, and were injured through such absenting of themselves by the journeymen, so leaving their labors and duties, against their wish.

For amending and allaying the which grievances and dissensions, the Mayor and Aldermen commanded that six of the said serving-men should attend in the name of the whole of the alleged Fraternity, and communicate with six or eight of the master saddlers aforesaid etc.; both parties to be here, before the said Mayor and Aldermen, on the 19th day of July then next ensuing, to make report to the Court as to such agreement between them as aforesaid. And further, the Mayor and Aldermen strictly forbade the said serving-men in any manner to hold any meeting thereafter at Stratford aforesaid, or elsewhere without the liberty of the said city, on pain of forfeiture of all that unto our Lord the King, and to the said city, they might forfeit.

On which 19th day of July, came here as well the masters aforesaid as the governors of the serving-men; and presented to the Mayor and

Aldermen a certain petition, in these words:—

"Gilbert Dustone, William Gylowe, John Clay, John Hiltone, William Berigge, and Nicholas Mason, do speak on behalf of all their Fraternity, and do beg of the Wardens of the Saddlers, that they may have and use all the points which heretofore they have used."

Which petition having been read and heard, and divers reasons by the said masters unto the Mayor and Aldermen shown, it was determined that the serving-men in the trade aforesaid should in future be under the governance and rule of the masters of such trade; the same as the serving-men in other trades in the same city are wont, and of right are bound, to be; and that in future they should have no fraternity, meetings, or covins, or other unlawful things, under a penalty etc. And that the said masters must properly treat and govern their serving-men in the trade, in such manner as the serving-men in like trades in the City have been wont to be properly treated and governed. And that if any serving-men should in future wish to make complaint to the Mayor and Aldermen, for the time being, as to any grievance unduly inflicted upon him by the masters aforesaid, such Mayor and Aldermen would give to him his due and speedy meed of justice as to the same.

4. Organizational Disputes: Craftsmen vs. Traders, Douai 1244–1250.

Friction was possible not only within a guild but also between separate guilds or between the craftsmen of different towns. The following edicts are from the town of Douai in Flanders.[8]

(1244) 1. The edict is made that no one be so bold in all this town, either man or woman burgess, or man servant or maid servant, that he be a party to a revolt; and whoever does this will incur a forfeit of £60, and will be banished from the town for a year. And if any one has been a party to a revolt, let him make reparation, under forfeit of £60, and banishment from the town for a year.

2. And whoever should take part in a combination against the town, of whatever craft he may be, shall incur the same forfeit. In the year 1244, the month of January.

(1247) 1. And the edict is made that no one be so bold, either man or woman, if he take, or cause to be taken, cloth of Douai, or linsey-woolsey, in bolts or lengths, or any kind, outside of the town to sell, that he engage in cloth making, or that he be a partner or associate of a cloth maker, either man or woman.

2. And the merchant, man or woman, who should trespass in this shall incur a forfeit of £50 and be banished from the town, and shall lose the right to trade for one year.

3. And the cloth maker, man or woman, who should be a partner or associate of theirs shall incur the same forfeit of £50 and shall be banished from the town, and shall not be allowed to make cloth for a year.

4. And the merchant, man or woman, who takes cloth or linsey-woolsey, or causes them to be taken out of the town, whether it be for selling or trading, know that they may have but one associate for a single kind of merchandise.

5. And he who should trespass in this shall incur a forfeit of £50 and shall be banished from the city, and may not trade nor take an indirect part in trading for a year.

6. And if he seek ways and means to it in any manner whatsoever, and if he be convicted of it, he shall incur a forfeit of £50 and shall be banished, and shall lose the right to trade for a year.

7. And every burgess, man or woman, who has associates in these affairs of more than one person in one transaction shall release them before the coming feast of the nativity of St. John the Baptist under the same forfeit.

8. And no cloth maker, man or woman, may take cloth or linsey-woolsey, or cause them to be taken, to sell if it is not according to the permission of the sheriffs.

9. And if they take them away by their permission they shall agree to export cloth for one year.

10. And the cloth maker, man or woman, who should do otherwise shall incur a forfeit of £50 and shall be banished from the town, and shall lose his craft for one year.

These edicts were proclaimed in the year '47, the second day before the feast of Our Lady in March, and these edicts shall apply for five years.

[*Circa, 1250, Sheriffs' edict concerning the right of foreigners in the matter of dyeing.*]

1. The edict is made that no dyer be so bold that he dye wool in a caldron if it belong to a foreign man or woman, under forfeit of £10 and banishment from the town.

2. And let no man or woman who is a resident in this town cause such kind of wool to be dyed for a foreign man or woman under the same forfeit.

[*Sheriffs' edict forbidding the dyeing of materials which have not been woven and dressed in the town, circa 1250.*]

1. The edict is made that no dyer be so bold that he dye cloth or blankets if they have not been woven and dressed in this town, under forfeit of £50 and banishment from the town for a year.

2. And the man or woman who owns the cloth or blankets shall lose them.

3. And if a burgess, man or woman, cause

such cloths or blankets to be dyed by deceit, he shall incur the forfeit of the dyer.

4. And the dyer shall be acquitted if he has testimony which the sheriffs accept that the man or woman had told him the cloth or blankets had been woven and dressed in this town.

[*Sheriffs' edict forbidding all deceit in wool and in dye materials, circa 1250.*]

1. The edict is made that no one be so bold, either man or woman, in all this town that he commit fraud in woolen cloth or linsey-woolsey.

2. And let no one be so bold, either man or woman, that he commit fraud concerning dye materials.

3. And let no dyer commit fraud concerning his dye for the sake of money.

4. And whoever should trespass in any of the above edicts shall incur a forfeit of £50, and shall be banished from the town, and shall lose his craft for a year.

5. And the dye-maker who is a party to such operations will incur a forfeit of £50 and shall

be banished one year from the town, and shall lose his craft.

6. And whoever should seek ways and means to break any of these edicts shall incur the same forfeit.

[*Sheriffs' edict regulating the method of hiring and the days and hours of work of journeyman weavers.*]

1. The edict is made that no weaver or others of the same trade be so bold that they hire a workman for weaving, nor form combinations in the market place at Ville Neuve, nor elsewhere, within the jurisdiction of this town, under penalty of 20 solidi forfeit. And whoever should allow himself to be hired, or forms a combination, shall incur a forfeit of 10 solidi.

2. And let the workmen begin their work when the first mass is sung at St. Peter's; and let them cease work when the upholsterers stop work. And on Saturday, and the eve of the Feast of the Apostles, let them stop work at precisely noon, under penalty of 20 solidi.

Part II. ECONOMIC ORGANIZATION: CREDIT AND CONTROL

In the emergence of more complex forms of economic organization, the facilities for mobilizing the more movable, monetary resources are just as important as the division of labor in industry. The first section below includes some of the instruments which the Middle Ages developed for the conduct of long-term or distant financial negotiations, and indicates something of the environment conditioning these arrangements. Since economic organization never grows in a vacuum but is always subject to many controls, the second section shows the nature, extent, and purpose of various regulatory activities.

A. MONEY AND CREDIT

Something of the variety and degree of cooperation to be found in medieval industrial organization has already been seen. These enterprises, particularly one as far-flung in its ramifications as the cloth industry or as slow in its completion as overseas trade, often demanded more capital for a longer period than a single individual possessed. Accordingly, myriad devices were employed to join together two or more persons in a common venture. Illustrations of a few of the more usual types of partnership follow.

1. *The Business Unit: A Loan, 1192.* A simple loan represents a business practice so venerable that it had almost better be studied as a part of human nature. Yet the line which divides aid to a friend in need from an investment or partnership merits examination. The following document describes a loan made at Genoa.[9]

Alberto Balbo of Saint Peter of Arena agrees that he will give to Gandulf of Raalvengo [both small towns near Genoa] £12½ in Genoese money, which Gandulf lent out of love, on or before the first of next March under the penalty

of paying double should he fail to pay by then. At the store of the Fornarii 28 January 1192. Witnesses Otto of Langasco, Jordan Ricerio, Henry Porco.

2. *The Business Unit: A Commenda, 1086.* One of the most widely used types of partnerships was the *Commenda.* Known to the ancient world in a slightly different form (the sea loan), the *Commenda* was common practice in the Italian cities by 1100. The one which follows concerns a voyage between Genoa and Alexandria.[10]

Ogerio Aragano and Ogerio Aguzzino witnesses. I, Alberto Ceclieto, have received in form of *commenda* from you, Bellobruno of Castello, £100 in Genoese money, which I shall take to Alexandria for the purpose of trading, and from there, should I wish, to Ceuta, [Morocco] and I am to return to Genoa without any other change in my route. I am to send either to you or your designated agent the capital and the profit from this venture, and after the capital has been deducted, I am to keep one quarter of the profit.

I swear on the Holy Gospels to keep safe, watch over, and increase the *commenda*, etc., and to turn over and give to you or to your designated representative the capital and profit of the venture in good faith and with no deceit; and furthermore not to spend more than two shillings for expenses during the whole voyage.

Done at Genoa in the castle, at the house of Bellobruno, in the year 1086, in the third indiction and the ninth day before the end of September.

3. *The Business Unit: Partnership, 1191.* The following document illustrates another type of partnership which became common practice in Italy during the twelfth century.[11]

In the house of Ingo Longo, 11 October 1191. Witnesses Fredenzo Ontardo, William Rava.

Lanfranco Lizano in partnership with Isoberto agrees to carry £152 of the money of Isoberto and £76 of his own to Septa [Ceuta], and from there wherever he shall think best for the purpose of trading in good faith. On his return to Genoa Isoberto promises to give to Lanfranco or his designated agent his share of whatever profit God may give together with his capital. When each has got his capital back, the profit is to be divided equally. Lanfranco may send the money back to Genoa to Isoberto, should it seem best, provided there are witnesses.

4. *The Business Unit: A Barcelona Bank, 1460.* Banking was obviously an enterprise where considerable capital could be used. Some of the outstanding bankers, like the Medici of Florence or the Fuggers of Augsburg, were large companies of many members. Below are the articles of partnership for a private bank in Barcelona in 1460.[12]

In the name of our Lord God and of the glorious Virgin and Madonna, St. Mary, and all the saints in Paradise who wish to be addressed in the same company.

Articles made, God willing, between the Honorable Galceran de Strelrich, Knight, and the Lady Francina, his wife, as parties of the first part; and Don Guillem Bages, merchant and citizen of Barcelona, as party of the second part.

I. First, said Mossignor Galceran de Strelrich and his wife contribute in cash six hundred pounds, Barcelona, which they proposed to invest in a bank which, God willing, the same Guillem Bages is to establish in his house at the street corner in front of the slaughter house. All the gains whether from the exchange of florins or other coins for silver and copper, and all the profits from the funds employed in woolen or linen cloth, fish, salt, oil, and other merchandise shall belong to said bank common to the partnership. The said Guillem promises well, loyally, and safely to rule and administer the said bank, seeking for it all the possible profits and avoiding all the dangers; keeping good, loyal and true account of all the affairs of the said bank.

II. It is also agreed that the expenses of the partnership shall be taken from the common funds in so far as they are incurred in respect of duties, brokerage fees, and gratuities. All the other charges and expenses shall be borne by the said Guillem, that is to say the rent of the house and shop. All the profits which God may give for any cause or reason shall be divided between the parties, one half of the net profits to each; that is the said Mossignor Strelrich and his wife shall have one half of the profits and the said Guillem Bages shall have the other half, the two halves being made equal.

III. It is also agreed that the said Guillem shall put into the company two hundred pounds which with the six hundred put in by the said Mossignor Strelrich and his wife shall be the foundation . . . and a common fund. All the profits of the eight hundred pounds shall be divided in halves as is described above. But it is understood and declared that from the moment that the said Guillem shall put in his share, that is the two hundred pounds, or any part thereof, he may take his share of the profits, that is the half and no more.

IV. It is also agreed that for any sums in excess of the said two hundred pounds which the said Guillem may wish to put into the business with the consent of the said Mossignor Strelrich and the lady his wife he shall draw profits per sou and pound in proportion to the other profits made on the other funds invested in the business. He may not use the funds except for exchange as stated above unless the said Mossignor Strelrich has given his explicit consent so that the business shall be a common fund with one profit. And if by chance the said Mossignor Strelrich and his wife should wish to put some other sum into the business, in such case the said Bages shall add a quarter of the amount contributed by the said Strelrich and his wife, that is to say, if Mossignor Strelrich and his wife put in four hundred pounds, the said Guillem shall put in one hundred pounds, which is one-fourth of four hundred pounds.

V. Also, the said partnership shall continue as long as it shall please the said Mossignor Strelrich and his wife and no longer, but it is understood and declared that if the said Mossignor Strelrich and his wife withdraw their funds they shall recover them subject to such gains and losses as may have occurred.

VI. Also, the said Guillem Bages promises and swears in good faith that he will not loan any of the funds of the said partnership and bank without security and should he do so, which God forbid, it shall be wholly at his cost unless the said Mossignor Galceran de Strelrich shall sign with his own hand at the foot of the loan when it shall be at his risk and loss as well as that of the said Guillem.

VII. Also, it is contained and agreed that in respect of the affairs which are to be transacted outside the bank or outside the house or outside the city the expenses and necessary costs shall be deducted from the net profit, one half from each share, and all the other expenses of the house and of the clerks and girls who tend shop to sell merchandise at retail shall be at the expense of the said Bages.

VIII. Also, it is agreed that the money which is at the desk controlled personally by the said Mossignor Strelrich and his wife shall not hereafter be employed in business unless it be gold or silver or foreign coin.

IX. Also, that each month, the said Guillem shall be obliged to determine the profit and give an account of it if the said Mossignor Strelrich shall wish it, and he shall make this statement well and loyally and as accurately as he can, avoiding all fraud and he shall swear so to do in the name of God and by the four holy gospels, touching them with his hands.

X. Also, it is agreed, that the funds which the said Mossignor Strelrich and his wife shall invest in said bank which may be deposited in the Bank of Deposit of the city shall stand in their name: likewise the funds which are transferred in the Bank of Deposit which are due for any reason on account of the said bank and affairs connected with it, all such sums shall be transferred to the credit of the said Mossignor Galceran de Strelrich and his wife and the whole account shall thus stand in the name of said Mossignor Galceran de Strelrich and his wife but they shall give a power of attorney to the said Guillem Bages, authorizing him to transfer funds in the banks, to withdraw cash, and to transact the business of the partnership with the aforesaid Bank of Deposit of the city and other banks. These are under the authority of the notary who drew the present contract. All the things written above were approved and the said Guillem Bages undertook to make no changes in the agreement. And for the security of the said Mossignor Galceran de Strelrich and his wife, the said Guillem Bages gave sureties who are to be held for all things promised by the said Bages to the said Mossignor Strelrich and his wife, both in respect of the sums invested by them and in respect of all other matters for which the said Bages is liable by virtue of the present articles.

Saturday, the 15th of March, 1460, the said Guillem Bages, principal, Isabel, his mother, signed the above articles in the presence of Leonardo Vernich of Auro Trovato and Ludovicus de Sanctafide, scrivener, inhabitants of Barcelona; on the same day and year there signed Pere Ballester, tailor and citizen, in the presence of Bartholomeu Roig, notary and citizen of Barcelona and Indomitus de Sanctafide, scrivener of Barcelona.

5. *The Business Instrument: Letter of Exchange, Genoa, 1202.* Many different media of exchange were employed in medieval Europe. Barter, both simple and complex, was common. Originally precious metals were used as a medium of exchange and as a general yardstick for comparative values. Although the total European supply of gold and silver suitable for coinage remained scanty until the sixteenth century brought more from the New World, an elaborate system of coinage was developed in the trading cities and the industrial areas. Since this coinage remained unstable in both value and acceptability, the perfection of means to effect payments at a distance with little or no exchange of coin proved vital to the growth of commerce. The following document is a letter of exchange between two merchants.[13]

I, John Ascherio, in my own name and in the name of my partnership, agree that I have received and have in my possession from you, Rondano of Rondani of Placentia, on your behalf and on behalf of your partners a certain sum of Genoese money. I yield my right to claim that I do not have said money or that it was not given to me, as well as all my other legal rights. In return for this money I promise by way of exchange to pay to you or your designated agent, either myself or through my designated agent, £ two hundred in the money of Provins [one of the Champagne fair towns] at the next fair of Troyes [Champagne] as payment in full. If the said fair should not be held, I shall pay at the time that it should have been held. Done at Genoa in front of the House of the Canons of St. Laurent where lived the late Aimus [a spice merchant] on 23 June 1202, in the late afternoon.

6. *The Risks Involved, 1312.* The perils which beset the medieval merchant can be seen in the document which follows, the court record before the Provost of Paris of an injured merchant.[14]

A case tried before the Provost of Paris, between Caute Bonafante on one side and William of Gascony, a transportation agent, on the other. Caute alleged against William in connection with this matter that William had received and had in his possession from him 64 bales of cloth worth £10,000 which were to be carried by said William from the City of Paris to Savona [near Genoa]. This was to be done by William at his own expense and with his own beasts, and for each bale of cloth which William had in his possession he received £10 of the money of Tour [the charge for transportation]. Caute alleged that it was clearly agreed between them in said contract that William for that price would take the bales of cloth along the direct road from Paris through Mâçon, and from Mâçon through the territory of Savoy to the mountain pass of Argentière, and from there through the territory of King Robert along the agreed route to the city of Savona and that he would not go by any other route or way, either by land or sea. These bales of cloth were to be delivered safe and sound within 35 days. And for the purpose of keeping this agreement William had clearly bound himself to the aforementioned Caute to pay double the value of said bales of cloth to Caute by way of penalty, together with all of the expenses that Caute might have or incur because of the failure of the agreement or if it should happen that William should act in any way contrary to the agreement.

Caute alleged as well that William by violating and breaking the provisions of the agreement had not taken the road agreed upon between them and had taken the cloth by another route or road; to wit through Mont Cenis and thence directly through the city and territory of Asti where there was a great war going on. In this territory William stated that he lost the bales of cloth—a thing which would not have happened, Caute alleged, if William had taken the cloth over the route that had been agreed upon. Hence, as the said 35 days within which William (in accordance with the provisions of the agreement which had been made) was to hand over and deliver the bales of cloth in the city of Savona, either to said Caute or to his appointed agent, had long elapsed, William should have brought the bales of cloth, handed them over, and delivered them to said Caute, in accordance with what had been agreed upon and likewise in accord with provisions of the legal document by which he had bound himself. On the contrary, by breaking the provisions of the agreement, William had done everything exactly the opposite from what he had agreed. Therefore, Caute asked that William should be condemned under the provisions of the agreement and be compelled to restore to Caute the 64 bales of cloth, together with as many again because of the double penalty clause, or else pay £20,000 (the value of said bales of cloth under the double penalty clause contained in the agreement between them) and likewise pay the £640 that William had in his possession and had received from Caute as his fee for the transporting which he had not done. He announces that he will sue for his expenses, his losses, and his interest at the proper time and place.

For his defense William brought many contrary allegations, and said that he personally had never entered into an agreement with Caute, but that it was true that on a certain day and hour in a certain place and in the presence of certain persons called together for the purpose an agreement was made between Caute in his [William's] name and in the name of certain other merchants and Gervase Martin in his own name and in the name of William himself and two other transportation agents to carry the said 64 bales of cloth from Paris to the city of Savona for the fee of £10 of money of Paris for each bale, and that in said contract and in the contracting of the agreement between them certain places were expressed and mentioned through which Gervase, William and the other partners were to take bales of cloth; to wit, through Mâçon and through Savoy and thence over the great direct royal road which was usual and customary to the city of Savona, just as was more fully stated and contained in the document of the court of Paris which was drawn up for the purpose.

In addition it had been agreed upon and determined between them that Caute was to turn over to them an assistant to go with them and show them the way or route over which they were to carry the bales of cloth; that Caute had given to them a certain servant by the name of Mathias and had given to him a copy or at least an affadavit of the document of the court of Paris on the subject, so that he could better show them the way which was designated in the document; and that Caute had ordered them to obey this assistant in all matters during the journey. William alleged also that according to what had been agreed upon the said transportation agents left Paris and took up their journey along with the assistant, and under his leadership they took the bales of cloth through Mâçon and Savoy and thence over the great royal road towards Savona according to what had been agreed upon and according to the way in which assistant in the name of Caute and his partners led them, and that about two leagues from Monte Acuto several armed men met them who said that Caute and his partners owed them a great sum of money. These armed men, against the wish of said transportation agents and the assistant, took the bales of cloth by violence and carried them off to their castle in Monte Acuto.

Therefore, as William himself alleged, since both he himself and his partners had well and carefully fulfilled the provisions of the agreement and had looked out for the interests of Caute as they had promised to do, and since the bales of cloth had been captured on the proper route and on the way to Savona, three days journey from Savona, through the fault of Caute and his partners without any blame or act on the part of the transportation agents themselves, William alleged that he ought by the decree of said court to be freed from the charge of Caute and that it should be declared that Caute had caused him to be arrested and detained in a strong prison and his goods to be seized without cause and that both he and his goods should be set free and that

Caute ought to recompense him for the loss and expense which he had sustained by reason of this arrest. The Provost, having heard both of its parties and evidence offered by the same, freed by his judgment said William from the charge of said Caute and punished Caute for the expense that he had caused to said William according to the custom of the court which is this: "he who cause a man to be falsely arrested shall pay expenses to the party arrested."

On the ground that this judgment was false and wrong, Caute has appealed to the king's court. Therefore, after hearing both sides in the appeal, after having seen through the king's court the dispositions of the witnesses in the course of the case, and after having more fully investigated the confessions of both sides and the documents and instruments produced by both sides by way of proof, by the judgment of the king's court we decree that the case was well judged and that Caute was wrong in making his appeal and that he shall make amends.

B.   REGULATION AND CONTROL

Economic activity free from all control remains in the realm of utopia. Something of the variety of medieval controls has already been seen. The documents which follow show who did the regulating and for what purposes.

1. *The Shearmen Regulate, London, 1350.* The following petition of the shearmen of London to the city should be studied in conjunction with the regulations of their brother shearmen of Arras (pp. 89–90).[15]

Unto the Mayor, Sheriffs, and Aldermen, of the City of London, show the good folks, the Shearmen, freemen of the same city, that whereas of late they showed unto you certain points touching their trade, to the profit of the people of the City and of the same trade, the which are entered and confirmed in the Chamber; and since then, by command of our Lord the King, among other trades of the City, you have examined the said trade, and set down for certain what they shall take for each piece of work touching the said trade; the which Ordinance you have caused to be cried and published in the City, and they do hold themselves well contented therewith; save only, that they desire that they may have their servants and journeymen at the same wages that they used to have; for in old time they were wont to have a man to work between the Feast of Christmas and Easter at 3d. per day and his table; and between Easter and St. John [24 June] at 4d. and his table; and from St. John to the Feast of St. Bartholomew [24 August] at 3d. and his table; and from the Feast of St. Bartholomew to Christ-

mas, in the case of a good workman, at 4d. and his table, for day and night. And now the said men will not work otherwise than by the cloth, and then do so greatly hurry over the same, that they do great damage to the folks to whom such cloths belong, by reason whereof, the masters in the said trade have great blame and abuse, and take less than they were wont to do. The masters in the said trade do therefore beg of you, that it will please you to order that the said men may be chastised, and commanded, under a certain penalty, to work according to the ancient usage, as before stated,—as matter of good feeling, and for the profit of the people.

2. *The Town Controls, London, 1327.* The following document is from the records of the city of London.[16]

A congregation of Richard de Betoigne, Mayor, John de Grantham, John de Caustone, Henry de Combemartyn, Reynald de Conduit, John de Prestone, and Hugh de Gartone, Aldermen, and Roger Chauntecler, one of the Sheriffs of London, held at the Guildhall, on Thursday in the week of Pentecost, that is, on the 4th day of June, A.D. 1327, and in the first year of the reign of King Edward, after the Conquest the Third.—

John Brid, baker, was attached to make answer as to certain falsehood, malice, and deceit, by him committed, to the nuisance of the common people; as to which, the Mayor, Aldermen, and Sheriffs of the City, were given to understand that the same John, for falsely and maliciously obtaining his own private advantage, did skilfully and artfully cause a certain hole to be made upon a table of his, called a "moldingboard," pertaining to his bakehouse, after the manner of a mouse-trap, in which mice are caught; there being a certain wicket warily provided for closing and opening such hole.

And when his neighbors and others, who were wont to bake their bread at his oven, came with their dough or material for making bread, the said John used to put such dough or other material upon the said table, called a "moldingboard," as aforesaid, and over the hole before-mentioned, for the purpose of making loaves therefrom, for baking; and such dough or material being so placed upon the table aforesaid, the same John had one of his household, ready provided for the same, sitting in secret beneath such table; which servant of his, so seated beneath the hole, and carefully opening it, piecemeal and bit by bit craftily withdrew some of the dough aforesaid, frequently collecting great quantities from such dough, falsely, wickedly, and maliciously; to the great loss of all his neighbors and persons living near, and of others, who had come to him with such dough to bake, and to the scandal and disgrace of the whole City, and, in especial, of the Mayor and Bailiffs for the safe-keeping of the assizes of the City assigned. Which hole, so found in his table aforesaid, was made of aforethought; and in like manner, a great quantity of such dough that had been drawn through the said hole, was found beneath the hole, and was by William de Hertynge, sergeant-at-mace, and Thomas de Morle, clerk of Richard de Rothinge, one of the Sheriffs of the City aforesaid, who had found such material or dough in the suspected place beforementioned, upon oath brought here into Court.

And the same John, here present in Court, being asked how he will acquit himself of the fraud, malice, and deceit aforesaid, personally in Court says that of such fraud, malice, and deceit, he is in no way guilty; and puts himself upon the country thereon, etc. Therefore, let inquisition as to the truth of the matter be made by the country, etc.

William atte Sele, John atte Barnette, Robert de Bertone, John de Polberowe, Robert de Brokesbourne, Roger de Miltone, and Richard de Honesdone, bakers, and Alice de Brightenoch, and Lucy de Pykeringe, bakeresses, in whose houses also, like tables, called "moldingboards," were found, with like holes, and with like dough beneath, as aforesaid, fraudulently and maliciously collected, were attached to make answer as to the fraud, malice, and deceit aforesaid, in like manner as above mentioned concerning the said John, etc. Who appeared; and each of them being singly arraigned as to the matters aforesaid, they say that they are in no way guilty, and put themselves upon the country, etc. Therefore let inquisition as to the truth of the matter be made, etc.

And hereupon, Richard le Mitere, Richard de Bitterle, William de Keyle, Adam de Bokelonde, Roger le Bere, Elyas Dycun, Geoffrey de Holewelle, William Pope, Richard Frere, John Thedmar, John atte Wodehouse, and Adam de Walpole, upon whom [as jurors] the said John and all the others had put themselves, being sworn, and having held converse and counsel hereon, appeared; and they say upon their oath, that the aforesaid John and all the others are guilty of all, as well as to the hole so suspected, and the dough drawn through such hole, as the other things charged against them; and that for long they have been wont to commit the said falsehood and deceit. Therefore it was adjudged that the said John and all the others should be committed to the jail of Newgate, etc.; and because, for lack of Aldermen, the Court was then unprepared further to give judgment thereon, a day was given, being the Saturday then next ensuing, etc.; and in the meantime, all the Aldermen, with twelve, eight, or six, of each Ward, according as the Ward was great or small, were to be summoned to be here present upon that day; to the end that then might be done what of right, and according to the custom of the City, ought to be done.

Afterwards, on the said Saturday, there came Richard, the Mayor aforesaid, Hamon de Chigwelle, Nicholas de Farndone, Reynald de Conduit, Hamon Godchepe, John de Prestone, John Priour, Thomas de Leyre, Richard Costantyn, John de Oxenford, Anketin de Gisorz, Henry de Combemartyn, Richard de Hakeney, John de Caustone, Hugh de Gartone, John Poyntel, and Adam de Salisbury, Aldermen, Roger Chauntecler and Richard de Rothynge, Sheriffs, and in like manner certain men summoned from each Ward, as set forth in the panel by the Sheriffs returned; and after counsel and treaty had been held among the Mayor and Aldermen, as to passing judgment upon the falsehood, malice, and deceit aforesaid; seeing that, although there is no one who prosecutes them, or any one of them, the said deed is, as it were, a certain species of theft, and that it is neither consonant with right nor pleasing to God that such falsehood, deceit, and malice, shall go unpunished; the more especially as all those who have come to the said bakers, to bake their bread, have been falsely, wickedly, and maliciously deceived, they themselves being wholly ignorant thereof, and have suffered no little loss thereby; it was agreed and ordained, that all those of the bakers aforesaid, beneath whose tables with holes dough had been found, should be put upon the pillory, with a certain quantity of such dough hung from their necks; and that those bakers in whose houses dough was not found beneath the tables aforesaid, should be put upon the pillory, but without dough hung from their necks; and that they should so remain upon the pillory until Vespers at St. Paul's in London should be ended.

And as to the two women aforesaid, because that they have husbands, namely, Alice William de Brechenoke for her husband, and Lucy aforesaid Hugh de Pykerynge for her husband, and this same has by their neighbors been attested; seeing too that the same Alice and Lucy allege that the said deed was not their deed;—it was agreed and ordained that they should be sent back to the Prison of Newgate, there to remain until as to them it should have been otherwise ordained; and that all such tables with holes, as aforesaid, should be thrown down and utterly destroyed, and from thenceforth not allowed to be made; and that if any one of the said bakers should in future be found acting with such deceit, falsehood, and malice, he should stand upon the pillory for one whole day, and afterwards abjure the City, so as at no future time to return thereto.

3. *The State Regulates: The Ordinance of Laborers, 1349.* By the fourteenth century England's size and insular position as well as certain facts in her earlier history had combined to give her an exceptional degree of unity and cohesiveness. The actions of the English government, when faced with the severe mid-century economic crisis, are unique for the time. The emergency demanded quick treatment, and the royal ordinance of 1349—the first document below— was confirmed and extended by a parliamentary act of 1351. In the second document are reproduced some of the presentments made by the jurors in the hundred of Chelmsford (Essex) in 1351 before the royal justices who were sent out to administer the act.[17]

(*The Ordinance of Laborers, 1349*) The King to the sheriff of Kent, greeting. Because a great part of the people and specially of the workmen and servants has now died in this plague, some, seeing the necessity of lords and the scarcity of servants, will not serve unless they receive excessive wages, and others preferring to beg in idleness rather than to seek their livelihood by labor: we, weighing the grave disadvantages which might arise from the dearth specially of tillers and workmen, have had deliberation and treaty hereon with the prelates and nobles and other learned men in session with us, by whose unanimous counsel we have thought fit to ordain that every man and woman of our realm of England, of whatsoever condition, free or servile, ablebodied and under the age of sixty years, not living by trade nor exercising a certain craft, nor having of his own whereof he shall be able to live, or land of his own, in the tilling whereof he shall be able to occupy himself, and not serving another man, shall be bound to serve him who shall require him, if he be required to serve in a suitable service, regard being had to his rank, and shall receive only the wages, liveries, hire or salaries which used to be offered in the places where he should serve in the twentieth year of our reign of England, or in the five or six common years last preceding; provided that lords be preferred to others in the bondmen or tenants of their lands so to be retained in their service; so however that such lords so retain as many as shall be necessary and not more; and if such a man or woman, so required to serve, refuse so to do, the same being proved by two trusty men before the sheriff, bailiff, lord, or constable of the town where this shall come to pass, he shall be taken forthwith by them or any of them and sent to the nearest jail, there to stay in strait keeping until he find security to serve in the form aforesaid.

And if a reaper, mower or other workman or servant, retained in the service of any man, withdraw from the said service without reasonable cause or licence before the end of the term agreed upon, he shall undergo the penalty of imprisonment, and none, under the same penalty, shall presume to receive or retain such an one in his service.

Furthermore no man shall pay or promise to pay to any man more wages, liveries, hire or salaries than is accustomed, as is aforesaid, nor shall any man in any wise demand or receive the same, under penalty of the double of that which shall be so paid, promised, demanded or received, to go to him who shall feel himself aggrieved hereby . . . and such prosecution shall be made in the court of the lord of the place where such a case shall befall; and if the lords of towns or manors shall presume in any wise to contravene our present ordinance, by themselves or their ministers, then prosecution shall be made against them in the form aforesaid in counties, wapentakes [division of a county] and ridings, or other such courts of ours. . . .

Moreover saddlers, skinners, tawyers [leather workers], shoemakers, tailors, smiths, carpenters, masons, tillers, boatmen, carters and other artificers and workmen whosoever shall not take for their labor and craft more than used to be paid to such in the twentieth year. . . .

Moreover butchers, fishermen, hostlers, brewers, bakers, poulterers and all other sellers of victuals whatsoever shall be bound to sell such victuals for a reasonable price, regard being had to the price at which such victuals are sold in the neighboring places; so that such sellers have a moderate profit and not excessive, as shall be reasonably required by the distance of the places wherefrom such victuals are carried; and if any man sell such victuals otherwise and be convicted thereof in the form aforesaid, he shall pay the double of that which he shall receive to him that suffered loss, or, for lack of such, to him who will prosecute in this behalf. . . .

And because many sturdy beggars, so long as they can live by begging for alms, refuse to labor, living in idleness and sin and sometimes by thefts and other crimes, no man, under the aforesaid penalty of imprisonment, shall presume under color of pity or alms to give anything to such as shall be able profitably to labor, or to cherish them in their sloth, that so they may be compelled to labor for the necessaries of life. . . .

The King to the venerable father in Christ, W. by the same grace bishop of Winchester, greeting. "Because a great part of the people," etc., as above, as far as "to labor for the necessaries of life," and then thus: and therefore we request you that you cause the premises to be proclaimed in the several churches and other places of your diocese where you shall deem expedient; commanding rectors, vicars of such churches, ministers and other your subjects that by salutary warnings they beseech and persuade their parishioners to labor and to keep the ordinances aforesaid, as instant necessity demands; and that you constrain the wage-earning chaplains of your said diocese, who, as is said, refuse in like manner to serve without excessive salary, and compel them, under penalty of suspension and interdict, to serve for the accustomed salary, as is expedient; and that you in no wise omit this as you love us and the common utility of our said realm. Witness as above.

By the King himself and the whole council.

The like letters of request are directed to the several bishops of England and to the guardian of the archbishopric of Canterbury, the see being vacant, under the same date.

(*Presentments Made Before the Justice of Laborers, 1351.*) [The twelve jurors] present that Arnulph le Hierde of Maldon, late servant of John Dodebroke from Michaelmas, 24 Edward III, until Michaelmas next following, 25 Edward III, for one year and for a quarter of a year next following and for the whole of that time, the said Arnulph took a quarter of wheat for twelve weeks and 5s. a year for his stipend. Further, he took from the feast of St. Peter's Chains [August 1] until Christmas in the same time 10s. beyond that which he took above; and hereupon the said Arnulph withdrew from his service before the

end of the term, to the damage of the said John of 40s. against the Statute, etc.

Trespass—Further, they present that Robert Grys of Danbury, potter, makes brass pots and sells them at threefold the price which he used [to take] against the Statute, etc., in oppression of the people.

Trespass—Further, they say that John Sextayn the younger, tailor, John Banestrat, tailor, Roger atte Tye of Great Baddow, take salaries for their labors from divers folk against the Statute, etc., and this threefold that which they used to take.

Trespass—Further, they say that William Denk, servant of Geoffrey le Smyth, took from the said Geoffrey 20s. a year, and is at his table, and was sworn before John de Sutton and his fellows to serve according to the Statute, etc., where he should not take but 8s., etc.

Trespass—Further, they present that Richard Smyth of Great Baddow commonly takes for his work double that which he used to take, against the Statute.

Trespass—Further, they present that John Plukkerose, William Smyth of Danbury and William Molt, shoemakers, of Great Baddow, make shoes and sell them at almost the price which they used [to take], against the Statute, etc., in oppression of the people.

Trespass—Further, they say that Alan, son of Sayer Banstrat of Great Baddow, sawyer, will not serve unless he take for his salary as much as two others take, against the Statute, etc., in oppression of the people. . . .

Grand Inquisition

Trespass—Further, they present that John Galion, vicar of Nazeing, will not minister to any the sacrament of marriage unless he have from each man 5s. or 6s., and in this manner by extortion the said John has taken from John Wakerild 4s. 10d., from William Gurteber 5s., from John Mabely 9s., and from many others to the sum of 20s., in oppression of the people by tort and against the peace. . . .

4. *The Church Regulates.* Business ethics and relationships in the Middle Ages were ultimately determined by the Church. The secular controls which have been seen were actually growing up under the shadow of the values for human conduct laid down by the Church. The first selection which follows is from the *Summa Theologica* of St. Thomas Aquinas (1225–1274). The second is from St. Antoninus (1389–1459), a popular and learned Dominican bishop of Florence. The "Philosopher" is Aristotle.[18]

(*St. Thomas on Buying, Selling, and Usury.*) We next have to consider the sins which have to do with voluntary exchanges, first, fraud committed in buying and selling; second, usury taken on loans. For in the case of other forms of voluntary exchange, no kind of sin is noted which is to be distinguished from rapine or theft. . . .

The value of a thing which is put to human use is measured by the price given; and for this purpose money was invented, as is explained in *Ethics*, V, 5. Hence, whether the price exceeds the value of a thing or conversely, the equality required by justice is lacking. Consequently, to sell dearer or to buy cheaper than a thing is worth is in itself unjust and unlawful.

We can speak of buying and selling in another sense, namely, the case where it accidentally turns out to the advantage of one and to the injury of the other; for example, when a man has great need of something, and another is injured if he is deprived of it; in such a case the just price will be one which not only takes into account the thing sold, but also the loss incurred by the seller in parting with it. And thus a thing may lawfully be sold for more than it is worth in itself, though not more than it is worth to its possessor. If, however, a man is greatly aided by something he has obtained from another, and the seller does not suffer any loss from doing without it, he ought not to charge more for it, since the advantage which accrues to the other is not due to the seller but to the condition of the buyer. Now no one has a right to sell to another what does not belong to him; though he may charge him for the loss he suffers. He, however, who derives great advantage from something received from another, may of his own accord pay the seller something in addition. This is a matter of honor. . . .

. . . it is the function of traders to devote themselves to exchanging goods. But, as the Philosopher says there are two kinds of exchange. One may be called natural and necessary, by means of which one thing is exchanged for another, or things for money to meet the needs of life, and this kind of trading is not the function of traders, but rather of household managers or of statesmen, who have to provide a family or a state with the necessaries of life. The other kind of exchange is that of money for money or of things for money, not to meet the needs of life, but to acquire gain; and this kind of trading seems to be the function of traders, according to the Philosopher. Now the first kind of exchange is praiseworthy, because it serves natural needs, but the second is justly condemned, because, in itself, it serves the desire for gain, which knows no limit but extends to infinity. Hence trading in itself is regarded as somewhat dishonorable, since it does not logically involve an honorable or necessary end. Gain, however, which

is the end of trading, though it does not logically involve anything honorable or necessary, does not logically involve anything sinful or contrary to virtue; hence there is no reason why gain may not be directed to some necessary or even honorable end; and so trading will be rendered lawful; as when a man uses moderate gains acquired in trade for the support of his household, or even to help the needy; or even when a man devotes himself to trade for the public welfare, lest there be a lack of the things necessary for the life of the country; and seeks gain, not as an end but as a reward for his efforts. . . .

In answer that to receive usury for money lent is, in itself, unjust, since it is a sale of what does not exist; whereby inequality obviously results, which is contrary to justice. . . .

Now money, according to the Philosopher was devised primarily for the purpose of effecting exchanges; and so the proper and principal use of money is the consumption or alienation of it, whereby it is expended in making purchases. Therefore, in itself, it is unlawful to receive a price for the use of money lent, which is called *usury;* and just as a man is bound to restore other things unjustly acquired, so he is bound to restore money received through usury.

. . . a lender may without sin contract with the borrower for compensation to cover the loss arising from the fact that he gives up something which belongs to him; for this is not selling the use of money, but avoiding loss; and it may be that the borrower avoids greater loss than the lender incurs; so that the borrower makes good the other's loss with advantage to himself. Compensation for loss, however, cannot be stipulated on the ground that the lender makes no profit on his money, because he should not sell what he does not yet possess, and which he may be prevented in various ways from getting.

. . . So, in the present question, it is also to be said that it is in no way lawful to induce a man to lend upon usury; one may, however, borrow upon usury from a man who is ready to do it and practices usury, provided it be for some good purpose, such as helping oneself or somebody else out of difficulty; just as it is also lawful for one who falls among robbers to point out what goods he has, in order to save his life, though the robbers commit sin in plundering him, like the ten men who said to Ishmael: "Kill us not, for we have stores in the field."

(*St. Antoninus on the Object of Gain.*) The object of gain is that by its means man may provide for himself and others according to their state. The object of providing for himself and others is that they may be able to live virtuously. The object of a virtuous life is the attainment of everlasting glory (I. i. 3, iii). . . . If the object of the trader is principally cupidity, which is the root of all evils, then certainly his trading will be evil. But that trade (as natural and necessary for the needs of human life) is, according to Aristotle, in itself praiseworthy which serves some good purpose—i.e., supplying the needs of human life. If, therefore, the trader seeks a moderate profit for the purpose of providing for himself and family according to the condition becoming to their state of life, or to enable him to aid the poor more generously, or even if he goes into commerce for the common good (lest, for example, the State should be without what its life requires), and consequently seeks a profit not as an ultimate end but merely as a wage of labor, he cannot in that case be condemned (II. i. 16, ii). . . . To acquire by labor the amount of food sufficient for preserving one's being requires only a moderate amount of time and a moderate amount of anxiety' (IV. xii. 3, i).

V

The English Monarchy under Edward I

EDWARD loved power. He would not have been so great a King as he was, if he had not estimated at its full value the kingly power that he inherited. It is only by clearly understanding this that we can appreciate the good faith and self-restraint implied in his keeping the engagements by which he was forced to limit the exercise of that power. . . . Believing in his own right, in his own power of governing, and in his own intention to govern well, he held fast to the last moment every point of his sovereign authority; but when he was compelled to accept a limit, he observed the limit. The good faith of a strong King is a safer guarantee of popular right than the helplessness of a weak one. Edward had, besides force and honesty, a clear perception of true policy, and such an intuitive knowledge of the needs of his people as could proceed only from a deep sympathy with them. The improvement of the laws, the definite organization of government, the definite arrangement of rights and jurisdictions, the definite elaboration of all departments, which mark the reign and make it the fit conclusion of a period of growth in all these matters, were unquestionably promoted, if not originated, by the personal action of the King.

William Stubbs

CONTENTS

QUESTIONS FOR STUDY

PART I

1. By an analysis of the articles of the Inquest, determine the major objectives of Edward in ordering the Inquest.
2. Who might welcome the Inquest? Who might resent it?
3. What do the articles of the Inquest indicate concerning the state of local government in 1274?
4. How many articles of the Inquest did the jurors of Totsmonslow answer?
5. If the Totsmonslow hundred roll may be taken as typical, was the Inquest worth while?
6. What aspects of local government irked the inhabitants of Totmonslow hundred?
7. What faults in local government were remedied by the Statute of Westminster?
8. Which articles of the Inquest can be connected with clauses in the Statute?
9. Why did the King issue the Statute of Gloucester? Did it have any connection with the answers to the Inquest?
10. "In his account of the Warenne case, Walter of Hemingburgh missed the point." Explain.
11. Of what value to the historian is Walter's account?
12. Why did the Earl of Surrey win his case?
13. What lines of defense did the Earl of Gloucester take?
14. What do the two law cases indicate about conditions in the period prior to Edward's reign?

PART II

15. For what reasons did Edward I summon Parliament?
16. Where did Parliament meet?
17. Who might be summoned to attend a meeting of Parliament?
18. How did writs of summons differ according to the persons to whom they were sent?
19. How did London elect representatives to Parliament?
20. What special arrangements did the King make prior to a meeting of Parliament?
21. What does the chronicle reveal about the types of business transacted at a meeting of Parliament?
22. Who presented petitions in Parliament? With what types of business did petitions deal?
23. What do the petitions and answers reveal about the power of the King? About the limitations of his power?
24. What do the answers to the petitions reveal about royal methods of administration?
25. How was a representative compensated for his attendance at Parliament? Why did representatives receive compensation but not bishops or barons?
26. The royal commission to the tax-collectors states that the representatives "courteously" granted a subsidy in 1296. Does this agree with the chronicler's account?
27. Compare the chronicle and the official documents as historical sources. What is the particular value of each?

[104]

Feudal government depended upon a complicated series of personal contracts, contracts which involved both land tenure and personal services. It had come into existence in a period of chaos and insecurity, when for the most part might made right and there seemed no better foundation for an orderly government than honorable agreements among strong men. Feudalism did not succeed in establishing perfect order in Western Europe, for complications of tenure often bred war, and the nature of feudal contracts left many matters open for dispute under a system in which combat was a recognized judicial process. But the feudal regime was a distinct advance over the conditions which produced it, while at the same time it contained the seeds of a more orderly and efficient form of government.

The seeds were the powers latent in the feudal king. On the one hand, as the successor to tribal chieftains, who theoretically derived authority from the Roman Empire, the king had inherited ill-defined powers of popular leadership. On the other the feudal system accorded him powers of lordship over the great vassals of the realm. The former endowed him with a claim to the highest position in the land, bound to protect and do justice to all his subjects. The latter gave him specific legal rights which could be exploited in detail: the services, aids, and incidents owing to a feudal lord. The full exploitation of his position and legal rights could make the king the powerful ruler of a centralized realm.

Circumstances and personal factors determined whether or not a king realized his potentialities. In the Empire the conflict with the Papacy had resulted, by the latter half of the thirteenth century, in the weakening of the power of the crown and the transfer of much of its strength, latent and actual, to the German nobility and the Italian towns. The centrifugal forces of feudalism had triumphed over the monarch, as Germany and Italy became congeries of petty sovereign entities in conflict with one another. During the same period in France and England, however, the king had emerged as the dominant power in the land, exploiting his inherent strength and extending his control over his subjects. And this result was being achieved by monarchs working toward centralization as a goal, despite baronial revolts, poor means of communication, and other inhibiting factors.

The process by which the French and English kings extended their control is of the utmost historical importance. For it was this process which, despite uneven development, was to build the strong monarchical state of the future. There were, it is true, many differences in the means employed by French and English rulers, for each kingdom possessed inherent peculiarities deriving from such factors as geography and previous historical development. But the general nature of the process in each kingdom was much the same. In this problem the reign of Edward I of England (1272–1307) has been chosen as a case study in some of the methods employed by a feudal king to improve and extend the royal power.

Edward Longshanks, as contemporaries called him, was a quick-tempered and ambitious man, with a passion for order and the strength of his own convictions. He had subdued the baronial revolt in his father's reign (1265) and restored tranquillity to a kingdom perennially upset since the days of King John. His father's death in 1272 found him on a crusade in the Holy Land, and it was two years before Edward reached England. After his return he immediately embarked upon the execution of policies which occupied the remaining thirty-one years of his reign. In foreign affairs he was determined to reduce Wales and Scotland to subjection. In domestic affairs his major concerns were to maintain stability and to keep and exploit his rights to the full.

For the pursuance of his domestic policies Edward inherited considerable governmental machinery from his predecessors. He possessed the right to summon the feudal council of his vassals for aid and advice whenever he thought fit. This council was frequently convened, especially in times of crisis; and in the reign of Henry III (1216–72), the king had occasionally summoned, in addition to the great barons and prelates, representatives from the counties and towns. Such representatives might be summoned when the king required extraordinary financial assistance. A meeting of the feudal council, with or without the representatives, was often vulgarly called a "parliament," a word meaning "talk" or "parley."

Edward's predecessors had also developed the practice of retaining certain members of the feudal council to form a permanent *curia* of administrators and justices, who performed the daily tasks of central government. In the course of time this permanent *curia* had become divided into four departments: the Chancery, office of the king's scribes, where was lodged the great seal used to validate royal documents; the Exchequer, office of royal finance, which also held a court to try cases involving the king's revenues; and the Courts of the King's Bench and Common Pleas, which tried cases in the common law brought up by royal writs. In addition to their routine duties, the administrators and justices of the permanent *curia* might be summoned to meet as a body in the king's presence, often as much as thrice a year, to constitute an extraordinary high court of justice to which his subjects might bring petitions for legal redress. Such an open joint session was also called a "parliament." During his reign Edward hit upon the idea of summoning both types of "parliament" to meet at the same time, which created the foundation of the representative lawmaking body which has been known as Parliament ever since.

Administrative offices, central law courts, and parliaments constituted the organs of central government. From this central government the king's authority radiated into the local communities of England, in part by means of the itinerant justices, or "justices in eyre." These men, who were technically members of the central law courts on tour or circuit ("eyre"), held special court sessions for all matters in which the king was concerned. But in the countryside there also existed a system of royal local government, much of which had been inherited by the Norman conquerors from their Anglo-Saxon predecessors. The kingdom was divided into counties, or shires, and each county was divided into smaller districts called hundreds. The royal official for the county was the sheriff. The sheriff's functions were various, but may be roughly analyzed as executive, fiscal, and judicial. He was responsible for the arrest and custody of criminals, for the empanelling of juries, and for the execution of writs; he collected the royal taxes and the royal debts; about once a month he presided over the shire court and twice a year he made his "tourn," in the course of which he visited each hundred and held court.

To help him in this work the sheriff had certain colleagues: coroners, whose functions were "to keep the pleas of the crown," that is, records of all crimes and other occurrences that involved crown rights in the shire; escheators, who looked after the king's feudal estates and interests in the shire, such as escheats, forfeitures, etc. The sheriff also had assistants of whom the most important was the hundred bailiff, who carried out the orders of the sheriff in the hundred, and in so doing was the man who performed most of the actual work of government there. The bailiff's job, like all others in the royal administration, was fairly lucrative, for he pocketed many fees and emoluments, and for his job he paid a yearly "farm," or rent to whomever had appointed him, either the sheriff or the lord of the hundred.

For some hundreds had feudal lords. Of the 678 hundreds in England in the
reign of Edward I, 358 were royal hundreds and 270 were in private hands. In the
past, kings had granted lordships of hundreds to their subjects by charter; sometimes, in troubled periods, subjects had acquired hundreds by usurpation. Furthermore, within a hundred there might exist certain "franchises" or "liberties" held
by feudal nobles or churchmen. These liberties were of various sorts: the right
to hold a court, to serve and return royal writs, to be exempt from certain fiscal
obligations, to have special hunting rights. In almost every instance, however,
a liberty was a source of profit for its holder, and represented a public function
in private hands.

The documents which follow introduce the student to some of the methods
employed by Edward I to extend and improve the royal government, in both central and local administration.

GLOSSARY

amercement: A pecuniary penalty like a modern fine.

assize: The term had several meanings. In these documents it means either the
   right to enforce regulations governing the price, quality, etc. of commodities
   (such as an assize of bread and ale), or an investigation by a sworn inquest.

banlieu: An area around a city, town, or monastery, distinguished and protected
   by certain privileges.

chases and warrens: A chase was an area, once part of a royal forest, which had
   been granted by the king to a private individual, or had been usurped. This
   area was exempt from the full force of the forest laws and such provisions of
   that law as were still binding were enforced, not by royal officials, but by
   the person holding the chase. The holder also had exclusive hunting rights.
   A warren carried with it exclusive rights of hunting lesser game such as hares
   and foxes.

distraint of knighthood: Requirement that those holding land of a certain annual
   value assume the rank and obligations of knighthood, or else pay a heavy
   fine.

eighth, tenth, twelfth, etc.: A tax levied on movable property, assessed at the
   rate of an eighth or other fraction of the value of movable property.

estreat: A true copy of any record.

franchise: Rights of jurisdiction and exemptions of various sorts enjoyed by feudal
   lords. Same as "liberties."

geldable: Liable to pay certain taxes, usually to the king.

liberty: An area in which a feudal noble possessed certain governmental rights.
   These rights varied according to the terms of the original royal charter granting the liberty (if there was such a charter), or according to custom. Same
   as "franchise."

mesne: A mesne lord was an intermediate lord, i.e., one who stood between a
   tenant and a higher lord.

murage: A toll levied for repairing or building public walls.

park: A piece of ground enclosed with a paling or hedge in which deer and other
   game were preserved for the owner of the land.

perambulation: The act of walking over the boundaries of a piece of territory
   (e.g., the royal forests) to determine them, or preserve evidence of them,
   and to see if any encroachments had been made upon them.

recognitors: Jurors impanelled on an assize.

replevin: Used in these documents in the sense of bail.

return of writs: A short account made by the sheriff or feudal lord of the manner in which he has executed a writ. The writ might be one ordering him to seize land or goods, and it was a valued right of many lords in their liberties.

sokemen: Those who held their land by free, as opposed to servile, tenure.

tally: A stick with notches which recorded the amount of a debt or of a payment.

vee de naam: A legal action arising from a particular kind of wrongful seizure of goods. Those who claimed the right to hold pleas of *vee de naam* claimed the right to try such cases.

view of frankpledge: According to the system of frankpledge all men in England were supposed to be enrolled in groups of ten. Each group was collectively responsible for producing any of its number who might be summoned to appear in court. Twice a year the sheriff held a "view of frankpledge," an inspection to make certain that all were properly enrolled. The right to hold view of frankpledge might also be held by a feudal noble.

vouchsafe to warrant: A legal process by which a tenant summoned the one from whom he obtained his land to come and guarantee title to the land.

wapentake: The name given to a hundred in several counties.

wreck of sea: Goods cast ashore from a wreck were forfeited to the crown, or to any person having the franchise of wreck of sea.

writ of attaint: A writ ordering an inquiry as to whether a jury of twelve men had given a false verdict, in order that the judgment might be reversed.

writ of novel disseisin: A writ, first used in the reign of Henry II, allowing a person alleging an eviction to have the case tried by a jury before a royal justice.

writ of pone: A writ used to carry a case from a lower to a higher court.

writ of prohibition: A writ from a superior court directing an inferior court to cease trying a case in process.

Part I. ASPECTS OF LOCAL GOVERNMENT UNDER EDWARD I

A. THE INQUEST OF 1274

The practice of holding inquests, or inquiries, was an old one in English history. Perhaps the most famous was that ordered by William the Conqueror in 1086, the answers to which went to make up Domesday Book. Whenever the king wanted facts about his kingdom he could order an inquest, either for the whole realm, or for a group of counties. On October 11, 1274, two months after his arrival in England to assume the government, Edward I ordered such an inquest. The country was divided into circuits (whether ten or eleven we do not know), each of which was visited by two commissioners. These commissioners summoned before them a jury (usually of twelve men) from each hundred, and these juries, on their oaths, answered the questions put to them.

The Articles of the Inquest. Thirty-nine questions were asked the jurors on all circuits, and additional questions were asked in certain counties. The articles which follow are selected from a typical list of such questions.[1]

1. How many and what demesne manors the king has in his hand in every county, that is, both of the ancient demesnes of the crown, and of escheats and purchases.

2. What manors, moreover, used to be in the hands of the kings who were the king's predecessors, and who hold them, by what warrant and since when, and by whom and how they were alienated.

3. Also concerning the lord king's fees and tenants; who hold them now from him in chief, how many fees each of them holds; what fees used to be held in chief of the king and now are held through a mesne lord, and by what mesne, and from what time they have been alienated, how and by whom.

4. Also concerning the lands of tenants of the ancient desmesne of the crown, whether free sokemen or serfs: whether held by deputies or by the tenants themselves, and by what deputies or tenants, and by whom they have been alienated, how and from what time.

5. Likewise inquiry shall be made concerning the farms of hundreds, wapentakes, ridings, cities and boroughs and of all other rents whatsoever and from what time.

6. Also how many hundreds, wapentakes and ridings are now in the lord king's hand, and how many and which are in the hands of others, from what time and by what warrant, and how much a year every hundred is worth.

7. Concerning ancient suits, customs, services and other things withdrawn from the lord king and from his ancestors; who withdrew them, and from what time; and who have appropriated to themselves such suits, customs, services and other things belonging of established custom to the lord king, from what time, and by what warrant.

8. Also, what other persons claim from the king to have return or estreats of writs, who hold pleas of *vee de naam,* who claim to have wreck of sea, and by what warrant, and other royal liberties such as gallows, the assizes of bread and ale and other things which belong to the crown; and from what time.

9. Also concerning those who have liberties granted to them by kings of England and have made use of them otherwise than they should have done; how, from what time and in what way.

10. Again concerning liberties which obstruct common justice and overturn the king's power, and by whom they were granted and since when.

11. Who, moreover, have recently appropriated to themselves free chases or warrens without warrant, and likewise who have had such chases and warrens from old time by the king's grant and have gone beyond their bounds and landmarks, and since when.

12. What persons also, whether lords or their seneschals or bailiffs of any kind or even the lord king's officials, have not upheld the execution of the lord king's commands or have even scorned to carry them out, or have hindered the doing of them in any way, since the time when the constitutions were made at Marlborough in the fifty-second year of the reign of the lord king Henry, father of the king that now is.

13. Again concerning all encroachments whatsoever upon the king or upon the royal dignity: by whom they have been made, how and from what time.

14. Concerning knights' fees, of whomsoever

held, and lands or holdings given or sold to monks or to other persons to the king's prejudice, by whom and from what time.

15. Concerning sheriffs who take gifts to consent to the concealment of felonies committed in their bailiwicks, or who neglect to attach such felons for favor to anyone, both within liberties and without. In like manner, concerning the clerks and other bailiffs of the sheriffs, concerning coroners and all their clerks and bailiffs: who have acted thus in the time of the lord king Henry since the battle of Evesham, and who in the time of the present lord king.

16. Concerning sheriffs and all manner of bailiffs who take gifts to remove recognitors from assizes and juries, and at what time.

17. Again, concerning sheriffs and all other manner of bailiffs who have amerced for default men summoned to make inquests by the lord king's command, when a sufficient number of persons had responded to the summons to make the inquest; how much and from whom they have taken on this pretext, and since when.

18. Again, concerning sheriffs who have handed over to extortionate bailiffs, oppressing the people beyond measure, hundreds, wapentakes or ridings at high farms, so that they may thus raise their own farms; who those bailiffs were, on whom they have inflicted such losses, and at what time.

19. Again, whereas sheriffs ought not to hold their tourn more than twice a year, who has held his tourn more often, and from what time. . . .

21. Again, who have by the power of their office troubled any maliciously and thus have extorted lands, rents or any other contributions, and from what time.

22. Who have received the command of the lord king to pay his debts, and have received part of the money from the creditors for paying the rest to them, and yet have had the whole sum allowed them in the Exchequer or elsewhere, and from what time.

23. Who have received monies owed to the king, or a part of them, and have not given the debtors quittance, both in the time of the lord king Henry and in the time of the lord king who now is.

24. Again, who have summoned any to be knighted, and have taken bribes from them to have respite; how much and from what time. And if any magnates or others have detained any to take up arms without the king's command, and from what time.

25. Again, if sheriffs or any bailiffs of any liberty whatsoever have not made summons in due manner, according to the form of the lord king's writ, or in any other way have fraudulently or inadequately executed the king's commands for prayer, for bribe or for favor, and from what time. . . .

27. Again, who have had felons in prison and have allowed them, for money, to get away and escape from prison free and unpunished; and who have extorted money for letting men out of prison on bail; when they have been bailed, and from what time.

28. Again, who have received any gifts or bribes for exercising or for not exercising or executing their offices, or have executed them or exceeded the bounds of the king's commands otherwise than belonged to their office, and from what date.

All these inquiries shall be made not only concerning sheriffs, coroners and their clerks, but also concerning the lords and bailiffs of all liberties whatsoever.

29. Again, what sheriffs or keepers of any of the lord king's castles or manors, or also what surveyors of such works wherever carried out by the king's command, have accounted for larger sums than they have rightly spent on them and have thereupon procured false allowances to be made to them. And likewise, who have retained or removed for their own use stone, timber or other things bought or provided for such works, and what and how much loss the lord king has thus suffered, and from what time.

30. Concerning escheators and subescheators occupying lands for the lord king who do waste and destruction in woods, parks, fishponds or warrens within the wardships committed to them by the lord king; how much, and in whose lands, and how and when.

31. Again concerning the same: if by occasion of such occupation they have unjustly taken the goods of the deceased or of the heirs into the lord king's hand till redeemed by them, and what and how much they have taken by way of such redemption, and what of it they have kept for themselves and at what time.

32. Again, concerning the same who have taken gifts from any for exercising or not exercising their office: how much, from whom, and at what time.

33. Again, concerning the same who have made inadequate valuations of any person's lands in favor of himself or of some other person to whom the custody of those lands ought to be given, sold or granted, thus deceiving the lord king; where, and how, and if they have received anything for doing this, and how much and when.

34. Again, concerning the same who for prayer, for bribe or for favor have agreed or advised that the lord king's wardships should be sold at a lesser price than they should be, by their true

value, or marriages of the heirs of tenants-in-chief, or marriages of widow ladies, married without the lord king's leave; what they have taken for this, how much, when, and since what time.

35. Again, concerning the same who have procured or permitted jurors of inquests into the age of heirs to declare that the heirs were of full age when they were not, whereby the lord king has lost the marriage and wardship of such heirs.

36. Again, concerning the same who have reserved for their own use wardships or marriages at a trifling price or by concealment from the lord king; what loss the lord king has thereby suffered, and since when.

37. Again, what sort of lands they have occupied, and for how long they have kept them in the hands of the lord king.

38. Again, concerning lands taken into the lord king's hands which ought not to have been taken, and afterwards restored, with their takings, by the lord king's command; whether they have restored the takings at the lord king's command or no.

B. AN ANSWER TO THE INQUEST

The answers of the jurors were written down on rolls, and these rolls, most of which have survived, are known as the Hundred Rolls. There follows the roll for Totmonslow, a hundred in the county of Stafford.

Hundred Roll, Totmonslow, county of Stafford.[2] An inquisition made in the county of Stafford, concerning the hundred of Totmonslow, before the commissioners of the lord the king, viz., Sir Richard of Fokeram and Osbert of Berescote, by a jury of the same hundred, viz., Sir Philip of Draycote, Roger of Verney, Richard of Acovere, Henry of Casterne, Benedict of Botertone, John of Berestord in Verselowe, Symon Basset, William Meverel in Ylum, Walter le Mareschal in Fenton, Richard of Stoke in Leye, Robert of Acovere in Denston, Robert of Chetelton, Robert of Gretewis, Richard of Rodeyert: who say that the Lord Edmund, the king's brother, holds the manor of Uttoxeter of the king *in capite* for one knight's fee; and John of Verdun held Crakemerch and Crethton for one knight's fee of the same Edmund and of the same manor; and Thomas of Ferars holds Lochesle of the same Edmund and of the same manor for one-fourth of a knight's fee, and the manor of Alton is held of the king *in capite* for one knight's fee, and is now in the king's hands by the death of John of Verdun; and Henry of Aldithelee holds of the same manor, i.e. (Alton), Aldithelee and Enedone, by the service of a knight's fee; and the abbey of Rowchester is held of the king in free alms and by feoffment of donors and by confirmation of the Lord King Henry, and it was of the fee of the Earl of Chester; and the Abbot of Deulacres holds the manor of Lek of the king *in capite,* and it used to be of the liberty of Chester; and the Abbot of Hulton holds Mixene, and it used to be held of the king in fee farm, viz., by the service of 5s., and a cartload of hay, and an iron fork paid to the manor of Penchul.

Of the farm of the hundreds, they say that William of Kaversewelle holds the hundred of Totmonslow by charter of the king for £10 yearly, and it is worth £10, and he held the same hundred sixteen years ago; and the barons of Alstonefield, viz., Henry of Aldithelee and his other co-heirs, give a mark annually to the sheriff for view of frankpledge, and the sheriff was accustomed to hold a court there annually, or receive a fine, and it was first withheld in the time of Hugh Despencer; and the Abbot of Rowchester gives 10s. for view of frankpledge; and the manor of Mayfield gives 20s. for the same; nevertheless the sheriff entered the said liberty after the Feast of St. Michael to hold a court there; and from Kingestone for view of frankpledge 3s. annually.

Of ancient suits or other things withheld from the king, they say that the tenants of the lands, viz., William of Wythilehe, Lawrence of Charpeclif, William of Padewick, and three others named, used to be geldable to the hundred, and it has been withdrawn for a long time, viz., from the time of Nicholas of Verdun, to his liberty of Alton; and other tenants, viz., Henry de le Athenehurst and four others named used to be geldable to the hundred, but are now appropriated to the liberty of the Abbot of Hulton, viz., to his manor of Brademore, by the power and the force of Henry of Aldithelee; and the grange of Dogge-Chedle used to be geldable to the hundred, and has now been appropriated to the abbey of Crokesdene for thirty years past; and the grange of Field used to be geldable, and is now appropriated by the Abbot of Deulacres; and it was alienated by Alina of St. Maur; and the above grange of Chedle was alienated by John of Saucheverel and by Henry his son; and Henry of Aldithelee holds a free court at Horton, and it is not known by what warrant, and it used to be geldable.

Of those who claim to have the return of

writs, etc., they say that Edmund the king's brother has gallows, and assize of bread and beer, at Uttoxeter, but it is not known by what warrant; and the Abbot of Rowchester has gallows, etc., by charter of donors, and by confirmation of King Henry; and the prior of Totteburi has gallows at Mayfield, it is not known by what warrant; and Geoffrey of Greselee has gallows at Kingeston, and assizes, etc., it is not known by what warrant; and the lord of Alton has gallows at Alton, and assizes, etc., it is not known by what warrant; and Henry of Aldithelee, Hugh le Despencer, and Warine of Vernun have gallows, etc., but it is not known by what warrant.

Of those who have liberties and use them otherwise than they ought, they say that the Abbot of Deulacres, Henry of Aldithelee, and the lord of Alton, have sergeanties, and they take by force and unjustly passage money through their demesne lands and elsewhere. Of those who have newly appropriated to themselves chases and warrens, they say that Sir John of Verdun appropriated to himself, after the war [i.e. the Baron's Revolt], a wood called Rinthay and Yornburi to his warren and free chase at Alton; and they used to be geldable to the hundred, and answer with the vill of Chedle; and the same John appropriated to himself a warren at Ramsor, of the bishop's fee; and it used to be a common chase for the whole country; and the same John appropriated to himself a warren at Wotton, it is not known by what warrant.

Of military fees diminished, etc., they say that the grange of Chedle and the grange of Field are alienated to the prejudice of the king.

Respecting sheriffs who took money to conceal felonies, they say that John Bareil took of William the provost of Bokenhale feloniously 100s., and John of Bromchulf, the bailiff of the hundred of Totmonslow, took 20s. of Robert of Lebenet feloniously, and also of many others of whose names they are ignorant; and William Rome, the bailiff of Henry of Aldithelee, has in his house at Alstonefield, Yun a felon and outlaw, who is brother to the said William; and John Bareil took a mark from Robert Oviet feloniously to conceal the same; and John Bareil took 40s. from Robert Bente to conceal him. And they say that all the sheriffs and sub-sheriffs took money from men indicted at their great hundred courts to admit them to bail, viz.: Hamon Lestrange and Leon his sub-sheriff, and William of Kavereswell and Walter of Hopton, and Urian of St. Pierre, Hugh of Mortimer, and Ralph of Mortimer; and Henry Owen, the bailiff of the Lord Edmund, took William the gardener, of Uttoxeter, and William of Deulacres of the same under an indictment of the magna curia of Uttoxeter, and sent them to the prison of Bruge, in the time of John Bareil; and there they refused to receive them, and sent them back to Uttoxeter; and Henry Owen took from them 20s. to admit them to bail. And they say that John Bareil when subsheriff took much money for removing men from assizes and juries, from many men of whose names they are ignorant; and John of Bromchulf took much money for the same whilst he was bailiff; and he took 12d. from Henry of Northwode, and from Adam of Hugebruge he took [no sum named].

And of those who took fines from persons summoned to make inquisition, they say that John of Bromchulf took fines from many of whose names they are ignorant; and Hervey of Leys, junior, took for the same an infinite quantity of money.

And they say that William of Kavereswelle sublet the hundred to John of Bromchulf for 20 marks annually, so that the said John had greatly vexed the people . . . for reaping in autumn, and the said John had a bailiff, Richard of Stanton, who had greatly vexed the country in this way.

And they say that whereas the sheriff ought not to make his tourn but twice a year, John Bareil held his tourn twice in one year, and in addition, Reginald the clerk of the same John held a tourn, and John of Bromchulf the bailiff of the hundred held a third hundred court in the same year, to the damage of the whole hundred. And of those who had acted maliciously under cover of their office, they say that Hamon Lestrange and Leo his sub-sheriff took Ralph of Burgo and imprisoned him at Stafford for a month and more, to the damage of the said Ralph of 20 marks; and the said Ralph was made to support six servants of the said Hamon for that time, who had inflicted upon him other enormities; and John Bareil the sub-sheriff took Richard of Swineschoch and imprisoned him, and took from him 20s.; and John of Bromchulf was one of twelve journeymen, and their clerk, and at a certain great tourn of the hundred in the time of Ralph of Mortimer, he had indicted William of Acovere without the assent of his associate jurors, and had caused him to be imprisoned, by which he had been damaged to the amount of 20 marks. And Henry the rector of the church of Blore, the bailiff of Henry of Aldithelee in Alstanefeld, took 10s. from William of Narendale; and John of Bromchulf took a certain maker of swords and imprisoned him, and took from him three swords, and afterwards released him spontaneously; and Alan Pes, the bailiff of John of Verdun of Alton, took six oxen and cows from Richard of Ruddeyert, and retained four of them, and for giving up two of them, took a mark from the said Richard; and Hamon le Strange, when sheriff, took

£20 from the whole county; and the same Hamon and Leo his sub-sheriff took forty head of cattle of the chattels of the Abbot of Hulton at Mixene, and drove them to Certeleye, and retained six of them there for the use of the castle; and John Bareil took from the Abbot of Deulacres 6 marks, and from Henry of St. Maur 2 marks.

And they say that the Lord Edmund, the king's brother, took 2 marks from Thomas of Ferars to distrain him to take knighthood, by the hands of Robert of Waldechef, the constable of Tutteburi.

And they say that William of Bromchulf took a mark from Margaret of Elkesdon for a writ of "pone," which she ought to have had for half a mark.

And of those who took money for executing their office, or for not executing it, they say that William of Chetelton, Bertram of Burgo, Robert Selwein, John of Charnes, coroners, took money for executing their offices, and were fined for it by the justices itinerant. And William Wyther the coroner took 2s. at Alstanesfelt for the death of Mathew . . . and the other coroners took 2s. or half a mark or more for every homicide.

C. THE RESULTS OF THE INQUEST: LEGISLATIVE ACTION

When the answers to the inquest were in the hands of the King and his council, it was up to them to take action. Where the answers showed that the system of local government was wrong or that confusion existed regarding royal rights, government action took the form of legislation. The King, whether acting in parliament or merely in council, issued certain statutes, declarations which then became the law of the land.

1. *The Statute of Westminster I, 1275.* A "general parliament" summoned by Edward in December, 1274, met at Westminster in April of the next year. The chief monument to its labors is to be found in fifty-one statutes, known collectively as the Statute of Westminster I.[3]

[*Preamble.*] These be the acts of King Edward, son to King Henry, made at his first parliament general after his coronation, on the Monday of Easter week, the third year of his reign, by his council and by the assent of archbishops, bishops, abbots, priors, earls, barons, and all the commonalty of the realm, being thither summoned. Because our lord the King had great zeal and desire to redress the state of the realm in such things as required amendment for the common profit of Holy Church, and of the realm, and because the state of the Holy Church had been evil kept, and the prelates and religious persons of the land grieved many ways, and the people otherwise treated than they ought to be, and the peace less kept, and the laws less used, and the offenders less punished, than they ought to be, by reason whereof the people of the land feared the less to offend, the King hath ordained and established these acts underwritten, which he intendeth to be necessary and profitable unto the whole realm. . . .

Pursuit of felons. And forasmuch as the peace of this realm hath been weakly kept heretofore for lack of quick and fresh pursuit after felons in due manner, and because of franchises, where felons are received: it is provided, that all generally be ready and apparelled, at the commandment and summons of sheriffs, and at the cry of the country, to pursue and arrest felons, when any need is, as well within franchise as without; and they that will not so do, and thereof be attainted, shall make a grievous fine to the King: and if default be found in the lord of the franchise, the King shall take the same franchise to himself; and if default be in the bailiff, he shall have one year's imprisonment, and after shall make a grievous fine; and if he have not whereof, he shall have imprisonment of two years. And if the sheriff, coroner, or any bailiff, within such franchise or without, for reward, or for prayer, or for fear or for any manner of affinity, conceal, consent, or procure to conceal the felonies done in their liberties, or otherwise will not attach nor arrest such felons there, . . . or otherwise will not do their office for favor borne to such misdoers, and be attainted thereof, they shall have one year's imprisonment, and after make a grievous fine at the King's pleasure, if they have wherewith; and if they have not whereof, they shall have imprisonment of three years. . . .

Prisoners and bail. And forasmuch as sheriffs, and other, which have taken and kept in prison persons accused of felony, and divers times have let out by replevin such as were not replevisable, and have kept in prison such as were replevisable, because they would gain of the one party, and grieve the other: and forasmuch as before this time, it was not determined which persons were replevisable, and which not, but only those that were taken for the death of man, or by commandment of the King, or of his justices: . . .

It is provided, and by the King commanded, that such prisoners as before were outlawed, and they which have abjured the realm, . . . and those which have broken the King's prison, thieves openly defamed and known, . . . and such as be taken for house-burning feloniously done, or for false money, or for counterfeiting the King's seal, or persons excommunicate, taken at the request of the bishop, or for manifest offenses, or for treason touching the King himself, shall be in no wise replevisable by the common writ, nor without writ.

But such as be indicted of larceny, by inquests taken before sheriffs or bailiffs by their office, or of light suspicion, or for petty larceny that amounteth not above the value of twelve-pence (if they were not guilty of some larceny aforetime, or guilty of receipt of felons, or of commandment, or force, or of aid in felony done; or guilty of some other trespass for which one ought not to lose life nor member,) . . . shall from henceforth be let out by sufficient surety, whereof the sheriff will be answerable, and that without giving aught of their goods.

And if the sheriff, or any other, let any go at large by surety that is not replevisable, if he be sheriff or constable or any other bailiff of fee, which hath keeping of prisons, and thereof be attainted, he shall lose his fee and office for ever. And if the under-sheriff, constable, or bailiff of such as have fee for keeping of prisons, do it contrary to the will of his lord, or any other bailiff being not of fee, they shall have three years imprisonment, and make fine at the King's pleasure. And if any withhold prisoners replevisable, after that they have offered sufficient surety, he shall pay a grievous amercement to the King; and if he take any reward for the deliverance of such, he shall pay double to the prisoner, and also shall pay a grievous amercement to the King. . . .

Assessing of common fines on the county. Forasmuch as the common fine and amercement of the whole county in eyre of the justices for false judgments, or for other trespass, is unjustly assessed by sheriffs . . . in the shires, so that the sum is many times increased, and the parcels [of land] otherwise assessed than they ought to be, to the damage of the people, which be many times paid to the sheriffs . . . which do not acquit the payers. It is provided, and the King wills, that from henceforth such sums shall be assessed before the justices in eyre, before their departure, by the oath of knights and other honest men, upon all such as ought to pay; and the justices, shall cause the parcels to be put into their estreats, which shall be delivered up unto the exchequer, and not the whole sum. . . .

Sheriffs, &c, receiving the King's debts shall acquit the debtor. In right of the sheriffs, or other, which answer by their own hands unto the exchequer, and which have received the King's father's debts, or the King's own debts before this time, and have not acquitted the debtors in the exchequer: it is provided, that the King shall send good and lawful men through every shire, to hear such as will complain thereof, and to determine the matters there that all such as can prove that they have paid, shall be thereof acquitted for ever, whether the sheriffs or other be living or dead, in a certain form that shall be delivered them; and such as have not so done, if they be living, shall be grievously punished; and if they be dead, their heirs shall answer, and be charged with the debt.

And the King hath commanded, that sheriffs and other aforesaid shall from henceforth lawfully acquit the debtors at the next accounting after they have received such debts; and then the debt shall be allowed in the exchequer, so that it shall no more come in the summons; and if the sheriff otherwise do, and thereof be attainted, he shall pay to the plaintiff thrice as much as he hath received, and shall make fine at the King's pleasure.

And let every sheriff take heed, that he have such a receiver, for whom he will answer; for the King will be recompensed of all, of the sheriffs and their heirs. And if any other, that is answerable to the exchequer by his own hands so do, he shall render thrice so much to the plaintiff, and make fine in like manner. And it is ordered that the sheriffs shall make tallies to all such as have paid their debt to the King, and that the summons of the exchequer be showed to all debtors that demand a sight thereof, without denying to any, and that without taking any reward, and without giving any thing; and he that doth contrary, the King shall punish him grievously. . . .

Unlawful disseisin by escheators, &c. It is provided also, that no escheator, sheriff, nor other bailiff of the King, by color of his office, without special warrant or commandment or authority certain pertaining to his office, disseise any man of his freehold, nor of any thing belonging to his freehold; and if any do, it shall be at the election of the disseisee, whether that the King by office shall cause it to be amended at his complaint, or that he will sue at the common law by a writ of novel disseisin; and he that is attainted thereof shall pay double damages to the plaintiff, and shall be grievously amerced unto the King. . . .

Extortions by the King's officers. And that no sheriff, nor other King's officer, take any reward to do his office, but shall be paid of that which they take of the King; and he that so doth, shall yield twice as much, and shall be punished at the King's pleasure. . . .

Excess of Jurisdiction in Franchises. Of great men and their bailiffs, and others, the King's officers only excepted unto whom especial authority is given, which at the complaint of some, or by their own authority, attach others passing through their jurisdiction with their goods compelling them to answer before them upon contracts, covenants, and trespasses, done out of their power and their jurisdiction, where indeed they hold nothing of them, nor with the franchise, where their power is, in prejudice of the King and his crown, and to the damage of the people: it is provided, that none from henceforth so do; and if any do, he shall pay to him, that by this occasion shall be attached, his damages double, and shall be grievously amerced to the King. . . .

2. *The Statute of Gloucester, 1278.* In August, 1278, at Gloucester, the King in council determined to hold a general eyre, or circuit of the royal justices throughout the realm. The Statute of Gloucester, selections of which are printed below, was to form the statutory basis of part of their labors.[4]

The year of grace MCCLXXVIII, and the sixth of the reign of King Edward son of King Henry, at Gloucester, in the month of August, the King himself providing for the amendment of his realm, and for a fuller administration of justice, as the good of the kingly office requireth, having called unto him the more discreet persons of his kingdom, as well of the greater as of the less: it is established and ordained with one accord, that whereas the same kingdom, in many divers cases, as well of franchises as of other things, wherein aforetime the law hath failed, and to avoid the grievous damages and innumerable disinheritances which this default of the law hath caused to the people of the realm, hath need of divers additions to the law, and of new provisions, there-

fore the statutes, ordinances, and provisions under-written should be steadfastly observed by all the people of the kingdom.

Whereas the prelates, earls, barons, and others of the kingdom, claim to have divers franchises, for the examination and judgment whereof the King had appointed a day to the said prelates, earls, barons, and others: it is provided and granted with one accord, that the aforesaid prelates, earls, barons, and others, may use such sort of franchises, so that nothing accrue to them by usurpation or occupation, and that they occupy nothing against the King, until the next coming of the King through the county, or the next coming of the justices in eyre for common pleas into the same county, or until the King shall otherwise order: saving the King's right when he shall put the same in suit, according to what is contained in the King's writ. And hereof writs shall be issued to the sheriffs, bailiffs, and others, in behalf of every demandant; and the form of the writ shall be changed according to the diversity of the franchises that each man claimeth.

And the sheriffs shall cause it to be commonly proclaimed throughout their bailiwicks, that is to say, in cities, boroughs, market towns, and elsewhere, that all those who claim to have any franchises by the charters of the King's predecessors, kings of England, or in other manner, shall come before the King or before the justices in eyre, at a certain day and place, to show what sort of franchises they claim to have, and by what warrant.

D.   THE RESULTS OF THE INQUEST: JUDICIAL ACTION

The central government learned from the answers to the Inquest of 1274 what individuals had misconducted themselves. Governmental action then took the form of judicial action. Royal justices were sent to a locality which complained, for example, of a dishonest bailiff, to conduct a judicial investigation of the offender. Our records of these trials are scanty; often the justices carried with them the original rolls containing the answers to the Inquest, and on them would note down what action was taken. Thus we find annotations such as "He was convicted," "He was hanged," or "He has died" in the margins of the Hundred Rolls. For another kind of case, however, the records are much more substantial. Many of the so-called *quo warranto* pleas, which stem from both the Inquest and the Statute of Gloucester, survive, and from them we can learn in detail what action was taken by Edward's justices. In addition, the chroniclers of the period have something to say of the *quo warranto* proceedings.

1. *A Chronicler's Account.* The following selection is from the *Chronicon* of Walter of Hemingburgh, a canon of a priory in northern Yorkshire. This portion of the work was probably written sometime between 1304 and 1313.[5]

In the year of our Lord 1278, a fortnight after the feast of St. John the Baptist, the King held

his parliament at Gloucester and issued what is called the statute of Gloucester containing fifteen clauses. In August he made the statute of *quo warranto.* . . .

Soon after he disquieted some of the magnates of the land by means of his justices, who sought to know by what warrant they held their lands. If they had no good warrant, he took possession of their lands. Among the rest Earl Warenne was summoned before the king's justices and asked by what warrant he held. He produced an ancient and rusty sword, and cried, "Here, my lords, here is my warrant! My ancestors came over with William the bastard and conquered their lands by the sword, and I will defend those same lands by the sword against any, whosoever he may be, who seeks to occupy them. For the King did not conquer and subdue the land by himself, but my ancestors were his partners and helpers." Other magnates adhered to him and his argument, and went off angry and in disorder. When the King heard of this he feared for himself, and ceased from his mistaken policy. Besides, soon after the Welsh rose in rebellion, and the King had great need of his magnates. So when the King was holding a certain parliament, and the sons of the magnates were standing in his presence at vespers, he said to them, "What were you talking about while I was in consultation with your fathers?" And one answered, "You will not be angry if we tell you the truth?" "No," said the King. "Sire, we were saying this:—

> The king desires our money,
> The queen our manors too,
> The writ of 'By what warrant'
> Will make a sad to-do."

2. *The King* versus *the Earl of Surrey*. The defendant in the following law case was a great noble, John of Warenne, Earl of Surrey, the same Earl Warenne mentioned by the chronicler in the preceding selection. The case, one of several *quo warranto* proceedings in which the Earl was a party, was tried before the justice in the Sussex eyre of June, 1279.[6]

John of Warenne, Earl of Surrey, was summoned to be here on this day to show by what warrant he claimed to have free warren and chase in the following manors of [64 are named] in the county [of Sussex]. And William of Giselham, who conducted the case for the King, said that William of Warenne, father of the present Earl, had seized the rights of warren and chase in these manors from lord King Henry, father of the present King, and the rights which the present Earl holds he has merely seized to the loss of the lord King.

And the Earl came and denied both the force and the injury. He said that William of Warenne, his father, (whose heir he was) held the barony and honor of Lewes with the feudal rights and the rights of warren, etc., and that all of the liberties aforementioned were added and joined to that barony and honor which William held from the lord King Henry as a tenant and chief, and

without premeditation King Henry, by reason of this, had received his homage. And in this homage William had died seised of the rights of warren and chase as well as all the liberties added and joined to the aforesaid barony and honor [of Lewes]. After William's death the barony and honor (with the liberties) came into the hands of King Henry by reason of the wardship of John [the present Earl] who was under age. And during the whole time of this wardship, which was seventeen years and more, King Henry was in possession of the rights of warren and chase, in as much as these belonged to the aforesaid barony and honor.

And Earl John said that when he came of age, King Henry restored to him this barony and honor together with all the liberties including rights of chase, and all of them were restored to him in the same state as his father William had held them when he died. And the Earl said that King Henry accepted his homage for the barony and the things pertaining to it, and gave it to him in seisin on his own account. And in like manner the present lord King [Edward] had received his homage for the barony and for all things pertaining to it.

By that warrant he claims to have warren and chase in the aforementioned manors. . . . And though the present King seeks judgment for the said barony and honor, the Earl asks whether King Edward should not be the warrant against himself for the reasons mentioned before. And if the court considered that this [claim] was not sufficient he was prepared to reply, etc.

Later, in the octave of St. Martin [Dec. 18], the Earl came to Chichester and said that in [the manors in question] he himself had his own parks, and asked whether the King had any claim on these parks. And William of Giselham, the King's attorney, said that these parks had nothing to do with the present case.

The Earl said that all his ancestors had adhered strictly to the Kings of England. And he said that because at the time of departure from Normandy his ancestors, who had been Counts of Warenne there, were unwilling to adhere to the King of France and for this reason had lost their Norman lands. In consequence King John of England, by way of recompense, gave to the Earl's ancestors more land [in England] and granted that they and their heirs should hold all those lands, thus given, from the King himself, and also any lands which they might obtain. And they were to have the right of warren because their name was Warenne.

And the Earl said that his father had held all those rights of chase and warren in the manors in which he claimed to have them even before King Henry had assumed the governance of the realm.

Therefore the Earl said that his father had made no seizure from King Henry nor from the present King. And he asked that an inquest be made that it were so. And William of Giselham, who conducted the case for the King, similarly asked that an inquest be made.

Accordingly the case went to the jury and the sheriff was ordered to have a jury elected in his presence. And [twelve jurors, the first six being listed as "knights," the remainder as "lords of manors"] were selected with the consent of William of Heure, the King's attorney, and with the consent of the Earl.

And these jurors declared upon their oath that even before King Henry was crowned King, William of Warenne, Earl of Surrey, the father of the present Earl, had possessed all the said liberties of chase and warren belonging to the honor and barony of Lewes. And they held that Earl William had not seized or usurped anything either from King Henry or from the present King. . . .

And because it was agreed by the jury that Earl William had made use of these rights of chase and warren in the aforementioned manors before the coronation of King Henry; and because Earl William had not seized or usurped anything from King Henry or the present King, it was decided that the King could not seize by his writ.

And Earl John of Warenne was left in possession of these rights indefinitely.

3. *The King* versus *the Earl of Gloucester.* Gilbert of Clare, ninth Earl of Clare, seventh Earl of Hertford, and eighth Earl of Gloucester was one of the greatest magnates in England. He had possessions and feudal franchises in almost every county in England, but the law case which follows concerns two hundreds in Kent. This case was heard at Canterbury in January, 1279.[7]

Gilbert of Clare, Earl of Gloucester and Hertford was summoned to answer the King on a plea by what warrant he holds the hundreds of Watleston and Littlefield in the county of Kent. And with regard to this, William of Giselham, who conducted the case for the King, said that in the time of King Henry father of the present King, these hundreds were annexed and joined to that county just as other hundreds which are now in the hand of the King, and that Gilbert of Clare holds them only through the removal which Gilbert of Clare, grandfather of the present Gilbert, made against Henry the King.

And the Earl, by Roger of Moleton his attorney, by writ of the King now came and said that his grandfather Gilbert of Clare held these hundreds as appurtenant to the banlieu of Tonbridge and that after his death Richard his son was under age and became the ward of the Blessed Edmund, Archbishop of Canterbury at that time. And the Archbishop was seised of the honor of Tonbridge together with the aforesaid hundreds, and held them by reason of the wardship of Richard. And when this Richard had come of age, Edmund restored to him the honor and the hundreds as his right and inheritance. And he said Richard held these hundreds all his life, and died seised thereof in feudal lordship. After the death of Richard these hundreds came into the hands of Boniface, Archbishop of Canterbury, by reason of his wardship of Gilbert, who on the death of Richard his father was under age. And when Gilbert had come of age, Boniface restored to him the hundreds as his right and inheritance which descended to him by hereditary right after the death of Richard his father. Wherefore Gilbert said that by that warrant he held the said hundreds, of which his grandfather and his father, whose heir he is, died seised in feudal lordship and he, after their death entered into the same as their heir. And the Earl, when asked if he wished to show some other warrant for these hundreds, said not as far as this writ is concerned, but when the King shall sue out another writ against him, in which the King is named a party and made a party seeking the same hundreds, he (Gilbert) was sufficiently prepared to show some other warrant.

And William of Giselham, who conducted the case for the King, prayed judgment inasmuch as the Earl did not deny that King Henry, father of the present King, was seised of the aforesaid hundreds in his time, nor deny that at that time the hundreds were annexed and joined to the county, at which time they were withdrawn from the hands of King Henry, which withdrawal had been continuous up to now from the time of Gilbert, grandfather of the present Earl. And he sought judgment if that which the present Earl now says—that Gilbert and Richard his ancestors died seised of said hundreds in feudal lordship, and that he as their heir entered into the same by hereditary descent—was able to be a warrant for retaining the hundreds. Moreover he demands judgment against the present Earl as one without defense unless he wished to show some other warrant to this writ.

And the Earl said that it seemed to him that he had shown a sufficient warrant to this writ inasmuch as he was summoned to show only by what warrant he held said hundreds, nor was it expressed in that writ to whom he ought to answer nor to whom he ought to show warrant, because neither the King nor any one else was a party to him for seeking the hundreds. And he sought judgment on the writ on the point as to whether he ought to answer the King on such a writ and show another warrant, inasmuch as the King was not named a party in it.

And William of Giselham said that the writ was an old original writ, provided for and formed from olden time, nor was it used nor ought to be used in the case of anyone other than the King, and therefore it was not necessary that the King be named in such a writ from the fact that his name is understood for the reason that the writ would not be applicable in the case of anyone else. And inasmuch as the Earl did not and could not deny that the hundreds were in the hands of King Henry as appurtenant to his crown, and had been withdrawn from the King's hands in the time of Gilbert his grandfather, the question was if the continuation of that withdrawal constituted a sufficient warrant for the Earl to retain these hundreds. And as to this he sought a decisive judgment in favor of the King. He said, moreover, just as he had said before, that King Henry in his life-time had been seised of the hundreds as appurtenant to his crown, and that they had been geldable just as other hundreds in that county, and that they had been withdrawn by Gilbert the grandfather of the present Earl and that the present Earl holds them thus withdrawn. And that this is so, he offered to prove for the king in any way the court should wish. And because the Earl sought judgment as to the insufficiency of that writ, and it was clear that the writ was good and well conceived, . . . nor is any warrant sufficient for holding royal liberties of this sort except it be ancient custom from time immemorial or a special royal act—which on the part of the said Earl was not shown in evidence—a discussion with the King and his council having been had on the aforesaid matters, it was said to the Earl that the ancient original writ was good and well conceived, and that he must make answer to it, and must show some warrant other than that already shown, if it seemed expedient to him.

Then the Earl made further reply, and said that the aforesaid hundreds were of the honor of Tonbridge, and appurtenant to it, and that he held them of the church of Christ at Canterbury, and of the Archbishop of that place, and he vouched thence to warranty John Peckham, Archbishop of Canterbury by the aid of the court, and he prayed that he be summoned into court.

And William of Giselham on behalf of the King said that he ought not to vouch to warranty the said Archbishop, because hundreds of this sort are a royal liberty, for which liberty there is no warrant other than ancient custom from time out of mind or a special act of the prince, but nothing of this was shown on the part of the Earl. He said, moreover, just as he said earlier, that these hundreds had been in the hands of King Henry, geldable just as other hundreds of that

county appurtenant to his crown, and from his hands they had been withdrawn by Gilbert the grandfather of the present Earl, and so continued successively up to now, nor after this withdrawal were the predecessors of the said Archbishop ever in seisin of these hundreds to make them able to bind to warranty themselves and their successors. So he sought judgment for the King if—touching the withdrawal, illegal seizure and intrusion of his ancestors—he was able to vouch anyone to warranty, especially when to vouch his own warranty no reply was made to the King or to his writ, because he was summoned only to show by what warrant etc.

Afterwards the said Earl came and desisted from asserting the warranty aforesaid and all that he had said previously, and he said that at the time of the foundation of the church of Christ in Canterbury and before, at a date earlier than legal memory, the honor of Tonbridge, together with the hundreds in question, had been in the hands of his ancestors. Wherefore he said that by that warrant he holds said hundreds, namely that he and his ancestors in the time aforesaid, and before, were in seisin of the same as of right, and thus from heir to heir successively they came to his hands as their heir. And that such was his right and that he holds them by such warrant he offered to prove as the court should decide.

And William of Giselham said as he had said before that King Henry was seised of said hundreds as of right, appurtenant to his crown, and that they had been joined to the county of Kent and geldable with the county, until the grandfather of the present Earl usurped them from King Henry and took them from his hands. And that this was so, he sought on behalf of the King that the matter might be inquired into by the country [i.e., go to a jury]. And the Earl by his attorney likewise. Therefore it was ordered a jury be sworn.

And . . . [the twelve] jurors chosen with the consent of the parties, said that in truth the said hundreds had been in the hands of King Henry as his right and they had pertained to his crown and had been geldable with the county, and that one William le Smallwriter had held them to farm from the then sheriff of Kent. And they said that Gilbert of Clare, grandfather of the present Earl, so treated William le Smallwriter that William handed over to him the hundreds to farm for an annual rent of 40 shillings. And the jurors said that by that delivery Gilbert had died seised of the hundreds and by no other right. After whose death Richard his son and heir, entered into the same hundreds and died seised thereof, to whom succeeded the present Earl who now holds them withdrawn. And they said that the right of Gilbert, the present Earl, to these hundreds is such as is aforesaid, and not otherwise, and that the King has greater right in the hundreds than has Gilbert.

And therefore it was decided that the King should recover his seisin thereof in such form as the jurors said.

Part II.   PARLIAMENT UNDER EDWARD I

No single meeting of Parliament under Edward I can be accurately termed typical of all those that met during his reign. Historians have called that of 1295 the "Model Parliament," since in many ways it most closely approximated the Parliaments of later periods. But Edward I does not seem to have considered it a model, nor does he seem to have been concerned with maintaining doctrinaire uniformity. The materials in this part have been chosen, therefore, to represent the institution of Parliament as it existed in the later years of Edward's reign, rather than any single meeting of the institution.

A.   PRELIMINARIES TO A MEETING OF PARLIAMENT

1. *Writs of Summons.* When the King had decided to hold a Parliament, he ordered the Chancery to issue writs of summons for those whom he wished to attend. The following writs show who might be summoned and also the reasons for which these particular Parliaments were held.[8]

(*To an archbishop, 1295*) The King to the venerable father in Christ Robert, by the same grace Archbishop of Canterbury, primate of all England, greeting. As a most just law, established by the careful providence of sacred princes, exhorts and decrees that what affects all, by all should be approved, so also, very evidently should common danger be met by means provided in common. You know sufficiently well, and it is now as we believe, divulged through all regions of the world, how the King of France fraudulently and craftily deprives us of our land of Gascony, by withholding it unjustly from us. Now, however, not satisfied with the before-mentioned fraud and injustice, having gathered together for the conquest of our kingdom a very great fleet, and an abounding multitude of warriors, with which he has made a hostile attack on our kingdom and the inhabitants of the same kingdom, he now proposes to destroy the English language altogether from the earth if his power should correspond to the detestable proposition of the contemplated injustice, which God forbid.

Because, therefore, darts seen beforehand do less injury, and your interest especially, as that of other fellow citizens of the same realm, is concerned in this affair, we command you, strictly enjoining you in the fidelity and love in which you are bound to us, that on the Lord's day next after the feast of St. Martin, in the approaching winter, you be present in person at Westminster; citing beforehand the dean and chapter of your church, the archdeacons and all the clergy of your diocese, causing the same dean and archdeacons in their own persons, and the said chapter by one suitable proctor, and the said clergy by two, to be present along with you, having full and sufficient power of themselves from the chapter and clergy, for considering, ordaining and providing along with us and with the rest of the prelates and principal men and other inhabitants of our kingdom how the dangers and threatened evils of this kind are to be met. Witness the King at Wangham, the thirtieth day of September.

[Identical summons were sent to the two archbishops and eighteen bishops, and, with the omission of the last paragraph, to seventy abbots.]

(*To an earl, 1295*) The King to his beloved and faithful relative, Edmund, Earl of Cornwall, greeting. Because we wish to have a consultation and meeting with you and with the rest of the principal men of our kingdom, as to provision for remedies against the dangers which in these days are threatening our whole kingdom; we command you, strictly enjoining you in the fidelity and love in which you are bound to us, that on the Lord's day next after the feast of St. Martin, in the approaching winter, you be present in person at Westminster, for considering, ordaining and doing along with us and with the prelates, and the rest of the principal men and other inhabitants of our kingdom, as may be necessary for meeting dangers of this kind.

Witness the King at Canterbury, the first of October.

[Similar summons were sent to seven earls and forty-one barons.]

(*To a royal official, 1299*) The King, to his faithful and beloved Philip of Willoughby, Chancellor of his Exchequer, greeting.

Since, for the safety of our crown and the common advantage of the people of our realm, we wish to hold a parliament at London on the second Sunday of Lent and to have a consultation and meeting with you and the rest of our council upon matters especially touching us and our kingdom; we command you, strictly enjoining you in the fidelity and love in which you are bound to us, that you be personally present at the said time and place to consult with us and the rest of our council and to give your advice. And under no circumstances fail to do this.

Witness the King at Berwick-on-Tweed, the twenty-ninth day of December.

[Similar summons were sent to thirty-seven other royal officials.]

(*To a royal justice, 1300*) The King to his beloved and faithful Walter of Gloucester, greetings.

Since, for the common benefit of the people of our realm, we have recently granted that the Charter of the Forest be strictly observed in all its articles, by assigning you and others of our faithful men in every county of the realm in which our forests exist to make a perambulation of these forests:

And so that this perambulation, clearly and carefully made, may be reported to us before any action be taken thereon, and so that our oath, the rights of the English crown, and our claims and accounts may be kept safe as well as the claims and accounts of all others:

We now for the first time permit you and our other faithful men to report to us what you have done in this matter. . . .

And since . . . we wish to have a consultation and meeting with the prelates, earls, barons, magnates and other men of the community of the realm concerning both this matter and certain other arduous matters touching us and our realm:

We strictly enjoin and command you to be with us and the prelates and magnates aforesaid at our parliament [at Lincoln] in the octave of St. Hilary next [20 Jan. 1301], to discuss these matters with them and give your advice; bringing with you all the perambulations of the forest which we have caused to be made by you and your agents assigned to this purpose in the various counties of our kingdom and all other things pertaining to the perambulations. And under no circumstance fail to do this.

Witness the King at La Rose, the twenty-ninth day of September.

[Similar writs were sent to seventeen other royal officials.]

(*To a sheriff, 1295*) The King to the sheriff of Northamptonshire. Since we intend to have a consultation and meeting with the earls, barons and other principal men of our kingdom with regard to providing remedies against the dangers which are in these days threatening the same kingdom; and on that account have commanded them to be with us on the Lord's Day next after the feast of St. Martin in the approaching winter, at Westminster, to consider, ordain, and do as may be necessary for the avoidance of these dangers; we strictly require you to cause two knights from the aforesaid county, two citizens from each city in the same county, and two burgesses from each borough, of those who are especially discreet and capable of laboring, to be elected without delay, and to cause them to come to us at the aforesaid time and place.

Moreover, the said knights are to have full and sufficient power for themselves and for the community of the aforesaid county, and the said citizens and burgesses for themselves and the community of the aforesaid cities and boroughs separately, then and there for doing what shall be ordained by the common council in the premises; so that the aforesaid business shall not remain unfinished in any way for defect of this power. And you shall have there the names of the knights, citizens and burgesses and this writ.

Witness the King at Canterbury on the third day of October.

[Identical summons were sent to the sheriffs of each county.]

(*To a sheriff, 1297*) The King to the sheriff of Yorkshire, greeting.

Since, for the relief of all the inhabitants and people of our kingdom, and in consideration of the eighth which is to be levied on all the goods of each layman throughout the whole kingdom on account of the urgent situation existing between our kingdom and the French; we have granted to confirm and strictly to keep the Great Charter of the liberties of England and the Charter of the liberties of the Forest, and to concede to all and sundry in our kingdom letters patent stating that the levy of the said eighth shall not result to their prejudice, servitude, or disinheritance in the use and custom of the future:

We order and firmly enjoin that without delay you cause to be elected two of the most upright and law-abiding knights of the county; and they are to have full power for themselves and the whole county. You are to have them go to our most dear son Edward, our lieutenant in England, and they must go to our son at London by the octave of St. Michael next at the latest [6 Oct. 1297], there to receive the charter by which we confirmed the said charter and our letters patent on behalf of the community in the form stated, and there to do whatever else is ordered by our son and our council. Under no circumstances fail to do this, and have this writ there.

Witness Edward, son of the King, at St. Paul's in London, on the fifteenth day of September.

[Similar writs were sent to every sheriff in England.]

(*To a city, 1296.*) On the Wednesday before the next feast of St. Hilary in the twenty-fourth year of the reign of King Edward [26 Sept. 1296] a writ of the lord King was issued in these words:

"Edward, by the grace of God, etc., to the mayor and aldermen of London. Since, with the earls, barons, and other lords of our realm, we must provide remedies against the dangers which in these days threaten our kingdom, we wish to have a consultation and meeting. We have therefore commanded them to be with us on the day after All Soul's Day next [3 Nov. 1296] at Bury St. Edmunds, to discuss, ordain, and accomplish what is necessary to avoid these dangers and to take safe and useful counsel concerning the status of our realm.

"We strictly order and enjoin that from the said city you have two of the most discreet citizens of the community of the said city elected without delay, and that you have them come to us at said time and place. And the said citizens are to have full and sufficient power, both for themselves and for the community of the said city to do what will be ordered there for the common good in these matters; lest by their lack of power of this sort the matters aforesaid should in any way remain undone. And also have there the names of the citizens and this writ.

"Witness myself in person at Berwick-on-Tweed, the twenty-sixth day of August. . . ."

In accordance with that command, all the aldermen of that city and four men from each ward of that city were called together. By the unanimous consent and assent of them all, Stephen Ashway and William of Hereford were elected to go to the parliament of the Lord King at Bury St. Edmunds. And by the assent of all, they were granted twenty shillings each day for their expenses while going and coming back.

2. *Royal Orders and Proclamations.* The issuance of writs of summons was followed by royal orders to various officials, commanding them to make proclamations or take certain measures concerning matters involved in the holding of a Parliament. Printed below are several such royal orders.[9]

(*Order to two sheriffs, 1305.*) The King to the sheriffs of Surrey and Sussex, greeting.

Since we wish to be provided with grain for the expenditure of our hospitality at our next Parliament at Westminster on the Sunday after the feast of St. Matthew the Apostle next [28 Feb.], we order you without delay to purchase two hundred quarters [1600 bushels] of grain at a definite price from the wealthier men in your bailiwick who have more than enough for this purpose, and

to make tallies between them and you for our needs regarding the said expenditure, and to have the grain carted and carried to Westminster without delay, at the very latest by the said Sunday. Fail not to do this as you cherish yourself and your possessions.

And we wish the said men to be paid for the grain out of the Wardrobe and that payment be made to them as soon as the grain has come into the hands of our receivers of supplies. In connection with the expenses you have incurred in the carting, we shall have due allowance made at our Exchequer on your account of the revenue of your bailiwick.

Witness the King at Walsingham, the second day of February.

(*Order to a sheriff, 1302.*) The King to the sheriff of Warwickshire, greeting.

Since we have summoned the earls, barons, and other magnates and lords of the realm to our coming Parliament on the octave of the nativity of St. John the Baptist next [1 July] to discuss with them certain arduous matters touching us and the status of our realm, we are therefore unwilling that any tournaments or jousts be held by anyone in this kingdom until this our said Parliament shall be fully and completely at an end.

We strictly enjoin and command you that, as soon as you have seen this letter, you make public proclamation in the cities, boroughs, trading towns, and other places in your bailiwick where it may seem expedient to you, especially at Warwick . . . , and cause it to be strictly forbidden to any knight, squire, or any one else, on pain of forfeit of life, limb, and all his possessions in this realm, to presume to engage in jousts or tournaments or to seek knightly adventures or to take up arms in any fashion.

Witness the King at Carmarthen, the thirteenth day of June.

(*Order to the Chancellor, 1305.*)

We bid you along with the treasurer, to whom we have issued a similar command, proclaim that all those who have petitions to deliver to us and our council at our forthcoming Parliament, shall deliver them day by day to those who are assigned to receive them between now and the first Sunday of Lent [the 7th of March] at the latest. And do you and the others of our Council in London 'deliver' [answer] as many of these petitions as you can before we come, so that no petitions shall come before us in person, save only those which cannot in anywise be 'delivered' without us, and these last you are to have well tried and examined and set in good order. This proclamation should be made in the great hall at Westminster, in the Chancery, before the justices of the bench, in the Guildhall, and in Westcheap, and the names of those who are to receive petitions must be declared. You are to let me know without delay in what manner you have fulfilled this command and whom you have appointed to receive the petitions.

Witness the King at Swaffingham, the fifth day of February, 1305.

(*A royal proclamation, 1305.*)

It was ordained by the King that Sir Gilbert of Roubiry, Master John of Caen, Sir John of Kirkby, and Master John Bush shall receive all the petitions of those who desire to deliver petitions at this Parliament at Westminster. And on this matter a proclamation was made by the command of the King in the Great Hall of Westminster, before the justices of the bench and at the Exchequer, in the Guildhall of London, and in Westcheap, in these words:

"All those who desire to present petitions at this next parliament shall deliver them from day to day, between now and the first Sunday of Lent [7 March] at the latest, to Sir Gilbert of Roubiry, Master John of Caen, Sir John of Kirkby, and Master John Bush, or to one of them, who are assigned to receive them between now and the next Sunday of Lent at the latest. And according to this ordinance and this proclamation, let them return all the petitions in the form aforesaid."

Thereafter the King appointed Sir William Inge, Master Richard of Havering, Sir Henry of Guildford, James of Dalileghe, and Master John of Weston to receive all the petitions which pertain to the realm of Scotland. And he also appointed the Bishop of Chester, the Earl of Lincoln, Sir Aymar of Valence, Sir John of Brittany, Sir John of Havering, Sir Arnold of Caupenne, the Prior of Le Mas, Master Peter Arnold of Vic, Master Peter Aimery, and Sir John of Sandale to receive and reply to all the petitions sent by the men of Gascony. And the King also appointed Sir John of Berwick, Sir Hervey of Stanton, William of Dene, William of Mortimer, and Roger of Beaufou to receive all the petitions from those of Ireland and the Isle of Guernsey and to reply to all those which can be answered without the King.

And all the petitions which pertain to the said lands of Scotland, Gascony, Ireland, and Guernsey shall presently be delivered to those assigned thereto by the aforesaid Gilbert of Roubiry, Master John of Caen, John of Kirkby, and Master John Bush in the form aforesaid.

[The receivers of petitions appointed in the above document were members of the permanent *curia,* often with interests in the localities concerned.]

B.   PARLIAMENTARY PROCEEDINGS

1. *The Accounts of a Chronicle.* The following are accounts of some of the Parliaments held in the last fifteen years of Edward's reign given in *The Flowers of History,* a chronicle attributed to a pseudonymous Matthew of Westminster but actually compiled by several monks at Westminster and St. Albans.[10]

(1294) Edward, King of England, held his Parliament at Westminster, after the feast of Pentecost, which was attended by John, King of Scotland, and by all the nobles of England; and at this Parliament were recited, in the hearing of all those then present, the reasons for the commencement and continuance of this war [with France], and the reports of the ambassadors; and also the promises which had been made of re-establishing peace in England. At which statement each of the ambassadors of the Lord the King showed his hand in all good faith, to the utmost of his power. At last, every one agreed to recover Guienne by force of arms. Then the King of Scotland granted to the King of England, for three years, the revenues of all his estates, which belonged to him by hereditary right, in the kingdom of England, as a subsidy toward the recovery of Guienne, contenting himself with those of Scotland alone. And the

other earls and nobles promised him aid from their resources. Therefore from that day forth all passage across the sea was forbidden, by which the merchants incurred heavy losses, and the scarcity and dearness of corn increased every day in the English territories. . . .

On the vigil of Saint Matthew the Apostle, all the clergy and laity having been assembled at Westminster, the King demanded of the whole church, throughout the whole kingdom of England, a moiety of all their possessions, both temporal and spiritual. But when this, which was a measure without a precedent in all ages, was heard of, the pontiffs and prelates were disturbed and alarmed, and groaning in anguish of spirit, not daring to offend or contradict the King, but consenting to the royal demands, they granted him a moiety of all their revenues which came in in one year. Which moiety, however, if they had thought more prudently and properly, and had not omitted to consult the Apostolic See, they would by no means have dared to grant to the King. Therefore, having arranged and appointed certain periods for this payment, they returned to their own homes.

And the King lost no time; but as soon as the first installments, according to the taxation of this previously taxed tithe had been paid, he ordered the goods of the secular knights to be taxed, and a tenth to be paid to him throughout all England. And he levied a tax for the relief of his necessities on all merchants, and on all citizens dwelling in their walled cities and market towns, to the amount of the sixth penny of all that they possessed. It is also said that Master William of Montfort, Dean of St. Paul's, in London, coming safe and sound to the court, in the hope of softening the disposition of the monarch, or, at all events, of lightening such an insupportable yoke of slavery, like a good son of the church, and coming before the King in order to deliver the speech which he had conceived in his mind, and which he had come to utter, became suddenly mute, and losing all the strength of his body, he fell down before the King and expired. But as the King passed over this event with indifferent eyes, and persisted the more vehemently in his demand, it was still uncertain how much every one was to pay to the King.

The consequence was, that different persons told different stories, varying from time to time; and so, after eating sour grapes, at last, when they were assembled in the refectory of the monks at Westminster, a knight, John Havering by name, rose up in the midst of them, and said, "My venerable men, this is the demand of the king—the annual moiety of the revenues of your churches. And if any one objects to this, let him rise up in the middle of this assembly, that his person may be recognized and taken note of, as he is guilty of treason against the King's peace." When they heard this, all the prelates were disturbed, and immediately agreed to the King's demands. . . .

(1295) Two days after the feast of the Apostles Peter and Paul, two cardinals were sent as legates *a latere* by the lord the pope, to reconcile and tranquillize the kingdoms of France and England, which were swelling against one another with mutual hatred. And when they had landed in England, the people received them with all due honor, and the chief body of his prelates and nobles was summoned by the King to meet at Westminster, on the fifth of August; and when they were assembled, the cardinals and bishops being seated all around, first of all, Edmund, the King's brother, and Master John of Lacy, in the King's presence, explained the beginning and moving cause of the destructive war which had been carried on, and the troubles which had existed, and the contempt of all the laws of nations with which the sailors of England had been treated; and how the King of England discharged himself from the homage previously due to the King of France. After this, when the cardinals demanded a proposal of the conditions of peace,

they were answered, that this could not be given in till the pleasure of the King of Germany had been consulted. On this, they next asked for a truce while the peace was under discussion, but could not obtain it. Then, in the third place, the violent band of sailors might be compelled to keep quiet. But even in this part of the business they met with no success.

And while they were thus laboring to bring about a peace, behold, in the darkness and silence of night, a piratical body of Frenchmen made an assault on Dover, and burnt a house of religious brethren, and several other houses near the seacoast, with fire-brands; and among other atrocities they slew a certain monk, named Thomas, a man of innocent and pure conversation from his childhood, by whom the Lord worketh some miracles. Then, when circumstances changed as aid came up, those who had ascended into the town having been beheaded, the rest, being terrified by the people who came forward to fight them, hid themselves in the gardens and in the caves; and only a few escaped out of a great number, who secretly regained their ships and embarked. And turning their backs and flying, when they arrived in their own country, they falsely boasted that they had got possession of the keys of Dover Castle.

Then the cardinals, not having succeeded in the business for which they had come, returned to Gaul. . . .

On the eve of the feast of Saint Andrew, the clergy, nobles, and laity having been summoned to Westminster, the King again requested that they would grant him a subsidy out of their substance, for the defense of the kingdom. And an eleventh was granted him from those who had paid a tenth the year before; and those who had paid a sixth that year, were now to contribute a seventh. Moreover, the Archbishop of Canterbury having been indulged with permission to confer with his suffragans on this subject, with their unanimous consent offered the King a tenth of all ecclesiastical property; which having been offered, but not accepted, the bishops returned a second time to consider of this matter. Therefore, the King seeing their firmness, sent to them a great man, fifty years of age, namely, the chief justice of the king's bench, and his subordinate officers, who said, "O bishop, the King says, I neither accept, nor will I accept your offering, but descend speedily and fulfil his will, granting him at least a fourth part, or a third."

But one Elias, the archbishop, did not descend with his clergy from their place; nor did the oxen who were supporting the ark of the covenant turn aside to the right hand or to the left. In the meantime, the King sent another man of fifty years of age, belonging to the chancery, and his subordinate officers, and they too made the same request that those who had been previously sent had made. But by all these measures the body of the clergy was not moved from their resolution, but as they had previously granted a tenth, they now repeated the offer. Therefore, the King seeing that his demand was beyond the ability of the clergy to grant, not wishing to afflict them, on the day after the feast of the Conception of the blessed Mary, he received their offering as if welcome. And the clergy received this as a good omen, and so Israel returned to their tents. . . .

(1296) Therefore, Edward, King of England, having traversed all the islands of Scotland, and taken the towns and castles, as no rebels showed themselves, summoned the prelates and nobles of his kingdom to meet in parliament at Saint Edmund's Bury, at the feast of Saint Martin, from whom he demanded a new talliage [tax]. And there was granted to him by the citizens and burgesses the eighth penny, and from the rest the twelfth penny was extorted. But on that occasion the clergy neither offered nor granted him anything. On which the King was indignant, and gave them time to deliberate on a better answer, which should be more welcome and acceptable to his will. And in the mean time he caused the doors of all the ecclesiastical barons to be sealed up. And while this was being done, the archbishop caused a bull from the Apostolic See to be published in all the cathedral churches, prohibiting on pain of excommunication, any contribution being granted to the King, or to any other prince, from the revenues of the church. . . .

On St. Hilary's day, the archbishop held his council with his fellow bishops and suffragans at London, in the church of Saint Paul. And after they had held a discussion for eight days on the King's demands, they could not find out any proper way or pretext for an exclusive sentence, which, through the discovery of any colorable title of any kind, any persons might contribute anything, even though many clerks and courtiers and officers of the court came, who gave their countenance to and advice in favor of the demands. All which was reported to the King by the bishops or other messengers. And the King being at once changed into a cruel tyrant, perverting all royal justice, having given his servants permission to seize for themselves all the best appointed equipages of any of the clergy, or members of religious orders whom they might meet, as if they were enemies, and having also prohibited all advocates skilled in his law, to plead before the barons of the exchequer, or any other secular judge, on behalf of any ecclesiastical person, thus decided that all ecclesiastics were unworthy of his peace. He also commanded every one who had received ordination, voluntarily to offer him a fifth part of their revenues, or else they would strip them, against their will, of all their property.

Some of those who had received the tonsure at once complied with this command, (being prelates in the King's court, but as to the care of souls manifest Pilates,) hoping by that conduct to bring over the minds of the rest. After which, at once the sheriffs laid hands upon and seized all the property of the clergy, whether movable or immovable, which were found on any lay fee, and confiscated them for the use of the King's treasury, all those liberties being all taken away, to their superabundant annoyance, which the predecessors of the King, the protectors of Christianity and authors of all good, had conferred upon the churches. And, what is more wicked and intolerable, their very estates were appraised, in order to be offered to purchasers with all due expedition; nor could the clergy ride out in safety, except in large companies, on account of the violence of the soldiery toward them, in consequence of the leave which had been given by the King. And all the property of the archbishop, both movable and otherwise, was taken possession of for the King's use. He, indeed, endured this patiently.

Therefore, while the clergy were suffering, as I have here related, in body, the King himself suffered in mind. And fear and grief seized all the prelates; for they were in the greatest perplexity, fearing that if they granted any thing, they would, by so doing, incur sentence of excommunication; and if they did not give, they would not be able to escape the merciless hands of the robbers. Worn out with this anxiety, anxious for themselves, and inconsolably afflicted on account of the flock committed to them, as having no means of support, while they were thus threatened with famine, they necessarily determined to return to the world, procuring the King's protection by a sacrifice of their property to a great extent. . . .

(1298) The King of England came to Westminster, on the twenty-ninth of March, and a terrible fire took place in the lesser hall of the palace, and the flame reached the roof, and being fanned by the wind, devoured the buildings of the neighboring abbey and the King's palace. The King leaving Westminster, proceeded to York, taking with him his barons of the exchequer, and his justiciaries of the King's bench, after the feast of the Holy Trinity, intending to hold a parliament with the nobles of the kingdom. From thence he moved onward, attended by a numerous company of earls, barons, and knights, determining to subdue the rebellious Scots. . . .

On the second Sunday in Lent, the King, having summoned the nobles to meet at Westminster, caused the conditions of peace which had been signed by the bull of Pope Boniface, as appointed arbiter between the Kings of France and England, and other bulls, too, affecting his position, to be recited to them. And all the laity and clergy assented to them. After which, the earls, barons, and prelates, requested the King to ratify the great charter of their liberties, and the one relating to the rights of the forest, as also to the disforestings which had already taken place, and to sanction and establish it. So he, having confirmed the two aforesaid charters, hardened his ears to their request of sanctioning the disforesting, and at twilight he quitted them, pretending that he was going some distance. But they, considering that he had left them, as a mark of contempt, returned to their own homes with great indignation. . . .

(1300) In the week after the feast of Saint Hilary, while the King was holding his parliament at Lincoln, the earls and barons complained of injurious and violent depredations which were committed in every direction by the ministers and household of the King. And, again, they requested that the liberties which were granted, as set forth in the great charter, should last from that time forth for ever in their original force. They also demanded that the disforestings, on account of which all the richer sort of the common people were distressed, and which had repeatedly been granted by the King, but had never hitherto been actually completed, should be ordered by him to be carried out, in accordance with his decree.

When these and some other articles had been demanded of the King with great earnestness, he procrastinated for several days; at last, seeing that the barons would not desist from the work which they had commenced, nor acquiesce in his necessary demands on other terms, answered that he was prepared to concede and ratify all that they requested, and anything else, also, which they might at any time demand and consider necessary to be confirmed. Therefore, the charters of their liberties were renewed, as also those concerning the forests; and both of them were ratified with the royal seal, and copies carried into every county in England. And when they were published before the people, the lord Archbishop of Canterbury, with the rest of his fellow-bishops, laid all the transgressors of them under the ban of the greater excommunication. Moreover, in return for the more effectual confirmation of these charters, the earls and barons granted to the King a fifteenth part of all their movables, to be paid on the feast of Saint Michael next ensuing. But Robert, Archbishop of Canterbury, would grant nothing on the part of the clergy, nor from the temporalities annexed to the church, without the special permission of the supreme pontiff. . . .

(1301) The same year, Pope Boniface having been instigated by the Scots, sent letters from himself to the King of England, asserting that the kingdom of Scotland belonged to the rightful estates of the Roman church, and that it was contrary to God and to justice, and to the prejudice of the Apostolic See, that the King of England was claiming its subjection to himself, alleging the reasons for this assertion. . . .

The King having, after some deliberation, convoked a council at Lincoln, for the purpose of framing a declaration of his rights, wrote back letters . . . as an answer to those from the Apostolic See. . . .

But as to the demand made by the pope, that if the King of England claimed any right over the kingdom of Scotland, or any part of it, he should send procurators instructed as to that point to the church of Rome, and full justice should be done him; to this demand the king did not choose to give an answer himself, but committed the affair to the earls and other nobles of the country, who on this point wrote letters to the lord the pope, of the following tenor. . . .

"To the most holy father in Christ, the lord Boniface, by Divine Providence, supreme pontiff of the holy Roman universal church, his devout sons, John, earl of Warenne, Thomas, earl of Lancaster, Radulph of Monthermer, earl of Gloucester and Hereford, Humphrey de Bohun, earl of Hertford and Essex and constable of England, Roger Bigot, earl of Norfolk and marshal of England, Guy, earl of Warwick &c., sending devout kisses of his blessed feet, &c.:

"The holy Roman mother church is the church by whose ministry the Catholic faith, as we firmly believe and hold, proceeds with such steadiness in its actions that it injures no one, but wishes to protect the rights of all persons uninjured. A general Parliament having been lately convoked by our most serene lord Edward, by the grace of God, the illustrious King of England, to meet at Lincoln, the said lord Edward, our King, caused to be produced, and carefully explained to us, some letters from the Apostolic See, which we on our part had received touching certain matters which relate to the condition and state of the kingdom. And when these letters had been heard and carefully understood, we perceived that some things surprising to our senses and hitherto unprecedented were contained in them.

"For we know, O most holy father, and it is notorious in these parts, and not unknown to other persons also, that from the first establishment of the kingdom of England, the Kings of that kingdom, both in the times of the Britons and of the Angles, have been possessed of the direct superior authority and dominion over the kingdom of Scotland, and have in successive ages had a right to the regulation of Scotland itself; nor does that kingdom, as to its temporalities, belong, nor has it at any time belonged, by any kind of right to your church before mentioned. Moreover, the aforesaid kingdom of Scotland has from ancient times been in feudal subjection to the progenitors of our aforesaid King, the Kings of England, and to himself, nor have the Kings of the kingdom of Scotland ever been subordinate or accustomed to be subject to any other sovereigns than the Kings of England. Nor have the Kings of England ever answered, nor have they been bound to answer, respecting their rights over the aforesaid kingdom, or any other of their temporalities, before any judge ecclesiastical or secular, according to the pre-eminence of the state of their royal dignity and custom inviolably observed in all ages.

"On which account, having carefully considered and deliberated on the contents of your aforesaid letters, the general harmonious and unanimous consent of all and each of us has been, and, by the favor of God, will be unalterably for the future, that the before-mentioned lord our King shall in no respect answer judicially before you respecting his rights over the kingdom of Scotland, or any other of his temporal possessions. Nor shall he in any way submit to a trial of them, or bring his aforesaid rights in question, or send procurators or ambassadors for that purpose to your presence, especially as such demands tend manifestly to the stripping him of his hereditary rights belonging to the crown of the kingdom of England, and to his royal dignity; and to the evident subversion of the constitution of the said kingdom, and to the prejudice of the liberties, customs, and native laws, to the observance and defense of which he and we are duly bound by the oath we have taken. And what we are now possessed of, we will, with the help of God, defend with all our might and all our power. Nor do we permit, nor will we in any way permit, as, indeed, we neither can nor ought, our lord the King to submit to the before-mentioned demands, being unusual, unjustifiable, prejudicial, and altogether unprecedented, nor would we permit it even if he were inclined himself to do so, or in the least to attempt it.

"Wherefore, we reverently and humbly entreat your holiness kindly to permit our lord the King aforesaid, who shows himself a Catholic among all the other princes of the earth, and a devout son of the Roman church, peaceably to possess his rights, and liberties, and customs, and laws, aforesaid, without diminution or disquietude, and to allow those rights to remain undisturbed. In testimony of which, our seals are appended to these present letters, on behalf both of ourselves and of the whole commonalty of the above-mentioned kingdom of England.

"Done and given at Lincoln, in the year of Our Lord thirteen hundred and one."

(1302) The King of England then, being desirous that a good peace should be made in his days, sent ambassadors of high rank to the King of France about Easter, to give him notice by their means of the resolutions to which he had come respecting peace and war. And, having received for answer that such important affairs could not be satisfactorily discussed unless twelve peers were assembled with full powers, which was not practicable at that moment, as the peers were now occupied in various places on account of the unexpected emergencies of the new war, but that they might expect that it could be done in a fortnight. And after this period had elapsed, the mayors of France assembled and answered the English ambassadors that they were not inclined to give a definite answer on the above-mentioned subject, without the presence of the Scottish confederates. Having received this answer, the ambassadors returned to England.

On this, the King held his Parliament at Westminster, on the first of July. And when they had had recounted to them the disappointing and evasive delays and procrastinating manoeuvres to which the ambassadors had been exposed, they determined to send the same persons back again, as news of the triumphant victory which the Flemings had gained over the French, had arrived; and the ambassadors now received for answer that the King of England ought to come in his own person, and that then an agreement about peace might well be come to between the two Kings, so that the powerful nobles and superiors of each kingdom might applaud it as advantageous to them, and the middle and lower classes might not be grieved at it. Therefore the King of England held his Parliament at Westminster, on the feast of the Translation of Saint Edward the King, where this answer was recited, and gave great offense. But it was decided positively by the council of the whole kingdom that the King should remain in his own dominions, and he was not permitted to leave England at the command or suggestion of the King of France. . . .

(1307) In the week after the festival of Saint Hilary [Jan. 13], the king held a Parliament at Carlisle, in which grave complaints were brought forward, by the chief nobles, of the oppressions of the churches and monasteries, by the manifold extortions of money lately introduced into the kingdom by the clerk of the lord the pope, Master William Teste; and the aforesaid clerk was commanded, by the unanimous decree of the earls and barons, not for the future to commit such oppression. Moreover, order was made that for the obtaining a remedy for these things, ambassadors appointed for the purpose should be sent to the pope.

In the same Parliament, some statutes were passed, affecting the members of religious orders, who had their chief houses in another kingdom. And there came to that Parliament, about the feast of Saint Peter, a certain cardinal of Sabionetta, Master Peter the Spaniard, having been sent by the pope as legate *a latere,* to perform the marriage which had been arranged between Edward, the eldest son of the King of England, and Isabella, the daughter of the King of France, as had been previously ordained by Pope Boniface, acting, as it were, as a mediator of peace. And he made answer, by the King, that he was ready to perform all that was commanded him, provided that the King of France, on his part, was willing to fulfil those engagements which depended on him. For the King of France, while he held Guienne, had given the castle which is called Mauleon to a certain knight, who still retained possession of it, and would not restore it at the command of the King of France. On which account, it is said, that that marriage was delayed to this time. Therefore, the cardinal returned to London, in order to await certain directions on this point, and to plunder the churches of England. For he wished, according to authority given in the bull, to receive from each church belonging to a cathedral, or convent, and from all regular and irregular churches and priories, twelve marks sterling. And from the rectories, eightpence out of his mark. But the clergy of England appealed against this exaction. And it was ordered by the King's council, that that cardinal ought not to have more than Cardinal Othobonus had formerly received, when he was legate in England, namely, the half of what was now demanded. . . .

2. *Petitions and Answers.* The official records of proceedings are contained in the *Rolls of Parliament,* which consist in large part of petitions and the answers made to them. Below are printed several types of petitions as they appear in the official records.[11]

(*Community of the Realm, 1301*) Bill of the prelates and lords delivered to the lord King on behalf of the whole community at the Parliament of Lincoln in the year aforesaid:

. . . Thus, if it please our lord the King, the said community is of the opinion that the two charters of liberties and of the forest should henceforth be completely observed in all particulars. [Answer] It expressly pleases the lord King.

And the statutes contrary to the said charters should be annulled and voided. [Answer] It expressly pleases.

And the power of the justices assigned to keep the charters in the counties should be defined by the counsel of the prelates, earls, and barons. [Answer] It tacitly pleases.

. . . And the offenses and trespasses committed by the King's ministers contrary to the tenor of the said charters . . . should henceforth cease. [Answer] It expressly pleases.

. . . On condition that the aforesaid matters be carried out and strictly done and established, the people of the realm grant him a fifteenth instead of the twentieth recently granted: provided that the matters aforesaid be carried out between now and the feast of St. Michael next; otherwise nothing should be levied. [Answer] It expressly pleases.

. . . And by virtue of the things aforesaid, the prelates of the Holy Church shall not under any circumstances dare to consent to the levying of any contribution upon their goods or the goods of the clergy contrary to the prohibition of the Apostolic See. [Answer] It has not pleased the King but the community of lords has approved.

(*The Poor Men of England, 1305*) To the petition of the poor men of the land of England, asking the King to give redress in the matter of the men serving on inquests, juries, and assizes, who are so commonly corrupted by gifts from the rich that no truth can be known from them, etc.; and also asking redress in the matter of the ordinaries [ecclesiastical judicial officers] who, to the prejudice of the crown, strive to take cognizance of pleas of debts, transgressions, and other matters pertaining to the crown, etc., and who take fines and payments therefor at their own will, etc.:—

It is answered thus: To the first, let them bring suit against jurors for convicting them by writ of attaint, etc. To the second, let them search diligently through the writs of prohibition in cases in which prohibition plays a part.

(*County of Norfolk, 1290*) The poor and middling men of the county of Norfolk, who are ruined by John of Brilond, prosecutor against them for the merchants of Lübeck, and who had been summoned to plead before the King in another Parliament, petition that the King assign judges to give them justice in the county, because the prosecution is so long drawn out and because they can not bring suit there [in Parliament] on account of their poverty.

[Answer] Let them bring their pleas before G. of Thornton and his fellow justices for the pleas of the crown, because they shall have no other judges.

(*County of Hertford, 1290*) The men of the county of Hertford beg that they may build a prison in the town of Hertford, from doing which William of Valence [Earl of Pembroke] hinders them, as it is said, to the King's loss and the county's vexation.

[Answer] The King granted it.

(*County of Cumberland, 1305*) To the petition of the community of Cumberland, seeking redress for that when the lord King by his writ commanded the sheriff of the county to provide the King's larder against the King's arrival in Scotland in the twenty-second year of his reign, the sheriff on pretext of the order took from the community a certain number of oats, and though he had an appropriation for them in his account, he paid nothing to the community:—

It is answered thus: Let suit be brought at the Exchequer, and if the sheriff has received an appropriation but has not paid, let him be punished by the established penalty and let him pay. But if otherwise let the Treasurer ordain what is proper.

(*Burgesses of Newcastle, 1305*) To the petition of the burgesses of Newcastle-on-Tyne, seeking redress because of the Prior of Tynemouth holds a fair by the King's concession there on the feast of St. Oswin in the autumn, lasting for fifteen days, to the prejudice of said town and the burgesses thereof and to the disinheritance of the King, as they say; because ships loaded with diverse wares (which were wont to come to the town of Newcastle, from which the King received the customs and dues and murages) now unload at Tynemouth, and the wares are there exposed for sale, since that place is nearer to the port of Tyne than is the town of Newcastle, which port indeed belongs to the King. Thus to the prior accrue the loading and unloading of wares at the port, and the sales of bread and wine and beer, to the prejudice of the King and the great loss of the merchants themselves. And in the nineteenth year of the reign of the present King in a suit brought before the King by the said burgesses, the prior lost thereof by way of consideration [a certain sum], etc.:—

It is answered thus: Let them have a writ from the Chancery to the effect that the two parties shall come together two weeks after Easter before the King, wherever he may be in England; and that the men of Newcastle and the Prior of Tynemouth shall likewise have their charters of privilege with them; and that the men of Newcastle shall meanwhile bring suit to Gilbert of Roubiry that they may have the process and judgment which earlier was made before the King in his Parliament, etc.

(*Merchants of England, 1290*) The merchants of England sought two thousand pounds damages from the Count of Flanders, by virtue of the convention made with the King at Mustrel, which damages they suffered by the seizure and detention in Flanders of their chattels valued at £10,000.

[Answer] The King can do nothing except to ask him [the Count] by a letter (which he granted) to satisfy them and cause them to be indemnified; because it is not recorded that any convention was made or discussed for paying damages, and because the Count can seek his damages from the English in the same way.

(*John of Thorp, 1305*) To the petition of John of Thorp, seeking redress because after the death of Thomas of Belhous, the King's escheator-beyond-Trent seized into the King's hands the said Thomas's manor of Nolaunde, which he had held from John by military service . . . :—

It was answered thus: Let him sue to have the inquisitions returned in Chancery brought before the King and his council at the end of Parliament. . . . Let it be ordered by writ of Chancery to the chancellor and barons of the Exchequer that all books, rolls, and other memoranda concerning the contentions in this petition be scrutinized, and let this inquisition be sent there [to parliament], and let justice be done.

(*Religious Orders, 1292*) Concerning the men of religious orders and others who seek to have their charters confirmed by the lord King and who present petitions for this purpose:—

The King orders that they all go to the Exchequer before the treasurer and barons, and let them make an end of the matter. Let the treasurer do what seems fitting to accomplish this, etc.

(*Hospital of St. Katherine, 1290*) The brothers and sisters of the hospital of St. Katherine petition that the King grant them the fifty shillings which King Henry, father of the present lord King, gave them annually, which they received for the soul of Sanchia, formerly Queen of Germany, that they might maintain a chapel in the tower of London where they celebrate [masses] for her soul; and the arrears of the same for ten years back.

[Answer] It is not found at the Exchequer that they received any of the said fifty shillings either in the time of King Henry or in the time of the present King, . . . and nothing is to be done in the matter.

(*Countess of Cornwall, 1298*) Touching the lands of the Countess of Cornwall, which were assigned to her for her sustenance by her lord, and from which she claims that she was ejected: it seemed to the council that the *Curia Regis* can not interfere in any arrangement made between the countess and her husband the earl.

(*Poor Alice, 1302*) Alice de la Chapele of the Isle of Guernsey begs the magnanimity, grace, and compassion of our Lord the King; for that she has taken thirty-five sheaves of various kinds of grain from the share-crop of our Lord the King, which sheaves were of little value, . . . so she begs in charity and compassion that grace be granted her upon her oath that she took them because of her poverty and to nourish her child.

[Answer] Let her have grace. Let the bailiffs certify the King concerning the cause and manner [of the theft], and if they find it as stated, the King concedes that it be done as is petitioned.

C.   CONCLUSION OF A PARLIAMENT

1. *A Proclamation of Prorogation, 1305.*[12]

Then after the twenty-first day of March was made a proclamation by the command of the King in these words:

"Archbishops, bishops, and other prelates, earls, barons, knights of the counties, citizens and burgesses and other men of the community, who have come here at the command of our lord the King to this Parliament:

"The King greatly thanks them for their coming and wills that for the present they return to their own lands, so that they be prepared to return quickly and without delay whenever they shall at another time be recalled; except for the bishops, earls and barons, justices and others who are of the council of our lord the King, who shall not depart without the special permission of the King. And those who have business to do, let them remain and pursue their business.

"And the knights who have come for the counties and the others who have come for the cities and boroughs, let them appear before Sir John of Kirkby [Remembrancer of the Exchequer], and he will have writs issued to them for their expenses to be repaid in their own lands. And the said John of Kirkby, by virtue of the above proclamation, shall deliver to the chancellor the names of the knights who came for the counties and the names of the others who came for the cities and boroughs, and he shall proclaim that all those who desire writs for repayment of their expenses, as aforesaid, shall sue there for their writs."

2. *A Royal Order, 1305.*[13]

Since it has been testified that William of Botereus of the county of Cornwallis came among the other knights by common summons to the royal Parliament at Westminster in the thirty-third year [of our reign], and stayed there on behalf of the community of the said county until ———— [date], and went home some time before the proclamation:

Let a writ of expenses be drawn up for him in the form in which it is done for others who came at this summons for the other counties of England. [Sealed with the royal privy seal.]

3. *A Writ of Expenses, 1300.*[14]

The King to the sheriff of Somerset, greeting.

We order you to cause the usual expense money to be paid from the community of the county to our beloved and faithful knights of that county, Gilbert of Bere and Hugh of Popham, who recently came at our command to Westminster to consult there with us upon divers matters especially touching us and the people of our realm, [to pay their expenses] for coming there to us, staying there, and returning home; as is the custom in similar cases at other times.

Witness the King at Westminster, the twentieth day of March.

[Similar writs sent to thirty-two other sheriffs for sixty-four other knights, and to twenty-one municipal officials for forty-two burgesses.]

4. *A Commission and Writ of Assistance, 1296.*[15]

The King to the knights, free tenants, and whole community of the county of Suffolk, greeting.

Since the earls, barons, knights, and others of our kingdom have courteously granted and conceded to us, by way of subsidy for our present war. . . , a twelfth of all their movable goods; and the citizens, burgesses, and other good men from every city and town and from all our royal domains . . . [have courteously granted] an eighth of all their movable goods . . . :

We, wishing to provide that the said twelfth and eighth be levied and collected with the smallest loss and burden to the people of our kingdom, have assigned our beloved and faithful Roger of Stoterly and Master Richard Lenebaud . . . to assess, levy, and collect the said twelfth and eighth in the said county, and to deliver them to the Exchequer, and there to pay them at the times written below: one half before the festival of the purification of the Virgin Mary next and the other half at the following festival of Pentecost.

And so we command you that you aid, counsel, advise, and assist said Roger and Richard in these matters . . . on our behalf.

Witness the King at La Neylaund, the sixteenth day of December.

VI
Carcassonne and Chartres: A Visual Approach to History

No kind of human activity is so permanent as the plastic arts, and nothing that survives from the past is so valuable as a clue to the history of civilization.

Herbert Read

CONTENTS

(The pictorial materials necessary for the study of this Problem may be obtained from the publisher.)

QUESTIONS FOR STUDY

PART I

1. What was the strategic geographical position of Carcassonne?

2. What types of city plans existed in the Middle Ages, and to what extent have they survived as types?

3. The typical medieval city was the result of gradual expansion beyond the city walls. To what extent can this be seen in Carcassonne and in Paris?

4. The typical medieval house served as a place of business or storage and as a domicile. How was this provided for in the arrangement of the house?

5. Identify the following technical terms:

Keep or "donjon"	Chemin de Rond	Trebuchet
Crenellations	Lisses	Siege Tower
Machicolations	Postern	"Chats"
Hourd	Portcullis	

6. How did the position and shape of the keep or "donjon" change as the castle developed?

7. What particular precautions were taken by the defenders?

8. What were the special techniques of the attackers?

PART II

9. Did the medieval church serve other functions than religious ones?

10. What were the advantages and disadvantages of Romanesque architecture?

11. To what extent did Gothic architecture satisfy the demands of the Christian religion?

12. Identify the following parts of the plan and structure:

Nave	Barrel Vault	Pinnacle
Transept	Ribbed Vault	Rose Window
Choir	Wall Buttress	Tracery
Chevet	Flying Buttress	Gargoyle

13. Select examples illustrating the four different mirrors as defined by Vincent of Beauvais.

14. "Medieval sculpture was both decorative and didactic." Select appropriate examples to prove this statement.

15. Contrast the different points of view expressed in Romanesque and Gothic sculpture.

16. To what extent was medieval sculpture integrated with the architecture? Compare this with modern sculpture and architecture.

17. What function did the stained glass serve in the architecture of the Gothic church?

INTRODUCTION TO THE PROBLEM

Previous problems have considered the evidence of texts alone. The written word, however, is not the only key to the past. The historian must be prepared to analyze and evaluate the physical remnants of society. Often these remnants are considered by succeeding generations as art. Sometimes the vestiges themselves are merely stones or nondescript fragments. The archaeologist can recreate the original objects or monuments from these fragments: the historian of art interprets the remains or the restorations, and by critical analysis sheds new light on the written accounts of the time.

As you have learned, volumes of texts are available for the study of medieval history. Without studying a city such as Carcassonne or a cathedral such as Chartres, it is difficult to achieve any understanding of the physical surroundings in which medieval society flourished. The meaning of the "chateau-fort," of the city walls, and of the cathedral—the "bible of the poor"—must be comprehended if we are to have any sense of the physical realities of medieval culture.

In order to understand these realities, the historian must learn to use such materials as buildings, sculpture, painting, and all the objects of use and pleasure. This he can do through plans, engravings, and photographs. He will need to know some of the terms used by architects, artists, and historians of art.

Like any historical event, the work of art is a fact in time. But unlike many historical events, the work of art is also an object in space. It is the visible, tangible expression of the thoughts and the feelings of powerful, orderly, and creative minds. We must learn to detect, observe, and describe the ways in which the work of art exists in time and space.

A special approach is therefore necessary. Among the visual documents assembled for your study are architects' plans and elevations, as well as airplane views and photographs of exteriors, interiors, and details. Also furnished below are the important dates in the history of Carcassonne and Chartres, an account of a siege in the thirteenth century, and Émile Mâle's method of interpreting medieval iconography. Remember, however, that visual materials are *primary historical sources* in and of themselves.

The questions for study are a guide to the pictures involved. Every question can be answered on the basis of the evidence presented. Study the pictures carefully, and answer the questions to the best of your ability. These questions are designed to accompany the various groups of pictures; they are available with the pictures, and they are printed here in these pages.

Carcassonne was founded in 636 B.C. and later became an important Roman settlement. Taken about 350 A.D. by the Franks, it was strongly fortified by the Visigoths in the fifth and sixth centuries. For over four hundred years its history is vague. It was not until about 1130 that the town walls were repaired and the château constructed. Besieged several times in the early thirteenth century Carcassonne became part of the royal domain in 1226. Louis IX and Philip III considered the town such an important outpost that from 1241 to 1285 they had it repaired, and new construction made it so nearly impregnable that it was never again taken by siege. It was restored to its present condition by Viollet-le-Duc in the latter part of the nineteenth century.

Chartres has been a religious center since pagan times. A well, still to be seen in the crypt of the Cathedral, was the focal point for Druid and other worship. Although a series of churches were erected on this site in the early Middle Ages, the existing building dates from the twelfth and thirteenth centuries. The western façade with its sculpture, the south (right) tower, and the base of the north (left) tower date from 1145–1155. A fire destroyed the town and all but the western portions of the cathedral in 1194. Rebuilding was begun immediately. Work progressed steadily and the cathedral was finished with all of its sculptural decoration and stained glass windows by about 1240. The most important subsequent addition was the spire of the north tower, finished in the sixteenth century. The cathedral stands today almost in its original condition.

Part I.   CARCASSONNE, A MEDIEVAL CITY AND FORTRESS

The pictures provide the student with most of his materials for study in this Part. One text, however, is reprinted below, the report by the town's commander to his Queen concerning the siege of Carcassonne in 1240.[1]

To the excellent and illustrious lady Blanche, by the grace of God Queen of France, Guillaume des Ormes, seneschal of Carcassonne, her humble, devoted and faithful servant, greetings.

Madame, Your Excellency is informed by this letter that the city of Carcassonne was besieged by the so-called viscount and his accomplices on Monday, the 17th of September, 1240. And immediately, those of us who were there, took from them the town of Graveillant, which is before the gate of Toulouse, and there we found a lot of timber, which was very useful to us. [This town extended from the barbacan of the city up to the corner of the aforementioned fortress.] The same day, our enemies took a mill, enabled to do so by the large number of men they had, and then Olivier de Termes, Bernard Hugon de Serre Longue, Géraud d'Aniort, and those who were with them camped between the edge of the city and the water, and the same day, aided by the trenches there and crossing the roads that were between them and ourselves, they barricaded themselves in so that we could not get at them.

On another side, between the bridge and the barbacan of the chateau, were Pierre de Fenouillet, Renaud du Puy, Guillaume Fort, Pierre de la Toure, and many others from Carcassonne. In both places they had so many archers that no one could get out of the city.

Then they trained a mangonel on our barbacan; and we immediately set up in the barbacan a very good Turkish stone-thrower, which sent projectiles towards the mangonel and around it; so that when they wished to shoot at us, and saw our stone-thrower being aimed at them, they fled and entirely abandoned their mangonel; and made trenches and barricades there. We too, after each time we had brought the stone-thrower into play, went back again, as we could not attack them, due to the trenches and the defenses they had erected.

Then, Madame, they began to tunnel towards the barbacan at the Narbonnaise gate; and immediately, having heard their work underground, we started a counter-mine, and made inside the barbacan a large, strong wall of stone, covering half the barbacan, and then they set a fire in the hole they had made, so that the wood being

burnt, part of the front of the barbacan collapsed.

They began to tunnel against another tower on the outside wall; we counter-mined, and were able to secure the hole they had made. They then began to tunnel between us and another wall, and they destroyed two battlements of the outside wall; but we made a good, strong barricade there between them and ourselves.

They also made a tunnel at the corner of the town, towards the bishop's house, and while tunneling they came, under one of the Saracen walls, up to the outside wall. But as soon as we noticed this we built a good, strong barricade between them and ourselves, and we counter-mined. Then they set fire to it and destroyed about 60 feet of our battlements. But immediately we built a good, strong barricade, and above it we built a bretèche with good slits in it, so that none of them dared approach us there.

They began too, Madame, to mine against the Rodez gate, and they kept at it, because they wanted to get to the inside wall, and they made a great hole; but we, having seen this, immediately made a great, strong barricade, both above and below it, and attacking them, seized the breach.

Know also, Madame, that from the start of the siege, they had not ceased sending attacks against us; but we had so many good archers, and men inspired to fight in self-defense, that in launching these attacks they suffered heavy losses.

Then, on Sunday, they assembled all their forces, and all attacked the barbacan below the castle. We went down to the barbacan and threw so many stones at them that we made them abandon the attack; a number of them were killed and wounded.

But the next Sunday, after St. Michael's Day, they launched a heavy attack at us; and we, by the grace of God and our men who fought well in self-defense, repulsed them; a number of them were killed and wounded; none of ours, thanks be to God, were either killed or mortally wounded. But then, on Monday, October 11, toward evening, they heard that your men, Madame, were coming to our aid, and they set fire to the houses in the town of Carcassonne. They completely destroyed the houses belonging to the Mineur brothers and the houses of St. Mary's monastery, which were in the town, to get the wood for their barricades. All those concerned with the siege left secretly that night, even those who lived in the town.

As for us, we were well prepared, thanks be to God, to await, Madame, your help; so that, during the siege, no one lacked food, no matter how poor he was; indeed, Madame, we had sufficient wheat and meat to wait a long time, if necessary, for your aid. Know, Madame, that these evil-doers, killed, the second day after their arrival, 33 priests and other clerics whom they found on entering the town; know, too, Madame, that the lord Pierre de Voisin, your high constable of Carcassonne, Raymond de Capendu, and

Gerard d'Ermenville behaved very well throughout this affair. And the high constable, by his vigilance, valor and presence of mind, distinguished himself above the others. As to other matters of this territory, Madame, we can tell you the rest when we arrive in your presence. Know then that they began to mine against us in seven places. We have counter-mined nearly everywhere, and have spared no pains. They started tunneling from their houses, so that we could tell nothing until they arrived at the outside walls.

Given at Carcassonne, October 13th, 1240.

Know, Madame, that the enemy have burnt the castles and unfortified towns which they encountered in their flight.

Part II. CHARTRES, THE MEDIEVAL CHURCH

The only text reproduced in this Part is from the work of a distinguished modern French student of the Middle Ages. In the section quoted below M. Mâle is suggesting a possible inspiration for much of the decoration of the cathedral. The student should test this theory for himself by examining the photographs of the sculpture and stained glass at Chartres.[2]

The thirteenth century was the century of encyclopaedias. At no other period have so many works appeared bearing the titles of *Summa*, *Speculum* or *Imago Mundi*. It was in this century that Thomas Aquinas co-ordinated the whole body of Christian doctrine, Jacobus de Voragine collected the most famous legends of the saints, Gulielmus Durandus epitomized all previous writers on the liturgy, and Vincent of Beauvais attempted to embrace universal knowledge. Christianity came to full consciousness of its own genius, and the conception of the universe which had been elaborated by previous centuries received complete expression. It was believed to be possible to raise the final edifice of human knowledge, and in the universities which had recently been founded throughout Europe—above all the young university of Paris—the work was carried on with enthusiasm.

While the doctors were constructing the intellectual edifice which was to shelter the whole of Christendom, the cathedral of stone was rising as its visible counterpart. It too in its fashion was a *Speculum*, a *Summa*, an *Imago Mundi* into which the Middle Age put all its most cherished convictions. These great churches are the most perfect known expression in art of the mind of an epoch. We shall attempt to show that in them a whole dogmatic scheme found expression in concrete form.

The difficulty lies in grouping in logical sequence the innumerable works of art which the

churches offer for our study. Surely we have hardly the right to dispose of the matter according to some arbitrary scheme which appears to us harmonious. It is necessary to discard modern habits of mind. If we impose our categories on medieval thought we run every risk of error, and for that reason we borrow our method of exposition from the Middle Age itself. The four books of Vincent of Beauvais' *Mirror* furnish us with the framework for the four divisions of our study of thirteenth-century art.

If Aquinas was the most powerful thinker of the Middle Ages, Vincent of Beauvais was certainly the most comprehensive. He might well be called an epitome of the knowledge of his day. A prodigious worker, he passed his life like the elder Pliny in reading and making extracts. He was called "librorum helluo," the devourer of books. St. Louis threw open to him the fine library containing virtually all the books procurable in the thirteenth century, and at times came to visit him at the abbey of Royaumont, where he loved to hear him talk of the wonders of the universe.

It was probably toward the middle of the century that Vincent of Beauvais published the great *Mirror*, the *Speculum majus*, which to his contemporaries seemed the supreme effort of human learning. Even today one cannot but admire so stupendous a work.

His learning was immense, yet it did not overwhelm him. The order he adopted was the most imposing which the Middle Age could conceive— the very plan of God as it appears in the Scriptures. Vincent of Beauvais' work is divided into four parts—the Mirror of Nature, the Mirror of Instruction, the Mirror of Morals, and the Mirror of History.

In the Mirror of Nature are reflected all natural phenomena in the order in which they were created by God. The Days of Creation mark the different chapters of this great encyclopaedia of nature. The four elements, the minerals, vegetables and animals are successively enumerated and described. All the truth and the error which had been transmitted by antiquity to the Middle Ages are found there. But it is naturally on the work of the sixth day—the creation of man— that Vincent of Beauvais dwells at greatest length, for man is the center of the universe and for him all things were made.

The Mirror of Instruction opens with the story of the Fall, the recital of the drama which explains the riddle of the universe. Man has fallen, and only through a Redeemer can he hope for salvation. Yet in his own strength he can begin to raise himself, and through knowledge to prepare for grace. There is in knowledge a quickening power, and to each of the seven Arts corresponds one of the seven Gifts of the Spirit. After expounding this large and humane doctrine Vincent of Beauvais passes in review all the different branches of knowledge; even the mechanical arts are included, for by the labor of his hands man begins the work of his redemption.

The Mirror of Morals is closely connected with the Mirror of Instruction, for the end of life is not to know but to act, and knowledge is but a means to virtue. Out of this springs a learned classification of the virtues and vices, in which the method, divisions and often the very expressions of Aquinas are found—for the *Speculum morale* is the *Summa* in abridged form.

The last division is the Mirror of History. We have studied human nature in the abstract, and we now turn to man himself, watching his progress under the eye of God. He invents arts and sciences, he struggles and suffers, choosing sometimes vice, sometimes virtue in the great battle of the soul which is the sum of the world's history. It is hardly necessary to observe that for Vincent of Beauvais, as for Augustine, Orosius, Gregory of Tours and all the historians of the Middle Ages,

true history is the history of the Church, the City of God, which begins with Abel the first just man. There is a chosen people and their history is the pillar of fire which lightens the darkness. The history of the pagan world is deserving of study only with reference to the other; it has merely value as a synchronism. It is true that Vincent of Beauvais did not scorn to tell of the revolution of empires, and even delighted in speaking of pagan philosophers, scholars, and poets, but such subjects are really incidental. The dominant thought of his book—the idea which gives it unity—is the unbroken line of saints of the Old and New Testaments. Through them and them alone the history of the world becomes coherent.

Thus was conceived this Encyclopaedia of the thirteenth century. In it the riddle of the universe finds solution. The plan is so comprehensive that the Middle Ages could conceive of nothing which it did not include, and until the Renaissance the following centuries found nothing to add to it.

Such a book is the surest guide that we can choose for our study of the great leading ideas which lay behind the art of the thirteenth century. Striking analogies are noticeable, for example, between the general economy of the *Speculum Majus* and the plan followed in the porches of the cathedral of Chartres. As was first pointed out by Didron in the authoritative introduction to his *Histoire de Dieu,* the innumerable figures which decorate the porches may well be grouped under the four heads of nature, instruction, morals and history. We do not know whether that great decorative scheme was directly inspired by Vincent of Beauvais' book with which it was almost contemporaneous, but it is obvious that the arrangement of the *Speculum Majus* belonged not to him but to the Middle Ages as a whole. It was the form which the thirteenth century imposed on all ordered thought. The same genius disposed the chapters of the *Mirror* and the sculpture of the cathedral. It is then legitimate to seek in the one the meaning of the other.

We shall therefore adopt the four great divisions of Vincent of Beauvais' work, and shall try to read the four books of the *Mirror* in the façades of the cathedrals. We shall find them all four represented, and shall decipher them in the order in which the encyclopaedist presents them. Each detail will in this way find its place, and the harmony of the whole will appear.

154

VII
The Mind of the Middle Ages

I DO not seek to know that I may believe, but I believe in order that I may understand.

St. Anselm (1033–1109)

CONTENTS

[139]

QUESTIONS FOR STUDY

Part I

1. What is the "theme and purpose" of Bishop Otto's chronicle?
2. What basic attitude is revealed by Bishop Otto's statement that "a devout rusticity is ever the friend of truth"?
3. What theory of causation lies behind Richard de Templo's interpretation of events?
4. What does Roger of Wendover believe is the purpose of reading history?
5. What points in common have Otto, Richard, and Roger?
6. What, according to John of Salisbury, is the relationship of the prince to God, the law, and the people?
7. What is John's distinction between a tyrant and a prince? Why do tyrants exist? How should they be dealt with?
8. What is the nature and form of the commonwealth described by John? What is the purpose of secular government?
9. Why, according to St. Thomas, do men live in society?
10. How does St. Thomas justify his statement that "the rule of one is more beneficial than the rule of many"?
11. If John of Salisbury and St. Thomas had read the "Song of the Battle of Lewes," with whom would each have sided? How would each have criticized the political argument of the author?
12. What clues does Chrétien de Troyes give as to the qualities of the ideal knight and ideal lady?
13. How do knight and lady behave toward each other in Chrétien's romances? What does *Aucassin and Nicolette* add to the picture given by Chrétien?
14. How did the knights in the army of St. Louis compare with the ideal?
15. Would St. Louis have approved of Sir Erec and Sir Yvain if they had been in his army?

Part II

16. What, according to St. Thomas, was the purpose of sacred science?
17. What is the relationship of sacred science to other sciences?
18. Upon what foundations does sacred science rest?
19. Is sufficient latitude permitted in the interpretation of Holy Scripture to allow of argument in sacred science?
20. Setting aside the personal bias in Abelard's autobiography, explain why he got into trouble with the church authorities.
21. What were the points of argument which arose in connection with the condemnation of Abelard's book? Why was there so much excitement about them?
22. What kind of theological disputation does St. Louis prescribe for laymen?
23. What were the sources of Bartholomew Anglicus' scientific knowledge?
24. What assumptions underlie Bartholomew's explanations of natural phenomena?
25. Summarize the basic elements of the medieval mind as evidenced in the documents of this Problem.

Behind the institutions of any historical period lies a complex fabric of ideas which is often called "the spirit of the times" or "the mind of the age." The men of the period are usually unconscious of its existence, for to them the pattern of this fabric of ideas is as natural as the composition of a familiar landscape. They cannot see it otherwise. It is an integral and assumed part of their existence. For the mind of an age is composed, not only of the articulated philosophy and faith of its people, but also of their unconscious attitudes and unquestioned assumptions. It is in short, the sum total of conceptions and preconceptions which impel the men of an age to order their lives in a manner peculiar to themselves.

Unconscious though men may be of its existence, the mind of an age is a very real thing. Intangible and changing imperceptibly with the passage of time, it nevertheless possesses sufficient solidity and stability to constitute a vital factor in the historical process. There is constant interaction between ideas and institutions, each helping to produce and modify the other, each in part the product of the economic and social conditions of the time. He who seeks understanding of an age can no more neglect its mind than he can ignore its economic structure, political institutions, or social organization. For ideas, to the men who possess them, are often more concrete than the tangible facts of objective existence.

To reconstruct the mind of a past age is to undertake a task requiring mental alertness and careful analysis. Written remains will usually state explicitly what is in the mind of an author and the first problem of the historian is to determine the author's precise meaning. But underlying an explicit statement may be a substratum of attitudes and assumptions of which the writer was unconscious or which he thought unnecessary to explain because he expected his readers to share them. The attitudes and assumptions of one age are often wholly foreign to another, and the historian must be alert to observe the character and composition of an unfamiliar substratum wherein may lie components of the mind of the age as vital as those which have been explicitly stated. At the same time, while eliciting the vital conceptions possessed by the men of a period, the historian must judiciously determine the correct emphasis to be placed upon each idea in relation to others. Otherwise he may, out of the right materials, recreate a pattern of thoughts unrecognizable to the men of the age.

The mind of the Middle Ages was a mosaic of firmly rooted beliefs and broad preconceptions. Medieval man had inherited much Greco-Roman learning, a Judaistic religion, a smattering of Arabic knowledge, and a mass of barbarian lore and custom. From these elements he evolved a culture and a characteristic state of mind. It was a synthetic creation, rather than an inventive one—not fashioned from newly discovered elements but molded from the variegated heritage of the past. Later ages have marvelled at the remarkable unity and completeness of the medieval mind. Disparate as were the elements of which it was made, it was all of a piece, strongly and perhaps uniquely integrated. Its firmness and integration make the medieval mind an excellent subject for historical analysis.

The student is already familiar with many materials which provide him with evidence of the mind of the Middle Ages. The documents which illustrate feudalism and the feudal monarchies, the church and medieval economy, all evince the state of mind which accompanied and underlay them. The documents in this problem—drawn from the central period of the Middle Ages, the twelfth and thirteenth centuries—provide more direct evidence for the reconstruction of the medieval mind. They are in part the writings of men who were stating what they believed and the presuppositions upon which their beliefs were based, and in part accounts of men and incidents which reveal the ideals and attitudes of the day.

The student should examine them to discover what knowledge medieval man possessed, what he considered important, what he thought about, and how he thought about it—so that, were the student transported back into the Middle Ages, like Mark Twain's Connecticut Yankee, he would have some understanding of the mind of the men he met as he now understands those of his own time.

THE PROBLEM

Part I.   ELEMENTS IN THE MEDIEVAL WORLD–VIEW

A.   PHILOSOPHY OF HISTORY

A vital element in the mind of an age is the prevailing theory of causation in human affairs. Men of all times have sought formulae to explain the course of history, a philosophy to account for the story of mankind as they know it. The philosophy of history which they evolve appears not only in their formal historical works but also in their interpretation of contemporary events, and it is likely to influence their daily actions in matters great and small. The materials in this section are drawn from chroniclers of the twelfth and thirteenth centuries to represent their philosophies of history.

1. *The Chronicle of Otto, Bishop of Freising, 1143–47.* Bishop Otto, an uncle of Emperor Frederick Barbarossa, entitled his chronicle of universal history *The Two Cities.* It has been called "the earliest philosophical treatment of history." Otto's preface to his work is printed below.[1]

In pondering long and often in my heart upon the changes and vicissitudes of temporal affairs and their varied and irregular issues, even as I hold that a wise man ought by no means to cleave to the things of time, so I find that it is by the faculty of reason alone that one must escape and find release from them. For it is the part of a wise man not to be whirled about after the manner of a revolving wheel, but through the stability of his powers to be firmly fashioned as a thing foursquare. Accordingly, since things are changeable and can never be at rest, what man in his right mind will deny that the wise man ought, as I have said, to depart from them to that city which stays at rest and abides to all eternity? This is the City of God, the heavenly Jerusalem, for which the children of God sigh while they are set in this land of sojourn, oppressed by the turmoil of the things of time as if they were oppressed by the Babylonian captivity. For, inasmuch as there are two cities—the one of time, the other of eternity; the one of the earth, earthy, the other of heaven, heavenly; the one of the devil, the other of Christ—ecclesiastical writers have declared that the former is Babylon, the latter Jerusalem.

But, whereas many of the Gentiles have written much regarding one of these cities, to hand down to posterity the great exploits of men of old (the many evidences of their merits, as they fancied), they have yet left to us the task of setting forth what, in the judgment of our writers, is rather the tale of human miseries. There are extant in this field the famous works of

Pompeius Trogus, Justin, Cornelius [Tacitus], Varro, Eusebius, Jerome, Orosius, Jordanes, and a great many others of our number, as well as of their array, whom it would take too long to enumerate; in those writings the discerning reader will be able to find not so much histories as pitiful tragedies made up of mortal woes. We believe that this has come to pass by what is surely a wise and proper dispensation of the Creator, in order that, whereas men in their folly desire to cleave to earthly and transitory things, they may be frightened away from them by their own vicissitudes, if by nothing else, so as to be directed by the wretchedness of this fleeting life from the creature to a knowledge of the Creator. But we, set down as it were at the end of time, do not so much read of the miseries of mortals in the books of the writers named above as find them for ourselves in consequence of the experiences of our own time. For, to pass over other things, the empire of the Romans, which in Daniel is compared to iron on account of its sole lordship— monarchy, the Greeks call it—over the whole world, a world subdued by war, has in consequence of so many fluctuations and changes, particularly in our day, become, instead of the noblest and the foremost, almost the last. So that, in the words of the poet, scarcely "a shadow of its mighty name remains." For being transferred from the City [Rome] to the Greeks [the Byzantine Empire], from the Greeks to the Franks, from the Franks to the Lombards, from the Lombards again to the German Franks, that empire not only became decrepit and senile through lapse of time, but also, like a once smooth pebble that has been rolled this way and that by the waters, contracted many a stain and developed many a defect. The world's misery is exhibited, therefore, even in the case of the chief power in the world, and Rome's fall foreshadows the dissolution of the whole structure. . . .

Since, then, the changeable nature of the world

[143]

is proved by this and like evidence, I thought it necessary . . . to compose a history whereby through God's favor I might display the miseries of the citizens of Babylon and also the glory of the kingdom of Christ to which the citizens of Jerusalem are to look forward with hope, and of which they are to have a foretaste even in this life. I have undertaken therefore to bring down as far as our own time, according to the ability that God has given me, the record of the conflicts and miseries of the one city, Babylon; and furthermore, not to be silent concerning our hopes regarding that other city, so far as I can gather hints from the Scriptures, but to make mention also of its citizens who are now sojourning in the worldly city. In this work I follow most of all those illustrious lights of the Church, Augustine and Orosius, and have planned to draw from their fountains what is pertinent to my theme and my purpose. The one of these [Augustine] has discoursed most keenly and eloquently on the origin and the progress of the glorious City of God and its ordained limits, setting forth how it has ever spread among the citizens of the world, and showing which of its citizens or princes stood forth preeminent in the various epochs of the princes or citizens of the world. The other, [Orosius] in answer to those who, uttering vain babblings, preferred the former times to Christian times, has composed a very valuable history of the fluctuations and wretched issues of human greatness, the wars and the hazards of wars, and the shifting of thrones, from the foundation of the world down to his own time. Following in their steps I have undertaken to speak of the Two Cities in such a way that we shall not lose the thread of history, that the devout reader may observe what is to be avoided in mundane affairs by reason of the countless miseries wrought by their unstable character, and that the studious and painstaking investigator may find a record of past happenings free from all obscurity.

Nor do I think that I shall be justly criticized if, coming after such great men—men so wise and so eloquent—I shall presume in spite of my ignorance to write, since I have both epitomized those things of which they themselves spoke profusely and at length, and have detailed, in however rude a style, the deeds which have been performed by citizens of the world since their time, whether to the advantage of the Church of God or to its hurt. Nor shall I believe that I ought to be assailed by that verse in which the writer of satire says: "All of us, taught or untaught, are everywhere writers of poems." For it is not because of indiscretion or frivolity, but out of devotion, which always knows how to excuse ignorance, that I, though I am without proper training, have ventured to undertake so arduous a task. Nor

can anyone rightfully accuse me of falsehood in matters which—compared with the customs of the present time—will appear incredible, since down to the days still fresh in our memory I have recorded nothing save what I found in the writings of trustworthy men, and then only a few instances out of many. For I should never hold the view that these men are to be held in contempt if certain of them have preserved in their writings the apostolic simplicity, for, as overshrewd subtlety sometimes kindles error, so a devout rusticity is ever the friend of truth.

As we are about to speak, then, concerning the sorrow-burdened insecurity of the one city and the blessed permanence of the other, let us call upon God, who endures with patience the turbulence and confusion of this world, and by the vision of Himself augments and glorifies the joyous peace of that other city, to the end that by His aid we may be able to say the things which are pleasing to Him.

2. *The Chronicle of Richard de Templo, c. 1210.* Richard was probably a chaplain of the Order of the Templars, who went on the Third Crusade (1189–92) and sometime thereafter composed his *Itinerary of King Richard,* an account of that colorful expedition to the Holy Land. Unlike Bishop Otto, Richard does not specifically outline his philosophy of history, but it may easily be discovered in the following selections from his chronicle.[2]

(*Saladin's Victory at Marescallia, 1187*) As our troops were marching to meet them, and the fatal day approached, a fearful vision was seen by the king's chamberlain, who dreamt that an eagle flew past the Christian army, bearing seven missiles and a balista in its talons, and crying with a loud voice, "Woe to thee, Jerusalem!" To explain the mystery of this vision, we need, I think, only take the words of Scripture; "The Lord hath bent his bow, and in it prepared the vessels of death." What are the seven missiles, but a figure for the seven sins by which that unhappy army was soon to perish? By this number, seven, may also be understood the number of punishments that impended over the Christians, which was some time after fulfilled by the event, that too faithful and terrible interpreter of omens. The battle had not begun, when, the armies having been drawn out at a short distance from Tiberias, at a place called the Marescallia, the Lord hemmed in his people with the sword, and as a punishment for the sins of men, gave over his inheritance to slaughter and devastation. What need I say more? Neither the plan of my work, nor the immensity of the calamity, allows me to find lamentations for all its details. However, to sum all up in few words, so many were slain there, so many wounded, and so many cast into prison, that the destruction of our people drew pity even from the enemies. That vivifying wood of the cross of our salvation, on which our Lord and Redeemer hung, and down whose shaft the holy blood of Christ flowed, the sign of which is adored by angels, venerated by men, and feared by devils, under whose protection our men have always been victors in war, alas! is now captured by the enemy, and the two bearers of the cross, the bishop of Acre, and the precentor of our Lord's tomb (the bishop of St. George), fell with it, the one slain, the other a prisoner. This was the second indignity, since Chosroes, king of the Persians, which that holy cross endured for our sins; it had redeemed us from the old yoke of captivity, and now it was captured from us, and soiled by the profane hands of the unbelievers.

Let him that hath intelligence consider how fierce must have been God's wrath, how great the iniquity of His servants, when unbelievers were deemed less unworthy than Christians to become its guardians. Nothing ever happened so lamentable in all ancient times; for neither the captivity of God's ark, nor that of the kings of Judah, can compare with the calamity of our own times, by which the king and the glorious cross are taken captive together. Of the other prisoners, whose number was both extraordinary and lamentable, part were reserved unhurt to be placed at the victor's disposal, part were dispatched with the sword, and so found a happy and short byroad to heaven! Among others was Reginald prince of Antioch: he was led into the presence of the sultan, and that tyrant, either following the impulse of his passion, or envious of the great excellence of the man, cut off with his own hand that veteran and aged head.

All the Templars also who were taken, except their master, he ordered to be decapitated, wishing utterly to exterminate those whom he knew to be valiant above all others in battle. O what faith, what fervor of mind was theirs! How many assumed the tonsure of the Templars, and flocked eagerly round their executioners, joyfully presenting their necks to the sword, in the pious fraud of this new costume! Among these soldiers of Christ was a Templar, named Nicholas, who had so induced others to aspire to martyrdom, that, by reason of their emulation to be beforehand with him, he could hardly succeed in first obtaining the mortal stroke which he coveted. Nor did the Divine mercy withhold its miraculous manifestation, for during the three following nights, when the bodies of the holy martyrs were lying still unburied, a ray of celestial light shone over them from above.

When the noise of battle had ceased, Saladin seeing prisoners carried off in all directions, and the ground on all sides covered with the slain, lifting up his eyes to heaven, gave thanks to God for the victory which he had gained. This was his practice in all cases; but at present among other things, he is reported to have said, that it was not his own power but our crimes which had given him the victory; and it was proved to be so by the character of the event. In other engagements, our army, however moderate in size, with the Divine aid, always conquered; but now, because we were not with God, nor God with us, our people were altogether defeated, even before the conflict, though they were reckoned at more than 1,000 knights and more than 20,000 footmen: so entirely had the whole force of the kingdom [Crusaders' Kingdom of Jerusalem] flocked together at the king's command to that fatal campaign, that those only remained to guard the cities and castles, whom weakness of sex or age rendered unfit to bear arms. This disastrous battle was fought on the day of the translation of St. Martin [1187], and in one moment all the glory of the kingdom passed from it and was extinguished.

(*Christian Victory at Iconium, 1190*) This splendid victory was not granted unworthily by the Divine excellence to His faithful servants: for they observed chastity in the camp, and discipline when under arms: in all, and above all, was the fear of the Lord; with all was the love of their neighbor; all were united in brotherly affection, as they were also companions in danger. The sultan, when the city was taken, seeing that there remained to him only the tower in which he was, sent hastily to the emperor. [Frederick Barbarossa], throwing all the blame upon his son, and professing his own innocence; promising, moreover, as much gold as he should demand, and whatsoever persons he should name as hostages for his observance of the treaty. The emperor, alas! too easy, accepted what was offered and gave what was asked: in this less worthy of praise, because he let go that man of blood and treachery whom he had almost in his possession, when it would have been more honorable to slay him than to keep alive so great an enemy to the Christian name.

(*Death of Frederick Barbarossa, 1190*) The victorious army now enters the Armenian territories: all rejoice at having quitted a hostile kingdom, and at their arrival in the country of the faithful. But, alas! a more fatal land awaits them, which is to extinguish the light and joy of all. Let man take thought and investigate, if he may, the counsels of the Lord, whose judgments are unfathomable. Things will occur sometimes to cause him astonishment, sometimes confusion, yet so that in every circumstance man may recognize the author of all things.

On the borders of Armenia there was a place, surrounded on one side by steep mountains, on the other side by the river Selesius. Whilst the sumpter-horses and baggage were passing this river, the victorious emperor [Frederick Barbarossa] halted. He was indeed an illustrious man, of stature moderately tall, with red hair and beard; his head was partly turning gray, his eyelids were prominent and his eyes sparkling; his cheeks short and wide; his breast and shoulders broad: in all other respects his form was manly. This great man, having halted some time, in consequence of the sumpter-horses crossing the river, became at last impatient of the delay; and wishing to accelerate the march, he prepared to cross the nearest part of the stream, so as to get in front of the sumpter-horses and be at liberty to proceed. O sea! O earth! O heaven! the ruler of the Roman empire, ever august, in whom the glory of ancient Rome again flourished, its honor again lived, and its power was augmented, was overwhelmed in the waters and perished! and though those who were near him hastened to his assistance, yet his aged spark of life was extinguished by a sudden though not premature death.

If love of swimming, as several have asserted, be said to have caused his death, yet the gravity of the man argues the contrary; nor does it merit belief that, a bad swimmer, he would have committed to the deceitful waters the safety of so many. The conscience is witness that death is less painful than the cause of death, but this is our consolation as it is written: the just, by whatever death he shall be surprised, will be refreshed. If the mountains of Gilboa, where the brave ones of Israel were slain, deserved to be deprived of the dew and rain, what imprecations may we not deservedly utter upon this fatal river, which overthrew a main pillar of all Christendom? There were some who said that the place had been marked by a fatality from ancient times, and that the nearest rock had long borne upon it these words inscribed, "Here the greatest of men shall perish."

The lamentable report of his death was spread around and filled all with dismay. If we search all the annals of antiquity, the traditions of history, and the fictions of romance, concerning the sorrows of mothers, the sighs of brides, or the distresses of men in general, the present grief will be found to be without example, never before known in any age, and surpassing all tears and lamentations. There were many of the emperor's domestics present, with some of his kinsmen and his son; but it was impossible to distinguish them amid the general lamentation, with which all and

each lamented the loss of their father and their lord. This, however, was a consolation to all, and they all returned thanks for it to Divine Providence, that he had not died within the territories of the infidels.

When his funeral-rites were performed, they left the fatal spot as soon as possible, bearing with them the body of the emperor adorned with royal magnificence, that it might be carried to Antioch. There the flesh, being boiled from the bones, reposes in the church of the Apostolic see, and the bones were conveyed by sea to Tyre, thence to be transported to Jerusalem. It was fit indeed and wonderfully contrived by God's providence, that one who had contended gloriously for Christ, should repose in the two principal churches of the Christian religion, for both of which he had been a champion,—part of him in the one, and part in the other,—the one that which our Lord's burial rendered the most distinguished, the other that which was honored by being the see of the chief of the apostles.

3. *The Chronicle of Roger of Wendover, c. 1235.* Nearly a century after Bishop Otto, the English monk, Roger of Wendover, wrote his *Flowers of History.* He made no attempt to work out a system of philosophy, but his preface, which follows, makes clear his approach to the events he describes.[8]

We have thought good briefly to note the chief events of past times, and to give the lineage of our Savior from the beginning, with the successions of certain kingdoms of the world and of their rulers, for the instruction of posterity, and to aid the diligence of the studious hearer. But, first, we will address a word to certain dull cavillers, who ask what need there is of recording men's lives and deaths, or the various chances which befall them; or of committing to writing the different prodigies of heaven, earth, and the elements? Now, we would have such persons know that the lives of good men in times past are set forth for the imitation of succeeding times; and that the examples of evil men, when such occur, are not to be followed, but to be shunned. Moreover, the prodigies and portentous occurrences of past days, whether in the way of pestilence, or in other chastisements of God's wrath, are not without admonition to the faithful. Therefore is the memory of them committed to writing, that if ever the like shall again occur, men may presently betake themselves to repentance, and by this remedy appease the divine vengeance.

For this cause, therefore, among many others, Moses, the law-giver, sets forth in the sacred history, the innocence of Abel, the envy of Cain, the sincerity of Job, the dissimulation of Esau, the malice of eleven of the sons of Israel, the goodness of Joseph the twelfth, the punishment of the five cities in their destruction by fire and brimstone, to the end that we may imitate the good, and carefully turn from the ways of the wicked; and this not only does Moses, but also all the writers of the sacred page, who, by commending virtue, and holding up vice to detestation, invite us to the love and fear of God. They are, therefore, not to be heeded, who say that books of chronicles, especially those by catholic authors, are unworthy of regard; for through them, whatever is necessary for human wisdom and salvation, the studious inquirer may be able to acquire by his memory, apprehend by his learning, and set forth by his eloquence.

The following work, then, is divided into two books, the first of which treats briefly of the Old Testament of the law of God, through five ages of the world, unto the coming of the Savior as the same are marked by Moses the law-giver, with the successions of the kings of the Gentiles and of their kingdoms, without which the law of God could not conveniently be set forth. For Luke, the evangelist, in writing the Gospel of Christ, made mention of Tiberius Caesar, and the kings of the Jewish nation, whose days and years were well known to all, to the end that the advent of the Savior among men, and His works, which were of

lowly origin, might come to the knowledge of all, by means of that which had more of splendor and notoriety; and this indeed was the way of almost all the writers of the sacred page, for the reasons above mentioned.

The second book of this work treats of the New Testament, commencing with the incarnation of Christ and His nativity, and notices every year, without omitting one, down to our times, on whom the ends of the world are come, which we will treat of more at large in its proper place. Nevertheless, for the sake of fastidious readers, who are easily wearied, we think it good to aim at brevity in this our history, to the end that while they experience delight in a short and pleasing narration, we may kindle in their minds a love of reading that which does not weary, and, from listless hearers and fastidious readers, convert them into diligent students. Finally, that which follows has been taken from the books of catholic writers worthy of credit, just as flowers of various colors are gathered from various fields, to the end that the very variety, noted in the diversity of the colors, may be grateful to the various minds of the readers, and by presenting some which each may relish, may suffice for the profit and entertainment of all.

B. POLITICAL THEORY

Though political machinery may not depend upon a theory of government for its practical operation, thinking men are often impelled to reach beyond contemporary practice to find a philosophic justification for the political institutions of their day. Thus, most men doubtless accepted feudal institutions without question, but academic reflection or actual political conflict, like that between Empire and Papacy, produced the expression of the fundamental concepts which lay behind medieval government. In this political philosophy are to be found some of the most cherished moral and ethical notions of the medieval mind. The selections below are characteristic of medieval political thought.

1. *The Political Theory of John of Salisbury.* A trained logician and prolific author, John of Salisbury also acquired considerable experience in political affairs as an adviser to two archbishops of Canterbury. To the second of these, St. Thomas à Becket, he dedicated his *Policraticus* or *Statesman's Book* (1159), a systematized exposition of the political lore he had acquired from classical texts, the Bible, and actual observation. Portions of this work are printed below.[4]

Between a tyrant and a prince there is this single or chief difference, that the latter obeys the law and rules the people by its dictates, accounting himself as but their servant. It is by virtue of the law that he makes good his claim to the foremost and chief place in the management of the

affairs of the commonwealth and in the bearing of its burdens; and his elevation over others consists in this, that whereas private men are held responsible only for their private affairs, on the prince fall the burdens of the whole community. Wherefore deservedly there is conferred on him, and gathered together in his hands, the power of all his subjects, to the end that he may be sufficient unto himself in seeking and bringing about the advantage of each individually, and of all; and to the end that the state of the human commonwealth may be ordered in the best possible manner, seeing that each and all are members one of another. Wherein we indeed but follow nature, the best guide of life; for nature has gathered together all the senses of her microcosma or little world, which is man, into the head, and has subjected all the members in obedience to it in such wise that they will all function properly so long as they follow the guidance of the head, and the head remains sane.

Therefore the prince stands on a pinnacle which is exalted and made splendid with all the great and high privileges which he deems necessary for himself. And rightly so, because nothing is more advantageous to the people than that the needs of the prince should be fully satisfied; since it is impossible that his will should be found opposed to justice. Therefore, according to the usual definition, the prince is the public power, and a kind of likeness on earth of the divine majesty. Beyond doubt a large share of the divine power is shown to be in princes by the fact that at their nod men bow their necks and for the most part offer up their heads to the axe to be struck off, and, as by a divine impulse, the prince is feared by each of those over whom he is set as an object of fear. And this I do not think could be, except as a result of the will of God. For all power is from the Lord God, and has been with Him always, and is from everlasting. The power which the prince has is therefore from God, for the power of God is never lost, nor severed from Him, but He merely exercises it through a subordinate hand, making all things teach His mercy or justice. "Who, therefore, resists the ruling power, resists the ordinance of God," in Whose hand is the authority of conferring that power, and when He so desires, of withdrawing it again, or diminishing it.

For it is not the ruler's own act when his will is turned to cruelty against his subjects, but it is rather the dispensation of God for His good pleasure to punish or chasten them. Thus during the Hunnish persecution, Attila, on being asked by the reverend bishop of a certain city who he was, replied, "I am Attila, the scourge of God." Whereupon it is written that the bishop adored him as representing the divine majesty. "Welcome," he said, "is the minister of God," and "Blessed is he that cometh in the name of the Lord," and with sighs and groans he unfastened the barred doors of the church, and admitted the persecutor through whom he attained straightway to the palm of martyrdom. For he dared not shut out the scourge of God, knowing that His beloved Son was scourged, and that the power of this scourge which had come upon himself was as nought except it came from God.

Princes should not deem that it detracts from their princely dignity to believe that the enactments of their own justice are not to be preferred to the justice of God, whose justice is an everlasting justice, and His law is equity. Now equity, as the learned jurists define it, is a certain fitness of things which compares all things rationally, and seeks to apply like rules of right and wrong to like cases, being impartially disposed toward all persons, and allotting to each that which belongs to him. Of this equity the interpreter is the law, to which the will and intention of equity and justice are known.

Therefore Chrysippus asserted that the power of the law extends over all things, both divine and human, and that it accordingly presides over all goods and ills, and is the ruler and guide of material things as well as of human beings. To which Papinian, a man most learned in the law, and Demosthenes, the great orator, seem to assent, subjecting all men to its obedience because all law is, as it were, a discovery, and a gift from God, a precept of wise men, the corrector of excesses of the will, the bond which knits together the fabric of the state, and the banisher of crime; and it is therefore fitting that all men should live according to it who lead their lives in a corporate political body. All are accordingly bound by the necessity of keeping the law, unless perchance there is any who can be thought to have been given the license of wrong-doing.

However, it is said that the prince is absolved from the obligations of the law; but this is not true in the sense that it is lawful for him to do unjust acts, but only in the sense that his character should be such as to cause him to practice equity not through fear of the penalties of the law but through love of justice; and should also be such as to cause him from the same motive to promote the advantage of the commonwealth, and in all things to prefer the good of others before his own private will. Who, indeed, in respect of public matters can properly speak of the will of the prince at all, since therein he may not lawfully have any will of his own apart from that which the law or equity enjoins, or the calculation of the common interest requires? For in these matters his will is to have the force of a judgment; and most properly that which pleases him therein has the force of law, because his decision may not be at variance with the intention of equity. "From thy countenance," says the Lord, "let my judgment go forth, let thine eyes look upon equity"; for the uncorrupted judge is one whose decision, from assiduous contemplation of equity, is the very likeness thereof.

The prince accordingly is the minister of the common interest and the bond-servant of equity, and he bears the public person in the sense that he punishes the wrongs and injuries of all, and all crimes, with even-handed equity. His rod and staff also, administered with wise moderation, restore irregularities and false departures to the straight path of equity, so that deservedly may the Spirit congratulate the power of the prince with the words, "Thy rod and thy staff, they have comforted me." His shield, too, is strong, but it is a shield for the protection of the weak, and one which wards off powerfully the darts of the wicked from the innocent. Those who derive the greatest advantage from his performance of the duties of his office are those who can do least for themselves, and his power is chiefly exercised against those who desire to do harm. Therefore not without reason he bears a sword, wherewith he sheds blood blamelessly, without becoming thereby a man of blood, and frequently puts men to death without incurring the name of guilt of homicide. . . .

This sword, then, the prince receives from the hand of the Church, although she herself has no sword of blood at all. Nevertheless she has this sword, but she uses it by the hand of the prince, upon whom she confers the power of bodily co-ercion, retaining to herself authority over spiritual things in the person of the pontiffs. The prince is, then, as it were, a minister of the priestly power, and one who exercises that side of the sacred offices which seems unworthy of the hands of the priesthood. For every office existing under, and concerned with the execution of, the sacred laws is really a religious office, but that is inferior which consists in punishing crimes, and which therefore seems to be typified in the person of the hangman. . . .

A commonwealth, according to Plutarch, is a certain body which is endowed with life by the benefit of divine favor, which acts at the prompt-ing of the highest equity, and is ruled by what may be called the moderating power of reason. Those things which establish and implant in us the practice of religion, and transmit to us the worship of God (here I do not follow Plutarch, who says "of the Gods") fill the place of the soul in the body of the commonwealth. And therefore those who preside over the practice of religion should be looked up to and venerated as the soul of the body. For who doubts that the minis-ters of God's holiness are His representatives? Furthermore, since the soul is, as it were, the prince of the body, and has rulership over the whole thereof, so those whom our author calls the prefects of religion preside over the entire body. . . .

The place of the head in the body of the com-monwealth is filled by the prince, who is subject only to God and to those who exercise His office and represent Him on earth, even as in the hu-man body the head is quickened and governed by the soul. The place of the heart is filled by the Senate, from which proceeds the initiation of good works and ill. The duties of eyes, ears, and tongue are claimed by the judges and the gov-ernors of provinces. Officials and soldiers corre-spond to the hands. Those who always attend upon the prince are likened to the sides. Financial officers and keepers (I speak now not of those who are in charge of the prisons, but of those who are keepers of the privy chest) may be com-pared with the stomach and intestines, which, if they become congested through excessive avidity, and retain too tenaciously their accumulations, generate innumerable and incurable diseases, so that through their ailment the whole body is threatened with destruction. The husbandmen correspond to the feet, which always cleave to the soil, and need the more especially the care and foresight of the head, since while they walk upon the earth doing service with their bodies, they meet the more often with stones of stumbling, and therefore deserve aid and protection all the more justly since it is they who raise, sustain, and move forward the weight of the entire body. Take away the support of the feet from the strongest body, and it cannot move forward by its own power, but must creep painfully and shamefully on its hands, or else be moved by means of brute animals. . . .

Let it suffice at present to have said so much concerning the unity of head and members, add-ing only what we have already premised, namely that an injury to the head, as we have said above, is brought home to all the members, and that a wound unjustly inflicted on any member tends to the injury of the head. Furthermore whatsoever is attempted foully and with malice against the head, or corporate community, of the members, is a crime of the greatest gravity and nearest to sacrilege; for as the latter is an attempt against God, so the former is an attack upon the prince, who is admitted to be as it were the likeness of deity upon earth. And therefore it is called the crime of lèse majesté. . . .

The acts are many which constitute the crime of lèse majesté, as for example if one conceives the death of the prince or magistrates, or has borne arms against his country, or, forsaking his prince, has deserted in a public war, or has in-cited or solicited the people to rebel against the commonwealth; or if by the act or criminal in-tent of any, the enemies of the people and com-monwealth are aided with supplies, armor, weap-ons, money, or any thing else whatsoever, or if, from being friends, they are turned into enemies of the commonwealth; or if by the criminal in-tent or act of any, it comes to pass that pledges or money are given against the commonwealth, or the people of a foreign country are perverted from their obedience to the commonwealth; like-wise he commits the crime who effects the escape of one who after confessing his guilt in court has on this account been thrown into chains; and many other acts of this nature, which it would be too long or impossible to enumerate.

But because the formula of fidelity or fealty ought herein above all else to be kept, there is language in the oath from which we can most conveniently learn a few of the acts which are not permitted. For a thing which is the opposite of something that is necessary is impossible, and by the same process of reasoning a thing which ought to be done is contradicted only by something that is not permitted. The formula of fealty, then, exacts the things which are inserted therein as being the necessary elements of loyalty, and expresses the latter by the words "sound," "safe," "honorable," "advantageous," "easy," "possible." If therefore, we are bound by fealty to anyone, we must not harm his soundness of body, or take from him the military resources upon which his safety depends, or presume to commit any act whereby his honor or advantage is diminished; neither is it lawful that that which is easy for him should be made difficult, or that which is possible impossible. Besides, one who holds a benefice from him whose liege man he is, owes to him aid and counsel in his undertakings; from which fact it is clearer than the sun how much is owed to the God of all, if so much is owed even to those to whom we are bound only by fealty. . . .

A tyrant, then, as the philosophers have described him, is one who oppresses the people by rulership based upon force, while he who rules in accordance with the laws is a prince. Law is the gift of God, the model of equity, a standard of justice, a likeness of the divine will, the guardian of well-being, a bond of union and solidarity between peoples, a rule defining duties, a barrier against the vices and the destroyer thereof, a punishment of violence and all wrong-doing. The law is assailed by force or by fraud, and, as it were, either wrecked by the fury of the lion or undermined by the wiles of the serpent. In whatever way this comes to pass, it is plain that it is the grace of God which is being assailed, and that it is God himself who in a sense is challenged to battle. The prince fights for the laws and the liberty of the people; the tyrant thinks nothing done unless he brings the laws to nought and reduces the people to slavery. Hence, the prince is a kind of likeness of divinity; and the tyrant, on the contrary, a likeness of the boldness of the Adversary, even of the wickedness of Lucifer, imitating him that sought to build his throne to the north and make himself like unto the Most High, with the exception of His goodness. . . .

The histories teach, however, that none should undertake the death of a tyrant who is bound to him by an oath or by the obligation of fealty. For we read that Sedechias, because he disregarded the sacred obligation of fealty, was led into captivity; and that in the case of another of the kings of Judah whose name escapes my memory, his eyes were plucked out because, falling into faithlessness, he did not keep before his sight God, to

Whom the oath is taken; since sureties for good behavior are justly given even to a tyrant.

But as for the use of poison, although I see it sometimes wrongfully adopted by infidels, I do not read that it is ever permitted by any law. Not that I do not believe that tyrants ought to be removed from our midst, but it should be done without loss of religion and honor. . . .

And surely the method of destroying tyrants which is the most useful and the safest, is for those who are oppressed to take refuge humbly in the protection of God's mercy, and lifting up undefiled hands to the Lord, to pray devoutly that the scourge wherewith they are afflicted may be turned aside from them. For the sins of transgressors are the strength of tyrants. . . .

Thus wickedness is always punished by the Lord; but sometimes it is His own, and at others it is a human hand, which He employs as a weapon wherewith to administer punishment to the unrighteous. . . .

2. *The Political Theory of St. Thomas Aquinas.* The rediscovery in the thirteenth century of the political writings of Aristotle led political theorists to reëvaluate their philosophy in the light of their new knowledge. Notable among them was the greatest of all medieval theologians, St. Thomas Aquinas, from whose work, *Concerning the Rule of Princes* (1266), the following selections are taken.[5]

If it is natural to man to live in a numerous society it is necessary that there should be provision for ruling such a society. Where there are many men and each seeks that which is agreeable to himself, the group will soon fall apart, unless there be some one who cares for those things which concern the good of the aggregate; just as the body of a man (or any other animal) would be destroyed if there were no controlling force in the body working for the common benefit of all the members. Thus Solomon says (Prov. xi. 14), "Where no counsel is, the people will fall." And this is reasonable; for what is individual (*proprium*) is not the same as that which is common; in private matters men differ, in common affairs they are united. Moreover, the interests of different people are diverse. It is, therefore, right that in addition to that which works to the private advantage of each there should be something which acts for the common good of the many; for in all things which are organized into a unity one is found to rule the other. In the universe of bodies, the first—that is, the astral, body rules all the others, according to the plan of divine providence; and all bodies are ruled by the rational creature. In a man, moreover, the soul rules the body, and within the soul the irascible and sensual parts are controlled by the reason. Among the members of the body one is chief—the heart, or the head, which rules the others. Thus there must be within every multitude a ruling power.

In some pursuits directed toward an end it is possible to proceed rightly or wrongly. There is a right and a wrong way in the government of a multitude. Anything is rightly directed when it is brought to its proper goal, and wrongly when it is guided to an unfitting end. The appropriate goal for a multitude of freemen is different from that for a multitude of slaves. He is free who lives for his own sake; he is a slave who exists for another. If a multitude of freemen is governed by a ruler for their common good, the government is right and just, and appropriate for freemen. If the government is directed not to the common good, but to the private good of the ruler, then it is unjust and perverted. The Lord threatens such a ruler, saying (Ezek. xxxiv. 2), "Woe be to the shepherds that do feed themselves! should not the shepherds feed the flocks?" Shepherds should seek the good of the flock, and every ruler the good of the multitude subject to him.

If an unjust government should be established by one man who in governing seeks his own benefit, and not that of the multitude committed to him, such a ruler is called a tyrant, a name derived from might (*fortitudine*), because he coerces with force, instead of ruling with justice; thus among the ancients some powerful persons were called tyrants. When an unjust government is founded, not by one, but by a few, it is called an *oligarchy*, which is the rule of a few who, for the sake of riches, oppress the people; it differs from a tyranny only in number. If the evil government be conducted by many, it is called a *democracy*, which is the rule of the common people who through force of numbers overwhelm the wealthy; the whole people here are as one tyrant. Just governments should be distinguished in the same manner. If just government is controlled by a multitude it is called by the general name of *polity*, as when a multitude of warriors rule within a state or province. If it is conducted by a few who are virtuous, it is called an *aristocracy*—which is the best dominion, or the government of the best, who are thus called *optimates*. If the just power belongs to one alone, he is properly called king; wherefore the Lord says (Ezek. xxxvii. 24), "Daniel my servant shall be king over them; and they all shall have one shepherd." Thus it is clearly manifest that from the nature of a king he is one who is set above, and that he should be a shepherd seeking the common good of the multitude and not his own.

Since it is fitting for man to live in a multitude because he is not sufficient unto himself with regard to the necessaries of life, the society of the multitude ought to be as much more perfect than life in isolation as it is in itself more sufficient in the necessaries of life. There is indeed a certain sufficiency for life in the family of one household, as much, that is, as is needed for natural acts of nutrition, reproduction of offspring, and other similar purposes. There is a sufficiency in one village, so far as the things belonging to one craft go. But in a city (*civitate*), which is a perfect community, there is everything that is required for all the necessaries of life; and still more sufficient is a province, when there is need for mutual assistance in fighting against common enemies. Therefore, the one who rules a perfect community—that is, a city or a province, is called by the title of king. The one who rules a house is called not king but *paterfamilias;* but he has a certain likeness to a king; so kings are sometimes called fathers of their people.

The aim of any ruler ought to be to secure the safety of that which he has undertaken to rule. Thus it is the duty of the pilot, by preserving his ship against the perils of the sea, to bring it uninjured to a port of safety. Now the good and safety of an associated multitude consist in the preservation of its unity, which is peace; if this be lost the advantages of social life vanish; nay more, the multitude in disagreement becomes a burden to itself. It is for this, therefore, that the ruler of a multitude ought especially to strive, that he may obtain the unity of peace. Nor is it right for him to debate whether he will maintain peace in the multitude subject to him, as it is not right for a physician to consider whether he will cure a patient intrusted to his care. For one ought to debate not concerning the end which it is his duty to seek but concerning the means to that end. Wherefore, the Apostle, commanding the unity of the faithful, says (Ephes. iv. 3), "Be solicitous to keep the unity of the Spirit in the bond of peace." The more efficacious is the government in preserving the unity of peace, the more useful will it be. For we regard that as more useful which leads more directly to a proposed end. And it is clear that unity can be more readily created by that which is one in itself than by a multiple agent, just as heat is produced most effectively by a body which is in itself hot or a source of heat. Therefore, the rule of one is more beneficial than the rule of many. . . .

Furthermore, those things which follow nature are best, for in every instance nature operates best. But all natural government is by one. Among the numerous members of the human body, there is one member, the heart, which controls all the others; and in the parts of the soul, one force rules supreme, namely, the reason. There is one king among bees; in the universe there is one God, the creator and ruler of all things. And this is reasonable. For every multitude is derived from one. Wherefore, if things of art imitate things of nature, and a work of art is by so much the better as it achieves similitude to what is in nature, then necessarily a human multitude is best governed by one. Experience proves the same thing. Those provinces and cities which are not ruled by one are beset with dissension and are buffeted about without any peace; thus here appears to be fulfilled the complaint of the Lord, who said, through His prophet (Jer. xii. 10), "Many pastors have destroyed my vineyard." On the other hand, the provinces and states which are ruled by one king enjoy peace, are strong in justice, and rejoice in affluence. Wherefore, the Lord, through His prophets, promised His people, as a great reward, that He would place over them one head, and that there should be one prince among them. . . .

Since the end of the life which we live well at present is heavenly happiness, it pertains to the duty of the king to make the life of the multitude good, in accordance with what is suitable for that heavenly happiness; he must command those things which lead to heavenly happiness and forbid their opposites, as far as possible. The way to true happiness and the obstructions on the way are revealed in the divine law, the teaching of which is the duty of priests. . . . The king, having learned the divine law, ought to study especially how the multitude subject to him may live well.

3. *The Political Theory of the Rebel English Barons.* That political theory was not a monopoly of academic philosophers was made evident during the English baronial revolt in the middle of the thirteenth century. Many of the English nobles rose against Henry III in 1259 because of his misgovernment and lavish gifts to foreign favorites. The rebels endeavored to place a council of their own number about the king to control his actions, and when this failed, civil war broke out. Though the king was eventually victorious, he suffered a severe defeat at Lewes in 1264. Shortly after this encounter appeared a Latin poem entitled "The Song of the Battle of Lewes," which reflects the political theory of the temporarily triumphant rebels. Portions of the poem follow.[6]

See! we touch the root of the disturbance of the kingdom about which we are writing, and of the dissension of the parties who fought the said battle; to different objects did they turn their aim. The king with his party wished to be thus free, and urged that he ought to be so, and was of necessity, or that deprived of a king's right he would cease to be king, unless he should do whatever he might wish; that the magnates of the realm had not to heed, whom he set over his own counties, or on whom he conferred the wardenship of castles, or whom he would have to show justice to his people; and he would have as chancellor and treasurer of his realm anyone soever at his own will, and counsellors of whatever nation, and various ministers at his own discretion, without the barons of England interfering in the king's acts, as "the command of the prince has the force of law"; and that what he might command of his own will would bind each.

For every earl also is thus his own master, giving aught of his own in what measure and to whom he will—castles, lands, and revenues, he entrusts to whom he will, and although he be a subject, the king permits it all. Wherein if he shall have done well, it is of profit to the doer, if not, he himself shall see to it; the king will not oppose him whilst injuring himself. Why is the prince made of worse condition, if the affairs of a baron, a knight, and a freeman are so managed? Wherefore they intrigue for the king to be made a servant, who wish to lessen his power, and to take away his dignity of prince; they wish to thrust down into wardship and subjection the royal power made captive through sedition, and to disinherit the king, that he may not have power to rule so fully as hitherto have done the kings who preceded him, who were in no wise subject to their own people, but managed their own affairs at their will, and conferred their own at their own pleasure. This is the king's pleading which seems true, and this allegation protects the right of the realm.

But now let my pen be turned to the opposite side. Let the proposal of the barons be subjoined to what has already been said; and when the parties have been heard let the statements be compared, and after comparison let them be closed by a definite termination, so that the truer part may be clear; the people are more prone to obey the more true. Therefore let the party of the barons now speak on its own behalf, and let it duly follow whither it is led by zeal. Which party in the first place openly makes protestation, that it devises naught against the royal honor or seeks anything contrary to it; nay, is zealous to reform and magnify the kingly state; just as, if the kingdom were devastated by enemies, it would not then be reformed without the barons, to whom this would be proper and suitable; and he who should then falsify himself, him the law would punish as guilty of perjury, as a betrayer of the king. He who can contribute aught of aid to the king's honor owes it to his lord, when he is in peril, when the kingdom is deformed as it were in extremity.

The king's adversaries are enemies who make

war, and counsellors who flatter the king, who by deceitful words mislead the prince, and with double tongues lead him into error; these are worse adversaries than the perverse, they make themselves out to be good, when they are misleaders, and they are procurers of their own honor; they deceive the unwary whom they render more careless through pleasant words, whence they are not guarded against but are looked on as speaking useful things. These can deceive more than can the open, as they know how to feign themselves as not hostile. What, if such wretches and such liars should cleave to the side of the prince, full of all malice, fraud and falsehood, pricked with the stings of envy they would devise a deed of wickedness, through which they might bend to their own ostentation the rights of the realm; and should fashion some hard arguments, which would gradually confound the community, crush and impoverish the commonalty of the people, and subvert and infatuate the kingdom, so that no one might be able to obtain justice unless he were willing to foster the pride of such men by means of money amply bestowed? Who would endure so great a wrong to be imagined? And if such men by their aims were to alter the realm, so as to supplant right by unright; and after trampling on the natives were to call in strangers, and were to subdue the kingdom to foreigners; were not to regard the magnates and nobles of the land, and were to put mean men in the highest place, and were to cast down and humble the great, were to pervert order and turn it upside down; were to abandon the best, be urgent on the worst; would not those who should do thus, lay waste the kingdom?

Although they might not be fighting with weapons of war from abroad, yet would they be contending with the devil's weapons, and pitifully violating the state of the realm, although their manner was different they would do no less damage. Whether the king consenting through misguidance, or not perceiving such deceit, were to approve such measures destructive to the kingdom; or whether the king out of malice were to do harm, by preferring his own power to the laws, or by abusing his strength on account of his opportunity; or if thus or otherwise the kingdom be wasted, or the kingdom be made utterly destitute, then ought the magnates of the kingdom to take care, that the land be purged of all errors. And if to them belongs the purging of error, and to them belongs provision the governess of customs, how would it not be lawful for them to take foresight lest any evil happen which might be harmful; which, after it may have happened, they ought to remove, lest of a sudden it make the unwary to grieve. Thus that none of the aforesaid things may come about, which may impede the forming of peace or good customs; but that the zeal of the skilled may come in, which may be more expedient to the interest of the many; why should not improvement be admitted wherein no corruption is mingled? For the clemency of the king, and the majesty of the king ought to approve endeavors which so temper baleful laws, that they be milder, and while less burdensome, be more welcome to God. For the oppression of the people pleases not God, nay rather does the compassion whereby the people may have leisure for God. . . . The Father of Truth both praises mercy more than judgment, and peace more than punishment. . . .

Since it is agreed that all this is lawful for the barons, it remains to reply to the reasonings of the king. The king wishes, by the removal of his guardians, to be free, and wishes not to be subject to his inferiors, but to be over them, to command his subjects and not to be commanded; nor does he wish to be humbled to those set in authority, for those, who are set in authority, are not set over the king, nay rather are men of distinction who support the right of the one; otherwise the king would not be without a rival but they, whom the king was under, would reign equally. Yet this incongruity which seems so great, may, with God's assistance, be easily solved. For we believe that God, through Whom we thus dissolve this doubt, desires the truth. One alone is called, and is King in truth, through Whom the world is ruled by pure majesty, Who needs not assistance whereby He may be able to reign, nay nor counsel, Who cannot err. Therefore all-powerful and knowing He excels in infinite glory all, to whom He has granted to rule His people under Him and as it were to reign, who are able to fail and able to err, and who cannot stand by their own strength and overcome their enemies by their own valor nor govern kingdoms by their own understanding, but go badly astray in the pathlessness of error; they need assistance that supports them, yea and counsel that keeps them right.

The king says: "I agree to thy reasoning, but the election of these men falls under my choice; I will associate with me whom I will, by whose defense I will govern all things; and if my own men be insufficient, have not understanding, or be not powerful, or if they be evil-wishers, and be not faithful, but may perchance be treacherous, I wish thee to make clear, why I ought to be constrained to certain persons, and from whom I have power to get better assistance." The reasoning on which matter is quickly declared, if it be considered what the constraining of the king is. All constraint does not deprive of liberty, nor does all restriction take away power. Those that are princes wish for free power, those that are lords wish not for wretched slavery. To what purpose does free law wish kings to be bound? That they may not be able to be stained by an adulterine law. And this constraining is not of slavery, but is the enlarging of kingly virtue.

So is the king's child preserved that he may not be hurt, yet he becomes not a slave when he is so constrained. Yea, thus also are the angel spirits constrained, who are confirmed that they be not apostate. For that the Author of all is not able to err, that the Beginning of all is not able to sin, is not impotence but the highest power, the great glory of God and His great majesty. Thus he who is able to fall, if he be guarded that he fall not, is aided by such guardianship to live freely; neither is such sustenance of slavery, but is the protectress of virtue. Therefore let the king like everything that is good, but let him not dare evil; this is the gift of God. They who guard the king, that he sin not when tempted, are themselves the servants of the king, to whom let him be truly grateful, because they free him from being made a slave, because they do not surpass him, by whom he is led. But whoever is truly king is truly free, if he rule himself and his kingdom rightly; let him know that all things are lawful for him which are fitted for ruling the kingdom, but not for destroying it. It is one thing to rule, which is the duty of a king, another to destroy by resisting the law. Law is so called from binding (*lex a ligando*), which is so perfectly described as the law of liberty, as it is freely served.

Let every king understand that he is the servant of God; let him love that only which is pleasing to Him; and let him seek His glory in ruling, not his own pride by despising his equals. Let the king, who wishes the kingdom which is put under him to obey him, render his duty to God, otherwise let him truly know that obedience is not due to him, who denies the service by which it is held of God. Again, let him know that the people is not his own but God's, and let him be profitable to it as a help. And he who is for a short time set over the people, is soon closed in marble and laid beneath the earth. . . .

The affairs of the commonalty are best managed if the realm is directed by the way of truth; and moreover, if the subjects seek to waste their own, those set over them can restrain their folly and rashness, that the power of the realm be not weakened through the insolence or stupidity of the foolish, and courage against the realm be given to its enemies. For when any member of the body is injured, the body is made of less strength; thus, granted that it may even be lawful for men to misuse their own, although it be harmful to the realm, many will soon follow the injurious liberty and so multiply the disgrace of error, as to cause loss to the whole. Nor ought that properly to be named liberty which unwisely permits the foolish to have dominion; but let liberty be limited by the bounds of right, and when those limits are despised let it be deemed error. Otherwise thou wilt say that the madman is free, although everything prosperous be hateful to him.

Therefore the king's pleading concerning his subjects carried whithersoever they will at their own pleasure, is through this sufficiently answered, sufficiently invalidated; while whoever is a subject is ruled by a greater, because we say that it is not lawful for any man to do whatever he wishes, but that each man has a lord to correct him in error, help him in well-doing, and raise him up whenever he falls. We give the first place to the commonalty.

We say also that law rules the dignity of the king; for we believe that law is a light, without which we infer that the guide goes astray. Law, whereby is ruled the world and the kingdoms of the world, is described as fiery, because it contains a mystery of deep meaning; it shines, burns, glows; fire by shining prevents wandering, it avails against cold, purifies, and reduces to ashes, some hard things it softens, and cooks what was raw, takes away numbness, and does many other good things. Sacred law supplies like gifts to the king. This wisdom Solomon asked for; its friendship he sought for with all his might. If the king be without this law, he will go astray; if he hold it not, he will err shamefully. Its presence gives right reigning, and its absence the disturbance of the realm. That law speaks thus: "By me kings reign, by me is justice shown to those who make laws." That stable law shall no king alter, but through it shall he strengthen his changing self. If he conform to this law he shall stand, and if he disagree with it he will stagger.

It is commonly said, "As the king wills, the law goes"; truth wills otherwise, for the law stands, the king falls. Truth and charity and the zeal of salvation are the integrity of law, the rule of virtue; truth is light, charity warmth, zeal burns: this variety of the law takes away all crime. Whatever the king determines, let it be consonant with these; for if he do otherwise the commons will be rendered sorrowful. The people will be confounded, if either the king's eye lacks truth, or if the prince's heart lacks charity, or does not always moderately fulfil its zeal with severity; these three being in support, let whatever pleases the king be done, but when they are in opposition, the king is resisting the law.

But kicking against the pricks hurts not; thus does the instruction of Paul from heaven teach us. So there will be no disinheritance of the king if provision be made in accordance with just law. For dissimulation will not change the law, the firm reason of which will stand without end.

Whence if anything useful has been long deferred, let it not be reprehended when it is late preferred.

And let the king prefer nothing of his own to the common weal, as though the safety of all gave way to him who is but one; for he is not set over them to live for himself, but so that this people which is put under him may be secure. Thou wilt know that the name of king is relative; thou wilt also understand that his name is protective; whence it was not lawful for him to live for himself alone, who ought by living to protect many;

he who wishes to live for himself ought not to be in command, but to dwell apart and be as one alone. It is the glory of a prince to save very many; with trouble to himself to relieve many; let him not therefore allege his own profit, but his regard for his subjects by whom he is trusted; if he shall have saved the kingdom, he has done what is the duty of a king; whatever he shall have done otherwise, in that he has failed. From this is the true theory of a king sufficiently plain, that the position of king is unknown to one who is at leisure for his individual interest.

C. SOCIAL VALUES OF THE UPPER CLASS

Men of different ages have placed different values on human qualities, laid down different sanctions for communal conduct, and established different social ideals. In these matters, as much as in the more philosophic aspects of thought, are to be found important features of the mind of an age. For here lie the bases for the attitudes and assumptions which guided everyday life. The following selections are illustrative of some of the characteristic social values of the upper class—the feudal nobility—in the twelfth and thirteenth centuries.

1. *The Knight of Romance.* Medieval ideals are often to be found in the romantic poetry of the era. Among the most popular romances were those of Chrétien de Troyes, who wrote at the court of Champagne in the third quarter of the twelfth century. His subjects were King Arthur and the Knights of the Round Table, who appeared as idealized forms of the feudal nobility of Chrétien's own time.[7]

(*Sir Erec.*) . . . After them there swiftly followed a knight, named Erec, who belonged to the Round Table, and had great fame at the court. Of all the knights that ever were there, never one received such praise; and he was so fair that nowhere in the world need one seek a fairer knight than he. He was very fair, brave, and courteous, though not yet twenty-five years old. Never was there a man of his age of greater knighthood. And what shall I say of his virtues? Mounted on his horse, and clad in an ermine mantle, he came galloping down the road, wearing a coat of splendid flowered silk which was made at Constantinople. He had put on hose of brocade, well made and cut, and when his golden spurs were well attached, he sat securely in his stirrups. He carried no arm with him but his sword. . . .

Entering a forest, they rode on without halting till hour of prime [dawn]. While they thus traversed the wood, they heard in the distance the cry of a damsel in great distress. When Erec heard the cry, he felt sure from the sound that it was the voice of one in trouble and in need of help. Straightway calling Enide, he says: "Lady, there is some maiden who goes through the wood calling aloud. I take it that she is in need of aid and succor. I am going to hasten in that direction and see what her trouble is. Do you dismount and await me here, while I go yonder." "Gladly, sire," she says. Leaving her alone, he makes his way until he found the damsel, who was going through the wood, lamenting her lover whom two giants had taken and were leading away with very cruel treatment. The maiden was rending her garments, and tearing her hair and her tender crimson face. Erec sees her and, wondering greatly, begs her to tell him why she cries and weeps so sore.

The maiden cries and sighs again, then sobbing, says: "Fair sire, it is no wonder if I grieve, for I wish I were dead. I neither love nor prize my life, for my lover has been led away prisoner by two wicked and cruel giants who are his mortal enemies. God! what shall I do? Woe is me! deprived of the best knight alive, the most noble and the most courteous. And now he is in great peril of death. This very day, and without cause, they will bring him to some vile death. Noble knight, for God's sake, I beg you to succor my lover, if now you can lend him any aid. You will not have to run far, for they must still be close by." "Damsel," says Erec, "I will follow them, since you request it, and rest assured that I shall do all within my power: either I shall be taken prisoner along with him, or I shall restore him to you safe and sound. If the giants let him live until I can find him, I intend to measure my strength with theirs." "Noble knight," the maiden said, "I shall always be your servant if you restore to me my lover. Now go in God's name, and make haste, I beseech you." "Which way lies their path?" "This way, my lord. Here is the path with the footprints." Then Erec started at a gallop, and told her to await him there. The maid commends him to the Lord, and prays God very fervently that He should give him force by His command to discomfit those who intend evil toward her lover.

Erec went off along the trail, spurring his horse in pursuit of the giants. He followed in pursuit of them until he caught sight of them before they emerged from the wood; he saw the knight with bare limbs mounted naked on a nag, his hands and feet bound as if he were arrested for highway robbery. The giants had no lances, shields or whetted swords; but they both had clubs and scourges, with which they were beating him so cruelly that already they had cut the skin on his back to the bone. Down his sides and flanks the blood ran, so that the nag was all covered with blood down to the belly. Erec came along alone after them. He was very sad and distressed about the knight whom he saw them treat so spitefully.

Between two woods in an open field he came up with them, and asks: "My lords," says he, "for what crime do you treat this man so ill and lead him along like a common thief? You are treating him too cruelly. You are driving him just as if he had been caught stealing. It is a monstrous insult to strip a knight naked, and then bind him and beat him so shamefully. Hand him over to me, I beg of you with all good-will and courtesy. I have no wish to demand him of you forcibly." "Vassal," they say, "what business is this of yours? You must be mad to make any demand of us. If you do not like it, try and improve matters." Erec replies: "Indeed, I like it not, and you shall not lead him away so easily. Since you have left the matter in my hands, I say whoever can get possession of him let him keep him. Take your positions. I challenge you. You shall not take him any farther before some blows have been dealt." "Vassal," they reply, "you are mad, indeed, to wish to measure your strength with us. If you were four instead of one, you would have no more strength against us than one lamb against two wolves." "I do not know how it will turn out," Erec replies; "if the sky falls and the earth melts, then many a lark will be caught. Many a man boasts loudly who is of little worth. On guard now, for I am going to attack you."

The giants were strong and fierce, and held in their clenched hands their big clubs tipped with iron. Erec went at them, lance in rest. He fears neither of them, in spite of their menace and their pride, and strikes the foremost of them through the eye so deep into the brain that the blood and brains spurt out at the back of his neck; that one lies dead and his heart stops beating. When the other saw him dead, he had reason

to be sorely grieved. Furious, he went to avenge him: with both hands he raised his club on high and thought to strike him squarely upon his unprotected head; but Erec watched the blow, and received it on his shield. Even so, the giant landed such a blow that it quite stunned him, and almost made him fall to earth from his steed. Erec covers himself with his shield and the giant, recovering himself, thinks to strike again quickly upon his head. But Erec had drawn his sword, and attacked him with such fierceness that the giant was severely handled: he strikes him so hard upon the neck that he splits him down to the saddlebow. He scatters his bowels upon the earth, and the body falls full length, split in two halves.

The knight weeps with joy and, worshipping, praises God who has sent him this aid. Then Erec unbound him, made him dress and arm himself, and mount one of the horses; the other he made him lead with his right hand, and asks him who he is. And he replied: "Noble knight, thou art my liege lord. I wish to regard thee as my lord, as by right I ought to do, for thou hast saved my life, which but now would have been cut off from my body with great torment and cruelty. What chance, fair gentle sire, in God's name, guided thee hither to me, to free me by thy courage from the hands of my enemies? Sire, I wish to do thee homage. Henceforth, I shall always accompany thee and serve thee as my lord." Erec sees that he is disposed to serve him gladly, if he may, and says: "Friend, for your service I have no desire; but you must know that I came hither to succor you at the instance of your lady, whom I found sorrowing in this wood. Because of you, she grieves and moans; for full of sorrow is her heart. I wish to present you to her now. As soon as I have reunited you with her, I shall continue my way alone; for you have no call to go with me."

(*Sir Yvain*) . . . For my courteous, bold, and excellent lord Yvain made them yield just as a falcon does the teal. And the men and women who had remained within the town declared as they watched the strife: "Ah, what a valiant knight! How he makes his enemies yield, and how fierce is his attack! He lays about him as a lion among the fallow deer, when he is impelled by need and hunger. Then, too, all our other knights are more brave and daring because of him, for, were it not for him alone, not a lance would have been splintered nor a sword drawn to strike. When such an excellent man is found he ought to be loved and dearly prized. See now how he proves himself, see how he maintains his place, see how he stains with blood his lance and bare sword, see how he presses the enemy and follows them up, how he comes boldly to attack them, then gives away and turns about; but he spends little time in giving away, and soon returns to the attack. See him in the fray again, how lightly he esteems his shield, which he allows to be cut in pieces mercilessly. Just see how keen he is to avenge the blows which are dealt at him. For, if some one should use all the forest of Argonne to make lances for him, I guess he would have none left by night. For he breaks all the lances that they place in his socket, and calls for more. And see how he wields the sword when he draws it! Roland never wrought such havoc with Durendal against the Turks at Ronceval or in Spain! If he had in his company some good companions like himself, the traitor, whose attack we are suffering, would retreat today discomfited, or would stand his ground only to find defeat."

Then they say that the woman would be blessed who should be loved by one who is so powerful in arms, and who above all others may be recognized as a taper among candles, as a moon among the stars, and as the sun above the moon. He so won the hearts of all that the prowess which they see in him made them wish that he had taken their lady to wife, and that he were master of the land. . . .

(*A Knightly Festival*) Mounted on great Spanish steeds, they all go to meet the King of Britain, saluting King Arthur first with great courtesy and then all his company. "Welcome," they say, "to this company, so full of honorable men! Blessed be he who brings them hither and presents us with such fair guests!" At the King's arrival the town resounds with the joyous welcome which they give. Silken stuffs are taken out and hung aloft as decorations, and they spread tapestries to walk upon and drape the streets with them, while they wait for the King's approach. And they make still another preparation, in covering the streets with awnings against the hot rays of the sun. Bells, horns, and trumpets cause the town to ring so that God's thunder could not have been heard. The maidens dance before him, flutes and pipes are played, kettle-drums, drums, and cymbals are beaten. On their part the nimble youths leap, and all strive to show their delight. With such evidence of their joy, they welcome the King fittingly.

And the lady came forth, dressed in imperial garb—a robe of fresh ermine—and upon her head she wore a diadem all ornamented with rubies. No cloud was there upon her face, but it was so gay and full of joy that she was more beautiful, I think, than any goddess. Around her the crowd pressed close, as they cried with one accord: "Welcome to the King of kings and lord of lords!" The King could not reply to all before he saw the lady coming toward him to hold his stirrup. However, he would not wait for this, but hastened to dismount himself as soon as he caught sight of her. Then she salutes him with these words: "Welcome a hundred thousand times to the King, my lord, and blessed be his nephew, my lord Gawain!" The King replies: "I wish all happiness and good luck to your fair body and your face, lovely creature!" Then clasping her around the waist, the King embraced her gaily and heartily, as she did him, throwing her arms about him. I will say no more of how gladly she welcomed them, but no one ever heard of any people who were so honorably received and served.

I might tell you much of the joy should I not be wasting words, but I wish to make brief mention of an acquaintance which was made in private between the moon and the sun. Do you know of whom I mean to speak? He who was lord of the knights, and who was renowned above them all, ought surely to be called the sun. I refer, of course, to my lord Gawain, for chivalry is enhanced by him just as when the morning sun sheds its rays abroad and lights all places where it shines. And I call her the moon, who cannot be otherwise because of her sense and courtesy. However, I call her so not only because of her good repute, but because her name is, in fact, Lunete.

The damsel's name was Lunete, and she was a charming brunette, prudent, clever, and polite. As her acquaintance grows with my lord Gawain, he values her highly and gives her his love as to his sweetheart, because she had saved from death his companion and friend; he places himself freely at her service. On her part she describes and relates to him with what difficulty she persuaded her mistress to take my lord Yvain as her husband, and how she protected him from the hands of those who were seeking him; how he was in their midst but they did not see him. My lord Gawain laughed aloud at this story of hers, and then he said: "Mademoiselle, when you need me and when you don't, such as I am, I place myself at your disposal. Never throw me off for some one else when you think you can improve your lot. I am yours, and do you be from now on my demoiselle!" "I thank you kindly, sire," she said.

While the acquaintance of these two was ripening thus, the others, too, were engaged in flirting. For there were perhaps ninety ladies there, each of whom was fair and charming, noble and polite, virtuous and prudent, and a lady of exalted birth, so the men could agreeably employ themselves in caressing and kissing them, and in talking to them and in gazing at them while they were seated by their side: that much satisfaction they had at least.

My lord Yvain is in high feather because the King is lodged with him. And the lady bestows such attention upon them all, as individuals and collectively, that some foolish person might suppose that the charming attentions which she showed them were dictated by love. But such persons may properly be rated as fools for thinking that a lady is in love with them just because she is courteous and speaks to some unfortunate fellow, and makes him happy and caresses him. A fool is made happy by fair words, and is very easily taken in.

That entire week they spent in gaiety; forest and stream offered plenty of sport for any one who desired it. And whoever wished to see the land which had come into the hands of my lord Yvain with the lady whom he had married, could go to enjoy himself at one of the castles which stood within a radius of two, three, or four leagues. When the King had stayed as long as he chose, he made ready to depart.

But during the week they had all begged urgently, and with all the insistence at their command, that they might take away my lord Yvain with them. "What? Will you be one of those," said my lord Gawain to him, "who degenerate after marriage? Cursed be he by Saint Mary who marries and then degenerates! Whoever has a fair lady as his mistress or his wife should be the better for it, and it is not right that her affection should be bestowed on him after his worth and reputation are gone. Surely you, too, would have cause to regret her love if you grew soft, for a woman quickly withdraws her love, and rightly so, and despises him who degenerates in any way when he has become lord of the realm. Now ought your fame to be increased! Slip off the bridle and halter and come to the tournament with me, that no one may say that you are jealous. Now you must no longer hesitate to frequent the lists, to share in the onslaught, and to contend with force, whatever effort it may cost! Inaction produces indifference.

"But, really, you must come, for I shall be in your company. Have a care that our comradeship shall not fail through any fault of yours, fair companion; for my part you may count on me. It is strange how a man sets store by the life of ease which has no end. Pleasures grow sweeter through postponement; and a little pleasure, when delayed, is much sweeter to the taste than a great pleasure enjoyed at once. The sweets of a love which develops late are like a fire in a green bush; for the longer one delays in lighting it the greater will be the heat it yields, and the longer will its force endure. One may easily fall into habits which it is very difficult to shake off, for when one desires to do so, he finds he has lost the power. Don't misunderstand my words, my friend; if I had such a fair mistress as you have, I call God and His saints to witness, I should leave her most reluctantly; indeed, I should doubtless be infatu-

ated. But a man may give another counsel, which he would not take himself, just as the preachers, who are deceitful rascals, and preach and proclaim the right, but who do not follow it themselves."

My lord Gawain spoke at such length and so urgently that he promised him that he would go; but he said that he must consult his lady and ask for her consent. Whether it be a foolish or prudent thing to do, he will not fail to ask her leave. . . .

2. *A Knightly Lover.* An incident from the thirteenth-century Provençal romance of *Aucassin and Nicolette* relates the effect of love upon a youthful knight.[8]

Nicolette was in prison, as you have listened and heard, in the chamber. The cry and the noise went through all the land and through all the country, that Nicolette was lost. Some say that she is fled out of the land; and some say that the Count Garin of Beaucaire has had her slain. Whoever may have rejoiced at it, Aucassin was not glad; but he went his way to the Viscount of the town, and addressed him:

"Sir Viscount, what have you done with Nicolette, my most sweet friend, the thing that I loved best in all the world? Have you carried her off, or stolen her away from me? Know well that if I die of this, vengeance will be demanded of you for it, and very right will it be. Since you will have slain me with your two hands; for you have taken from me the thing that I loved best in this world."

"Fair sir," said the Viscount, "now let it be! Nicolette is a captive maid, whom I brought from a foreign land, and I bought her with my money of Saracens; and I have reared her, and baptized her, and made her my god-daughter, and have cherished her; and one of these days I should have given her a young bachelor, who would have earned bread for her honorably. With this have you nothing to do; but take you the daughter of a king, or of a count. Moreover, what think you that you would have gained, if you had made her your paramour, or taken her to your bed? Very little would you have won by that, for all the days of Eternity would your soul be in Hell for it; since into Paradise you would never enter!"

"What have I to do in Paradise? I seek not to enter there, so that I have Nicolette my most sweet friend, whom I love so much. For none go to Paradise, but such folk as I will tell you. Those old priests go there, and those old cripples, and those maimed wretches, who grovel all day and all night before those altars and in those old crypts; and those folk clad in those old threadbare cloaks, and in those old rags and tatters, who are naked and barefoot and full of sores, who die of hunger and thirst and cold and miseries. These go to Paradise;

with them have I nothing to do, but to Hell will I go. For to Hell go the fine clerks and the fine knights, who have died in tourneys and in grand wars, and the brave soldiers and the noble men. With those will I go. And there too go the fair and gracious ladies who have friends two or three beside their lords; and there go the gold and the silver, and the vair and the grey; and there too go harpers and minstrels and the kings of the world. With those will I go, so that I have Nicolette, my most sweet friend, with me."

"Certès," said the Viscount, "to no purpose will you speak of it, since you will never see her again. And if you should speak to her, and your father knew it, he would burn both me and her in a fire, and you yourself might have the utmost fear."

"This troubles me!" said Aucassin.

He departs from the Viscount sad at heart.

> Aucassin has turned and passed,
> Sorrowful and sore down-cast,
> All for his bright-favored fere;
> None can counsel him nor cheer.
> To the palace he went home;
> There the outer steps he clomb,
> To a chamber entered in,
> And began to weep therein,
> And ado most doleful make,
> And lament for his love's sake.

> "Nicolette! thy pretty bearing!
> Pretty coming, pretty faring!
> Thy sweet speech and pretty joying,
> Pretty jesting, pretty toying,
> Pretty kissing, pretty coying!—
> For thee am I in such tene,
> And so ill bested,—I ween
> Never hence alive to wend,
> Sweet sister friend!"

Whilst Aucassin was in the chamber, and was bewailing Nicolette his friend, the Count Bougart of Valence, who had his war to carry on, did not forget it, but had summoned his men on foot and on horse, and advanced to assault the castle. And the cry arose and the noise; and the knights and the soldiers arm themselves, and rush to the gates and to the walls to defend the castle; and the townsfolk go up to the alures of the walls, and throw quarrels and sharpened stakes. While the attack was great and plenary, the Count Garin of Beaucaire came into the chamber where Aucassin was making moan and bewailing Nicolette his most sweet friend, whom he loved so much.

"Ah, son!" said he, "caitiff that thou art and miserable! In that thou seest assault made on thy castle, altogether the best and the strongest! And know that if thou lose it thou art disherited! Son, now take arms, and mount horse, and fight for thy land, and help thy men! Strike thou never a

man nor other thee, yet, if they see thee among them, they will fight better for their goods and their lives, and thy land and mine. And thou art so tall and so strong that thou art well able to do it, and do it thou oughtest."

"Father," said Aucassin, "what do you speak of now? Never God give me ought that I ask of Him, if I will be a knight, or mount horse, or go to onset wherein I may strike knight or other me, except you give me Nicolette my sweet friend, whom I love so much!"

"Son," said the father, "that cannot be! Rather would I endure to be utterly disherited, and to lose all that I have, than that thou shouldest ever have her to woman or to wife!"

He turned away. And when Aucassin saw him going away, he called him back.

"Father," said Aucassin, "come here! I will make a fair covenant with you!"

"And what is that, fair son?"

"I will take arms and go to the onset by such covenant,—that if God bring me back again safe and sound, you will let me see Nicolette, my sweet friend, long enough to have spoken two words or three to her, and to have kissed her one single time."

"I consent to it!" said the father.

He grants it him, and Aucassin was glad.

> Aucassin heard of the kiss
> Which shall on return be his.
> Had one given him of pure gold
> Marks a hundred thousand told,
> Not so blithe of heart he were.
> Rich array he bade them bear:
> They made ready for his wear.
> He put on a hauberk lined,
> Helmet on his head did bind,
> Girt his sword with hilt pure gold,
> Mounted on his charger bold;
> Spear and buckler then he took;
> At his two feet cast a look:
> They trod in the stirrups trim.
> Wondrous proud he carried him.
> His dear love he thought upon,
> And his good horse spurred anon,
> Who right eagerly went on.
> Through the gate he rode straightway,
> Into the fray.

3. Knights in the Army of St. Louis. The knight of reality often approached the ideal, and perhaps no medieval monarch strove more to uphold the ideal in practice than did the saintly King Louis IX of France. Below are selections from the account of St. Louis' crusade of 1248–54, written by the Sire de Joinville, who accompanied the king to the Holy Land.[9]

(*Worthy and Rash Knights*) I made mention just now of the worthy knights who were with the king, because he had with him eight, all good knights, who had performed gallant deeds of arms on both sides of the sea, and such knights were usually styled *bons chevaliers*. The names of the knights who were attached to the king's person were—Monseigneur Geoffrey de Sargines, Monseigneur Matthew de Marly, Monseigneur Philip de Nanteuil, Monseigneur Imbert de Beaujeu, Constable of France, who was not there, but outside the camp with the master of the cross-bowmen and the greater part of the king's sergeants-at-arms, to guard the camp from any damage the Turks might strive to do unto it.

Then it came to pass that Monseigneur Walter d'Antrèche armed himself in his tent at all points, and when he had mounted his horse, his shield suspended from his neck, and helm on head, he ordered the flaps of his tent to be raised, and spurred towards the Turks; and at the moment he started from his tent, all alone, his followers shouted, "Chatillon!" But it chanced that before he reached the Turks he fell, and his charger passed over his body and galloped on, caparisoned with his arms, to the enemy, because most of the Saracens were mounted on mares, wherefore the horse was drawn towards them. And those who witnessed it told how four Turks came up to Seigneur Walter, as he was lying on the ground, and, in passing him, struck him heavy blows with their maces. Then the constable of France, with some of the king's sergeants-at-arms rescued him, and carried him in their arms to his tent. When he came there he was speechless. Several of the camp surgeons and physicians went to him, and because it seemed to them that there was no danger of death, they bled him in both arms. At a late hour of the evening, Monseigneur Aubert de Nancy proposed to me that we should go and see him, as we had not yet done so, and he was a man of great renown and valor. As we entered his tent, his chamberlain came up to us, and begged us to walk softly for fear of awakening his master. We found him lying on a coverlid of miniver, and, as we approached his bed very softly, we saw that he was dead. When this was told to the king, he replied that he should not like to have a thousand such, because they would be wanting to act without waiting for his commands, as this one had done.

(*A Fierce Engagement*) There Monseigneur Hugh d'Escoz was wounded by three lance-thrusts in the face, and Monseigneur Raoul, and Monseigneur Frederick de Loupy received a lance-thrust between his shoulders, and the wound was so broad that the blood gushed from his body as through the bunghole of a cask. Monseigneur Erard de Siverey was wounded in the face by a sword, so that his nose fell upon his lip. Then I bethought me of Monseigneur St. James: "Fair Sir St. James, to whom I pray, help and succor me in this need." I had hardly finished my prayer when Monseigneur Erard de Siverey said to me: "Sir, if you think that neither I nor my heirs would incur reproach, I would go and seek succor for you from the Count of Anjou, whom I see there in the midst of the fields."

And I answered, "Sir Erard, it seems to me that you would do yourself much honor if you would go in quest of aid to save our lives, for your own is also in great peril." And I spoke truly, for he died of his wound. Then he consulted the other knights who were there, all of whom approved of the advice I had given him. When he heard that, he asked me to let go his horse, which I held with the others, and I did so. He went to the Count of Anjou, and begged him to come to the rescue of myself and my knights. A rich man who was with him tried to dissuade him, but the count told him he would do what my knight requested, and he turned his horse's head to come to our aid, and some of his sergeants spurred forward. When the Saracens beheld them, they quitted us.

In advance of these sergeants came Monseigneur Peter d'Auberive, sword in hand, and when they saw that the Saracens had left us, they charged a body of the enemy who had taken Monseigneur Raoul de Wanou, and delivered him out of their hands sorely wounded. While I was on foot with my knights, and wounded as I have already described, there came the king with the whole of his division, with loud shouts, and much noise of trumpets and cymbals, and he halted upon a raised causeway. Never have I seen so fine a knight, for he towered above all his people, out-topping them by the shoulders, a gilded helmet on his head, and a German sword in his hand. When he halted there, the good knights whom he had about his person, and whom I have already named, dashed into the midst of the Turks, with many other valiant knights who were in the king's own "battle." And it was truly a fine passage of arms, for no one drew bow or cross-bow, but it was a combat with sword and mace between the Turks and our people, who were all mingled together. . . .

(*Judgments of St. Louis*) You shall hear now of some of the judgments and sentences which I heard pronounced at Caesarea while the king tarried there.

In the first place we will tell you of a knight who was caught in a house of ill fame, and who was allowed to choose one of two things, according to the custom of the country. The alternative was this: either that the wanton should lead him through the camp in his shirt, shamefully bound by a rope, or that he should forfeit his horse and his arms, and be expelled from the camp. The knight left his horse and arms with the king, and went his way. I begged the king to give me the horse for a poor gentleman who was in the camp. And the king replied, that my request was not reasonable, for the horse was well worth eighty livres. "Why have you broken our compact by losing your temper about what I asked of you?"

The king answered laughing, "Ask for what you please, I will not lose my temper."

For all that, I did not get the horse for the poor gentleman.

The second judgment was in this wise. The knights of our "battle" were hunting a wild animal called a gazelle, which is something like a roebuck. The brethren of the Hospital [the "Knights Hospitallers," a chivalric order] rushed at our knights, hustled them, and drove them off. I complained to the master of the Hospital, who replied that he would do me justice according to the usage of the Holy Land, which was that he would make the brethren who had committed the outrage take their meals upon the ground, seated on their cloaks, until such time as those to whom the outrage had been offered should forgive them. The master kept his promise; and when we saw that they had eaten for some time upon their cloaks, I went to the master and found him at table, and I prayed him to allow the brethren to rise who were eating on their cloaks before him; and the knights to whom the wrong had been done also besought him. But he answered that he would do nothing of the kind, for he would not have the brethren offer insults to those who came on pilgrimage to the Holy Land. When I heard that I seated myself beside the brethren, and began to eat with them; and I told him I would not rise until the brethren also rose. He replied that I was putting violence upon him, and granted my request; and he made me and the knights who were with me, sit at meat with himself; and the brethren went to dine at table with their comrades.

A third judgment which I saw rendered at Caesarea was in this way. One of the king's sergeants having laid his hand upon a knight belonging to my corps, I went and complained to the king, who said that it seemed to him I might very well desist from my complaint, for the sergeant had only pushed the knight. I told him that I would not desist, and that if he did not do me justice I would leave his service, since his sergeants lifted their hands against knights. He then consented to do me justice after the usages of the country, which were such that the sergeant came to my tent barefooted, in his drawers, and without any other article of dress, and with a naked sword in his hand, and knelt down before the knight, and said to him, "Sir, I make reparation to you for having laid my hand upon you, and I have brought you this sword that you may cut off my hand, if so it please you." And I prayed the knight to pardon him, and he did so.

(*Knightly Qualities*) The Duke of Burgundy was a very brave knight, but he was never looked upon as wise, either with regard to God, or to this world. . . . Wherefore the great King Philip, when he was told that Count John of Chalons had a son, and that he was named Hugh, after the Duke of Burgundy, replied that he prayed God to make him a *preu homme*, like the duke, whose name he bore. They asked him why he had not said *prud' homme*, and he answered, "Because there is a great difference between *preu homme* and *prud' homme*, for there is many a *preu homme* knight in the lands both of Christians and Saracens, who never believed in God or His mother. Wherefore I say to you," he continued, "that God vouchsafes a great boon and grace to the Christian knight, whom He permits to be valiant in body, and whom He suffers to remain in His service, by preserving him from deadly sin. Whoso thus rules himself, deserves to be called *prud' homme*, because this prowess comes to him from God's bounteousness. While those of whom I spoke just now may be called *preux hommes*, because they are valiant in body, but do not fear either God or sin.

Part II.   LEARNING AND SCIENCE

A.   SCHOLASTICISM

The twelfth and thirteenth centuries saw the rise of the great universities of western Europe. Their system of study and writing, taken in its broadest sense, is comprehensively termed "scholasticism," but in most western universities all other studies were overshadowed by theology, "the queen of the sciences," and a medieval "scholastic" was generally a theologian. The emphasis upon theology gives the key to the fundamental doctrines that underlay all medieval thinking, for here lie the deepest philosophical reaches of the mind of the Middle Ages.

1. *The Nature and Extent of Medieval Theology.* The greatest of the medieval scholastics was St. Thomas Aquinas, whose political tract was cited in Part I; and his greatest work was the *Summa Theologica,* a voluminous compendium of sacred doctrine, written in the third quarter of the thirteenth century. The following passages are taken from the opening pages of this work, in which St. Thomas explains "The Nature and Extent of Sacred Doctrine." The first article is quoted in its entirety to illustrate the method of argument; the other articles have been quoted sufficiently to set forth the main points made by St. Thomas.[10]

FIRST ARTICLE.

WHETHER, BESIDES PHILOSOPHY, ANY FURTHER DOCTRINE IS REQUIRED?

We proceed thus to the First Article:—

Objection 1. It seems that, besides philosophical science, we have no need of any further knowledge. Man should not seek to know what is above reason: "Seek not the things that are too high for thee" (Eccles. iii. 22). But whatever is not above reason is fully treated of in philosophical science. Therefore any other knowledge besides philosophical science is superfluous.

Obj. 2. Further, knowledge can only be concerned with being, for nothing can be known, save what is true; and all that is, is true. But everything that is, is treated of in philosophical science—even God Himself; so that there is a part of philosophy called Theology, or the Divine Science, as Aristotle has proved. Therefore, besides philosophical science, there is no need of any further knowledge.

"On the contrary," it is said, "All Scripture inspired of God is profitable to teach, to reprove, to correct, to instruct in justice" (2 Tim. iii. 16). Scripture, inspired of God, is no part of philosophical science, which has been built up by human reason. Therefore it is useful that besides philosophical science there should be other knowledge—i.e., inspired of God.

I answer that it was necessary for man's salvation that there should be a knowledge revealed by God, besides philosophical science built up by human reason. Firstly, indeed, because man is ordained to God, as to an end that surpasses the grasp of his reason; "The eye hath not seen, besides Thee, O God, what things Thou hast prepared for them that wait for Thee" (Isa. lxiv. 4). But the end must first be known by men who are to direct their thoughts and actions to the end. Hence it was necessary for the salvation of man that certain truths which exceed human reason should be made known to him by Divine Revelation. Even as regards those truths about God which human reason could have discovered, it was necessary that man should be taught by a Divine Revelation; because the Truth about God such as reason could discover, would only be known by a few, and that after a long time, and with the admixture of many errors. Whereas man's whole salvation, which is in God, depends upon the knowledge of this Truth. Therefore, in order that the salvation of men might be brought about more fitly and more surely, it was necessary that they should be taught Divine Truths by Divine Revelation. It was therefore necessary that, besides philosophical science built up by reason, there should be a sacred science learnt through Revelation.

Reply Obj. 1. Although those things which are beyond man's knowledge may not be sought for by man through his reason, nevertheless, once they are revealed by God, they must be accepted by faith. Hence the sacred text continues, "For many things are shown to thee above the understanding of man" (Eccles. iii. 25). And in this the Sacred Science consists.

Reply Obj. 2. Sciences are differentiated according to the various means through which knowledge is obtained. The astronomer and the physicist both may prove the same conclusion—that the earth, for instance, is round: the astronomer by means of mathematics (i.e., abstracting from matter), but the physicist by means of matter itself. Hence there is no reason why those things which may be learnt from philosophical science, so far as they can be known by natural reason, may not also be taught us by another science so far as they fall within revelation. Hence theology included in Sacred Doctrine differs in kind from that theology which is part of philosophy.

SECOND ARTICLE.

WHETHER SACRED DOCTRINE IS A SCIENCE?

. . . Sacred Doctrine is a science. We must bear in mind that there are two kinds of sciences. There are some which proceed from a principle known by the light of the natural intelligence, such as arithmetic and geometry. There are some which proceed from principles known by the light of a higher science: thus the science of perspective proceeds from principles established by geometry, and music from principles established by arithmetic. So it is that Sacred Doctrine is a science, because it proceeds from principles established by the light of a higher science, namely, the science of God and the blessed. Hence, just as the musician accepts on authority the principles taught him by the mathematician; so sacred science is established on principles revealed by God.

THIRD ARTICLE.

WHETHER SACRED DOCTRINE IS ONE SCIENCE?

. . . Sacred Doctrine is one. The unity of a faculty or habit is to be gauged by its object, not, indeed, in its material aspect, but as regards the precise formality under which it is an object. For example, man, ass, stone, agree in the one precise formality of being colored; and color is the formal object of sight. Therefore, because Sacred Scripture considers things precisely under the formality of being divinely revealed, whatever has been divinely revealed possesses the one precise formality of the object of this science; and therefore is included under Sacred Doctrine as under one science.

FOURTH ARTICLE.

WHETHER SACRED DOCTRINE IS A PRACTICAL SCIENCE?

. . . Sacred Doctrine, being one, extends to things which belong to different philosophical sciences, because it considers in each, the same formal aspect (*ratio*), namely so far as they can be known through Divine Revelation. Hence, although among the philosophical sciences one is speculative and another practical, nevertheless Sacred Doctrine includes both; as God, by one and the same science, knows both Himself and His works. Still, it is rather speculative than practical, because it is more concerned with Divine Things than with human acts; though it does treat even of these latter, inasmuch as man is ordained by them to the perfect knowledge of God, in which consists eternal bliss. . . .

FIFTH ARTICLE.

WHETHER SACRED DOCTRINE IS NOBLER THAN OTHER SCIENCES?

. . . Since this science is partly speculative and partly practical, it transcends all other speculative and practical. One speculative science is said to be nobler than another, either by reason of its greater certitude, or by reason of the higher worth of its subject-matter. In both these respects this science surpasses other speculative sciences; in point of greater certitude, because other sciences derive their certitude from the natural light of human reason, which can err; whereas this derives its certitude from the light of the Divine Knowledge, which cannot be misled; in point of the higher worth of its subject-matter, because this science treats chiefly of those things which by their sublimity transcend human reason; while other sciences consider only those things which are within reason's grasp. Of the practical sciences, that one is nobler which is ordained to the further purpose. Political science is nobler than military science; for the good of the army is ordained to the good of the State. But the purpose of this science, in so far as it is practical, is eternal bliss; to which as to an ultimate end the purposes of every practical science are ordained. Hence it is clear that from every standpoint it is nobler than other sciences.

SIXTH ARTICLE.

WHETHER THIS DOCTRINE IS THE SAME AS WISDOM?

. . . This Doctrine is wisdom above all human wisdom; not merely in any one kind, but absolutely. For since it is the part of a wise man to arrange and to judge, and since lesser matters should be judged in the light of some higher principle, he is said to be wise in any one order who perfectly considers the highest principle in that order: as in the order of building he who plans the form of the house is called wise and the architect, in opposition to the inferior laborers who trim the wood and make ready the stones: "As a wise architect I have laid the foundation" (I Cor. iii. 10). Again, in the order of all human life, the prudent man is called wise, inasmuch as he orders his acts for a fitting purpose: "Wisdom is prudence to a man" (Prov. x. 23). Therefore he who considers absolutely the highest cause of the whole universe, who is God, is most of all called wise. Hence Wisdom is said to be the knowledge of Divine things, as Augustine says. But Sacred Doctrine essentially treats of God viewed as the highest cause—not only so far as He can be known through creatures just as philosophers knew Him—"That which is known of God is manifest in them" (Rom. i. 19) —but also so far as He is known to Himself alone and revealed to others. Hence Sacred Doctrine is especially called wisdom.

SEVENTH ARTICLE.

WHETHER GOD IS THE SUBJECT OF THIS SCIENCE?

. . . God is the subject of this science. The relation between a science and its subject is the same as that between a habit or faculty and its object. That is properly taken to be the object of a faculty under the formality of which all things are referred to that habit or faculty, as man and stone are referred to the faculty of sight as being colored. Hence colored things are the proper objects of sight. But in Sacred Science all things are treated of under the formality of God; either because they are God Himself; or because they refer to God as their beginning and end. Hence it follows that God is in very truth the subject of this science. This is clear also from the principles of this science, namely, the articles of Faith, for Faith is about God. The subject of the principles and of the whole science must be the same, since the whole science is contained virtually in its principles. Some, however, looking to what is treated of in this science, and not to the formality under which it is treated, have asserted the subject of this science to be something other than God—that is, either things and symbols, or the works of salvation or the whole Christ, as the head and members. Of all these things, in truth, we treat in this science, but so far as they have reference to God.

EIGHTH ARTICLE.

WHETHER SACRED SCIENCE IS A MATTER OF ARGUMENT?

. . . As other sciences do not argue in proof of their principles, but argue from their principles to demonstrate other truths in these sciences: so this Doctrine does not argue in proof of its principles, which are the articles of Faith, but from them it goes on to prove something else; as the Apostle from the Resurrection of Christ argues in proof of the general resurrection (I Cor. xv.). However, it is to be borne in mind, in regard to the philosophical sciences, that the inferior sciences neither prove their principles nor dispute with those that deny them, but leave this to a higher science; whereas the highest of them can dispute with one who denies its principles, if only the opponent will make some concessions of metaphysical principles; but if he concedes nothing, it can have no dispute with him, though it can answer his objections. Hence Sacred Science, since it has no science above itself, can dispute with one who denies its principles only if the opponent admits some at least of the truths obtained through Divine Revelation; as we can argue with heretics from texts in Holy Writ, and against those that deny one article of Faith we can argue from another. If our opponent believes nothing of Divine Revelation, there is no longer any means of proving the articles of Faith by reasoning, but only of answering his objections—if he has any—against Faith. Since Faith rests upon infallible truth, and since the contrary of a truth can never be demonstrated, it is clear that the arguments brought against Faith cannot be strict demonstrations; but difficulties that can be answered.

NINTH ARTICLE.

WHETHER HOLY SCRIPTURE SHOULD USE METAPHORS?

. . . It is befitting Holy Writ to put forward Divine and spiritual truths by means of comparisons with material things. God provides for everything according to the capacity of its nature. It is natural to man to attain to intellectual truths through sensible objects, because all our knowledge originates from sense. Hence in Holy Writ spiritual truths are fittingly taught under the likeness of material things. This is what Dionysius says: "We cannot be enlightened by the Divine rays except they be hidden within the coverings of many sacred veils." It is also befitting Holy Writ, which is proposed to all without distinction of persons—"To the wise and to the unwise I am made a debtor" (Rom. i. 14)—that spiritual truths be expounded by means of figures taken from material things, in order that thereby even the simple who are unable to grasp intellectual things of themselves may be able to understand it.

TENTH ARTICLE.

WHETHER IN HOLY SCRIPTURE THE WORD HAS SEVERAL INTERPRETATIONS?

. . . The author of Holy Writ is God, in whose power it is to signify His meaning, not by words only (as man also can do), but also by things themselves. So, whereas in every other science things are signified by words, this science has the property, that the things signified by the words have themselves also a signification. Therefore that first signification whereby words signify things belongs to the first interpretation, the historical or literal. That signification whereby things signified by words have themselves also a signification is called the spiritual interpretation, which is based on the literal interpretation, and presupposes it. This spiritual interpretation has a three-fold division. As the Apostle says (Heb. vii.) the Old Law is a figure of the New Law, and "the New Law itself (Dionysius says) is a figure of future glory." In the New Law, whatever our Head has done is a type of what we ought to do. Therefore, so far as the things of the Old Law signify the things of the New Law, there is the allegorical interpretation; so far as the things done in Christ, or so far as the things which signify Christ, are types of what we ought to do, there is the moral interpretation. So far as they signify what relates to eternal glory, there is the anagogical interpretation. Since the literal sense is that which the author intends, and since the author of Holy Writ is God, Who by one act comprehends all things by His intellect, it is not unfitting (as Augustine says) if, even according to the literal sense, one word in Holy Writ should have several interpretations.

2. *A Theological Dispute.* The intense interest in theological matters inevitably led the scholastics into disputes over the interpretation of doctrine. The subjects of these debates and the approach of the debaters provide a clear insight into the nature and workings of the scholastic mind. The following selection is taken from *Historia Calamitatum*, the autobiography of Peter Abelard, an exceptionally tempestuous theologian. Here he describes his part in the Council of Soissons, which took place in 1121, a century and a half before Aquinas wrote the *Summa*.[11]

It so happened that at the outset I devoted myself to analyzing the basis of our faith through illustrations based on human understanding, and I wrote for my students a certain tract on the unity and trinity of God. This I did because they were always seeking for rational and philosophical explanations, asking rather for reasons they could understand than for mere words, saying that it was futile to utter words which the intellect could not possibly follow, that nothing could be believed unless it could first be understood, and that it was absurd for any one to preach to others a thing which neither he himself nor those whom he sought to teach could comprehend. Our Lord Himself maintained this same thing when He said: "They are blind leaders of the blind" (Matthew. xv. 14).

Now a great many people saw and read this tract, and it became exceedingly popular, its clearness appealing particularly to all who sought information on this subject. And since the questions involved are generally considered the most difficult of all, their complexity is taken as the measure of the subtlety of him who succeeds in answering them. As a result, my rivals became furiously angry, and summoned a council to take action against me, the chief instigators therein being my two intriguing enemies of former days, Alberic and Lotulphe. These two, now that both William and Anselm, our erstwhile teachers, were dead, were greedy to reign in their stead, and, so to speak, to succeed them as heirs. While they were directing the school at Rheims, they managed by repeated hints to stir up their archbishop, Rodolphe, against me, for the purpose of holding a meeting, or rather an ecclesiastical council, at Soissons, provided they could secure the approval of Conon, Bishop of Praeneste, at that time papal legate in France. Their plan was to summon me to be present at this council, bringing with me the famous book I had written regarding the Trinity. In all this, indeed, they were successful, and the thing happened according to their wishes.

Before I reached Soissons, however, these two rivals of mine so foully slandered me with both clergy and the public that on the day of my arrival the people came near to stoning me and the few students of mine who had accompanied me thither. The cause of their anger was that they had been led to believe that I had preached and written to prove the existence of three gods. No

sooner had I reached the city, therefore, than I went forthwith to the legate; to him I submitted my book for examination and judgment, declaring that if I had written anything repugnant to the Catholic faith, I was quite ready to correct it or otherwise to make satisfactory amends. The legate directed me to refer my book to the archbishop and to those same two rivals of mine, to the end that my accusers might also be my judges. So in my case was fulfilled the saying: "Even our enemies are our judges" (Deut. xxxii. 31).

These three, then, took my book and pawed it over and examined it minutely, but could find nothing therein which they dared to use as the basis for a public accusation against me. Accordingly they put off the condemnation of the book until the close of the council, despite their eagerness to bring it about. For my part, every day before the council convened I publicly discussed the Catholic faith in the light of what I had written, and all who heard me were enthusiastic in their approval alike of the frankness and the logic of my words. When the public and the clergy had thus learned something of the real character of my teaching, they began to say to one another: "Behold, now he speaks openly, and no one brings any charge against him. And this council, summoned, as we have heard, chiefly to take action upon his case, is drawing toward its end. Did the judges realize that the error might be theirs rather than his?"

As a result of all this, my rivals grew more angry day by day. On one occasion Alberic, accompanied by some of his students, came to me for the purpose of intimidating me, and, after a few bland words, said that he was amazed at something he had found in my book, to the effect that, although God had begotten God, I denied that God had begotten Himself, since there was only one God. I answered unhesitatingly: "I can give you an explanation of this if you wish it." "Nay," he replied, "I care nothing for human explanation or reasoning in such matters, but only for the words of authority." "Very well," I said; "turn the pages of my book and you will find the authority likewise." The book was at hand, for he had brought it with him. I turned to the passage I had in mind, which he had either not discovered or else passed over as containing nothing injurious to me. And it was God's will that I quickly found what I sought. This was the following sentence, under the heading "Augustine, On the Trinity, Book I": "Whosoever believes that it is within the power of God to beget Himself is sorely in error; this power is not in God, neither is it in any created thing, spiritual or corporeal. For there is nothing that can give birth to itself."

When those of his followers who were present heard this, they were amazed and much embarrassed. He himself, in order to keep his countenance, said: "Certainly, I understand all that." Then I added: "What I have to say further on this subject is by no means new, but apparently it has nothing to do with the case at issue, since you have asked for the word of authority only, and not for explanations. If, however, you care to consider logical explanations, I am prepared to demonstrate that, according to Augustine's statement, you have yourself fallen into a heresy in believing that a father can possibly be his own son." When Alberic heard this he was almost beside himself with rage, and straightway resorted to threats, asserting that neither my explanations nor my citations of authority would avail me aught in this case. With this he left me.

On the last day of the council, before the session convened, the legate and the archbishop deliberated with my rivals and sundry others as to what should be done about me and my book, this being the chief reason for their having come together. And since they had discovered nothing either in my speech or in what I had hitherto written which would give them a case against me, they were all reduced to silence, or at the most to maligning me in whispers. Then Geoffroi, Bishop of Chartres, who excelled the other bishops alike in the sincerity of his religion and in the importance of his see, spoke thus:

"You know, my lords, all who are gathered here, the doctrine of this man, what it is, and his ability, which has brought him many followers in every field to which he has devoted himself. You know how greatly he has lessened the renown of other teachers, both his masters and our own, and how he has spread as it were the offshoots of his vine from sea to sea. Now, if you impose a lightly considered judgment on him, as I cannot believe you will, you well know that even if mayhap you are in the right there are many who will be angered thereby, and that he will have no lack of defenders. Remember above all that we have found nothing in this book of his that lies before us whereon any open accusation can be based. Indeed it is true, as Jerome says: 'Fortitude openly displayed always creates rivals, and the lightning strikes the highest peaks.' Have a care, then, lest by violent action you only increase his fame, and lest we do more hurt to ourselves through envy than to him through justice. A false report, as that same wise man reminds us, is easily crushed, and a man's later life gives testimony as to his earlier deeds. If, then, you are disposed to take canonical action against him, his doctrine or his writings must be brought forward as evidence, and he must have free opportunity to answer his questioners. In that case, if he is found guilty or if he confesses his error, his lips can be wholly sealed. Consider the words of the blessed Nico-

demus, who, desiring to free Our Lord Himself, said: 'Doth our law judge any man before it hear him and know what he doeth?'" (John. vii. 51).

When my rivals heard this they cried out in protest, saying: "This is wise counsel, forsooth, that we should strive against the wordiness of this man, whose arguments, or rather, sophistries, the whole world cannot resist!" And yet, methinks, it was far more difficult to strive against Christ Himself, for Whom, nevertheless, Nicodemus demanded a hearing in accordance with the dictates of the law. When the bishop could not win their assent to his proposals, he tried in another way to curb their hatred, saying that for the discussion of such an important case the few who were present were not enough, and that this matter required a more thorough examination. His further suggestion was that my abbot, who was there present, should take me back with him to our abbey, in other words to the monastery of St. Denis, and that there a large convocation of learned men should determine, on the basis of a careful investigation, what ought to be done. To this last proposal the legate consented, as did all the others.

Then the legate arose to celebrate mass before entering the council, and through the bishop sent me the permission which had been determined on, authorizing me to return to my monastery and there await such action as might be finally taken. But my rivals, perceiving that they would accomplish nothing if the trial were to be held outside of their own diocese, and in a place where they could have little influence on the verdict, and in truth having small wish that justice should be done, persuaded the archbishop that it would be a grave insult to him to transfer this case to another court, and that it would be dangerous for him if by chance I should thus be acquitted. They likewise went to the legate, and succeeded in so changing his opinion that finally they induced him to frame a new sentence, whereby he agreed to condemn my book without any further inquiry, to burn it forthwith in the sight of all, and to confine me for a year in another monastery. The argument they used was that it sufficed for the condemnation of my book that I had presumed to read it in public without the approval either of the Roman pontiff or of the Church, and that, furthermore, I had given it to many to be transcribed. Methinks it would be a notable blessing to the Christian faith if there were more who displayed a like presumption. The legate, however, being less skilled in law than he should have been, relied chiefly on the advice of the archbishop, and he, in turn, on that of my rivals. When the Bishop of Chartres got wind of this, he reported the whole conspiracy to me, and strongly urged me to endure meekly the manifest violence of their enmity. He bade me not to doubt that this violence would in the end react upon them and prove a blessing to me, and counseled me to have no fear of the confinement in a monastery, knowing that within a few days the legate himself, who was now acting under compulsion, would after his departure set me free. And thus he consoled me as best he might, mingling his tears with mine.

Straightway upon my summons I went to the council, and there, without further examination or debate, did they compel me with my own hand to cast that memorable book of mine into the flames. Although my enemies appeared to have nothing to say while the book was burning, one of them muttered something about having seen it written therein that God the Father was alone omnipotent. This reached the ears of the legate, who replied in astonishment that he could not believe that even a child would make so absurd a blunder. "Our common faith," he said, "holds and sets forth that the Three are alike omnipotent." A certain Tirric, a schoolmaster, hearing this, sarcastically added the Athanasian phrase, "And yet there are not three omnipotent Persons, but only One."

This man's bishop forthwith began to censure him, bidding him desist from such treasonable talk, but he boldly stood his ground, and said, as if quoting the words of Daniel: "Are ye such fools, ye sons of Israel, that without examination or knowledge of the truth ye have condemned a daughter of Israel? Return again to the place of judgment (Daniel. xiii. 48—The History of Susanna) and there give judgment on the judge himself. You have set up this judge, forsooth, for the instruction of faith and the correction of error, and yet, when he ought to give judgment, he condemns himself out of his own mouth. Set free today, with the help of God's mercy, one who is manifestly innocent, even as Susanna was freed of old from her false accusers."

Thereupon the archbishop arose and confirmed the legate's statement, but changed the wording thereof, as indeed was most fitting. "It is God's truth," he said, "that the Father is omnipotent, the Son is omnipotent, the Holy Spirit is omnipotent. And whosoever dissents from this is openly in error, and must not be listened to. Nevertheless, if it be your pleasure, it would be well that this our brother should publicly state before us all the faith that is in him, to the end that, according to its deserts, it may either be approved or else condemned and corrected."

When, however, I fain would have arisen to profess and set forth my faith, in order that I might express in my own words that which was in my heart, my enemies declared that it was not needful for me to do more than recite the Athanasian Symbol, a thing which any boy might do

as well as I. And lest I should allege ignorance, pretending that I did not know the words by heart, they had a copy of it set before me to read. And read it I did as best I could for my groans and sighs and tears. Thereupon, as if I had been a convicted criminal, I was handed over to the Abbot of St. Médard, who was there present, and led to his monastery as to a prison. And with this the council was immediately dissolved.

3. *Laymen and Theology.* In the following selection from the biography of St. Louis, Joinville gives a layman's approach to theological disputation.[12] The king and the knight had been together on a Holy Land crusade.

The sainted king recounted to me how certain persons from among the Albigenses went to the Count de Montfort, who at that time was holding their country for the king, and said to him that they had come to see the body of our Lord, which had become flesh and blood in the hands of the priest. And he said to them:—

"Go and see it, you who do not believe in it. For my part, I believe firmly all that the holy Church tells us about the sacrament of the altar. And do you know," added the count, "what I shall gain by believing in this mortal life all that the holy Church teaches us? I shall have a crown in the heavens rather than the angels who behold Him face to face—for which reason they cannot help believing in Him."

He related to me how there had been a great conference of clergy and Jews at the monastery of Cluny. There was a knight there to whom the abbot had given food for the love of God, and he asked the abbot to let him have the first word, a request that was granted with some reluctance. Then he stood up, and resting upon his crutches, asked that they would cause the greatest clerk and greatest rabbi of the Jews to come to him; and they did so. And he asked the following question:

"Master," said the knight, "I ask you if you believe that the Virgin Mary, who carried God in her womb and in her arms, was a virgin and yet mother of God."

And the Jew replied that of all that he believed nothing at all. Then the knight answered that truly he had acted like a madman in entering her church and her house, when he neither believed in her nor loved her.

"And verily," added the knight, "you shall pay for it."

Thereupon he lifted up his crutch and struck the Jew on the ear, and knocked him down. The Jews then took to flight, and carried off their wounded rabbi, and that was the end of the conference. Then the abbot went up to the knight and told him that he had committed a great folly. But the knight replied that the abbot had been guilty of a greater folly in summoning such a conference; for before the conference would have been brought to an end there were a great many Christians there who would have gone away unbelievers because they would not have properly understood the Jews.

"Therefore, I tell you," said the king, "that no one, if he is not a very clever clerk, ought to dispute with them; but a layman, when he hears the Christian law evil spoken of, should not defend that law save only with his sword, which he ought to run into the infidel's belly as far as it will go."

B.   NATURAL SCIENCE

Though theology was considered the most important subject of study, medieval scholars also turned their minds to natural science. Since medieval culture was synthetic rather than experimental and inventive, scientific knowledge was drawn more from ancient manuscripts than from observation. The materials in this section are illustrative of medieval man's knowledge of and approach to nature.

Medieval Scientific Knowledge. One of the most popular volumes of the Middle Ages was an encyclopedia called *De Proprietatibus Rerum* ("Concerning the Properties of Things"), written about 1260 by a Franciscan friar, Bartholomew Anglicus. The following selections are representative of Bartholomew's scientific knowledge in several different fields.[13]

Elements are simple, and the least particles of a body that is compound. And it is called least touching us, for it is not perceived by wits of feeling. For it is the least part and last in undoing of the body, as it is first in composition. And is called simple, not for an element is simple without any composition, but for it hath no parts that compound it, that be diverse in kind and in number as some medlied bodies have: as it fareth in metals of the which some parts be diverse; for some part is air, and some is earth. But each part of fire is fire, and so of others. Elements are four, and so there are four qualities of elements, of the which every body is composed and made as of matter. The four elements are Earth, Water, Fire, and Air, of the which each hath his proper qualities. Four be called the first and principal qualities, that is, hot, cold, dry, and moist: they are called the first qualities because they slide first from the elements into the things made of elements. Two of these qualities are called Active— heat and coldness. The others are dry and wetness and are called Passive. . . .

Heliotrope is a precious stone, and is green, and sprinkled with red drops, and veins of the color of blood. If it be put in water before the sunbeams, it maketh the water seethe in the vessel that it is in, and resolveth it as it were into mist, and soon after it is resolved into rain-drops. Also it seemeth that this same stone may do wonders, for if it be put in a basin with clear water, it changeth the sunbeams by rebounding of the air, and seemeth to shadow them, and breedeth in the air red and sanguine color, as though the sun

were in eclipse and darkened. An herb of the same name, with certain enchantments, doth beguile the sight of men that look thereon, and maketh a man that beareth it not to be seen. . . .

The sapphire is a precious stone, and is blue in color, most like to heaven in fair weather, and clear, and is best among precious stones, and most apt and able to fingers of kings. Its virtue is contrary to venom and quencheth it every deal. And if thou put an addercop [spider] in a box, and hold a very sapphire of Ind at the mouth of the box any while, by virtue thereof the addercop is overcome and dieth, as it were suddenly. And this same I have seen proved oft in many and divers places. . . .

The spittle of a man fasting hath a manner strength of privy infection. For it grieveth and hurteth the blood of a beast, if it come into a bleeding wound, and is medlied with the blood. And that, peradventure, is, as saith Avicenna, by reason of rawness. For raw humor medlied with blood that hath perfect digestion, is contrary thereto in its quality, and disturbeth the temperance thereof, as authors say. And therefore it is that holy men tell that the spittle of a fasting man slayeth serpents and adders, and is venom to venomous beasts, as saith Basil. . . .

The liver hath name, for fire hath place therein, that passeth up anon to the brain, and cometh thence to the eyes, and to the other wits and limbs. And the liver, by its heat, draweth woose and juice and turneth it into blood, and serveth the body and members therewith, to the use of feeding. In the liver is the place of voluptuousness and liking of the flesh. The ends of the liver hight fibra, for they are straight and passing as tongs, and beclip the stomach, and give heat to digestion of meat: and they hight fibra, because the necromancers brought them to the altars of their god Phoebus and offered them there, and then they had answers. . . .

The liver is the chief fundament of kindly virtue, and greatest helper of the first digestion in the stomach, and the liver maketh perfectly the second digestion in the stomach, in the hollowness of its own substance, and departeth clean and pured, from unclean and unpured, and sendeth feeding to all the members, and exciteth love or bodily lust, and receiveth divers passions. Then the liver is a noble and precious member, by whose alteration the body is altered, and the liver sendeth feeding and virtues of feeding to the other members, to the nether without mean, and to the other, by mean of the heart.

Some men ween, that the milt is cause of laughing. For by the spleen we are moved to laugh, by the gall we are wroth, by the heart we are wise, by the brain we feel, by the liver we love. . . .

If the crocodile findeth a man by the brim of the water, or by the cliff, he slayeth him if he may, and then he weepeth upon him, and swalloweth him at the last.

The Dragon is most greatest of all serpents, and oft he is drawn out of his den, and riseth up into the air, and the air is moved by him, and also the sea swelleth against his venom, and he hath a crest with a little mouth, and draweth his breath at small pipes and straight, and reareth his tongue, and hath teeth like a saw, and hath strength, and not only in teeth, but also in his tail, and grieveth both with biting and with stinging, and hath not so much venom as other serpents: for to the end to slay anything, to him venom is not needful, for whom he findeth he slayeth, and the elephant is not secure of him, for all his greatness of body. Oft four or five of them fasten their tails together, and rear up their heads, and sail over sea and over rivers to get good meat.

Between elephants and dragons is everlasting fighting, for the dragon with his tail bindeth and spanneth the elephant, and the elephant with his foot and with his nose throweth down the dragon, and the dragon bindeth and spanneth the elephant's legs, and maketh him fall, but the dragon buyeth it full sore: for while he slayeth the elephant, the elephant falleth upon him and slayeth him. Also the elephant seeing the dragon upon a tree, busieth him to break the tree to smite the dragon, and the dragon leapeth upon the elephant, and busieth him to bite him between the nostrils, and assaileth the elephant's eyes, and maketh him blind sometime, and leapeth upon him sometime behind and biteth him and sucketh his blood. And at the last after long fighting the elephant waxeth feeble for great blindness, in so much that he fallen upon the dragon, and slayeth in his dying the dragon that him slayeth.

The cause why the dragon desireth his blood, is coldness of the elephant's blood, by the which the dragon desireth to cool himself. Jerome saith, that the dragon is a full thirsty beast, insomuch that unneth he may have water enough to quench his great thirst; and openeth his mouth therefore against the wind, to quench the burning of his thirst in that wise. Therefore when he seeth ships sail in the sea in great wind, he flieth against the sail to take their cold wind, and overthroweth the ship sometimes for greatness of body, and strong rose against the sail. And when the shipmen see the dragon come nigh, and know his coming by the water that swelleth ayenge him, they strike the sail anon, and scape in that wise.

VIII
Geographical Horizons

THE Widder Douglas always told me the earth was round like a ball, but I never took any stock in a lot of them superstitions o' hers, and of course I paid no attention to that one, because I could see myself that the world was the shape of a plate, and flat. I used to go up on the hill, and take a look around and prove it for myself, because I reckon the best way to get a sure thing on a fact is to go and examine for yourself, and not take anybody's say-so. But I had to give in now that the widder was right. That is, she was right as to the rest of the world, but she warn't right about the part our village is in; that part is the shape of a plate, and flat, I take my oath!

Tom Sawyer Abroad

CONTENTS

[171]

QUESTIONS FOR STUDY

PART I

1. *To be handed in at class.* Draw a sketch map of the world as described in the *Polychronicon* of Ranulf Higden. On this sketch map locate the following:

Europe	Africa	River Thanays	Paradise
Asia	River Nile	India	Pillars of Hercules

2. Describe the cosmology of the Middle Ages. What seem to have been some of the sources for this medieval conception of the Universe?

3. Compare the attitudes of Mandeville and Pegolotti towards the Far East and its marvels.

PART II

4. What were the reasons which led Prince Henry the Navigator to act as a patron of discovery?

5. Compare the motives of the explorers as described by Barlow and Hakluyt (in the *Voyages*) with those of Prince Henry.

6. Contrast the geographical horizons of Higden and Galvano.

7. How does Hakluyt's attitude to the world differ from that of Higden?

8. What geographical authorities served as guides for the early explorers?

9. For what reasons did Hakluyt urge the English to attempt Western discoveries?

The face of the earth is the stage upon which the drama of history is enacted. To study history without a knowledge of its setting is to attend a play blind-folded. The surface, sub-surface, and climate of the earth exercise upon man's development an inexorable influence, the effect of which he can modify only to a limited extent through technological development. But man's environment, the world around him, remains one of the most important of historical determinants.

The influence of geography can be seen at work in many ways. Not only do the greater land masses of the earth lie north of the equator, but also these masses are largely within the temperate zone. South of the equator, on the other hand, the land masses are smaller and lie for the most part in the tropics, whose climate is much less conducive to energetic activity. Geography thus helps to explain the historic location of the most dynamic and powerful civilizations of the world in the northern hemisphere.

In a more restricted sense the facts of geography can be seen shaping the course of the great discoveries of the fifteenth and sixteenth centuries, to be encountered in the second half of this problem. The very pattern of these voyages remains at least partially a mystery without a knowledge of the winds and currents of the world's oceans. The Dutch and the English, with the advantage of their heavier ships, were able in turn to circumvent the Portuguese monopoly of the earlier route to the fabulous Indies by rounding the Cape and running before the west winds of the "roaring forties." When they had reached the longitude of Java, they worked the trade winds into the archipelago through the Straits of Sunda between Java and Sumatra. And finally, the whole outburst of exploring activity was in a sense a function of the technology of maritime Europe, since it slowly but dramatically equipped the seafarers of Europe to open up the world.

The effect of geography on history may also be seen at work in a more indirect fashion. Scholars frequently point to geographic influence upon art, religion, political institutions, and racial characteristics. The pagan northman's hell was frigid; the hell of the primitive desert dweller was torrid. The latter's environment has always impressed upon him the vastness and singleness of the universe, a fact which helps to explain the frequency of monotheistic religion among nomads and desert peoples. This effect of environment on people is colorfully expressed in the Indians' belief that only "mad-dogs and Englishmen go out in the noon-day sun."

Another facet of the relationship of geography to history—namely, what man at successive epochs in his history has thought his world to be—is of equal importance to the historian. His geographical concepts, which are constantly changing, have been not merely a product of man's civilization but also a major factor in the development of his philosophy and religion, his arts and science. For man's conception of his relation to his gods and to nature is in great part dependent upon his conception of his world, which is, in turn, a function of his knowledge of the earth. The geographical horizon of a civilization has thus ever been limited.

This sense of space has varied greatly in different ages in the world's history. Primitive peoples were at all times limited literally by the physical horizon of the area in which they struggled to survive. The next stage, regional sense of space, appeared in the ancient world, particularly among the Romans, whose "geography" centered on the known world of the Mediterranean basin with little knowledge and less concern for the area beyond Rome's frontiers.

Obviously, the complex role of geography in the historical process cannot be fully appraised in the compass of a single problem; such an appraisal requires continuous attention, throughout the study of history. The purpose of this Problem is specific: to examine the geographic horizons of the Middle Ages and of the Age of Discovery which followed. It is intended first to inquire into the knowledge of the world possessed by the men of the period in which flourished feudalism, scholasticism, and the Church Universal; then to observe the transition to a period in which Europe's geographical horizons expanded from something more than a regional sense of space.

Part I.   THE GEOGRAPHY OF THE MIDDLE AGES

The Middle Ages possessed a wealth of geographical information. Chroniclers, scholastics, travellers, and scientists included quantities of data on the world and the universe in their writings. Frequently maps of the world are attempted in monastic manuscripts. The following selections from medieval geographical authorities reveal man's attitude to his world and the extent of his geographical horizon.

A.   THE SOURCES OF MEDIEVAL GEOGRAPHICAL KNOWLEDGE

His life and work in the world around him remained always the silent inspiration for much of the geographical knowledge of medieval man. But his world-view was derived also from the written records at his disposal.

1. *The Bible and the Church Fathers.* The Bible was of primary importance as a source of geographical and cosmological lore in the Middle Ages. Among the Church Fathers St. Augustine (345–450) in Book XVI, Chapter 9, *The City of God* discusses one of the more controversial questions in medieval cosmology: "whether there be any inhabitants of the earth called the Antipodes." [1]

(*Genesis, I, 6–17*) And God said, Let there be a firmament in the midst of the waters, and let it divide the waters from the waters. And God made the firmament and divided the waters which were under the firmament from the waters which were above the firmament: and it was so. And God called the firmament Heaven. . . . And God said, Let the waters under the heaven be gathered together unto one place, and let the dry land appear: and it was so. And God called the dry land Earth; and the gathering together of the water called the Seas. . . . And God said, Let there be lights in the firmament of the heaven to divide the day from the night; and let them be for signs, and for seasons, and for days, and years. . . . And God made two great lights; the greater light to rule the day, and the lesser light to rule the night: he made the stars also. And God set them in the firmament of the heaven to give light upon the earth. . . .

(*Acts, XVII, 24–26*) God that made the world and all things therein, seeing that He is Lord of heaven and earth, dwelleth not in temples made with hands; . . . And hath made of one blood all nations of men for to dwell on all the face of the earth, and hath determined the times before appointed, and the bounds of their habitation.

(*Ezekiel, V, 5*) Thus said the Lord God; This is Jerusalem: and I have set it in the midst of the nations and countries that are round about her.

(*St. Augustine*) But whereas they fable of a people that inhabit that land where the sun rises, when it sets with us, and go with their feet toward ours, it is incredible. They have no authority for it, but only conjecture that such a thing may be, because the earth hangs within the orbs of heaven, and each part of the world is above and below alike, and thence they gather that the other hemisphere cannot want inhabitants. Now they consider not that although that it be globous as ours is, yet it may be all covered with sea: and if it be bare, yet it follows not, that it is inhabited, seeing that the Scripture (that proves all that it says to be true, by the true events that it presages) never makes any mention of any such thing. And it were absurd to say that men might sail over that huge ocean and go and dwell there or that the race of the first man might people that part also.

2. *The Etymologies of Isidore of Seville (fl. 600–636)* Although the vogue for encyclopedias in the early Middle Ages is a subject in itself, they indicate to the student something of the intellectual condition of the times. The writer of the *Etymologies*, from which the following selections are taken, was an orthodox Spanish bishop who set out to preserve all the information, as he says, "about all that ought to be known." The twenty books of the *Etymologies* cover everything from grammar, rhetoric, and logic to man, the universe and household utensils. His geographical information, together with the rest of his work, became the standard work of reference for much of the Middle Ages.[2]

Book III Chapter 29. On the universe and its name.

1. *Mundus* (the universe) is that which is made up of the heavens and earth and the sea and all the heavenly bodies. And it is called *mundus* for the reason that it is always in *motion.* For no repose is granted to its elements.

Chapter 30. On the form of the universe.

1. The form of the universe is described as follows: as the universe rises toward the region of the north, so it slopes away toward the south; its head and face, as it were, is the east, and its back part the north.

Chapter 31. On the heavens and their name.

1. The philosophers have asserted that the heavens are round, in rapid motion, and made of fire, and that they are called by this name (*coelum*) because they have the forms of the stars fixed on them, like a dish with figures in relief (*coelatum*).

2. For God decked them with bright lights, and filled them with the glowing circles of the sun and moon, and adorned them with the glittering images of flashing stars.

Chapter 32. On the situation of the celestial sphere.

1. The sphere of the heavens is rounded and its center is the earth, equally shut in on every side. This sphere, they say, has neither beginning nor end, for the reason that being rounded like a circle it is not easily perceived where it begins or where it ends.

2. The philosophers have brought in the theory of seven heavens of the universe, that is, globes with planets moving harmoniously, and they assert that by their circles all things are bound together, and they think that these, being connected, and, as it were, fitted to one another, move backward and are borne with definite motions in contrary directions.

Chapter 33. On the motion of the same.

1. The sphere revolves on two axes, of which one is the northern, which never sets, and is called Boreas; the other is the southern, which is never seen, and is called Austronotius.

2. On these two poles the sphere of heaven moves, they say, and with its motion the stars fixed in it pass from the east all the way around to the west, the *septentriones* near the point of rest describing smaller circles.

Chapter 34. On the course of the same sphere.

1. The sphere of heaven, [moving] from the east towards the west, turns once in a day and night, in the space of twenty-four hours, within which the sun completes his swift revolving course over the lands and under the earth.

Chapter 35. On the swiftness of the heavens.

1. With such swiftness is the sphere of heaven said to run, that if the stars did not run against its headlong course in order to delay it, it would destroy the universe.

Chapter 36. On the axis of the heavens.

1. The axis is a straight line north, which passes through the center of the globe of the sphere, and is called axis because the sphere revolves on it like a wheel, or it may be because the Wain [constellation shaped like a wagon] is there.

Chapter 37. On the poles of the heavens.

1. The poles are little circles which run on the axis. Of these one is the northern which never sets and is called Boreas; the other is the southern which is never seen, and is called Austronotius.

Chapter 38. On the cardines of the heavens.

1. The *cardines* of the heavens are the ends of the axis, and are called *cardines* (hinges) because the heavens turn on them, or because they turn like the heart (*cor*).

Chapter 40. On the gates of the heavens.

1. There are two gates of the heavens, the east and the west. For by one the sun appears, by the other he retires.

Chapter 42. On the four parts of the heavens.

1. The *climata* of the heavens, that is, the tracts or parts, are four, of which the first part is the eastern, where some stars rise; the second, the western, where some stars set; the third, the northern, where the sun comes in the longer days; the fourth, the southern, where the sun comes in the time of the longer nights. . . .

4. There are also other *climata* of the heavens, seven in number, as if seven lines from east to west, under which the manners of men are dissimilar, and animals of different species appear; they are named from certain famous places, of which the first is Meroe; the second, Siene; the third, Catachoras, that is Africa; the fourth, Rhodus; the fifth, Hellespontus; the sixth, Mesopontus; the seventh, Boristhenes.

Chapter 43. On the hemispheres.

1. A hemisphere is half a sphere. The hemisphere above the earth is that part of the heavens the whole of which is seen by us; the hemisphere under the earth is that which cannot be seen as long as it is under the earth.

Chapter 44. On the five circles of the heavens.

1. There are five zones in the heavens, according to the differences of which certain parts of the earth are inhabitable, because of their moderate temperature, and certain parts are uninhabitable because of extremes of heat and cold.

And these are called zones or circles for the reason that they exist on the circumference of the sphere.

2. The first of these circles is called the Arctic, because the constellations of the Arcti are visible enclosed within it; the second is called the summer tropic, because in this circle the sun makes summer in northern regions, and does not pass beyond it but immediately returns, and from this it is called tropic.

3. The third circle is called *equinoctialis* in Latin, for the reason that when the sun comes to this circle it makes equal day and night and by this circle the sphere is seen to be equally divided. The fourth circle is called Antarctic, for the reason that it is opposite to the circle which we call Arctic.

4. The fifth circle is called the winter tropic which in the Latin is *hiemalis* or *brumalis*, because when the sun comes to this circle it makes winter for those who are in the north and summer for those who dwell in the parts of the south.

Chapter 47. On the size of the sun.

1. The size of the sun is greater than that of the earth and so from the moment when it rises it appears equally to east and west at the same time. And as to its appearing to us about a cubit in width, it is necessary to reflect how far the sun is from the earth, which distance causes it to seem small to us.

Chapter 48. On the size of the moon.

1. The size of the moon also is said to be less than that of the sun. For since the sun is higher than the moon and still appears to us larger than the moon, if it should approach near to us it would be plainly seen to be much larger than the moon. Just as the sun is larger than the earth, so the earth is in some degree larger than the moon.

Chapter 49. On the nature of the sun.

1. The sun, being made of fire, heats to a whiter glow because of the excessive speed of its circular motion. And its fire, philosophers declare, is fed with water, and it receives the virtue of light and heat from an element opposed to it. Whence we see that it is often wet and dewy.

Book XIII Chapter 12. On the waters.

2. The two most powerful elements of human-life are fire and water, whence they who are forbidden fire and water are seriously punished.

3. The element of water is master of all the rest. For the waters temper the heavens, fertilize the earth, incorporate air in their exhalations, climb aloft and claim the heavens; for what is more marvelous than the waters keeping their place in the heavens!

4. It is too small a thing to come to such a height; they carry with them thither swarms of fishes; pouring forth, they are the cause of all growth on the earth. They produce fruits, they make fruit trees and herbs grow, they scour away filth, wash away sin, and give drink to all living things.

Chapter 13. On the different qualities of waters.

5. Linus, a fountain of Arcadia, does not allow miscarriages to take place. In Sicily are two springs, of which one makes the sterile woman fertile, the other makes the fertile, sterile. In Thessaly are two rivers; they say that sheep drinking from one become black; from the other, white; from both, parti-colored. . . .

10. Hot springs in Sardinia cure the eyes; they betray thieves, for their guilt is revealed by blindness. They say there is a spring in Epirus in which lighted torches are extinguished, and torches that are extinguished are lighted. Among the Garamantes they say there is a spring so cold in the daytime that it cannot be drunk, so hot at night that it cannot be touched.

Chapter 14. On the sea.

2. . . . The depth of the sea varies; still the level of its surface is invariable.

3. Moreover that the sea does not increase, though it receives all streams and all springs, is accounted for in this way; partly that its very greatness does not feel the waters flowing in; secondly, because the bitter water consumes the fresh that is added, or that the clouds draw up much water to themselves, or that the winds carry it off, and the sun partly dries it up; lastly, because the water leaks through certain secret holes in the earth, and turns and runs back to the sources of rivers and to the springs.

B. THE EXTENT OF MEDIEVAL GEOGRAPHICAL KNOWLEDGE

The *Polychronicon* of Ranulf Higden, an English Benedictine monk, is an universal history prefaced by a long summary of the geographical knowledge of the fourteenth century. The following selections from his work provide a good indication of the world as it seemed to the more educated man of the time.[3]

. . . all the world hath 30 famous seas, 72 isles, 40 famous hills, 78 provinces, 370 noble cities, 57 great rivers, and 125 different nations. The circumference of this world is 300 and 15 times 100,000 paces [about 31,500 miles]. The length of the habitable earth from east to west, that is from Inde to the Pillars of Hercules in the Gaditan Sea [Atlantic Ocean], is 8 times 5 times 103 score and 18 miles [82,418 miles]. . . . The breadth of the earth from south to north, that is from the gulf of Ethiopia, land of the black men, to the source of the river called the Thanays [Don], is less than half the length aforesaid, and it containeth 50 times 462 miles. Also it is found that the deepest place in the Mediterranean Sea containeth the space of 15 furlongs by a plumb of lead. . . . Then, half the thickness of the earth inward and downright is 3,245 miles and somewhat over, about half a mile. So if Hell is in the middle of the earth downright, we may know how many miles it is to Hell.

For the division of the earth, it is to be known that the great sea of ocean surroundeth the earth all about, and the earth is divided into 3 great parts, namely Asia, Europe, and Africa. These 3 parts be not all even and alike in muchness; for Asia, one of the three, containeth half the earth, and stretcheth from the south by the east to the north, and is enclosed about with the sea of ocean, but it endeth westward at the great sea. Its ends be the mouth of the river Nile in the south and of the river Thanays [Don] in the north. That other part, Europe, stretcheth downward from the river Thanays by the north ocean to the coasts of Spain, and joineth the great sea by east and south, and endeth in the island called Gades [Cadiz]. Africa, the third part, stretcheth from the west to the south anon to the coast of Egypt, and these two parts, Africa and Europe, be parted in twain by an arm of the sea. . . . Asia is most in quantity, Europe is less but equal in number of people. But Africa is least of all the three parts both in place and number of people; and therefore some men, that knoweth men and lands, account but two parts of the earth only, Asia and Europe; and they account Africa a part of Europe; for Africa is narrow in breadth,

and evil doers, corrupt air, and wild and venemous beasts dwell therein.

. . . wise men conclude that the earthly Paradise [Garden of Eden] is in the uttermost end of the east, and that it is a great country of the earth no less than Inde or Egypt: a place large and convenable for all mankind to live in, if mankind had not sinned. . . . There is health, for the air is neither too hot nor too cold, so that nothing that liveth may die therein . . . Every tree therein is sweet to eat and fair to see. Therein is comfort and security. . . . Our way to Paradise is completely blocked because of the sin of our forefather; and it is closed about with a wall of fire, the burning of which archeth to Heaven, as some men opine. Paradise is closed with that wall to keep out mankind; angels stand on that wall to guard Paradise, that no evil spirits may come therein.

. . . Inde hath many kings and people. Some people till the earth, some use merchandise, some follow knighthood and chivalry, and some be great clerks. . . . There be men of five cubits height that neither languish nor die. Also there be men of the measure of one cubit called pygmies, who beget children when three years of age and grow old in five years. Also there be Satyrs and other divers men, grisly and awesome in shape. . . . Also some hath heads like hounds, and the voice they maketh is liker to an hound's barking than to a man's voice. . . . Others there be that have no mouths and live by odor and smells. . . . In some parts of Inde be men that have the soles of their feet overturned and eight fingers on one hand. . . . That land beareth corn twice a year, bringeth forth men of spotted color, and hath in it nightingales, elephants, pepper, precious stones, beryls, chrysophrase, carbuncles, adamants, and hills of gold. Nevertheless it is impossible to go to them because of dragons and griffons and monstrous giants. . . .

C.   THE QUALITY OF MEDIEVAL GEOGRAPHICAL KNOWLEDGE

Earlier documents have provided considerable evidence on the nature and accuracy of medieval geographical knowledge. The documents in this section provide more direct testimony to the extremes of fact and fancy to be found in the geographical lore of the Middle Ages.

1. *The Travels of Sir John Mandeville.* The *Travels,* which date from the first half of the fourteenth century, are now known to represent an ingenious compilation of earlier travels. Nevertheless, the intrinsic value of the book remains, for it furnishes an entertaining picture of the world as the simple layman saw it—vast, mysterious, and ever-wonderful to behold.[4]

There be also in that country [Indo-China] a kind of snails that be so great, that many persons may lodge them in their shells, as men would do in a little house. And other snails there be that be full great but not so huge as the other. And of these snails, and of great white worms that have black heads that be as great as a man's thigh, and some less as great worms that men find there in woods, men make viand royal for the king and for other great lords. And if a man that is married die in that country, men bury his wife with him all quick; for men say there, that it is reason that she make him company in that other world as she did in this. . . .

Also when the emperor [of Cathay] goeth from one country to another, as I have told you here before, and he pass through cities and towns, every man maketh a fire before his door, and putteth therein powder of good gums that be sweet smelling, for to make good savor to the emperor. And all the people kneel down against him, and do him great reverence. And there, where religious Christian men dwell, as they do in many cities in the land, they go before him with procession with cross and holy water, and they sing, *Veni creator spiritus!* with an high voice, and go towards him.

And when he heareth them, he commandeth to his lords to ride beside him, that the religious men may come to him. And when they be nigh him with the cross, then he doth adown his galiot that sits on his head in manner of a chaplet, that is made of gold and precious stones and great pearls, and it is so rich, that men prize it to the value of a realm in that country. And then he kneeleth to the cross. And then the prelate of the religious men saith before him certain orisons, and giveth him a blessing with the cross; and he inclineth to the blessing full devoutly. And then the prelate giveth him some manner fruit, to the number of nine, in a platter of silver, with pears or apples, or other manner fruit. And he taketh one.

And then men give to the other lords that be about him. For the custom is such, that no stranger shall come before him, but if he give him some manner thing, after the old law that saith, *Nemo accedat in conspectu meo vacuus.* And then the emperor saith to the religious men, that they withdraw them again, that they be neither hurt nor harmed of the great multitude of horses that come behind him. And also, in the same manner, do the religious men that dwell there, to the empresses that pass by them, and to his eldest son. And to every of them they present fruit.

And ye shall understand, that the people that he hath so many hosts of, about him and about his wives and his son, they dwell not continually with him. But always, when him liketh, they be sent for. And after, when they have done, they return to their own households, save only they that be dwelling with him in household for to serve him and his wives and his sons for to govern his household. And albeit, that the others be departed from him after that they have performed their service, yet there abideth continually with

him in court 50,000 men at horse and 200,000 men a foot, without minstrels and those that keep wild beasts and divers birds, of the which I have told you the number before.

Under the firmament is not so great a lord, ne so mighty, ne so rich as is the great Chan; not Prester John, that is emperor of the high Ind, ne the Soldan of Babylon, ne the Emperor of Persia. All these ne be not in comparison to the great Chan, neither of might, ne of noblesse, ne of royalty, ne of riches; for in all these he passeth all earthly princes. Wherefore it is great harm that he believeth not faithfully in God. And natheles he will gladly hear speak of God. And he suffereth well that Christian men dwell in his lordship, and that men of his faith be made Christian men if they will, throughout all his country; for he defendeth no man to hold no law other than him liketh.

In that country some men hath an hundred wives, some sixty, some more, some less. And they take the next of their kin to their wives, save only that they out-take their mothers, their daughters, and their sisters of the mother's side; but their sisters on the father's side of another woman they may well take, and their brothers' wives also after their death, and their step-mothers also in the same wise.

The folk of that country use all long clothes without furs. And they be clothed with precious cloths of Tartary, and of cloths of gold. And their clothes be slit at the side, and they be fastened with laces of silk. And they clothe them also with pilches, and the hide without; and they use neither cape ne hood. And in the same manner as the men go, the women go, so that no man may unneth know the men from the women, save only those women that be married, that bear the token upon their heads of a man's foot, in sign that they be under man's foot and under subjection of man.

And their wives ne dwell not together, but every of them by herself; and the husband may lie with whom of them that him liketh. Everych hath his house, both man and woman. And their houses be made round of staves, and it hath a round window above that giveth them light, and also that serveth for deliverance of smoke. And the heling of their houses and the walls and the doors be all of wood. And when they go to war, they lead their houses with them upon chariots, as men do tents or pavilions. And they make their fire in the midst of their houses. . . .

2. *Pegolotti's Book of Descriptions, c. 1340.* It has been said that the century from 1245 to 1345 was unique in the history of medieval travel, for the two great centers of the civilized world, Cathay and Christendom, were

brought into more intimate contact than they had been since the days of Alexander or would be again until the Great Voyages. While the Italian merchants who had formerly dealt with western outposts of the eastern trade in the Levant chaffered, "Italian friars said Mass in the ports and cities of India and China." The friars and the Poles led the way in the thirteenth century, and the latter's travels throughout the vast empire of Kubla Khan remain the great travel epic of the Middle Ages. The implications of the knowledge thus afforded can be traced in the writings of the merchant-travelers of Venice and Genoa who followed these pioneers. One of them, Francesco Pegolotti, a factor for the Bardi banking house of Florence, represented his firm in Cyprus and Armenia. He wrote the handbook quoted below for his fellow merchants about 1340.[5]

CHAPTER I. Information regarding the journey to Cathay, for such as will go by Tana [Genoese trading post on the sea of Azov] and come back with goods.

In the first place, from Tana to Gittarchan [Astrakhan] may be twenty-five days with an ox-wagon, and from ten to twelve days with a horse-wagon. On the road you will find plenty of *Moccols* [Mongols], that is to say, of *gens d'armes*. And from Gittarchan to Sara may be a day by river, and from Sara to Saracanco, also by river, eight days. You can do this either by land or by water; but by water you will be at less charge for your merchandise.

From Saracanco to Organci may be twenty days' journey in camel-wagon. It will be well for anyone travelling with merchandise to go to Organci, for in that city there is a ready sale for goods. From Organci to Oltrarre is thirty-five to forty days in camel-wagons. But if when you leave Saracanco you go direct to Oltrarre, it is a journey of fifty days only, and if you have no merchandise it will be better to go this way than to go by Organci.

From Oltrarre to Armalec is forty-five days' journey with pack-asses, and every day you find Moccols. And from Armalec to Camexu is seventy days with asses, and from Camexu until you come to a river called . . . is forty-five days on horse-back; and then you can go down the river to Cassai, and there you can dispose of the *sommi* of silver that you have with you, for that is a most active place of business. After getting to Cassai you carry on with the money which you get for the *sommi* of silver which you sell there; and this money is made of paper, and is called *balishi*. And four pieces of this money are worth one *sommo* of silver in the province of Cathay. And from Cassai to Gamalec [Cambalec], which is the capital city of the country of Cathay, is thirty days' journey.

CHAPTER II. Things needful for merchants who desire to make the journey to Cathay above described.

In the first place, you must let your beard grow long and not shave. And at Tana you should furnish yourself with a dragoman. And you must not try to save money in the matter of dragomen by taking a bad one instead of a good one. For the additional wages of the good one will not cost you so much as you will save by having him. And besides the dragoman it will be well to take at least two good men servants, who are acquainted with the Cumanian tongue. And if the merchant likes to take a woman with him from Tana, he can do so; if he does not like to take one there is no obligation, only if he does take one he will be kept much more comfortably than if he does not take one. Howbeit, if he do take one, it will be well that she be acquainted with the Cumanian tongue as well as the men.

And from Tana travelling to Gittarchan you should take with you twenty-five days' provisions, that is to say, flour and salt fish, for as to meat you will find enough of it at all the places along the road. And so also at all the chief stations noted in going from one country to another in the route, according to the number of days set down above, you should furnish yourself with flour and salt fish; other things you will find in sufficiency, and especially meat.

The road you travel from Tana to Cathay is perfectly safe, whether by day or night, according to what the merchants say who have used it. Only if the merchant, in going or coming, should die upon the road, everything belonging to him will become perquisite of the lord of the country in which he dies, and the officers of the lord will take possession of all. And in like manner if he die in Cathay. But if his brother be with him, or an intimate friend and comrade calling himself his brother, then to such an one they will surrender the property of the deceased, and so it will be rescued.

And there is another danger: this is when the lord of the country dies, and before the new lord who is to have the lordship is proclaimed; during such intervals there have sometimes been irregularities practised on the Franks, and other foreigners. (They call *Franks* all the Christians of these parts from Romania westward.) And neither will the roads be safe to travel until the other lord be proclaimed who is to reign in room of him who is deceased.

Cathay is a province which contained a multitude of cities and towns. Among others there is one in particular, that is to say the capital city, to which is great resort of merchants, and in which there is a vast amount of trade; and this city is called Cambalec. And the said city hath a circuit of one hundred miles, and is all full of people and houses and of dwellers in the said city.

You may calculate that a merchant with a dragoman, and with two men servants, and with goods to the value of twenty-five thousand golden florins, should spend on his way to Cathay from sixty to eighty *sommi* of silver, and not more if he manage well; and for all the road back again from Cathay to Tana, including the expenses of living and the pay of servants, and all other charges, the cost will be about five *sommi* per head of pack animals, or something less. And you may reckon the *sommo* to be worth five golden florins. You may reckon also that each ox-wagon will require one ox, and will carry ten cantars Genoese weight; and the camel-wagon will require three camels, and will carry thirty cantars Genoese weight; and the horse-wagon will require one horse, and will commonly carry six and half cantars of silk, at 250 Genoese pounds to the cantar. And a bale of silk may be reckoned at between 110 and 115 Genoese pounds.

You may reckon also that from Tana to Sara the road is less safe than on any other part of the journey; and yet even when this part of the road is at its worst, if you are some sixty men in the company you will go as safely as if you were in your own house.

Anyone from Genoa or from Venice, wishing to go to the places above-named, and to make the journey to Cathay, should carry linens with him, and if he visit Organci he will dispose of these well. In Organci he should purchase *sommi* of silver, and with these he should proceed with-out making any further investment, unless it be some bales of the very finest stuffs which go in small bulk, and cost no more for carriage that coarser stuffs would do.

Merchants who travel this road can ride on horseback or on asses, or mounted in any way that they list to be mounted.

Whatever silver the merchants may carry with them as far as Cathay the lord of Cathay will take from them and put into his treasury. And to merchants who thus bring silver they give that paper money of theirs in exchange. This is of yellow paper, stamped with the seal of the lord aforesaid. And this money is called *balishi,* and with this money you can readily buy silk and all other merchandise that you have a desire to buy. And all the people of the country are bound to receive it. And yet you shall not pay a higher price for your goods because your money is of paper. And of the said paper money there are three kinds, one being worth more than another, according to the value which has been established for each by that lord.

And you may reckon that you can buy for one *sommo* of silver nineteen or twenty pounds of Cathay silk, when reduced to Genoese weight, and that the *sommo* should weigh eight and a half ounces of Genoa, and should be of the alloy of eleven ounces and seventeen deniers to the pound.

You may reckon also that in Cathay you should get three or three and a half pieces of damasked silk for a *sommo;* and from three and a half to five pieces of *nacchetti* of silk and gold, likewise for a *sommo* of silver.

Part II. THE AGE OF DISCOVERY

The rate and extent of geographical advance which began in fifteenth-century Europe was little short of revolutionary. Although a multitude of factors—political, economic, and technological—contributed to this development, two specifically geographical stimuli may be singled out. The first was academic in character—the scholarly revival of classical and medieval geographical lore. The second was the mariners of the seaports of western Europe, whose voyages into the unknown helped roll back the curtain. Early successes turned interest into enthusiasm and with some navigation became a consuming passion. The European states did not drop their religious quarrels and dynastic wars, but the exploits of adventurous explorers in the fifteenth and sixteenth centuries were of such significance for the development of western civilization that the historians have often termed this period the Age of Discovery.

A. PORTUGAL PIONEERS

Prince Henry the Navigator (1394–1460), a younger son of the Portuguese royal house, was among the first great patrons of exploration. Eschewing politics, marriage, and the court, he devoted his whole energy to the promotion of geographical and navigational knowledge. In him and under his auspices were profitably blended the academic and nautical strains whose union meant so much for geographical progress. Henry's labors were recorded in the contemporary *Chronicles of Azurara,* a selection from which is given below.[6]

The reasons which led the Infante to seek the lands of Guinea; how this enterprise was begun, and how Gil Eannes was the first to round Cape Bojador.

We consider that we know things when we know him who has accomplished them and the object for which they were accomplished. In the foregoing chapters we have shown you the Infante Dom Henrique as chief artisan of these things in making him known to you as well as was in our power; and in this chapter it is proper that you should know why he accomplished these things.

You must take good note that the magnanimity of this prince constrained him always to begin, and lead to a good conclusion, high exploits; and for this reason, after the taking of Ceuta, he had always at sea ships armed against the Infidels. And because he desired to know what lands there were beyond the Canary Isles and a cape which was called Bojador, for up to that time no one knew, whether by writing or the memory of any man, what there might be beyond this cape.

Some believed that St. Brandan had passed it; others said that two galleys had gone thither and had never returned. But it seems to us that this cannot be in any way true, for it is not credible that if the said galleys had gone thither, other ships would not have undertaken to discover what had become of them. And the Infante Dom Henrique desired to know the truth of this; for it seemed to him that if he or some other lord did not essay to discover this, no sailor or merchant would undertake this effort, for it is very sure that these do not think to navigate otherwhere than to places where they already know that they will find their profit. And seeing that no other prince was concerning himself with the matter, he sent his own ships to these countries in order to acquire certitude, and this for the service of God and of the King Dom Duarte, his brother and seigneur, who was reigning at this time. And this was the first reason of his enterprise.

And the second was the thought that if in these territories there should be any population of Christians, or any harbors where men could enter without peril, they could bring back to the realm many merchandises at little cost, by reason that there would be no other persons on these coasts who would negotiate with them; and that in like manner one could carry to these regions merchandise of the realm, of which the traffic would be of great profit to the natives.

The third reason was founded on this: that it was said that the power of the Moors of this land of Africa was very much greater than was generally thought, and that there were among them neither Christians nor other races. And

because every wise man is moved by desire to know the strength of his enemy, the Infante devised means to send his people in quest of information, in order to know the full extent of the Infidels' power.

The fourth reason was this: during one and thirty years of battles with the Moors the Infante had never found Christian king or seigneur, outside this kingdom, who, for the love of Our Lord Jesus Christ, was willing to aid him in this war. He desired to know whether in those regions there might be any Christian princes in whom the charity and love of Christ were strong enough to cause them to aid him against these enemies of the faith.

The fifth reason was his great desire to increase the holy faith in Our Lord Jesus Christ, and to lead to this faith all souls desirous of being saved, recognizing that the whole mystery of the Incarnation, the death, and the passion of Our Lord Jesus Christ took place to this end: namely, that lost souls should be saved; and the Infante was fain, by his efforts and his expenditure, to lead these souls into the true path, understanding that man could render the Lord no greater service. For if God has promised a hundred treasures in return for one, it is just that we should believe that for so many treasures—which is to say, for so many souls which were saved by the agency of this prince—there would be in the Kingdom of God as many hundreds of rewards, which would permit his soul, after this life, to be glorified in the celestial kingdom. For myself, who am writing this history, I have seen so many men and women of these regions converted to the holy faith that, even if this prince were pagan, the prayers of these men and women would be enough to save him. And I have seen not only these people, but also their children and their grandchildren; and they had all become true Christians, as though the Divine grace were awaiting in them the moment when they were given clear knowledge of themselves.

[The writer concludes this chapter with a sixth reason, from which, it seems to him, all the others proceed: the astrological reason, on which he enlarges, giving copious explanations, finally arriving at the conclusion that, according to the disposition of the planets:]

. . . this prince was bound to engage in great and noble conquests, and above all was he bound to attempt the discovery of things which were hidden from other men, and secret . . . and all his exploits and conquests would be loyally accomplished, giving full satisfaction to his King and seigneur.

[The Infante Dom Henrique, having completed his preparations in his town of Sagres, began to send his caravels and his men along the western coast of Africa, with the mission of rounding Cape Bojador, and bringing back word to him as to what they found beyond this limit, which no man until then had passed.]

. . . However, although many set out—and they were men who had won fair renown by their exploits in the trade of arms—none dared go beyond this cape. . . .

And this, to tell truth, was not by reason of any lack of courage or goodwill, but because they had to do with a thing entirely novel, which was yet mingled with ancient legends which had existed for generations among the mariners of the Spains. And although these legends were deceitful, the idea of discovering if they were true seemed full of menace; and it was doubtful who would be the first to be willing to risk his life in such an adventure.

"How shall we pass beyond the limits established by our elders?" they said. "What profit can the Infante win from the loss of our souls and our bodies? for plainly we should be as men taking their own lives. Have there not been in the Spains other princes or lords as desirous as the Infante of knowing these things? It is very sure that among so many such noble princes and lords, who have accomplished such high exploits, by which their memories are honored, some one of them all must have had the thought of such an enterprise. But assuredly perceiving the peril, and no hope of honor or profit, he ceased to think of it. This is clear," said the mariners; "beyond this cape there is no one, there is no population; the land is no less sandy than the deserts of Libya, where is no water at all, neither trees nor green herbs; and the sea is so shallow that at a league from the shore its depth is hardly a fathom. The tides are so strong that the ships which pass the cape will never be able to return. . . ."

. . . This dread was great in these mariners, threatened not alone by fear but by the shadow of fear. And this was the cause of great expense, since for twelve years the Infante continued his effort, sending his ships to these regions each year, with great expense to his revenue; and none of these ships dared to go beyond the cape, although they returned with honor, since to make up for the fact that they had not accomplished the mission with which their lord had charged them, some of them descended upon the coast of Granada, and others sailed upon the sea of the Levant until they made great capture of Infidels, with which they returned honorably to the kingdom.

. . . The Infante always welcomed with great patience the captains of the ships which he had sent to seek out these countries, never showing them any resentment, listening graciously to the tale of their adventures, and rewarding them as those who were serving him well. And immediately he sent them back again to make the same voyage, them or others of his household, upon his armed ships, insisting more and more strongly upon the mission to be accomplished, and promising each time greater rewards to those who should bring him the intelligence he desired.

And at last, after twelve years of effort, the Infante had a barque fitted out, appointing the captain his squire Gil Eannes, whom he afterwards knighted and rewarded largely. This captain made the same voyage that the others had made, and overcome by the same dread did not pass beyond the Canary Isles, where he took captives, and returned to the kingdom. And this took place in the year 1433 of Jesus Christ. But the following year the Infante again had the same barque fitted out, and sending for Gil Eannes, and speaking with him alone, he recommended him strongly to do all that was possible to go beyond the cape; and that even if he did no more on this voyage, that would seem to him sufficient.

"You cannot meet there a peril so great," said the Infante, "that the hope of reward shall not be even greater. In truth, I marvel at these imaginings which have possessed you all, and of matters so uncertain. If these things possessed any authority, even though that authority were small, I might still find excuse for you; but I am astonished to think that you have them from the opinion of some few mariners who know only the navigation of Flanders and other ports to which they are accustomed to resort, and do not know how to handle a compass or make use of a chart of the seas. Have, therefore, no fear of their opinion in undertaking your voyage, because, with the grace of God, you shall derive therefrom only honor and profit."

The Infante was possessed of great authority; his remonstrances, even the lightest, were for wise men of great weight. And this was proved on this occasion, for having heard these words Gil Eannes promised himself resolutely that he would never again appear before his lord without having accomplished the mission with which he had been charged. And it was even so, for on this voyage, disdaining all peril, he passed beyond the cape, where he found matters very different from what he and others had imagined. . . .

And on his return he related to the Infante how the voyage had passed; having lowered a small boat into the sea, he had approached the shore and had landed without finding any person or sign of population. "And because it seemed to me," said Gil Eannes, "that I ought to bring back some token of this country, since I was there, I gathered these plants, which in our kingdom we call roses of St. Mary."

He having thus related to the Infante the account of his voyage, the Infante straightway had a barinal fitted out, in which he sent Affonso Gonçalves Baldaya, his cup-bearer, and also Gil Eannes, in his caravel, commanding them to return thither, as indeed they did; and they found lands without habitations, but with imprints of the feet of men and camels. And because such were the orders they had received, or of necessity, they returned with this news, without having done any other thing worthy of being recounted.

B.   THE REST FOLLOW

The industrious activities of the Portuguese were soon imitated by the Spanish in the fifteenth century, and there followed the well known discoveries and conquests of da Gama, Columbus, Cortez, Pizarro, and their fellow *conquistadores*. The other nations of Europe soon took a lively interest in exploration.

1. *Roger Barlow, A Brief Somme of Geographie; 1540–41:* Roger Barlow, a wealthy English merchant, put together in this volume the results of his reading and his own experiences overseas for the purpose of persuading King Henry VIII to take an interest in discovering and establishing an all-English trade route to the East Indies. After a careful description of the world, he concluded his work with the following paragraphs.[7]

Now by this your Grace may well perceive what part of the universe is discovered and what there resteth for to discover. It is clearly seen by the cosmographia that, of the four parts of the world, the three parts be discovered. For out of Spain they sail all the Indies and seas occidental, and from Portugal they sail all the Indies and seas oriental. So that between the way of the orient and the way of the occident, they have compassed all the world; the one departing from Spain toward occident, and the other out of Portugal toward orient, they have met together. And also by the way of the meridian there is a great part discovered by the Spaniards; so there resteth this way of the north only for to discover, which resteth on to your Grace's charge, for that the situation of this realm toward that part is more apt than any other. . . .

And for such an enterprise no man should think upon the cost in comparison to the great profit that may thereby succeed, nor think the labor great where so much profit, honor, and glory may follow unto this our natural realm and king. And as for jeopardies and perils, this way of navigation well considered and pondered shall seem much less peril than all the other navigations, as it may be proved by very evident reasons. . . .

How much more should men count us for fearful and of little stomach to leave off such an enterprise which may be done with continual light [by sailing over the north pole]. Much more, passing this little space of navigation, which is accounted dangerous, may be 400 leagues before they come to the pole, and other as much after they have passed the pole, it is clear that from thenceforward the seas and land are temperate, as it is here in England. And then it shall be in the will of them that discover to choose the cold countries, temperate, or hot, in the degree that they will.

For once past the pole, they may choose at their pleasure to decline to what part they list, for if they will take toward the orient, they shall enjoy of the regions of the Tartars, which have their borders to the south. And from thence following the coast, they shall go to the lands of China, and from thence forward to the Cathay Oriental, which is of the main land the most oriental counting from our habitation. And if from thence they will continue their navigation, following the coast which turneth toward occident, they shall come to Malacca and from thence to all the Indies that we call oriental. And so continuing that coast, they may come home by the Cape of Good Hope, and so to have gone most round about the world.

And if they will sail, in passing the pole, toward occident, they shall go on the back side of all the new found land that is discovered by your Grace's subjects, till they come into the South Sea on the back side of the Indies Occidental. And so continuing their navigation, they may turn by the Strait of Magellan unto this realm, and so to compass the world about by that part.

And if in passing the Pole Arctic, they will sail straight toward the Pole Antarctic, they shall incline to the lands and islands that have their situation between the Tropics and the Equinoctial, which without doubt be the richest lands and islands in the world; for all the gold, spices, aromatics, and precious stones, with all other things that we have in estimation, from thence they come. And beside all this yet, the convenience of this navigation by this way is of so great advantage over the other navigations in shorting of half the way, for the other must sail by great circuits and compasses, and these shall sail by straight ways and lines.

2. *The Discoveries of the World, 1555:* Shortly after Barlow finished his treatise, Antonio Galvano, a Portuguese colonial administrator, wrote a summary of *The Discoveries of the World,* in which he gave the following estimate of the progress of exploration up to 1555.[8]

Now I gather by all the precedent discoveries, that the whole earth is in circuit 360 degrees according to the geometry thereof: and to every degree the ancient writers allow 17 leagues and a half, which amount unto 6,300 leagues [the moderns make the degree 16⅔, making 6,000 leagues], yet I take it that every degree is just 17 leagues, so that the circuit of the earth is about 6,200. However it be, all is discovered and sailed from the east unto the west almost even as the sun compasseth it: but from the south to the north there is great difference; for towards the north pole there is found discovered no more than 77 or 78 degrees, which come to 1326 leagues: and towards the south pole there is discovered from the equinoctial to 52 or 53 degrees, that is, to the strait which Magellan passed through (which amounteth to about 900 leagues); and putting both these said main sums together, they amount to 2226 leagues. Now take so many out of 6300 leagues, there remaineth as yet undiscovered (north and south above the space of) 4000 leagues.

3. *Hakluyt's Voyages, 1589:* After more than a century of overseas conquest by the nations of western Europe, an English geography scholar named Richard Hakluyt (1553–1616) set himself the task of collecting and publishing the narratives of all noteworthy expeditions made until his time. The first edition of his great work, *The Principal Navigations, Voyages, and Discoveries of the English Nation,* appeared in 1589, and thereafter his work was frequently reprinted. The following selections are taken from Hakluyt's preface to the second edition, 1598.[9]

For (to contain myself only within the bounds of this present discourse, and in the midst thereof to begin) will it not in all posterity be as great a renown unto our English nation, to have been the first discoverers of a Sea beyond the North cape (never certainly known before) and of a convenient passage into the huge Empire of Russia by the bay of St. Nicolas and the river of Dvina; as for the Portuguese to have found a Sea beyond the Cape of Good Hope, and so consequently a passage by Sea into the East Indies; or for the Italians and Spaniards to have discovered unknown lands so many hundred leagues Westward and Southwestward of the straits of Gibraltar, and of the pillars of Hercules? Be it granted that the renowned Portuguese Vasco da Gama traversed the main Ocean Southward of Africa: Did not Richard Chanceler and his mates perform the like Northward of Europe? Suppose that Columbus that noble and high-spirited Genoese escried unknown lands to the Westward of Europe and Africa: Did not the valiant English knight Sir Hugh Willoughby; did not the famous pilots Stephen Burrough, Arthur Pet, and Charles Jackman accoast Nova Zembla, Colgoieve, and Vaigatz to the North of Europe and Asia?

Howbeit you will say perhaps, not with the like golden success, not with such deductions of Colonies, nor attaining of conquests. True it is, that our success hath not been correspondent unto theirs: yet in this our attempt the uncertainty of finding was far greater, and the difficulty and danger of searching was no whit less. For hath not Herodotus (a man for his time, most skillful and judicial in Cosmography, who writ above 2000 years ago) in his fourth book called Melpomene, signified unto the Portuguese in plain terms: that Africa, except the small Isthmus between the Arabian gulf and the Mediterranean sea, was on all sides environed with the Ocean? . . .

And what should I speak of the Spaniards? Was not divine Plato (who lived so many ages ago, and plainly described their West Indies under the name of Atlantis) was not he (I say) instead of a Cosmographer unto them? Were not those Carthaginians . . . to stir them up, and prick them forward unto their Western discoveries; yea, to be their chief loads-man and pilot?

Since, therefore these two worthy Nations had those bright lamps of learning (I mean the most ancient and best philosophers, historiographers and geographers) to show them light; and the lode-star of experience (to wit those great exploits and voyages laid up in store and recorded) whereby to shape their course: what great attempt might they not presume to undertake? But alas our English nation, at the first setting forth for their Northeastern discovery, were either altogether destitute of such clear lights and inducements, or if they had any inkling at all, it was as misty as they found the Northern seas, and so obscure and ambiguous, that it was meet rather to deter them, then to give them encouragement.

But besides the foresaid uncertainty, into what dangers and difficulties they plunged themselves, *Animus meminisse horret,* I tremble to recount. For first they were to expose themselves unto the rigor of the stern and uncouth Northern seas, and to make trial of the swelling waves and boisterous winds which there commonly do surge and blow: then were they to sail by the ragged and perilous coast of Norway, to frequent the unhaunted shores of Finmark, to double the dreadful and misty North cape, to bear with Willoughbies land, to run along within kenning of the countries of Lapland and Carelia, and as it were to open and unlock the seven-fold mouth of Dvina. Moreover, in their Northeasterly navigations, upon the seas and by the coasts of Condura, Colgoieve, Petzora, Joughoria, Samoedia, Nova Zembla, &c. and their passing and return through the straits of Vaigatz, unto what drifts of snow and mountains of ice even in June, July, and August, unto what hideous overfalls, uncertain currents, dark mists, and fogs, and divers other fearful inconveniences they were subject and in danger of, I wish you rather to learn out of the voyages of Sir Hugh Willoughbie, Stephen Burrough, Arthur Pet and the rest, than to expect in this place an endless catalogue thereof.

And here by the way I cannot but highly commend the great industry and magnanimity of the Hollanders, who within these few years have discovered to 78 yea (as themselves affirm) to 81 degrees of Northerly latitude: yet with this proviso; that our English nation led them the dance, broke the ice before them, and gave good leave to light their candle at our torch.

But now it is high time for us to weigh our anchor, to hoist up our sails, to get clear of these boistrous, frosty, and misty seas, and with all speed to direct our course for the mild, lightsome, temperate, and warm Atlantic Ocean, over which the Spaniards and Portuguese have made so many pleasant prosperous and golden voyages. And albeit I cannot deny, that both of them in their East and West Indian navigations have endured many tempests, dangers and shipwrecks: yet this dare I boldly affirm; first that a great number of them have satisfied their fame-thirsty and gold-thirsty minds with that reputation and wealth, which made all perils and misadventures seem tolerable unto them; and secondly, that their first attempts (which in this comparison I do only stand upon) were no whit more difficult and dangerous, than ours to the Northeast.

For admit that the way was much longer, yet was it never barred with ice, mist, or darkness, but was at all seasons of the year open and navigable; yea and that for the most part with fortunate and fit gales of wind. Moreover they had no foreign prince to intercept or molest them, but their own towns, islands, and main lands to succor them. The Spaniards had the Canary Isles: and so had the Portuguese the Isles of the Azores, of Porto Santo, of Madeira, of Cape Verde, the castle of Mina, the fruitful and profitable Isle of St. Thomas, being all of them conveniently situated, and well fraught with commodities. And had they not continual and yearly trade in some one part or other of Africa, for getting of slaves, for sugar, for elephants' teeth, grains, silver, gold, and other precious wares, which served as allurements to draw them on by little and little, and as props to stay them from giving over their attempts? . . .

And here had I almost forgotten to put the reader in mind of that learned and philosophical treatise of the true state of Iceland, and so consequently of the Northern Seas and regions lying that way: wherein a great number of none of the meanest historiographers and cosmographers of later times, as namely, Munster, Gemma Frisius, Zieglerus, Krantzius, Saxo Grammaticus, Olaus Magnus, Peucerus and others, are by evident arguments convinced of manifold errors: that is to say, as touching the true situation and Northerly latitude of that Island, and of the distance thereof from other places; touching the length of days in summer and of nights in winter, of the temperature of the land and sea, of the time and manner of the congealing, continuance, and thawing of the ice in those seas, of the first discovery and inhabiting of that island, of the first planting of Christianity there, as likewise of the continual flaming of mountains, strange qualities of fountains, of hell-mouth, and of purgatory which those authors have fondly written and imagined to be there. All which treatise ought to be the more acceptable; first in that it hath brought sound truth with it; and secondly, in that it cometh from that far Northern climate which most men would suppose could not afford any one so learned a patron for itself.

IX

The Renaissance in Italy

THERE is a certain justification for my plan of life. It may be only glory that we seek here, but I persuade myself that, so long as we remain here, that is right. Another glory awaits us in heaven and he who reaches there will not wish even to think of earthly fame. So this is the natural order, that among mortals the care of things mortal should come first; to the transitory will then succeed the eternal; from the first to the second is the natural progression.

Petrarch (1304–74)

CONTENTS

[187]

QUESTIONS FOR STUDY

PART I

1. How would a medieval ascetic have viewed the Genoa described by Aeneas Silvius Piccolomini?

2. What particular human qualities does Piccolomini single out for praise? What impresses him most about the city?

3. Why did Petrarch read the classic authors?

4. What is Petrarch's attitude to Cicero? How does it differ from that of the "old man" in the debate?

5. How does Salutati justify secular studies?

6. Why did Leonardo Bruni desert the law to study under Chrysoloras?

7. What does the description of the Duke of Urbino's library reveal about the interests of a Humanist book-lover? How did the Duke treat his books?

8. What were the content and purpose of Humanist education, as described by Guarino?

9. How does Guarino's approach to knowledge differ from that of St. Thomas Aquinas?

10. Why did Cellini love antiquities?

11. How did Cellini's approach to art differ from that of a medieval sculptor?

12. What did Aretino find enjoyable?

13. Having read the documents in Part I, formulate a definition of Humanism.

14. "They [the Humanists] shifted authorities, rather than freed men from them." Do you agree with this judgment?

PART II

15. Why did Cellini write his autobiography?

16. What made Alberti admirable in the eyes of his biographer?

17. What was the position of the artist in Renaissance society?

18. How did Nicolo Perotto obtain preferment in the Church?

19. What were the qualifications of the ideal courtier? How many were carried over from the medieval ideals?

20. How did Renaissance types differ from those of the Middle Ages? From those of today?

The Renaissance has been called "the most intractable problem child of historiography."[1] For the term, which means literally "Rebirth," is used to characterize both the period in history which immediately followed the Middle Ages, and an intellectual movement on a broad scale, which appeared in western Europe as the Middle Ages drew to a close. Among the basic difficulties in dealing with this "problem child," therefore, are to delimit accurately the historical period to which the term applies, and to determine the nature and character of the intellectual movement.

Any attempt to set precise terminal dates for the Renaissance involves the delicate decision as to the point at which one age ends and another begins. History flows continuously, and the transition from age to age is gradual and often imperceptible. Moreover, history flows unevenly, and some areas of the world make the transition to a new age considerably in advance of others. Thus, the terminal dates of an historical period can be stated only approximately and with careful qualifications as to locale.

Now in one sense the transition from Middle Ages to Renaissance was a transformation of the basis of western culture from a rural agrarian economy to an urban commercial economy. Viewed in this way, the Renaissance was the fulfillment of the promise of the Middle Ages, for the small and often insecure medieval town grew to be the dynamic economic factor in western civilization; and the point at which the men and methods of the city came to dominate those of the countryside was the dividing line between the two ages. The transformation occurred first in Italy. Here the medieval towns, which had grown wealthy on the Mediterranean trade that revived with the launching of the Crusades, became the prosperous center of a network of trade routes extending all over Europe. In the general neighborhood of the year 1300 Italy had come to be dominated by her vigorous city-states. That date may be taken as the beginning of the Renaissance.

The transition was delayed by a century or more in northern Europe. The towns of the northern countries, unable to exploit fully the commercial advantages of their geographical positions until after the great voyages of discovery, developed more slowly than those of Italy. But by the latter half of the fifteenth century it was clear that the Middle Ages had closed and the Renaissance begun in the north. The Hanseatic League of German cities grew opulent on the Baltic trade; the Netherlands flourished as the entrepôt of the west; and the towns of France and England throve and expanded with the aid and protection of their kings. Thus the age of the Renaissance came gradually into being in the fourteenth and fifteenth centuries. By the end of the sixteenth century the Renaissance had drawn to a close, as further developments and new factors effected the transition to the modern age. Thus, at its greatest extent, the Renaissance is said to span the years from 1300 to 1600.

To determine the nature and character of the Renaissance as an intellectual movement is also a task of considerable complexity. For it was a movement which vitally affected a wide range of man's activities. On the one hand, it touched the development of the fine arts: painting, sculpture, and architecture. On the other, it touched many fields of thought: education, literature, and philosophy. The movement is alternately termed Humanism. But though it can be denominated by a word, it cannot so easily be defined. Its manifold character demands careful investigation and analysis.

The purpose of this problem is to arrive at a definition of Humanism by the examination of documents illustrating the growth of the movement in Italy.

Humanism first appeared in the writings of Italian authors in the fourteenth and fifteenth centuries. Inspired by their own works, they first spoke of themselves as leading a *Rinascimento* or Renaissance, and throughout much of the period they held the position of leadership in the Humanist movement. Men of other lands caught the spirit of Humanism from Italy, which enjoyed a cultural pre-eminence unequalled since the days of ancient Rome. The documents in the following pages are selected from the works of prominent writers in the three centuries of the Italian Renaissance.

Part I.   ITALIAN HUMANISM

A.   THE SETTING OF THE HUMANIST MOVEMENT

Genoa in 1432. The milieu in which the Humanist movement took place—the cities of Italy—is pictured in the following document. It is a selection from a letter written by Aeneas Silvius Piccolomini (afterwards Pope Pius II), in which he describes the city of Genoa in 1432.[2] He had traveled widely on the continent, also visiting England.

Would you were with me! You would see a city which has no equal anywhere on earth. It lies upon a hill over which rude mountains tower, while the lower city is washed by the waves of the sea. The harbor is bow-shaped so that the storms can not do the ships any harm. . . . It constitutes thus a thoroughly reliable anchorage sought by ships big as hills, triremes and countless other craft. And what a coming and going there is! From the east they hail and from the west, so that you may see daily people of the most different sort with unimaginable rough manners and customs and traders with every conceivable ware. Right at the shore arise the most magnificent palaces, heaven-scaling, built of marble, decorated with columns and often too with sculptures. Under them runs an arcade for the length of a thousand steps where every conceivable object is for sale.

The rest of the city winds upward along the side of the hill. In this section the houses are so large and distinguished that a king or a prince might be content with any one of them. For they are all of royal magnificence though they stand closely together and the streets are narrow to the point of permitting only two or three people to pass abreast. The churches, beautiful as they are, do not seem to me to be worthy of such a city. However, they are not without splendor and boast more particularly some handsome sepulchral monuments in honor of deceased noblemen. Certain relics enjoy considerable veneration. I examined the emerald bowl, from which, according to the legend, our Savior ate with his disciples, and found it marvelously luminous. The city is notably well supplied with water from mountain sources which is distributed to the individual houses and is of especial excellence of taste.

Now as to the life and customs of the popula-

tion. The men are substantial, well-grown, and impressive, carry themselves proudly and are in fact proud. They are a gifted folk, not likely to be found inferior to any other people in the quality of their mind. Strenuous labors, night-watches, and self-denials they bear easily. Their deeds of bravery at sea are incredible; incredible too the perils they confront and the difficulties they master. Our helmsman, a certain Ottobono Imperiali, who has been living at sea now for twenty-three years, has never slept between walls, and never, as he told us, did he change his clothes, even when he was drenched with water. The advantages that come with profits and riches offer compensation for past hardships. In case of a war at sea one does well to take their experience and skill into account, for victory depends solely on them. Should they desire it, victory is certain; should they be contrary-minded, there is no prospect of success since they are the lords of the sea and every one trembles before them.

They dress nobly and elegantly. As for their women, they let them do as they please, for rather may it be said that the women wield the scepter than the other way about. They are not afflicted with thirst for education, though they learn languages as they need them. For other elements of the Liberal Arts they have little use, except as a possible relief from business. Every man selects a woman to whom he pays court. A strange thing is that they maintain irregular relations with other men's wives and at the same time are not in the least offended with the carryings-on of their own wives. Thus it happens that the women of this city enjoy great freedom; indeed it would not be an exaggeration to designate Genoa as the paradise of women. . . . Their dresses are luxurious, loaded with gold and silver trimmings and with jewels. On their fingers sparkle emeralds and diamonds supplied by India and Persia. For where it is a question of adornment they fear no expense. They bother neither about the household nor about needle and dishes, for every house enjoys abundant service. I remember a woman who was not even a woman of rank—when her son-in-law asked her what she had prepared for his breakfast, she made answer that she had not been in the kitchen for seven years. These women are all very easy-going, refuse to make an effort, and do not wait for the holidays to enjoy themselves with their admirers. They are always showing themselves in their best clothes. Indeed the more I reflect upon this city, the more I am convinced that Venus in our time no longer dwells in Cyprus or on Cytheron but in this city of Genoa. Here seems to me to be her shrine. . . .

Even the nuns are not held to a rigorous stand-ard. They go about at pleasure whither they will. It is incredible that this should not distract them from their purpose. Nor do they, as is said to be the case with us [i.e., the Sienese], curse their parents who confined them in the cloister. They are very numerous and much more merry than the married women, evidently because they do not bear the yoke of matrimony. . . .

B. THE CULT OF THE CLASSICS

1. *Petrarch on Homer.* Francesco Petrarca (1304–74), or, as he is commonly known, Petrarch, was the most famous of the earliest Humanists in Italy. He was born in Arezzo, whence his family had been exiled from Florence, and spent much of his life in the towns of Italy and southern France. He was destined for the law, but his introduction to the Latin classics, particularly Cicero and Vergil, so charmed him that he forsook law and embraced literature. He produced much, in both Latin and the vernacular, which won him such fame throughout Europe that in 1341 Rome revived an old office by conferring upon Petrarch the crown of poet laureate. Following is a selection from one of Petrarch's letters, the spirit and content of which are typical of early Humanism.[3]

You ask me finally to lend you the copy of Homer that was on sale at Padua, if, as you suppose, I have purchased it; since, you say, I have for a long time possessed another copy; so that our friend Leo may translate it from Greek into Latin for your benefit and for the benefit of our other studious compatriots. I saw this book, but neglected the opportunity of acquiring it, because it seemed inferior to my own. It can easily be had with the aid of the person to whom I owe my friendship with Leo; a letter from that source would be all-powerful in the matter, and I will myself write him.

If by chance the book escape us, which seems to me very unlikely, I will let you have mine. I have been always fond of this particular translation and of Greek literature in general, and if fortune had not frowned upon my beginnings, in the sad death of my excellent master, I should be perhaps today something more than a Greek still at his alphabet. I approve with all my heart and strength your enterprise, for I regret and am indignant that an ancient translation, presumably the work of Cicero, the commencement of which Horace inserted in his *Ars Poetica,* should have been lost to the Latin world, together with many other works. It angers me to see so much solicitude for the bad and so much neglect of the good.

But what is there to be done? We must be resigned. If the zeal of strangers shall come to rouse us from our lethargy, then may the Muses and our Apollo help it on! The Chinese, the Arabs and the Red Sea offer in my eyes no more valuable merchandise [*merx*]. I am not unaware of what I say. I know that this nominative [*merx*] is not used to-day by our grammarians; but it was used by the ancients, possibly not by the very earliest, whose style the ignorance of our times blushes to imitate; but by those nearest to us and the first in science and ability, whom blind and loquacious pride has not yet dared to set aside. In their writings, and notably in Horace, I remember that the nominative of which I speak is often found. Let us put it again into use, I beg of you, if we may; for I do not know why we should not dare to recall from unmerited exile this word banished from the Latin country, and introduce it into the tongue to which we are devoting all our time.

I wish to take this opportunity of warning you of one thing, lest later on I should regret having passed it over in silence. If, as you say, the translation is to be made literally in prose, listen for a moment to the opinion of St. Jerome as expressed in his preface to the book, *De Temporibus,* by Eusebius of Caesarea, which he translated into Latin. Here are the very words of this great man, well acquainted with these two languages, and indeed with many others, and of especial fame for his art of translating: "If any one," he says, "refuses to believe that translation lessens the peculiar charm of the original, let him render Homer into Latin, word for word; I will say further, let him translate it into prose in his own tongue, and he will see a ridiculous array and the most eloquent of poets transformed into a stammerer." I tell you this for your own good, while it is yet time, in order that so important a work may not prove useless.

As for me, I wish the work to be done, whether well or ill. I am so famished for literature that just as he who is ravenously hungry is not inclined to quarrel with the cook's art, so I await with lively impatience whatever dishes are to be set before my soul. And in truth, the morsel in which the same Leo, translating into Latin prose the beginning of Homer, has given me a foretaste of the whole work, although it confirms the sentiment of St. Jerome, does not displease me. It possesses, in fact, a secret charm, as certain viands, which have failed to take a moulded shape, although they are lacking in form, nevertheless preserve their taste and odor. May he continue with the aid of Heaven, and may he give us Homer, who has been lost to us!

In asking of me the volume of Plato which I have with me, and which escaped the fire at my trans-Alpine country house, you give me proof of your ardor, and I shall hold this book at your disposal, whenever the time shall come. I wish to aid with all my power such noble enterprises. But beware lest it should be unbecoming to unite in one bundle these two great princes of Greece, lest the weight of these two spirits should overwhelm mortal shoulders. Let your messenger undertake, with God's aid, one of the two, and first him who has written many centuries before the other. Farewell. (Milan, Aug. 18, 1360.)

2. *Petrarch on Cicero.* Following is another of Petrarch's letters, in which he describes the scholarly labors of a Humanist.[4]

Your copy of Cicero has been in my possession four years and more. There is a good reason, though, for so long a delay; namely, the great scarcity of copyists who understand such work. It is a state of affairs that has resulted in an incredible loss to scholarship. Books that by their nature are a little hard to understand are no longer multiplied, and have ceased to be generally intelligible, and so have sunk into utter neglect, and in the end have perished. This age of ours consequently has let fall, bit by bit, some of the richest and sweetest fruits that the tree of knowledge has yielded; has thrown away the results of the vigils and labors of the most illustrious men of genius,—things of more value, I am almost tempted to say, than anything else in the whole world. . . .

But I must return to your Cicero. I could not do without it, and the incompetence of the copyists would not let me possess it. What was left for me but to rely on my own resources, and press these weary fingers and this worn and ragged pen into the service? The plan that I followed was this. I want you to know it, in case you should ever have to grapple with a similar task. Not a single word did I read except as I wrote. But how is that, I hear some one say; did you write without knowing what it was that you were writing? Ah! but from the very first it was enough for me to know that it was a work of Tullius, and an extremely rare one too. And then as soon as I was fairly started, I found at every step so much sweetness and charm, and felt so strong a desire to advance, that the only difficulty which I experienced in reading and writing at the same time came from the fact that my pen could not cover the ground so rapidly as I wanted it to, whereas my expectation had been rather that it would outstrip my eyes, and that my ardor for writing would be chilled by the slowness of my reading.

So the pen held back the eye, and the eye drove on the pen, and I covered page after page, delighting in my task, and committing many and many a passage to memory as I wrote. For just in proportion as the writing is slower than the reading does the passage make a deep impression and cling to the mind. . . .

And yet I must confess that I did finally reach a point in my copying where I was overcome by weariness; not mental, for how unlikely that would be where Cicero was concerned, but the sort of fatigue that springs from excessive manual labor. I began to feel doubtful about this plan that I was following, and to regret having undertaken a task for which I had not been trained; when suddenly I came across a place where Cicero tells how he himself copied the orations of—someone or other; just who it was I do not know, but certainly no Tullius, for there is but one such man, one such voice, one such mind. These are his words: "You say that you have been in the habit of reading the orations of Cassius in your idle moments. But I," he jestingly adds, with his customary disregard of his adversary's feelings, "have made a practice of *copying* them, so that I might *have* no idle moments."

As I read this passage I grew hot with shame, like a modest young soldier who hears the voice of his beloved leader rebuking him. I said to myself, "So Cicero copied orations that another wrote, and you are not ready to copy his? What ardor! what scholarly devotion! what reverence for a man of godlike genius!" These thoughts were a spur to me, and I pushed on, with all my doubts dispelled. If ever from my darkness there shall come a single ray that can enhance the splendor of the reputation which his heavenly eloquence has won for him, it will proceed in no slight measure from the fact that I was so captivated by his ineffable sweetness that I did a thing in itself most irksome with such delight and eagerness that I scarcely knew I was doing it at all.

So then at last your Cicero has the happiness of returning to you, bearing you my thanks. And yet he also stays, very willingly, with me; a dear friend to whom I give the credit of being almost the only man of letters for whose sake I would go to the length of spending my time, when the difficulties of life are pressing on me so sharply and inexorably and the cares pertaining to my literary labors make the longest life seem far too short, in transcribing compositions not my own.

I may have done such things in former days, when I thought myself rich in time, and had not learned how stealthily it slips away: but I now know that this is of all our riches the most uncertain and fleeting; the years are closing in upon me now, and there is no longer any room for deviation from the beaten path. I am forced to practise strict economy; I only hope that I have not begun too late. But Cicero! he assuredly is worthy of a part of even the little that I still have left. Farewell.

3. *A Humanist Debate on Cicero.* In the following passage, Petrarch describes how he introduced two critical letters he had written on Cicero into a heated scholarly debate in 1351.[5]

These two [letters] you read while the others listened; and then the strife of words grew warmer. Some approved of what I had written, admitting that Cicero deserved my censure. But the old man stood his ground more stubbornly even than before. He was so blinded by love of his hero and by the brightness of his name that he preferred to praise him even when he was in the wrong; to embrace faults and virtues together rather than make any exceptions. He would not be thought to condemn anything at all in so great a man. So instead of answering our arguments he rang the changes again and again upon the splendor of Cicero's fame, letting authority usurp the place of reason. He would stretch out his hand and say imploringly: "Gently, I beg you, gently with my Cicero." And when we asked him if he found it impossible to believe that Cicero had made mistakes, he would close his eyes and turn his face away and exclaim with a groan, as if he had been smitten, "Alas! alas! Is my beloved Cicero accused of doing wrong?" just as if he were speaking not of a man but of some god. I asked him accordingly whether in his opinion Tullius was a god or a man like others. "A god," he replied; and then realizing what he had said, he added, "a god of eloquence."

4. *Salutati on Secular Studies.* Notable among the early Humanists was Coluccio Salutati (1331–1406), who, though for thirty years chancellor of the city of Florence, found time for considerable literary output. Following is a selection from a letter he wrote to a certain Brother John of San Miniato in 1406.[6]

I read recently, Venerable Father in Christ, the letter which you wrote to that very dear son of mine, Angelo Corbinelli, and was greatly amused by it. You are trying, according to your habit, to draw him away from poetry and secular studies; or, to put it more exactly, to frighten him away

from them. Whether you are right in so doing is your affair, and I leave you to the reproaches of my distinguished friend, John of Ravenna, and the many others who hold a contrary opinion [that is, the whole body of the humanists]. . . .

What right have you, I beg you, to forbid my friend Angelo to indulge his taste for oratory, poetry, and philosophy? What rights have you over any one outside your monastery? True, it is right for you and for every one to encourage and even command that which is honorable and to prohibit the contrary, but what is there in these things which makes it right to forbid them? I know and read daily in St. Jerome, St. Ambrose, and St. Augustine splendid passages from the philosophers and orators and verses from the poets which shine out like stars from those most sacred writings, and I do not suppose you condemn this in them as a crime. If things true and holy, decorous and beautiful, are found in those doctors [of the Church] and may be read there without harm, why should these same things be called profane and infamous in the original writings of their authors? Why are they forbidden to us if they were permitted to holy doctors? . . .

5. *Bruni on Greek Letters.* A friend and admirer of Salutati, Leonardo Bruni (1370–1444) was inspired by him to pursue classical studies. In the following selection from Bruni's *History of His Own Times in Italy* he describes an event that extended Humanist study of the ancients.[7]

Then first came the knowledge of Greek letters, which for seven hundred years had been lost among us. It was the Byzantine, Chrysoloras, a nobleman in his own country and most skilled in literature, who brought Greek learning back to us. Because his country was invaded by the Turks, he came by sea to Venice; but as soon as his fame went abroad, he was cordially invited and eagerly besought to come to Florence on a public salary to spread his abundant riches before the youth of the city. [This took place in 1396.] At that time I was studying Civil Law. But my nature was afire with the love of learning and I had already given no little time to dialectic and rhetoric. Therefore at the coming of Chrysoloras I was divided in my mind, feeling that it was a shame to desert the Law and no less wrong to let slip such an occasion for learning Greek. And often with youthful impulsiveness I addressed myself thus: "When you are privileged to gaze upon and have converse with Homer, Plato, and Demosthenes as well as the other poets, philosophers, and orators of whom such wonderful things are reported, and when you might saturate yourself with their admirable teachings, will you turn your back and flee? Will you permit this opportunity, divinely offered you, to slip by? For seven hundred years now no one in Italy has been in possession of Greek and yet we agree that all knowledge comes from that source. What great advancement of knowledge, enlargement of fame, and increase of pleasure will come to you from an acquaintance with this tongue! There are everywhere quantities of doctors of the Civil Law and the opportunity of completing your study in this field will not fail you. However,

should the one and only doctor of Greek letters disappear, there will be no one from whom to acquire them."

Overcome at last by these arguments, I gave myself to Chrysoloras and developed such ardor that whatever I learned by day, I revolved with myself in the night while asleep. I had many fellow-students, two of the number who were particularly proficient belonging to the Florentine nobility. . . .

C. THE CULT OF BOOK COLLECTING

The Library of Frederick, Duke of Urbino. One aspect of Humanism was the love of books. The following description of the library of Frederick, Duke of Urbino (1422–82), written by a contemporary Florentine bookseller, indicates the nature and extent of the interests of a book lover of that day.[8]

We come now to consider in what high esteem the Duke held all Greek and Latin writers, sacred as well as secular. He alone had a mind to do what no one had done for a thousand years or more; that is, to create the finest library since ancient times. He spared neither cost nor labor, and when he knew of a fine book, whether in Italy or not, he would send for it. It is now fourteen or more years ago since he began the library, and he always employed, in Urbino, in Florence and in other places, thirty or forty scribes in his service. He took the only way to make a fine library like this: by beginning with the Latin poets, with any comments on the same which might seem merited; next the orators, with the works of Tully and all Latin writers and grammarians of merit; so that not one of the leading writers in this faculty should be wanted. He sought also all the known works on history in Latin, and not only those, but likewise the histories of Greek writers done into Latin, and the orators as well. The Duke also desired to have every work on moral and natural philosophy in Latin, or in Latin translations from Greek.

As to the sacred Doctors in Latin, he had the works of all four, and what a noble set of letters and writings we have here; bought without regard of cost. After the four Doctors, he was set on having the works of St. Bernard and of all the Doctors of old, without exception, Tertullian, Hilarius, Remigius, Hugh de St. Victor, Isidore, Anselm, Rabanus and all the rest. After Latin works came Greek writings done into Latin, Dionysius the Areopagite, Basil, Cyril, Gregory, Nazianzen, John of Damascus, John Chrysostom, Gregory of Nicea, all the works of Eusebius, of

Ephrem the monk, and of Origen, an excellent writer. Coming to the Latin Doctors in philosophy and theology, all the works of Thomas Aquinas, and of Albertus Magnus; of Alexander ab Alexandro, of Scotus, of Bonaventura, of Richard of Mediavilla, of the Archbishop of Antoninus and of all the recognized modern Doctors, down to the *Conformità* of St. Francis: all the works on civil law in the finest text, the lectures of Bartolo written on goat-skin.

He had an edition of the Bible made in two most beautiful volumes, illustrated in the finest possible manner and bound in gold brocade with rich silver fittings. It was given this rich form as the chief of all writings. With it are all the commentaries of the Master of the Sentences, of Nicola di Lira, and of all the Greek and Latin Doctors, together with the literal glossary of Nicola di Lira. Likewise all the writers on astrology, geometry, arithmetic, architecture and *De re Militari;* books on painting, sculpture, music and canon law, and all the texts and lectures on the *Summa* of Ostiensis and other works in the same faculty. In medicine all the works of Avicenna, Hippocrates, Galen, the *Continenti* of Almansor and the complete works of Averroes in logic and natural philosophy. A volume of all the Councils, held since ancient times, and the logical, philosophical and musical works of Boethius.

There were all the works of modern writers beginning with Pope Pius; of Petrarch and Dante in Latin and in the vulgar tongue, of Boccaccio in Latin; of Coluccio and of Lionardo d'Arezzo, original and translations; of Fra Ambrogio, of Giannozzo Manetti and Guerrino; the prose and poetical works of Panormita, and Francesco Filelfo, and Campano; as well as everything written by Perrotto, Maffeo Vegio, Nicolò Secondino (who was interpreter of Greek and Latin at the Council of the Greeks in Florence), Pontano, Bartolomeo Fazi, Gasparino, Pietro Paolo Vergerio, Giovanni Argiropolo (which includes the Philosophy and Logic of Aristotle and the Politics besides), Francesco Barbaro, Lionardo Giustiniano, Donato Acciaiuoli, Alamanno, Rinuccini, Cristofano da Prato, Vecchio, Poggio, Giovanni Tortello, Francesco d'Arezzo and Lorenzo Valla.

He added to the books written by ancient and modern doctors on all the faculties all the books known in Greek, also the complete works of Aristotle and Plato (written on the finest goatskin) ; of Homer in one volume, the *Iliad,* the *Odyssey,* and the *Batrachomiomachia;* of Sophocles, Pindar and Menander, and all the other Greek poets; a fine volume of Plutarch's lives and his moral works, the *Cosmography* of Ptolemy illustrated in Greek, and the writings of Herodotus, Pausanius, Thucydides, Polybius, Demosthenes, Æschines and Plotinus. All the Greek comments, such as those upon Aristotle, the *Physica de Plantis* and Theophrastus; all the Greek vocabulists—Greek into Latin; the works of Hippocrates, Galen, Xenophon, St. Basil, St. John Chrysostom, St. Athanasius, St. John Damascenas, St. Gregory Nazianzen, St. Gregory of Nicea, Origen, Dionysius the Areopagite, John Climacus, St. Ephrem the monk, Æneas the Sophist, the Collations of John Cassianus, the book of Paradise, *Vitae sanctorum patrum ex Ægypto,* the Life of Barlaam and Josaphat, a wonderful psalter in Hebrew, Greek and Latin, verse by verse, and all the Greek works on geometry, arithmetic, and astrology.

Finding that he lacked a vast number of Greek books by various writers, he sent to seek them so that nothing in that tongue which could be found should be lacking; also whatever books which were to be had in Hebrew, beginning with the Bible and all those dealt with by the Rabbi Moses and other commentators. And besides the Holy Scriptures, there are books in Hebrew on medicine, philosophy and the other faculties.

The Duke, having completed this noble work at the great cost of thirty thousand ducats, beside the many other excellent provisions that he made, determined to give every writer a worthy finish by binding his work in scarlet and silver. Beginning with the Bible, as the chief, he had it covered with gold brocade, and then he bound in scarlet and silver the Greek and Latin doctors and philosophers, the histories, the books on medicine and the modern doctors, a rich and magnificent sight. In this library all the books are superlatively good, and written with the pen, and had there been one printed volume it would have been ashamed in such company. They were beautifully illuminated and written on parchment.

This library is remarkable amongst all others in that, taking the works of all writers, sacred and profane, original and translated, there will be found not a single imperfect folio. No other library can show the like, for in all of them the works of certain authors will be wanting in places. A short time before the Duke went to Ferrara it chanced that I was in Urbino with His Lordship, and I had with me the catalogues of the principal Italian libraries: of the papal library, of those of San Marco at Florence, of Pavia, and even of that of the University of Oxford, which I had procured from England. On comparing them with that of the Duke I remarked how they all failed in one respect; to wit, they possessed the same work in many examples, but lacked the other writings of the author; nor had they writers in all the faculties like this library.

D.   Humanist Education

Guarino on Teaching and Studying. Battista Guarino (1370–1460) was, like his father, the head of a famous academy at Ferrara. In *De Ordine Docendi et Studendi,* 1459, Guarino laid down the educational principles upon which he and his father conducted the academy.[9]

In offering this short treatise for your acceptance, I am fully aware that you need no incentive to regard the pursuit of letters as the most worthy object of your ambition. But you may find what I have written a not unwelcome reminder of our past intercourse, whilst it may prove of use to other readers into whose hands it may fall. For I have had in view not only students anxious for guidance in their private reading, but masters in search of some definite principles of method in teaching the classics. Hence I have treated both of Greek and of Latin letters and am confident that the course I have laid down will prove a thoroughly satisfactory training in literature and scholarship. I should remind you that the conclusions presented in this little work are not the result of my own experience only. It is indeed a summary of the theory and practice of several scholars, and especially does it represent the doctrine of my father, Guarino of Verona; so much so, that you may suppose him to be writing to you by my pen and giving you the fruit of his long and ripe experience in teaching. May I hope that you will yourself prove to be one more example of the high worth of his precepts?

Let me, at the outset, begin with a caution. No master can endow a careless and indifferent nature with the true passion for learning. That a young man must acquire for himself. But once the taste begins to develop, then in Ovid's words "the more we drink, the more we thirst." For when the mind has begun to enjoy the pleasures of learning, the passion for fuller and deeper knowledge will grow from day to day. But there can be no proficiency in studies unless there be first the desire to excel. Wherefore let a young man set forward eagerly in quest of those true, honorable, and enduring treasures of the mind which neither disease nor death has power to destroy. Riches, which adventurers seek by land and sea, too often win men to pleasure rather than to learning; for self-indulgence is a snare from whose enticements it is the bounden duty of parents to ween their children, by kind words, or by severity if need arise. Perchance then in later years the echo of a father's wise advice may linger and may avail in the hour of temptation. . . .

As regards the course of study. From the first, stress must be laid upon distinct and sustained enunciation, both in speaking and in reading. But at the same time utterance must be perfectly natural; if affected or exaggerated the effect is unpleasing. The foundation of education must be laid in grammar. Unless this be thoroughly learnt, subsequent progress is uncertain,—a house built upon treacherous ground. . . .

Now these rules can be most satisfactorily learnt from the Compendium written by my father which briefly sets out the more important laws of composition. In using this or a similar textbook the pupil must be practised both in written and in oral exercises. Only by rapid practise in oral composition can fluency and readiness be gained. And this will be further secured if the class is accustomed to speak in Latin. . . .

I have said that ability to write Latin verse is one of the essential marks of an educated person. I wish now to indicate a second, which is of at least equal importance, namely, familiarity with the language and literature of Greece. The time has come when we must speak with no uncertain voice upon this vital requirement of scholarship. I am well aware that those who are ignorant of the Greek tongue decry its necessity for reasons which are sufficiently evident. But I can allow no doubt to remain as to my own conviction that, without a knowledge of Greek, Latin scholarship itself is, in any real sense, impossible. . . .

But whilst a beginning is being thus made with Greek, continued progress must at the same time be secured in Latin. For instance, the broader rules of grammar which sufficed in the earlier stages must give place to a more complete study of structure, such as we find in Priscian, and irregularities or exceptions, hitherto ignored, must be duly noted. At the same time the Epistles of Cicero should be taken in hand for purposes of declamation. Committed to memory they serve as one of the finest possible aids to purity, directness, and facility of style, and supply admirable matter in no less admirable form for adaptation to our own uses. Yet I would not be understood to claim the *Letters* of Cicero as alone offering a sufficient training in style. For distinction of style is the fruit of a far wider field of study. To quote Horace:

> Of writing well, be sure, the secret lies
> In wisdom: therefore study to be wise.

But we are now passing from the first, or elementary to the second, or more advanced, stage of grammar which I called "historices" and which is concerned with the study of continuous prose authors, more particularly the historians. Here we begin with a short but comprehensive view of general history, which will include that of the Roman people by such writers as Justin or Valerius Maximus. The latter author is also valuable as affording actual illustrations of virtuous precepts couched in attractive style. The scholar will now devote his attentions to the historians in regular order. By their aid he will learn to understand the manners, laws, and institutions of different types of nations, and will examine the varying fortune of individuals and states, the sources of their success and failure, their strength and their weakness. . . .

Side by side with the study of history a careful reading of the poets will be taken in hand. The true significance of poetic fiction will now be appreciated. It consists, as Cicero says, in the exhibition of the realities of our own life under the form of imaginary persons and situations. Thus Jerome could employ Terence in bringing home his exhortations to temperance. Let us not forget that Virgil as a subject of deep and regular study must always stand not first, but alone. Here we have the express authority of Augustine, who urges the supreme claim of the great poet to our life-long companionship. Lucian may perhaps with good reason be postponed to a later stage. Quintilian regarded him as the "rhetorical poet"; and undoubtedly his poem has much affinity with certain aspects of the forensic art. There is a certain strain of the keen debator in particular portions of his work. So I should advise that Virgil be followed by Statius, whose *Thebais,* fashioned upon the *Aeneid,* will be found easy reading. The *Metamorphoses* of Ovid form a useful introduction to the systematic knowledge of mythology—a subject of wide literary application and as such deserves close attention.

The course of study which I have thus far sketched out will prove an admirable preparation for that further branch of scholarship which constitutes rhetoric, including the thorough examination of the great monuments of eloquence. . . . The first work to claim our attention in this subject is the *Rhetoric* of Cicero, in which we find all the points of oratory concisely but comprehensively set forth. The other rhetorical writings of Cicero will follow; and the principles therein laid down must be examined in the light of his own speeches. Indeed the student of eloquence must have his Cicero constantly in his hand; the simplicity, the lofty moral standard, the practical temper of his writings render them a peculiarly noble training for a public speaker. Nor should the admirable Quintilian be neglected in this same connection.

It will be desirable also to include the elements of logic in our course of studies, and with that the *Ethics* of Aristotle and the *Dialogues* of Plato. For these are necessary aids to the proper understanding of Cicero. . . .

Before I bring this short treatise to a close I would urge you to consider the function of letters as an adornment of leisure. Cicero, as you may remember, declares learning to be the inspiration of youth, the delight of age, the ornament of happy fortunes, the solace of adversity. A recreation in the study, abroad it is no hindrance. In our work, in our leisure, whether we keep vigil or whether we court sleep, letters are ever at hand as our surest resource. Do we seek refreshment for our minds? Where can we find it more happily than in a pursuit which affords alike utility and delight? If others seek recreation in dice, in ball-play, in the theatre, do you seek it in acquir-

ing knowledge. There you will see nothing which you may not admire; you will hear nothing which you would gladly forget. For good books give no offense, call forth no rebuke; they will stir you, but with no empty hopes, no vain fears. Finally, through books, and books alone, will your converse be with the best and greatest, nay, even with the mighty dead themselves. . . .

Let us, then, heeding these great names, see to it that we allow not our short working years to pass idly away. To each species of creatures has been allotted a peculiar and instinctive gift. To horses galloping, to birds flying comes naturally. To man is given the desire to learn. Hence what the Greeks called παιδεία, we call *studia humanitatis*. For learning and training in virtue are peculiar to man; therefore our forefathers called them *humanitas*, the pursuits and activities proper to mankind. And no branch of knowledge embraces so wide a range of subjects as that learning which I have here attempted to describe.

I will end as I began. If this little work fulfills, perhaps more than fulfills, the promise which I held out, it is because it does but exhibit that order and method of study which my learned and revered father has followed for so many years in his own school. For as from the Trojan Horse of old the Greek heroes spread over the captured city, so from that famous Academy of my father has proceeded the greater number of those scholars who have carried learning, not merely throughout Italy, but far beyond her borders.

E.   THE CULT OF ANTIQUITY

Cellini on Antique Remains. Besides an interest in ancient literature, the Humanists had an enormous enthusiasm for the physical remains of Greek and Roman civilization. The following selections from the autobiography of the famous goldsmith and sculptor, Benvenuto Cellini (1500–71), illustrate this enthusiasm for the antique.[10]

[Rome] At this period, when I was still a youth of about twenty-three years of age, a pestilential disease broke out of such unparalleled virulence that there died in Rome many thousands per day. Somewhat terrified by this, I began to take up certain amusements such as my fancy directed, caused moreover by a circumstance that I shall relate. For I enjoyed on feast-days visiting the antiquities [of the city], copying them either in wax models or by drawing from them; and since these said antiquities are all in ruins, and amid these same ruins build a great

many pigeons, the desire came upon me to employ against them my fowling-piece; and in order to avoid intercourse with anyone, being afraid of the plague, I put my gun upon the shoulder of my boy Pagolino, and he and I went alone to the said ruins. It resulted therefore that very many times I returned laden with very plump pigeons. I did not care to load my gun with more than a single ball, and it was therefore by real skill in that art that I made such large bags. I had a straight fowling-piece made by my own hands; and (so bright was it) both within and without there was never seen a mirror like it. I made besides with my own hands the finest gunpowder, in the composition of which I discovered the finest secrets that have ever up to today been discovered by anyone. . . .

By means of this diversion of mine, I acquired the friendship of certain curiosity-hunters who watched out for those Lombard peasants, who came to Rome at that season to till the vines.

These latter in the course of their tilling the earth often found antique medals, agates, chrysoprases, cornelians, cameos; they found besides precious stones, that is to say, emeralds, sapphires, diamonds, and rubies. These same curio-hunters sometimes got from those peasants for very small sums some of these things; for which I—meeting these curio-hunters occasionally, nay, very often—gave as many gold *scudi* for a thing which they had frequently just bought for scarcely as many pence (*giuli*). This circumstance, exclusive of the great profit that I procured out of it, which was tenfold or more, set me besides in high favor with almost all the Roman cardinals.

Of these objects I will only speak of the notable and rarest examples. There fell into my hands, among so many other things, a dolphin's head as large as a big balloting bean. Amongst the other treasures, not only was this the most beautiful, but nature in this case had far surpassed art; for this emerald was of such fine color that the man who bought it of me for some tens of *scudi* had it set after the fashion of an ordinary stone to wear in a ring; set thus he sold it for some hundreds. I had besides another variety of stone: this was a head made of the most beautiful topaz that the world ever saw. In this object art had equalled nature. It was as big as a large filbert, and the head upon it was as well executed as it is possible to imagine: it represented *Minerva*. There was besides another stone differing from these. This was a cameo; upon it was cut a *Hercules binding the three-jawed Cerberus*. This was of such beauty and fashioned with such fine skill, that our great Michelagniolo protested that he had never seen anything so wonderful. There were besides, among many bronze medals, one that fell into my hands, upon which was the head of *Jove*. This medal was much larger than any that I had ever seen. The head was so beautifully executed that such a medal had never been seen. It had a most beautiful reverse side, with some small figures likewise superbly executed. . . .

[Florence] One feast day among others I went into the Palace after dinner, and when I came up into the Hall of the Clock I saw the door of the Wardrobe open; and when I approached it a little the duke [of Florence, Cosimo de' Medici] called to me, and, with a kindly greeting, said to me: "You are welcome indeed. Look at this chest which has been sent as a present to me by the lord Stefano of Pilestina! Open it, and let us see what the thing is." Having immediately opened it, I said to the Duke: "My Lord! this is a figure in Greek marble, and a wondrous thing. I tell you that for a boy's figure I do not recollect that I have ever seen among the antiques so fine a work, nor one of so beautiful a fashion. Wherefore I offer to Your Most Illustrious Excellency

to restore it, and the head and the arms and the feet. And I will make an eagle in order that it may be labeled as a *Ganymede*. And although it is not customary for me to patch up statues—for that is the art of certain bunglers, who do it very badly—yet the excellence of this great master calls me to assist him." The Duke was pleased that the statue was so beautiful, and asked me many questions, saying to me: "Tell me distinctly, my Benvenuto! in what consists the great talent of this master, which causes you so much admiration." Thereupon I demonstrated to His Most Illustrious Excellency after the best method that I knew in order to make him understand such beauty, and the intellectual skill, and the rare manner [of the fragment]; upon which questions I discoursed very much and I did it the more willingly, realizing that therein His Excellency took very great pleasure.

While I was thus agreeably entertaining the Duke, it chanced that a page went out of the Wardrobe, and as the said [page] went out Bandinello [a rival sculptor] entered. When the Duke saw him he was half disturbed, and with a severe expression he said to him: "What are you doing here?" The said Bandinello, without making any other reply, immediately cast his eyes upon that chest, wherein lay the said uncovered statue, and with one of his evil chuckles, shaking his head, he said, turning towards the Duke: "My Lord! These are some of those things of which I have so often spoken to Your Most Illustrious Excellency. Know that these ancient [sculptors] understood nothing at all about anatomy, and for this reason their works are quite full of faults." I remained quiet and paid no attention to anything that he was saying; rather I had turned my back on him.

Directly that this animal had finished his disagreeable chatterings, the Duke said: "Oh! Benvenuto! This is exactly the opposite to that which you with so many fine arguments have but now so well demonstrated to me. Therefore defend it a little." At these words of the Duke, conveyed to me with so much charm, I immediately responded, and said: "My Lord! Your Most Illustrious Excellency ought to know that Baccio Bandinelli is composed entirely of evil, and so he always has been: in such a way that whatever he gazed upon, to his disapproving eyes immediately, although the thing may be altogether good in a superlative degree, it is immediately converted into the worst evil. But I who am drawn only towards the good, perceive the truth more divinely; in such a fashion that what I have said to Your Most Illustrious Excellency about this most beautiful statue is altogether the simple truth, and that which Bandinello has said is altogether that evil of which alone he is composed."

The Duke stood listening to me with much pleasure; and while I was saying these things Bandinello fidgeted and made the ugliest grimaces of his countenance—which was [itself] the most ugly—that it is possible to imagine in the world. The Duke immediately moved away, proceeding through certain lower chambers and the said Bandinello followed him. And the Chamberlain took me by the cloak and led me after him. And thus we followed the Duke, so that when His Most Illustrious Excellency reached a certain chamber he sat down, and both Bandinello and I stood, one upon the right, and the other upon the left, of His Most Illustrious Excellency. I remained silent, and those who were around us—several servants of His Excellency—all gazed fixedly at Bandinello, somewhat sniggering with one another at those words which I had uttered in that chamber above. So the said Bandinello began to chatter, and he said: "My Lord! When I uncovered my *Hercules and Cacus* I certainly believe that more than one hundred ballads were made upon me, which they say were the worst that one could possibly imagine in the world from this mob."

I thereupon answered and said: "My Lord, when our Michelagniolo Buonaroti unveiled his Sacristy, where may be seen so many beautiful figures, this admirable and talented School, the friend of truth and of the excellent, made more than one hundred sonnets upon him, competing with one another which could speak the best of him. And so just as that work of Bandinello's deserved so much ill said as he says has been spoken about it, so that of Buonaroti deserved as much good as was said of him." At these words of mine Bandinello fell into such a fury that he was bursting, and he turned to me and said: "And what do you know that you can say about it?" "I will tell you if you have sufficient patience to know how to listen to me." Says he: "Speak up then now." The Duke and the others who were there, all listened eagerly.

I began, and in the first place I said: "Do you know that it pains me to have to tell you of the defects of that work of yours; but I will not speak of such things, rather I will tell you all that this most talented School says about it." And because this wretched man kept now saying something disagreeable, and now moving about his hands and his feet, he caused me to fall into such a rage that I began in a much more unpleasant manner than I should have done if he had acted otherwise.

"This talented School says that if one were to shave the hair off *Hercules*, there would not remain noddle sufficient to contain his brain; and that as regards that face of his one would not know whether it was the countenance of a man or of a lion-ox: and that he is not paying any attention to what he is doing: and that it is badly attached to its neck, with so little skill and with so bad a grace, that one has never seen anything worse: and that those two ugly shoulders of his resemble the two pommels of an ass's packsaddle; and that his breasts and the rest of his muscles are not copied from those of a man, but are drawn from an old sack full of melons, which has been set upright propped against a wall. So [also] the loins seem to be copied from a sack full of long gourds; one does not know by what method the two legs are attached to that ugly body; for one does not know upon which leg he is standing, or upon which he is making any display of pressure: still less does he appear to be resting upon both, as it is customary sometimes for those masters who know something about the representation [of figures]. It is easy to see that he is falling forward more than a third of a *braccio* [balance]; for this alone is the greatest and most intolerable fault that those wretched masters of the common herd commit. Of the arms they say that they are both stretched downwards without any grace: nor is there any artistic sense to be perceived in them, as if you had never seen living nudes: and that the right leg of *Hercules* and that of *Cacus* make a mixture in the calves of their legs; so that if one of the two were removed from the other, not only one of them, but rather both would remain without calves at that point where they touch: and they say that one of the feet of *Hercules* is buried and the other appears to have fire under it."

The man could not restrain himself to be patient, so that I might tell him also the great defects of *Cacus*. For one thing was that I was speaking truly, and another was that I was making it known clearly to the Duke and to the others who were in our presence, so that they made very great expressions and acts of astonishment, and then realized that I was telling the very truth. All at once this wretched man said: "Ah! you wicked lying tongue! Oh! where do you leave my design?" I replied "that he who designs well can never work out that design badly. Consequently I can believe that your design is like your work." Now when he saw from those ducal and other countenances that with their looks and with their gestures they were despising him, he allowed himself to be too much overcome by his insolence, and turning towards me with his most hideous ugly face, he all of a sudden said to me: "Oh! be silent! You b. . . . b. . . . you!"

F. THE CULT OF BEAUTY

1. *Cellini and the Pope's Button.* Love of the antique inspired men of the Renaissance to the creation of new things of beauty. The passage from Benvenuto Cellini's autobiography quoted below reveals the Renaissance approach to art and the artist.[11]

[Cellini had been engaged to reset some jewels for Pope Clement VII.] Since that was not, however, a work in which I could gain great reputation, the pope was resolved, he said, to employ me in an undertaking of the last importance, in which I should have opportunity of displaying my abilities. "The work I have in mind," he added, "is the button for the pontifical cape, which is made round, and in the form of a trencher and as big as a small trencher; in this I would have God the Father represented in half relievo, and in the midst of it I would have the edge of the large diamond set, with many other jewels of the greatest value. Go then and draw a fine design of it." Thereupon he caused all his jewels to be shown me, and I left him, highly pleased with my success.

[Several of Cellini's rivals, hearing of this undertaking, had a number of other designs made, which were submitted to the pope at the same time as his.] It so fell out that all those who had drawn those designs had laid the fine large and beautiful diamond in the middle of the breast of God the Father. The pope, who was a person of great genius, having noticed this blunder, would proceed no farther in examining their performances. After he had examined about ten, he threw the rest upon the ground and desired me to give him my model, that he might see whether I had committed the same mistake. Thereupon I came forward and opened a little round box, when instantly there seemed to flash from it a luster which dazzled the pope himself, and he cried out with a loud voice, "Benvenuto, had you been my very self, you could not have designed this with greater propriety." Then calling to Trojano, his gentleman of the bedchamber, he ordered him to fetch five hundred ducats.

Whilst they were bringing the money, he examined more minutely the ingenious artifice by which I had placed that fine diamond and God the Father in a proper position. I had laid the diamond exactly in the middle of the work, and over it I represented God the Father sitting in a sort of free, easy attitude, which suited admirably well with the rest of the piece, and did not in the least crowd the diamond; his right hand was lifted up, giving his blessing. Under the diamond I had drawn three little boys, who supported it

with their arms raised aloft. Round it was a number of figures of boys placed amongst other glittering jewels. The remainder of God the Father was covered with a cloak which wantoned in the wind, from whence issued several figures of boys, with other striking ornaments, most beautiful to behold.

[While Cellini was engaged on this work and other orders for the pope, his brother was killed in a street brawl between some soldiers and young gallants, such as occurred almost daily on any provocation, or none.] Meanwhile I exerted my utmost efforts to finish the work in gold which I was employed in by Pope Clement; still thinking day and night of the musketeer that shot my brother. Perceiving that my solicitude and anxious desire of revenge deprived me both of sleep and appetite, which threw me into a lingering disorder, and not caring to have recourse to any treacherous or dishonorable means, one evening I prepared to put an end to my disquietude.

Just after sunset, as this musketeer stood at his door with his sword in his hand, when he had done supper, I with great address came close up to him with a long dagger and gave him a violent back-handed stroke which I had aimed at his neck; that instant he turned about, and the blow falling directly upon his left shoulder, broke the whole bone of it; upon which he dropped his sword, quite overcome by the pain, and took to his heels. I pursued and in four steps came up with him, when, raising the dagger over his head which he lowered down, I hit exactly upon his collar bone and the middle of the neck; the weapon penetrated so deep into both that though I made a great effort to recover it again, I found it impossible; for at that same instant there issued out of a neighboring house four soldiers, with their swords drawn, so that I was obliged to draw mine also in my own defense.

[He takes refuge with his protector, Duke Alexander de' Medici, in whose palace he stays under cover for eight days. At the end of that time the pope sends for him, the messenger saying that the pope] knew all that had happened, that his Holiness was very much my friend, and desired me to go on with my business without giving myself any uneasiness. When I came into the presence of the pontiff, he frowned on me very much, and with angry looks seemed to reprimand me; but, upon viewing my performance, his countenance grew serene and he praised me highly, telling me that I had done a great deal in a short time; then looking attentively at me, he said, "Now that you have recovered your health, Benvenuto, take care of yourself." I understood his meaning, and told him that I should not neglect his advice.

2. *Letters of Aretino.* Another aspect of Humanist love of beauty is to be found in the following selections from the letters of Pietro Aretino (1492–1556). He was a biting satirist, whose sharp pen caused his banishment from both Arezzo and Rome and caused him to take up his residence at Venice, where he lived on the bounty of patrons who infinitely preferred supporting him to becoming the subjects of his satire.[12]

(*To his landlord.*) I should think it a sin of ingratitude, gentle sir, if I did not repay with praise a part of my debt to the divine site on which your house is built and where I dwell with the utmost pleasure in life, for it is set in a place which neither hither nor thither nor higher nor lower could better. Certainly, whoever built it gave it the most proper and pre-eminent place on the whole Grand Canal, and, as this is the patriarch of all avenues and Venice the Pope of all cities, I may truthfully say that I enjoy the most beautiful street and the most delightful view in the world. I never go to the window but I see thousands of people and as many gondolas going to market. The *piazze* to my right are the Beccarie and the Pescaria; on the left, the Bridge and the Fondaco dei Tedeschi; while, facing them both, rises the Rialto, crowded with traders. Here I see boats full of grapes, game and birds in the shops, and kitchen gardens on the pavements. Rivers and irrigated fields I no longer care to see, now that I can watch the water at dawn covered with every manner of thing that is in season. It is a joy to study the bearers of this grand plenty of fruits and greens and to watch them dispensing them to the porters who carry them to their stalls.

But all this is nothing to the sight of twenty or twenty-five sail-boats, heaped up with melons like a little island, and the multitude thronging about them to reckon and weigh and smell their beauty. Of the beautiful housewives shining in silks and gold and jewels, and seated proudly under the poop, I will say nothing, lest I slight their pomp. But I will say that I hold my sides when I listen to the boatmen shouting, jeering, and roaring at those who are rowed by lackeys without scarlet hose. And what man could hold his water if he saw, as Giulio Camillo and I saw, a boatload of Germans upset in the dead of winter, just as they came out of a tavern? Giulio is a wag and he says that the side-door of this house, being dark, narrow, and brutal to climb, is like the terrible name I have made for myself by venting the truth; but he adds: anyone who knows

me finds in my pure, frank, and natural friendship the same calm contentment that he feels when he comes out on the portico of my palace and leans on my balcony. Moreover, to add to the delight of my eye, here are the orange groves that gild the base of the Palazzo dei Camerlinghi on one side, and on the other the *rio* and bridge of San Giovanni Grisostomo; and the winter sun cannot rise without saluting my bed, my study, my kitchen; my chambers, and my hall. . . .

In sum, if I could satisfy touch and the other senses as I satisfy sight, the house would be a heaven, for I enjoy every recreation here that can please the eye. Nor must I forget the great gentlemen, both foreign and native, who pass my door, nor my heavenly rapture when the Bucentaur goes by, nor the regattas, nor the festivals which convert the Canal into a continual triumph for my eye, which is lord of all it surveys. And what shall I say of the lights which appear in the evening like scattered stars? Or of the night music which tickles my ear with sweet harmonies? It would be easier to describe your profound judgment in letters and public affairs than to exhaust the delights that I enjoy merely in gazing. Therefore, if there be any faint breath of talent in the trifles I have written, I owe it to the influence, neither of shadow nor of light nor yet of verdure nor of violets, but to the joy I feel in the airy felicity of your mansion, in which God grant me to number, in vigor and health, the years a respectable man may hope to live.

(*To Titian.*) My dear gossip, having in contempt of my custom supped alone, or rather in company of this tedious fever which lets me relish no food, I rose from table, surfeited with the despondency with which I sat down to it. And resting both arms flat on the window-sill, and leaning my whole body on it, I abandoned myself to the marvellous spectacle of the multitude of boats. . . . And when the crowds had dispersed, I, like a man weary of himself and with nothing to occupy his mind, raised my eyes to the heavens which, since God made them, were never so lovely with light and shadow. The atmosphere was such as men like myself, who envy you because they cannot be you, would render it. First, the buildings in the foreground, although of stone, seemed to be of some plastic material; and beyond them you beheld the air, in some parts pure and alive, in other murky and sallow.

Fancy, too, how I marvelled at the clouds, dense with moisture, lying half in the foreground over the roofs and half in the gloaming, for on the right everything was a *sfumato* darkening down into gray-black. I was spellbound by the variety of hues they revealed. The nearest burned with the embers of the sunset; the farthest glowed with a dimmer, leaden hue. Ah, how beautifully the hand of Nature hatched the air, making it fade and recede from the palaces, as Titian does in his landscapes! Here was a blue-green and there a green-blue, truly conceived by the caprice of Nature, that master of masters! She melted and modelled with light and shadow in a manner which made me exclaim more than once: O Titian, where are you? Upon my word, if you had painted what I report, you would confound men with the wonder that astounded me; and in gazing on what I have told you I nourished my soul on it, for the wonder of such paintings does not endure.

Part II.   TYPES OF THE ITALIAN RENAISSANCE

The Humanist movement produced many colorful individuals. An examination of their lives gives a clear insight into the effect of the Renaissance upon man's approach to living and the things of this world. Three selections in this part, therefore, are drawn from the lives of notable Renaissance types, and a fourth represents the ideal man as the age envisaged him.

A.   THE ARTIST AS AN INDIVIDUALIST

Following are the opening passages from the autobiography of Benvenuto Cellini, the famous sculptor and goldsmith, whose work was quoted in other connections in the first part of this problem.[13]

All men of every sort, who have done anything that is meritorious, or that indeed resembles merit, ought, if they be truthful persons and of good report, to set forth their lives with their own hand: but they should not commence so noble an undertaking before they have passed the age of forty years. Recognizing such a fact, now that I have travelled along my life's span for full fifty-eight years, and am in Florence, my native place, whilst recalling the many afflictions which befall those who live, and being troubled with these same afflictions less than I have ever been before up to this age: even it would seem to me that I am in greater content of mind and health of body that I have ever been in times past: and remembering certain agreeable blessings and certain incalculable calamities; looking back upon these I am struck with astonishment that I should have arrived at this age of 58 years, in which I am, by the grace of God, so happily proceeding onwards.

Although these men, inasmuch as they have labored with the very smallest trace of merit, have made themselves known to the world, the fact alone ought to be sufficient for them, that they see themselves men of mark; but because they must live in the same manner as others live, we experience in this respect a certain amount of worldly curiosity, which arises upon many different points. The first duty is to make known to others that the hero traces his descent from persons of merit and very ancient lineage. I am called Benvenuto Cellini, the son of Giovanni d'Andrea di Christofano Cellini; my mother was Elisabetta, daughter of Stefano Granacci: and both of them were Florentine citizens.

We find it set out in the chronicles made by our most ancient and reliable Florentines, according to what Giovanni Villani writes, that we may observe how the city of Florence is constructed in imitation of the beautiful city of Rome, and some traces may be discovered of the Colosseum and of the Baths. These traces are near to Santa Croce; the Capital was where the Mercato Vecchio stands today; the Rotonda is entirely standing, which was made for a temple of Mars, and today is dedicated to our patron, San Giovanni. That this was so can be very clearly seen and cannot be denied: but the said edifices are much smaller than those in Rome. They say that the man who caused them to be built was Julius Caesar, together with certain other Roman nobles, who having conquered and taken Fiesole, erected a city on that spot; and each of them undertook one of these remarkable structures. Julius Caesar had a brave chief captain who was called Fiorino da Cellino (which is a fortress about two miles from Monte Fiasconi). This Fiorino having taken up his abode below Fiesole, on the spot where Florence now is, in order to be near the river Arno for the convenience of his army, all his soldiers and such other persons as had dealings with this said captain used to say: "Let us go to Fiorenze," because the said captain bore the name of Fiorino, and because in that place where he had his said dwelling, from the natural features of the place, there grew a vast quantity of flowers. So in giving a commencement to the city, since this seemed to Julius Caesar a most beautiful name, and one appropriately given to it, and because flowers bring good omen, he gave this name of Fiorenze to the said city; and in order besides to confer a sort of favor upon his brave captain; since he liked him so much the more, because he had drawn him from a very humble condition, and because so brave a man had been created by himself. . . .

We find that there are some of our Cellini in Ravenna, the most ancient city in Italy, and there they are great nobles; they are also in Pisa, and I have found them in many places throughout Christendom; and in this very State there also remain some of the stock, addicted, moreover, to the profession of arms; for it is not so many years back that a youth named Luca Cellini, a beardless lad, entered into combat with a soldier, a skilled and very valiant man, who had fought on previous occasions in the lists, called Francesco da Vicorati. This Luca, by his own valor, sword in hand, conquered and slew him with so much bravery and skill, that he made every one marvel, since they had expected the opposite result. So that I boast of having my descent from brave men.

Now as regards such honor as I have acquired for my house, under the known conditions of our life today and by means of my profession, which is not a matter of great consequence, I will speak of it in its own place, glorying much more in that having been born in humble circumstances I have added some honorable foundation to my family, than if I had sprung from high lineage and by base qualities had stained or extinguished it. I will therefore commence with how it pleased God that I should be born.

B. THE ARTIST-SCHOLAR

The following account of the life and talents of Leon Battista Alberti (1404–72) is taken from Giorgio Vasari's *Lives of Seventy of the Most Eminent Painters, Sculptors, and Architects*. Vasari, a contemporary of Cellini, was himself a talented painter, but he is remembered more as a biographer. His life of Alberti reveals the versatility of the Renaissance artist.[14]

The knowledge of letters and the study of the sciences are without doubt of the utmost value to all, and offer the most important advantages to every artist who takes pleasure therein; but most of all they are serviceable to sculptors, painters, and architects, for whom they prepare the path to various inventions in all the works executed by them; and be the natural qualities of a man what they may, his judgment can never be brought to perfection if he be deprived of the advantages resulting from the accompaniment of learning. . . . Since theory, when separated from practice, is, for the most part, found to avail very little; but when theory and practice chance to be happily united in the same person, nothing can be more suitable to the life and vocation of artists, as well because art is rendered much richer and more perfect by the aid of science, as because the councils and writings of learned artists have, in themselves, a greater efficacy, and obtain a higher degree of credit, than can be accorded to the words or works of those who know nothing beyond the simple process they use, and which they put in practice, well or ill, as it may chance.

Now that all this is true is seen clearly in the instance of Leon Battista Alberti, who, having given his attention to the study of Latin as well as to that of architecture, perspective, and painting, has left behind him books, written in such a manner, that no artist of later times has been able to surpass him in his style and other qualities as an author, while there have been numbers, much more distinguished than himself in the practice of art, although it is very generally supposed (such is the force of his writings, and so extensive has been their influence on the pens and words of the learned, his contemporaries and others), that he was, in fact, superior to all those who have, on the contrary, greatly surpassed him in their works. We are thus taught, by experience, that, in so far as regards name and fame, the written word is that which, of all things has the most effectual force, the most vivid life, and the longest duration; for books make their way to all places, and everywhere they obtain the credence of men, provided they be truthful and written in the spirit of candor. We are therefore not to be surprised if we find the renowned Leon Battista to be better known by his writings than by the works of his hand.

This master was born in Florence, of the most noble family of the Alberti, concerning which we have already spoken in another place. He gave his attention, not only to the acquirement of knowledge in the world of art generally, and to the examination of works of antiquity in their proportions, etc., but also, and much more fully, to writing on these subjects, to which he was by nature more inclined than to the practice of art.

Leon Battista was well versed in arithmetic, and a very good geometrician; he wrote ten books respecting architecture in the Latin tongue, which were published in 1481; they may now be read in the Florentine language, having been translated by the Rev. Messer Cosimo Bartoli, provost of San Giovanni, in Florence. He likewise wrote three books on painting, now translated into the Tuscan by Messer Ludovico Domenichi, and composed a dissertation of tractile forces, containing rules for measuring heights. Leon Battista was moreover the author of the *Libri della vita civile*, with some other works of an amatory character, in prose and verse: he was the first who attempted to apply Latin measures to Italian verse. . . .

At the time when Nicholas V had thrown the city of Rome into utter confusion with his peculiar manner of building, Leon Battista Alberti arrived in that city, where, by means of his intimate friend Biondo da Forli, he became known to the pontiff. The latter had previously availed himself of the counsel of Bernardo Rossellino, a Florentine sculptor and architect, as will be related in the life of Antonio, his brother; and Bernardo, having commenced the restoration of the papal palace, with other works in Santa Maria Maggiore, thenceforward proceeded by the advice of Leon Battista, such being the will of the Pope. Thus the pontiff with the counsel of one of these two, and the execution of the other, brought many useful and praiseworthy labors to conclusion: among these was the Fountain of the Acqua Vergine, which had been ruined, and was restored by him. He likewise caused the fountain of the Piazza de' Trevi to be decorated with the marble ornaments which we now see there, among which are the arms of Pope Nicholas himself, and those of the Roman people. . . .

It is said that the same architect produced the design for the palace and gardens, erected by the Rucellai family in the Via della Scala, an edifice constructed with much judgment, and which is therefore exceedingly commodious. Besides many other convenient arrangements, there are two galleries or *loggie*, one towards the south, the other to the west, both very beautiful, and raised upon the columns without arches; which method is the true and proper one, according to the ancients, because the architraves, which are placed immediately upon the capitals of the columns, stand level, while a rectangular body, such as is the arch turned into a vault in the upper part, cannot stand on a round column, without having the angles out of square or awry; this considered, the best mode of construction requires that the architraves should be placed upon the columns, or that, when it is resolved to construct arches, the master should employ pillars instead of columns. . . .

Leon Battista Alberti was a man of refined habits and praiseworthy life, a friend of distinguished men, liberal and courteous to all. He lived honorably and like a gentleman, as he was, all the course of his life, and finally, having attained to a tolerably mature age, he departed content and tranquil to a better life, leaving behind him a most honorable name.

C. THE SCHOLAR-CHURCHMAN

The life of Nicolò Perotto (d. 1430), which follows, was written by Vespasiano da Bisticci, a Florentine bookseller who recorded the lives of many of the notable Humanists with whom he came into contact in his business.[15]

Messer Nicolò Perotto, born of poor parentage, was learned in Greek and Latin, having been sent in his youth to study under Guerino at Ferrara, where by his ready intellect he soon became a fine scholar and master of an elegant style in writing. While he was at Ferrara, William Gray, Bishop of Ely, and of royal descent, was also a student there, and, having been told of the good qualities of Messer Nicolò, he asked him to lodge with him. He was so conscious of the virtues of Nicolò that he gave him as much as he needed for the purchase of books.

After several years of assiduous study had passed, the King of England wrote to Gray and directed him to go to Rome as his proctor, whereupon he took Nicolò in his train. Here Gray was fully occupied with his duties, and Nicolò, being anxious to go on with his Greek studies, although he was already well versed in the language, begged his patron to arrange with Cardinal Niceno that he might acquire still fuller knowledge of it. When he learned Nicolò's wishes Gray procured his admission to the cardinal's house when he was twenty years old. Here he studied Greek day and night till he became a profound scholar, and the cardinal, who was greatly attached to men of worth, showed him much favor and affection. He ultimately determined to become a priest, and by the cardinal's aid he got a benefice. His father was very poor, but Nicolò, who enjoyed certain emoluments and was able to live well, managed to have him made a *cavaliere* whereby he obtained an income from the state. Thus he was able to do good service to his family.

Messer Nicolò won great honor at the court for his writings, and the beauty of his style. Pope Nicolas, having seen some of his compositions, begged him to translate *Polibio Megalopolitano* from Greek into Latin, which work he executed with such skill that all who read it were astonished, declaring that no writer during the present pontificate had written with such elegance and erudition. He then presented it to the Pope, who, when he saw it, was so greatly pleased that he gave Nicolò a purse of six hundred ducats. This work was of such excellence that, when it appeared in Florence, Messer Poggio and other scholars of the time praised it highly. It happened that, before this, Messer Poggio had differed sharply with Messer Nicolò, but now—so great is the power of truth—he was constrained to praise it unreservedly, saying he had never read a finer or more coherent style.

This work brought him fame at the court of Rome and throughout Italy. He spent several years in Rome and had charge of the household of the Cardinal of Niceno. Nevertheless, he still found time for study, and when the bishopric of Sipontino became vacant the Pope gave it to him. Then, when he had established a suitable household for himself, he found posts for his father and all his brothers. He translated several works of St. Basil, *De Odio et Invidia,* Plutarch's

De fortuna populi Romani et Virtute Alexandri, and others. He wrote a book on the rules of verse, and a grammar for the use of Latin students. Last, he wrote a great and intricate work on all the Latin and Greek authors which, though he called it the *Commento di Marziale,* is really an alphabetical list of all Latin writers, and much longer than the ten books of Livy, a work which he was able to complete without grammar or vocabulary so great was his knowledge of Latin. He wrote it at the request of the Duke of Urbino, who afterwards preserved him from disaster.

Up to the time of Pope Sixtus, Nicolò was very prosperous, and was nominated to several state offices, but this Pope at once began to persecute him; to lay hands on him, to rob him of all he had and even worse. And if the Duke of Urbino had not remembered him favorably and had not come to his rescue—like a protector of all men of merit—he would have fared badly. As it was Nicolò was only saved because the Duke had a strong hold over the Pope. Nicolò was in no respect culpable, he was only attacked through envy and jealousy. He lost heavily through this molestation and, finding himself debarred from all enjoyment of the fruit of his labor, he fell ill of grief and died. He left a number of writings which are not mentioned here.

D. THE COURTIER

One of the most famous works of the Renaissance was *The Book of the Courtier* by Baldassare Castiglione (1478–1529). Written in 1508, the book reports conversations held in the court of the Duke of Urbino. Castiglione was himself a diplomat and courtier, and the following selections from his work indicate the ideal of the early sixteenth century.[16]

". . . I would that this evening's game might be, that we select some one of the company and give him the task of portraying a perfect Courtier, explaining all the conditions and special qualities requisite in one who deserves this title; and as to those things that shall not appear sound, let everyone be allowed to contradict as in the schools of the philosophers it is allowed to contradict anyone who proposes a thesis. . . ."

"I wish, then, that this Courtier of ours should be nobly born and of gentle race; because it is far less unseemly for one of ignoble birth to fail in worthy deeds, than for one of noble birth, who, if he strays from the path of his predecessors, stains his family name, and not only fails to achieve but loses what has been achieved already; for noble birth is like a bright lamp that manifests and makes visible good and evil deeds, and kindles and stimulates to virtue both by fear of shame and by hope of praise. And since this splendor of nobility does not illumine the deeds

of the humbly born, they lack that stimulus and fear of shame, nor do they feel any obligation to advance beyond what their predecessors have done; while to the nobly born it seems a reproach not to reach at least the goal set them by their ancestors. . . ."

"It is true that, by favor of the stars or of nature, some men are endowed at birth with such graces that they seem not to have been born, but rather as if some god had formed them with his very hands and adorned them with every excellence of mind and body. So too there are many men so foolish and rude that one cannot but think that nature brought them into the world out of contempt or mockery. Just as these can usually accomplish little even with constant diligence and good training, so with slight pains those others reach the highest summit of excellence. And to give you an instance: you see my lord Don Ippolito d'Este, Cardinal of Ferrara, who has enjoyed such fortune from his birth, that his person, his aspect, his words, and all his movements are so disposed and imbued with this grace, that—although he is young—he exhibits among the most aged prelates such weight of character that he seems fitter to teach than to be taught; likewise in conversation with men and women of every rank, in games, in pleasantry and in banter, he has a certain sweetness and manners so gracious, that whoso speaks with him or even sees him, must needs remain attached to him forever.

"But to return to our subject: I say that there is a middle state between perfect grace on the one hand and senseless folly on the other; and those who are not thus perfectly endowed by nature, with study and toil can in great part polish and amend their natural defects. Besides his noble birth, then, I would have the Courtier favored in this regard also, and endowed by nature not only with talent and beauty of person and feature, but with a certain grace and (as we say) air that shall make him at first sight pleasing and agreeable to all who see him; and I would have this an ornament that should dispose and unite all his actions, and in his outward aspect give promise of whatever is worthy the society and favor of every great lord."

Here, without waiting longer, my lord Gaspar Pallavicino said:

"In order that our game may have the form prescribed, and that we may not seem to slight the privilege given us to contradict, I say that this nobility of birth does not appear to me so essential in the Courtier; and if I thought I were saying what was new to any of us, I should cite instances of many men born of the noblest blood who have been full of vices; and on the other hand, of many men among the humbly born who by their virtue have made their posterity illustrious. And if what you just said be true, namely that there is in everything this occult influence of the original seed, then we should all be in the same case, because we had the same origin, nor would any man be more noble than another. But as to our differences and grades of eminence and obscurity, I believe there are many other causes: among which I rate fortune to be chief; for we see her holding sway in all mundane affairs, often amusing herself by lifting to heaven whom she pleases (although wholly without merit), and burying in the depths those most worthy to be exalted.

"I quite agree with what you say as to the good fortune of those endowed from birth with advantages of mind and body: but this is seen as well among the humbly born, since nature has no such subtle distinctions as these; and often, as I said, the highest gifts of nature are found among the most obscure. Therefore, since this nobility of birth is won neither by talent nor by strength nor by craft, and is rather the merit of our predecessors than our own, it seems to me too extravagant to maintain that if our Courtier's parents be humbly born, all his good qualities are spoiled, and that all those other qualifications that you mentioned do not avail to raise him to the summit of perfection; I mean talent, beauty of feature, comeliness of person, and that grace which makes him always charming to everyone at first sight. . . ."

"But to come to some details, I am of opinion that the principal and true profession of the Courtier ought to be that of arms; which I would have him follow actively above all else, and be known among others as bold and strong, and loyal to whomsoever he serves. And he will win a reputation for these good qualities by exercising them at all times and in all places, since one may never fail in this without severest censure. And just as among women, their fair fame once sullied never recovers its first luster, so the reputation of a gentleman who bears arms, if once it be in the least tarnished with cowardice or other disgrace, remains forever infamous before the world and full of ignominy. Therefore the more our Courtier excels in this art, the more he will be worthy of praise; and yet I do not deem essential in him that perfect knowledge of things and those other qualities that befit a commander; since this would be too wide a sea, let us be content, as we have said, with perfect loyalty and unconquered courage, and that he be always seen to possess them. . . .

"Not that we would have him look so fierce, or go about blustering, or say that he has taken his cuirass to wife, or threaten with those grim scowls that we have often seen in Berto; because to such men as this, one might justly say that which a brave lady jestingly said in gentle company to one whom I will not name at present; who, being invited by her out of compliment to dance, refused not only that, but to listen to the music, and many other entertainments proposed to him,—saying always that such silly trifles were not his business; so that at last the lady said, 'What is your business, then?' He replied with a sour look, 'To fight.' Then the lady at once said, 'Now that you are in no war and out of fighting trim, I should think it were a good thing to have yourself well oiled, and to stow yourself with all your battle harness in a closet until you be needed, lest you grow more rusty than you are'; and so, amid much laughter from the bystanders, she left the discomfited fellow to his silly presumption.

"Therefore let the man we are seeking be very bold, stern, and always among the first, where the enemy are to be seen; and in every other place, gentle, modest, reserved, above all things avoiding ostentation and that impudent self-praise by which men ever excite hatred and disgust in all who hear them."

Then my lord Gaspar replied:

"As for me, I have known few men excellent in anything whatever, who do not praise themselves; and it seems to me that this may well be permitted them; for when anyone who feels himself to be of worth, sees that he is not known to the ignorant by his works, he is offended that his worth should lie buried, and needs must in some way hold it up to view, in order that he may not be cheated of the fame that is the true reward of worthy effort. Thus among the ancient authors, whoever carries weight seldom fails to praise himself. They indeed are insufferable who do this without desert, but such we do not presume our Courtier to be."

The Count then said:

"If you heard what I said, it was impudent and indiscriminate self-praise that I censured: and as you say, we surely ought not to form a bad opinion of a brave man who praises himself modestly, nay we ought rather to regard such praise as better evidence than if it came from the mouth of others. I say, however, that he, who in praising himself runs into no error and incurs no annoyance or envy at the hands of those that hear him, is a very discreet man indeed and merits praise from others in addition to that which he bestows upon himself; because it is a very difficult matter."

Then my lord Gaspar said:

"You must teach us that."

The Count replied:

"Among the ancient authors there is no lack of those who have taught it; but to my thinking, the whole art consists in saying things in such a way that they shall not seem to be said to that end, but let fall so naturally that it was impossible not to say them, and while seeming always to avoid self-praise, yet to achieve it; but not after the manner of those boasters, who open their mouths and let the words come forth haphazard. Like one of our friends a few days ago, who, being quite run through the thigh with a spear at Pisa, said he thought it was a fly that had stung him; and another man said he kept no mirror in his room because, when angry, he became so terrible to look at, that the sight of himself would have frightened him too much."

Everyone laughed at this, but messer Cesare Gonzaga added:

"Why do you laugh? Do you not know that Alexander the Great, on hearing the opinion of a philosopher to be that there was an infinite number of worlds, began to weep, and being asked why he wept, replied, 'Because I have not yet conquered one of them'; as if he would fain have vanquished all? Does not this seem to you a greater boast than that about the fly-sting?"

Then the Count said:

"Yes, and Alexander was a greater man than he who made the other speech. But extraordinary men are surely to be pardoned when they assume much; for he who has great things to do must needs have daring to do them, and confidence in himself, and must not be abject or mean in spirit, yet very modest in speech, showing less confidence in himself than he has, lest his self-confidence lead to rashness."

The Count now paused a little, and messer Bernardo Bibbiena said, laughing:

"I remember what you said earlier, that this Courtier of ours must be endowed by nature with beauty of countenance and person, and with a grace that shall make him so agreeable. Grace and beauty of countenance I think I certainly possess, and this is the reason why so many ladies are ardently in love with me, as you know; but I am rather doubtful as to the beauty of my person, especially as regards these legs of mine, which seem to me decidedly less well proportioned than I should wish: as to my bust and other members however, I am quite content. Pray, now, describe a little more in particular the sort of body that the Courtier is to have, so that I may dismiss this doubt and set my mind at rest."

After some laughter at this, the Count continued:

"Of a certainty that grace of countenance can be truly said to be yours, nor need I cite further example than this to show what manner of thing it is, for we unquestioningly perceive your aspect to be most agreeable and pleasing to everyone, albeit the lineaments of it are not very delicate. Still it is of a manly cast and at the same time full of grace; and this characteristic is to be found in many different types of countenance. And of such sort I would have our Courtier's aspect; not so soft and effeminate as is sought by many, who not only curl their hair and pluck their brows, but gloss their faces with all those arts employed by the most wanton and unchaste women in the world; and in their walk, posture and every act, they seem so limp and languid that their limbs are like to fall apart; and they pronounce their words so mournfully that they appear about to expire upon the spot: and the more they find themselves with men of rank, the more they affect such tricks. Since nature has not made them women, as they seem to wish to appear and be, they should be treated not as good women but as public harlots, and driven not merely from the courts of great lords but from the society of honest men.

"Then coming to the bodily frame, I say it is enough if this be neither extremely short nor tall, for both of these conditions excite a certain contemptuous surprise, and men of either sort are gazed upon in much the same way that we gaze on monsters. Yet if we must offend in one of the two extremes, it is preferable to fall a little short of the just measure of height than to exceed it, for besides often being dull of intellect, men thus huge of body are also unfit for every exercise of agility, which thing I should much wish in the Courtier. And so would I have him well built and shapely of limb, and would have him show strength and lightness and suppleness, and know all bodily exercises that befit a man of war: whereof I think the first should be to handle every sort of weapon well on foot and on horse, to understand the advantages of each, and especially to be familiar with those weapons that are ordinarily used among gentlemen; for besides the use of them in war, where such subtlety in contrivance is perhaps not needful, there frequently arise differences between one gentleman and another, which afterwards result in duels often fought with such weapons as happen at the moment to be within reach: thus knowledge of this kind is a very safe thing. Nor am I one of those who say that skill is forgotten in the hour of need; for he whose skill forsakes him at such a time, indeed gives token that he has already lost heart and head through fear.

"Moreover I deem it very important to know how to wrestle, for it is a great help in the use of all kinds of weapons on foot. Then, both for his own sake and for that of his friends, he must understand the quarrels and differences that may arise, and must be quick to seize an advantage, always showing courage and prudence in all things. Nor should he be too ready to fight except when honor demands it; for besides the great danger that the uncertainty of fate entails, he who rushes into such affairs recklessly and without urgent cause, merits the severest censure even though he be successful. But when he finds himself so far engaged that he cannot withdraw without reproach, he ought to be most deliberate, both in the preliminaries to the duel and in the duel itself, and always show readiness and daring. . . .

"Even in time of peace weapons are often used in various exercises, and gentlemen appear in public shows before the people and ladies and great lords. For this reason I would have our Courtier a perfect horseman in every kind of seat; and besides understanding horses and what pertains to riding, I would have him use all possible care and diligence to lift himself a little beyond the rest in everything, so that he may be ever recognized as eminent above all others.

And as we read of Alcibiades that he surpassed all the nations with whom he lived, each in their particular province, so I would have this Courtier of ours excel all others, and each in that which is most their profession. And as it is the especial pride of the Italians to ride well with the rein, to govern wild horses with consummate skill, and to play at tilting and jousting,—in these things let him be among the best of the Italians. In tourneys and in the arts of defence and attack, let him shine among the best in France. In stick-throwing, bull-fighting, and in casting spears and darts, let him excel among the Spaniards. But above everything he should temper all his movements with a certain good judgment and grace, if he wishes to merit that universal favor which is so greatly prized.

"There are also many other exercises, which although not immediately dependent upon arms, yet are closely connected therewith, and greatly foster manly sturdiness; and one of the chief among these seems to me to be the chase, because it bears a certain likeness to war: and truly it is an amusement for great lords and befitting a man at court, and furthermore it is seen to have been much cultivated among the ancients. It is fitting also to know how to swim, to leap, to run, to throw stones, for besides the use that may be made of this in war, a man often has occasion to show what he can do in such matters; whence good esteem is to be won, especially with the multitude, who must be taken into account withal. Another admirable exercise, and one very befitting a man at court, is the game of tennis, in which are well shown the disposition of the body, the quickness and suppleness of every member, and all those qualities that are seen in nearly every other exercise. Nor less highly do I esteem vaulting on horse, which although it be fatiguing and difficult, makes a man very light and dexterous more than any other thing; and besides its utility, if this lightness is accompanied by grace, it is to my thinking a finer show than any of the others.

"Our Courtier having once become more than fairly expert in these exercises, I think he should leave the others on one side: such as turning somersaults, rope-walking, and the like, which savor of the mountebank and little befit a gentleman.

"But since one cannot devote himself to such fatiguing exercises continually, and since repetition becomes very tiresome and abates the admiration felt for what is rare, we must always diversify our life with various occupations. For this reason I would have our Courtier sometimes descend to quieter and more tranquil exercises, and in order to escape envy and to entertain himself agreeably with everyone, let him do whatever others do, yet never departing from praiseworthy deeds, and governing himself with that good judgment which will keep him from all folly; but let him laugh, jest, banter, frolic, and dance, yet in such fashion that he shall always appear genial and discreet, and that everything he may do or say shall be stamped with grace. . . ."

"I would have him more than passably accomplished in letters, at least in those studies that are called the humanities, and conversant not only with the Latin language but with the Greek, for the sake of the many different things that have been admirably written therein. Let him be well versed in the poets, and not less in the orators and historians, and also proficient in writing verse and prose, especially in this vulgar tongue of ours; for besides the enjoyment he will find in it, he will by this means never lack agreeable entertainment with ladies, who are usually fond of such things. And if other occupations or want of study prevent his reaching such perfection as to render his writings worthy of great praise, let him be careful to suppress them so that others may not laugh at him, and let him show them only to a friend whom he can trust: because they will at least be of this service to him, that the exercise will enable him to judge the work of others. For it very rarely happens that a man who is not accustomed to write, however learned he may be, can ever quite appreciate the toil and industry of writers, or taste the sweetness and excellence of style, and those latent niceties that are often found in the ancients.

"Moreover these studies will also make him fluent, and as Aristippus said to the tyrant, confident and assured in speaking with everyone. . . ."

"My lords, you must know that I am not content with the Courtier unless he be also a musician and unless, besides understanding and being able to read notes, he can play upon divers instruments. For if we consider rightly, there is to be found no rest from toil or medicine for the troubled spirit more becoming and praiseworthy in time of leisure, than this; and especially in courts, where besides the relief from tedium that music affords us all, many things are done to please the ladies, whose tender and gentle spirit is easily penetrated by harmony and filled with sweetness. Thus it is no marvel that in both ancient and modern times they have always been inclined to favor musicians, and have found refreshing spiritual food in music. . . ."

". . . I wish to discuss another matter, which I deem of great importance and therefore think our Courtier ought by no means to omit: and this is to know how to draw and to have acquaintance with the very art of painting.

"And do not marvel that I desire this art, which today may seem to savor of the artisan and little to befit a gentleman; for I remember having read that the ancients, especially throughout Greece, had their boys of gentle birth study painting in school as an honorable and necessary thing, and it was admitted to the first rank of the liberal arts; while by public edict they forbade that it be taught to slaves. Among the Romans too, it was held in highest honor, and the very noble family of the Fabii took their name from it; for the first Fabius was given the name *Pictor,* because,—being indeed a most excellent painter, and so devoted to painting that when he painted the walls of the temple of Health,—he inscribed his own name thereon; for although he was born of a family thus renowned and honored with so many consular titles, triumphs and other dignities, and although he was a man of letters and learned in the law, and numbered among the orators,—yet he thought to add splendor and ornament to his fame by leaving a memorial that he had been a painter. Nor is there lack of many other men of illustrious family, celebrated in this art; which besides being very noble and worthy in itself, is of great utility, and especially in war for drawing places, sites, rivers, bridges, rocks, fortresses, and the like; since however well we may keep them in memory (which is very difficult), we cannot show them to others.

"And truly he who does not esteem this art, seems to me very unreasonable; for this universal fabric that we see,—with the vast heaven so richly adorned with shining stars, and in the midst the earth girdled by the seas, varied with mountains, valleys and rivers, and bedecked with so many divers trees, beautiful flowers and grasses, —may be said to be a great and noble picture, composed by the hand of nature and of God; and whoever is able to imitate it, seems to me deserving of great praise: nor can it be imitated without knowledge of many things, as he knows well who tries. Hence the ancients greatly prized both the art and the artist, which thus attained the summit of highest excellence; very sure proof of which may be found in the antique marble and bronze statues that yet are seen. And although painting is different from sculpture, both the one and the other spring from the same source, which is good design. Therefore, as the statues are divine, so we may believe the pictures were also; the more indeed because they are susceptible of greater skill."

X

The Reformation

Luther at Worms is the most pregnant and momentous fact in our history. . . . The great fact which we have to recognize is that with all the intensity of his passion for authority he did more than any single man to make modern history the development of revolution.

Lord Acton

CONTENTS

[211]

QUESTIONS FOR STUDY

PART I

1. Why is the sin of simony particularly dangerous for the well-being of the Church?

2. Why was Pope Pius concerned with the behavior of Cardinal Rodrigo Borgia?

3. "Erasmus laid the egg that Luther hatched." Explain.

4. What is an indulgence?

5. How does the Lutheran formula for salvation differ from that of the Catholic Church?

6. It is often said that Luther was essentially a medieval man, despite the fact that he lived in the Renaissance. What justification is there for this statement?

7. How does Luther's concept of the Christian Church as an organization differ from that of the Papacy?

8. Compare the attitudes of Luther and Calvin toward God and the means to salvation.

PART II

9. What is Luther's attitude toward temporal power? What factors in German history and German conditions in Luther's time helped to shape his ideas on church and state?

10. According to the Augsburg settlement, what determined the religion of the individual German?

11. What aspects of the Augsburg settlement might cause trouble for the future?

12. Is there any difference between the attitudes of Luther and Calvin on civil government?

13. In what sense did Knox extend the arguments of Calvin concerning civil government to their logical conclusion? What would the Papacy have said of Knox's arguments?

14. What, according to Knox, is the source of "right knowledge?"

15. How did Calvin's economic theories differ from those of medieval churchmen?

16. What did the Reformation contribute to the growth of the spirit of capitalism?

INTRODUCTION TO THE PROBLEM

Throughout the Middle Ages the Roman Catholic Church had frequently been obliged to face the attacks of heretics, anticlericals, and reformers. The Church thus had long experience with inimical movements, and usually it had met such challenges by adopting reforms, reconciling dissenters, or suppressing and destroying its opponents. The reform movements of the early sixteenth century appeared at first to be similar to those of the past and subject to similar treatment. The anticlerical agitation which preceded Luther's revolt seemed little different from the anticlericalism endemic in the Middle Ages and even the Humanist satires upon the Church had their medieval parallels. By many contemporaries the storm over indulgences in Germany was thought to be only another "monkish quarrel." But it soon became evident that the reform movement initiated by Martin Luther in 1517 was proceeding beyond mere condemnation of clerical abuses to an assault upon the most cherished fundamentals of Catholic dogma. It became equally evident that the reformers were supported by forces difficult to suppress or destroy because they were derived from the dynamics of the economic, political, and intellectual attitudes of the day. The Reformation thus became a complex movement involving such widespread elements as economic doctrine, political theory, and state policy, and one of its results was a series of international and civil wars which embroiled Europe for over a century.

One must constantly bear in mind, however, that despite its many-sided character the Reformation was first of all a religious movement. The concern of its leaders was primarily with the soul of the individual, and the most striking feature of the Reformation was the change in relationship between the individual and what had been the unique source of religious authority in the Middle Ages, the Church. This change, which had the effect of actually releasing large groups from the authority of the Church, was so drastic that some historians have preferred the title "Protestant Revolt" to "Protestant Reformation." This breach in the monopoly of the Catholic Church was accomplished originally by theologians like Luther who believed that certain accepted doctrines had been misstated or misinterpreted by the Church. Originally Luther had no desire to leave the Church or to start a new church of his own. He desired to reform the Church; specifically his hope was that his own interpretation of certain doctrines would be pronounced valid. It was the unwillingness of the Church to accept this interpretation, and Luther's refusal to recant and bow to the authority of the Church which made the attempted reformation an actual revolt.

Inherent in the religious revolt were the basic political issues involving Church and State which had agitated popes, kings, and philosophers during the Middle Ages. "What should be the relationship between the reformed churches and the secular magistrate? How does the State stand in relation to the new religion of the reformers?" The protestants could not escape these questions. Indeed, the reformers had often to answer them under circumstances as difficult and confusing as in the days of Gregory VII, Innocent III, and Boniface VIII. The princes of Europe were also deeply concerned to find a solution to the problem of their relation to the "spiritual arm" in a world in which there were several religions rather than one, and the religious Reformation thereby became inextricably involved in the domestic and international politics of the day. This involvement forced the reformers to enunciate political theories, theories which were often in opposition to those previously developed by the Catholic Church.

Then, too, the Reformation must be studied as a revolt not only against the religious and political doctrines of the Church, but also against its economic precepts. In Problem IV the student has already been introduced to the basic economic doctrines of the Church. These doctrines had been developed in the period before the rise of the towns, and despite the radical alterations brought about by the revival of trade in the eleventh century, the fundamental attitude of the Church toward economic activity remained unchanged. Moreover, its economic doctrines were inextricably interwoven with its religious dogma, and while an assault upon the one did not necessarily mean an assault upon the other, once the Church's formula for salvation had been so pugnaciously questioned it was only to be expected that the lag of its economic doctrine behind economic fact would invite attack upon the Church's attitude toward trade.

The documents which follow are intended to introduce the student to some of the religious, political, and economic problems raised by the Reformation.

THE PROBLEM

Part I.   THE RELIGIOUS ASPECT

A.   ANTICLERICALISM

The Babylonian Captivity (1309–1376) and the Great Schism (1378–1417) gave grounds for an increase of long-standing anticlerical feeling, and the reputedly "scandalous lives of the clergy" in the fifteenth century, though perhaps no more "scandalous" than during earlier periods, fostered popular discontent with the Church. The documents which follow reveal the nature of anticlericalism and the Church's understanding of the problem.

1. *The Incidence of Simony.* The following selection is from the contemporary *History of the Council of Constance* (1414–1418) written by Theodoric Vrie, an Augustinian friar. The lament is put in the mouth of Christ.[1]

The supreme pontiffs, as I know, are elected through avarice and simony, and likewise the other bishops are ordained for gold. These, in turn, will not ordain those below them, the priests, deacons, sub-deacons and acolytes, except a strict agreement be first drawn up. Of this mammon of unrighteousness the bishops, the real rulers, and the chapters, each has his part. The once accepted proverb, "Freely give for freely ye have received," is now most vilely perverted: "Freely I have not received, nor will I freely give, for I have bought my bishopric for a great price, and must indemnify myself impiously for my untoward outlay. I will not ordain you as priest except for money. I purchased the sacrament of ordination when I became a bishop and I propose to sell you the same sacred sign and seal of ordination. By beseeching and by gold, I have gained my office, for beseeching and for gold do I sell you your place. Refuse the amount I demand and you shall not become a priest."

If Simon Magus were now alive he might buy with money not only the Holy Ghost, but God the Father, and Me, the Son of God. But favor is bought from the ungrateful who do not the works of grace, for grace must give freely, but if bought and not given, grace is no longer grace. But why say more? The bishops who take money for ordination become lepers with Gehasi. Those ordained do, by their bribery, condemn themselves to perdition with Simon Magus, to whom Peter said, "Thy money perish with thee."

2. *A Papal Admonition.* The following letter was written by Pope Pius II to Cardinal Rodrigo Borgia (later Pope Alexander VI) on June 11, 1460.[2]

Dear Son: We have learned that your Worthiness, forgetful of the high office with which you are invested, was present from the seventeenth to the twenty-second hour, four days ago, in the gardens of John de Bichis, where there were several women of Siena, women wholly given over to worldly vanities. Your companion was one of your colleagues whom his years, if not the honor of the Apostolic See, ought to have reminded of his duty. We have heard that the dance was indulged in in all wantonness; none of the allurements of love were lacking, and you conducted yourself in a wholly worldly manner. Shame forbids mention of all that took place, for not only the things themselves but their very names are unworthy of your rank. In order that your lust might be all the more unrestrained, the husbands, fathers, brothers, and kinsmen of the young women and girls were not invited to be present. You and a few servants were the leaders and inspirers of this orgy. It is said that nothing is now talked of in Siena but your vanity, which is the subject of universal ridicule. Certain it is that here at the baths, where Churchmen and the laity are very numerous, your name is on every one's tongue.

Our displeasure is beyond words, for your conduct has brought the holy state and office into disgrace; the people will say that they make us rich and great, not that we may live a blameless life, but that we may have means to gratify our passions. This is the reason the princes and the powers despise us and the laity mock us; this is why our own mode of living is thrown in our face when we reprove others. Contempt is the lot of Christ's vicar because he seems to tolerate these actions. You, dear son, have charge of the bishopric of Valencia, the most important in Spain; you are a chancellor of the Church, and what renders your conduct all the more reprehensible is the fact that you have a seat among the cardinals, with the Pope, as advisors of the Holy See. We leave it to you whether it is be-

Leo made 50,000 ducats
@ 5 annually from sale[?]
2000 offices . Sixtus[?]. So annual =10%? purchase price[?]

coming to your dignity to court young women, and to send those whom you love fruits and wine, and during the whole day to give no thought to anything but sensual pleasures.

People blame us on your account, and the memory of your blessed uncle, Calixtus, likewise suffers, and many say he did wrong in heaping honors upon you. If you try to excuse yourself on the ground of your youth, I say to you: you are no longer so young as not to see what duties your offices impose upon you. A cardinal should be above reproach and an example of right living before the eyes of all men, and then we should have just grounds for anger when temporal princes bestow uncomplimentary epithets upon us; when they dispute with us the possession of our property and force us to submit ourselves to their will.

Of a truth we inflict these wounds upon ourselves, and we ourselves are the cause of these troubles, since we by our conduct are daily

diminishing the authority of the Church. Our punishment for it in this world is dishonor, and in the world to come well deserved torment. May, therefore, your good sense place a restraint on these frivolities, and may you never lose sight of your dignity; then people will not call you a vain gallant among men.

If this occurs again we shall be compelled to show that it was contrary to our exhortation, and that it caused us great pain; and our censure will not pass over you without causing you to blush. We have always loved you and thought you worthy of our protection as a man of an earnest and modest character. Therefore, conduct yourself henceforth so that we may retain this opinion of you, and may behold in you only the example of a well ordered life. Your years, which are not such as to preclude improvement, permit us to admonish you paternally. As for your companion, should his years not warrant it, we shall not be so charitable.

B.   HUMANISM AND THE CHURCH

Many of the Humanists, especially those of Northern Europe, turned their eyes back not only to classical pagan writings but also to the Bible as a piece of antique literature. The study of Hebrew was revived in order that the Old Testament might be read in the original, and scholars in the universities of Germany, France, and England enthusiastically undertook biblical research. These "Christian Humanists" found in the Bible a simpler form of Christianity than they saw in the Church of Rome and were led thereby to the advocacy of a religion shorn of medieval trappings and scholastic subtlety. By far the greatest and most cosmopolitan of the northern Humanists was Desiderius Erasmus of Rotterdam (1466–1536). A peripatetic scholar, he wandered about France, Flanders, Italy and Germany. For five years he taught at Cambridge in England, and he published numerous volumes of his own as well as a Greek edition of the New Testament. Among the most famous of his writings is *The Praise of Folly* (1509–10), a gentle satire on human foibles in which he ridicules various aspects of the Church and its beliefs. The selections below are representative passages from that work.[3]

Erasmus, The Praise of Folly.

. . . Closely related are those who have reached the foolish but comforting belief that if they gaze on a picture of Polyphemus-Christopher, they will not die that day; or that whoever speaks the right words to an image of Barbara will return unharmed from battle; or that a novena to Erasmus, with proper prayers and candles, will shortly make one rich. In St. George they have turned up another Hercules or Hippolytus. They all but adore his horse, which is piously studded and ornamented, and they ingratiate themselves by small gifts. To swear by St. George's brass helmets is an oath for a king.

Then, what shall I say of those who happily delude themselves with forged pardons for their sins? They calculate the time to be spent in Purgatory down to the year, month, day, and hour,

as if from a fool-proof mathematical table. There are also those who propose to get everything they desire by relying on magical charms and prayers devised by some pious imposter for the sake of his soul, or for profit. They will have wealth, honor, pleasure, plenty, good health, long life, a vigorous old age, and at last, a place next to Christ in heaven. However, they don't want that seat of honor until the very last minute; celestial pleasures may come only when worldly pleasures, hung on to with tooth and nail, finally depart.

I picture a business man, a soldier, or a judge taking from all his loot one small coin as a proper expiation for the infinite evil of his life. He thinks it possible to buy up, like notes, so many perjuries, rapes, debauches, fights, murders, frauds, lies and treacheries. Having done this, he feels free to start with a clean slate on a new round of sin. How foolish also—and how happy

—are those who expect something more than the highest happiness if they repeat daily the seven verses of the Psalms. These are the verses believed to have been pointed out to St. Bernard by the devil. He was a merry fellow but not very shrewd, since his tongue was loosened by the saint's trick.

Things like that are so foolish that I am almost ashamed of them myself; yet they are accepted not only by the laity but by the professors of theology themselves. The same thing on a larger scale occurs when sections of the country set up regional saints, and assign peculiar rites and powers to each one. One gives relief from toothache, another aids women in labor, a third recovers stolen goods, a fourth succors the shipwrecked, and still another watches over the sheep—the list is too long to finish. Some are helpful in a number of difficulties, especially the Virgin Mother, whom the common people honor more than they do the Son.

Do men ask anything but folly from these saints? Among all the gifts hanging from the walls and even from the ceilings of churches, have you ever seen one in payment for an escape from folly, or for making the giver wiser? One person has escaped from drowning. Another has lived after being run through. This fellow had the good luck or the nerve to leave the battlefield, allowing the others to fight. Another was delivered from the shadow of the gallows by the patron saint of thieves so that he could continue to relieve those who are burdened with too much wealth. . . .

The life of Christians everywhere runs over with such nonsense. Superstitions are allowed and even promoted by the priests; they do not regret anything so profitable. Imagine, in the midst of this, some insolent wise men speaking the real truth: "You will not die badly if you live well. Your sins are redeemed if to the payment of money you add tears, vigils, prayers, fastings, and hatred of evil, and if you change your whole way of living. The saints will favor you if you imitate them. . . ."

Perhaps it would be wise to pass over the theologians in silence. That short-tempered and supercilious crew is as unpleasant to deal with as Lake Camarina or *Anagyris foetida*. They may attack me with an army of six hundred syllogisms; and if I do not recant, they will proclaim me a heretic. With this thunderbolt they terrify the people they don't like. They are extremely reluctant to acknowledge my benefits to them, which are nevertheless considerable. Their opinion of themselves is so great that they behave as if they were already in heaven; they look down pityingly on other men as so many worms.

Next to the theologians in happiness are those who commonly call themselves "the religious" and "monks." Both are complete misnomers, since most of them stay as far away from religion as possible, and no people are seen more often in public. These monks would be very doleful if I did not relieve them in many ways. They are so detested that it is considered bad luck if one crosses your path, and yet they are highly pleased with themselves. They cannot read, and so they consider it the height of piety to have no contact with literature. In church, when they bray out the psalms they have memorized without understanding, they think they are anointing God's ears with the blandest oil. Most of them capitalize on their dirt and poverty by whining for food from door to door. They push into inns, ships, and public conveyances, to the great disadvantage of the regular beggars . . .

Most of them consider one heaven an inadequate reward for their devotion to ceremony and traditional details. They forget that Christ will condemn all of this and will call for a reckoning of that which He has prescribed, namely, charity. One monk will then present his belly, swollen with all the fish he has eaten, and another will dump out a peck of prayers. One will count up his many fasts, and explain that his almost bursting paunch was caused by a single light lunch. Another will offer enough ceremonies to fill seven ships. Another will glory in the fact that for sixty years he has never touched money, unless his fingers were protected by double gloves. Another will throw down a cowl so dirty and greasy that not even a sailor would wear it. . . .

Here Christ will interrupt these otherwise endless boasts, and exclaim: "Whence come this new race of Jews? I acknowledge only one commandment as truly mine, and of that I hear nothing. Speakingly openly and without parables, I long ago promised my Father's inheritance, not to cowls, prayers, or fasts, but to works of charity. Nor do I accept any who boast of their own good works . . ." Imagine the look on their faces when they hear these words and see sailors and teamsters preferred above them. In the meantime, however, they are happy enough with my assistance.

C.   THE LUTHERAN REFORMATION

Martin Luther (1483–1546), the prime mover of the German Reformation, was a Saxon miner's son who became an Augustinian monk. His intense piety and scholarly bent led him to the profession of teaching, and by 1511 he was established as a Biblical lecturer at the University of Wittenberg in Saxony. Though exceptionally devout, and ardent in ascetic practices, he found no inner peace in his faith, and his continual strivings for spiritual contentment, during which he read not only the Bible, but widely among the "Christian Humanists," drove him toward doctrines contrary to those of the Church. Specifically he came to examine critically the Catholic doctrine of Indulgences, and it was the practice of this doctrine which led him to take the first step away from Rome.

The circumstances were these: in 1517 Pope Leo X needed money to complete the basilica of St. Peter's at Rome. At the same time the Archbishop Mainz needed money to repay a large debt incurred by the necessity of purchasing a Papal dispensation confirming him in the uncanonical possession of his archbishopric. To serve these financial needs the Pope authorized the archbishop to undertake a general sale of indulgences within his diocese. As the chief agent for the sale the archbishop chose an energetic Dominican named John Tetzel, who conducted an intensive campaign with little regard for theological exactitude. The unvarnished commercialism of Tetzel's methods (he established a categorical table of prices for particular sins) goaded Luther into action, and he chose to protest what he considered a flagrant abuse by publishing the Ninety-five Theses.

1. *The Doctrine of Indulgences.* The doctrinal basis of the issuance of indulgences was definitely stated in the bull *Unigenitus* issued by Pope Clement VI in 1343, selections from which follow. In the bull *Salvator Noster* (1476) the doctrine was extended to souls in purgatory.[4]

The Only-begotten Son of God deigned to come down from His Father's bosom into the womb of His mother, in whom and from whom by an ineffable union He joined the substance of our mortal nature to His godhead, in unity of Person; uniting what was permanent with what was transitory, which He assumed in order that He might be able to redeem fallen man and for him make satisfaction to God the Father. For when the fullness of time came, God sent His own Son, made under the law, born of a woman, that He might redeem them that were under the law, that they might receive the adoption of sons.

For He Himself having been made for us by God, wisdom, righteousness, sanctification, and redemption [I Cor. i. 30], not through the blood of goats or calves, but through His own blood entered once for all into the holy place, having obtained eternal redemption [Heb. ix. 12]. For not with corruptible things, with silver and gold, did He redeem us, but with the precious blood of Himself, a lamb without spot or blemish [I Pet. i. 18 sq.], the precious blood which He is known to have shed as an innocent victim on the altar of the cross, not a mere drop of blood (although, because of its union with the Word, that would have sufficed for the redemption of the whole human race), but as it were a copious flood, so that from the sole of the foot to the crown of the head there was found no soundness in Him [Is. i. 6].

Wherefore therefrom (so that the pitifulness of such an effusion be not rendered idle, useless or superfluous) how great a treasure did the holy Father acquire for the Church Militant, wishing to enrich His sons with treasure, that so men might have an infinite treasure, and those who avail themselves thereof are made partakers of God's friendship. Now this treasure is not hidden in a napkin nor buried in a field, but He entrusted it to be healthfully dispensed—through blessed Peter, bearer of heaven's keys, and his successors as vicars on earth—to the faithful, for fitting and reasonable causes, now for total, now for partial remission of punishment due for temporal sins, as well generally as specially (as they should understand it to be expedient with God), and to be applied in mercy to them that are truly penitent and have confessed.

And to this heap of treasure the merits of the blessed Mother of God and of all the elect, from the first just man to the last, are known to have supplied their increment: and no diminution or washing away of this treasure is in any wise to be feared, as well because of the infinite merits of Christ (as aforesaid) as because the more men are drawn to righteousness as a result of its application by so much the more does the heap of merits increase. . . .

2. *The Sale of Indulgences.* An indulgence was not considered efficacious unless its possessor were truly "contrite in heart" and had "made oral confession," but many vendors of indulgences were apt to gloss over these requirements. The following passage describes the activities of John Tetzel in the year 1512. It was written by Frederick Mecum or Myconius, then a member of the Franciscan order at Annaberg.[5]

He gained by his preaching in Germany an immense sum of money, all of which he sent to Rome; and especially at the new mining works at St. Annaberg, where I, Frederick Mecum, heard him for two years, a large sum was collected. It is incredible what this ignorant and impudent monk gave out. He said that if a Christian had slept with his mother, and placed the sum of money in the Pope's indulgence chest, the Pope had power in Heaven and earth to forgive the sin, and if he forgave it, God must do so also. Item—if they contributed readily, and bought grace and indulgence, all the hills of St. Annaberg would become pure massive silver. Item—so soon as the coin rang in the chest, the soul for whom the money was paid would go straightway to Heaven.

The indulgence was so highly prized, that when the commissary entered a city, the Bull was borne on a satin or gold-embroidered cushion, and all the priests and monks, the town council, schoolmaster, scholars, men, women, maidens, and children, went out to meet him with banners and tapers, with songs, and procession. Then all the bells were rung, all the organs played; he was conducted into the church, a red cross was erected in the midst of the church, and the Pope's banner displayed; in short, God Himself could not have been welcomed and entertained with greater honor.

It is incredible what this ignorant monk gave out in speaking and preaching. He gave sealed letters stating that even the sins which a man might wish to do hereafter were forgiven. The Pope had more power than all the apostles, all the angels and saints, even than the Virgin Mary Herself. For these were all subject to Christ, but the Pope was equal to Christ. After His ascension into Heaven Christ had nothing more to do with the government of the Church till the last day, but had entrusted all to the Pope as His vicar and vicegerent.

3. *The Ninety-five Theses.* In protest against the sale of indulgences, Luther, on October 31, 1517, posted his Ninety-five Theses on the door of the castle church in Wittenberg. In doing so, he followed the approved medieval academic custom of publishing a declaration upon which he invited public disputation with other scholars.[6]

DISPUTATION OF DR. MARTIN LUTHER CONCERNING PENITENCE AND INDULGENCES

In the desire and with the purpose of elucidating the truth, a disputation will be held on the underwritten propositions at Wittenberg, under the presidency of the Reverend Father Martin Luther, Monk of the Order of St. Augustine, Master of Arts and of Sacred Theology, and ordinary Reader of the same in that place. He therefore asks those who cannot be present and discuss the subject with us orally, to do so by letter in their absence. In the name of our Lord Jesus Christ. Amen.

1. Our Lord and Master Jesus Christ in saying: "Repent ye," etc., intended that the whole life of believers should be penitence.

2. This word cannot be understood of sacramental penance, that is, of the confession and satisfaction which are performed under the ministry of priests.

3. It does not, however, refer solely to inward penitence; nay such inward penitence is naught, unless it outwardly produces various mortifications of the flesh.

4. The penalty thus continues as long as the hatred of self—that is, true inward penitence—continues; namely, till our entrance into the kingdom of heaven.

5. The Pope has neither the will nor the power to remit any penalties, except those which he has imposed by his own authority, or by that of the canons.

6. The Pope has no power to remit any guilt, except by declaring and warranting it to have been remitted by God; or at most by remitting cases reserved for himself; in which cases, if his power were despised, guilt would certainly remain. . . .

20. Therefore the Pope, when he speaks of the plenary remission of all penalties, does not mean simply of all, but only of those imposed by himself.

21. Thus those preachers of indulgences are in error who say that, by the indulgences of the Pope, a man is loosed and saved from all punishment.

22. For in fact he remits to souls in purgatory no penalty which they would have had to pay in this life according to the canons.

23. If any entire remission of all penalties can be granted to any one, it is certain that it is granted to none but the most perfect, that is, to very few.

24. Hence the greater part of the people must needs be deceived by this indiscriminate and high-sounding promise of release from penalties. . . .

27. They preach mad, who say that the soul flies out of purgatory as soon as the money thrown into the chest rattles.

28. It is certain that, when the money rattles in the chest, avarice and gain may be increased, but the suffrage of the Church depends on the will of God alone. . . .

32. Those who believe that, through letters of pardon, they are made sure of their own salvation, will be eternally damned along with their teachers.

33. We must especially beware of those who say that these pardons from the Pope are that inestimable gift of God by which man is reconciled to God.

34. For the grace conveyed by these pardons

has respect only to the penalties of sacramental satisfaction, which are of human appointment.

35. They preach no Christian doctrine, who teach that contrition is not necessary for those who buy souls out of purgatory or buy confessional licenses.

36. Every Christian who feels true compunction has of right plenary remission of pain and guilt, even without letters of pardon.

37. Every true Christian, whether living or dead, has a share in all the benefits of Christ and of the Church, given him by God, even without letters of pardon. . . .

42. Christians should be taught that it is not the mind of the Pope that the buying of pardons is to be in any way compared to works of mercy.

43. Christians should be taught that he who gives to a poor man, or lends to a needy man, does better than if he bought pardons. . . .

50. Christians should be taught that, if the Pope were acquainted with the exactions of the preachers of pardons, he would prefer that the Basilica of St. Peter should be burnt to ashes, than that it should be built up with the skin, flesh, and bones of his sheep. . . .

52. Vain is the hope of salvation through letters of pardon, even if a commissary—nay, the Pope himself—were to pledge his own soul for them. . . .

56. The treasures of the Church, whence the Pope grants indulgences, are neither sufficiently named nor known among the people of Christ.

57. It is clear that they are at least not temporal treasures, for these are not so readily lavished, but only accumulated, by many of the preachers.

58. Nor are they the merits of Christ and of the saints, for these, independently of the Pope, are always working grace to the inner man, and the cross, death, and hell to the outer man. . . .

62. The true treasure of the Church is the Holy Gospel of the glory and grace of God. . . .

65. Hence the treasures of the Gospel are nets, wherewith of old they fished for the men of riches.

66. The treasures of indulgences are nets, wherewith they now fish for the riches of men. . . .

75. To think that Papal pardons have such power that they could absolve a man even if—by an impossibility—he had violated the Mother of God, is madness.

76. We affirm on the contrary that Papal pardons cannot take away even the least of venial sins, as regards its guilt. . . .

83. Again; why do funeral masses and anniversary masses for the deceased continue, and why does not the Pope return, or permit the withdrawal of the funds bequeathed for this purpose, since it is a wrong to pray for those who are already redeemed . . . ?

86. Again; why does not the Pope, whose riches are at this day more ample than those of the wealthiest of the wealthy, build the one Basilica of St. Peter with his own money, rather than with that of poor believers . . . ?

92. Away then with all those prophets who say to the people of Christ: "Peace, peace," and there is no peace.

93. Blessed be all those prophets, who say to the people of Christ: "The cross, the cross," and there is no cross.

94. Christians should be exhorted to strive to follow Christ their head through pains, deaths, and hells.

95. And thus trust to enter heaven through many tribulations, rather than in the security of peace.

PROTESTATION

I, Martin Luther, Doctor, of the Order of Monks at Wittenberg, desire to testify publicly that certain propositions against pontifical indulgences, as they call them, have been put forth by me. Now although, up to the present time, neither this most celebrated and renowned school of ours, nor any civil or ecclesiastical power has condemned me, yet there are, as I hear, some men of headlong and audacious spirit, who dare to pronounce me a heretic, as though the matter had been thoroughly looked into and studied. But on my part, as I have often done before, so now too I implore all men, by the faith of Christ, either to point out to me a better way, if such a way has been divinely revealed to any, or at least to submit their opinion to the judgment of God and of the Church. For I am neither so rash as to wish that my sole opinion should be preferred to that of all other men, nor so senseless as to be willing that the word of God should be made to give place to fables, devised by human reason.

4. *Luther on Christian Liberty.* The publication of the Theses did not go unchallenged by the Church. After considerable correspondence between Luther and the Papal Curia, in June, 1520, the Pope issued a bull of excommunication which, however, allowed Luther sixty days in which to recant his errors and submit to the Papal authority. This action only inflamed the choleric temper of the reformer, and in the summer of 1520 he issued three great reform treatises. Excerpts from one of these tracts, *On Christian Liberty,* are printed below.[7]

. . . That I may open, then, an easier way for the ignorant—for these alone I am trying to serve—I first lay down these two propositions, concerning spiritual liberty and servitude.

A Christian man is the most free lord of all, and subject to none; a Christian man is the most dutiful servant of all, and subject to every one.

Although these statements appear contradictory, yet, when they are found to agree together, they will be highly serviceable to my purpose. They are both the statements of Paul himself, who says: "Though I be free from all men, yet have I made myself servant unto all" (I Cor. ix. 19), and: "Owe no man anything, but to love one another." (Rom. xiii. 8.) Now love is by its own nature dutiful and obedient to the beloved object. Thus even Christ, though Lord of all things, was yet made of a woman; made under the law; at once free and a servant; at once in the form of God and in the form of a servant.

Let us examine the subject on a deeper and less simple principle. Man is composed of a twofold nature, a spiritual and a bodily. As regards the spiritual nature, which they name the soul, he is called the spiritual, inward, new man; as regards the bodily nature, which they name the flesh, he is called the fleshly, outward, old man. The Apostle speaks of this: "Though our outward man perish, yet the inward man is renewed day by day." (II Cor. iv. 16.) The result of this diversity is, that in the Scriptures opposing statements are made concerning the same man; the fact being that in the same man these two men are opposed to one another; the flesh lusting against the spirit, and the spirit against the flesh. (Gal. v. 17.) . . .

And so it will profit nothing that the body should be adorned with sacred vestments, or dwell in holy places, or be occupied in sacred offices, or pray, fast, and abstain from certain meats, or do whatever works can be done through the body and in the body. Something widely different will be necessary for the justification and liberty of the soul, since the things I have spoken of can be done by any impious person, and only hypocrites are produced by devotion to these things. On the other hand, it will not at all injure the soul that the body should be clothed in profane raiment, should dwell in profane places, should eat and drink in the ordinary fashion, should not pray aloud, and should leave undone all the things abovementioned, which may be done by hypocrites.

And, to cast everything aside, even speculations, meditations, and whatever things can be performed by the exertions of the soul itself, are of no profit. One thing, and one alone, is necessary for life, justification, and Christian liberty; and that is the most holy word of God, the Gospel of Christ, as He says: "I am the resurrection and the life; he that believeth in me shall not die

eternally" (John xi. 25); and also (John viii. 36) "If the Son shall make you free, ye shall be free indeed"; and (Matt. iv. 4) "Man shall not live by bread alone, but by every word that proceedeth out of the mouth of God."

Let us therefore hold it for certain and firmly established that the soul can do without everything, except the word of God, without which none at all of its wants are provided for. But, having the word, it is rich and wants for nothing; since that is the word of life, of truth, of light, of peace, of justification, of salvation, of joy, of liberty, of wisdom, of virtue, of grace, of glory, and of every good thing. It is on this account that the prophet in a whole psalm (Ps. cxix.), and in many other places, sighs for and calls upon the word of God with so many groanings and words. . . .

But you will ask:—"What is this word, and by what means is it to be used, since there are so many words of God?" I answer, the Apostle Paul (Rom. i.) explains what it is, namely, the Gospel of God, concerning His Son, incarnate, suffering, risen, and glorified through the Spirit, the sanctifier. To preach Christ is to feed the soul, to justify it, to set it free, and to save it, if it believes the preaching. For faith alone, and the efficacious use of the word of God, bring salvation. "If thou shalt confess with thy mouth the Lord Jesus, and shalt believe in thine heart that God hath raised him from the dead, thou shalt be saved." (Rom. x. 9.) And again: "Christ is the end of the law for righteousness to every one that believeth" (Rom. x. 4); and "The just shall live by faith." (Rom. i. 17.) For the word of God cannot be received and honored by any works, but by faith alone. Hence it is clear that, as the soul needs the word alone for life and justification, so it is justified by faith alone and not by any works. For if it could be justified by any other means, it would have no need of the word, nor consequently of faith. . . .

Since then this faith can reign only in the inward man, as it is said: "With the heart man believeth unto righteousness" (Rom. x. 10); and since it alone justifies, it is evident that by no outward work or labor can the inward man be at all justified, made free, and saved; and that no works whatever have any relation to him. And so, on the other hand, it is solely by impiety and incredulity of heart that he becomes guilty, and a slave of sin, deserving condemnation; not by any outward sin or work.

Therefore the first care of every Christian ought to be, to lay aside all reliance on works, and strengthen his faith alone more and more, and by it grow in the knowledge, not of works, but of Christ Jesus, who has suffered and risen again for him; as Peter teaches, when he makes no other work to be a Christian one. Thus Christ, when the Jews asked Him what they should do that they might work the works of God, rejected the multitude of works, with which He saw that they were puffed up, and commanded them one thing only, saying: "This is the work of God, that ye believe on him whom He hath sent, for him hath God the Father sealed." (John vi. 27, 29.)

Hence a right faith in Christ is an incomparable treasure, carrying with it universal salvation, and preserving from all evil, as it is said: "He that believeth and is baptized shall be saved; but he that believeth not shall be damned." (Mark xvi. 16.) Isaiah, looking to this treasure, predicted: "The consumption decreed shall overflow with righteousness. For the Lord God of hosts shall make a consumption, even determined, in the midst of the land." (Is. x. 22, 23.) As if he said:— "Faith, which is the brief and complete fulfilling of the law, will fill those who believe with such righteousness, that they will need nothing else for justification." Thus too Paul says: "For with the heart man believeth unto righteousness." (Rom. x. 10.)

But you ask how it can be the fact that faith alone justifies, and affords without works so great a treasure of good things, when so many works, ceremonies, and laws are prescribed to us in the Scriptures. I answer: before all things bear in mind what I have said, that faith alone without works justifies, sets free, and saves. . . .

Thus the believing soul, by the pledge of its faith in Christ, becomes free from all sin, fearless of death, safe from hell, and endowed with the eternal righteousness, life, and salvation of its husband Christ. Thus he presents to himself a glorious bride, without spot or wrinkle, cleansing her with the washing of water by the word; that is, by faith in the word of life, righteousness, and salvation. Thus he betroths her unto himself "in faithfulness, in righteousness, and in judgment, and in loving-kindness, and in mercies." (Hosea ii. 19, 20.) . . .

But, that we may have a wider view of that grace which our inner man has in Christ, we must know that in the Old Testament God sanctified to Himself every first-born male. The birthright was of great value, giving a superiority over the rest by the double honor of priesthood and kingship. For the first-born brother was priest and lord of all the rest.

Under this figure was foreshown Christ, the true and only first-born of God the Father and of the Virgin Mary, and a true king and priest, not in a fleshly and earthly sense. For His kingdom is not of this world; it is in heavenly and spiritual things that He reigns and acts as priest; and these are righteousness, truth, wisdom, peace, salvation, &c. Not but that all things, even those

of earth and hell, are subject to Him—for otherwise how could He defend and save us from them?—but it is not in these, nor by these, that His kingdom stands.

So too His priesthood does not consist in the outward display of vestments and gestures, as did the human priesthood of Aaron and our ecclesiastical priesthood at this day, but in spiritual things, wherein, in His invisible office, He intercedes for us with God in heaven, and there offers Himself, and performs all the duties of a priest; as Paul describes Him to the Hebrews under the figure of Melchizedek. Nor does He only pray and intercede for us; He also teaches us inwardly in the spirit with the living teachings of His Spirit. Now these are the two special offices of a priest, as is figured to us in the case of fleshly priests, by visible prayers and sermons.

As Christ by His birthright has obtained these two dignities, so He imparts and communicates them to every believer in Him, under that law of matrimony of which we have spoken above, by which all that is the husband's is also the wife's. Hence all we who believe on Christ are kings and priests in Christ, as it is said: "Ye are a chosen generation, a royal priesthood, an holy nation, a peculiar people; that ye should show forth the praises of him who hath called you out of darkness into his marvellous light." (I Pet. ii. 9.)

These two things stand thus. First, as regards kingship, every Christian is by faith so exalted above all things, that, in spiritual power, he is completely lord of all things; so that nothing whatever can do him any hurt; yea, all things are subject to him, and are compelled to be subservient to his salvation. Thus Paul says: "All things work together for good to them who are the called" (Rom. viii. 28) ; and also; "Whether life, or death, or things present, or things to come: all are yours; and ye are Christ's." (I Cor. iii. 22, 23.)

Not that in the sense of corporeal power any one among Christians has been appointed to possess and rule all things, according to the mad and senseless idea of certain ecclesiastics. That is the office of kings, princes, and men upon earth. In the experience of life we see that we are subjected to all things, and suffer many things, even death. Yea, the more of a Christian any man is, to so many the more evils, sufferings, and deaths is he subject; as we see in the first place in Christ the first-born, and in all His holy brethren.

This is a spiritual power, which rules in the midst of enemies, and is powerful in the midst of distresses. And this is nothing else than that strength is made perfect in my weakness, and that I can turn all things to the profit of my salvation; so that even the cross and death are compelled to serve me and to work together for my salvation. This is a lofty and eminent dignity, a true and almighty dominion, a spiritual empire, in which there is nothing so good, nothing so bad, as not to work together for my good, if only I believe. And yet there is nothing of which I have need—for faith alone suffices for my salvation—unless that, in it, faith may exercise the power and empire of its liberty. This is the inestimable power and liberty of Christians.

Nor are we only kings and the freest of all men, but also priests for ever, a dignity far higher than kingship, because by that priesthood we are worthy to appear before God, to pray for others, and to teach one another mutually the things which are of God. For these are the duties of priests, and they cannot possibly be permitted to any unbeliever. Christ has obtained for us this favor, if we believe in Him, that, just as we are His brethren, and co-heirs and fellow kings with Him, so we should be also fellow priests with Him, and venture with confidence, through the spirit of faith, to come into the presence of God, and cry "Abba, Father!" and to pray for one another, and to do all things which we see done and figured in the visible and corporeal office of priesthood. But to an unbelieving person nothing renders service or works for good. He himself is in servitude to all things, and all things turn out for evil to him, because he uses all things in an impious way for his own advantage, and not for the glory of God. And thus he is not a priest, but a profane person, whose prayers are turned into sin; nor does he ever appear in the presence of God, because God does not hear sinners. . . .

Here you will ask: "If all who are in the Church are priests, by what character are those, whom we now call priests, to be distinguished from the laity?" I reply: By the use of these words, "priest," "clergy," "spiritual person," "ecclesiastic," an injustice has been done, since they have been transferred from the remaining body of Christians to those few, who are now, by a hurtful custom, called ecclesiastics. For Holy Scripture makes no distinction between them, except that those, who are now boastfully called popes, bishops, and lords, it calls ministers, servants, and stewards, who are to serve the rest in the ministry of the Word, for teaching the faith of Christ and the liberty of believers. For though it is true that we are all equally priests, yet we cannot, nor, if we could, ought we all to minister and teach publicly. Thus Paul says: "Let a man so account of us as of the ministers of Christ, and stewards of the mysteries of God." (I Cor. iv. 1.)

This bad system has now issued in such a pompous display of power, and such a terrible tyranny, that no earthly government can be compared to it, as if the laity were something else than Christians. Through this perversion of things it has happened that the knowledge of Christian grace, of faith, of liberty, and altogether of Christ, has utterly perished, and has been succeeded by an intolerable bondage to human works and laws; and, according to the Lamentations of Jeremiah, we have become the slaves of the vilest men on earth, who abuse our misery to all the disgraceful and ignominious purposes of their own will. . . .

Let it suffice to say this concerning the inner man and its liberty, and concerning that righteousness of faith, which needs neither laws nor good works; nay, they are even hurtful to it, if any one pretends to be justified by them.

And now let us turn to the other part, to the outward man. Here we shall give an answer to all those who, taking offense at the word of faith and at what I have asserted, say: "If faith does everything, and by itself suffices for justification, why then are good works commanded? Are we then to take our ease and do no works, content with faith?" Not so, impious men, I reply; not so. That would indeed really be the case, if we were thoroughly and completely inner and spiritual persons; but that will not happen until the last day, when the dead shall be raised. As long as we live in the flesh, we are but beginning and making advances in that which shall be completed in a future life. On this account the Apostle calls that which we have in this life, the first-fruits of the Spirit. (Rom. viii. 23.) In future we shall have the tenths, and the fullness of the Spirit. To this part belongs the fact I have stated before, that the Christian is the servant of all and subject to all. For in that part in which he is free, he does no works, but in that in which he is a servant, he does all works. Let us see on what principle this is so.

Although, as I have said, inwardly, and according to the spirit, a man is amply enough justified by faith, having all that he requires to have, except that this very faith and abundance ought to increase from day to day, even till the future life; still he remains in this mortal life upon earth, in which it is necessary that he should rule his own body, and have intercourse with men. Here then works begin; here he must not take his ease; here he must give heed to exercise his body by fastings, watchings, labor, and other moderate discipline, so that it may be subdued to the spirit, and obey and conform itself to the inner man and faith, and not rebel against them nor hinder them, as is its nature to do if it is not kept under. For the inner man, being conformed to God, and created after the image of God through faith, rejoices and delights itself in Christ, in whom such blessings have been conferred on it; and hence has only this task before it, to serve God with joy and for nought in free love.

In doing this he offends that contrary will in his own flesh, which is striving to serve the world, and to seek its own gratification. This the spirit of faith cannot and will not bear; but applies itself with cheerfulness and zeal to keep it down and restrain it; as Paul says: "I delight in the law of God after the inward man; but I see another law in my members, warring against the law of my mind, and bringing me into captivity to the law of sin." (Rom. vii. 22, 23.) And again: "I keep under my body, and bring it into subjection, lest that by any means, when I have preached to others, I myself should be a castaway." (I Cor. ix. 27.) And: "They that are Christ's have crucified the flesh with the affections and lusts." (Gal. v. 24.)

These works, however, must not be done with any notion that by them a man can be justified before God—for faith, which alone is righteousness before God, will not bear with this false notion—but solely with this purpose, that the body may be brought into subjection, and be purified from its evil lusts, so that our eyes may be turned only to purging away those lusts. For when the soul has been cleansed by faith and made to love God, it would have all things to be cleansed in like manner; and especially its own body, so that all things might unite with it in the love and praise of God. Thus it comes that, from the requirements of his own body, a man cannot take his ease, but is compelled on its account to do many good works, that he may bring it into subjection. Yet these works are not the means of his justification before God; he does them out of disinterested love to the service of God; looking to no other end than to do what is well-pleasing to Him whom he desires to obey most dutifully in all things.

On this principle every man may easily instruct himself in what measure, and with what distinctions, he ought to chasten his own body. He will fast, watch, and labor, just as much as he sees to suffice for keeping down the wantonness and concupiscence of the body. But those who pretend to be justified by works are looking, not to the mortification of their lusts, but only to the works themselves; thinking that, if they can accomplish as many works and as great ones as possible, all is well with them, and they are justified. Sometimes they even injure their brain, and extinguish nature, or at least make it useless. This is enormous folly, and ignorance of Christian life and faith, when a man seeks, without faith, to be justified and saved by works. . . .

True then are these two sayings: Good works do not make a good man, but a good man does good works. Bad works do not make a bad man, but a bad man does bad works. Thus it is always necessary that the substance or person should be good before any good works can be done, and that good works should follow and proceed from a good person. As Christ says: "A good tree cannot bring forth evil fruit, neither can a corrupt tree bring forth good fruit." (Matt. vii. 18.) Now it is clear that the fruit does not bear the tree, nor does the tree grow on the fruit; but, on the contrary, the trees bear the fruit and the fruit grows on the trees. . . .

Here is the truly Christian life; here is faith really working by love; when a man applies himself with joy and love to the works of that freest servitude, in which he serves others voluntarily and for naught; himself abundantly satisfied in the fullness and riches of his own faith.

5. *Luther on the Sacraments.* In *The Babylonian Captivity of the Church,* the second of Luther's tracts to appear in the summer of 1520, the author attacked the sacramental system of the Catholic Church and defined his own stand.[8]

. . . To begin. I must deny that there are seven Sacraments, and must lay it down, for the time being, that there are only three, baptism, penance, and the bread, and that by the Court of Rome all these have been brought into miserable bondage, and the Church despoiled of all her liberty. And yet, if I were to speak according to the usage of Scripture, I should hold that there was only one sacrament, and three sacramental signs. . . .

It has seemed best, however, to consider as sacraments, properly so called, those promises which have signs annexed to them. The rest, as they are not attached to signs, are simple promises. It follows that, if we speak with perfect accuracy, there are only two sacraments in the Church of God, baptism and the bread; since it is in these alone that we see both a sign divinely instituted and a promise of remission of sins. The sacrament of penance, which I have reckoned along with these two, is without any visible and divinely appointed sign; and is nothing else, as I have said, than a way and means of return to baptism. Not even the schoolmen can say that penitence agrees with their definition; since they themselves ascribe to every sacrament a visible sign, which enables the senses to apprehend the form of that effect which the sacrament works invisibly. Now penitence or absolution has no such sign; and therefore they will be compelled by their own definition either to say that penitence is not one of the sacraments, and thus to diminish their number, or else to bring forward another definition of a sacrament.

Baptism, however, which we have assigned to

the whole of life, will properly suffice for all the sacraments which we are to use in life; while the bread is truly the sacrament of the dying and departing, since in it we commemorate the departure of Christ from this world, that we may imitate Him. Let us then so distribute these two sacraments that baptism may be allotted to the beginning and to the whole course of life, and the bread to its end and to death; and let the Christian, while in this vile body, exercise himself in both, until, being fully baptized and strengthened, he shall pass out of this world, as one born into a new and eternal life, and destined to eat with Christ in the kingdom of His Father, as He promised at the Last Supper, saying: "I say unto you, I will not drink of the fruit of the vine until the kingdom of God shall come." (Luke xxii. 18.) Thus it is evident that Christ instituted the sacrament of the bread that we might receive the life which is to come; and then, when the purpose of each sacrament shall have been fulfilled, both baptism and the bread will cease.

6. *Luther at the Diet of Worms, 1521.* In consequence of Luther's refusal to recant, the Pope issued a bull of excommunication and required the Emperor Charles V to execute it. Charles, however, in deference to the wishes of many of the German princes, summoned Luther before the Imperial Diet, then in session at Worms, for examination. On April 17th he appeared before the Diet and acknowledged the authorship of his controversial writings. When asked to recant his errors he asked for time to consider and was given twenty-four hours. On the next day he appeared again and was interrogated by Dr. Ecken, official of the archbishopric of Trier. The account which follows was written by Luther himself shortly afterward.[9]

. . . [Dr. Ecken asked Luther.] Do you wish to defend the books which are recognized as your work? Or to retract anything contained in them? . . .

[Luther replied.] Most Serene Lord Emperor, Most Illustrious Princes, Most Gracious Lords . . . I beseech you to grant a gracious hearing to my plea, which, I trust, will be a plea of justice and truth; and if through my inexperience I neglect to give to any their proper titles or in any way offend against the etiquette of the court in my manners or behavior, be kind enough to forgive me, I beg, since I am a man who has spent his life not in courts but in the cells of a monastery; a man who can say of himself only this, that to this day I have thought and written in simplicity of heart, solely with a view to the glory of God and the pure instruction of Christ's faithful people. . . .

. . . Your Imperial Majesty and Your Lordships: I ask you to observe that my books are not all of the same kind.

There are some in which I have dealt with piety in faith and morals with such simplicity and so agreeably with the Gospels that my adversaries themselves are compelled to admit them useful, harmless, and clearly worth reading by a Christian. Even the Bull, harsh and cruel though it is, makes some of my books harmless, although it condemns them also, by a judgment downright monstrous. If I should begin to recant here, what, I beseech you, would I be doing but condemning, alone among mortals, that truth which is admitted by friends and foes alike, in an unaided struggle against universal consent?

The second kind consists in those writings levelled against the papacy and the doctrine of the papists, as against those who by their wicked doctrines and precedents have laid waste Christendom by doing harm to the souls and the bodies of men. No one can either deny or conceal this, for universal experience and world-wide grievances are witnesses to the fact that through the Pope's laws and through man-made teachings the consciences of the faithful have been most pitifully ensnared, troubled, and racked in torment, and also that their goods and possessions have been devoured (especially amongst this famous German nation) by unbelievable tyranny, and are to this day being devoured without end in shameful fashion; and that though they themselves by their own laws take care to provide that the Pope's laws and doctrines which are contrary to the Gospel or the teachings of the Fathers are to be considered as erroneous and reprobate. If then I recant these, the only effect will be to add strength to such tyranny, to open not the windows but the main doors to such blasphemy, which will thereupon stalk farther and more widely than it has hitherto dared. . . .

The third kind consists of those books which I have written against private individuals, so-called; against those, that is, who have exerted themselves in defense of the Roman tyranny and to the overthrow of that piety which I have taught. I confess that I have been more harsh against them than befits my religious vows and my profession. For I do not make myself out to be any kind of saint, nor am I now contending about my conduct but about Christian doctrine. But it is not in my power to recant them, because that recantation would give that tyranny and blasphemy an occasion to lord it over those whom I defend and to rage against God's people more violently than ever.

However, since I am a man and not God, I

cannot provide my writings with any other defense than that which my Lord Jesus Christ provided for His teaching. When He had been interrogated concerning His teaching before Annas and had received a buffet from a servant, He said: "If I have spoken evil, bear witness of the evil." If the Lord Himself, who knew that He could not err, did not refuse to listen to witness against His teaching, even from a worthless slave, how much more ought I, scum that I am, capable of naught but error, to seek and to wait for any who may wish to bear witness against my teaching.

And so, through the mercy of God, I ask Your Imperial Majesty, and Your Illustrious Lordships, or anyone of any degree, to bear witness, to overthrow my errors, to defeat them by the writings of the Prophets or by the Gospels; for I shall be most ready, if I be better instructed, to recant any error, and I shall be the first in casting my writings into the fire. . . .

Thereupon the Orator of the Empire, in a tone of upbraiding, said that his answer was not to the point, and that there should be no calling into question of matters on which condemnations and decisions had before been passed by Councils. He was being asked for a plain reply, without subtlety or sophistry, to this question: Was he prepared to recant, or no?

Luther then replied: Your Imperial Majesty and Your Lordships demand a simple answer. Here it is, plain and unvarnished. Unless I am convicted of error by the testimony of Scripture or (since I put no trust in the unsupported authority of Pope or of councils, since it is plain that they have often erred and often contradicted themselves) by manifest reasoning I stand convicted by the Scriptures to which I have appealed, and my conscience is taken captive by God's word, I cannot and will not recant anything, for to act against our conscience is neither safe for us, nor open to us.

On this I take my stand. I can do no other. God help me.

Amen.

D. THE CALVINIST REFORMATION

John Calvin (1509–1564), the leader of the Reformation in Switzerland, was the son of a French ecclesiastic and was trained in both theology and the law. In 1534 he mysteriously underwent a sudden conversion from Catholicism to a new form of Christian faith, which he expounded in *The Institute of the Christian Religion,* first published in 1536. Although Calvin later revised this work and wrote many other volumes, his theology remained essentially unchanged. While Calvin's theology and system of church government had great influence on most protestant sects they were especially important in what came to be called Presbyterianism.

1. *Calvinist Theology.* The following selections from the *Institutes* concern the basic problems of salvation and grace.[10]

. . . Original sin, therefore, appears to be an hereditary pravity and corruption of our nature, diffused through all the parts of the soul . . .

Wherefore those who have defined original sin as a privation of the original righteousness, which we ought to possess, though they comprise the whole of the subject, yet have not used language sufficiently expressive of its operation and influence. For our nature is not only destitute of all good, but is so fertile in all evils that it cannot remain inactive. Those who have called it *concupiscence* have used an expression not improper, if it were only added, which is far from being conceded by most persons, that every thing in man, the understanding and will, the soul and body, is polluted and engrossed by this concupiscence; or, to express it more briefly, that man is of himself nothing else but concupiscence. . . .

The fathers are sometimes too scrupulous on this subject, and afraid of a simple confession of the truth, lest they should afford an occasion to impiety to speak irreverently and reproachfully of the works of God. Though I highly approve this sobriety, yet I think we are in no danger, if we simply maintain what the Scripture delivers. Even Augustine at one time was not free from this scrupulosity; as when he says that hardening and blinding belong not to the operation, but to the prescience of God. But these subtleties are inconsistent with numerous expressions of the Scripture, which evidently import some intervention of God beyond mere foreknowledge. . . .

So also what they advance concerning permission is too weak to be supported. God is very frequently said to blind and harden the reprobate, and to turn, incline, and influence their hearts, as I have elsewhere more fully stated. But it affords no explication of the nature of this influence to resort to prescience or permission. We answer, therefore, that it operates in two ways. For, since, when His light is removed, nothing remains but darkness and blindness; since, when His Spirit is withdrawn, our hearts harden into stones; since, when His direction ceases, they are warped into obliquity; He is properly said to blind, harden, and incline those whom He deprives of the power of seeing, obeying, and acting aright. The second way, which is much more consistent with strict propriety of language, is, when, for the execution of His judgments, He, by means of Satan, the minister of His wrath, directs their counsels to what He pleases, and excites their wills and strengthens their efforts. . . .

Predestination, by which God adopts some to the hope of life, and adjudges others to eternal death, no one, desirous of the credit of piety, dares absolutely to deny. But it is involved in many cavils, especially by those who make foreknowledge the cause of it. We maintain, that both belong to God; but it is preposterous to represent one as dependent on the other.

When we attribute foreknowledge to God, we mean that all things have ever been, and perpetually remain, before His eyes, so that to His knowledge nothing is future or past, but all things are present; and present in such a manner, that He does not merely conceive of them from ideas formed in His mind, as things remembered by us appear present to our minds, but really beholds and sees them as if actually placed before Him. And this foreknowledge extends to the whole world, and to all the creatures. Predestination we call the eternal decree of God, by which He has determined in himself, what He would have to become of every individual of mankind. For they are not all created with a similar destiny; but eternal life is foreordained for some, and eternal damnation for others. Every man, therefore, being created for one or the other of these ends, we say, he is predestinated either to life or to death.

(*Concerning Sacraments*) . . . In the first place, it is necessary to consider what a sacrament is. Now, I think it will be a simple and appropriate definition, if we say that it is an outward sign, by which the Lord seals in our consciences the promises of His good-will toward us, to support the weakness of our faith; and we on our part testify our piety toward Him, in His presence and that of angels, as well as before men. It may, however, be more briefly defined, in other words, by calling it a testimony of the grace of God toward us, confirmed by an outward sign, with a reciprocal attestation of our piety toward Him.

(*Concerning the Lord's Supper*) . . . Now, that holy participation of His flesh and blood, by which Christ communicates His life to us, just as if He actually penetrated every part of our frame, in the sacred supper He also testifies and seals; and that not by the exhibition of a vain or ineffectual sign, but by the exertion of the energy of His Spirit, by which He accomplishes that which He promises. And the thing signified He exhibits and offers to all who come to that spiritual banquet; though it is advantageously enjoyed by believers alone, who receive such great goodness with true faith and gratitude of mind. . . . If it be true that the visible sign is given to us to seal the donation of the invisible substance, we ought to entertain a confident assurance, that in receiving the symbol of His body, we at the same time truly receive the body itself.

2. *Calvinist Morality.* Calvin endeavored, with considerable success, to impose a strict moral code in the territory in which his religion prevailed. The selections which follow are ordinances issued in 1547 for the regulation of churches dependent on Geneva.[11]

Concerning the Times of Assembling at Church

That the temples be closed for the rest of the time, in order that no one shall enter therein out of hours, impelled thereto by superstition; and if anyone be found engaged in any special act of devotion therein or near by he shall be admonished for it: if it be found to be of a superstitious nature for which simple correction is inadequate then he shall be chastised.

Blasphemy

Whoever shall have blasphemed, swearing by the body or by the blood of our Lord, or in similar manner, he shall be made to kiss the earth for the first offense; for the second to pay 5 sous, and for the third 6 sous, and for the last offense be put in the pillory for one hour.

Drunkenness

1. That no one shall invite another to drink under penalty of 3 sous.
2. That taverns shall be closed during the sermon, under penalty that the tavern-keeper shall pay 3 sous, and whoever may be found therein shall pay the same amount.
3. If anyone be found intoxicated he shall pay for the first offense 3 sous and shall be remanded to the consistory; for the second offense he shall be held to pay the sum of 6 sous, and for the third 10 sous and be put in prison. . . .
4. That no one shall make festivals under penalty of 10 sous.

Songs and Dances

If anyone sing immoral, dissolute or outrageous songs, or dance the *virollet* or other dance, he shall be put in prison for three days and then sent to the consistory.

Usury

That no one shall take upon interest or profit more than five per cent., upon penalty of confiscation of the principal and of being condemned to make restitution as the case may demand.

Games

That no one shall play at any dissolute game or at any game whatsoever it may be, neither for gold or silver nor for any excessive stake, upon penalty of 5 sous and forfeiture of stake played for.

Part II. THE POLITICAL AND ECONOMIC ASPECTS

A. POLITICAL THEORY AND POLITICS IN GERMANY

Luther had no sooner raised the standard of religious revolt than he was obliged to face the political implications of his work. Though politically inexperienced and primarily concerned with religious matters, he was driven by German princes and peasants alike to devote considerable attention to the relations of Church and State and of the Christian believer and the State. The following selections indicate the trend of Lutheran political thought and show the temporary solution of the problem reached in Germany in 1555.

1. *An Address to the German Nobility, 1520.* In this pamphlet, one of the three "primary works" written in the summer of 1520, Luther expounded his nascent political theories to the Emperor and princes of the Holy Roman Empire.[12]

To his most Serene and Mighty Imperial Majesty, and to the Christian Nobility of the German Nation.

Dr. MARTINUS LUTHER

The grace and might of God be with you, Most Serene Majesty! most gracious, well beloved gentlemen!

It is not out of mere arrogance and perversity that I, a single poor man, have taken upon me to address your lordships. The distress and misery that oppress all the Christian estates, more especially in Germany, have led not only myself, but every one else, to cry aloud and to ask for help, and have now forced me too, to cry out and to ask, if God would give His Spirit to any one, to reach a hand to His wretched people. Councils have often put forward some remedy, but through the cunning of certain men it has been adroitly frustrated, and the evils have become worse; whose malice and wickedness I will now, by the help of God, expose, so that, being known, they may henceforth cease to be so obstructive and injurious. God has given us a young and noble sovereign, and by this has roused hope in many hearts: now it is right that we too should do what we can, and make good use of time and grace. . . .

The Romanists have, with great adroitness, drawn three walls round themselves, with which

they have hitherto protected themselves, so that no one could reform them, whereby all Christendom has fallen terribly.

Firstly, if pressed by the temporal power, they have affirmed and maintained that the temporal power has no jurisdiction over them, but on the contrary that the spiritual power is above the temporal.

Secondly, if it were proposed to admonish them with the Scriptures, they objected that no one may interpret the Scriptures but the Pope.

Thirdly, if they are threatened with a Council, they pretend that no one may call a Council but the Pope.

Thus they have secretly stolen our three rods, so that they may be unpunished, and entrenched themselves behind these three walls, to act with all wickedness and malice, as we now see. . . .

Now may God help us, and give us one of those trumpets, that overthrew the walls of Jericho, so that we may blow down these walls of straw and paper, and that we may set free our Christian rods, for the chastisement of sin, and expose the craft and deceit of the devil, so that we may amend ourselves by punishment and again obtain God's favor. . . .

Let us, in the first place, attack the first wall.

It has been devised, that the Pope, bishops, priests and monks are called the Spiritual Estate; Princes, lords, artificers and peasants, are the Temporal Estate; which is a very fine, hypocritical device. But let no one be made afraid by it; and that for this reason: That all Christians are truly of the Spiritual Estate, and there is no difference among them, save of office alone. As St. Paul says (I Cor. xii), we are all one body, though each member does its own work, to serve the others. This is because we have one baptism, one gospel, one faith, and are all Christians alike; for baptism, gospel and faith, these alone make Spiritual and Christian people. . . .

And to put the matter even more plainly; if a little company of pious Christian laymen were taken prisoners and carried away to a desert, and had not among them a priest consecrated by a bishop, and were there to agree to elect one of them, married or unmarried, and were to order him to baptize, to celebrate the mass, to absolve and to preach; this man would as truly be a priest, as if all the bishops and all the Popes had consecrated him. That is why in cases of necessity every man can baptize and absolve, which would not be possible if we were not all priests. This great grace and virtue of baptism and of the Christian Estate, they have almost destroyed and made us forget by their ecclesiastical law. . . .

Since then the temporal power is baptized as we are, and has the same faith and gospel, we must allow it to be priest and bishop, and account its office an office that is proper and useful to the Christian community. . . .

It follows then, that between laymen and priests, princes and bishops, or as they call it, between spiritual and temporal persons, the only real difference is one of office and function, and not of estate. . . .

Now see, what a Christian doctrine is this: that the temporal authority is not above the clergy, and may not punish it. This is, as if one were to say, the hand may not help, though the eye is in grievous suffering. . . . Nay, the nobler the member, the more the rest are bound to help it. Therefore I say: forasmuch as the temporal power has been ordained by God for the punishment of the bad, and the protection of the good, therefore we must let it do its duty throughout the whole Christian body, without respect of persons: whether it strike popes, bishops, priests, monks, or nuns. . . .

. . . Thus we Germans have been prettily taught German: whilst we expected to become lords, we have become the servants of the most crafty tyrants; we have the name, title and arms of the Empire, but the Pope has the treasure, authority, law and freedom; thus whilst the Pope eats the kernel, he leaves us the empty shells to play with. . . . Because the Pope crowns or makes the Emperor, it does not follow that he is above him; for the prophet, St. Samuel, anointed and crowned King Saul and David, at God's command, and was yet subject to them. And the prophet Nathan anointed King Solomon, and yet was not placed over him. . . . Therefore let the German Emperor be a true free Emperor, and let not his authority or his sword be overborne by these blind pretenses of the Pope's sycophants,

as if they were to be exceptions, and be above the temporal sword in all things.

2. *On Secular Authority, 1523.* Dissatisfied with the reaction to his earlier pamphlet, Luther was impelled to clarify his views on the relationship between secular and spiritual authority.[13]

. . . For this reason God has ordained the two governments; the spiritual, which by the Holy Spirit under Christ makes Christians and pious people; the secular, which restrains the unchristian and wicked so that they must needs keep the peace outwardly, even against their will. So Paul interprets the secular sword, Romans xiii, and says it is not a terror to good works, but to the evil. And Peter says it is for the punishment of evil doers. . . .

For this reason these two kingdoms must be sharply distinguished, and both be permitted to remain; the one to produce piety, the other to bring about eternal peace and prevent evil deeds; neither is sufficient in the world without the other. For no one can become pious before God by means of the secular government, without Christ's spiritual rule. Hence Christ's rule does not extend over all, but Christians are always in the minority and are in the midst of non-Christians. Where there is only secular rule or law, there, of necessity, is sheer hypocrisy, though the commandments be God's very own. Without the Holy Spirit in the heart no one becomes really pious, he may do as fine works as he will. Where, on the other hand, the spiritual government rules alone over land and people, there evil is given free rein and the door is opened for every kind of knavery; for the natural world cannot receive or comprehend spiritual things. . . .

But perhaps you will say, since Christians do not need the secular sword and the law, why does Paul say to all Christians, in Romans xiii, "Let all souls be subject to power and authority?" And St. Peter says, "Be subject to every human ordinance," etc., as quoted above. I answer, as I have said, that Christians, among themselves and by and for themselves, need no law or sword, since it is neither necessary nor profitable for them. Since, however, a true Christian lives and labors on earth not for himself, but for his neighbor, therefore the whole spirit of his life impels him to do even that which he need not do, but which is profitable and necessary for his neighbor. Because the sword is a very great benefit and necessary to the whole world, to preserve peace, to punish sin and to prevent evil, he submits most willingly to the rule of the sword, pays tax, honors those in authority, serves, helps, and does all he can to further the government, that it may be sustained and held in honor and fear. Although he needs none of these things for himself and it is not necessary for him to do them, yet he considers what is for the good and profit of others, as Paul teaches in Ephesians v.

He serves the State as he performs all other works of love, which he himself does not need. He visits the sick, not that he may be made well; feeds no one because he himself needs food; so he also serves the State not because he needs it, but because others need it,—that they may be protected and that the wicked may not become worse. He loses nothing by this, and such service in no way harms him, and yet it is of great profit to the world. If he did not do it, he would be acting not as a Christian but contrary even to love, and would also be setting a bad example to others, who like him would not submit to authority, though they were no Christians. In this way the Gospel would be brought into disrepute, as though it taught rebellion and made self-willed people, unwilling to benefit or serve any one, when in reality it makes a Christian the servant of every one. Thus in Matthew xvii, Christ gave the tribute money that He might not offend them, although He did not need to do it. . . .

Worldly government has laws which extend no farther than to life and property and what is external upon earth. For over the soul God can and will let no one rule but Himself. Therefore, where temporal power presumes to prescribe laws for the soul, it encroaches upon God's government and only misleads and destroys the souls. We desire to make this so clear that every one shall grasp it, and that our junkers, the princes and bishops, may see what fools they are when they seek to coerce the people with their laws and commandments into believing one thing or another.

3. *Peace of Augsburg, 1555.* The civil war in Germany between Catholic and Protestant factions was finally concluded pragmatically at Augsburg under the aegis of Charles V just before his abdication.[14]

And in order that such peace, which is especially necessary in view of the divided religions, as is seen from the causes before mentioned, and is demanded by the sad necessity of the Holy Roman Empire of the German nation,

may be the better established and made secure and enduring between his Roman Imperial Majesty and us, on the one hand, and the electors, princes, and states of the Holy Empire of the German nation on the other, therefore his Imperial Majesty, and we, and the electors, princes, and states of the Holy Empire will not make war upon any state of the empire on account of the Augsburg Confession and the doctrine, religion, and faith of the same, nor injure nor do violence to those states that hold it, nor force them, against their conscience, knowledge, and will, to abandon the religion, faith, church usages, ordinances, and ceremonies of the Augsburg Confession, where these have been established, or may hereafter be established, in their principalities, lands, and dominions. Nor shall we, through mandate or in any other way, trouble or disparage them, but shall let them quietly and peacefully enjoy their religion, faith, church usages, ordinances, and ceremonies, as well as their possessions, real and personal property, lands, people, dominions, governments, honors, and rights . . .

On the other hand, the estates that have accepted the Augsburg Confession shall suffer his Imperial Majesty, us, and the electors, princes, and other estates of the Holy Empire, adhering to the old religion, to abide in like manner by their religion, faith, church usages, ordinances, and ceremonies. They shall also leave undisturbed their possessions, real and personal property, lands, people, dominions, government, honors, and rights, rents interest, and tithes. . . .

But all others who are not adherents of either of the above-mentioned religions are not included in this peace, but shall be altogether excluded. . . .

No state shall urge another state, or the subjects of the same, to embrace its religion.

But when our subjects and those of the electors, princes, and states, adhering to the old religion or to the Augsburg Confession, wish, for the sake of their religion, to go with wife and children to another place in the lands, principalities, and cities of the electors, princes, and estates of the Holy Empire, and settle there, such going and coming, and the sale of property and goods, in return for reasonable compensation for serfdom and arrears of taxes . . '. shall be everywhere unhindered, permitted, and granted. . . .

B.   CALVINISM AND THE STATE

1. *Calvin, On Civil Government.* John Calvin saw a close connection between religion and politics, and the *Institutes* contains a chapter entitled "On Civil Government." The following selections from that chapter

illustrate the political ideas behind the Genevan Theocracy.[15]

Having already stated that man is the subject of two kinds of government, and having sufficiently discussed that which is situated in the soul, or the inner man, and relates to eternal life, —we are, in this chapter, to say something of the other kind, which relates to civil justice, and the regulation of the external conduct. For, though the nature of this argument seems to have no connection with the spiritual doctrine of faith which I have undertaken to discuss, the sequel will show that I have sufficient reason for connecting them together, and, indeed, that necessity obliges me to it; especially since, on the one hand, infatuated and barbarous men madly endeavor to subvert this ordinance established by God; and, on the other hand, the flatterers of princes, extolling their power beyond all just bounds, hesitate not to oppose it to the authority of God Himself. Unless both these errors be resisted the purity of the faith will be destroyed. . . .

But for speaking of the exercise of civil polity, there will be another place more suitable. At present we only wish it to be understood, that to entertain a thought of its extermination, is inhuman barbarism; it is equally as necessary to mankind as bread and water, light and air, and far more excellent. For it not only tends to secure the accommodations arising from all these things, that men may breathe, eat, drink, and be sustained in life, though it comprehends all these things while it causes them to live together, yet, I say, this is not its only tendency; its objects also are, that idolatry, sacrileges against the name of God, blasphemies against His truth, and other offenses against religion, may not openly appear and be disseminated among the people; that the public tranquillity may not be disturbed; that every person may enjoy his property without molestation; that men may transact their business together without fraud or injustice; that integrity and modesty may be cultivated among them; in short, that there may be a public form of religion among Christians, and that humanity may be maintained among men.

Nor let any one think it strange that I now refer to human polity the charge of the due maintenance of religion, which I may appear to have placed beyond the jurisdiction of men. For I do not allow men to make laws respecting religion and the worship of God now, any more than I did before; though I approve of civil government, which provides that the true religion which is contained in the law of God, be not violated, and polluted by public blasphemies, with impunity. . . .

It now remains for us, as we proposed, in the last place, to examine what advantage the common society of Christians derives from laws, judgments, and magistrates; with which is connected another question—what honor private persons ought to render to magistrates, and how far their obedience ought to extend. . . .

We owe these sentiments of affection and reverence to all our rulers, whatever their characters may be; which I the more frequently repeat, that we may learn not to scrutinize the persons themselves, but may be satisfied with knowing that they are invested by the will of the Lord with that function, upon which He has impressed an inviolable majesty. But it will be said, that rulers owe mutual duties to their subjects. That I have already confessed. But he who infers from this that obedience ought to be rendered to none but just rulers, is a very bad reasoner. . . .

Wherefore, if we are inhumanly harassed by a cruel prince; if we are rapaciously plundered by an avaricious or luxurious one; if we are neglected by an indolent one; or if we are persecuted, on account of piety, by an impious and sacrilegious one,—let us first call to mind our transgressions against God, which He undoubtedly chastises by these scourges. Thus our impatience will be restrained by humility. Let us, in the next place, consider that it is not our province to remedy these evils, and that nothing remains for us, but to implore the aid of the Lord, in whose hand are the hearts of kings and the revolutions of kingdoms. It is "God" who "standeth in the congregation of the mighty," and "judgeth among the gods"; Whose presence shall confound and crush all kings and judges of the earth who shall not have kissed His Son; "that decree unrighteous decrees, to turn aside the needy from judgment, and to take away the right from the poor, that widows may be their prey, and that they may rob the fatherless. . . ."

But in the obedience which we have shown to be due to the authority of governors, it is always necessary to make one exception, and that is entitled to our first attention,—that it do not seduce us from obedience to Him, to Whose will the desires of all kings ought to be subject, to Whose decrees all their commands ought to yield, to Whose majesty all their scepters ought to submit. And, indeed, how preposterous it would be for us, with a view to satisfy men, to incur the displeasure of Him on whose account we yield obedience to men! The Lord, therefore, is the King of Kings; Who, when He has opened His sacred mouth, is to be heard alone, above all, for all, and before all; in the next place, we are subject to those men who preside over us; but no otherwise than in Him. If they command any thing against Him, it ought not to have the least attention; nor, in this case, ought we to pay any regard to all that dignity attached to magistrates; to which no injury is done when it is subjected to the unrivalled and supreme power of God. . . .

2. *Calvinism in Scotland.* Calvin's ideas were brought to Scotland by John Knox (1505–1572), who applied them to practical politics in the reign of Mary, Queen of Scots, a Catholic. The following description of one of Knox's arguments with the queen is taken from his *History of the Reformation in Scotland.* In it Knox speaks of himself in the third person, but otherwise he is hardly retiring.[16]

Whether it was by counsel of others, or the queen's own desire, we know not; but the queen spake with John Knox, and had long reasoning with him, none being present, except the lord James—two gentlemen stood in the other end of the house. The sum of their reasoning was this. . . .

"But yet," said she, "ye have taught the people to receive another religion, than their princes can allow: and how can that doctrine be of God, seeing, that God commands subjects to obey their princes?"

"Madam," said he, "as that right religion takes neither original nor authority from worldly princes, but from the eternal God alone, so are not subjects bound to frame their religion according to the appetite of their princes; for oft it is, that princes are the most ignorant of all others in God's true religion, as we may read as well in the histories before the death of Christ Jesus, as after. If all the seed of Abraham should have been of the religion of Pharoah, to whom they were long subjects, I pray you, madam, what religion should there have been in the world? For, if all men, in the days of the apostles, should have been of the religion of the Roman emperors, what religion should have been upon the face of the earth? Daniel and his fellows were subjects to Nebuchadnezzar, and unto Darius, and yet, madam, they would not be of their religion, neither of the one nor of the other: for the three children said, 'We make it known unto thee, O king, that we will not worship thy gods.' And Daniel did pray publicly unto his God, against the express commandment of the king. And so, madam, ye may perceive, that subjects are not bound to the religion of their princes, albeit they are commanded to give them obedience."

"Yea," said she, "none of those men raised the sword against their princes." "Yet, madam," said he, "ye cannot deny but that they resisted: for these that obey not the commandments that are given, in some sort they resist." "But yet," said she, "they resisted not by the sword." "God," said he, "madam, had not given unto them the power and the means." "Think ye," said she, "that subjects having power may resist their princes?" "If their princes exceed their bounds," said he,

"madam, and do against that wherefore they should be obeyed, it is no doubt but they may be resisted, even by power. . . .

At these words, the queen stood as it were amazed, more than a quarter of an hour; her countenance altered, so that lord James began to entreat her, and to demand, "What has offended you, madam?" At length, she said, "Well, then, I perceive, that my subjects shall obey you, and not me; and shall do what they list, and not what I command: and so must I be subject to them, and not they to me." "God forbid," answered he, "that ever I take upon me to command any to obey me, or yet to set subjects at liberty to do what pleases them. But my travail is, that both princes and subjects obey God. And think not," said he, "madam, that wrong is done unto you, when you are willed to be subject unto God: for, it is He that subjects the people under princes, and causes obedience to be given unto them; yea, God craves of kings, 'That they be, as it were, foster-fathers to His kirk, and commands queens to be nurses unto His people.' And this subjection, madam, unto God, and unto His troubled kirk, is the greatest dignity that flesh can get upon the face of the earth, for it shall carry them to everlasting glory."

"Yea," said she, "but ye are not the kirk that I will nurse. I will defend the kirk of Rome, for it is, I think, the true kirk of God."

"Your will," said he, "madam, is no reason; neither doth your thought make that Roman harlot to be the true and immaculate spouse of Jesus Christ. And wonder not, madam, that I call Rome a harlot; for that kirk is altogether polluted with all kind of spiritual fornication, as well in doctrine as in manners. Yea, madam, I offer myself farther to prove, that the kirk of the Jews, that crucified Christ Jesus, when that they manifestly denied the Son of God, was not so far degenerated from the ordinances and statutes which God gave by Moses and Aaron unto His people, as that the kirk of Rome is declined, and more than five hundred years hath declined from the purity of that religion, which the apostles taught and planted."

"My conscience," said she, "is not so." "Conscience, madam," said he, "requires knowledge; and I fear that right knowledge you have none." "But," said she, "I have both heard and read." "So, madam," said he, "did the Jews who crucified Christ Jesus, read both the law and the prophets, and heard the same interpreted after their manner. Have ye heard," said he, "any teach, but such as the pope and the cardinals have allowed? And ye may be assured, that such will speak nothing to offend their own estate." "Ye interpret the scriptures," said she, "in one manner, and they in another; whom shall I believe, and who shall be judge?" "You shall believe God," said he, "that plainly speaketh in His word: and farther than the word teacheth you, you neither shall believe the one nor the other. The word of God is plain in the self; and if there appear any obscurity in any place, the Holy Ghost, who is never contrarious to Himself, explains the same more clearly in other places: so that there can remain no doubt, but unto such as will remain obstinately ignorant."

C.   Calvinist Economic Theory

The most radical departure from Catholic economic doctrine was made by **Calvin** and his followers. Although they did not entirely reject medieval ethical standards, they developed a wholly different approach to the problems of trade and commerce. This new approach was in part, at least, caused by the enormous changes in European economic life which had occurred since the scholastic philosophers had defined the Church's economic theories.

1. *Calvin on the Calling.* The following selections are taken from the chapter in the *Institutes* entitled "The Right Use of the Present Life and its Supports." [17]

By such principles, the Scripture also fully instructs us in the right use of terrestrial blessings—a thing that ought not to be neglected in a plan for the regulation of life. For if we must live, we must also use the necessary supports of life; nor can we avoid even those things which appear to subserve our pleasures rather than our necessities. It behooves us, therefore, to observe moderation, that we may use them with a pure conscience, whether for necessity or for pleasure. This the Lord prescribes in His word, when He teaches us, that to His servants the present life is like a pilgrimage, in which they are travelling toward the celestial kingdom. If we are only to pass through the earth, we ought undoubtedly to make such a use of its blessings as will rather assist than retard us in our journey. . . .

It must be laid down as a principle, that the use of the gifts of God is not erroneous, when it is directed to the same end for which the Creator Himself has created and appointed them for us; since He has created them for our benefit, not for our injury. Wherefore, no one will observe a more proper rule, than he who shall diligently regard this end. Now, if we consider for what end He has created the various kinds of aliment, we shall find that He intended to provide not only for our necessity, but likewise for our pleasure and delight. . . .

Let us discard, therefore, that inhuman philosophy which, allowing no use of the creatures but what is absolutely necessary, not only malignantly deprives us of the lawful enjoyment of the Divine beneficence, but which cannot be embraced till it has despoiled man of all his senses, and reduced him to a senseless block. But, on the other hand, we must, with equal diligence, oppose the licentiousness of the flesh;

which, unless it be rigidly restrained, transgresses every bound. : . . .

The other rule will be, That persons whose liberty is small should learn to be patient under their privations, that they may not be tormented with an immoderate desire of riches. They who observe this moderation, have attained no small proficiency in the school of the Lord, as he who has made no proficiency in this point can scarcely give any proof of his being a disciple of Christ. For besides that an inordinate desire of earthly things is accompanied by most other vices, he who is impatient under penury, in abundance generally betrays the opposite passion. By this I mean, that he who is ashamed of a mean garment, will be proud of a splendid one; he who, not content with a slender meal, is disquieted with the desire of a more sumptuous one, would also intemperately abuse those dainties, should they fall to his lot; he who bears a private and mean condition with discontent and disquietude, would not abstain from pride and arrogance, should he rise to eminence and honors. Let all, therefore, who are sincere in the practice of piety, earnestly endeavor to learn, after the apostolic example, "both to be full and to be hungry, both to abound and to suffer need."

The Scripture has also a third rule, by which it regulates the use of earthly things; of which something was said, when we treated of the precepts of charity. For it states, that while all these things are given to us by the Divine goodness, and appointed for our benefit, they are, as it were, deposits intrusted to our care, of which we must one day give an account. We ought, therefore, to manage them in such a manner that this alarm may be incessantly sounding in our ears, "Give an account of thy stewardship." Let it also be remembered by whom this account is demanded; that it is by him who has so highly recommended abstinence, sobriety, frugality, and modesty; who abhors profusion, pride, ostentation, and vanity; who approves of no other

Be satisfied

management of his blessings, than such as is connected with charity; who has with his own mouth already condemned all those pleasures which seduce the heart from chastity and purity, or tend to impair the understanding.

Lastly, it is to be remarked, that the Lord commands every one of us, in all the actions of life, to regard his vocation. For He knows with what great inquietude the human mind is inflamed, with what desultory levity it is hurried hither and thither, and how insatiable is its ambition to grasp different things at once. Therefore, to prevent universal confusion being produced by our folly and temerity, He has appointed to all their particular duties in different spheres of life. And that no one might rashly transgress the limits prescribed, He has styled such spheres of life *vocations, or callings*. Every individual's line of life, therefore, is, as it were, a post assigned him by the Lord, that he may not wander about in uncertainty all his days. And so necessary is this distinction, that in His sight all our actions are estimated according to it, and often very differently from the sentence of human reason and philosophy.

There is no exploit esteemed more honorable, even among philosophers, than to deliver our country from tyranny; but the voice of the celestial Judge openly condemns the private man who lays violent hands on a tyrant. It is not my design, however, to stay to enumerate examples. It is sufficient if we know that the principle and foundation of right conduct in every case is the vocation of the Lord, and that he who disregards it will never keep the right way in the duties of his station. He may sometimes, perhaps, achieve something apparently laudable; but however it may appear in the eyes of men, it will be rejected at the throne of God; besides which, there will be no consistency between the various parts of his life.

Our life, therefore, will then be best regulated, when it is directed to this mark; since no one will be impelled by his own temerity to attempt more than is compatible with his calling, because he will know that it is unlawful to transgress the bounds assigned to him. He that is in obscurity will lead a private life without discontent, so as not to desert the station in which God has placed him.

It will also be no small alleviation of his cares, labors, troubles, and other burdens, when a man knows that in all these things he has God for his guide. The magistrate will execute his office with greater pleasure, the father of a family will confine himself to his duty with more satisfaction, and all, in their respective spheres of life, will bear and surmount the inconveniences, cares, disappointments, and anxieties which befall them,

when they shall be persuaded that every individual has his burden laid upon him by God. Hence also will arise peculiar consolation, since there will be no employment so mean and sordid (provided we follow our vocation) as not to appear truly respectable, and be deemed highly important in the sight of God.

2. *Baxter on Labor and Riches.* Richard Baxter (1615–1691) was perhaps England's most notable Presbyterian divine. The following selections are from his *Christian Directory* (1673), a work designed to provide the layman with practical and complete advice on moral and ethical problems.[18]

Take special heed that the common Thief, your carnal self either Personal or in your Relations, do not rob God of His expected due, and devour that which He requireth. It is not for nothing that God calleth for the first fruits: Honor the Lord with thy substance, and with the first fruits of all thine increase: so shall thy Barns be filled with plenty, and thy Presses shall burst forth with new wine. . . .

Public service is God's greatest service. To neglect this, and say, I will pray and meditate, is as if your servant should refuse your greatest work, and tie himself to some lesser easy part: And God hath commanded you some way or other to labor for your daily bread, and not to live as drones on the sweat of others only. Innocent Adam was put into the Garden of Eden to dress it: And fallen man must eat his bread in the sweat of his brows: Gen. 3. 19. And he that will not work must be forbidden to eat, 2 Thes. 3. 6, 10, 12. And indeed it is necessary to our selves, for the health of our bodies, which will grow diseased with idleness; and for the help of our souls, which will fail if the body fail: And man in flesh must have work for his body as well as for his soul: And he that will do nothing but pray and meditate, it's like will (by sickness or Melancholy) be disabled e're long either to pray or meditate: Unless he have a body extraordinary strong. . . .

Take heed of Idleness, and be wholly taken up in diligent business, of your lawful callings, when you are not exercised in the more immediate service of God. . . .

It is lawful and meet to look at the commodity of your Calling in the third place, (that is, after the public good, and after your personal good of soul and bodily health.) Though it is said, Prov. 23. 4. Labor not to be rich: the meaning is, that you make not Riches your chief end: Riches for our fleshly ends must not ultimately be intended or sought. But in subordination to higher things they may: That is, you may labor in that manner as tendeth most to your success and lawful gain:

You are bound to improve all your Master's Talents: But then your end must be, that you may be the better provided to do God service, and may do the more good with what you have. If God show you a way in which you may lawfully get more than in another way, (without wrong to your soul, or to any other) if you refuse this, and choose the less gainful way, you cross one of the ends of your Calling, and you refuse to be God's Steward, and to accept His gifts, and use them for Him when He requireth it: You may labor to be Rich for God, though not for the flesh and sin. . . .

Idleness usually bringeth Poverty: And it is a just and merciful chastisement of God to cure the sin: But such can have little comfort in their wants; nor expect that others should pity them as they would do the diligent. Yea, many when by idleness they are brought to poverty, by poverty are brought to murmuring and stealing, to the ruin both of soul, and body, and family, and reputation.

XI
The New Monarchy

THE motive of domination became a reigning force in Europe; for it was an idea which monarchy would not willingly let fall after it had received a religious and an international consideration. For centuries it was constantly asserted as a claim of necessity and of right. It was the supreme manifestation of the modern state according to the image which Machiavelli had set up, the state that suffers neither limit nor equality, and is bound by no duty to nations or to men, that thrives on destruction and sanctifies whatever things contributed to increase of power.

Lord Acton

CONTENTS

QUESTIONS FOR STUDY

PART I

1. Why shouldn't you, as a private citizen, be reading *The Prince?*

2. Compare the authorities invoked by Machiavelli to prove his arguments with those used by political thinkers in the Middle Ages.

3. What is Machiavelli's opinion of mankind? Why is it fundamental to his system of politics? How does it compare with the medieval concept of man?

4. What, in Machiavelli's view, determined whether a prince's action was good or bad? Would St. Thomas Aquinas have agreed with this method of determining the good? What would he have suggested instead?

5. What is Machiavelli's conception of the workings of the historical process?

6. In Chapter Fifteen, what does Machiavelli consider to be novel or original in his approach to politics?

7. What similarities, either in approach or method, do you find between Bodin and Machiavelli?

8. Compare what you imagine would have been the reactions of a feudal noble, Pope Gregory VII, Luther, and Calvin to Bodin's concept of sovereignty.

PART II

9. What was the mercantilist objection to inclosures?

10. The dialogue on inclosures brings out what basic mercantilist attitude concerning the relation of the prosperity of the individual to that of the state?

11. Which of the activities of the Derbyshire justices were serving mercantilist ends?

12. In evaluating the accounts of the English merchants, what must the historian keep in mind?

13. What was the relation between mercantilism and war?

14. A study of the map of Europe reveals that England enjoyed certain geographic advantages of site and location over her continental rivals (Venice, Portugal, Spain, Holland) in the race for overseas trade. What were these advantages?

15. In what sense is the author of the *Discourse on Corporations* attacking the very root of mercantilism?

16. How well does Cecil's legislative program represent Mun's mercantilist principles?

17. What seems to have been the long-run purpose of mercantilist regulation?

18. Why is a favorable balance of trade vital to Mun? How does he propose to obtain it?

19. The mercantilists never asked themselves the question: "What shall we do with our money?" Would Mun have had an answer to this question?

Although their roots lay deep in the past, the monarchies of Western Europe in the fifteenth, sixteenth, and seventeenth centuries were sufficiently novel in organization and purpose to warrant the adjective "new" which historians have since applied to them. Externally, the emergence of these centralized dynastic states as definite entities, each with interests of its own, frequently brought them into open war as well as peaceful rivalry. And to dynastic sources of conflict the sixteenth century added Protestantism, commerce, and empire. The ruler of the day thus had to find means of building a kingdom strong enough to survive unending competition. Since events had determined that "the rule of one royal lion" was preferable "to that of a pack of feudal wolves," how then must a ruler act in order that he might truly be a "royal lion" rather than a majestic popinjay or a princely jackass? What policies made a royal lion powerful enough to hold his own and to prosper in the lion's den of western Europe?

Because Niccolo Machiavelli (1469–1527) offers some spectacular answers to these questions, the first Part of this Problem begins with selections from his handbook for rulers, *The Prince*. But in order to evaluate Machiavelli's contribution to the problems of government, the student must understand three vital factors: the political inheritance of the Middle Ages, the environment of sixteenth century Italy which so conditioned Machiavelli's thinking, and Machiavelli's definition of the purpose of the state's activity—the true end of any political theory.

The universal ideal of the Middle Ages, the *Respublica Christiana,* had at one time seemed both real and realizable. But this single universal society, ultimately subject to a single divine authority, seemed increasingly out of touch with the realities of fifteenth- and sixteenth-century Europe. A growing number of secular princes were actually contesting for the fragments of a dismembered Christendom, while the thinkers were still preoccupied with these visions. And their thoughts on politics, which like all other medieval fields of study had been ultimately subject to theology, had grown well away from contemporary reality.

This was perhaps nowhere more apparent than in the Italy of Machiavelli's time. Far from possessing any unity, it was split up into numerous little states, within which in the course of the fifteenth century the stern hand of a despot had often proved the only alternative to the wastefulness of civil war. This was the case in most of the city states of the north, and even the popes at Rome followed the accepted pattern of despotism. Yet another tendency in Renaissance Italy was symbolized by the presence of foreign powers in the peninsula. Since 1435 a branch of the Spanish royal family had ruled Naples and Sicily, and the internecine rivalry produced by Italy's lack of unity had made her militarily so impotent as to invite further intervention. The invasion of Charles VIII of France in 1494 inaugurated a series of alien inroads which made Italy the cockpit of Renaissance Europe. This environment, with all its internal anarchy and attraction for the foreign aggressor, was only too well known to Machiavelli who had a career in the foreign service of the Florentine Republic. It is this reality which conditions the approach, scope, and conclusion of the *Prince.*

The treatise must thus first be studied as a description of an existing political system. But in as much as Machiavelli intended to write a handbook for an Italian prince, his analysis of Italian politics, and particularly the lessons which he derived therefrom lend more than a descriptive importance to the work. He went at the problem with a hard-bitten, secular realism that was in sharp contrast to the wishful thinking which had inspired medieval excursions into political thought. Limited and unsystematic though the book may be, it inaugurated the modern period in political thought. The book has become a classic and its author a synonym for craft and duplicity. For in the words of Lord Acton, "the authentic interpreter of Machiavelli is the whole of later history."

This mention of his fame and notoriety brings up the third factor in any assessment of Machiavelli as a political philosopher. He must be studied historically, as a product of a certain environment; he must be studied for his contributions, in analysis and method, to the science of politics; and finally he must be studied for his understanding of the principles underlying the state. Here politics moves over into the domain of the philospher and moralist. For ultimately moral values are inseparable from any political theory. Indeed the divine purpose of all political activity was the only justification for all medieval thought about the state. Although Machiavelli breaks dramatically with this tradition and although at first sight he may appear to have been preoccupied with the mere mechanics of statecraft, he could not help but indicate what he actually considered the state to be or what its purpose ought to be. It is at this level that his influence has been perhaps most significant. For all modern power politics trace their descent back to *The Prince*. The student, as he reads Machiavelli's tract, therefore must seek to understand this operative ideal which inspired the state according to Machiavelli as well as his historically conditioned analysis of the main springs of political action.

The remainder of Part I consists of selections from the *Six Books Concerning the State*, by the Frenchman, Jean Bodin (1530–1596). Unlike the realistic but unsystematic observations of *The Prince*, Bodin's work is truly political theory. Although he was influenced by the confusion of the French wars of religion, his real search was for a comprehensive political system. To this task he brought wide-ranging interests in history and economics and practical experience as a lawyer, professor of law, and public servant in the estates of his province and the royal courts.

The passages chosen concern one of Bodin's most novel and influential ideas. In the Middle Ages the concept of sovereignty had been subject to a variety of limitations; in Bodin's hands it began to assume that omnipotence which was to become the hallmark of the modern state. Such a theory was as necessary as Machiavelli's new approach to the reality of politics to the emergence of the new territorial, national state.

The second half of the Problem is concerned with the economic side of state-making in the sixteenth century. As was the case with Machiavelli and Bodin the break with the past is the dominant factor. In the first place a major shift in the economic center of gravity of western Europe was taking place. In the same way that the Mediterranean had been the economic center of the ancient world, or the line from north Italy through the south German trading towns was the axis of medieval economy, the maritime states of the west assumed in the sixteenth century the economic hegemony of Europe. Spain, Portugal, Holland, and England had been, in a sense, on the fringe of medieval Europe; overseas activity was now plummeting them into the lead. In the second place, the state was rapidly overtaking the town as the dynamic factor in economic life, and increased governmental activity meant increased governmental expense. The feudal king, like the rest of his barons, had ideally at least lived off the income of his own lands but the "new" monarchies required in war and peace vastly increased, more steady, and more calculable revenues. Finally, the influx of precious metals from the New World, lowering the value of money, was underlining these fiscal difficulties.

These changes in the nature of economic activity were paralleled by changes in economic outlook and theory. The student has already encountered the moral, otherworldly attitude of a medieval authority like St. Thomas Aquinas towards economic activity. From the fourteenth century onwards these ideas were changing under the impact of events, and a reading of seventeenth-century Englishman Thomas Mun, in Part II, will indicate the veritable revolution which had taken place.

The economic theory and practise which developed in the "new" monarchies was called "mercantilism." Extending as it did over three centuries in time and most of western Europe in space, mercantilism was never uniform or unchanging. But certain common assumptions can be distinguished for all so-called mercantilistic doctrine and action, which assumptions in turn derive from the changing conditions in Europe between 1450 and 1750. The nature of this theory and of the techniques so practised make up the second Part of this Problem.

Part I.   MACHIAVELLI AND BODIN

A.   THE PRINCE

The Prince was the product of Machiavelli's exile from Florence and public service. For almost twenty years, from 1494 to 1512, he had been busy as a diplomat in the service of the Republic. The return of the Medici in 1512 meant exile from his native city, and as time showed, an end to his public employment. The first product of this new leisure was the essay, *The Prince,* which was not published until after his death. Its purpose is made clear with only a modicum of polite restraint in the first section quoted below. The first eleven chapters of the work describe the various kinds of principalities as Machiavelli distinguishes them—civil, religious, hereditary, those acquired by arms or ability or good fortune, and those acquired by wickedness. Then follow three chapters on the armed forces and the act of war as far as they concern the prince. Chapters XV–XXIII provide a detailed analysis of the conduct proper to a prince. The last three concern primarily contemporary Italy and Machiavelli's solutions for its troubles.[1]

(*Preface*) Niccolo Machiavelli to the Magnificent Lorenzo di Piero de' Medici: Those who strive to obtain the good graces of a prince are accustomed to come before him with such things as they hold most precious, or in which they see him take most delight: whence one often sees horses, arms, cloth of gold, precious stones, and similar ornaments presented to princes, worthy of their greatness.

Desiring therefore to present myself to your Magnificence with some testimony of my devotion towards you, I have not found among my possessions anything which I hold more dear than, or value so much as, the knowledge of the actions of great men, acquired by long experience in contemporary affairs, and a continual study of antiquity; which, having reflected upon it with great and prolonged diligence, I now send, digested into a little volume, to your Magnificence. . . .

Seventh Chapter. Concerning New Principalities which are Acquired Either by The Arms of Others or by Good Fortune: Those who solely by good fortune become princes from being private citizens have little trouble in rising, but much in keeping atop; they have not any difficulties on the way up, because they fly, but they have many when they reach the summit. Such are those to whom some state is given either for money or by the favor of him who bestows it; as happened to many in Greece, in the cities of Ionia and of the Hellespont, where princes were made by Darius, in order that they might hold the cities both for his security and his glory; as also were those emperors who, by the corruption of the soldiers, from being citizens came to empire. Such stand simply upon the goodwill and the fortune of him who has elevated them—two most inconstant and unstable things. Neither have they the knowledge requisite for the position; because, unless they are men of great worth and ability, it is not reasonable to expect that they should know how to command, having always lived in a private condition; besides, they cannot hold it because they have not forces which they can keep friendly and faithful.

States that rise unexpectedly, then, like all other things in nature which are born and grow rapidly, cannot have their foundations and correspondencies fixed in such a way that the first storm will not overthrow them; unless, as is said, those who unexpectedly become princes are men of so much ability that they know they have to be prepared at once to hold that which fortune has thrown into their laps, and that those foundations, which others have laid *before* they became princes, they must lay *afterwards.*

Concerning these two methods of rising to be a prince by ability or fortune, I wish to adduce two examples within our own recollection, and these are Francesco Sforza and Cesare Borgia. Francesco, by proper means and with great ability, from being a private person rose to be Duke of Milan, and that which he had acquired with a thousand anxieties he kept with little trouble. On the other hand, Cesare Borgia, called by the people Duke Valentino, acquired his state during the ascendency of his father, and on its decline he lost it, notwithstanding that he had taken every measure and done all that ought to be done by a wise and able man to fix firmly his roots in the states which the arms and fortunes of others had bestowed on him.

Because, as is stated above, he who has not first laid his foundations may be able with great ability to lay them afterwards, but they will be laid with trouble to the architect and danger to the building. If, therefore, all the steps taken by the duke be considered, it will be seen that he laid solid foundations for his future power, and I do not consider it superfluous to discuss them, because I do not know what better precepts to give a new prince than the example of his actions; and if his dispositions were of no avail, that was not his fault, but the extraordinary and extreme malignity of fortune.

Alexander the Sixth, in wishing to aggrandize the duke, his son, had many immediate and prospective difficulties. Firstly, he did not see his way to make him master of any state that was not a state of the Church; and if he was willing to rob the Church he knew that the Duke of Milan and the Venetians would not consent, because Faenza and Rimini were already under the protection of the Venetians. Besides this, he saw the arms of Italy, especially those by which he might have been assisted, in hands that would fear the aggrandizement of the Pope, namely, the Orsini and the Colonnesi and their following. It behooved him, therefore, to upset this state of affairs and embroil the powers, so as to make himself securely master of part of their states. This was easy for him to do, because he found the Venetians, moved by other reasons, inclined to bring back the French into Italy; he would not only not oppose this, but he would render it more easy by dissolving the former marriage of King Louis. Therefore the king came into Italy with the assistance of the Venetians and the consent of Alexander. He was no sooner in Milan than the Pope had soldiers from him for the attempt on the Romagna, which yielded to him on the reputation of the king. The duke, therefore, having acquired the Romagna and beaten the Colonnesi, while wishing to hold that and to advance further, was hindered by two things: the one, his forces did not appear loyal to him, the other, the goodwill of France: that is to say, he feared that the forces of the Orsini, which he was using, would not stand to him, that not only might they hinder him from winning more, but might themselves seize what he had won, and that the king might also do the same. Of the Orsini he had a warning when, after taking Faenza and attacking Bologna, he saw them go very unwillingly to that attack. And as to the king, he learned his mind when he himself, after taking the Duchy of Urbino, attacked Tuscany, and the king made him desist from that under-

taking; hence the duke decided to depend no more upon the arms and the luck of others.

For the first thing he weakened the Orsini and Colonnesi parties in Rome, by gaining to himself all their adherents who were gentlemen, making them his gentlemen, giving them good pay, and, according to their rank, honoring them with office and command in such a way that in a few months all attachment to the factions was destroyed and turned entirely to the duke. After this he awaited an opportunity to crush the Orsini, having scattered the adherents of the Colonna house. This came to him soon and he used it well; for the Orsini, perceiving at length that the aggrandizement of the duke and the Church was ruin to them, called a meeting at Magione in Perugia. From this sprung the rebellion at Urbino and the tumults in the Romagna, with endless dangers to the duke, all of which he overcame with the help of the French. Having restored his authority, not to leave it at risk by trusting either to the French or other outside forces, he had recourse to his wiles, and he knew so well how to conceal his mind that, by the mediation of Signor Pagolo—whom the duke did not fail to secure with all kinds of attentions, giving him money, apparel, and horses— the Orsini were reconciled, so that their simplicity brought them into his power at Sinigalia. Having exterminated the leaders, and turned their partisans into his friends, the duke had laid sufficiently good foundations to his power, having all the Romagna and the Duchy of Urbino; and the people now beginning to appreciate their prosperity, he gained them all over to himself. And as this point is worthy of notice, and to be imitated by others, I am not willing to leave it out.

When the duke occupied the Romagna he found it under the rule of weak masters, who rather plundered their subjects than ruled them, and gave them more cause for disunion than for union, so that the country was full of robbery, quarrels, and every kind of violence; and so, wishing to bring back peace and obedience to authority, he considered it necessary to give it a good governor. Thereupon he promoted Messer Ramiro d'Orco, a swift and cruel man, to whom he gave the fullest power. This man in a short time restored peace and unity with the greatest success. Afterwards the duke considered that it was not advisable to confer such excessive authority, for he had no doubt but that it would become odious, so he set up a court of judgment in the country, under a most excellent president, wherein all cities had their advocates. And because he knew that the past severity had caused some hatred against himself, so, to clear himself in the minds of the people, and gain them entirely to himself, he desired to show that, if any cruelty had been practised, it had not originated with him, but in the natural sternness of the minister. Under this pretence he took Ramiro, and one morning caused him to be executed and left on the piazza at Cesena with the block and a bloody knife at his side. The barbarity of this spectacle caused the people to be at once satisfied and dismayed.

But let us return whence we started. I say that the duke, finding himself now sufficiently powerful and partly secured from immediate dangers by having armed himself in his own way, and having in a great measure crushed those forces in his vicinity that could injure him if he wished to proceed with his conquest, had next to consider France, for he knew that the king, who too late was aware of his mistake, would not support him. And from this time he began to seek new alliances and to temporize with France in the expedition which she was making towards the kingdom of Naples against the Spaniards who were besieging Gaeta. It was his intention to secure himself against them, and this he would have quickly accomplished had Alexander lived.

Such was his line of action as to present affairs. But as to the future he had to fear, in the first place, that a new successor to the Church might not be friendly to him and might seek to take from him that which Alexander had given him, so he decided to act in four ways. Firstly, by exterminating the families of those lords whom he had despoiled, so as to take away that pretext from the Pope. Secondly, by winning to himself all the gentlemen of Rome, so as to be able to curb the Pope with their aid, as has been observed. Thirdly, by converting the college [of Cardinals] more to himself. Fourthly, by acquiring so much power before the Pope should die that he could by his own measures resist the first shock. Of these four things, at the death of Alexander, he had accomplished three. For he had killed as many of the dispossessed lords as he could lay hands on, and few had escaped; he had won over the Roman gentlemen, and he had the most numerous party in the college. And as to any fresh acquisition, he intended to become master of Tuscany, for he already possessed Perugia and Piombino, and Pisa was under his protection. And as he had no longer to study France (for the French were already driven out of the kingdom of Naples by the Spaniards, and in this way both were compelled to buy his goodwill), he pounced down upon Pisa. After this, Lucca and Siena yielded at once, partly through hatred and partly through fear of the Florentines; and the Florentines would have had no remedy had he continued to prosper, as he was prospering the year that Alexander died, for he had acquired so

much power and reputation that he would have stood by himself, and no longer have depended on the luck and forces of others, but solely on his own power and ability.

But Alexander died five years after he had first drawn the sword. He left the duke with the state of Romagna alone consolidated, with the rest in the air, between two most powerful hostile armies, and sick unto death. Yet there were in the duke such boldness and ability, and he knew so well how men are to be won or lost, and so firm were the foundations which in so short a time he had laid, that if he had not had those armies on his back, or if he had been in good health, he would have overcome all difficulties. And it is seen that his foundations were good, for the Romagna awaited him for more than a month. In Rome, although but half alive, he remained secure; and whilst the Baglioni, the Vitelli, and the Orsini might come to Rome, they could not effect anything against him. If he could not have made Pope him whom he wished, at least the one whom he did not wish would not have been elected. But if he had been in sound health at the death of Alexander, everything would have been easy to him. On the day that Julius the Second was elected, he told me that he had thought of everything that might occur at the death of his father, and had provided a remedy for all, except that he had never anticipated that, when the death did happen, he himself would be on the point to die.

When all the actions of the duke are recalled, I do not know how to blame him, but rather it appears to me, as I have said, that I ought to offer him for imitation to all those who, by the fortune or the arms of others, are raised to government. Because he, having a lofty spirit and far-reaching aims, could not have regulated his conduct otherwise, and only the shortness of the life of Alexander and his own sickness frustrated his designs. Therefore, he who considers it necessary to secure himself in his new principality, to win friends, to overcome either by force or fraud, to make himself beloved and feared by the people, to be followed and revered by the soldiers, to exterminate those who had power or reason to hurt him, to change the old order of things for new, to be severe and gracious, magnanimous and liberal, to destroy a disloyal soldiery and to create new, to maintain friendship with kings and princes in such a way that they must help him with zeal and offend with caution, cannot find a more lively example than the actions of this man.

Only can he be blamed for the election of Julius the Second, in whom he made a bad choice, because, as is said, not being able to elect a Pope to his own mind, he could have hindered any other from being elected Pope; and he ought never to have consented to the election of any cardinal whom he had injured or who had cause to fear him if they became pontiffs. For men injure either from fear or hatred. Those whom he had injured, amongst others, were San Pietro ad Vincula, Colonna, San Giorgio, and Ascanio. The rest, in becoming Pope, had to fear him, Rouen and the Spaniards excepted; the latter from their relationship and obligations, the former from his influence, the kingdom of France having relations with him. Therefore, above everything, the duke ought to have created a Spaniard Pope, and, failing him, he ought to have consented to Rouen and not San Pietro ad Vincula. He who believes that new benefits will cause great personages to forget old injuries is deceived. Therefore, the duke erred in his choice, and it was the cause of his ultimate ruin. . . .

Eleventh Chapter. Concerning Ecclesiastical Principalities: It only remains now to speak of ecclesiastical principalities, touching which all difficulties are prior to getting possession, because they are acquired either by capacity or good fortune, and they can be held without either; for they are sustained by the ancient ordinances of religion, which are so all-powerful, and of such a character that the principalities may be held no matter how their princes behave and live. These princes alone have states and do not defend them, they have subjects and do not rule them; and the states, although unguarded, are not taken from them, and the subjects, although not ruled, do not care, and they have neither the desire nor the ability to alienate themselves. Such principalities only are secure and happy. But being upheld by powers, to which the human mind cannot reach, I shall speak no more of them, because, being exalted and maintained by God, it would be the act of a presumptuous and rash man to discuss them. . . .

Fifteenth Chapter. Concerning Things for Which Men, and Especially Princes, Are Praised or Blamed: It remains now to see what ought to be the rules of conduct for a prince towards subject and friends. And as I know that many have written on this point, I expect I shall be considered presumptuous in mentioning it again, especially as in discussing it I shall depart from the methods of other people. But, it being my intention to write a thing which shall be useful to him who apprehends it, it appears to me more appropriate to follow up the real truth of a matter than the imagination of it; for many have pictured republics and principalities which in fact have never been known or seen, because how one lives is so far distant from how one ought to live, that he who neglects what is done for what ought to be done, sooner effects his

ruin than his preservation; for a man who wishes to act entirely up to his professions of virtue soon meets with what destroys him among so much that is evil.

Hence it is necessary for a prince wishing to hold his own to know how to do wrong, and to make use of it or not according to necessity. Therefore, putting on one side imaginary things concerning a prince, and discussing those which are real, I say that all men when they are spoken of, and chiefly princes for being more highly placed, are remarkable for some of those qualities which bring them either blame or praise; and thus it is that one is reputed liberal, another miserly, using a Tuscan term (because an avaricious person in our language is still he who desires to possess by robbery, whilst we call one miserly who deprives himself too much of the use of his own); one is reputed generous, one rapacious; one cruel, one compassionate; one faithless, another faithful; one effeminate and cowardly, another bold and brave; one affable, another haughty; one lascivious, another chaste; one sincere, another cunning; one hard, another easy; one grave, another frivolous; one religious, another unbelieving, and the like. And I know that every one will confess that it would be most praiseworthy in a prince to exhibit all the above qualities that are considered good; but because they can neither be entirely possessed nor observed, for human conditions do not permit it, it is necessary for him to be sufficiently prudent that he may know how to avoid the reproach of those vices which would lose him his state; and also to keep himself, if it be possible, from those which would not lose him it; but this not being possible, he may with less hesitation abandon himself to them. And again, he need not make himself uneasy at incurring a reproach for those vices without which the state can only be saved with difficulty, for if everything is considered carefully, it will be found that something which looks like virtue, if followed, would be his ruin; whilst something else, which looks like vice, yet followed brings him security and prosperity. . . .

Sixteenth Chapter. Concerning Liberality and Meanness: Commencing then with the first of the above-named characteristics, I say that it would be well to be reputed liberal. Nevertheless, liberality exercised in a way that does not bring you the reputation for it, injures you; for if one exercises it honestly and as it should be exercised, it may not become known, and you will not avoid the reproach of its opposite. Therefore, any one wishing to maintain among men the name of liberal is obliged to avoid no attribute of magnificence; so that a prince thus inclined will consume in such acts all his property, and will be compelled in the end, if he wish to maintain the name of liberal, to unduly weigh down his people, and tax them, and do everything he can to get money. This will soon make him odious to his subjects, and becoming poor he will be little valued by any one; thus, with his liberality, having offended many and rewarded few, he is affected by the very first trouble and imperilled by whatever may be the first danger; recognizing this himself, and wishing to draw back from it, he runs at once into the reproach of being miserly.

Therefore, a prince, not being able to exercise this virtue of liberality in such a way that it is recognized, except to his cost, if he is wise he ought not to fear the reputation of being mean, for in time he will come to be more considered than if liberal, seeing that with his economy his revenues are enough, that he can defend himself against all attacks, and is able to engage in enterprises without burdening his people; thus it comes to pass that he exercises liberality towards all from whom he does not take, who are numberless, and meanness towards those to whom he does not give, who are few.

We have not seen great things done in our time except by those who have been considered mean; the rest have failed. Pope Julius the Second was assisted in reaching the papacy by a reputation for liberality, yet he did not strive afterwards to keep it up, when he made war on the King of France; and he made many wars without imposing any extraordinary tax on his subjects; for he supplied his additional expenses out of his long thriftiness. The present King of Spain would not have undertaken or conquered in so many enterprises if he had been reputed liberal. A prince, therefore, provided that he has not to rob his subjects, that he can defend himself, that he does not become poor and abject, that he is not forced to become rapacious, ought to hold of little account a reputation for being mean, for it is one of those vices which will enable him to govern. . . .

Seventeenth Chapter. Concerning Cruelty and Clemency, and Whether it is Better to be Loved than Feared: Coming now to the other qualities mentioned above, I say that every prince ought to desire to be considered clement and not cruel. Nevertheless he ought to take care not to misuse this clemency. Cesare Borgia was considered cruel; notwithstanding, his cruelty reconciled the Romagna, unified it, and restored it to peace and loyalty. And if this be rightly considered, he will be seen to have been much more merciful than the Florentine people, who, to avoid a reputation for cruelty, permitted Pistoia to be destroyed. Therefore a prince, so long as he keeps his subjects united and loyal, ought not to mind the reproach of cruelty; because with a few examples he will be more merciful than those who, through too much mercy, allow disorders to arise, from which follow murder or robbery; for these are wont to injure the whole people, whilst those executions which originate with a prince offend the individual only.

And of all princes, it is impossible for the new prince to avoid the imputation of cruelty, owing to new states being full of dangers. Hence Virgil, through the mouth of Dido, excuses the inhumanity of her reign owing to its being new, saying: —

*Res dura, et regni novitas me talia cogunt
Moliri, et late fines custode tueri.*

Nevertheless he ought to be slow to believe and to act, nor should he himself show fear, but proceed in a temperate manner with prudence and humanity, so that too much confidence may not make him incautious and too much distrust render him intolerable.

Upon this a question arises: whether it be better to be loved than feared or feared than loved? It may be answered that one should wish to be both, but, because it is difficult to unite them in one person, it is much safer to be feared than loved, when, of the two, either must be dispensed with. Because this is to be asserted in general of men, that they are ungrateful, fickle, false, cowards, covetous, and as long as you succeed they are yours entirely; they will offer you their blood, property, life, and children, as is said above, when the need is far distant; but when it approaches they turn against you. And that prince who, relying entirely on their promises, has neglected other precautions, is ruined; because friendships that are obtained by payments, and not by greatness or nobility of mind, may indeed be earned, but they are not secured, and in time of need cannot be relied upon; and men have less scruple in offending one who is beloved than one who is feared, for love is preserved by the link of obligation which, owing to the baseness of men, is broken at every opportunity for their advantage; but fear preserves you by a dread of punishment which never fails.

Nevertheless a prince ought to inspire fear in such a way that, if he does not win love, he avoids hatred; because he can endure very well being feared whilst he is not hated, which will always be as long as he abstains from the property of his citizens and subjects and from their women. But when it is necessary for him to proceed against the life of some one, he must do it on proper justification and for manifest cause, but above all things he must keep his hands off the property of others, because men more quickly forget the death of their father than the loss of their patrimony. Besides, pretexts for taking away the property are never wanting; for he who has once begun to live by robbery will always find pretexts for seizing what belongs to others; but reasons for taking life, on the contrary, are more difficult to find and sooner lapse. But when a prince is with his army, and has under control a multitude of soldiers, then it is quite necessary for him to disregard the reputation of cruelty, for without it he would never hold his army united or disposed to its duties. . . .

Eighteenth Chapter. Concerning the Way in Which Princes Should Keep Faith: Every one admits how praiseworthy it is in a prince to keep faith, and to live with integrity and not with craft. Nevertheless our experience has been that those princes who have done great things have held good faith of little account, and have known how to circumvent the intellect of men by craft, and in the end have overcome those who have relied on their word. You must know there are two ways of contesting, the one by the law, the other by force; the first method is proper to men, the second to beasts; but because the first is frequently not sufficient, it is necessary to have recourse to the second. Therefore it is necessary for a prince to understand how to avail himself of the beast and the man. This has been figuratively taught to princes by ancient writers, who describe how Achilles and many other princes of old were given to the Centaur Chiron to nurse, who brought them up in his discipline; which means solely that, as they had for a teacher one who was half beast and half man, so it is necessary for a prince to know how to make use of both natures, and that one without the other is not durable. A prince, therefore, being compelled knowingly to adopt the beast, ought to choose the fox and the lion; because the lion cannot defend himself against snares and the fox cannot defend himself against wolves. Therefore, it is necessary to be a fox to discover the snares and a lion to terrify the wolves. Those who rely simply on the lion do not understand what they are about. Therefore a wise lord cannot, nor ought he to, keep faith when such observance may be turned against him, and when the reasons that caused him to pledge it exist no longer. If men were entirely good this precept would not hold, but because they are bad, and will not keep faith with you, you too are bound not to observe it with them. Nor will there ever be wanting to a prince legitimate reasons to excuse this non-observance. Of this endless modern examples could be given, showing how many treaties and engagements have been made void and of no effect through the faithlessness of princes; and he who has known best how to employ the fox has succeeded best.

But it is necessary to know well how to disguise this characteristic, and to be a great pretender and dissembler; and men are so simple, and so subject to present necessities, that he who seeks to deceive will always find some one who will allow himself to be deceived. One recent example I cannot pass over in silence. Alexander the Sixth did nothing else but deceive men, nor ever thought of doing otherwise, and he always found victims; for there never was a man who had greater power in asserting, or who with greater oaths would affirm a thing, yet would observe it less; nevertheless his deceits always succeeded according to his wishes, because he well understood this side of mankind.

Therefore it is unnecessary for a prince to have all the good qualities I have enumerated, but it is very necessary to appear to have them. And I shall dare to say this also, that to have them and always to observe them is injurious, and that to appear merciful, faithful, humane, religious, upright, and to be so, but with a mind so framed that should you require not to be so, you may be able and know how to change to the opposite.

And you have to understand this, that a prince, especially a new one, cannot observe all those things for which men are esteemed, being often forced, in order to maintain the state, to act contrary to fidelity, friendship, humanity, and religion. Therefore it is necessary for him to have a mind ready to turn itself accordingly as the winds and variations of fortune force it, yet, as I have said above, not to diverge from the good if he can avoid doing so, but, if compelled, then to know how to set about it.

For this reason a prince ought to take care that he never lets anything slip from his lips that is not replete with the above-named five qualities, that he may appear to him who sees and hears him altogether merciful, faithful, humane, upright, and religious. There is nothing more necessary to appear to have than this last quality, inasmuch as men judge generally more by the eye than by the hand, because it belongs to everybody to see you, to few to come in touch with you. Every one sees what you appear to be, few really know what you are, and those few dare not oppose themselves to the opinion of the many, who have the majesty of the state to defend them; and in the actions of all men, and especially of princes, which it is not prudent to challenge, one judges by the result.

For that reason, let a prince have the credit of conquering and holding his state, the means will always be considered honest, and he will be praised by everybody; because the vulgar are always taken by what a thing seems to be and by what comes of it; and in the world there are only the vulgar, for the few find a place there only when the many have no ground to rest on.

One prince of the present time, whom it is not

well to name, never preaches anything else but peace and good faith, and to both he is most hostile, and either, if he had kept it, would have deprived him of reputation and kingdom many a time.

Nineteenth Chapter. That One Should Avoid Being Despised and Hated: Now, concerning the characteristics of which mention is made above, I have spoken of the more important ones, the others I wish to discuss briefly under this generality, that the prince must consider, as has been in part said before, how to avoid those things which will make him hated or contemptible; and as often as he shall have succeeded he will have fulfilled his part, and he need not fear any danger in other reproaches.

It makes him hated above all things, as I have said, to be rapacious, and to be a violater of the property and women of his subjects, from both of which he must abstain. And when neither their property nor honor is touched, the majority of men live content, and he has only to contend with the ambition of a few, whom he can curb with ease in many ways.

It makes him contemptible to be considered fickle, frivolous, effeminate, mean-spirited, irresolute, from all of which a prince should guard himself as from a rock; and he should endeavor to show in his actions greatness, courage, gravity, and fortitude; and in his private dealings with his subjects let him show that his judgments are irrevocable, and maintain himself in such reputation that no one can hope either to deceive him or to get round him.

That prince is highly esteemed who conveys this impression of himself, and he who is highly esteemed is not easily conspired against; for, provided it is well known that he is an excellent man and revered by his people, he can only be attacked with difficulty. For this reason a prince ought to have two fears, one from within, on account of his subjects, the other from without, on account of external powers. From the latter he is defended by being well armed and having good allies, and if he is well armed he will have good friends, and affairs will always remain quiet within when they are quiet without, unless they should have been already disturbed by conspiracy; and even should affairs outside be disturbed, if he has carried out his preparations and has lived as I have said, as long as he does not despair, he will resist every attack, as I said Nabis the Spartan did.

But concerning his subjects, when affairs outside are disturbed he has only to fear that they will conspire secretly, from which a prince can easily secure himself by avoiding being hated and despised, and by keeping the people satisfied with him, which it is most necessary for him to

accomplish, as I said above at length. And one of the most efficacious remedies that a prince can have against conspiracies is not to be hated and despised by the people, for he who conspires against a prince always expects to please them by his removal; but when the conspirator can only look forward to offending them, he will not have the courage to take such a course, for the difficulties that confront a conspirator are infinite. And as experience shows, many have been the conspiracies, but few have been successful; because he who conspires cannot act alone, nor can he take a companion except from those whom he believes to be malcontents, and as soon as you have opened your mind to a malcontent you have given him the material with which to content himself, for by denouncing you he can look for every advantage; so that, seeing the gain from this course to be assured, and seeing the other to be doubtful and full of dangers, he must be a very rare friend, or a thoroughly obstinate enemy of the prince, to keep faith with you.

And to reduce the matter into a small compass, I say that, on the side of the conspirator, there is nothing but fear, jealousy, prospect of punishment to terrify him; but on the side of the prince there is the majesty of the principality, the laws, the protection of friends and the state to defend him; so that, adding to all these things the popular goodwill, it is impossible that any one should be so rash as to conspire. For whereas in general the conspirator has to fear before the execution of his plot, in this case he has also to fear the sequel to the crime; because on account of it he has the people for an enemy, and thus cannot hope for any escape.

Endless examples could be given on this subject, but I will be content with one, brought to pass within the memory of our fathers. Messer Annibale Bentivogli, who was prince in Bologna (grandfather of the present Annibale), having been murdered by the Canneschi, who had conspired against him, not one of his family survived but Messer Giovanni, who was in childhood: immediately after his assassination the people rose and murdered all the Canneschi. This sprung from the popular goodwill which the house of Bentivogli enjoyed in those days in Bologna; which was so great that, although none remained there after the death of Annibale who were able to rule the state, the Bolognese, having information that there was one of the Bentivogli family in Florence, who up to that time had been considered the son of a blacksmith, sent to Florence for him and gave him the government of their city, and it was ruled by him until Messer Giovanni came in due course to the government.

For this reason I consider that a prince ought to reckon conspiracies of little account when his people hold him in esteem; but when it is hostile to him, and bears hatred towards him, he ought to fear everything and everybody. And well-ordered states and wise princes have taken every care not to drive the nobles to desperation, and to keep the people satisfied and contented, for this is one of the most important objects a prince can have.

Among the best ordered and governed kingdoms of our times is France, and in it are found many good institutions on which depend the liberty and security of the king; of these the first is the parliament and its authority, because he who founded the kingdom, knowing the ambition of the nobility and their boldness, considered that a bit in their mouths would be necessary to hold them in; and, on the other side, knowing the hatred of the people, founded in fear, against the nobles, he wished to protect them, yet he was not anxious for this to be the particular care of the king; therefore, to take away the reproach which he would be liable to from the nobles for favoring the people, and from the people for favoring the nobles, he set up an arbiter, who should be one who could beat down the great and favor the lesser without reproach to the king. Neither could you have a better or a more prudent arrangement, or a greater source of security to the king and kingdom. From this one can draw another important conclusion, that princes ought to leave affairs of reproach to the management of others, and keep those of grace in their own hands. And further, I consider that a prince ought to cherish the nobles, but not so as to make himself hated by the people.

It may appear, perhaps, to some who have examined the lives and deaths of the Roman emperors that many of them would be an example contrary to my opinion, seeing that some of them lived nobly and showed great qualities of soul, nevertheless they have lost their empire or have been killed by subjects who have conspired against them. Wishing, therefore, to answer these objections, I will recall the characters of some of the emperors, and will show that the causes of their ruin were not different to those alleged by me; at the same time I will only submit for consideration those things that are noteworthy to him who studies the affairs of those times. . . .

But returning to the subject of our discourse, I say that whoever will consider it will acknowledge that either hatred or contempt has been fatal to the above-named emperors, and it will be recognized also how it happened that, a number of them acting in one way and a number in another, only one in each way came to a happy end and the rest to unhappy ones. Because it would have been useless and dangerous for Pertinax and Alexander, being new princes, to imitate Marcus,

who was heir to the principality; and likewise it would have been utterly destructive to Caracalla, Commodus, and Maximinus, to have imitated Severus, they not having sufficient valor to enable them to tread in his footsteps. Therefore a prince, new to the principality, cannot imitate the actions of Marcus, nor, again, is it necessary to follow those of Severus, but he ought to take from Severus those parts which are necessary to found his state, and from Marcus those which are proper and glorious to keep a state that may already be stable and firm. . . .

Twenty-First Chapter. How a Prince Should Conduct Himself so as to Gain Renown: Nothing makes a prince so much esteemed as great enterprises and setting a fine example. We have in our time Ferdinand of Aragon, the present King of Spain. He can almost be called a new prince, because he has risen, by fame and glory, from being an insignificant king to be the foremost king in Christendom; and if you will consider his deeds you will find them all great and some of them extraordinary. In the beginning of his reign he attacked Granada, and this enterprise was the foundation of his dominions. He did this quietly at first and without any fear of hindrance, for he held the minds of the barons of Castille occupied in thinking of the war and not anticipating any innovations; thus they did not perceive that by these means he was acquiring power and authority over them. He was able with the money of the Church and of the people to sustain his armies, and by that long war to lay the foundation for the military skill which has since distinguished him. Further, always using religion as a plea, so as to undertake greater schemes, he devoted himself with a pious cruelty to driving out and clearing his kingdom of the Moors; nor could there be a more admirable example, nor one more rare. Under this same cloak he assailed Africa, he came down on Italy, he has finally attacked France; and thus his achievements and designs have always been great, and have kept the minds of his people in suspense and admiration and occupied with the issue of them. And his actions have arisen in such a way, one out of the other, that men have never been given time to work steadily against him.

Again, it much assists a prince to set unusual examples in internal affairs, similar to those which are related of Messer Bernabo da Milano, who, when he had the opportunity, by any one in civil life doing some extraordinary thing, either good or bad, would take some method of rewarding or punishing him, which would be much spoken about. And a prince ought, above all things, always to endeavor in every action to gain for himself the reputation of being a great and remarkable man.

A prince is also respected when he is either a true friend or a downright enemy, that is to say, when, without any reservation, he declares himself in favour of one party against the other; which course will always be more advantageous than standing neutral; because if two of your powerful neighbors come to blows, they are of such a character that, if one of them conquers, you have either to fear him or not. In either case it will always be more advantageous for you to declare yourself and to make war strenuously; because, in the first case, if you do not declare yourself, you will invariably fall a prey to the conqueror, to the pleasure and satisfaction of him who has been conquered, and you will have no reasons to offer, nor anything to protect or to shelter you. Because he who conquers does not want doubtful friends who will not aid him in the time of trial; and he who loses will not harbor you because you did not willingly, sword in hand, court his fate.

Antiochus went into Greece, being sent for by the Aetolians to drive out the Romans. He sent envoys to the Acheans, who were friends of the Romans, exhorting them to remain neutral; and on the other hand the Romans urged them to take up arms. This question came to be discussed in the council of the Acheans, where the legate of Antiochus urged them to stand neutral. To this the Roman legate answered: "As for that which has been said, that it is better and more advantageous for your state not to interfere in our war, nothing can be more erroneous; because by not interfering you will be left, without favor or consideration, the guerdon of the conqueror." Thus it will always happen that he who is not your friend will demand your neutrality, whilst he who is your friend will entreat you to declare yourself with arms. And irresolute princes, to avoid present dangers, generally follow the neutral path, and are generally ruined. But when a prince declares himself gallantly in favor of one side, if the party with whom he allies himself conquers, although the victor may be powerful and may have him at his mercy, yet he is indebted to him, and there is established a bond of amity; and men are never so shameless as to become a monument of ingratitude by oppressing you. Victories after all are never so complete that the victor must not show some regard, especially to justice. But if he with whom you ally yourself loses, you may be sheltered by him, and whilst he is able he may aid you, and you become companions in a fortune that may rise again.

In the second case, when those who fight are of such a character that you have no anxiety as to who may conquer, so much the more is it greater prudence to be allied, because you assist at the destruction of one by the aid of another, who, if he had been wise, would have saved him; and conquering, as it is impossible that he should not with your assistance, he remains at your discretion. And here it is to be noted that a prince ought to take care never to make an alliance with one more powerful than himself for the purpose of attacking others, unless necessity compels him, as is said above; because if he conquers you are at his discretion, and princes ought to avoid as much as possible being at the discretion of any one. The Venetians joined with France against the Duke of Milan, and this alliance, which caused their ruin, could have been avoided. But when it cannot be avoided, as happened to the Florentines when the Pope and Spain sent armies to attack Lombardy, then in such a case, for the above reasons, the prince ought to favor one of the parties.

Never let any government imagine that it can choose perfectly safe courses; rather let it expect to have to take very doubtful ones, because it is found in ordinary affairs that one never seeks to avoid one trouble without running into another; but prudence consists in knowing how to distinguish the character of troubles, and for choice to take the lesser evil.

A prince ought also to show himself a patron of ability, and to honor the proficient in every art. At the same time he should encourage his citizens to practice their callings peaceably, both in commerce and agriculture, and in every other following, so that the one should not be deterred from improving his possessions for fear lest they be taken away from him or another from opening up trade for fear of taxes; but the prince ought to offer rewards to whoever wishes to do these things and designs in any way to honor his city or state.

Further, he ought to entertain the people with festivals and spectacles at convenient seasons of the year; and as every city is divided into guilds or into societies, he ought to hold such bodies in esteem, and associate with them sometimes, and show himself an example of courtesy and liberality; nevertheless, always maintaining the majesty of his rank, for this he must never consent to abate in anything.

Twenty-Second Chapter. Concerning the Secretaries of Princes: The choice of servants is of no little importance to a prince, and they are good or not according to the discrimination of the prince. And the first opinion which one forms of a prince, and of his understanding, is by observing the men he has around him; and when they are capable and faithful he may always be considered wise, because he has known how to recognize the capable and to keep them faithful. But when they are otherwise one cannot form a good opinion of him, for the prime error which he made was in choosing them.

There were none who knew Messer Antonio da Venafro as the servant of Pandolfo Petrucci, Prince of Siena, who would not consider Pandolfo to be a very clever man in having Venafro for his servant. Because there are three classes of intellects: one which comprehends by itself; another which appreciates what others comprehend; and a third which neither comprehends by itself nor by the showing of others; the first is the most excellent, the second is good, the third is useless. Therefore, it follows necessarily that, if Pandolfo was not in the first rank, he was in the second, for whenever one has judgment to know good or bad when it is said and done, although he himself may not have the initiative, yet he can recognize the good and the bad in his servant, and the one he can praise and the other correct; thus the servant cannot hope to deceive him, and is kept honest.

But to enable a prince to form an opinion of his servant there is one test which never fails; when you see the servant thinking more of his own interests than of yours, and seeking inwardly his own profit in everything, such a man will never make a good servant, nor will you ever be able to trust him; because he who has the state of another in his hands ought never to think of himself, but always of his prince, and never pay any attention to matters in which the prince is not concerned.

On the other hand, to keep his servant honest the prince ought to study him, honoring him, enriching him, doing him kindnesses, sharing with him the honors and cares; and at the same time let him see that he cannot stand alone, so that many honors may not make him desire more, many riches make him wish for more, and that many cares may make him dread changes. When, therefore, servants, and princes towards servants, are thus disposed, they can trust each other, but when it is otherwise, the end will always be disastrous for either one or the other.

Twenty-Third Chapter. How Flatterers Should Be Avoided: I do not wish to leave out an important branch of this subject, for it is a danger from which princes are with difficulty preserved, unless they are very careful and discriminating. It is that of flatterers, of whom courts are full, because men are so self-complacent in their own affairs, and in a way so deceived in them, that they are preserved with difficulty from this pest, and if they wish to defend themselves they run the danger of falling into contempt. Because there is no other way of guarding oneself from flatterers except letting men understand that to tell you the truth does not offend you; but when every

one may tell you the truth, respect for you abates.

Therefore a wise prince ought to hold a third course by choosing the wise men in his state, and giving to them only the liberty of speaking the truth to him, and then only of those things of which he inquires, and of none others; but he ought to question them upon everything, and listen to their opinions, and afterwards form his own conclusions. With these councillors, separately and collectively, he ought to carry himself in such a way that each of them should know that, the more freely he shall speak, the more he shall be preferred; outside of these, he should listen to no one, pursue the thing resolved on, and be steadfast in his resolutions. He who does otherwise is either overthrown by flatterers, or is so often changed by varying opinions that he falls into contempt.

I wish on this subject to adduce a modern example. Fra Luca, the man of affairs to Maximilian, the present emperor, speaking of his majesty, said: He consulted with no one, yet never got his own way in anything. This arose because of his following a practice the opposite to the above; for the emperor is a secretive man—he does not communicate his designs to any one, nor does he receive opinions on them. But as in carrying them into effect they become revealed and known, they are at once obstructed by those men whom he has around him, and he, being pliant, is diverted from them. Hence it follows that those things he does one day he undoes the next, and no one ever understands what he wishes or intends to do, and no one can rely on his resolutions.

A prince, therefore, ought always to take counsel, but only when he wishes and not when others wish; he ought rather to discourage every one from offering advice unless he asks it; but, however, he ought to be a constant inquirer, and afterwards a patient listener concerning the things of which he inquired; also, on learning that any one, on any consideration, has not told him the truth, he should let his anger be felt.

And if there are some who think that a prince who conveys an impression of his wisdom is not so through his own ability, but through the good advisers that he has around him, beyond doubt they are deceived, because this is an axiom which never fails: that a prince who is not wise himself will never take good advice, unless by chance he has yielded his affairs entirely to one person who happens to be a very prudent man. In this case indeed he may be well governed, but it would not be for long, because such a governor would in a short time take away his state from him.

But if a prince who is not experienced should take counsel from more than one he will never get united counsels, nor will he know how to unite them. Each of the counsellors will think of his own interests, and the prince will not know how to control them or to see through them. And they are not to be found otherwise, because men will always prove untrue to you unless they are kept honest by constraint. Therefore it must be inferred that good counsels, whencesoever they come, are born of the wisdom of the prince, and not the wisdom of the prince from good counsels. . . .

Twenty-Fifth Chapter. What Fortune Can Effect in Human Affairs, and How to Withstand Her: It is not unknown to me how many men have had, and still have, the opinion that the affairs of the world are in such wise governed by fortune and by God that men with their wisdom cannot direct them and that no one can even help them; and because of this they would have us believe that it is not necessary to labor much in affairs, but to let chance govern them. This opinion has been more credited in our times because of the great changes in affairs which have been seen, and may still be seen, every day, beyond all human conjecture. Sometimes pondering over this, I am in some degree inclined to their opinion. Nevertheless, not to extinguish our free will, I hold it to be true that fortune is the arbiter of one half of our actions, but that she still leaves us to direct the other half, or perhaps a little less.

I compare her to one of those raging rivers, which when in flood overflows the plains, sweeping away trees and buildings, bearing away the soil from place to place; everything flies before it, all yield to its violence, without being able in any way to withstand it; and yet, though its nature be such, it does not follow therefore, that men, when the weather becomes fair, shall not make provision, both with defenses and barriers, in such a manner that, rising again, the waters may pass away by canal, and their force be neither so unrestrained nor so dangerous. So it happens with fortune, who shows her power where valor has not prepared to resist her, and thither she turns her forces where she knows that barriers and defenses have not been raised to constrain her.

And if you will consider Italy, which is the seat of these changes, and which has given to them their impulse, you will see it to be an open country, without barriers and without any defense. For if it had been defended by proper valor, as are Germany, Spain, and France, either this invasion would not have made the great changes it has made or it would not have come at all. And this I consider enough to say concerning resistance to fortune in general.

But confining myself more to the particular, I say that a prince may be seen happy to-day and ruined tomorrow without having shown any change of disposition or character. This, I believe, arises firstly from causes that have already been discussed at length, namely, that the prince who relies entirely upon fortune is lost when it changes. I believe also that he will be successful who directs his actions according to the spirit of the times, and that he whose actions do not accord with the times will not be successful. Because men are seen, in affairs that lead to the end which every man has before him, namely, glory and riches, to get there by various methods; one with caution, another with haste; one by force, another by skill; one by patience, another by its opposite; and each one succeeds in reaching the goal by a different method. One can also see of two cautious men the one attain his end, the other fail; and similarly, two men by different observances are equally successful, the one being cautious, the other impetuous; all this arises from nothing else than whether or not they conform in their methods to the spirit of the times. This follows from what I have said, that two men working differently bring about the same effect, and of two working similarly, one attains his object and the other does not.

Changes in estate also issue from this, for if, to one who governs himself with caution and patience, times and affairs converge in such a way that his administration is successful, his fortune is made; but if times and affairs change, he is ruined if he does not change his course of action. But a man is not often found sufficiently circumspect to know how to accommodate himself to the change, both because he cannot deviate from what nature inclines him to, and also because, having always prospered by acting in one way, he cannot be persuaded that it is well to leave it; and, therefore, the cautious man, when it is time to turn adventurous does not know how to do it, hence he is ruined; but had he changed his conduct with the times fortune would not have changed.

Pope Julius the Second went to work impetuously in all his affairs, and found the times and circumstances conform so well to that line of action that he always met with success. Consider his first enterprise against Bologna, Messer Giovanni Bentivogli being still alive. The Venetians were not agreeable to it, nor was the King of Spain, and he had the enterprise still under discussion with the King of France; nevertheless he personally entered upon the expedition with his accustomed boldness and energy, a move which made Spain and the Venetians stand irresolute and passive, the latter from fear, the former from desire to recover all the kingdom of Naples; on the other hand, he drew after him the King of France, because that king, having observed the movement, and desiring to make the Pope his friend so as to humble the Venetians, found it impossible to refuse him soldiers without manifestly offending him. Therefore Julius with his impetuous action accomplished what no other pontiff with simple human wisdom could have done; for if he had waited in Rome until he could get away, with his plans arranged and everything fixed, as any other pontiff would have done, he would never have succeeded. Because the King of France would have made a thousand excuses, and the others would have raised a thousand fears.

I will leave his other actions alone, as they were all alike, and they all succeeded, for the shortness of his life did not let him experience the contrary; but if circumstances had arisen which required him to go cautiously, his ruin would have followed, because he would never have deviated from those ways to which nature inclined him.

I conclude therefore that, fortune being changeful and mankind steadfast in their ways, so long as the two are in agreement men are successful, but unsuccessful when they fall out. For my part I consider that it is better to be adventurous than cautious, because fortune is a woman, and if you wish to keep her under it is necessary to beat and ill-use her; and it is seen that she allows herself to be mastered by the adventurous rather than by those who go to work more coldly. She is, therefore, always, woman-like, a lover of young men because they are less cautious, more violent, and with more audacity command her.

B.   BODIN ON THE NATURE AND FUNCTIONS OF SOVEREIGNTY

The Six Books Concerning the State first appeared in French in 1576. The book systematically considers such general problems as the "principal end of a well-ordered commonwealth" as well as the more detailed questions of institutions and forms of government. It is Bodin's practice to announce an idea and then illustrate his arguments by evidence drawn from ancient and modern history. In the following selection he is analysing the central problem of sovereignty.[2]

Sovereignty is supreme power over citizens and subjects, unrestrained by laws. . . . Since we have already defined the state as the rightful government of a number of families in their common affairs, with a supreme and perpetual power, it should now be explained what is meant by supreme and perpetual power. We say that the power must be perpetual; for supreme power over citizens may be given to some one or several not perpetually, but for a brief period at the expiration of which the authority ceases. Such persons cannot be called sovereign rulers; they are rather custodians of sovereignty until such time as the sovereign prince or people may withdraw the power intrusted, of which they are the true owners and possessors, as those who have lent or pawned their goods to another; just as those who have conferred upon others powers of judgment and command for a certain time, or to be withdrawn at will, do not cease to be masters and possessors of the jurisdiction and authority. So the jurist has said that the prefect of the Roman emperor surrendered his authority upon demand of the magistrate. It makes no difference whether greater or less power is thus conferred; for if the high power conceded by a prince to his lieutenant to be withdrawn at will, be called sovereignty, the power might be used against the prince himself, to whom nothing but an empty title would then remain; so also a servant might command his master, than which nothing more absurd can be imagined. When authority is granted to a magistrate or to a private individual the person of the prince is always excepted. Whatever authority the sovereign gives to another is less than that which he reserves to himself by virtue of his sovereignty; and he is never so divested of his sovereignty that he may not undertake an examination of the affairs committed to his magistrates or officers, by way of prevention, concurrence, or challenge, or that he may not withdraw power altogether from them. Wherefore, the Roman dictator, the harmosts of the Lacedaemonians, the esymnet of Thessaly, the archons of Malta, or the ancient bailly of Florence (when it had popular government), or those who among us are called regents, or any magistrate or officer to whom is conceded power which though supreme is not perpetual—no such official can be said to have sovereignty.

But suppose that supreme power, unlimited by laws, and without protest or appeal, be granted by the people to some one or few, shall we say that the latter have sovereignty? For he has sovereignty who, after God, acknowledges no one greater than himself. I hold that sovereignty resides not in such persons, but in the people, at whose pleasure they hold their power, or to whom they must return their authority at the expiration of the period designated. The people cannot be considered as having divested themselves of their power when they intrust supreme authority, unrestrained by laws, to one or a few, if the commitment is for a certain period of time, or at the pleasure of the people; for in either case the holders of the supreme authority must render account of their doings to the prince or people, who, being sovereign, are required to give account to no one, save immortal God. What if supreme power be conferred for a period of ten years; as in Athens one archon, whom they called judge, stood thus preëminent in power in the city? Still the sovereignty of the state did not rest in him; he was rather curator or deputy for the people, and had to render account to them. What if the high power of which I speak be given to one or more for a year, with no requirement that account of their actions be given to any one? So the Cnidians every year chose sixty citizens whom they called *amymones,* that is, men superior to any limitation or censure. Sovereignty, nevertheless, was not in them, since they were compelled, at the expiration of the year, to surrender their authority.

But what if the people have given supreme and perpetual power to any one for life: If the power is given unlimited by laws, and without the name of magistrate, deputy, governor, or guardian, and not at the pleasure of any one, certainly it must be confessed that sovereign rights have been conceded to such a one. The people in such case have despoiled themselves of their authority, in order to give to another all the privileges of sovereignty, without conditions; in like manner as any one might by pure gift surrender to another the ownership and possession of his property; such a perfect donation contains no conditions.

As a prince is bound by no laws of his predecessor, much less is he bound by his own laws. One man may receive a command from another, but no man can command himself. Pomponius says that no obligation can exist if it must receive its sanction from the will of him who makes the promise; this shows conclusively that a prince can in no way be bound by his own laws and orders. As the Pope, according to the jurists, cannot bind his own hands, so the supreme prince, or even the lowest magistrate, or a private person, cannot issue commands to himself. Thus we see at the end of every law, "because it has so pleased us," in order that all may understand that laws, however just in themselves, depend for their force solely upon the will of him who makes the law.

As for the laws of God and of nature, princes and people are equally bound by them, so that no one who attempts to abrogate or weaken them can escape the judgments of divine sovereignty. What we have said as to the freedom of sovereignty from the binding force of law does not have reference to divine or natural law. That Pope who best of all knew the rights of sovereignty and who brought under his sway almost all Christian emperors and princes, said "sovereignty pertains to him who can derogate from ordinary law"; the latter expression I interpret to mean the laws of the country. But is a prince bound by the laws of his country if he has sworn to observe them? Here it is necessary to make a distinction. If the prince has sworn to himself, no obligation exists; he is not bound by an oath made to himself; just as private persons are not bound by oaths which they make in mutual contract, if the contract be such as the law does not make binding, however honorably the agreements may have been made. If a prince swears to another ruler not to abrogate the laws made by himself or by his predecessors, he is bound, if the prince to whom he makes the promise has interest in the matter. . . .

Likewise we say that a prince who has made sworn promises to his subjects is bound by them, if the promises are reasonable; but this is true not because he has sworn or because he is bound by his own laws, but because any one is bound by his just covenants, if they are made with another who has any interest, whether the promises be made with or without oath. Moreover, as a private person may be relieved of his obligation if he has been circumvented by fraud, deceit, error, or threat, so a prince may be released not only in those cases which tend to impair his sovereignty, but also where his private convenience and domestic affairs are disturbed.

This, then, I hold: A prince may abrogate, modify, or replace a law made by himself and without the consent of his subjects; such action is fully permissible where justice seems to demand it; the abrogation, modification, or substitution, however, must not be obscure or ambiguous, but must be set forth in clear detail. If there is no probable reason for abrogating the law, he is acting contrary to the duty of a good prince in seeking such abrogation. However, he is not bound by any obligation assumed by his predecessors, further than what is compatible with his own interest. . . .

We must not confuse laws and contracts. Law depends upon the will of him who holds supreme power in the state, and who can bind subjects by his law, but cannot bind himself. A contract between a prince and his subjects has mutual binding force, so that it cannot be departed from save with the consent of both parties; in this the prince seems to have nothing above his subjects, except that the purpose of a law to which he has sworn having ceased to exist, he is no longer bound either by the law or by the oath which he took with regard to the law. A well-advised prince will not suffer himself to be bound by oath to observe the laws, for in such case he does not possess the supreme authority in the commonwealth.

As to laws concerning the supreme power, the prince cannot abrogate or modify them, since they are attached to the very sovereignty with which he is clothed; such as the Salic law, which is the foundation of our monarchy.

The sovereignty of a prince is manifest in the fact that when the estates and orders of the people, with humble mien, present their requests to him they are exercising no authority of commanding, forbidding, or concurring; but the prince by his own judgment and will directs everything; whatever he desires and orders has the force of law. The opinion of those who in books scattered broadcast have written that the king is bound by the popular command, must be disregarded; such doctrine furnishes seditious men with material for revolutionary plots, and leads to disturbance in the commonwealth. No reasonable ground can be adduced why subjects should control princes, or why power should be attributed to popular assemblies—except in the infancy, madness, or captivity of the prince, when a guardian or deputy may be created by the suffrages of the people. If princes were restrained by laws made by these assemblies or by the commands of the people, the power of the prince would be worthless and the royal name a vain thing.

The approval and promulgation of laws, which is commonly done in an assembly or senate, does not imply that the sovereignty of the realm resides in such assembly or senate, but only a species of authority without which laws issued by the king might be called in question at his death, or before the senate when it acts judicially. I hold, therefore, that the sovereignty of the prince is in no degree diminished by calling together the assemblies or estates, though indeed a prince grants many things to the assembled people which he would not so readily grant to individuals; this is because the voices of individuals are not heard so clearly as the voice of the multitude; or it is because the prince, accustomed to use the eyes and ears of others, in the assembly sees and hears the people directly, and so, impelled by shame, religious fear, or his own good disposition, he grants their requests. But the highest privilege of sovereignty consists primarily in giving laws not only to individuals but also to the people as a whole, without their consent.

We may hold that a king who by lawful right assumes the kingship is bound by the contracts and promises of his predecessors, in so far as such contracts were made for the benefit of the commonwealth. This is especially true if they were made with the judgment and consent of the entire people or of the greater assemblies; for their good faith is at stake, which it is not only appropriate but necessary for the king to respect, even though the state may be harmed thereby. But when a prince has contracted with strangers or with citizens concerning matters pertaining to the commonwealth without the consent of the people, if serious injury would come upon the commonwealth from the performance of the contracts, his successor is not bound by them, especially if he obtains his authority through election by the people or the senate; in such case he has received none of his privileges from his predecessor. It would be otherwise if he had acquired authority by grant from another; then he would be bound by the latter's promises, unless express exception had been made. But by whatever right a prince obtains his authority, whether by law, testament, popular election, or lot, it is just to fulfil those obligations which were undertaken for the good of the state. Otherwise it would be permissible for him, through evil practices, contrary to the laws of nature, to draw profit to himself out of hardships endured by others. It is of concern to the citizenship to keep the public faith to the best of its ability, lest when the state is in extreme danger all means of relief should be cut off. . . .

But why, some one may ask, are the foregoing distinctions necessary, since all princes are bound by the law of nations? For in that law compacts and testaments are included. This is not true, if we mean every kind of contract or testament. But admitting it to be true, it does not follow that a prince is more bound by the law of nations than by his own laws, except in so far as the former are in agreement with the laws of nature and of God; to these latter laws all that we have said concerning the obligation of princes must be referred. If certain of the laws of nations are unjust, the prince may abrogate them and forbid his subjects to follow them. This we showed in relation to slavery; this institution was established in many states, by pernicious examples, yet in accord with the law of almost every nation; but through salutary decrees of several princes it has been abolished, in conformity to the laws of nature. What has been said of one thing may be extended to other things of like kind; for a proviso in the whole argumentation is that nothing be sanctioned which is contrary to the laws of God or of nature. For if justice is the end of the law, and law is the command of the prince, and the prince is the image of the almighty God, then the laws of the prince should bear the stamp of divine laws.

The first and principal function of sovereignty is to give laws to the citizens generally and individually, and, it must be added, not necessarily with the consent of superiors, equals, or inferiors. If the consent of superiors is required, then the prince is clearly a subject; if he must have the consent of equals, then others share his authority; if the consent of inferiors—the people or the senate—is necessary, then he lacks supreme authority. . . .

It may be objected that custom does not get its power from the judgment or command of the prince, and yet has almost the force of law, so that it would seem that the prince is master of law, the people of custom. Custom, insensibly, yet with the full compliance of all, passes gradually into the character of men, and acquires force with the lapse of time. Law, on the other hand, comes forth in one moment at the order of him who has the power to command, and often in opposition to the desire and approval of those whom it governs. Wherefore, Chrysostom likens law to a tyrant and custom to a king. Moreover, the power of law is far greater than that of custom, for customs may be superseded by laws, but laws are not supplanted by customs; it is within the power and function of magistrates to restore the operation of laws which by custom are obsolescent. Custom proposes neither rewards nor penalties; laws carry one or the other, unless it be a permissive law which nullifies the penalty of some other law. In short, a custom has compelling force only as long as the prince, by adding his endorsement and sanction to the custom, makes it a law.

It is thus clear that laws and customs depend for their force upon the will of those who hold supreme power in the state. This first and chief mark of sovereignty is, therefore, of such sort that it cannot be transferred to subjects, though the prince or people sometimes confer upon one of the citizens the power to frame laws, which then have the same force as if they had been framed by the prince himself. The Lacedaemonians bestowed such power upon Lycurgus, the Athenians upon Solon; each stood as deputy for his state, and the fulfilment of his function depended upon the pleasure not of himself but of the people; his legislation had no force save as the people confirmed it by their assent. The former composed and wrote the laws, the people enacted and commanded them.

Under this supreme power of ordaining and abrogating laws, it is clear that all other functions of sovereignty are included; so that it may be truly said that supreme authority in the state is comprised in this one thing—namely, to give laws to all and each of the citizens, and to receive none from them. For to declare war or make peace, though seeming to involve what is alien to the term law, is yet accomplished by law, that is by decree of the supreme power. It is also the prerogative of sovereignty to receive appeals from the highest magistrates, to confer authority upon the greater magistrates and to withdraw it from them, to allow exemption from taxes, to bestow other immunities, to grant dispensations from the laws, to exercise power of life and death, to fix the value, name and form of money, to compel all citizens to observe their oaths: all of these attributes are derived from the supreme power of commanding and forbidding—that is, from the authority to give law to the citizens collectively and individually, and to receive law from no one save immortal God. A duke, therefore, who gives laws to all his subjects, but receives law from the emperor, Pope, or king, or has a co-partner in authority, lacks sovereignty.

Part II. MERCANTILISM: THEORY AND PRACTICE

The documents which follow illustrate the critical nature of the economic change that was revolutionizing Tudor and early Stuart England, the actions of the government to meet this crisis, and the theory which motivated this action. England provides an excellent laboratory for the study of mercantilism in action, for the island kingdom not only experienced the economic growing pains that stimulated the activity of the period but she also began the sixteenth century with a good start along the road to the mercantilist ideal. England's island position and the consequent territorial unity had long facilitated the task of the English kings, and the tradition of vigorous state action, when faced with a national crisis, as the policy of the government in 1349–51 had showed, was early established. Thus, with the accession of the Tudors in 1485 the "new" monarchy found the way clear for a new burst of government activity.

A. AGRICULTURE AND THE COMMON WEAL

As had been the case in the Middle Ages economic change had immediate repercussions on the basic agrarian economy of sixteenth century England. These effects were sufficiently profound to stimulate comment among the more reflective members of the society, and, ultimately, to call forth legislative action.

1. *The State of the Nation, 1549*. The selections which follow are from *The Common Weal of England* (circa 1549), whose unknown author has made use of the device of a dialogue between a Husbandman (farmer), a Capper (hat-maker), a Merchant, and a Knight to convey his observations. Inclosures, referred to in the document, consisted in the appropriation of common land which had either lain waste, or, as was more likely in the sixteenth century, had been a part of the common fields, to the sole use of one person.[3]

Husbandman: Marry, these inclosures do undo us all, for they make us pay dearer for our land that we occupy; all is taken up for pastures, either for sheep or for grazing of cattle. So that I have known of late a dozen ploughs within less compass than 6 miles about me laid down within these seven years; and where forty persons had their living, now one man and his shepherd hath all. Which thing is not the least cause of these uproars, for by these inclosures men do lack livings and be idle: and therefore for very necessity they are desirous of a change, being in hope to come thereby to somewhat, and well assured, howsoever it befall with them, it cannot be no harder with them than it was before. Moreover all things are so dear that by their daily labor they are not able to live.

Capper: I have well experience thereof, for I am fain to give my journeyman 2d. a day more than I was wont to do, and yet they say they cannot sufficiently live thereon. And by reason of such dearth as ye speak of, we that are artificers can keep few or no apprentices like as we were wont to do. Therefore the city, which was heretofore well inhabited and wealthy (as ye know every one of you) is fallen for lack of occupiers to great disolation and poverty.

Merchant: So the most part of all the towns of England, London excepted, and not only the good towns are decayed sore in their houses, streets, and other buildings, but also the country in their highways, and bridges: for such poverty reigneth everywhere that few men have so much to spare as they may give anything to the reparation of such ways and bridges.

And albeit there be many things laid down now that to foretimes were occasions of much expenses as stage plays, interludes, May games, wakes, revels, wagers at shooting, and besides that, pardons, pilgrimages, offerings, and many such other things, yet I perceive we be never the wealthier, but rather the poorer. Whereof it belongs, I cannot tell, for there is such a general dearth of all things as I never knew the like, not only of things growing in this Realm, but also of all other merchandise that we buy beyond the seas; as silks, wines, oils, wood, madder, iron, steel, wax, flax, linen cloth, fustians, worsteds, coverlets, carpets, and all arrases, and tapestry, spices of all sorts, and all haberdash wares, as paper both white and brown, glasses both drinking and looking, as for glazing of windows, pins, needles, knives, daggers, hats, caps, buttons and laces; I wot well all these do cost me more now by a third than they did but seven years ago.

Then, all kinds of victuals are as dear or dearer again, and no cause of God's part thereof, as far as I can perceive; for I never saw more plenty of corn, grass and cattle of all sort, than we have at this present, and have had these three years past continually, thanked be our Lord. If these inclosures be the cause thereof, or any other thing else, it were pity it were not removed.

Knight: Since we have plenty of things of corn and cattle as ye say, then it should not seem this dearth should be brought about of these inclosures; for it is not by scarceness of corn that we have this dearth, for thanks be to God, corn is good cheap. It cannot be the occasion of the dearth of cattle; for inclosures is the thing that nourisheth most of any others; yet I confess there is a wonderful dearth of all things; and that do I, and all men of my sort, feel most grief in, which have no wares to sell, or occupation to live by, but only our lands.

For you all three, I mean you my neighbors, the husbandman, and you mister merchant, and you good man Capper, and all sorts of artificers, may save themselves metely well; for as much as all things are dearer than they were, so much do you arise in the price of your wares and occupations that you sell again; but we have nothing to sell, whereby we might advance the price thereof, to countervail those things that we must buy again.

Husbandman: Yes: you raise the price of your lands, and you take farms also and pastures into your hands, which was wont to be poor men's livings, such as I am, and gentlemen ought to live only upon their lands.

Merchant and Capper: On my soul, ye say truth, quoth the merchantman, and the Capper also said no less, adding thereto, that it was never merry with poor men since gentlemen became graziers; for they cannot nowadays find their apprentices and servants meat and drink, but it cost them almost double as much as it did aforetime. And now we are scant able to live without debt or to keep any servants at all, except it be an apprentice or two, and therefore the journeyman, what of your occupation, and what of clothiers or other occupations, being forced to be without work are, the most part of these rude people that make these uproars abroad. And need, as you know, hath no boot. . . .

Capper: Marry, these inclosures and great pastures are a great cause whereby men do turn their arable land, being a living for divers poor men before time, now to one man's hand. And where both corn of all sorts, and also cattle of all kind, were reared afore time, now there is nothing but only sheep. And instead of some hundred or two hundred persons that had their livings thereon, now there be but three or four shepherds, and the Master only, that hath a living thereon.

Doctor: You touch a matter that is much to be considered, albeit I take not that only to be the cause of this dearth at this time. And I think it to be the most occasion, of any thing ye spake of yet, of these wild and unhappy uproars amongst us; for by reason of these inclosures many of the King's subjects have no ground to live upon, as they have had afore time, and occupations be not always set on work all alike; and therefore the people still increasing, and their livings diminished, it must needs come to pass that a great part of the people shall be idle and lack livings; and hunger is a better thing to bear. Wherefore, when they lack they must murmur against them that have plenty, and so stir up these tumults.

Knight: Experience should seem plainly to prove that inclosures should be profitable and not hurtful to the Common Weal; for we see that countries where most inclosures be, are most wealthy, as Essex, Kent, Devonshire and such. And I heard a civilian once say that it was taken for a maxim in his law, this saying, that which is possessed of many is neglected of all; and experience showeth that tenants in common be not so good husbands, as when every man hath his part in several.

Doctor: I mean not all inclosures, nor yet all commons, but only of such inclosures as turneth commonly arable fields into pastures; and violent inclosures, without recompense of them that have right to come therein; for if land were severally inclosed, to the intent to continue husbandry thereon, and every man, that had right to common, had for his portion a piece of the same to himself inclosed, I think no harm but rather good should come thereof. But it would not suddenly be done; for there be many a thousand cottagers in England, which, having no lands to live of their own but their handy labors, and some refreshing upon the said commons, if they were suddenly thrust out from that commodity might make a great tumult and discord in the Commonwealth. And

percase also, if men were suffered to inclose their grounds, under pretense to keep it still in tillage, within a while after they would turn all to pasture, as we see they do now too fast, more is the pity.

Knight: If they find more profit thereby than otherwise, why should they not?

Doctor: I can tell you well enough why they should not, for they may not purchase themselves profit by that that may be hurtful to others. But how to bring them that they would not do so, is all the better; for so long as they find more profit by pasture than by tillage, they will still inclose, and turn arable lands to pasture.

2. *Parliament Reacts, 1597–1601.* The statute book bears eloquent witness to the constant concern of the Tudor government for what has since been labelled "the agrarian problem of the sixteenth century." In the first selection below, the House of Commons debates an act of tillage in 1597, the eleventh of a list of similar acts passed between 1489 and 1597. In the second selection the Commons considers the repeal of the 1597 act in 1601; it remained on the statute book, nevertheless, until 1863.[4]

(*November 5, 1597. A Debate upon Inclosures.*) Mr. Francis Bacon spoke first, and made a motion against inclosures and depopulations of towns and houses for husbandry and tillage. And to this purpose he brought in, as he termed it, two Bills not drawn with a polished pen, but with a polished heart, free from affection and affectation. And because former laws are medicines of our understanding, he said that he had perused the preambles of former statutes, and by these did see the inconvenience of this matter, being then scarce out of the shell, to be now full opened. And he said, that the overflowing, of the people here, makes a shrinking and abate elsewhere; and that these two mischiefs, though they be exceeding great, yet they seem the less, because *Qui mala cum multis patimur.* And though it may be thought ill and very prejudicial to lords that have inclosed great grounds, and pulled down even whole towns, and converted them to sheep pasture, yet considering the increase of people and the benefit of the Commonwealth, I doubt not but every man will deem the revival of former moth-eaten laws in this point a praiseworthy thing. For in matters of policy, ill is not to be thought ill; if it bringeth forth good. For inclosure of grounds brings depopulation, which brings first idleness, secondly decay of tillage, thirdly subversion of houses, and decay of charity, and charges to the poor, fourthly impoverishing the state of this Realm.

A law for the taking away of such inconveniences is not to be thought ill or hurtful to the general state. And I would be sorry to see within this Kingdom, that piece of Ovid's verse prove true, *Iam seges ubi Troia fuit;* so in England, instead of a whole town full of people, nought but green fields, but a shepherd and his dog.

In the end of the said speech, Mr. Bacon did move the House that a Committee might be appointed to consider the said matter touching inclosures. Which done, Sir John Fortescue, Chancellor of the Exchequer, in like manner shared his opinion of the case, much answerable to the said speech of the said Mr. Bacon; and so moving for a Committee to that end, the House did nominate all the Privy Council being members of this House, all the Knights of the Counties, and all the citizens of the cities returned into this present parliament. Mr. Finch, showing sundry great and horrible abuses of idle and vagrant persons greatly offensive both to God and the world; and further showing the extreme and miserable estate of the Godly and honest sort of the poor subjects of this Realm, moved for a Committee of this House to be selected for consideration to be had for the redress thereof; whereupon the same was referred to the former Committee. . . .

(*December 9, 1601. A Debate on the Repeal of Restrictive Legislation.*) A motion was made for the repeal of the former Statute of Tillage.

Sir Walter Raleigh said: "I think this law fit to be repealed; for many poor men are not able to find seed to sow as much as they are bound to plough, which they must do, or incur the penalty of the law. And therefore I think the best course is to set it at liberty, and have every man free, which is the desire of a true Englishman."

Mr. Secretary Cecil said: "I do not dwell in the country. I am not acquainted with the plough; but I think that whoever doth not maintain the plough, destroys this Kingdom. My motion, therefore shall be that this law may not be repealed, except former laws may be in force and revived. Say that a glut of corn should be, have we not sufficient remedy by transportation, which is allowable by the policy of all nations.

"If in Edward I's time a law was made for the maintenance of the fry of fish, and in Henry VII's time for the preservation of the eggs of wild fowl, shall we now throw away a law of far more consequence and import? If we debar tillage, we give scope to the depopulator; and thus if the poor being thrust out of their houses go to dwell with others, straight we catch them with the Statute of Inmates; if they wander abroad, they are in danger of the Statute of the poor to be whipt. So by this means undo this Statute, and you endanger many thousands. 'Today is the teacher of tomorrow.' If former times have made us wise to make a law, let these latter times warn us to preserve so good a law."

B. INDUSTRY AND THE COMMON WEAL

The wool trade and later the cloth industry had given an almost modern complexity to the economic life of late medieval England. By the sixteenth century England was undergoing the pleasant and the unpleasant experiences which inevitably accompany the reconciliation of an agrarian past with a predominantly commercial and industrial future.

1. *Government Concern, 1559.* England had had a long tradition of state action in the economic sphere. The extent of this activity under the Tudors is illustrated by the selection which follows, the legislative program of William Cecil, Queen Elizabeth's first minister, as projected for the first meeting of parliament in 1559. Such legislation as the Statute of Apprentices (1563) carried out much of this plan so far as it concerned the hiring and paying of workmen and apprentices.[5]

1. *Vagabonds.* That the statute 1 Edward VI, Chap. 3, concerning idle persons and vagabonds being made slaves, now repealed, be revived, with additions.

2. *Laborers and Servants.* That the statutes 12 Richard II, Chap. 3, "that no servant or laborer at the end of his term depart out of the hundred or place where he dwells etc.," and 13 Richard II, Chap. 8, ordering the justices at every session to appoint by proclamation the wages of workers, etc., be confirmed with the addition "that no man hereafter receive into service any servant without a testimonial from the master he last dwelt with, sealed with a parish seal kept by the constable or churchwarden, witnessing he left with the free license of his master, penalty £10." So, by the need of the masters, servants may be reduced to obedience, which shall reduce obedience to the Prince and to God also; by the looseness of the time no other remedy is left but by awe of law to acquaint men with virtue again, whereby the Reformation of religion may be brought in credit, with the amendment of manners, the want whereof hath been imputed as a thing grown by the liberty of the Gospel, etc.

3. *Husbandry.* That the statutes, 4 Henry VII, Chap. 9, "for re-edifying houses of husbandry, and to avoid the decay of towns and villages," and 5 Edward VI, Chap. 5, "for maintenance of husbandry and tillage," be put in execution.

4. *Purchase of Lands.* No husbandman, yeoman or artificer to purchase above £5 by the year of inheritance; . . . save in cities, towns and boroughs, for their better repair; one mansion house only to be purchased over and above the said yearly value. The common purchasing thereof is the ground of dearth of victuals, raising of rents, etc.

5. *Merchants.* No merchant to purchase above £50 a year of inheritance, except aldermen and sheriffs of London, who, because they approach to the degree of knighthood, may purchase to the value of £200.

6. *Apprentices.* None to be received apprentice except his father spend 40s. a year of freehold, nor to be apprenticed to a merchant except his father spend £10 a year of freehold, or be descended from a gentleman or merchant. Through the idleness of those professions so many embrace them that they are only a cloak for vagabonds and thieves, and there is such a decay of husbandry that masters cannot get skillful servants to till the ground without unreasonable wages, etc. . . .

10. That the statutes 3 Henry IV, Chap. 9, and 3 Henry VII, Chap. 8 for keeping gold and silver and for increase of the commodities of the realm, ordaining that any merchant stranger bringing in merchandise sell it within three months and employ the money therefore received in England by exchange upon the commodities of the realm, etc.; and the statute 1 Richard III, Chap. 9, that no stranger host or sojourn with a stranger of another country, be revived and executed. The Italians above all other to be taken heed of, for they in all times pass to go to and fro everywhere and for themselves serve all princes at once, and with their perfumed gloves and wanton presents, and gold enough to boot if need be, work what they list and lick the fat even from our beards.

11. *Haberdashers' wares.* That the statute 3 Edward IV, Chap. 4, ordaining that no merchant, English or stranger, bring into the realm caps, pins, points, dice, gilt stirrups, etc., be revived; for they are not only false and deceitful wares, rather serving for the gaze than any good use, but for such trifles they filch from us the chief and substantial staple wares of the realm, where the people might be better employed in making them, if we will needs have them, and then for our precious commodities we shall receive things of price again.

12. *Wines.* That the statute 40 Edward III, Chap. 8, be revived, ordaining that no Englishman fetch or buy any wines in Gascony or France, but have them brought into the realm by Gascons for the profit of the realm. For they are not able to live two years together without making their sale hither, and we are well able to forbear their wines for ever, whereby our fine gold being yearly at 100,000 at the least which is carried into France by Englishmen shall be kept still within the realm, and we shall rule the price alike of our commodities and their wines, and so make the French King afeared to break friendship with us, etc. . . .

24. *Navy.* If any object against the articles aforesaid touching wine and merchandise, that they will decay the navy, it may be answered that England was never in so great wealth and strength both by sea and land as when those laws were observed; there are new navigations since found out, which will alone maintain as great a navy, e.g. those to Guinea, to Barbary, to Muscovy, yea, the navigation into Flanders, Antwerp and Spain, was not then half so much used as now; besides, there may be still a course into France for their woad, salt and canvas, though if the law made for sowing hemp and flax were executed and provision made for growing woad and madder in the realm, as by some men's diligence it is already practised, which growth is here found better than that from beyond the seas, we should not need to seek into France for it. Besides Flanders has enough; no country robbeth England so much as France.

25. *Fishing.* Let the old course of fishing be maintained by the straitest observation of fish days, for policy sake; so the sea coasts shall be strong with men and habitations and the fleet flourish more than ever.

    2. *Government Activity, 1631.* The central government, the sheriffs, and the local justices of the peace were always the chief instruments of Tudor paternalism. The following document is the report of the justices of Derbyshire to the high sheriff of the county in 1631. After his break with parliament in 1629, the Stuart king, Charles I, proceeded to attempt to rule solely through the executive branch of the government, thus reviving in a more intensive form the practise of the Tudors.[6]

Sir,

    In pursuit of the orders and directions given us in command as well by the printed book as also by several letters sent unto us from the right honorable the lords of Her Majesty's most honorable Privy Council, we, whose names are hereunder written, having within our allotment the wapentake or hundred of Wirksworth, have had monthly meetings within the said hundred and have summoned both the high constable, petty constables, churchwardens, and overseers of the poor within that division and hundred to appear before us.

1. And first we have made diligent inquiry how all the said officers and others have done their duties in execution of the laws mentioned in the Commission, and what persons have offended against any of them, and punished such as we have found faulty.

2. We have taken care that the lords and parishioners of every town relieve the poor thereof, and they are not suffered to straggle or beg up and down either in their parishes or elsewhere. But such poor as have transgressed have been punished according to law, and the impotent poor there are carefully relieved. We have also taken especial care that both the stewards of leets [local manorial courts] and ourselves in particular have taken care for the reformation of abuses in bakers, alehousekeepers, breaking of assize, forestallers and regrators, against tradesmen of all sorts for selling with underweight, and have made search in market towns and other places and taken away and burned very many false weights and measures, and taken order for the punishing of the said offenders.

3. We have made special inquiry of such poor children as are fit to be bound apprentices to husbandry and otherwise, and of such as are fit to take apprentices, and therein we have taken such course as by law is required. And we find none refuse to take apprentices, being thereunto required.

4. We do not find upon our inquiry that the statute for laborers and ordering of wages is deluded, . . .

5. The weekly taxations for relief of the poor in these times of scarcity is raised to higher rates, and we have further observed the course appointed in the fifth article.

6. We have taken order the petty constables within our said division are chosen of the ablest parishioners.

7. Watches in the night and warding by day are appointed in every town for apprehension of rogues and for good order, and we have taken order to punish such as we have found faulty.

8. We have taken care that the high constable doth his duty in presenting to us the defaults of the petty constables for not punishing the rogues and in presenting to us the defaulters.

9. We find none presented to us that live out of service and refuse to work for reasonable wages.

10. We have one House of Correction at Ashborn within our wapentake, which is near the town prison, where such as are committed are kept to work.

11. We have punished several persons for harboring rogues in their barns and outhouses, and have observed the further directions of the eleventh article.

12. We have had care to see that all defects and defaults in the amending of highways be redressed, and the defaulters have been presented to the next quarter sessions and punished.

And as touching their lordships' letters and orders directed concerning corn and inclosures, we do at our monthly meetings take a strict account that the former orders therein taken by us in pursuit thereof be duly observed and put in execution, and particularly none sell such corn (as they are appointed to sell out of the market) but to the poor of the said parish. And neither the petty constable nor any other officer can (as they inform us) present any engrossers of corn, etc., or forestallers of markets.

The prices of corn (considering the times) are not on our markets in our opinion unreasonable, but are as follow, viz., wheat for the strike 5s., four peck making a strike, rye 4s., barley 3s. 4d., malt 5s., peas 4s., oats 2s. 6d.

We have made especial inquiry touching inclosures made within these two years, but find very few within our division, for the most of our wapentake hath been long since inclosed. Howsoever some few hath been presented, which we have commanded to throw down, and have stayed the proceedings of such inclosures as have been lately begun and are not finished.

We have no maltmakers in this wapentake but for their own use.

We have put down a full third part of all the alehouses within this wapentake; yet there are so great a multitude of poor miners within this wapentake that we are enforced to leave more alehousekeepers than otherwise we would.

We have taken order for the binding all cooks, alehousekeepers, victuallers and butchers within this hundred that they neither dress nor suffer to be dressed or eaten any flesh during the time of Lent or other days prohibited, and our recognizances to that purpose do remain with the Clerk of the Peace, to be by him certified according to the statute.
John Fitzherbert
Chr. Fulwood.

C.   COMMERCE AND THE PUBLIC WEAL

A dynamic factor in the economic life of sixteenth century Europe was overseas trade. In every country which had any chance in the race, all the resources, whether under state intervention or private enterprise, entered into this competition for the trade of the world.

1. *The Export Trade, 1586.* The following document from the records of the privy council illustrates the role of cloth exports in the economy of Tudor England. The council has just heard a case between some clothiers, or middlemen, from the clothing counties of western England and the Merchant Adventurers, an association of English merchants who were engaged during the sixteenth century in wresting from the Hanse, or German merchants, the monopoly of trade with the Low Countries. The Merchants of the Staple, also referred to in the document, were an older group of English merchants originally engaged in exporting English wool (as opposed to cloth) .[7]

Upon hearing of such reports as were made in writing of the complaints of sundry clothiers in Gloucestershire, Wiltshire, and Somersetshire for lack of sales of their clothes at Blackwell Hall in such number and at such prices as they were lately accustomed to the Merchant Adventurers, whereby they were in some part forced to decay their workmen, and in like manner of the answers of the Merchant Adventurers for their defense, and having Mr. Attorney General, who was fully instructed for the clothiers, and the Governor of the Merchant Adventurers with some of his company present, who also were heard at good length each against the other, it was at length by the Council concluded as a matter most necessary in this time for many respects, and especially for keeping of a great multitude of poor people in work by continuance of drapery in the aforesaid counties, that the clothiers should not lack the ordinary market of their clothes at London for default of reasonable sales thereof to the merchants; and thereupon it was determined that the clothiers should be commanded to recontinue their former trade, and that if they should ordinarily bring to the markets at Blackwell Hall such sorts and number of clothes as they were in former seasons of the months of the year accustomed to do, and in like manner the Merchant Adventurers should also buy the same at such reasonable prices as they were accustomed to do without any fraud or delay. And though the Merchants alleged that they had great numbers of clothes lying on their hands here in London and on shipboard not sold, yet they declared to the Council that upon a former motion made to them they had already agreed to take up on interest a good sum of money on their common charge, with which money they would buy up all such clothes weekly as the particular merchants for lack of ready money should not be able to buy, so as the clothiers would charge them with no greater num-

ber than usually they were accustomed, and that their clothes should be merchantable, and then they gave assurance in words that there should be no cause for the clothiers to leave their work unoccupied, nor to complain for lack of reasonable sales. But forasmuch as it might be doubted that either on the clothiers' part or of the merchants', in respect of the diversity of their clothes and their prices, there might arise some controversy whereby there might be some stay of sale, it was by the Council determined that certain persons of understanding and of indifference towards both parties should be charged weekly to see to the order of the markets for the said clothes, and should make report to the Council of the utterance of the clothes; and if there were by them found any lack of sale, they should either by their persuasions remedy the same where the default should be, or else if they could not so conveniently do, they should report their opinions thereof, that by authority from Her Majesty the defaults might be reformed, either in the clothiers or the merchants. And it was also further declared [to] the Merchant Adventurers, that if by their want of buying there should be found any unnecessary stay, for remedy thereof there should be liberty given to any of the Merchants of the Staple to buy any clothes weekly from Friday after 12 of the clock all that day, and on Saturday also during the continuance of the market to buy any clothes, and the same to transport into any parts beyond the seas to be paid to Her Majesty as the Merchant Adventurers ought to do; and if thereby also the clothiers should not have reasonable sales for lack of buyers there should be liberty given at those market times, that is, for the afternoon on every Friday and the forenoon on every Saturday, for any merchant, English or strangers, to buy any such clothes, and the same also to transport over the seas, paying all duties and customs for the same. And their Lordships furthermore declared to the merchants that if the default of the sales of clothes should be found to be in them, whereby the people should not be set a-work, they were otherwise to move Her Majesty that such means might be used by her permission that they doubted not but there should be plenty of buyers and transporters found for the remedy of any such lack to ensue. And, finally, their Lordships ordered that there should be letters sent to the Lords Lieutenants, Sheriffs, and Justices of the forsaid shires to advertise the clothiers what care Her Majesty had of their case, and what order was taken with the Merchant Adventurers for their relief, and therefore to charge them to recontinue their usual trade for their clothing, and for the setting of the people on work as they were accustomed to do.

2. *The Second Levant Company Charter,
1592.* Although the English government
never exercised as strict a control in overseas
enterprise as was the case in sixteenth century Spain or seventeenth century France,
English trading ventures and colonizing proj-
ects received royal approval in the form of
charters to private companies. Shortly after
1570 the English began their battle with the
Venetians for a share of the eastern Mediterranean or Levant trade. In 1529 the original English Levant Company was granted its
second charter, some of the text of which follows.[8]

Elizabeth by the grace of God Queen of England, France, and Ireland, defender of the faith
&c. To all our officers, ministers and subjects, and
to all other people as well within this our realm
of England, as else where under our obeisance
and jurisdiction or otherwise unto whom these
our letters shall be seen, showed, or read, greeting.

Where our well beloved subjects, Edward Osborne knight, alderman of our city of London,
William Hareborne Esquire, and Richard Staper
of our said city, merchant, have by great adventure and industry with their great cost and
charges by the space of sundry late years traveled,
and caused travel to be taken as well by secret
and good means, as by dangerous ways and passages both by land and sea to find out and set
open a trade of merchandise and traffic into the
lands, islands, dominions, and territories of the
great Turk, commonly called the Grand Signor,
not before that time in the memory of any man
now living known to be commonly used and fre-
quented by way of merchandise by any the merchants or other subjects of us or our progenitors:
And also have by their like good means and industry and great charges procured of the said
Grand Signor in our name, amity, safety and freedom for trade and traffic of merchandise to be
used and continued by our subjects within his
said dominions, whereby we perceive and find
that both many good actions have been done and
performed, and hereafter are likely continually
to be done and performed for the peace of Christendom: Namely by the relief and discharge of
many Christians which have been, and which
hereafter may happen to be in thraldom and
bondage under the said Grand Signor and his
vassals or subjects. And also good and profitable
vent and utterance of the commodities of our
realm, and sundry other great benefits to the
advancement of our honor and dignity royal, the
maintenance of our navy, the increase of our customs, and the revenues of our Crown, and generally the great wealth of our whole realm. . . .

Know ye, that hereupon we greatly tendering

the wealth of our people and the encouragement
of them and other our loving subjects in their
good enterprises for the advancement of lawful
traffic to the benefit of our common wealth, have
of our special grace, certain knowledge, and mere
motion given and granted, and by these presents
for us, our heirs, and successors, do give and
grant unto our said trusty and well beloved subjects Edward Osborne knight, [then follows a
list of 62 merchants] . . . and servants of them
and of every of them, which have been or hereafter shall be employed in the said trade by the
space of four years or upwards by themselves,
their servants, factors or deputies, shall and may
by the space of twelve years from the day of the
date of these our letters patent freely traffic, and
use the trade of merchandise as well by sea as by
land into and from the dominions of the said
Grand Signor, and into and from Venice, Zante,
Candie and Zephalonia, and other the dominions
of the Signory and state of Venice, and also by
land through the countries of the said Grand
Signor into and from the East Indies, lately discovered by John Newberie, Ralph Fitch, William
Leech, and James Storie, sent with our letters to
that purpose at the proper costs and charge of
the said merchants . . .

And furthermore we of our ample and abundant grace, mere motion, and certain knowledge
have granted, and by these presents for us our
heirs and successors do grant unto the said Governors and company of merchants of the Levant,
that they and such only as be and shall be of that
company, shall for the said term of twelve years
have, use, and enjoy the whole and only trade
and traffic, and the whole entire and only liberty, use, and privilege of trading and trafficing,
and using feat of merchandising by and through
the Levant seas otherwise called the Mediterranean seas into and from the said dominions of
the Grand Signor, and dominions of the state
of Venice; and by and through the said Grand
Signor's dominions to and from such other places
in the East Indies discovered as aforesaid. . . .

3. *Commercial Rivalry, 1599–1603.* Something of the structure of English commercial
enterprise, as well as the nature of contemporary commercial rivalry, is illustrated by the
selections which follow.[9]

(*August 21, 1599. From the Venetian Ambassador in Constantinople to the Doge and Senate.*) After waiting a long time for the Queen of
England's present to the Sultan, they say that the
ship [*Hector*], which is bringing it has at last
passed the Dardanelles. It brings a cargo of
woollen cloth and other high-class goods; and
the letters patent confirming the English Agent
here as Ambassador of the Queen. He is making

preparations for the liveries of a numerous suite, and shows that he intends to live in a great state.

The Turks are much pleased with the arrival of this ship, as they consider it a confirmation of their alliance with England, which they consider is highly important for holding the King of Spain in check. The English, who know their advantage, will make all profit out of it, and will find a ready assent to all their demands, especially if they are accompanied by gifts, of which they are very liberal. If the trade in woollen cloth especially makes way here, as is expected, on account of its excellence and its appearance, in which the Turks delight, the Venetian trade will receive a great blow. The English would open factories through the entire Turkish Empire, as I am told they have done in Syria and Alexandria, and will obtain any concessions they care to ask for.

(*March 20, 1603. The Venetian Secretary in London to the Doge and Senate.*) . . . I must not omit to say that the English through their rapacity and cruelty have become odious to all nations. With Spain they are at open war, and are already plundering her and upsetting the India trade. They are continually robbing with violence the French, whom they encounter on the long stretches of open sea. They cannot sail at present to Poland and Prussia, because the Danish Straits are blocked against them. In Germany, at Hamburg, Lübeck, and other ports, for example, they are detested; because the German merchants still claim their ancient privileges of their exchange house in London, of which they were deprived by the Queen a few years ago, merely with the view to foster English and restrict foreign commerce. . . .

With the Flemish they have little accord on account of the Spanish War, but also for natural reasons; for the Flemish trade in the Levant has grown to such proportions that the English trade is considerably diminished. . . .

Then, inside the Straits of Gibraltar, how can the English be endured, seeing clearly that under the guise of merchants, they plunder in the very vitals of foreign dominions all the shipping they find? . . .

Hence both those who command, and those who execute, here in England, see quite clearly how great, how universal, and how just is the hatred which all nations, nay, all peoples, we might say, bear to the English, for they are the disturbers of the whole world.

And yet, with all this they not only do not take any steps to remedy the mischief, but in a certain sense they glory that the English name should become formidable just in this way. For whereas the Kings of England, down to Henry VII and Henry VIII were wont to keep up a fleet of one hundred ships in full pay as a defense, now the Queen's ships [in commission] do not amount to more than fifteen or sixteen, as her revenue cannot support a greater charge; and so the whole of the strength and repute of the nation rests on the vast numbers of small privateers, which are supported and increase to that dangerous extent which everyone recognizes; and to ensure this support, the privateers make the ministers partners in the profits, without the risk of a penny in the fitting out, but only a share in the prizes, which are adjudged by judges placed there by the ministers themselves.

(*Antwerp, July 1600, The representative of the German bankers, the Fuggers, to the home office in Augsburg.*) From Holland and Zeeland we get written tidings that four ships from the East Indies and others from the West Indies have again sailed into Plymouth in England, heavily laden with spices. Altogether they have brought ninety loads of pepper, which are estimated at fully £324,000. In addition cloves and cinnamon. Besides this nine similar ships are expected in Zeeland, Amsterdam and Rotterdam. The consignment of the two ships which have recently come from the Moluccas amounts to 620,000 pounds of nutmeg, 65,000 pounds of mace, 35,000 pounds of cloves and 700 pounds of pepper, which altogether is estimated at 230,000 Flemish pounds in gold bars. . . . It is said that six ships more are due to sail for the East Indies, namely, four of the Old Company and two of the New. This voyage is thus becoming quite common, and very harmful to the Spaniards, because voyages in Portuguese and Spanish territory are decided upon in Holland and Zeeland. From Emden comes news that a ship has arrived there from Pernambucco in Brazil, whose crew say that the fleet of the States General [Dutch] have taken two castles in Brazil with seven ships, then sailed to the town and seized seven to eight thousand chests of sugar.

4. *Corporate Activity and the Public Interest, 1587–89.* The internal, as opposed to the external, impact of the great, corporate trading ventures is seen in the selections which follow from an essay by an unknown English writer in 1587–89, *A Discourse on Corporations.*[10]

A corporation is a uniting of a society using one trade, mystery, or occupation into one body by the Prince or sovereign, which has authority to make laws and ordinances touching such trade, mystery, or occupation, whereunto every member of the same is subject. . . .

Of these corporations some concern foreign traffic and some our trades at home.

First I put down for a maxim that all monopolies have been condemned by all politic men and in all well-governed commonwealths, as a cause of all dearth and scarcity in the same, contrary to the nature and kind of all societies which first grow into towns and cities to be in safety and to live in plenty and cheapness.

For a monopoly is an engrossment of the commodities into the hands of one or few, whereby the sole buying and selling of the same is brought into few hands, which ought to be free and common to all the citizens of the same commonwealth. . . . For where there be few sellers and many buyers, there of necessity must be highness of price at the will of the seller, wherein the rulers ought to have great care. For those kingdoms continue longest and people best where most men feel plenty and few feel want, wherein, whatsoever may be replied to the contrary, he who will read stories of time past may observe republics and commonwealths to have continued longer than kingdoms and kings longer than tyrants. . . .

But that any societies should have the prerogative above the rest of the nation to traffic the seas [is] against common right and the law, under which we are born, and is our inheritance and ought not to be taken from any members of the same state without apparent utility and profit of the whole body of the commonwealth. . . .

Lest perchance it might be conceived of me that I do utterly condemn all manner of bodies public and societies, I am wholly of the opinion that all societies and bodies public being foreign and all universal corporations as of towns, cities, and boroughs, are unprofitable and very hurtful to the commonwealth. Private societies, and companies such as concern mysteries and consist in buying and selling, as merchants, grocers, etc., bring more harm than good to the public wealth. But corporations which concern manual occupations, as smiths, carpenters, armorers, and such other, wherein is used and exercised the labor and work of the hands, are not only profitable, but also very needful, that order be taken that no man be admitted to public practise and profession of the same arts till he hath served in the same, and be allowed of the masters and wardens of the companies to be an able and a sufficient man to deal truly and skillfully in the science that he professeth.

D.   THE DOCTRINE OF MERCANTILISM

A warning has already been given concerning the danger of singling out any rigid, orthodox system of mercantilistic doctrine. Circumstances, time, and place, as they have been studied in the preceding selections, were the determining factors. But Thomas Mun (1571–1641), in his *England's Treasure by Foreign Trade,* provides a typically mercantilistic description of the nature and source of a state's prosperity. Mun, who departed considerably from the older theories which had limited wealth to the accumulation of treasure, was a prosperous merchant and a Director of the East India Company. His book was written about 1630 for the instruction of his son, but was not published until after his death.[11]

Although a kingdom may be enriched by gifts received, or by purchase taken from some other nations, yet these are things uncertain and of small consideration when they happen. The ordinary means therefore to increase our wealth and treasure is by foreign trade, wherein we must ever observe this rule; to sell more to strangers yearly than we consume of theirs in value. For suppose that when this kingdom is plentifully served with the cloth, lead, tin, iron, fish and other native commodities, we do yearly export the overplus to foreign countries to the value of twenty two hundred thousand pounds; by which means we are enabled beyond the seas to buy and bring in foreign wares for our use and consumptions, to the value of twenty hundred thousand pounds. By this order duly kept in our trading, we may rest assured that the kingdom shall be enriched yearly two hundred thousand pounds, which must be brought to us in so much treasure; because that part of our stock which is not returned to us in wares must necessarily be brought home in treasure.

For in this case it cometh to pass in the stock of a kingdom, as in the estate of a private man; who is supposed to have one thousand pounds yearly revenue and two thousand pounds of ready money in his chest. If such a man through excess shall spend one thousand five hundred pounds per annum, all his ready money will be gone in four years; and in the like time his said money will be doubled if he take a frugal course to spend but five hundred pounds per annum; which rule never faileth likewise in the commonwealth, but in some cases (of no great moment) which I will hereafter declare, when I shall show by whom and in what manner this balance of the kingdom's account ought to be drawn up yearly, or so often as it shall please the state to discover how much we gain or lose by trade with foreign nations. But first I will say something concerning those ways and means which will increase our exportations and diminish our importations of wares; which being done, I will then set down some other arguments both affirmative and negative to strengthen that which is here declared, and thereby to show that all the other means which are commonly supposed to enrich the kingdom with treasure are altogether insufficient and mere fallacies.

The revenue or stock of a kingdom by which it is provided of foreign wares is either natural or artificial. The natural wealth is so much only as can be spared from our own use and necessities to be exported unto strangers. The artificial consists in our manufactures and industrious trading with foreign commodities, concerning which I will set down such particulars as may serve for the cause we have in hand.

1. First, although this realm be already exceeding rich by nature, yet might it be much increased by laying the waste grounds (which are infinite) into such employments as should no way hinder the present revenues of other manured lands, but hereby to supply ourselves and prevent the importations of hemp, flax, cordage, tobacco, and divers other things which now we fetch from strangers to our great impoverishing.

2. We may likewise diminish our importations, if we would soberly refrain from excessive consumption of foreign wares in our diet and raiment.

3. In our exportations we must not only regard our own superfluities, but also we must consider our neighbors' necessities, that so upon the wares which they cannot want, nor yet be furnished thereof elsewhere, we may (besides the sale of the materials) gain so much of the manufacture as we can, and also endeavor to sell them dear, so far forth as the high price cause not a less sale in the quantity. . . . And on the other side a few years past, when by the excessive price of wools our cloth was exceeding dear, we lost at the least half our clothing for foreign parts, which since is no otherwise (well near) recovered again than by the great fall of price for wools and cloth. We find that twenty five in the hundred less in the price of these and some other wares, to the loss of private men's revenues, may raise above fifty upon the hundred in the quantity sold to the benefit of the public. For when cloth is dear, other nations do presently practise clothing, and we know they want neither art nor materials to this performance. But when by cheapness we drive them from this employment, and so in time obtain our dear price again, then do they also use their former remedy. . . .

4. The value of our exportations likewise may be much advanced when we perform it ourselves in our own ships, for then we get not only the price of our wares as they are worth here, but also the merchants' gains, the charges of insurance and freight to carry them beyond the seas. . . .

5. The frugal expending likewise of our own natural wealth might advance much yearly to be exported unto strangers; and if in our raiment we will be prodigal, yet let this be done with our own materials and manufactures, as cloth, lace, embroideries, cutworks, and the like, where the excess of the rich may be the employment of the poor, whose labors notwithstanding of this kind, would be more profitable for the commonwealth, if they were done to the use of strangers.

6. The fishing in His Majesty's seas of England, Scotland, and Ireland is our natural wealth, and would cost nothing but labor, which the Dutch bestow willingly, and thereby draw yearly a very great profit to themselves by serving many places of Christendom with our fish, for which they return and supply their wants both of foreign wares and money, besides the multitude of mariners and shipping. . . .

7. A staple or magazine for foreign corn, indigo, spices, raw-silks, cotton, wool, or any other commodity whatsoever, to be imported will increase shipping, trade, treasure, and the King's customs, by exporting them again where need shall require. . . .

8. Also we ought to esteem and cherish those trades which we have in remote or far countries, for besides the increase of shipping and mariners thereby, the wares also sent thither and received from thence are far more profitable unto the kingdom than by our trades near at hand. As for example; suppose pepper to be worth here two shillings the pound constantly, if then it be brought from the Dutch at Amsterdam, the merchant may give there twenty pence the pound, and gain well by the bargain; but if he fetch this pepper from the East Indies, he must not give above three pence the pound at the most, which is a mighty advantage. . . .

9. It would be very beneficial to export money as well as wares, being done in trade only, it would increase our treasure; but of this I write more largely in the next chapter to prove it plainly.

10. It were policy and profit for the state to suffer manufactures made of foreign materials to be exported custom-free, as velvets and all other wrought silks, fustians, thrown silks and the like, it would employ very many poor people, and much increase the value of our stock yearly issued into other countries, and it would (for this purpose) cause the more foreign materials to be brought in, to the improvement of His Majesty's Customs. But if any man allege the Dutch prov-

erb, Live and let others live; I answer, that the Dutchmen notwithstanding their own proverb do not only in these kingdoms, encroach upon our livings, but also in other foreign parts of our trade (where they have power) they do hinder and destroy us in our lawful course of living, hereby taking the bread out of our mouth, which we shall never prevent by plucking the pot from their nose, as of late years too many of us do practise to the great hurt and dishonor of this famous nation. We ought rather to imitate former times in taking sober and worthy courses more pleasing to God and suitable to our ancient reputation. . . .

11. It is needful also not to charge the native commodities with too great customs, lest by endearing them to the stranger's use, it hinder their sale. And especially foreign wares brought in to be transported again should be favored, for otherwise that manner of trading (so much importing the good of the Commonwealth) cannot prosper nor subsist. . . .

12. Lastly, in all things we must endeavor to make the most we can of our own, whether it be natural or artificial. And forasmuch as the people which live by the arts are far more in number than they who are masters of the fruits, we ought the more carefully to maintain those endeavors of the multitude, in whom doth consist the greatest strength and riches both of King and Kingdom; for where the people are many, and the arts good, there the traffic must be great, and the country rich . . .

If we duly consider England's largeness, beauty, fertility, strength, both by sea and land, in multitude of warlike people, horses, ships, ammunition, advantageous situation for defense and trade, number of sea-ports and harbors, which are of difficult access to enemies, and of easy outlet to the inhabitants' wealth by excellent fleece-wools, iron, lead, tin, saffron, corn, victuals, hides, wax, and other natural endowments, we shall find this kingdom capable to sit as master of a monarchy. For what greater glory and advantage can any powerful nation have, than to be thus richly and naturally possessed of all things needful for food, raiment, war, and peace, not only for its own plentiful use, but also to supply the wants of other nations, in such a measure, that much money may be thereby gotten yearly, to make the happiness complete. For experience telleth us, that notwithstanding that excessive consumption of this Kingdom alone, to say nothing of Scotland, there is exported *communibus annis* [in an average year] of our own native commodities for the value of twenty two hundred

thousand pounds sterling, or somewhat more; so that if we were not too much affected to pride, monstrous fashions, and riot, above all other nations, one million and an half of pounds might plentifully supply our unnecessary wants (as I may term them) of silks, sugars, spices, fruits, and all others; so that seven hundred thousand pounds might be yearly treasured up in money to make the Kingdom exceeding rich and powerful in short time. But this great plenty which we enjoy, makes us a people not only vicious and excessive, wasteful of the means we have, but also improvident and careless of much other wealth that shamefully we lose, which is the fishing in His Majesty's seas of England, Scotland, and Ireland, being of no less consequence than all our other riches which we export and sell to strangers, whilst in the mean time (through lewd idleness) great multitudes of our people cheat, roar, rob, hang, beg, cant, pine and perish, which by this means and maintenance might be much increased, to the further wealth and strength of these Kingdoms, especially by sea, for our own safety and terror of our enemies. The endeavors of the industrious Dutch do give sufficient testimony of this truth, to our great shame, and no less peril, if it have not a timely prevention: for, whilst we leave our wanted honorable exercises and studies, following our pleasures, and of late years besetting ourselves with pipe and pot, in a beastly manner, sucking smoke, and drinking healths, until death stares many in the face; the said Dutch have well-near left this swinish vice, and taken up our wanted valor, which we have often so well performed both by sea and land, and particularly in their defense, although they are not now so thankful as to acknowledge the same. The sum of all is this, that the general leprosy of our piping, potting, feasting, fashions, and mis-spending of our time in idleness and pleasure (contrary to the Law of God, and the use of other nations) hath made us effeminate in our bodies, weak in our knowledge, poor in our treasure, declined in our valor, unfortunate in our enterprises, and condemned by our enemies. I write the more of these excesses, because they do so greatly waste our wealth, which is the main subject of this whole book's discourse: and indeed our wealth might be a rare discourse for all Christendom to admire and fear, if we would but add art to nature, our labor to our natural means; the neglect whereof hath given a notable advantage to other nations, and especially to the Hollanders, whereof I will briefly say something in the next place. . . .

XII

Rights and Liberties in Stuart England

For the people. And truly I desire their liberty and freedom as much as anybody whomsoever. But I must tell you that their liberty and freedom consists in having of government; those laws by which their life and their goods may be most their own. It is not for having share in government, Sir, that is nothing pertaining to them. A subject and a sovereign are clean different things, and therefore until they do that, I mean, that you do put the people in that liberty as I say, certainly they will never enjoy themselves. . . . If I would have given way to an arbitrary way, for to have all laws changed according to the power of the sword, I needed not to have come here. And, therefore, I tell you, and I pray God it be not laid to your charge, that I am the martyr of the people.

Charles I on the Scaffold

CONTENTS

QUESTIONS FOR STUDY

PART I

1. Why did the Commons draw up the Apology of 1604? What is their attitude to the king?

2. What basic claims do the Commons make in the Apology of 1604?

3. What are the points at issue between king and Commons in 1610? Do you see any basis for reconciliation of their fundamental differences?

4. What new issues appeared in the Parliament of 1621? To what fundamental point were the issues finally reduced?

5. What special significance is there in the king's action of 30 December 1621?

6. What does the scene of 2 March 1629 indicate about the level to which the dispute between king and Commons had been reduced?

7. To what authorities did the Commons appeal in their claims of rights and liberties? To what authorities did the king appeal? Did either authority deny the validity of the authorities of the other?

8. In your opinion did either party (king or Parliament) shift its position between 1604 and 1629?

PART II

9. What are the differences in means and ends among Fifth Monarchy Men, Diggers, and Levellers? To what authorities do these groups appeal in support of their theories? How do they differ from the authorities invoked by Parliament from 1604 to 1629?

10. To what extent are the arguments of these groups influenced by the part they claim to have played in the rebellion? To what extent are they a reaction against the government of the Stuarts?

11. Which party's theories are most clearly reflected in the Agreement of the People in 1647?

12. What is the basic issue in dispute between Ireton and his opponents in the Putney debates?

13. Analyze the Army Debates to determine to what party the speakers belonged.

14. "The basic tenets of modern democracy were conceived in the Puritan rebellion." Is this an accurate statement?

Political thought in the Middle Ages was largely concerned with the rights and duties of rulers. John of Salisbury and St. Thomas Aquinas directed their attention primarily to the prince and his activities. They paid scant regard to the subject, who was expected to obey the law and fulfill the duties of the place in society to which he had been born. The prince, it is true, was obligated to do justice to his subjects and govern for their welfare, but God might send evil rulers to govern them ill for their sins, and tyrannicide was at best a doubtful expedient. The political writers of the Renaissance also gave little thought to the governed. The subject in the Machiavellian state, for example, was the merest pawn in the hands of the prince who treated his citizenry in whatever manner seemed expedient to prevent rebellion. The subject deserved no more consideration than the threat of revolt could command.

The political implications of the individualism inherent in the Protestant Reformation, however, tended to focus thinking more upon ruled as well as ruler. Luther proclaimed the liberty of the Christian man, insisting upon his right to follow the dictates of his conscience. Calvin asserted that a princely command against true religion was not to be obeyed, and Knox carried the Calvinist argument to its logical conclusion by his declaration of the right of rebellion against a wrongful prince. Such arguments naturally provoked new speculation as to the relationship between ruler and subject. The religious wars of the sixteenth century were an added stimulus to political speculation of this sort. The Protestants developed theories based on the rights of the individual to justify their revolt from the Church, while the Jesuits laid emphasis upon popular rights for the use of Catholics persecuted by Protestant princes.

By the beginning of the seventeenth century, when the greatest intensity of religious conflict had passed, the interest in the rights of subjects was smothered in the practical politics of the state-building on the Continent. Rulers considered any clamor for individual political rights to be productive of anarchy and a hindrance to the creation of a strong state. They strove to gather all political power into their own hands and to suppress popular institutions as threats to their control of government. The Estates General in France and the Cortes in Spain fell into disuse, and the Diet of the Holy Roman Empire became little more than a debating chamber for the German princes. The rulers reacted strongly against the chaos engendered, as they thought, by the claims of subjects against the state in the era of religious wars.

In England the story was different. Under Elizabeth the English emerged as a Protestant nation, with an increasing tendency toward Calvinist doctrine. Tudor despotism was based on popularity, and the crown, instead of suppressing Parliament, used it to gain public support. Parliament therefore survived, as representative bodies on the Continent did not, to become an arena in which the subject could lay claim to what he believed to be his rights and to protest any infringement of them. By the standards of the day, the mild Tudor régime dealt gently with the forward subject, and notions of the subject's rights in practical politics were allowed to grow under the shade of royal benevolence.

The advent of the Stuarts in 1603 was accompanied by greater friction between the crown and its subjects. The claims of the king concerning the powers inherent in his prerogative seemed incompatible with the rights claimed by Parliament for the people, and the first twenty-five years of Stuart rule were marked by continual clashes between the king and the House of Commons. So irreconcilable did the two parties seem that from 1629 to 1640 Charles I endeavored to rule without Parliament on the model of a continental prince. But in 1640 he was forced to give up the experiment, and the summoning of Parliament in that year set the stage for new clashes and eventual civil war. The outbreak of civil war in 1642 provoked anew the discussion of popular rights, as the rebels, sectaries, statesmen, and soldiers sought a basis upon which to rebuild the state which was torn by internal strife.

The purpose of this Problem is to examine two important stages in the development of political liberties in England: first, the period from 1604 to 1629 when Parliament struggled with James I and Charles I to establish certain rights of the subject; and second, the period of civil war and interregnum from 1642 to 1660 when earlier claims of right were expanded into political theories based on popular liberties.

Part I.   PREROGATIVE AND PARLIAMENT

The latter years of Elizabeth's reign were not free from friction between parliament and the crown, but matters never came to a serious crisis. Parliament displayed great restraint and forbearance in its dealings with the aged queen, and Elizabeth, on her part, was a master of tact and diplomacy. Always more interested in substance than form, she knew when she must be firm, when to give in, when and how to postpone an issue to avoid a grave quarrel. Her successors, the Stuarts, lacked her charm and insight. James I, with his rolling eyes, oversized tongue, and stumbling gait, was an unimpressive figure of a king; and as the author of a tract on government, he looked upon himself as an authority in matters of state in addition to being a monarch. Charles I, though handsome and dignified, was haughty and unbending in all his dealings. Moreover, James and Charles inherited many of the vexing issues which Elizabeth had postponed, and Parliament was less inclined to accord them the respect and indulgence shown to the old queen. The result was increasing friction between crown and Parliament, produced in large part by their differing interpretations of their rights and duties, which finally culminated in civil war. The documents in this part make clear the nature of the quarrel and the positions of the protagonists.

A.   THE PARLIAMENT OF 1604

Serious differences arose in James' first Parliament. The House of Commons showed a strong disinclination to follow the king's wishes, and on 30 May 1604 he took occasion to deliver a formal rebuke in person. The Commons thereupon appointed a committee to draw up a remonstrance, which was done and presented to the House on 20 June. There is no record of how it was made known to the king, but it is clear that James possessed knowledge of it. The remonstrance is printed below.[1]

FORM OF APOLOGY AND SATISFACTION, June 1604

Most gracious Sovereign, We cannot but with much joy and thankfulness of mind acknowledge your Majesty's great graciousness in declaring lately unto us by the mouth of our Speaker that you rested now satisfied with our doings.

We know, and with great thankfulness to God acknowledge, that He hath given us a King of such understanding and wisdom as is rare to find in any prince in the world.

Howbeit, seeing no human wisdom, how great soever, can pierce into the particularities of the rights and customs of people or of the sayings and doings of particular persons but by tract of experience and faithful report of such as know them (which it hath pleased your Majesty's princely mouth to deliver), what grief, what anguish of mind hath it been unto us at some time in presence to hear, and so in other things to find and feel by effect, your gracious Majesty (to the extreme prejudice of all your subjects of England, and in particular of this House of the Commons thereof) so greatly wronged by misinformation as well touching the estate of the one as the

privileges of the other, and their several proceedings during this Parliament: Which misinformations, though apparent in themselves and to your subjects most injurious, yet have we in some humble and dutiful respect rather hitherto complained of amongst ourselves than presumed to discover and oppose against your Majesty. . . .

With all humble and due respect to your Majesty our Sovereign Lord and Head, against those misinformations we most truly avouch,

First, That our privileges and liberties are our right and due inheritance, no less than our very lands and goods.

Secondly, That they cannot be withheld from us, denied, or impaired, but with apparent wrong to the whole state of the realm.

Thirdly, And that our making of request in the entrance of Parliament to enjoy our privilege is an act only of manners, and doth weaken our right no more than our suing to the King for our lands by petition. . . .

Fourthly, We avouch also, That our House is a Court of Record, and so ever esteemed.

Fifthly, That there is not the highest standing Court in this land that ought to enter into competency, either for dignity or authority, with this High Court of Parliament, which with your Majesty's royal assent gives laws to other Courts but from other Courts receives neither laws nor orders.

Sixthly and lastly, We avouch that the House of Commons is the sole proper judge of return of all such writs and of the election of all such members as belong to it, without which the freedom of election were not entire: And that the Chancery, though a standing Court under your Majesty, be to send out those writs and receive the returns and to preserve them, yet the same is done only for the use of the Parliament, over which neither the Chancery nor any other Court ever had or ought to have any manner of jurisdiction. . . .

The rights of the liberties of the Commons of England consisteth chiefly in these three things:

First, That the shires, cities, and boroughs of England, by representation to be present, have free choice of such persons as they shall put in trust to represent them.

Secondly, That the persons chosen, during the time of the Parliament as also of their access and recess, be free from restraint, arrest, and imprisonment.

Thirdly, That in Parliament they may speak freely their consciences without check and controlment, doing the same with due reverence to the Sovereign Court of Parliament, that is, to your Majesty and both the Houses, who all in this case make but one politic body whereof your Highness is the Head. . . .

There remaineth, dread Sovereign, yet one part of our duty at this present which faithfulness of heart, not presumption, doth press. We stand not in place to speak or do things pleasing; our care is and must be to confirm the love and tie the hearts of your subjects the commons most firmly to your Majesty. Herein lieth the means of our well deserving of both. There was never prince entered with greater love, with greater joy and applause of all his people. This love, this joy, let it flourish in their hearts for ever. Let no suspicion have access to their fearful thoughts that their privileges, which they think by your Majesty should be protected, should now by sinister informations or counsel be violated or impaired, or that those which with dutiful respects to your Majesty speak freely for the right and good of their country shall be oppressed or disgraced.

Let your Majesty be pleased to receive public information from your Commons in Parliament as to the civil estate and government, for private informations pass often by practice: the voice of the people, in the things of their knowledge, is said to be as the voice of God. And if your Majesty shall vouchsafe, at your best pleasure and leisure, to enter into your gracious consideration of our petition for the ease of these burdens under which your whole people have of long time mourned, hoping for relief by your Majesty, then may you be assured to be possessed of their hearts, and if of their hearts, of all they can do or have.

And so we your Majesty's most humble and loyal subjects, whose ancestors have with great loyalty, readiness, and joyfulness served your famous progenitors, Kings and Queens of this Realm, shall with like loyalty and joy, both we and our posterity, serve your Majesty and your most royal issue for ever, with our lives, lands, and goods, and all other our abilities, and by all means endeavor to procure your Majesty honor, with all plenty, tranquillity, content, joy, and felicity.

B. THE PARLIAMENT OF 1610

Six years later the issue between crown and Parliament was sharpened by an exchange of communications between king and Commons. Following are three documents which indicate the points for which each party was contending at that stage of the quarrel.

1. *The King's Speech to the Parliament, March 1610.*[2]

The state of Monarchy is the supremest thing upon earth; for kings are not only God's lieutenants upon earth and sit upon God's throne, but even by God himself they are called gods. There be three principal similitudes that illustrate the state of Monarchy: one taken out of the Word of God and the two other out of the grounds of policy and philosophy. In the Scriptures kings are called gods, and so their power after a certain relation compared to the Divine power. Kings are also compared to the fathers of families, for a king is truly *parens patriae*, the politic father of his people. And lastly, kings are compared to the head of this microcosm of the body of man.

Kings are justly called gods for that they exercise a manner or resemblance of Divine power upon earth; for if you will consider the attributes to God you shall see how they agree in the person of a king. God hath power to create or destroy, make or unmake, at his pleasure; to give life or send death; to judge all, and to be judged nor accomptable to none; to raise low things and to make high things low at his pleasure; and to God are both soul and body due. And the like power have kings: they make and unmake their subjects; they have power of raising and casting down; of life and of death; judges over all their subjects and in all causes, and yet accomptable to none but God only. They have power to exalt low things and abase high things, and make of their subjects like men at the chess, a pawn to take a bishop or a knight, and to cry up or down any of their subjects as they do their money. And to the king is due both the affection of the soul and the service of the body of his subjects. . . .

As for the father of a family, they had of old under the Law of Nature *patriam potestatem,* which was *potestatem vitae et necis,* over their children or family (I mean such fathers of families as were the lineal heirs of those families whereof kings did originally come), for kings had their first original from them who planted and spread themselves in colonies through the world. Now a father may dispose of his inheritance to his children at his pleasure, yea, even disinherit the eldest upon just occasions and prefer the youngest, according to his liking; make them beggars or rich at his pleasure; restrain or banish out of his presence, as he finds them give cause of offense, or restore them in favor again with the penitent sinner. So may the king deal with his subjects.

And lastly, as for the head of the natural body, the head hath the power of directing all the members of the body to that use which the judgment in the head thinks most convenient. It may apply sharp cures or cut off corrupt members, let blood in what proportion it thinks fit and as the body may spare; but yet is all this power ordained by God *ad aedificationem, non ad destructionem.* For although God have power as well of destruction as of creation or maintenance, yet will it not agree with the wisdom of God to exercise his power in the destruction of nature and overturning the whole frame of things, since his creatures were made that his glory might thereby be the better expressed; so were he a foolish father that would disinherit or destroy his children without a cause or leave off the careful education of them; and it were an idle head that would in place of physic so poison or phlebotomize the body as might breed a dangerous distemper or destruction thereof.

But now in these our times we are to distinguish between the state of kings in their first original and between the state of settled kings and monarchs that do at this time govern in civil kingdoms; for even as God, during the time of the Old Testament, spake by oracles and wrought by miracles, yet how soon it pleased Him to settle a Church which was bought and redeemed by the blood of His only Son Christ, then was there a cessation of both; He ever after governing His people and Church within the limits of His revealed will. So in the first original of kings, whereof some had their beginning by conquest and some by election of the people, their wills at that time served for law; yet how soon kingdoms began to be settled in civility and policy, then did kings set down their minds by laws, which are properly made by the king only, but at the rogation of the people, the king's grant being obtained thereunto.

And so the king became to be *Lex loquens* after a sort, binding himself by a double oath to the observation of the fundamental laws of his kingdom: tacitly, as by being a king, and so bound to protect as well the people as the laws of his kingdom, and expressly, by his oath at his coronation; so as every just king in a settled kingdom is bound to observe that paction made to his people by his laws in framing his government agreeable thereunto, according to that paction which God made with Noë after the Deluge, "Hereafter seed-time and harvest, cold and heat, summer and winter, and day and night shall not cease so long as the earth remains."

And therefore a king governing in a settled kingdom leaves to be a king and degenerates into a tyrant as soon as he leaves off to rule according to his laws. In which case the king's conscience may speak unto him as the poor widow said to Philip of Macedon: "Either govern according to your law, *aut ne Rex sis.*" And though no Christian man ought to allow any rebellion of people against their Prince, yet doth God never leave kings unpunished when they transgress these limits, for in that same Psalm where God saith to kings, *Vos Dii estis,* he immediately thereafter concludes, "But ye shall die like men." The higher we are placed, the greater shall our fall be. *Ut casus sic dolor:* the taller the trees be, the more in danger of the wind; and the tempest bears sorest upon the highest mountains.

Therefore all kings that are not tyrants or perjured will be glad to bound themselves within the limits of their laws, and they that persuade them the contrary are vipers and pests, both against them and the commonwealth. For it is a great difference between a king's government in a settled State and what kings in their original power might do *in individuo vago.* As for my part, I thank God I have ever given good proof that I never had intention to the contrary; and I am sure to go to my grave with that reputation and comfort, that never king was in all his time more careful to have his laws duly observed, and himself to govern thereafter, than I.

I conclude then this point touching the power of kings with this axiom of Divinity, That as to dispute what God may do is blasphemy, but *quid vult Deus,* that divines may lawfully and do ordinarily dispute and discuss, for to dispute *a posse ad esse* is both against Logic and Divinity, so is it sedition in subjects to dispute what a king may do in the height of his power; but just kings will ever be willing to declare what they will do, if they will not incur the curse of God. I will not be content that my power be disputed upon, but I shall ever be willing to make the reason appear of all my doings, and rule my actions according to my laws.

2. *The Petition of Right, May 1610.*[3]

Most gracious Sovereign, Whereas your Majesty's most humble subjects the Commons assembled in Parliament have received, first by message and since by speech from your Majesty a commandment of restraint from debating in Parliament your Majesty's right of imposing upon your subjects' goods exported or imported out of or into this realm, yet allowing us to examine the grievance of those impositions in regard to quantity, time, and other circumstances of disproportion thereto incident; we your said humble subjects, nothing doubting but that your Majesty had no intent by that commandment to infringe the ancient and fundamental right of the liberty of the Parliament in point of exact discussing of all matters concerning them and their possessions, goods, and rights whatsoever (which yet we cannot but conceive to be done in effect by this commandment), do with all humble duty make this remonstrance to your Majesty.

First, we hold it an ancient, general, and undoubted right of Parliament to debate freely all matters which do properly concern the subject and his right or state; which freedom of debate being once foreclosed, the essence of the liberty of Parliament is withal dissolved.

And whereas in this case the subjects' right on the one side and your Majesty's prerogative on the other cannot possibly be severed in debate of either, we allege that your Majesty's prerogatives of that kind concerning directly the subject's right and interest are daily handled and discussed in all Courts at Westminster, and have been ever freely debated upon all fit occasions, both in this and all former Parliaments, without restraint: Which being forbidden, it is impossible for the subject either to know or to maintain his right and property to his own lands and goods, though never so just and manifest.

It may farther please your most excellent Majesty to understand that we have no mind to impugn, but a desire to inform ourselves of, your Highness's prerogative in that point, which, if ever, is now most necessary to be known; and though it were to no other purpose, yet to satisfy the generality of your Majesty's subjects, who finding themselves much grieved by these new impositions do languish in much sorrow and discomfort.

These reasons, dread Sovereign, being the proper reasons of Parliament, do plead for the upholding of this our ancient right and liberty. Howbeit, seeing it hath pleased your Majesty to insist upon that judgment in the Exchequer as being direction sufficient for us without farther examination, upon great desire of leaving your Majesty unsatisfied in no one point of our intents and proceedings, we profess touching that judgment that we neither do nor will take upon us to reverse it; but our desire is, to know the reasons whereupon the same was grounded, and the rather for that a general conceit is had that the reasons of that judgment may be extended much farther, even to the utter ruin of the ancient liberty of this kingdom and of your subjects' right of propriety of their lands and goods.

Then for the judgment itself, being the first and last that ever was given in that kind, for aught appearing unto us, and being only in one case and against one man, it can bind in law no other but that person, and is also reversible by writ of error granted heretofore by Act of Parliament, and neither he nor any other subject is debarred by it from trying his right in the same or like case in any of your Majesty's Courts of Record at Westminster.

Lastly, we nothing doubt but our intended proceeding in a full examination of the right, nature, and measure of these new impositions (if this restraint had not come between) should have been so orderly and moderately carried, and so applied to the manifold necessity of these times, and given your Majesty so true a view of the state and right of your subjects, that it would have been much to your Majesty's content and satisfaction (which we most desire), and removed all cause of fears and jealousies from the loyal hearts of your subjects, which is (as it ought to be) our careful endeavor; whereas, contrariwise, in that other way directed by your Majesty we cannot safely proceed without concluding for ever the right of the subject, which without due examination thereof we may not do.

We therefore, your Highness's loyal and dutiful Commons, not swerving from the approved steps of our ancestors, most humbly and instantly beseech your gracious Majesty that without offense to the same we may, according to the undoubted right and liberty of Parliament, proceed in our intended course of a full examination of these new impositions; that so we may cheerfully pass on to your Majesty's business, from which this stop hath by diversion so long withheld us. And we your Majesty's most humble, faithful, and loyal subjects shall ever (according to our bounden duty) pray for your Majesty's long and happy reign over us.

3. *The Petition of Grievances, July 1610.*[4]

Among many other points of happiness and freedom which your Majesty's subjects of this kingdom have enjoyed under your royal progenitors, kings and queens of this realm, there is none which they have accounted more dear and precious than this, to be guided and governed by certain rule of law, which giveth both to the Head and members that which of right belongeth to them, and not by any uncertain or arbitrary form of government. Which, as it hath proceeded from the original and constitution and temperature of this Estate, so hath it been the principal means of upholding the same in such sort as that their kings have been just, beloved, happy, and glorious, and the kingdom itself peaceable, flourishing, and durable so many ages.

And the effect as well of the contentment that the subjects of this kingdom have taken in this form of government as also of the love, respect, and duty which they have by reason of the same rendered unto their princes may appear in this, That they have, as occasion hath required, yielded more extraordinary and voluntary contributions to assist their kings than the subjects of any other known kingdom whatsoever. Out of this root hath grown the indubitable right of the people of this kingdom not to be made subject to any punishment that shall extend to their lives, lands, bodies, or goods, other than such as are ordained by the common laws of this land or the Statutes made by their common consent in Parliament.

Nevertheless it is apparent both that proclamations have been of late years much more frequent than heretofore, and that they are extended not only to the liberty but also to the goods, inheritances, and livelihood of men: some of them tending to alter some points of the law and make them new; other some made shortly after a session of Parliament for matter directly rejected in the same session; others appointing punishments to be inflicted before lawful trial and conviction; some containing penalties in form of penal statutes; some referring the punishment of offenders to the Courts of arbitrary discretion, which have laid heavy and grievous censures upon the delinquents; some, as the proclamation for search, accompanied with letters commanding inquiry to be made against the transgressors at the Quarter Sessions; and some vouching former proclamations to countenance and warrant the latter: as by a catalogue hereunder written more particularly appeareth.

By reason whereof there is a general fear conceived and spread amongst your Majesty's people that proclamations will by degrees grow up and increase to the strength and nature of laws; whereby not only that ancient happiness, freedom, will be as much blemished (if not quite taken away) which their ancestors have so long enjoyed, but the same may also (in process of time) bring a new form of arbitrary government upon the realm. And this our fear is the more increased by occasion as well of certain books lately published, which ascribe a greater power to proclamations than heretofore hath been conceived to belong unto them, as also of the care taken to reduce all the proclamations made since your Majesty's reign into one volume, and to print them in such form as Acts of Parliament formerly have been and still are used to be, which seemeth to imply a purpose to give them more reputation and more establishment than heretofore they have had.

C. THE PARLIAMENT OF 1621

After another failure in 1614, James I did not again summon Parliament until 1621. In that year he found himself urgently in need of funds, for it was a year of depression, and James' foreign policy required money. His son-in-law's election as the first Protestant king of Bohemia had precipitated the Thirty Years' War, and James wished to support his relative against the Catholic assault. At the same time James sought the friendship of Catholic Spain, England's old enemy, for he hoped to marry his son to the Spanish Infanta. This policy involved toleration of the English Catholics, a move designed to placate Spain but also calculated to irritate the Protestant English. The meeting of Parliament therefore brought on a renewal of its clashes with the king, and after months in session Parliament was prorogued in a flurry of sharp exchanges between crown and Commons. The following documents are the outstanding papers in the last two weeks of the session.

1. *Petition of the House of Commons, 3 December 1621.*[5]

Most gracious and dread Sovereign: We, your Majesty's most humble and loyal subjects, the knights, citizens and burgesses now assembled in parliament . . . finding how ill your Majesty's goodness hath been requited by princes of different religion, who even in time of treaty have taken opportunities to advance their own ends, tending to the subversion of religion, and disadvantage of your affairs and the estate of your children; by reason whereof your ill-affected subjects at home, the popish recusants, have taken too much encouragement, and are dangerously increased in their number and in their insolencies, we cannot but be sensible thereof, and therefore humbly represent what we conceive to be the causes of so great and growing mischiefs, and what be the remedies.

1. The vigilancy and ambition of the Pope of Rome and his dearest son; the one aiming at as large a temporal monarchy, as the other at a spiritual supremacy. 2. The devilish positions and doctrines whereon popery is built and taught with authority to their followers, for the advancement of their temporal ends. 3. The distressed and miserable estate of the professors of our religion in foreign parts. 4. The disastrous accidents to your Majesty's children abroad. . . . 5. The strange confederacy of the princes of the popish religion. . . . 6. The great and many armies raised and maintained at the charge of the King of Spain, the chief of that league. 7. The expectation of the popish recusants of the match with Spain, and feeding themselves with great hopes of the consequences thereof. 8. The interposing of foreign princes and their agents in the behalf of popish recusants. . . . 9. The open and usual resort to the houses and, which is worse, to the chapels of foreign ambassadors. 10. Their more than usual concourse to the city, and their frequent conventicles and conferences there. 11. The education of their children in many several seminaries and houses of their religion in foreign parts, appropriated to the English fugitives. 12. The grants of their just forfeitures . . . transferred or compounded for at such mean rates, as will amount to little less than a toleration. 13. The licentious printing and dispersing of popish and seditious books, even in the time of parliament. 14. The swarms of priests and Jesuits, the common incendiaries of all Christendom, dispersed in all parts of your kingdom.

And from these causes, as bitter roots, we humbly offer to your Majesty that we foresee and fear there will necessarily follow very dangerous effects both to church and state. For, 1. The popish religion is incompatible with ours, in respect of their positions. 2. It draweth with it an unavoidable dependency on foreign princes. 3. It openeth too wide a gap for popularity to any who shall draw too great a party. 4. It hath a restless spirit, and will strive by these gradations: if it once get but a connivance, it will press for a toleration; if that should be obtained, they must have an equality; from thence they will aspire to superiority, and will never rest till they get a subversion of the true religion.

The remedies against these growing evils, which in all humility we offer unto your most excellent Majesty, are these. 1. That, seeing this inevitable necessity is fallen upon your Majesty which no wisdom or providence of a peaceable and pious king can avoid, your Majesty would not omit this just occasion, speedily and effectually to take your sword into your hand. 2. That once undertaken upon so honorable and just grounds, your Majesty would resolve to pursue and more publicly avow the aiding of those of our religion in foreign parts; which doubtless would reunite the princes and states of the union, by these disasters disheartened and disbanded.

2. *The King's Letter to the Commons, 3 December 1621.* Having heard about this petition from the Spanish ambassador, James did not wait for its formal presentation, but immediately dispatched this reply to the speaker of the Commons.[6]

Mr. Speaker: We have heard by divers reports, to our great grief, that our distance from the Houses of Parliament, caused by our indisposition of health, hath emboldened some fiery and popular spirits of some of the House of Commons to argue and debate publicly of the matters far above their reach and capacity, tending to our high dishonor and breach of prerogative royal. These are therefore to command you to make known in our name unto the House, that none therein shall presume henceforth to meddle with anything concerning our government or deep matters of state, and namely, not to deal with our dearest son's match with the daughter of Spain, or to touch the honor of that king or any other our friends and confederates: and also not to meddle with any men's particulars, which have their due motion in our ordinary courts of justice.

And whereas we hear that they have sent a message to Sir Edwin Sandys, to know the reasons of his late restraint [he was imprisoned with others on June 16 and released on July 16] you shall in our name resolve them, that it was not for any misdemeanor of his in Parliament. . . . we think ourselves very free and able to punish any man's misdemeanors in parliament as well during their sitting as after, which we mean not to spare hereafter upon any occasion of any man's insolent behaviour there that shall be ministered unto us. And, if they have already touched any of these points which we have forbidden, in any petition of theirs . . . except they reform it before it comes to our hands, we will not deign the hearing nor answering of it.

3. *Petition of the House of Commons, 9 December 1621.* Upon receipt of the king's letter, the Commons refused to transact any business until the question of their privileges had been settled. They therefore drew up a second petition and sent it with a deputation of members to King James.[7]

Most dread and gracious Sovereign: We your most humble and loyal subjects, the knights, citizens and burgesses assembled in the Commons House of Parliament . . . in all humbleness beseech your most excellent Majesty that the loyalty and dutifulness of as faithful and loving subjects as ever served or lived under a gracious sovereign may not undeservedly suffer by the misinformation of partial and uncertain reports, which are ever unfaithful intelligencers; but that your Majesty would, in the clearness of your own judgment, first vouchsafe to understand from ourselves, and not from others, what our humble Declaration and Petition (resolved upon by the universal voice of the House and proposed, with your gracious favour, to be presented unto your sacred Majesty) doth contain. [A summary of the petition of 3 December follows.] . . .

This being the effect of that we had formerly resolved upon, and these the occasions and reasons inducing the same, our humble suit to your Majesty and confidence is, That your Majesty will be graciously pleased to receive, at the hands of these our messengers, our former humble Declaration and Petition, and vouchsafe to read and favorably to interpret the same: . . .

And whereas your Majesty, by the general words of your letter, seemeth to restrain us from intermeddling with matters of government or particulars which have their motion in the courts of justice, the generality of which words, in the largeness of the extent thereof (as we hope beyond your Majesty's intention) might involve those things which are the proper subjects of parliamentary occasions and discourse:

And whereas your Majesty doth seem to abridge us of the ancient liberty of parliament for freedom of speech, jurisdiction and just censure of the House, and other proceedings there (wherein, we trust in God, we shall never transgress the bounds of loyal and dutiful subjects) a liberty which we assure ourselves so wise and just a king will not infringe, the same being our ancient and undoubted right and an inheritance received from our ancestors, without which we cannot freely debate nor clearly discern of things in question before us, nor truly inform your Majesty. . . .

4. *The King's Reply, 10 December 1621.* James received the deputation tactfully and gave its members the following reply.[8]

. . . Now whereas, in the very beginning of this your apology, you tax us, in fair terms, of trusting uncertain reports and partial informations concerning your proceedings, we wish you to remember that we are an old and experienced king, needing no such lessons, being, in our conscience, freest of any king alive from hearing or trusting idle reports; which so many of your House as are nearest us can bear witness unto you, if you would give as good ear to them as you do to some tribunitial orators among you. . . .

In the body of your petition, you usurp upon our prerogative royal and meddle with things far above your reach, and then in the conclusion you protest the contrary; as if a robber would take a man's purse and then protest he meant not to rob him. . . . And touching your excuse of not determining anything concerning the match of our dearest son, but only to tell your opinion and lay it down at our feet, first we desire to know how you could have presumed to determine in that point without committing of high treason? . . . And as to your request that we would now receive your former petition, we wonder what could make you presume that we would receive it, whereas in our former letter we plainly declared the contrary unto you. And therefore we have justly rejected that suit of yours, for what have you left unattempted in the highest points of sovereignty in that petition of yours, except the striking of coin? . . . These are unfit things to be handled in parliament, except your king should require it of you: . . . and therefore, *ne sutor ultra crepidam.* . . .

And although we cannot allow of the style, calling it *your ancient and undoubted right and inheritance,* but could rather have wished that ye had said that your privileges were derived from the grace and permission of our ancestors and us (for most of them grow from precedents, which shows rather a toleration than inheritance), yet we are pleased to give you our royal assurance, that as long as you contain yourself within the limits of your duty, we will be as careful to maintain and preserve your lawful liberties and privileges, as ever any of our predecessors were, nay, as to preserve our own royal prerogative; so as your House shall only have need to beware to trench upon the prerogative of the crown; which would enforce us, or any just king, to retrench them of their privileges, that would pare his prerogative and flowers of the crown: but of this, we hope, there shall never be cause given.

5. *Protestation of The House of Commons, 18 December 1621.* Unmollified by the royal answer, the Commons restated their position once more on the day before the king prorogued Parliament. Their resolution is printed below.[9]

The Commons now assembled in parliament, being justly occasioned thereunto, concerning sundry liberties, franchises and privileges of parliament amongst others here mentioned, do make this protestation following: That the liberties, franchises, privileges and jurisdictions of parliament are the ancient and undoubted birthright and inheritance of the subjects of England; and that the arduous and urgent affairs concerning the king, state and defense of the realm, and of the church of England and the maintenance and making of laws, and redress of mischiefs and grievances which daily happen within this realm, are proper subjects and matter of counsel and debate in parliament: and that in the handling and proceeding of those businesses every member of the House of Parliament hath, and of right ought to have, freedom of speech, to propound, treat, reason and bring to conclusion the same. . . .

6. *The King's Answer to the Protestation, 30 December 1621.* When Parliament had been prorogued for Christmas, the following scene was enacted in the royal council chamber.[10]

His most Excellent Majesty coming this day to the Council, the Prince His Highness, and all the Lords and others of his Majesty's Privy Council sitting about him, and all the Judges then in London, which were six in number, there attending upon His Majesty; the Clerk of the Commons House of Parliament was called for, and commanded to produce his Journal Book, wherein was noted, and entries made of most passages that were in the Commons House of Parliament; and amongst other things there was written down the form of a protestation concerning sundry Liberties, Privileges and Franchises of Parliament; with which form of protestation His Majesty was justly offended.

Nevertheless His Majesty, in a most gracious manner, there expressed that he never means to deny that House of Commons any lawful privileges that ever they had enjoyed; but whatsoever privileges or liberties they had by any law or statute, the same should be inviolably preserved unto them; and whatsoever privileges they enjoyed by custom, or uncontrolled and lawful precedent, His Majesty would be careful to pre-

serve. But this protestation of the Commons House, so contrived and carried as it was, His Majesty thought fit to be razed out of all Memorials, and utterly to be annihilated, both in respect of the manner by which it was gained and the matter therein contained.

For the manner of getting it, first in respect of the time: for after such time as His Majesty, out of His Princely grace, and to take away all mistakings, had directed his letters to Secretary Calvert, dated at Royston, 16 December, and therein had so explained himself in the point of maintaining the privileges of the House of Commons, as that most of the said House rested fully satisfied, and freed from any scruple of having their liberties impeached; and after that, by His Majesty's Letters, directed to the Speaker, dated 18 December, being Tuesday, His Majesty, at the humble suit of the House of Commons, condescended to make this meeting a session before Christmas, and for that purpose had assigned Saturday following.

Now upon this very Tuesday, and while the messengers from the House of Commons were with His Majesty at Theobalds, to return thanks unto His Majesty, and therewith an excuse from them not to make it a session, in respect of the strait of time whereunto they were driven, which deferment His Majesty admitted of at their desires, and thereupon gave orders for the adjournment of the parliament until the eighth of February next, which was the first day formerly appointed by His Majesty for the meeting together of the parliament. And whilst their messengers were with His Majesty, and had received a gracious answer to return unto their houses, even that afternoon, a committee was procured to be made for taking their liberties into consideration.

And this afternoon a protestation was made (to whom appears not) concerning their liberties; and at six o'clock at night, by candlelight, the same protestation was brought into the House by the committee, and at that time of night it was called upon to be put to the Question, there not being the third part of the House then present, whereas in all matters of weight, their usual custom is, to put nothing of importance to the Question, till the house be full. And at this time many of them that were present, expected the Question would have been deferred to another day, and a fuller house, and some then present stood up to have spoken to it but could not be seen or heard in that darkness and confusion.

Now for the matter of the protestation, it is penned in such ambiguous and general words, the Rights and Prerogatives annexed to the Imperial Crown; the claim of some privileges being grounded upon the words of the Writ for assembling the Parliament, wherein some words, viz. *Ardiis Regni,* are cunningly mentioned; but the word *quibusdam,* which restraineth the generality to such particular cases, as His Majesty pleaseth to consult with them upon, is purposely omitted.

These things considered, His Majesty did, this present day, in full assembly of his Council, and in the presence of the Judges, declare the said protestation to be invalid, annulled, void and of no effect. And did further, *manu sua propria,* take the said protestation out of the Journal Book of the Clerk of the Commons House of Parliament, and commanded an Act of Council to be made thereupon, and this Act to be entered in the Register of Council causes.

D. THE PARLIAMENT OF 1629

A temporary reconciliation of crown and parliament in the last year of James' reign was followed by even more severe clashes when Charles I ascended the throne in 1625. The quarrel came to center more and more upon the question of taxation, for the king required greater supplies than parliament would vote, and the king felt obliged to resort to non-parliamentary taxation, especially the customs levies of tonnage and poundage. The Commons hoped to have settled the issue by forcing the king to assent to the Petition of Right in 1628, but Charles continued to collect the hated imposts and gave further offense to an increasingly Puritan parliament by his support of the Arminian or high-church clergy. The parliament which met in 1629, therefore, proved exceedingly recalcitrant, and when the alarmed king endeavored to cut short their discussions, the incident described below was enacted. Following this scene, Charles embarked upon his experiment of rule without parliament, which eventually led to civil war.[11]

The Agitation of the [Lower] House of Parliament on the last Day of their Sitting being the 2 of March 1628.

This day, being the last day of the Assembly, as soon as prayers were ended the Speaker went into the Chair, and delivered the King's command for the adjournment of the House until Tuesday sevennight following.

The House returned him answer, that it was not the office of the Speaker to deliver any such command unto them, but for the adjournment of the House it did properly belong unto themselves; and after they had settled some things they thought fit and convenient to be spoken of they would satisfy the King.

The Speaker told them that he had an express command from the King as soon as he had delivered his message to rise; and upon that he left the Chair, but was by force drawn to it again by Mr. ˙Denzil Holles, son to the Earl of Clare, Mr. Valentine, and others. And Mr. Holles, notwithstanding the endeavors of Sir Thomas Edmondes, Sir Humphrey May, and other Privy Councillors to free the Speaker from the Chair, swore, God's wounds, he should sit still until they pleased to rise.

Here *Sir John Eliot* began in a rhetorical oration to inveigh against the Lord Treasurer and the Bishop of Winchester, saying he could prove the Lord Treasurer to be a great instrument in the innovation of Religion, and innovation of the liberties of the House; and offered a Remonstrance to the House wherein he said, he could prove him to be the great enemy of the Commonwealth, saying that he had traced him in all his actions, and withal that if ever it were his fortune to meet again in this honorable assembly, he protested (as he was a gentleman) that where he now left, he would begin again.

The Remonstrance, being refused by the Speaker and the Clerk, was restored to his hands and by him read.

The House then required the Speaker to put the business in hand to the question which he again denying and urging the King's command was checked by *Mr. Selden* who told him he had ever loved his person well, but he could not choose but much blame him now that he being the servant of the House should refuse their command under any color whatsoever; and that this his obstinacy would grow a precedent to posterity if it should go unpunished. For that hereafter if we shall meet with a dishonest Speaker (as we cannot promise ourselves to the contrary) he might under pretense of the King's command refuse to propose the business and intendment of the House; and therefore wished him to proceed.

The Speaker with abundance of tears answered, I will not say, I will not, but I dare not; desiring that they would not command his ruin therein; that he had been their faithful servant, and would gladly sacrifice his life for the good of his country; but he durst not sin against the express command of his Sovereign.

Yet notwithstanding the Speaker's extremity of weeping and supplicatory oration quaintly eloquent, *Sir Peter Heyman* (a gentleman of his own country) bitterly inveighed against him, and told him he was sorry he was a Kentish man, and that he was a disgrace to his country, and a blot to a noble family, and that all the inconveniences that should follow, yea, their destruction, should be derived to posterity as the issue of his baseness, by whom he should be remembered with scorn and disdain. And that he for his part (since he would not be persuaded to do his duty) thought it fit he should be called to the Bar, and a new Speaker chosen in the meantime, since neither advice nor threats would prevail.

Then they required Mr. Holles to read certain Articles as the Protestations of the House, which were jointly, as they were read, allowed with a loud *Yea* by the House. The effect of which Articles are as followeth, *viz.:—*

First, Whosoever shall bring in innovation in Religion, or by favor or countenance, seek to extend or introduce Popery or Arminianism or other opinions disagreeing from the true and orthodox Church, shall be reputed a capital enemy of this Kingdom and Commonwealth.

Secondly, Whosoever shall counsel or advise the taking and levying of the Subsidies of Tonnage and Poundage, not being granted by Parliament, or shall be an actor or instrument therein, shall be likewise reputed an innovator in the government, and a capital enemy to this Kingdom and Commonwealth.

Thirdly, If any merchant or person whatsoever shall voluntarily yield or pay the said subsidies of Tonnage and Poundage, not being granted by Parliament, he shall likewise be reputed a betrayer of the liberties of England and an Enemy of the same.

These being read and allowed of, the House rose up after they had sitten down two hours.

The King hearing that the House continued to sit (notwithstanding his command for the adjourning thereof) sent a messenger for the serjeant with the mace, which being taken from the table there can be no further proceeding; but the serjeant was by the House stayed, and the key of the door taken from him, and given to a gentleman of the House to keep. After this the King sent Maxwell (the usher) with the black rod for the dissolution of Parliament, but being informed that neither he nor his message would be received by the House, the King grew into much rage and passion, and sent for the Captain of the Pensioners and Guard to force the door, but the rising of the House prevented the bloodshed that might have been spilt.

Notwithstanding the Parliament was but as yet adjourned until that day seven-night, being the tenth of March, yet were the principal gentlemen attached by pursuivants, some the next morning; and on Wednesday by order from the Council-board sent to sundry prisons.

Part II.   CONSCIENCE AND COMMONWEALTH

The period from 1642 to 1660 was rife with political speculation. Once the standard of battle had been raised, the question of how to define the liberties for which men fought was added to the old question of how to secure the legal rights of the subject in the machinery of state. For it very quickly became evident that the rebels were far from being united upon the aims of the revolution. The concrete legal rights for which the Commons had striven between 1604 and 1629 seemed to be but a small part of the general liberties for which men were now willing to lay down their lives. Hence appeared a multitude of writings, in which different rebels explained their political ideals. The documents in this part are illustrative of the ferment of political ideas during the interregnum.

A.   SECTS AND PARTIES

Puritan insistence on liberty of conscience encouraged men to make their own interpretations of religion and law. The inevitable result was a multiplicity of sects and parties, each convinced of the correctness of its own doctrines. Many of these groups developed political creeds which had a considerable effect upon experiments in government under Commonwealth and Protectorate. In this section are included the doctrines of three of the outstanding sects and parties.

1. *The Fifth Monarchy Men.* This sect based its political creed upon an interpretation of the second chapter of Daniel, from which was evolved a rather confused but highly moral program for the government of men. The following documents explain the doctrines of the Fifth Monarchy Men, who also called themselves The Saints.[12]

(*The Fifth Monarchy Text*) And in the second year of the reign of Nebuchadnezzar, Nebuchadnezzar dreamed dreams, wherewith his spirit was troubled, and his sleep brake from him. Then the king commanded to call the magicians, and the astrologers, and the sorcerers, and the Chaldeans, for to show the king his dreams. So they came and stood before the king. And the king said unto them, I have dreamed a dream, and my spirit was troubled to know the dream. Then spake the Chaldeans to the king in Syriac, O king, live for ever: tell thy servants the dream, and we will show the interpretation. The king answered and said to the Chaldeans, The thing is gone from me: if ye will not make known unto me the dream, with the interpretation thereof, ye shall be cut in pieces, and your houses shall be made a dunghill. . . .

And the decree went forth that the wise men should be slain; and they sought Daniel and his fellows to be slain. Then Daniel answered with counsel and wisdom to Arioch the captain of the king's guard, which was gone forth to slay the wise men of Babylon: He answered and said to Arioch the king's captain, Why is the decree so hasty from the king? Then Arioch made the thing known to Daniel. Then Daniel went in, and desired of the king that he would give him time, and that he would show the king the interpretation. Then Daniel went to his house and made the thing known to Hananiah, Mishael, and Azariah, his companions: That they would desire mercies of the God of heaven concerning this secret; that Daniel and his fellows should not perish with the rest of the wise men of Babylon. Then was the secret revealed unto Daniel in a night vision. Then Daniel blessed the God of heaven. . . .

Therefore Daniel went in unto Arioch, whom the king had ordained to destroy the wise men of Babylon: he went and said thus unto him; Destroy not the wise men of Babylon: bring me in before the king, and I will show unto the king the interpretation. Then Arioch brought in Daniel before the king in haste, and said thus unto him, I have found a man of the captives of Judah, that will make known unto the king the interpretation. The king answered and said to Daniel whose name was Belteshazzar, Art thou able to make known unto me the dream which I have seen, and the interpretation thereof? Daniel answered in the presence of the king, and said, The secret which the king hath demanded cannot the wise men, the astrologers, the magicians, the soothsayers, show unto the king; But there is a God in heaven that revealeth secrets, and maketh known to the king Nebuchadnezzar what shall be in the latter days. Thy dream, and the visions of thy head upon thy bed, are these: . . .

Thou, O king, sawest, and behold a great image. This great image, whose brightness was excellent, stood before thee, and the form thereof was terrible. This image's head was of fine gold, his breast and his arms of silver, his belly and his thighs of brass, his legs of iron, his feet part of iron and part of clay. Thou sawest till that a stone was cut out without hands, which smote the image upon his feet that were of iron and clay, and brake them to pieces. Then was the iron, the clay, the brass, the silver, and the gold, broken to pieces together, and became like the chaff of the summer threshing floors; and the wind carried them away, that no place was found for them: and the stone that smote the image became a great mountain, and filled the whole earth.

This is the dream; and we will tell the interpretation thereof before the king. Thou, O king, art a king of kings: for the God of heaven hath given thee a kingdom, power, and strength, and glory. And wheresoever the children of men dwell, the beasts of the field and the fowls of the heaven hath he given into thine hand, and hath made thee ruler over them all. Thou art this head of gold. And after three shall arise another kingdom inferior to thee, and another third kingdom of brass, which shall bear rule over all the earth. And the fourth kingdom shall be strong as iron: forasmuch as iron breaketh in pieces and subdueth all things: and as iron that breaketh all these, shall it break in pieces and bruise. And whereas thou sawest the feet and toes, part of potters' clay, and part of iron, the kingdom shall be divided; but there shall be in it of the strength of the iron, forasmuch as thou sawest the iron mixed with miry clay. And as the toes of the feet were part of iron, and part of clay, so the kingdom shall be partly strong, and partly broken.

And whereas thou sawest iron mixed with miry clay, they shall mingle themselves with the seed of men: but they shall not cleave one to another, even as iron is not mixed with clay. And in the days of these kings shall the God of heaven set up a kingdom, which shall never be destroyed: and the kingdom shall not be left to other people, but it shall break in pieces and consume all these kingdoms, and it shall stand for ever. Forasmuch as thou sawest that the stone was cut out of the mountain without hands, and that it brake in pieces the iron, the brass, the clay, the silver, and the gold; the great God hath made known to the king what shall come to pass hereafter: and the dream is certain, and the interpretation thereof sure.

(*The Fifth Monarchy Interpretation*) How this Fifth Monarchy must enter in? A word to that: 1. Gradually, the Stone cut without hands grows by degrees greater and greater till it fill the whole earth . . . Dan. 2. The Stone is this Fifth Monarchy cut out without men's hands, which must break a pieces all the other Monarchies never more to rise. The fourth Monarchy is breaking up apace and will suddenly tumble and kick his heels in the air. . . .

Why this Fifth Monarchy hastens so? Amongst other things I pick out two, as First, for the Redemption of the people; Luke 21. 28, lift up your heads for your redemption draweth nigh. . . . But our Redemption will be 1. From Ecclesiastic Bondage, Decrees, Councils, Orders and Ordinances, of Pope, Priest, Prelate, or the like. The whore shall be stripped stark naked and made desolate. Rev. 17. 16. . . . 2. From Civil Bondage and slavery, or those bloody, base, unjust, accursed tyrannical laws and sin-monopolizing Lawyers, as (now) oppress and afflict the people.

(The Fifth Monarchy Men Protest to Lord Protector Cromwell, 1655) . . . But in pursuance of our duty to God, our fellow members and countrymen, as we are Christians, having a right to the things of Christ, and as we are men, having a right to our native privileges, we do declare our real apprehensions and consciences, which (to the great grief of some of us) we have so long concealed, waiting if God might by his providence alter our minds.

First, that the sins and present condition of this nation hold parallel in many things with the old Israelites, after the mighty wonders of God shewed unto them in their great deliverance out of Egypt. For instance, they and we have soon forgotten God our Savior, and the great works which He did, we have not set our hearts aright, and our spirits have not been steadfast with God, but have gone back, and dealt treacherously, and turned aside like a deceitful bow; and not trusting to His salvation have provoked the Lord to anger with our inventions, so that men have dominion over our bodies, and over our cattle at their pleasure, and we are in great distress, for this is a day of trouble, and of blasphemy, for the children are come to the birth, and there is not strength to bring forth,

Secondly, that blessed cause, and those noble principles propounded and prosecuted by the old parliament, and the good people of this nation (in the maintaining of which God did miraculously appear) are now altogether laid aside and lost, and another cause and interest (quite contrary as we conceive) espoused and maintained; for then the advancement of Christ's kingdom, the extirpation of popery and popish innovations, the privileges of parliament, the liberty of the subjects, and an equal distinction of justice were declared and fought for, and tyranny, oppression, injustice, arbitrariness, destroying the privileges of parliaments we declared and engaged against: but how far some men have now receded from,

and acted contrarily to the dishonor of God, scandal of religion, great grief of many faithful men, and the strengthening of the wicked in their principles, and justifying their practices, we leave to the consideration of those that are sober and wise.

Thirdly, moreover the unadvised and unwarrantable changing of the government and swearing thereunto, doth (as we judge) put a necessity upon the chief undertaker thereof, to overthrow the very foundation of a commonwealth; and to maintain the things comprised in the said instrument (whether right or wrong)? and to turn the very edge and dint of his sword against the faces and bowels of such as should or shall declare their consciences contrary thereunto.

Fourthly, as a consequence and fruit of this forbidden tree, many of the choice servants of God and faithful of the nation (some noblemen, gentlemen, ministers of the gospel, soldiers, &c.) are imprisoned without knowing their accusers, or having so much liberty as was granted by the heathens to the apostles, or the benefit of a fair and public trial, according to the fundamental laws of this nation.

Fifthly, under pretense of necessity still to continue the heavy burdens of taxes, customs, excise, &c. upon the nation without (yea contrary to) the consent of the people represented in parliament, and contrary to their own instrument.

Sixthly, notwithstanding all the fair pretenses and promises of reformation; yet what abominable and horrible impieties, injustice, and oppression are there couched and covered under this new form, from the head to the tail (as the prophet saith), treading in the very footsteps of their predecessors; witness the receiving of the honors, profits, customs, benefits, tenths, and firstfruits coming in formerly to the crown; the exalting of sons, servants, friends, and favorites (though some of them known for wicked men) to the highest places and greatest preferment, which the good rulers of old, as Gideon, Nehemiah and others did not so, because of the fear of the Lord, and the bondage that was heavy upon the people; witness also the unreasonableness of the army to have so many officers, which might easily be reduced to a lesser number, and both officers and soldiers for many years to receive their pay, (even in a time of peace) when the poor peasants or tenants (who pay but ten shilling rent per ann.) do pay out of their penury, to maintain them in their pomp and luxury. . . .

Lastly, we do declare and publish to all from our hearts and souls, that those of us that had any hand in joining with the parliament and army heretofore, had no other design against the late king and his party, save as they were enemies to our Lord Christ, his kingdom and people, hinderers of his work, and oppressors of the nation, and that it never came into our hearts to think or intend the pulling down of one person to set up another, or one unrighteous power to promote another: but we aimed as primarily at the glory of God, so likewise at the general good of the nation, and particular benefit and just liberty of every man; and it grieves us, that any just cause is given them to stumble at professors, or complain that they are deprived of their freedom, and several ways more oppressed, than in the days of the wicked kings.

We do also believe in our heart that (though the worst things are not without God's permission and providence) yet that this government is not of God's approbation, or taken up by His counsel, or according to His word; and therefore we do utterly disclaim having any hand or heart in it, and for the contrivers and undertakers thereof, we suspect and judge them to be great transgressors therein; and so much the more, because they are professors of religion, and declarers, engagers, and fighters against the very things they now practise: and it is most evident to us, that they thereby build again, what before they did destroy, and in so doing they render themselves and the cause, religion, name, and people of God abominable to the heathens, papists, and profane enemies, which is a grief to our souls to consider.

We do also detest the practices of those men in imprisoning the saints of God, for their consciences and testimony, and just men, who stand for moral and just principles, and the freedom of the nation and people, and their breaking off parliaments to effect their own design. We also from our souls witness against their new modelling of ministers, (as antichristian) and keeping up parishes and tithes, (as popish innovations) and we disclaim all adherence to, owning of, or joining with these men in their ways. And do withdraw, and desire all the Lord's people to withdraw from these men, as those that are guilty of the sins of the later days, and that have left following the Lord, and that God's people should avoid their sin, lest they partake with them in their plagues. Thus concluding our testimony, we subscribe our names hereunto. [There follow 321 signatures.]

2. *The Diggers.* Shortly after the execution of the king, the curious sect of the Diggers first made its appearance under the leadership of a dynamic figure named Gerrard Winstanley. The following documents explain their views and activities.[13]

(*Information of one Henry Sanders to the Council of State, 16 April, 1649*) Informeth, that on Sunday was sennight last, there was one Everard, once of the army but was cashiered, who termeth himself a prophet, one Stewer and Col-

ten, and two more, all living at Cobham, came to St. George's Hill in Surrey, and began to dig on that side the hill next to Campe Close, and sowed the ground with parsnips, carrots, and beans. On Monday following they were there again, being increased in their number, and on the next day, being Tuesday, they fired the heath, and burned at least forty rood of heath, which is a very great prejudice to the town.

On Friday last they came again, between twenty and thirty, and wrought all day at digging. They did then intend to have two or three ploughs at work, but they had not furnished themselves with seed-corn, which they did on Saturday at Kingston. They invite all to come in and help them, and promise them meat, drink, and clothes. They do threaten to pull down and level all park pales, and lay open, and intend to plant there very shortly. They give out they will be four or five thousand within ten days, and threaten the neighboring people there, that they will make them all come up to the hills and work: and forewarn them suffering their cattle to come near the plantation; if they do, they will cut their legs off. It is feared they have some design in hand.

(*Council of State to Lord Fairfax, 16 April, 1649*) My Lord,—By the narrative enclosed your Lordship will be informed of what relation hath been made to this Council of a disorderly and tumultuous sort of people assembling themselves together not far from Oatlands, at a place called St. George's Hill; and although the pretense of their being there by them avowed may seem very ridiculous, yet that conflux of people may be a beginning whence things of a greater and more dangerous consequence may grow, to the disturbance of the peace and quiet of the Commonwealth. We therefore recommend it to your Lordship's care that some force of horse may be sent to Cobham in Surrey and thereabouts, with orders to disperse the people so met, and to prevent the like for the future, that a malignant and disaffected party may not under color of such ridiculous people have any opportunity to rendezvous themselves in order to do a greater mischief.

(*Captain Gladman to Lord Fairfax, 19 April, 1649*) Sir,—According to your order I marched towards St. George's Hill and sent four men before to bring certain intelligence to me; as they went they met with Mr. Winstanley and Mr. Everard (which are the chief men that have persuaded these people to do what they have done). And when I had enquired of them and of the officers that lie at Kingston, I saw there was no need to march any further. I cannot hear that there have been above twenty of them together since they first undertook the business. Mr. Winstanley and Mr. Everard have engaged both to be with you this day: I believe you will be glad to be rid of them again, especially Everard, who is no other than a mad man. Sir, I intend to go with two or three men to St. George's Hill this day, and persuade these people to leave this employment if I can, and if then I see no more danger than now I do, I shall march back again to London tomorrow. . . . Indeed the business is not worth the writing nor yet taking notice of: I wonder the Council of State should be so abused with informations. . . .

(*Gerrard Winstanley to Lord Fairfax, 9 June, 1649*) When you were at our works upon the hill, we told you many of the country people that were offended at first begin now to be moderate, and to see righteousness in our work, and to own it, excepting one or two covetous freeholders, that would have all the commons to themselves, and that would uphold the Norman tyranny over us, which by the victory that you have got over the Norman successor is plucked up by the roots, therefore ought to be cast away. And we expect that these our angry neighbors, whom we never wronged nor will not wrong, will in time see their furious rashness to be their folly, and become moderate, to speak and carry themselves like men rationally, and leave off pushing with their horns like beasts; they shall have no cause to say we wrong them unless they count us wrongers of them for seeking a livelihood out of the common land of England by our righteous labor, which is our freedom, as we are Englishmen equal with them, and rather our freedom than theirs, because they are elder brothers and freeholders and call the enclosures their own land, and we are younger brothers and the poor oppressed, and the common lands are called ours by their own confession.

We told you (upon a question you put to us) that we were not against any that would have magistrates and laws to govern, as the nations of the world are governed, but as for our parts we shall need neither the one nor the other in that nature of government; for as our land is common, so our cattle is to be common, and our corn and fruits of the earth common, and are not to be bought and sold among us, but to remain a standing portion of livelihood to us and our children, without that cheating entanglement of buying and selling, and we shall not arrest one another.

And then, what need have we of imprisoning, whipping, or hanging laws to bring one another into bondage? and we know that none of those that are subject to this righteous law dares arrest or enslave his brother for or about the objects of the earth, because the earth is made by our creator to be a common treasury of livelihood to one equal with another, without respect of persons. . . .

And as for spiritual teachings, we leave every man to stand and fall to his own master: if the power of covetousness be his master or king that rules in his heart, let him stand and fall to him; if the power of love and righteousness be his master or king that rules in his heart, let him stand and fall to him; let the bodies of men act love, humility, and righteousness one towards another, and let the spirit of righteousness be the teacher, ruler, and judge both in us and over us; and by thus doing we shall honor our father, the spirit that gave us our being. And we shall honor our mother the earth, by laboring her in righteousness, and leaving her free from oppression and bondage. . . .

I affirm (and I challenge you to disprove) that the earth was made to be a common treasury of livelihood for all, without respect of persons, and was not made to be bought and sold: and that mankind in all his branches is the lord over the beasts, birds, fishes, and the earth, and was not made to acknowledge any of his own kind to be his teacher and ruler, but the spirit of righteousness only his maker, and to walk in his light, and so to live in peace, and this being a truth, as it is, then none ought to be lords or landlords over another, but the earth is free for every son and daughter of mankind, to live free upon.

(*Gerrard Winstanley to Lord Fairfax, 8 December, 1649*) Now Sir, the end of our digging and ploughing upon the common land is this, that we and all the impoverished poor in the land may get a comfortable livelihood by our righteous labors thereupon; which we conceive we have a true right unto, (I speak in the name of all the poor commoners) by virtue of the conquest over the king, for while he was in power he was the successor of William the Conquerer, and held the land as a conquerer from us, and all Lords of Manors held title to the common lands from him; but seeing the common people of England by joint consent of person and purse, have cast out Charles our Norman oppressor, we have by this victory recovered ourselves from under his Norman yoke, and the land now is to return into the joint hands of those who have conquered, that is the commoners, and the land is to be held no longer from the use of them by the hand of any who will uphold the Norman and kingly power still; and if so, then we that are impoverished by sticking to the Parliament and you, shall lose the benefit of all our taxes, free quarter, and blood, and remain slaves still to the kingly power in the hands of Lords of Manors, which we have cast out of the hands of Charles.

Therefore we poor oppressed Commoners claim freedom in the common land, by virtue of the

Parliament's promises and engagement, and of the armies acting; for we did believe and rely thereupon, being as we conceive it a firm bargain between you and us; for you and the Parliament in effect said to us, "Give us your taxes, free quarter, excise, and adventure your lives with us to cast out the oppressor Charles, and we will make you a free people"; therefore by the law of contract as we expected was firmly made and confirmed on our part by performance, we claim this freedom to enjoy the common land for our livelihood, for we have bought it by our blood and money.

Secondly, we claim this freedom by equality in the conquest over the king, for the Parliament told us what they did, they did it for the safety and peace of the whole nation; the army told us they fought not for themselves, but for the safety and peace of the whole Nation; and you and we joined our forces together to procure our freedom, and have obtained it; therefore if there be a spoil of the common land to be gathered, as there is, it is to be equally divided between you that went to war, and we that stayed at home and paid you, that is, as the Gentry have their inclosure free to themselves, so we the poor impoverished commoners claim freedom in the common land by virtue of this conquest over the king, which is gotten by our joint consent.

Thirdly, we know that England cannot be a free Commonwealth, unless all the poor commoners have a free use and benefit of the land, for if this freedom be not granted, we that are the poor commoners are in a worse case than we were in the king's days, for then we had some estate about us, though we were under oppression, but now our estates are spent to purchase freedom, and we are under oppression still of Lords of Manors' tyranny; therefore [unless] we that are poor commoners have some part of the land to live upon freely, as well as the gentry, it cannot be a common wealth, neither can the kingly power be removed so long as this kingly power in the hands of Lords of Manors rules over us.

Now Sir, if you and the Council will quietly grant us this freedom, which is our own right, and set us free from the kingly power of Lords of Manors, that violently now as in the king's days hold the commons from us (as if we had obtained no conquest at all over the kingly power), then the poor that lie under the great burden of poverty, and are always complaining for want, and their miseries increased because they see no means of relief found out, and therefore cry out continually to you and the Parliament for relief and to make good your promises, will be quieted.

<u>We desire no more of you than freedom to</u> <u>work, and to enjoy the benefit of our labors—for</u> <u>here is wasteland enough and to spare to supply</u> <u>all our wants</u>—but if you deny this freedom, then in righteousness we must raise collections for the poor out of the estates, and a mass of money will not supply their wants; because many are in want that are ashamed to take collection money, and therefore they are desperate, and will rather rob and steal, and disturb the land, and others that are ashamed to beg would do any work for to live, as it is the case of many of our diggers that have been good housekeepers; but if this freedom were granted to improve the common lands then there would be a supply to answer every one's inquiry, and the murmurings of the people against you and the Parliament would cease, and within a few years we should have no beggars nor idle persons in the land.

Secondly, hereby England would be enriched with all commodity within itself which they each would afford; and truly this is a stain to Christian religion in England, that we have so much land lying waste, and so many starve for want; and further, if this freedom be granted, the whole land will be united in love and strength, that if a foreign enemy like an army of rats and mice come to take our inheritance from us, we shall all rise as one man to defend it.

Then lastly, if you will grant the poor commoners this quiet freedom to improve the common land for our livelihood, we shall rejoice in you and the army in protecting our work, and we and our work will be ready to secure that, and we hope there will not be any kingly power over us, to rule at will and we to be slaves, as the power has been, but that you will rule in love as Moses and Joshua did the Children of Israel before any kingly power came in, and that the Parliament will be as the Elders of Israel, chosen freely by the people to advise for and assist both you and us.

And thus in the name of the rest of these called Diggers and Commoners through the land, I have in short declared our mind and cause to you in the light of righteousness, which will prove all these reports made against us to be false and destructive to the uniting of England into peace.

Per me Gerrard Winstanley for myself and in the behalf of all my fellow Commoners.

3. *The Levellers.* This group was the product of the fearless and tempestuous John Lilburne (1618–57). Whipped, pilloried, and imprisoned in 1637 by the Star Chamber, he was later released by the Long Parliament on a motion by Oliver Cromwell. Lilburne's political doctrines, widely disseminated by means of pamphlets, were highly popular with the soldiers in the parliamentary army

and attracted to him a small group of personal followers who were called Levellers. But his condemnation of the revolutionary government incurred the displeasure of Parliament and Cromwell, who again imprisoned him for several years. Lilburne's own writings are diffuse and filled with comments on the passing interests of the moment but the central ideas, developed by Lilburne and his followers during the civil wars, were succinctly summarized in the following pamphlet, written in 1659 and entitled *The Leveller, or The Principles and Maxims Concerning Government and Religion, Which are Asserted by Those That are Commonly Called Levellers.*[14]

. . . But to satisfy such as desire to know what they are, who are now for destruction's sake (though formerly by their enemies scandalously) called "levellers," and what their designs are, I shall tell you their fundamental doctrines or maxims concerning our government; and from thence you may make a true judgment of all their plots, and either fear them or favor them accordingly.

I. First, they assert it as fundamental that the government of England ought to be by laws, and, not by men; they say the laws ought to be the protectors and preservers under God of all our persons and estates, and that every man may challenge that protection as his right, without a ticket from a major general, and live under that protection and safely, without fear of a red-coat, or a pursuivant from Whitehall. They say that Englishmen ought to fear nothing but God and the breach of the laws, not to depend upon the will of a court and their council for the security of themselves and their estates. They say the laws ought to judge of all offenses and offenders, and all penalties and punishments to be inflicted upon criminals, and that the pleasure of his highness, or his council, ought not to make whom they please offenders, and punish and imprison whom they please, and during their pleasure. . . .

II. The Levellers' second maxim, or principle about government, is that all the laws, levies of monies, war and peace, ought to be made by the people's deputies in parliament, to be chosen by them successively at certain periods of time; and that no council-table, orders, or ordinances, or court proclamations [ought] to bind the peoples' persons or estates; 'tis the first principle of a people's liberty that they shall not be bound but by their own consent, and this our ancestors left to England as its undoubted right, that no laws to bind our persons or estates could be imposed upon us against our wills; and they challenged it as their native right, not to be controlled in mak-

ing such laws as concerned their common right and interests, as may appear by the parliament's records in the time of Edward the second and Richard the second.

The Levellers say that those whose interests are in all things one with the whole people's, are the only proper uninterested judges of what laws are most fit to preserve and provide for that common interest: such are the people in parliament rightly constituted and methodized, and they may be depended upon to provide remedies for the people's grievances because they themselves are sharers in every common grievance; and they will be naturally led to study the common good, because they shall share in it. . . .

III. The Levellers assert it as another principle that every man of what quality or condition, place or office whatsoever, ought to be equally subject to the laws. Every man, say they, high and low, rich and poor, must be accountable to the laws, and either obey them or suffer the penalties ordained for the transgressors; there ought to be no more respect of persons in the execution of the laws than is with God himself if the law be transgressed; no regard should be had who is the offender, but of what kind, nature, and degree is the offense: 'tis destructive to the end of a government by law that any magistrate or other should be exempt from the obedience or justice of the laws; it dissolves the government *ipso facto* and exposeth all the people to rapine and oppression without security of their persons and estates, for which the laws are intended.

Therefore, say they, great thieves and little must alike to the gallows, and the meanest man as readily and easily obtain justice and relief of any injury and oppression against the greatest as he shall do against the lowest of the people; and therefore, say they, it ought not to be in the power of any single person to defend himself from the impartial stroke of the laws, or to pervert justice by force; and that brings in their fourth principle, viz.

IV. That the people ought to be formed into such a constant military posture, by and under the commands of their parliament, that by their own strength they may be able to compel every man to be subject to the laws, and to defend their country from foreigners, and enforce right and justice from them upon all emergent occasions. No government can stand without force of arms, to subdue such as shall rebel against the laws and to defend their territories from the rapine and violence of strangers; and the people must either hire mercenary soldiers to be the guardians of their laws and their country, or take the care upon themselves, by disposing themselves into a posture of arms, that may make them ready and able to be their own guard.

Now say the Levellers, 'tis neither prudent nor safe that the people's armies should be put into mercenary soldiers' hands. What reason can induce any people to believe that their laws, estates, liberties and lives shall be more secure in the hands of mercenaries than in their own? Who can think his estate, his liberty, or his life in safety, when he knows they are all at the mercy and will of hirelings, that are led by no other motive than that of profit or pay to serve them, and may be led by any proposal or temptation of greater profit or pay to desert them? . . .

These four foregoing maxims contain the sum of all the Levellers' doctrine about our government in externals (whose principles without naming one of them have been rendered so prodigious and of such dangerous consequence); but let the reader judge whether the liberty, happiness, and security of every Englishman be not sought in the endeavors to establish those foundations of equal justice and safety; neither can they be charged herein with novelty or inconstancy, the same fundamentals of government having been claimed by our ancestors as their right for many hundred years. . . .

But the designers of oppression having also thrown dirt in the faces of those whom they have named Levellers in the matters of religion, and aspersed them sometimes as Jesuits, sometimes as notorious heretics, and sometimes as licentious atheists, men of no religion, 'tis necessary that I should acquaint the reader with their principles that relate unto religion; I do not mean to give an account of their faith, for the men branded with the name of Levellers are and may be under several dispensations of light and knowledge in spiritual things, in which they do not one judge the other; yet they are all professors of the Christian reformed religion, and do all agree in these general opinions about religion and the power of men over it.

First, they say that all true religion in men is founded upon the inward consent of their understandings and hearts to the truths revealed, and that the understanding is so free that 'tis not in the power of men to compel it to or restrain it from a consent; nothing but the irresistible evidence of a truth can gain a consent; and when the evidence is clear to any man's understanding, he himself (much less another howsoever potent) cannot so much as suspend an assent. Therefore no man can compel another to be religious, or by force or terror constrain the people to be of the true religion.

Secondly, they say, that the last dictate of every man's understanding in matters of faith and God's worship, is the last voice of God to him, and obligeth him to practise accordingly. If a man be erroneously informed, yet the mis-conceptions he hath of truth bind him to practise erroneously; and should he resist that seeming light (though it should be in truth darkness), his sin would be much greater and of worse consequence than if he follows by his actions his erroneous conceptions. Therefore the only means to promote the true religion under any government is to endeavor rightly to inform the people's consciences, by whose dictates God commands them to be guided; and therefore Christ ordained the preaching of the Gospel as the outward means for converting souls, faith coming by hearing; and He also ordained spiritual ordinances for the conviction, instruction and punishment of erroneous and heretical persons, the scripture commanding the erroneous to be instructed with the spirit of meekness, and admonished privately, publicly, etc. And Christ never mentioned any penalties to be inflicted on the bodies or purses of unbelievers because of their unbelief.

Thirdly, Levellers say that there are two parts of true religion: the first consists in the right conceptions and receptions of God, as He is revealed by Christ, and sincere adoration of Him in the heart or spirit, and the expressions or declarations of that worship outwardly, in and by the use of those ordinances that are appointed by Christ for that purpose. The second part of it consists in works or righteousness and mercy towards all men, done in obedience to the will of God and in imitation of His justice and goodness to the whole world. . . .

Fourthly, they say that nothing is more destructive to true religion, nor of worse consequence to human society than the quarrels of nations or persons about their difference of faith and worship, and the use of force and punishments, each to compel the other to be of his belief. It cannot be denied that God, in His infinite secret wisdom, is pleased to cause His spirit to enlighten men's minds with several degrees of light, and to suffer many to remain in darkness, which be afterwards also enlightened: and therefore their faith and worship, if it be sincere, must necessarily and unavoidably differ, according to the different root of light upon which it grows. . . .

Now I heartily wish that my countrymen may not be mistaken in my candid intentions in giving them this account. I mean not to court them, as Absalom did his father's subjects, to make them believe that those called Levellers would use them better than others, if power was trusted in their hands: for our age hath given me experience that power to enslave the people ought not to be entrusted in any man's hands, upon the fairest pretenses and most solemn oaths that that power shall be used to establish their freedom.

And it is the Levellers' doctrine that the government ought to be settled upon such equal foundations of common right and freedom that no man, or number of men, in the nation, should have the power to invade or disturb the common freedom, or the common course of impartial justice, and therefore that every authority ought to be of small continuance, and the several authorities to be so balanced each by other, that without such an agreement of men, against their own interest, as human prudence cannot think possible, the people cannot suffer any common injury.

But my meaning in this is only to prevent the division of my countrymen into parties, with animosities each against others, by the cozenage of names or scandals; when, it may be, they would otherwise join hands and hearts for their common rights and liberties, if they understood each others' minds, and could converse each with other, without prejudice, because of the names

whereby each hath usually called the others. It is a threadbare plot of tyrants to divide the people into parties, that they may more easily master them.

But I wish that my countrymen would unite in the equal principles of common right, and hearken to reason, with clearness of mind, whosoever offers it; not regarding whether he that speaks it is called a Leveller, or a Sectary, or an Anabaptist, or a Presbyter, or a Cavalier, but considering what he says; and then the number of hands to defend our liberties and properties would be so numerous that the ambition of one, or a few, could not hope for success in attempting a tyranny over us. And if this poor paper may have such an effect, that my countrymen be not deluded with the idle scandal of Levelling, cast upon honest men, into an opposition of their own welfare, I and many that agree in the publication of this, shall have our ends.

B. THE ARMY DEBATES

After the campaign of 1644, Parliament ordered the reconstitution of its army on "a new model": strict discipline, prompt pay, and reliance upon the principle that he who prays best fights best. So effective was the New Model Army that by 1647 the royal forces had been defeated and the king made a prisoner. Fearful of its own creation, Parliament then ordered the break-up of the army with arrears of pay outstanding, but the New Model refused to disband. Instead, the regiments chose "agitators" or representatives to meet with its officers in a General Council of the Army to present their grievances and consider the problems of a return to peaceful government. The debates of the General Council began in October 1647, and during the next two years the Council provided a sounding board, in some ways more effective than Parliament, for the expression of the political thought stimulated by the civil war.

1. *The Agreement of the People, October 1647.* The more radical "agitators" presented the following document to the General Council as a program for the reconstitution of the government.[15]

1. That the People of England being at this day very unequally distributed by Counties, Cities, and Boroughs, for the election of their Deputies in Parliament, ought to be more indifferently proportioned, according to the number of the Inhabitants; the circumstances whereof, for number, place, and manner, are to be set down before the end of this present Parliament.

2. That to prevent the many inconveniences apparently arising from the long continuance of the same persons in authority, this present Parliament be dissolved upon the last day of September, which shall be in the year of our Lord 1648.

3. That the People do of course choose themselves a Parliament once in two years, *viz.,* upon the first Thursday in every second March, after the manner as shall be prescribed before the end

of this Parliament, to begin to sit upon the first Thursday in April following at Westminster, or such other place as shall be appointed from time to time by the preceding Representatives; and to continue till the last day of September, then next ensuing and no longer.

4. That the power of this and all future Representatives of the Nation is inferior only to theirs who chose them, and doth extend, without the consent or concurrence of any other person or persons: to the enacting, altering and repealing of Laws: to the erecting and abolishing of Offices and Courts: to the appointing, removing and calling to account Magistrates, and Officers of all degrees; to the making war and peace, to the treating with Foreign States; and generally, to whatsoever is not expressly, or impliedly reserved by the represented to themselves.

Which are as followeth:

1. That matters of Religion, and the ways of God's Worship, are not at all intrusted by us to any humane power, because therein we cannot remit or exceed a tittle of what our Consciences

[margin handwritten note: Strong Leveller influence.]

dictate to be the mind of God, without wilful sin: nevertheless the public way of instructing the Nation (so it be not compulsive) is referred to their discretion.

2. That the matter of impressing and constraining any of us to serve in the wars, is against our freedom; and therefore we do not allow it in our Representatives; the rather, because money (the sinews of war) being always at their disposal, they can never want numbers of men, apt enough to engage in any just cause.

3. That after the dissolution of this Parliament, no person be at any time questioned for any thing said or done, in reference to the late public differences, otherwise than in execution of the Judgments of the present Representatives, or House of Commons.

4. That in all Laws made, or to be made, every person may be bound alike, and that no tenure, Estate, Charter, Degree, Birth or place, do confer any exemption from the ordinary course of Legal proceedings, whereunto others are subjected.

5. That as the Laws ought to be equal, so they must be good, and not evidently destructive to the safety and well-being of the People. These things we declare to be our *native rights*, and therefore are agreed and resolved to maintain them with our utmost possibilities, against all opposition whatsoever, being compelled thereunto, not only by the examples of our Ancestors, whose blood was often spent in vain for the recovery of their Freedoms. . . .

2. *The Putney Debates, October 1647.* Following is a selection from the debates in the General Council of the Army at Putney on the first article of the Agreement of the People.[16]

Ireton: The exception that lies in it is this. It is said, they are to be distributed according to the number of the inhabitants: "The people of England," etc. And this doth make me think that the meaning is, that every man that is an inhabitant is to be equally considered, and to have an equal voice in the election of these representers, the persons that are for the general Representative; and if that be the meaning, then I have something to say against it. But if it be only those people that by the civil constitution of this kingdom, which is original and fundamental, and beyond which I am sure no memory of record does go— . . .

Rainborough: I desired that those that had engaged in it might be included. For really I think that the poorest he that is in England hath a life to live, as the greatest he; and therefore truly, sir, I think it's clear that every man that is to live under a government ought first by his own consent to put himself under that government; and I do think that the poorest man in England is not

at all bound in a strict sense to that government that he hath not had a voice to put himself under; and I am confident that, when I have heard the reasons against it, something will be said to answer those reasons, insomuch that I should doubt whether he was an Englishman or no, that should be doubting of these things.

Ireton: That's the meaning of this, "according to the number of the inhabitants"?

Give me leave to tell you, that if you make this the rule I think you must fly for refuge to an absolute natural right, and you must deny all civil right; and I am sure it will come to that in the consequence. This I perceive is pressed as that which is so essential and due: the right of the people of this kingdom, and as they are the people of this kingdom, distinct and divided from other people, and that we must for this right lay aside all other considerations; this is so just, this is so due, this is so right to them. And that those that they do thus choose must have such a power of binding all, and loosing all, according to those limitations, this is pressed as so due, and so just, as it is argued, that it is an engagement paramount to all others; and you must for it lay aside all others; if you have engaged any otherwise you must break it. We must so look upon these as thus held out to us; so it was held out by the gentlemen that brought it yesterday.

For my part, I think it is no right at all. I think that no person hath a right to an interest or share in the disposing of the affairs of this kingdom, and in determining or choosing those that shall determine what laws we shall be ruled by here—no person hath a right to this, that hath not a permanent fixed interest in this kingdom, and those persons together are properly the represented of this kingdom, and consequently are also to make up the representers of this kingdom, who taken together do comprehend whatsoever is of real or permanent interest in the kingdom. And I am sure otherwise I cannot tell what any man can say why a foreigner coming in amongst us—or as many as will come in amongst us, or by force or otherwise settling themselves here . . . —why they should not as well lay claim to it as any other.

We talk of birthright. Truly by birthright there is thus much claim. Men may justly have by birthright, by their very being born in England, that we should not seclude them out of England, that we should not refuse to give them air and place and ground, and the freedom of the highways and other things, to live amongst us—not any man that is born here, though by his birth there come nothing at all (that is part of the permanent interest of this kingdom) to him. That I think is due to a man by birth. But that by a man's being born here he shall have a share in that power that shall dispose of the lands here, and of all things here, I do not think it a sufficient ground.

I am sure if we look upon that which is the utmost (within any man's view) of what was originally the constitution of this kingdom, upon that which is most radical and fundamental, and which if you take away, there is no man hath any land, any goods, or any civil interest, that is this: that those that choose the representers for the making of laws by which this state and kingdom are to be governed, are the persons who, taken together, do comprehend the local interest of this kingdom; that is, the persons in whom all land lies, and those in corporations in whom all trading lies. This is the most fundamental constitution of this kingdom and that which if you do not allow, you allow none at all. This constitution hath limited and determined it that only those shall have voices in elections.

It is true, as was said by a gentleman near me, the meanest man in England ought to have a voice in the election of the government he lives under—but only if he has some local interest. I say this: that those that have the meanest local interest—that man that hath but forty shillings a year, he *hath* as great voice in the election of a knight for the shire as he that hath ten thousand a year, or more if he had never so much; and therefore there is that regard had to it. But this local interest, still the constitution of this government hath had an eye to and what other government hath not an eye to this? It doth not relate to the interest of the kingdom if it do not lay the foundation of the power that's given to the representers, in those who have a permanent and a local interest in the kingdom, and who taken all together do comprehend the whole interest of the kingdom.

There is all the reason and justice that can be, in this: if I will come to live in a kingdom, being a foreigner to it, or live in a kingdom, having no permanent interest in it, and if I will desire as a stranger, or claim as one freeborn here, the air, the free passage of highways, the protection of laws, and all such things—if I will either desire them or claim them, then I (if I have no permanent interest in that kingdom) must submit to those laws and those rules which they shall choose, who, taken together, do comprehend the whole interest of the kingdom. And if we shall go to take away this, we shall plainly go to take away all property and interest that any man hath either in land by inheritance, or in estate by possession, or anything else—I say, if you take away this fundamental part of the civil constitution.

Rainborough: Truly, sir, I am of the same opinion I was, and am resolved to keep it till I know reason why I should not. I confess my memory is bad, and therefore I am fain to make use of my pen. I remember that, in a former speech which this gentleman brought before this meeting he was saying that in some cases he should not value whether there were a king or no king, whether lords or no lords, whether a property or no property. For my part I differ in that. I do very much care whether there be a king or no king, lords or no lords, property or no property; and I think if we do not all care we shall all have none of these very shortly.

But as to this present business. I do hear nothing at all that can convince me, why any man that is born in England ought not to have his voice in election of burgesses. It is said that if a man have not a permanent interest, he can have no claim; and that we must be no freer than the laws will let us be, and that there is no law in any chronicle will let us be freer than that we now enjoy. Something was said to this yesterday. I do think that the main cause why Almighty God gave men reason, it was that they should make use of that reason, and that they should improve it for that end and purpose that God gave it them. And truly, I think that half a loaf is better than none if a man be hungry: this gift of reason without other property may seem a small thing, yet I think there is nothing that God hath given a man that any one else can take from him.

And therefore I say, that either it must be the Law of God or the Law of Man that must prohibit the meanest man in the kingdom to have this benefit as well as the greatest. I do not find anything in the Law of God, that a lord shall choose twenty burgesses, and a gentleman but two, or a poor man shall choose none: I find no such thing in the Law of Nature, nor in the Law of Nations. But I do find that all Englishmen must be subject to English laws, and I do verily believe that there is no man but will say that the foundation of all law lies in the people, and if it lie in the people, I am to seek for this exemption.

And truly I have thought something else: in what a miserable distressed condition would many a man that hath fought for the Parliament in this quarrel, be! I will be bound to say that many a man whose zeal and affection to God and this kingdom hath carried him forth in this cause, hath so spent his estate that, in the way the state and the Army are going, he shall not hold up his head, if when his estate is lost, and not worth forty shillings a year, a man shall not have any interest. And there are many other ways by which the estates men have (if that be the rule which God in his providence does use) to fall to decay.

A man, when he hath an estate, hath an interest in making laws, but when he hath none, he hath no power in it; so that a man cannot lose that which he hath for the maintenance of his family, but he must also lose that which God and nature hath given him! And therefore I do think, and am still of the same opinion, that every man born in England cannot, ought not, neither by the Law of God nor the Law of Nature, to be exempted from the choice of those who are to make laws for him to live under, and for him, for aught I know, to lose his life under. And therefore I think there can be no great stick in this.

Truly I think that there is not this day reigning in England a greater fruit or effect of tyranny than this very thing would produce. Truly I know nothing free but only the knight of the shire, nor do I know anything in a parliamentary way that is clear from the height and fulness of tyranny, but only that. As for this of corporations which you also mentioned, it is as contrary to freedom as may be. For, sir, what is it? The King he grants a patent under the Broad Seal of England to such a corporation to send burgesses, he grants to such a city to send burgesses. When a poor base corporation from the King's grant shall send two burgesses, when five hundred men of estate shall not send one, when those that are to make their laws are called by the King, or cannot act but by such a call, truly I think that the people of England have little freedom.

Ireton: I think there was nothing that I said to give you occasion to think that I did contend for this, that such a corporation as that should have the electing of a man to the Parliament. I think I agreed to this matter, that all should be equally distributed. But the question is, whether it should be distributed to all persons, or whether the same persons that are the electors now should be the electors still, and it be equally distributed amongst *them.* I do not see anybody else that makes this objection; and if nobody else be sensible of it I shall soon have done.

Only I shall a little crave your leave to represent the consequences of it, and clear myself from one thing that was misrepresented by the gentleman that sat next me. I think, if the gentleman remember himself, he cannot but remember that what I said was to this effect: that if I saw the hand of God leading so far as to destroy King, and destroy Lords, and destroy property, and leave no such thing at all amongst us, I should acquiesce in it; and so I did not care if no king, no lords, or no property should be, in comparison of the tender care that I have of the honor of God, and of the people of God, whose good name is so much concerned in this Army. This I did deliver so, and not absolutely.

All the main thing that I speak for, is because I would have an eye to property. I hope we do not come to contend for victory—but let every man consider with himself that he do not go that way to take away all property. For here is the case of the most fundamental part of the constitution of the kingdom, which if you take away, you take away all by that. Here men of this and this quality are determined to be the electors of men to the Parliament, and they are all those who have any permanent interest in the kingdom, and who, taken together, do comprehend the whole permanent, local interest of the kingdom.

I mean by permanent and local, that it is not able to be removed anywhere else. As for instance, he that hath a freehold, and that freehold cannot be removed out of the kingdom; and so there's a freeman of a corporation, a place which hath the privilege of a market and trading, which if you should allow to all places equally, I do not see how you could preserve any peace in the kingdom, and that is the reason why in the constitution we have but some few market towns.

Now those people that have freeholds and those that are the freemen of corporations, were looked upon by the former constitution to comprehend the permanent interest of the kingdom. For first, he that hath his livelihood by his trade, and by his freedom of trading in such a corporation, which he cannot exercise in another, he is tied to that place, for his livelihood depends upon it. And secondly, that man hath an interest, hath a permanent interest there, upon which he may live, and live a freeman without dependence. These things the constitution of this kingdom hath looked at.

Now I wish we may all consider of what right you will challenge that all the people should have right to elections. Is it by the right of nature? If you will hold forth that as your ground, then I think you must deny all property too, and this is my reason. For thus: by that same right of nature (whatever it be) that you pretend, by which you can say, one man hath an equal right with another to the choosing of him that shall govern him—by the same right of nature, he hath the same equal right in any goods he sees—meat, drink, clothes—to take and use them for his sustenance. He hath a freedom to the land, to take the ground, to exercise it, till it; he hath the same freedom to anything that any one doth account himself to have any propriety in.

Why now I say then, if you, against the most fundamental part of the civil constitution (which I have now declared), will plead the Law of Nature, that a man should (paramount to this, and contrary to this) have a power of choosing those men that shall determine what shall be law in this state, though he himself have no permanent interest in the state, but whatever interest he hath he may carry about with him—if this be allowed, because by the right of nature we are free, we are equal, one man must have as much voice as another, then show me what step or difference there is, why I may not by the same right take your property though not of necessity to sustain nature. It is for my better being, and the better settlement of the kingdom? Possibly not for it, neither: possibly I may not have so real a regard to the peace of the kingdom as that man who hath a permanent interest in it. He that is here today and gone tomorrow, I do not see that he hath such a permanent interest.

Since you cannot plead to it by anything but the Law of Nature, or for anything but for the end of better being, and since that better being is not certain, and what is more, destructive to another; upon these grounds, if you do, paramount to all constitutions, hold up this Law of Nature, I would fain have any man show me their bounds, where you will end, and why you should not take away all property.

Rainborough: I shall now be a little more free and open with you than I was before. I wish we were all true-hearted, and that we did all carry ourselves with integrity. If I did mistrust you I would not use such asseverations. I think it doth go on mistrust, and things are thought too readily matters of reflection, that were never intended. For my part, as I think, *you* forgot something that was in *my* speech, and you do not only yourselves believe that some men are inclining to anarchy, but you would make all men believe that. And, sir, to say because a man pleads that every man hath a voice by right of nature, that therefore it destroys by the same argument all property—this is to forget the Law of God. That there's a property, the Law of God says it; else why hath God made that law, *Thou shalt not steal?*

I am a poor man, therefore I must be oppressed: If I have no interest in the kingdom, I must suffer by all their laws be they right or wrong. Nay thus: a gentleman lives in a country and hath three or four lordships, as some men have (God knows how they got them); and when a Parliament is called he must be a Parliament-man; and it may be he sees some poor men, they live near this man, he can crush them—I have known an invasion to make sure he hath turned the poor men out of doors; and I would fain know whether the potency of rich men do not this, and so keep them under the greatest tyranny that was ever thought of in the world. And therefore I think that to that it is fully answered: God hath set down that thing as to propriety with this law of his, *Thou shalt not steal.* And for my part I am against any such thought, and, as for yourselves, I wish you would not make the world believe that we are for anarchy.

Cromwell: I know nothing but this, that they that are the most yielding have the greatest wisdom; but really, sir, this is not right as it should

be. No man says that you have a mind to anarchy, but that the consequence of this rule tends to anarchy, must end in anarchy, for where is there any bound or limit set if you take away this limit, that men that have no interest but the interest of breathing shall have no voice in elections? Therefore I am confident on't, we should not be so hot with one another.

Rainborough: I know that some particular men we debate with believe we are for anarchy. . . .

I do very well remember that the gentleman in the window said that, if it were so, there were no propriety to be had, because five parts of the nation, the poor people, are now excluded and would then come in. So one on the other side said that, if it were otherwise, then rich men only shall be chosen. Then, I say, the one part shall make hewers of wood and drawers of water of the other five, and so the greatest part of the nation be enslaved. Truly I think we are still where we were; and I do not hear any argument given but only that it is the present law of the kingdom. I say still, what shall become of those many men that have laid out themselves for the Parliament of England in this present war, that have ruined themselves by fighting, by hazarding all they had? They are Englishmen. They have now nothing to say for themselves. . . .

Ireton: I cannot consent so far. As I said before: when I see the hand of God destroying King, and Lords, and Commons too, or any foundation of human constitution, when I see God hath done it, I shall, I hope, comfortably acquiesce in it. But first, I cannot give my consent to it, because it is not good. And secondly, as I desire that this Army should have regard to engagements wherever they are lawful, so I would have them regard to this as well: that they should not bring that scandal upon the name of God and the Saints, that those that call themselves by that name, those whom God hath owned and appeared with—that we should represent ourselves to the world as men so far from being of that peaceable spirit which is suitable to the Gospel, as we should have bought peace of the world upon such terms —as we would not have peace in the world but upon such terms—as should destroy all property.

If the principle upon which you move this alteration, or the ground upon which you press that we should make the alteration, do destroy all kind of property or whatsoever a man hath by human constitution, I cannot consent to it. The Law of God doth not give me a property, nor the Law of Nature, but property is of human constitution. I have a property and this I shall enjoy. Constitution founds property. If either the thing itself that you press or the consequence of that you press do destroy property, though I shall acquiesce in having no property, yet I cannot give my heart or hand to it; because it is a thing evil in itself and scandalous to the world, and I desire this Army may be free from both.

Sexby: I see that though liberty were our end, there is a degeneration from it. We have engaged in this kingdom and ventured our lives, and it was all for this: to recover our birthrights and privileges as Englishmen; and by the arguments urged there is none. There are many thousands of us soldiers that have ventured our lives; we have had little propriety in the kingdom as to our estates, yet we have had a birthright. But it seems now, except a man hath a fixed estate, in this kingdom, he hath no right in this kingdom. I wonder we were so much deceived. If we had not a right to the kingdom, we were mere mercenary soldiers. There are many in my condition, that have as good a condition as I have; it may be little estate they have at present, and yet they have as much a birthright as those two who are their lawgivers, as any in this place.

I shall tell you in a word my resolution. I am resolved to give my birthright to none. Whatsoever may come in the way, and whatsoever may be thought, I will give it to none. If this thing be denied the poor, that with so much pressing after they have sought, it will be the greater scandal. There was one thing spoken to this effect: that if the poor and those in low condition were given their birthright it would be the destruction of this kingdom. I think this was but a distrust of Providence. I do think the poor and meaner of this kingdom—I speak as in relation to the condition of soldiers, in which we are—have been the means of the preservation of this kingdom. I say, in their stations, and really I think to their utmost possibility; and their lives had not been held dear for the purchasing the good of the kingdom. And now they demand the birthright for which they fought. Those that act to this end are as free from anarchy or confusion as those that oppose it, and they have the Law of God and the law of their conscience with them.

But truly I shall only sum up in this. I desire that we may not spend so much time upon these things. We must be plain. When men come to understand these things, they will not lose that which they have contended for. That which I shall beseech you is to come to a determination of this question. . . .

Ireton: I have declared that you will alter that constitution from a better to a worse, from a just thing to a thing that is less just in my apprehension; and I will not repeat the reasons of that, but refer to what I have declared before. To me, if there were nothing but this, that there is a constitution, and that constitution which is the very last constitution, which if you take away you leave nothing of constitution, and consequently nothing of right or property, it would be enough. I would not go to alter this, though a man could propound that which in some respects might be better, unless it could be demonstrated to me that this were unlawful, or that this were destructive. Truly, therefore, I say for my part, to go on a sudden to make such a limitation as that to inhabitants in general, is to make no limitation at all. If you do extend the latitude of the constitution so far that any man shall have a voice in election who has not that interest in this kingdom that is permanent and fixed, who hath not that interest upon which he may have his freedom in this kingdom without dependence, you will put it into the hands of men to choose, not of men desirous to preserve their liberty, but of men who will give it away.

I am confident, our discontent and dissatisfaction if ever they do well, they do in this. If there be anything at all that is a foundation of liberty it is this, that those who shall choose the lawmakers shall be men freed from dependence upon others. I have a thing put into my heart which I cannot but speak. I profess I am afraid that if we, from such apprehensions as these are of an imaginable right of nature opposite to constitution, if we will contend and hazard the breaking of peace upon this business of that enlargement, I think if we, from imaginations and conceits, will go about to hazard the peace of the kingdom, to alter the constitution in such a point, I am afraid we shall find the hand of God will follow it and we shall see that liberty which we so much talk of, and have so much contended for, shall be nothing at all by this our contending for it, by our putting it into the hands of those men that will give it away when they have it.

XIII

The Anatomy of Absolutism

L̶E métier de roi est grand, noble, et délicieux.

Louis XIV

CONTENTS

[297]

QUESTIONS FOR STUDY

Part I

1. What practical objections might be raised to Bossuet's theory of kingship? What theoretical objections?

2. How does Bossuet's theory of kingship compare with that of James I of England?

3. Evaluate the writings of St. Simon as source material for the reign of Louis XIV. What were the particular advantages possessed by the author? With what reservations must his work be read?

4. What sort of man was Louis XIV? How did he view his duties as king?

5. Why did Louis XIV surround himself with court ceremonial? Why did he build the palace at Versailles?

Part II

6. How did Louis XIV perform his duties as king?

7. What was the general structure of central and local government in absolutist France?

8. What were the strengths and weaknesses of the French royal administration and finance? In what sense were finance and administrative efficiency inextricably linked?

9. From an examination of Colbert's correspondence, what do you discover to have been the purpose of his administration?

10. Why is Colbert's memorandum of 1663 of peculiar value to the historian?

11. What was the role of religion in an absolute monarchy?

12. What was Colbert's attitude to the economic life of the nation? How does it compare with that of the English statesmen of the sixteenth century?

13. Why did the state found and support the Gobelins' tapestry factory?

14. What was Colbert's opinion of the French businessman? Does this opinion reflect the prevailing mercantilist theory of the day?

15. From a study of the location of the town of Gueret (marked with an ⊗ on the four maps on p. 310), ascertain the complications involved in the relationship of Gueret with Paris and the rest of France, and in the administration of Gueret by the central government.

16. After examining the documents in this problem, how efficient, how absolute, and how centralized do you consider the French monarchy to have been?

[298]

During the reign of Louis XIV (1643–1715) the Capetian monarchy reached the highest point in its seven hundred years' history. Louis' government was the culmination of that royal policy, inaugurated in the eleventh century, which had guided France in the direction of strong, centralized government under a quasi-divine monarch. To create this government had been no easy task. Since the days when Robert the Pious had worked miracles and touched for the "king's evil" destiny had put some fools and some madmen on the throne, and there had been many reversals in Capetian fortunes.

For the problems confronted by French kings in the Middle Ages were largely the same as those which had to be solved by ambitious monarchs in England and in the Empire. To exercise control within his kingdom the monarch had to reduce the powers and pretensions of the great feudal magnates—a reduction complicated, in the case of the French king, by the fact that his greatest vassal was also the King of England. This process may be regarded, in part, as a recovery of the royal powers which existed in pre-feudal days. But this recovery of power presented a new problem: the necessity of developing non-feudal organs of administration through which to exercise the newly-won authority. In France this development was reaching completion in the first half of the seventeenth century.

Another and very potent rival of royal authority was the Church. In France, as in the other European states, the monarchs had to meet the claims of universal authority asserted by the great medieval popes. By the period of the early Renaissance this rivalry had been successfully resolved by the rulers of France, but the Reformation presented them with new rivals, the Protestants. For almost half a century France was disrupted by Wars of Religion, and the peace effected after the accession of Henry IV in 1594 left the French Protestants with military and political privileges scarcely compatible with the ideal of a strong, centralized royal government.

But the fortunes of the French monarch were secured during the first half of the seventeenth century by the work of two great ministers of the crown, Cardinal Richelieu and Cardinal Mazarin. Their task was not easy. During the minorities of Louis XIII and Louis XIV the country relapsed into civil war, and powerful neighbors—particularly Spain—were ready to profit by French disunion. But when, at the death of Mazarin in 1661, Louis XIV assumed control, he possessed the most powerful French monarchy yet known in history.

This monarchy was at the same time the most powerful state in Europe. France had emerged predominant at the Congress at Westphalia; and the Peace of the Pyrenees (1659) had set the seal upon a predominance which extended beyond the sphere of international politics. For not only did the other Western peoples fear and admire French might. France set the style for Europe in government and war, literature and art, manners and taste. Other monarchs and petty princes imitated Louis XIV's court and copied his palace of Versailles. His army and his diplomatic service were models for rival states. French literature was *à la mode*, and the French tongue attained a position as the polite language of diplomacy. The hegemony of France was cultural as well as political.

In the realm which was thus the envy and terror of Europe, the King enjoyed unrivalled prestige and preëminence. Louis XIV looked upon himself, and was regarded by his subjects, as an absolute monarch who ruled by divine right. His person was the embodiment of the state and the epitome of French hegemony in every sphere.

The purpose of this Problem is to dissect the anatomy of absolutism by examining several important aspects of the monarchy of Louis XIV. To comprehend the true nature of divine right government, of which Louis' state was the most shining example, it is necessary to understand the part played by the personality of the ruler, the justification for absolute rule, the structure of the government, and the policies pursued by the monarch and his ministers. The documents which follow provide an insight into these questions.

Part I. THE GRAND MONARCH

A. THE THEORY OF MONARCHY

> Jacques Bossuet, Bishop of Meaux, was one of the most prominent churchmen in France. An accomplished preacher, he was no less renowned for his erudition, and in 1670 he was chosen to be the tutor of the only son of Louis XIV. For his pupil's instruction he wrote a tract entitled *Politics drawn from the Very Words of Holy Scripture*, selections from which follow.[1]

Bossuet on Kingship.

It appears from all this that the person of the king is sacred, and that to attack him in any way is sacrilege. God has the kings anointed by his prophets with the holy unction in like manner as he has bishops and altars anointed. But even without the external application in thus being anointed, they are by their very office the representatives of the divine majesty deputed by Providence for the execution of His purposes. . . .

There is something religious in the respect accorded to a prince. The service of God and the respect for kings are bound together. St. Peter unites these two duties when he says, "Fear God. Honor the king." . . .

But kings, although their power comes from on high, as has been said, should not regard themselves as masters of that power to use it at their pleasure. . . . They must employ it with fear and self-restraint, as a thing coming from God, and of which God will demand an account. . . .

Kings should tremble then as they use the power God has granted them; and let them think how horrible is the sacrilege if they use for evil a power which comes from God. We behold kings seated upon the throne of the Lord, bearing in their hand the sword which God himself has given them. What profanation, what arrogance, for the unjust king to sit on God's throne to render decrees contrary to his laws and to use the sword which God has put in his hand for deeds of violence and to slay his children! . . .

The royal power is absolute. With the aim of making this truth hateful and insufferable, many writers have tried to confound absolute government with arbitrary government. But no two things could be more unlike, as we shall show when we come to speak of justice.

The prince need render account of his acts to no one. "I counsel thee to keep the king's commandment, and that in regard of the oath of God.

Be not hasty to go out of his sight: stand not on an evil thing for he doeth whatsoever pleaseth him. Where the word of a king is, there is power: and who may say unto him, What doest thou? Whoso keepeth the commandment shall feel no evil thing." Without this absolute authority the king could neither do good nor repress evil. It is necessary that his power be such that no one can hope to escape him, and, finally, the only protection of individuals against the public authority should be their innocence. This conforms with the teaching of St. Paul: "Wilt thou then not be afraid of the power? Do that which is good."

I do not call majesty that pomp which surrounds kings or that exterior magnificence which dazzles the vulgar. That is but the reflection of majesty and not majesty itself. Majesty is the image of the grandeur of God in the prince.

God is infinite, God is all. The prince, as prince, is not regarded as a private person: he is a public personage, all the state is in him; the will of all the people is included in his. As all perfection and all strength are united in God, so all the power of individuals is united in the person of the prince. What grandeur that a single man should embody so much!

The power of God makes itself felt in a moment from one extremity of the earth to another. Royal power works at the same time throughout all the realm. It holds all the realm in position, as God holds the earth. Should God withdraw his hand, the earth would fall to pieces; should the king's authority cease in the realm, all would be in confusion.

Look at the prince in his cabinet. Thence go out the orders which cause the magistrates and the captains, the citizens and the soldiers, the provinces and the armies on land and on sea, to work in concert. He is the image of God, who, seated on his throne high in the heavens, makes all nature move. . . .

Finally, let us put together the things so great and so august which we have said about royal authority. Behold an immense people united in a single person; behold this holy power, paternal and absolute; behold the secret cause which governs the whole body of the state, contained in a single head: you see the image of God in the king, and you have the idea of royal majesty. God is holiness itself, goodness itself, and power itself. In these things lies the majesty of God. In the image of these things lies the majesty of the prince.

So great is this majesty that it cannot reside in the prince as in its source; it is borrowed from God, who gives it to him for the good of the people, for whom it is good to be checked by a superior force. Something of divinity itself is attached to princes and inspires fear in the people. The king should not forget this. "I have said,"—and it is God who speaks,—"I have said, Ye are

gods; and all of you are children of the Most High. But ye shall die like men, and fall like one of the princes." "I have said, Ye are gods"; that is to say, you have in your authority, and you bear on your forehead, a divine imprint. "You are the children of the Most High"; it is he who has established your power for the good of mankind. But, O gods of flesh and blood, gods of clay and dust, "ye shall die like men, and fall like princes." Grandeur separates men for a little time, but a common fall makes them all equal at the end.

O kings, exercise your power then boldly, for it is divine and salutary for human kind, but exercise it with humility. You are endowed with it from without. At bottom it leaves you feeble, it leaves you mortal, it leaves you sinners, and charges you before God with a very heavy account.

B. THE MONARCH

Louis de Ronvray, Duc de Saint-Simon (1675–1755), was an indifferent soldier and diplomat, but the prince of gossips. He was passionately interested in everything that went on at the French court, and, being an indefatigable writer, recorded most of his interests. A keen observer, though by no means free from prejudice, his description of Louis XIV is the most vivid which we have. The following passages are from his *Parallèle des Trois Premiers Rois Bourbons* written in 1746, and from his *Memoirs*.[2]

1. *A Portrait of the King.*

The king's great qualities shone more brilliantly by reason of an exterior so unique and incomparable as to lend infinite distinction to his slightest actions; the very figure of a hero, so impregnated with a natural but most imposing majesty that it appeared even in his most insignificant gestures and movements, without arrogance but with simple gravity; proportions such as a sculptor would choose to model; a perfect countenance and the grandest air and mien ever vouchsafed to man; all these advantages enhanced by a natural grace which enveloped all his actions with a singular charm which has never perhaps been equaled. He was as dignified and majestic in his dressing gown as when dressed in robes of state, or on horseback at the head of his troops.

He excelled in all sorts of exercise and liked to have every facility for it. No fatigue nor stress of weather made any impression on that heroic figure and bearing; drenched with rain or snow, pierced with cold, bathed in sweat or covered with dust, he was always the same. I have often observed with admiration that except in the most extreme and exceptional weather nothing prevented his spending considerable time out of doors every day.

A voice whose tones corresponded with the rest of his person; the ability to speak well and to listen with quick comprehension; much reserve of manner adjusted with exactness to the quality of

different persons; a courtesy always grave, always dignified, always distinguished, and suited to the age, rank, and sex of each individual, and, for the ladies, always an air of natural gallantry. So much for his exterior, which has never been equaled nor even approached.

In whatever did not concern what he believed to be his rightful authority and prerogative, he showed a natural kindness of heart and a sense of justice which made one regret the education, the flatteries, the artifice which resulted in preventing him from being his real self except on the rare occasions when he gave way to some natural impulse and showed that,—prerogative aside, which choked and stifled everything,—he loved truth, justice, order, reason,—that he loved even to let himself be vanquished. . . .

Louis XIV was made for a brilliant court. In the midst of other men, his figure, his courage, his grace, his beauty, his grand mien, even the tone of his voice and the majestic and natural charm of all his person, distinguished him till his death as the King Bee, and showed that if he had only been born a simple private gentleman, he would equally have excelled in fêtes, pleasures, and gallantry. . . .

He reigned, indeed, in little things; the great he could never reach: even in the former, too, he was often governed. The superior ability of his early ministers and his early generals soon wearied him. He liked nobody to be in any way superior to him. Thus he chose his ministers, not for their knowledge, but for their ignorance; not for their capacity, but for their want of it. He liked to form them, as he said; liked to teach them even the most trifling things. It was the same with his generals. He took credit to himself for instructing them; wished it to be thought that from his cabinet he commanded and directed all his armies.

Naturally fond of trifles, he unceasingly occupied himself with the most petty details of his troops, his household, his mansions; would even instruct his cooks, who received, like novices, lessons they had known by heart for years. This vanity, this unmeasured and unreasonable love of admiration, was his ruin. His ministers, his generals, his mistresses, his courtiers, soon perceived his weakness. They praised him with emulation and spoiled him. Praises, or to say truth, flattery, pleased him to such an extent, that the coarsest was well received, the vilest even better relished. It was the sole means by which you could approach him. . . .

It was his vanity, his desire for glory, that led him, soon after the death of the King of Spain, to make that event the pretext for war; in spite of the renunciations so recently made, so carefully stipulated, in the marriage contract. He marched into Flanders; his conquests there were rapid; the passage of the Rhine was admirable; the triple alliance of England, Sweden, and Holland only animated him. In the midst of winter he took Franche-Comté, by restoring which at the peace of Aix-la-Chapelle, he preserved his conquests in Flanders. All was flourishing then in the state. Riches everywhere. Colbert had placed the finances, the navy, commerce, manufactures, letters even, upon the highest point; and this age, like that of Augustus, produced in abundance illustrious men of all kinds,—even those illustrious only in pleasures. . . .

He was exceedingly jealous of the attention paid to him. Not only did he notice the presence of the most distinguished courtiers, but those of inferior degree also. He looked to the right and to the left, not only upon rising but upon going to bed, at his meals, in passing through his apartments, or his gardens of Versailles, where alone the courtiers were allowed to follow him; he saw and noticed everybody; not one escaped him, not even those who hoped to remain unnoticed. He marked well all absentees from the court, found out the reason of their absence, and never lost an opportunity of acting towards them as the occasion might seem to justify. With some of the courtiers (the most distinguished), it was a demerit not to make the court their ordinary abode; with others 'twas a fault to come but rarely; for those who never or scarcely ever came it was certain disgrace. When their names were in any way

mentioned, "I do not know them," the King would reply haughtily. Those who presented themselves but seldom were thus characterized: "They are people I never see"; these decrees were irrevocable. He could not bear people who liked Paris.

Louis XIV took great pains to be well informed of all that passed everywhere; in the public places, in the private houses, in society and familiar intercourse. His spies and tell-tales were infinite. He had them of all species; many who were ignorant that their information reached him; others who knew it; others who wrote to him direct, sending their letters through channels he indicated; and all these letters were seen by him alone, and always before everything else; others who sometimes spoke to him secretly in his cabinet, entering by the back stairs. These unknown means ruined an infinite number of people of all classes, who never could discover the cause; often ruined them very unjustly; for the King, once prejudiced, never altered his opinion, or so rarely, that nothing was more rare.

He had, too, another fault, very dangerous for others and often for himself, since it deprived him of good subjects. He had an excellent memory; in this way, that if he saw a man who, twenty years before, perhaps, had in some manner offended him, he did not forget the man, though he might forget the offense. This was enough, however, to exclude the person from all favor. The representations of a minister, of a general, of his confessor even, could not move the King. He would not yield.

The most cruel means by which the King was informed of what was passing—for many years before anybody knew it—was that of opening letters. The promptitude and dexterity with which they were opened passed understanding. He saw extracts from all the letters in which there were passages that the chiefs of the post-office, and then the minister who governed it, thought ought to go before him; entire letters, too, were sent to him, when their contents seemed to justify the sending. Thus the chiefs of the post, nay, the principal clerks were in a position to suppose what they pleased and against whom they pleased. A word of contempt against the King or the government, a joke, a detached phrase, was enough. It is incredible how many people, justly or unjustly, were more or less ruined, always without resource, without trial, and without knowing why. The secret was impenetrable; for nothing ever cost the King less than profound silence and dissimulation. . . .

2. *The King Arises.*[3]

At eight o'clock the chief *valet de chambre* on duty, who alone had slept in the royal chamber, and who had dressed himself, awoke the King.

The chief physician, the chief surgeon, and the nurse (as long as she lived) entered at the same time. . . . At quarter past the hour the grand chamberlain was called and all those who had what was called the *grandes entrées*. The chamberlain drew back the curtains which had been closed again, and presented the holy water from the vase, at the head of the bed. These gentlemen stayed but a moment, and that was the time to speak to the King, if anyone had anything to ask of him; in which case the rest stood aside. When, contrary to custom, nobody had aught to say, they were there but for a few moments. He who had opened the curtains and presented the holy water, presented also a prayerbook.

Then all passed into the cabinet of the council. A very short religious service being over, the King called, and they re-entered. The same officer gave him his dressing-gown; immediately after, other privileged courtiers entered, and then everybody, in time to find the King putting on his shoes and stockings, for he did almost everything himself and with address and grace. Every other day we saw him shave himself; and he had a little short wig in which he always appeared, even in bed. . . . No toilet table was near him; he had simply a mirror held before him.

As soon as he was dressed, he prayed to God, at the side of his bed, where all the clergy knelt, the cardinals without cushions, all the laity remaining standing; and the captain of the guards came to the balustrade during the prayer, after which the King passed into his cabinet. He found there a very numerous company, for it included everybody in any office. He gave orders to each for the day; thus within less than ten minutes it was known what he meant to do; and then all this crowd left directly. . . .

All the court meantime waited for the king in the gallery, the captain of the guard being alone in the chamber, seated at the door of the cabinet. . . . During this pause the King gave audiences, when he wished to accord any, and gave secret interviews to foreign ministers. They were called "secret" simply to distinguish them from the uncommon ones by the bedsides.

3. *The King Dines.*[4]

The dinner was always *au petit couvert,* that is, the King ate by himself in his chamber upon a square table in front of the middle window. It was more or less abundant, for he ordered in the morning whether it was to be "a little," or "very little" service. But even at this last, there were always many dishes, and three courses without counting the fruit. The dinner being ready, the principal courtiers entered; then all who were known; and the first gentlemen of the chamber on duty, informed the King.

I have seen, but very rarely, Monseigneur and his sons standing at their dinners, the King not offering them a seat. I have continually seen there the Princes of the blood and the cardinals. I have often seen there also Monsieur, either on arriving from St. Cloud to see the King, or arriving from the Council of Despatches (the only one he entered), give the King his napkin and remain standing. A little while afterwards, the King, seeing that he did not go away, asked him if he would not sit down; he bowed, and the King ordered a seat to be brought for him. A stool was put behind him. Some moments after the King said, "Nay then, sit down, my brother." Monsieur bowed and seated himself until the end of the dinner, when he presented the napkin.

4. *The King Retires.*[5]

At ten o'clock his supper was served. The captain of the guard announced this to him. . . . This supper was always on a grand scale, the royal household at table, and a large number of courtiers and ladies present, sitting or standing. . . .

After supper the King stood some moments, his back to the balustrade of the foot of his bed, encircled by all his court; then, with bows to the ladies, passed into his cabinet, where on arriving, he gave his orders. He passed a little less than an hour there, seated in an armchair. . . .

The King, wishing to retire, went and fed his dogs; then said good night, passed into his chamber, where he said his prayers, as in the morning, and undressed. He said good night with an inclination of the head, and while everybody was leaving the room stood at the corner of the mantelpiece, where he gave the order to the colonel of the guards alone. Then commenced what was called the *petit coucher*, at which only specially privileged persons remained. They did not leave until he got into bed.

C. THE SETTING OF MONARCHY: VERSAILLES

The setting of the French monarchy was the great palace at Versailles, situated twelve miles south of Paris. Louis XIII had built a small hunting lodge there, but it was his son who was responsible for the palace where, after 1682, he made his residence and from which the government of France was directed. The construction of the palace took forty-seven years, and cost nearly sixty-six million livres.

1. *Why Louis Built Versailles.* In the following selection from his *Memoirs,* Saint Simon gives his explanation for the building of Versailles.[6]

He early showed a disinclination for Paris. The troubles that had taken place there during the minority made him regard the place as dangerous; he wished, too, to render himself venerable by hiding himself from the eyes of the multitude: all these considerations fixed in him at St. Germains soon after the death of the Queen, his mother. It was to that place he began to attract the world by fêtes and gallantries, and by making it felt that he wished to be often seen.

His love for Madame de la Vallière, which was at first kept secret, occasioned frequent excursions to Versailles, then a little card castle, which had been built by Louis XIII—annoyed, and his suite still more so, at being frequently obliged to sleep in a wretched inn there, after he had been out hunting in the forest of Saint Leger. That monarch rarely slept at Versailles more than one night, and then from necessity; the King, his son, slept there, so that he might be more in private with his mistress, pleasures unknown to the hero and just man, worthy son of Saint Louis, who built the little château.

These excursions of Louis XIV by degrees gave birth to those immense buildings he erected at Versailles; and their convenience for a numerous court, so different from the apartments at St. Germains, led him to take up his abode there entirely shortly after the death of the Queen. He built an infinite number of apartments, which were asked for by those who wished to pay their court to him; whereas at St. Germains nearly everybody was obliged to lodge in the town, and the few who found accommodations at the château were strangely inconvenienced.

The frequent fêtes, the private promenades at Versailles, the journeys, were means on which the King seized in order to distinguish or mortify the courtiers, and thus render them more assiduous in pleasing him. He felt that of real favors he had not enough to bestow; in order to keep up the spirit of devotion, he therefore unceasingly invented all sorts of ideal ones, little preferences and petty distinctions, which answered his purpose as well.

2. *The Wonders of Versailles.* In 1684 an English publisher brought out a translation of a little French book published in Paris three years earlier. Its title was *An Historical Explanation of What there is most remarkable in that Wonder of the World, The French King's Royal House at Versailles.* A few selections follow.[7]

Instructions to the Reader. For a more clear understanding of the explication of the subjects of painting which compose this work, you must know that as the sun makes the body of the King's device, and that Apollo and the sun are the same thing, this deity is represented in many places at Versailles. In the garden near the canal, at the basin of Apollo, it's the sun when he riseth, and seems to issue from the sea. At the grottos of Apollo, which are opposite to it, is the same sun when he is setting in the bosom of Thetis, where he is washed and refreshed by the nymphs, from the labors which he has undergone during his course. In the apartments of the house you will see him accompanied with all that has affinity with him. On the front of the house, which looks into the garden, he divides the year with Diana his sister, where they communicate their mild influences to the earth, that it may produce all sorts of plants.

The subjects of painting which complete the ornament of the ceiling pieces are heroes and illustrious men, taken from history and from fable, who have merited the titles of generous and great men, of fathers of the people, of liberal, just, august, and victorious persons, who have possessed all the virtues which have been seen to appear with admiration in the person of our great monarch, since the happy course of his reign; so that all that is seen of remarkable [*sic*] in the house and in the garden, has always a relation to the great actions of his majesty. It's for this reason that I have been obliged to make those acquainted with it that do not know it. . . .

Italy must now yield to France the prize and garland which it has borne away hitherto from all the nations of the earth in what regards the excellency of architecture, the beauty of carving, the magnificence of painting, the art of gardening, the structure of fountains, and the invention of aqueducts.

Versailles alone suffices to secure forever to France the glory it has at present, in surpassing all other kingdoms in the science of buildings; and it is beholding for this high esteem to the grandeur and magnificence of Louis the Great, its invincible monarch.

This magnanimous prince has cherished arts even to so high a point, and has known so well to cultivate them among the noise of arms, that peace, which is the mother of both sciences and arts, to testify its gratitude, has built him the most magnificent palace of the world; to the end it might there receive him, as it were in its bosom, when he returns from his enemies loaded with laurels and trophies.

It's into this royal and charming house that you are invited to come, you people of the earth, who are curious and learned; you shall see there the ancient and the new Rome; you shall see there all that the world has ever had of beautiful and surprising [sic]; admire there the skill, the knowledge, the design, and the curiousness of the workmen; admire there the grandeur, the sumptuousness, the magnificence and the liberality of the prince; and own that Versailles eclipses all the enchanted palaces of history and of fable.

When you are at Versailles, and are come to the end of the great walk of elms, it cannot be but the beautiful aspect of the house will charm your spirit, and seize all your senses, and convert the force of them all into the sight and imagination. Pause you a little at the first iron grate of the forecourt, to see there the two stone pieces, the one on the right of the house, representing the victories of France over Spain, denoted by the lion, and the other on the left, the victories over Germany, denoted by the eagle. The Sieur Girardon made the figure on the right, and the Sieur de Mercy that on the left.

From this grate you pass as far as the gilded grate, where you will see at the entrance a sun of gold on a trophy of arms, with two pieces of stone figures on the two sides. On the right it's Abundance, and on the left Peace, who burns with a torch a trophy of arms, and holds in her left hand a caduceum, which is the symbol of prudence, eloquence, and command.

When you have passed this gilded grate, turn on the left hand; you will see at the end of the right wing of the house, on six pillars, six deities, three of the earth, and three of the water. The deities of the earth are Ceres, who carries ears of corn; Flora who carries flowers; and Pomona fruits. The deities of the water are Thetis and Galatea, with Neptune in the midst. When you have seen these six statues, look afterward on your right, at the end of the left wing of the house, you will see on six pillars six other deities, three of the air, and three of the fire. The deities of the air are Iris, who represents the rainbow with her veil, Juno with a peacock by her side, and Zephirus. The deities of the fire are Vulcan in the midst of Cyclopes, who are Brontes and Steropes.

When these twelve pagan deities were set up, who represent the four elements, regard was had to that place where are all the offices of his majesty belonging to the mouth; the four elements being those who by their mixture compose all the food proper for nourishment; the earth gives flowers, fruits, and animals; the water gives fish; the air furnishes birds; and the good fire acts the good cook.

Advance yourself now as far as the basin, which is in the middle of the little court of the house and look on the pediment of the front of the house, you will see two figures. The one, which is on the right, represents Hercules, or France, who reposes after having overcome the Hydra, that is to say, the great number of enemies which it has defeated in these last wars. The Hydra is denoted there by the dragon: Spain by the lion; and all the other forces by the bull, which signifies also the River Rhine. Hercules overcame the river Achelous under the figure of a bull, from which he took away a horn, whence issued abundance, and our French Hercules having overcome the forces of the Rhine, and the Rhine itself, there is come of it peace and abundance. This figure was made by the Sieur Girardon. And the other figure which is on the left, represents Mars or France victorious over Spain and Germany. This figure was made by the Sieur de Mercy.

Under these two figures, on the balustrade of the little house, you will see eighteen figures of stone, each of eight foot in height, representing in general the virtues of the King. . . .

When you have considered all these figures, if you will enter into the apartment of the baths, you must pass through the door which is under the last statue you saw. This apartment is dedicated to Magnificence, and makes one of the seven wonders of Versailles. The first piece of the low apartment of the baths is remarkable for the picture in the midst of the ceiling, where there is represented a Flora. It will be changed, and in its place there will be put a Mars, reposing himself from the toils of war, from whom Venus takes the helmet from off the head, showing him peace. . . .

The sixth piece of the apartment of the baths is also considerable for the picture in the midst of the ceiling which represents an Apollo driving away tempests and storms by shooting darts. By the darts of Apollo are understood the rays of the sun, which dissipate clouds and mists; this alludes to the King, who by his prudence, justice, and power exterminates from his kingdom the errors, crimes, and seditions which malice and ignorance might there form. The picture for the chimneypiece is a Daphne, who being pursued by Apollo, is changed into a laurel, after having triumphed over this god. . . . When you have seen this last apartment of the baths, you must return back as you came, to make an end of admiring the magnificence of these places, and ascend afterwards into the King's apartments, which are over the baths, and which make the second wonder of Versailles. . . .

The third wonder of Versailles is the great marble staircase, which eclipses all that Greece and Italy have ever had of wonderful. For besides the gold and the azure which shine there from all parts, the work surpasses in it the matter. M. le Brun, whom we may call the most excellent painter of the age, painted the ceiling piece. We see there among other things, the nations of the four parts of the world, who admire the beauty of Versailles, and the heroic exploits of our great monarch, and on their part, they draw on themselves the admiration of all that are curious and learned, so beautiful and natural they are. . . .

The fifth wonder of Versailles is the gallery of M. le Brun, first painter to the King, and head of the Royal Academy of Painters. This gallery is not yet finished; it will be in a little time. M. le Brun has there surpassed himself in the design and project which he has made in it; there is not any figure which is not a masterpiece of art. This admirable man, whom we ought to place in the rank of Raphaels and Michael Angelos, takes a grand care to represent there the high exploits and heroic actions of our great monarch. . . .

D.   THE MONARCH AT WORK

1. *Louis Takes up the Reins of Government.* On March 9th, 1661, Cardinal Mazarin died. Louis summoned a meeting of his council for the next day. This meeting is described by the Comte de Brienne in the selections from his *Memoirs* which follow.[8]

The next day [March 10th, 1661] at precisely seven o'clock in the morning, I entered the King's apartments, according to his orders. I told His Majesty that the chancellor and my colleagues had arrived. "One moment," he said, searching in a casket. He took from it a paper, and putting on it the provisions for the government of Brittany which I had presented him, he said, "After the council, go to see my mother the Queen and tell her that you have delivered these provisions." He pointed them out with his finger. "Tell the council to come in," he said.

I went out, and, approaching the chancellor, I told him that he could enter. "And you also, messieurs," I added, "the King demands your presence." . . . We were then eight in all, namely: the Chancellor, the Superintendant, my father, M. de Lionne, M. de la Vrillière, M. Duplesus-Guenegand, M. Le Tellier and myself. The king uncovered and then put his hat back on, and standing before his chair, addressed the chancellor.

"Monsieur," he said, "I have had you meet with my ministers and my Secretaries of State in order to inform you that until now I have been willing to let my affairs be managed by the late Cardinal; it is now time that I manage them myself. You will assist me with your advice when I ask you for it. Beyond the routine of the chancery which I do not intend to change, I ask and order you, my lord Chancellor, to seal nothing except by my orders, or without having consulted me, unless a Secretary of State has brought the documents to be sealed from me." . . . Finally the King turned to us and said, "And you, my Secretaries of State, I order you to sign nothing, not even a letter of protection nor a passport, without my command; to render your accounts to me personally each day; and to show favor to no one in your monthly reports." . . .

"The scene has changed. In the government of my realm, in the regulation of my finances, and in my dealings with foreign powers, I shall have other principles than those of the late Cardinal. You know my wishes, gentlemen; it now remains for you to execute them." Nothing more was said, and the council adjourned.

2. *King, Councils, and Ministers.* In the central administration, France was in a transitional stage between the older type of hereditary, feudal administrative system and a more modern type based on function. The historic advisers of the crown, Ministers of State, who had no special departmental functions still existed, though their number was limited to seven or eight. Of increasing importance were the Secretaries of State (War, Foreign Affairs, etc.), who represented the new functional administration though, paradoxically enough, each still administered a certain region of France as well. The Secretaries met in councils. The Council of State was the center of the whole government. It discussed foreign affairs and high policy. The Council of Despatches corresponded to a Department of the Interior. A third council, the Council of Finance, concerned itself with taxation and revenue. There were other councils, all of which met with the King as chairman. In the following selections Saint-Simon describes Louis's working week and his relations with his ministers.[9]

On Sunday and often on Monday, there was a Council of State; on Tuesday a Finance Council; on Wednesday Council of State; on Saturday Finance Council. Rarely were two held in one day or any on Thursday or Friday. Once or twice a month there was a Council of Despatches on Monday morning; but the order that the Secretaries of State took every morning between the King's rising and his mass, much abridged this kind of business. All the ministers were seated according to rank, except at the council of despatches, where all stood except the sons of France, the Chancellor, and the Duc de Beauvilliers.

Thursday morning was almost always blank.

It was the day for audiences that the King wished to give—often unknown to any—back stair audiences. It was also the grand day taken advantage of by the bastards, the valets, etc., because the King had nothing to do. On Friday after the mass the King was with his confessor, and the length of their audiences was limited by nothing, and might last until dinner. At Fontainebleau on the mornings when there was no council, the King usually passed from mass to Madame de Maintenon's and so at Trianon and Marly. It was the time of their *tête-à-tête* without interruption. Often on the days when there was no council the dinner hour was advanced, more or less for the chase or the promenade. The ordinary hour was one o'clock; if the council still lasted, then the dinner waited and nothing was said to the King. . . .

He [Louis XIV] followed two maxims all his life after he became master on the death of Cardinal Mazarin. One, which was very sound, was to have no more first minister, and never to admit to his Council any Cardinal, Bishop, or any ecclesiastic, who, in his opinion (which is quite true), might want to make themselves masters of all, if they were Cardinals; if they were not Cardinals, they would sacrifice anything in the effort so.

The other maxim was far from good: this was to include in the Councils only men of mediocre strength and ability; anything higher overshadowed him; most of all he feared nobles, who he thought would try to impose upon him, take too much, or improve their station. Also, there was awkwardness involved in dismissing them, thereby making dissatisfied a host of relatives. To find them back on their feet by their own efforts after having been dismissed was another strong reason against having them in the first place. He wanted people who owed everything to their posts as secretary of state, or controllers of finance, or ministers; whom he could treat as he willed and fire when and how he wanted; who, being nothing in themselves, would fall back into the obscurity whence he had pulled them. Since they

would realize this, they would bend every effort to serve him well and to please him. He so persevered in this design that from his accession to power to his death, in fifty years he only included one person of gentle birth in his Council. . . .

These wise heads [the ministers] had already sized up the King: little common sense, an almost unbelievable ignorance; a scorn for everybody and everything; a thirst for grandeur, power, and glory, which went so far as to brook no rival; a fear of being ruled amounting to a boasting that he was not ruled; a jealous desire to do everything and run everything; and all the confidence which an intelligent court, filled with bright men and women, could give a person lacking in common sense and knowledge. His contact with this court, while Mazarin was in power, only had a superficial effect on him. His ministers did not hesitate to capitalize on this character. They infatuated him with the idea of his greatness and power in order to exercise this power themselves, as well as to monopolize it. They used this means to bring all other power under them, and to raise themselves up in comparison with the real nobles by persuading the King that all authority besides their own was a usurpation of his power, which they were only administering.

In order to keep him from mistrusting the government, and at the same time to keep control entirely to themselves, they overwhelmed him with little details, especially since he revelled in petty things. He went after these last with avidity and was able to persuade himself that he alone ruled and did everything himself. Thus the important, big affairs, as well as the more important details, remained in their hands, this fact being concealed by the other details with which they amused him. But even with these precautions they did not feel too sure. His kindness and essential sense of fairness disturbed them and also the access to the King possessed by the most important or the favorite nobles meant that he might be enlightened, thus foiling them. They managed therefore to persuade the King that this accessibility was contrary to his greatness. . . .

Part II.   THE ADMINISTRATION OF THE MONARCHY

The first part of the problem was concerned mainly with the theory and setting of absolute monarchy. The documents in this part seek to demonstrate how the absolute monarchy actually operated. Since this is an extremely broad subject, only certain aspects have been selected, namely, the working of the government in central and in local administration, and the relationships of the government with religion and the economy.

A.   THE WEB OF GOVERNMENT

1. *The Establishment of the Intendants.* Beneath these councils at the center, Richelieu

and Louis XIV pursued the same policy of subordinating provincial and local government that had motivated their predecessors. The *Intendants,* constituted by Richelieu, were the new instrument for the realization of this policy. In his *Political Testament* (1642) the Cardinal described them as follows: [10]

Although it was desirable that the officials already established locally to provide justice for all perform their functions so well that no recourse need be made to any extraordinary commission to keep them at their job: nevertheless this is so much to hope for that I daresay that, to keep this great state in the degree of discipline and control essential for its welfare, one could hardly do better than to send from time to time into the provinces courts composed of carefully chosen counsellors of state and *Maîtres des Requêtes* [old-established royal officials who had been employed since the mid-sixteenth century on provincial trips of inspection].

Since it is impossible to send such groups at the same time into all the provinces . . . I think it would be very useful to send often into the provinces these carefully chosen *Conseillers d'État* or *Maîtres des Requêtes,* not only to function as *Intendants de Justice* in the capital towns (a step which will be of more help to their vanity than to their usefulness for the public) but also to go into all corners of the provinces to inquire after the conduct of the judicial and financial officials; to see if the taxes raised correspond with the *ordonnances,* and if the tax receivers are guilty of annoying the people with any injustice; to discover how the nobility conducts itself and to stop all disorder and, especially, all violence on the part of the rich or powerful who may be mistreating the weak or poor subjects of the King.

2. *Local Government, Colbert's Program, 1663.* In 1661 the young King appointed Jean-Baptiste Colbert as intendant, or chief financial officer of the crown. Colbert, who held this and many other economic and financial posts until his death in 1683, was of middle-class origin like most of Louis' counsellors. His great passion was administration, in all its multifarious detail, as the way to the greater efficiency of the government and, ultimately, to the increased prosperity of France. The document which follows contains Colbert's instructions, in 1663 shortly after his taking office, to the itinerant justices who are about to depart into the provinces to survey the state of the realm. From it the student can reconstruct the administrative organization and, what is more important, Colbert's sober appraisal of its performance.[11]

The King wishing to be clearly informed concerning the state of the provinces of his realm,

His Majesty has ordered that this memorandum be sent to the *maîtres des requêtes* [itinerant justices] so that they may set themselves, each within the confines of his own district, to ascertain carefully and exactly the following information.

Maps. It is necessary that the itinerant justices investigate the maps which have been made of each province or generality, verifying with care those which are good, and, in the case of those which are not exactly done, or which are not full enough, that they find some capable and intelligent person to redraw them. If they can find no person capable of this work they should make full reports, which His Majesty will put in the hands of M. Sanson, his mapmaker. Furthermore in these reports the said itinerant justices should take care that the distinction between the four types of administrative divisions of the country—ecclesiastical, military, judicial and financial—are clearly made, not only in general, but in detail and with the subdivisions of each indicated, so that [His Majesty] may know:

For Ecclesiastical Government: The dioceses, distinguished one from another; in each diocese, the archdeaconries and arch presbyteries; the names of all the parishes in each division, so that the total number in the dioceses will be revealed; the abbeys and other benefices, with a distinction between those which are under the authority of the bishops and those which are exempt; and in the case of those having jurisdiction over extended areas or over parishes that they be mentioned as well.

For Military Government: The lines of division between the different military governments be distinctly made; that all the parishes which are dependent on each government be clearly marked, and, in the case of governments overlapping, that this be mentioned.

For Justice: It is necessary to indicate the divisions between the territories of each *parlement,* and in the case where there are several (which is rare) it is necessary to make a distinction; then the distinction between the *bailliages,* the *presidencies* and the *royal justices* [old administrative divisions of the country].

For Finance: To distinguish between the *généralités,* the *élections,* and the *greniers à sel* [territorial divisions, each established for the collection of taxes]; and to take care above all in all the four types of governmental divisions to know the correct names of the cities, towns, and parishes, of which each of these general and particular divisions is composed.

While the itinerant justices will strive to know all these [administrative] divisions His Majesty desires that they make correct reports concerning

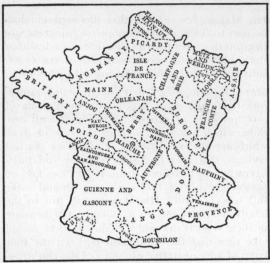

I. THE GOVERNMENTS

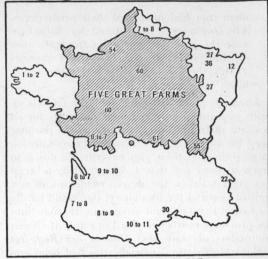

II. CUSTOMS AND SALT TAX

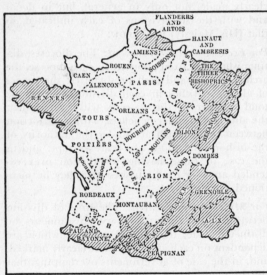

III. GENERALITES OR INTENDANCIES

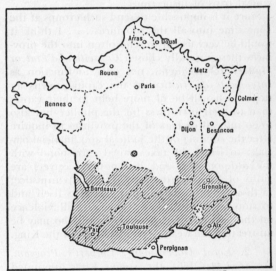

IV. PARLEMENTS AND LEGAL SYSTEMS

Map I shows the ancient administrative divisions for military purposes, the *gouvernements*. These units represented survivals of the older local administrative divisions of the *prévots*, *baíllis*, and *sénéchaux*. Map II shows the divisions of France for the purpose of taxation and customs. By the tariff of 1664 Colbert had begun the elimination of internal customs duties; the boundaries between his new free trade area (the Five Great Tax Farms) and the rest of France are indicated on the map. The numbers scattered over Map II represent the relative prices paid for the same amount of salt in various parts of France. This household necessity was an historic government monopoly. On Map III are shown the newer administrative division of the *generalité* or *intendancy*. Originally fiscal in purpose, these divisions had become the real center of local administration by 1700. Their character was hardly uniform, for some of them (the *pays d'état* with the diagonal marks on Map III) were provinces more recently incorporated into the monarchy and retained their local estates (*états*). In the rest of France (the *pays d'election*) there were no estates to interfere between the royal officials and their job. Map IV shows the major judicial divisions, between customary (feudal) and written (Roman) law (the region of Roman law is marked with diagonal lines on Map IV) and between the jurisdiction of the *parlements* of Paris and the various provincial *parlements* (which bear the name of capital city where they met).

[310]

all those things about which he wishes to be informed, namely:

Ecclesiastic: In regard to the Church, the names and numbers of dioceses; the cities, towns, villages, and parishes which are under their ecclesiastical jurisdiction, their temporal government and the towns and parishes of which this government is composed; particularly, if the bishop is temporal lord of the cathedral city; the name, age, estate, and disposition of the bishop; if he comes from that part of the country or not; if he makes his residence there; how he performs his episcopal visitations; what credit he has in his diocese, and what effect he might have in difficult times; what reputation he enjoys among his flock, if he confers the benefice of his chapter; if he is engaged in any lawsuit; the amount of his revenues; the names and the values of the benefices which he confers.

Besides that which concerns the bishops and all episcopal matters it is necessary to report the names and the numbers of all religious houses, secular and regular, which are in the province. . . . Whether before the reform [of the religious houses] [these houses] contained gentlemen of good family or not; whether there are among them any reformed monks; if formerly it were necessary to be of gentle birth to enter these abbeys, and whether one furnished proof of nobility or not; and what was the origin of the requirement. . . .

After having mentioned all endowed monasteries divided into their different orders, beginning with the Benedictine, it is necessary to do the same thing with respect to the endowed convents and after that with respect to the mendicant and non-endowed religious houses for men and women, so that by this complete explanation which His Majesty wishes he can know in truth and in general the revenue which his vessals and his subjects enjoy; the conduct of the principals who are charged with taking care of the safety of others and generally all that which concerns the ecclesiastical order, which is the first order of his kingdom.

Military Government: Concerning the military government, which concerns the nobility, which is the second order of his kingdom, although His Majesty knows all the talents of the governors and lieutenant-generals of his provinces he wishes nevertheless in order to make these reports complete that the itinerant justices begin their inquiry concerning the nobility and the name of the said governor general, his house and relationships in the province, whether they actually are in residence there; their good and bad conduct; if they are accused of taking money or of vexing the people in any other way; if these accusations

are probable; if the people complain of them; what credit they have among the nobility and the lower classes. And since the principal and most important application that His Majesty wishes the governors of provinces to do is to insist upon justice and prevent the suppression of the weak and the violence of the strong, His Majesty wishes to be particularly informed of the past conduct of these governors in order to judge what he should do in the future. In case that some violent outbreak happened in some province, His Majesty wishes to be informed in detail along with knowledge of how the governor conducted himself.

It is necessary to be informed of the same things with respect to the lieutenant-generals. After having examined that which concerns the governors and lieutenant-generals His Majesty wishes to be particularly informed of all that which concerns the nobility, namely the principal houses in each province, their relationships, their possessions, and the extent of their lands and lordships, their way of life and good conduct; if they commit violence on the inhabitants of their lands and in case that there has been committed any considerable thing which has not been punished His Majesty would be very glad to know the details; if they favor or hinder the process of royal justice in the *bailliages* and *presidencies;* their credit in the country both among the other gentlemen and among the common people. As far as the lesser nobility are concerned, it is well to know the number and names of the most accredited. Whether in general there are many of them who have been to the war or not; whether they cultivate the lands themselves or whether they rent them out to farmers, since one of the best evidences of their disposition is whether they go to war or live in their houses.

Concerning Justice: As far as that which concerns justice, in case there is a *parlement* or some other sovereign court in the province, it will be necessary that the itinerant justices examine carefully in general and in particular those who compose them. In general, it is necessary to inquire into their conduct during the minority of His Majesty, by what principles they had been regulated and how the leaders, whether they conducted themselves badly or well, acted. If the conduct was then bad [it is necessary] to know if the influence which might have since changed their attitudes are strong enough to keep them loyal and active in any future trouble or whether it is to be feared that they will fall again into the same evil ways.

And since it is assuredly the most important matter which there is to examine in the province, it will be good and even very necessary to know in detail the interests of the principal officers of these judicial bodies and particularly if those who led in the recent unpleasantness [the Fronde] are still living. . . . It is necessary first of all to be informed in detail of the kind of justice which that judicial body dispenses to the subjects of the King; if there is corruption or not; the cases and persons who are under suspicion. If the court has been guilty of any manifest injustice, which created any stir in the province or which resulted in the oppression of the weak in favor of any friend, relative, or any other vicious condition, His Majesty desires to be informed as well concerning the length of trials and any excessive judges' fees, not only in the superior courts but also in the lower courts, for it is necessary to know in detail concerning these two matters which can be such a burden to His Majesty's subjects.

Since these great judicial bodies have been established by Kings in order to administrate royal justice and since their principal object ought always to be to employ the authority vested in them in order to protect the weak against the strong, it is necessary to be informed if, in all cases of violence such as murder, assassination, or evil treatments committed by the gentlemen or the principal people of the province, they have maintained firmly the same authority and if they proceed without fear to instigate suit against and do strict justice to the guilty as they are supposed to do.

His Majesty, having often received complaints that the officers of the sovereign courts in diverse places sometimes make forced sales to themselves of the lands which are to provide their stipends. He will be very well pleased to be particularly informed of these cases or of anyone who practices this. It will be equally necessary to expose in the report all the resources in lands possessed by each one of the officers of the court. There remain the *gens du roi* [royal prosecutors], concerning whom it is very necessary to know the intentions and the competency, above all if they have enough strength to make applications and the necessary pursuits to uphold justice with vigor and severity, being absolutely necessary to have people in these positions who will not let themselves be swayed by any consideration of personal gain and still less of influence.

Finances: Concerning that which concerns finances in the provinces where there are *cours des aides* [courts having final jurisdiction over tax cases] it will be good to know the names of the officers, their merits and the relationships which they have in the provinces, particularly the first president, afterwards the other presidents, the principals of the court; what reputation they have in the province and their manner of dispensing justice; if there is any manifest corruption among them, if anyone has made any uproar one should be informed in detail. If the farmers and tax receivers are satisfied with the courts' firmness in sustaining them; if the people complain of any vexation on their part [the members of the *Cour des aides*] and complain that they do not keep the interests of the two parties to a case separate. Moreover, it is necessary to examine carefully the vexations which the people can suffer, whether by delays in law suits or by excessive legal fees. And for all these evils [it is necessary] to seek out convenient remedies and those which are as easy as possible.

Since one of the greatest surcharges suffered by the tax payer results from the creation of false nobles in the province who have been created partly by letters from the King and partly by simple decrees of the *cour des aides,* it is most important and necessary to discover convenient remedies for both of these evils. In regard to nobles created by letters of the King, His Majesty will consider the remedies which he can bring forward on the basis of the report which will be made to him concerning the number in each province and concerning the prejudice which the other subjects suffer. But in respect to the nobles made by decrees of the *cours des aides,* it is not only necessary to suppress them but also to find means to discover the root of this disorder so that it will be always suppressed in the future. . . .

Revenues of the King. It remains to examine the revenues of the King and that which concerns them. They consist in the crown lands which are all alienated and which in consequence produce no revenue; the tax-farms of the import and export duties, *aides* [excise taxes], *gabelles* [salt taxes], diverse other rights and tax-farms, and in *tailles* [property taxes]. Concerning these five kinds of revenue it is necessary to discover carefully how much His Majesty collects annually from each province. In respect to the import and export duties, one can easily know how many offices there are established in each and how much each office produces annually. In respect to the *aides,* how many are farmed out, either by the general farm of the whole province or by the particular farm in each district. In respect to the *gabelles,* it should be easy to learn whether the sale of salt has to be forced or whether it is voluntarily purchased. In respect to the *tailles,* the same.

After having discovered the value of all these different kinds of revenue and by this means all that which the king collects annually in the provinces, it will be necessary to examine in detail all the difficulties encountered in collecting and gathering them. Whether they cause any lessening of the revenues or are prejudicial to the people. Concerning import and export duties which are regulated by tariff schedules, it is nevertheless very necessary to hear the complaints and to inform oneself exactly if they are well founded; for better understanding it will be good to communicate their complaints to the directors and principals of the tax farms who are always in the province.

It will be very necessary on this point to make a particular study and to examine in detail the basis of the merchant's complaints and the answers of the tax farmers because the former were accustomed to make great complaints and to search out all imaginable means to defraud the rights of the farms and the latter not only seek to defend themselves but even to plague unnecessarily the merchants on occasion; and since that farm concerns commerce to the establishment of which up and down his kingdom His Majesty gives his care in all matters, it is necessary that the justices examine carefully all that which has to do with the subject in the province for the satisfaction of His Majesty and for the good and advancement of his people.

Concerning the *aides,* there is a general rule to observe on all kinds of taxes which are levied on the people, from which results assuredly either their surcharge or their relief, which consists in knowing well all those who are subject to them and if each pays his part according to his resources; since it is certain that by the inequality of charges, that is to say when the most powerful or the richest (because of the estate of which they are members) lighten or relieve themselves, the poor or the feeble find themselves overcharged; and that inequality causes in the provinces poverty, misery, and difficulty in the recovery of what is due the King, which increases the annoyance of the receivers or collectors of receipts, the sergeants, and generally all sorts of evils.

So that the collectors in the provinces ought always to have that fundamental maxim and that certain rule in their heads from which they should never depart [it is necessary] to understand the true resources of all those who are liable for the payment of these *aides, tailles, gabelles,* not only in general, that is to say, for the parishes and towns, but also for the principal inhabitants thereof, and to prevent all the powerful people of all classes in the provinces from imposing either on the community or on separate individuals in it. . . .

Aides. In regard to the *aides,* it is necessary to point out those lords [*seigneurs*] who have estab-lished on their lands the right of *banvin* [liquor license and wine tax] the greatest part of them without valid title. This results in considerable detriment to the farming of the *aides,* and it is necessary to have very exact information on this account in order to present the appropriate remedy in the official report to the justices.

It is well to observe, on this tax, that in many cases, not content with evading payment for these rights, some of the more powerful lords force the tax-farmers, by various means, to give up to them at very low costs the tax-farm for the cities and communities, whether they belong to them or whether they are in their neighborhood, at great profit.

Gabelles. Concerning the *gabelles,* as it is with the exception of those previously mentioned the most important tax-farm of the realm, there are a number of important things to observe.

In those provinces where the purchase of salt is voluntary, it is necessary to find out and to know the exact price, according to the distance from the sea and from rivers.

Moreover, it is necessary to know all the revenue rights of each customs officer, in excess of the base price, so that the cost to the people of each measure of salt may be reckoned exactly; in addition, it is necessary to determine the fashion in which the officials of each district [of the *gabelle*] render justice to the people and particularly, to find out the extent of the illicit salt-trade in each province, which is of so great consequence to the returns from this tax. . . .

Concerning the provincial taxes, it is necessary to determine whether the schedule of the above-mentioned tax has been long established and to see that it has not been changed; and, as the original schedule was established with reference to the number of inhabitants in each province or community, [it is necessary] to find out if that number has changed, whether through [the effects] of the war, or through changes in [the locations] of the fairs and markets, or through any of a number of other reasons which cause fluctuation in the population of various places and which may have caused the original schedule to be out of proportion to the number of inhabitants. . . .

Taille. Concerning the *taille,* it is necessary to find out, through means of the Royal Commissions, sent out each year by the local finance officer, and which the above-mentioned commissioners represent, how much the *taille* has amounted to in the preceding six years, in order to know exactly the increases and decreases granted by the King. Furthermore, through the annual reports of the local finance officers for these years, it is possible to determine whether they have kept close watch on the rise and fall in the *tailles* for each year; and if they have not done this, one should find out the reasons from the [Magistrates] themselves. . . .

Donations and Tolls. It remains to speak of the donations and the municipal Tolls of the cities which come under the heading of finances. It is necessary that the commissioners carefully inform themselves of the quantity of these tolls, which will be found in the letters-patent and the writs of concession of the last two or three leases which were granted, and [to examine] the accounts of the expenditure of these [tolls], in order to know whether they have been wisely or badly employed. . . .

Crown Lands [Domaines de la Couronne]. In order that no more need be said, in this instruction, concerning the Crown Lands, which are alienable, it is well and quite necessary that the commissioners obtain all the instructions and memoranda that they can during their sojourn in each province, in order to ascertain the true value of the amounts [*sommes*] for which they have been engaged.

The Situation of the Provinces. Having commented on all the things which must be known about the four units of governments of the provinces of the realm, it remains only to examine the advantages which His Majesty can obtain from each. To effect this, it is necessary that the commissioners examine carefully the mood and the spirit of the people of each province, each region and each city; if they are more inclined to war, agriculture, or commerce and manufacturing; if the provinces are maritime or not; and, in case they are maritime, the number of able seamen and their reputation as sailors; the condition of the soil; if it is completely under cultivation or if there are some uncultivated regions; if fertile or not, and what sort of crops it produces; if the inhabitants are industrious, and if they not only cultivate their land well, but if they understand good husbandry and use their lands in the most productive way; if there are forests in the province and what condition they are in; on this point, it is well to point out that His Majesty has drawn up a decree dealing with the reformation of the forests of the realm; what sort of trade and commerce, and what sort of manufactures, are present in each province.

[Colbert then makes certain general recommendations concerning commerce, shipping industry, canals, bridges, stud farms and counterfeit money.]

3. *Local Government and Central Government, 1671–82.* The following extracts from Colbert's voluminous and incessant correspondence with the local representatives of

the central administration give some idea of the size and success of his task.[12]

(*To the Count de Grignan, Lieutenant-General of Provence, Paris, 25 December, 1671.*) I have informed the King of the disorderly conduct in which the Assembly of the Towns of Provence has persisted; and, as His Majesty is not disposed to countenance it longer, he has given the orders necessary to prorogue it and, at the same time, has dispatched ten *lettres-de-cachet*, to commit the ten most discontented deputies to Granville, Cherbourg, Saint-Malo, Morlaix and Concarneau.

These orders and letters will be brought you by the First Gentleman in Ordinary of the King, and I think it superfluous to advise you to carry them out exactly and punctually, knowing with what zeal and earnestness you comport yourself in all that concerns the service of the King.

(*To the Same, Versailles, 31 December, 1671.*) I have made a complete report to the King of all which has transpired in the Assembly of the Towns of Provence since the 20th of the month. You will see, through the orders which His Majesty sends, how little pleased he is with the conduct of those who have served as deputies this year. And, as soon as His Majesty has accepted their offer of 450,000 livres, his desire is that, following the orders which you will receive, you send to the provinces of Normandy and Brittany ten of those deputies who have displayed the most ill-will toward the good of his service. All of Provence will see the troublous extremities in which the obstinacy of these deputies has placed them. I very much doubt whether His Majesty will see fit to call them together for a long time, and in any case, he will give them sufficient leisure to repent the bad conduct to which they held. However, with your own conduct, His Majesty is very satisfied.

(*To M. de Creil, Intendant of Rouen, Saint-Germain, 27 January, 1673.*) I have reported to the King the decrees of the *Cour des Aides* [financial courts] of Normandy and the fashion in which you have conducted the affairs of your department. I am obliged to inform you that His Majesty, not wishing to debase his prerogative, a small part of which he has confided to you, has set aside the decree of the *Cour des Aides*, has forbidden the finding of like judgments in the future, and has suspended the advocate-general. His Majesty has further ordered me to write you that he has found the explanations which you yourself made upon each one of the articles [of the decree] to be wrong in almost every respect; he has found that you have actually set up an additional court there, that barristers and solicitors plead before it, and that you or your subdelegates have administered those things which are properly within the jurisdiction of the magistrates [*élus*] and the *Cour des Aides*. He has therefore ordered me to add that if you do not remedy these errors and avoid them henceforth, he cannot maintain you in your present position.

In order to understand better what your functions should be, you ought to examine closely all the regulations dealing with the taxes and tax-farms, generally, and with all the ordinances treating the duties of commissioners in the provinces, and conduct yourself according to these rules without ever deviating from them. You have the power, set forth in the regulations, to levy *taxes d'office* [on jobs]; you can never lower them, only raise them, when it seems expedient to do so.

Concerning the collectors [of taxes], you should neither deviate from the import of the regulations, nor give orders which may be contrary to them, nor assign this power to any subdelegates.

You alone have the responsibility of seeing that the magistrates and the *Cour des Aides* interpret correctly and punctually the tax regulations; and when you find that they have departed from them, you should instruct the Council to take the necessary remedies and to give you those powers which His Majesty deems necessary for the good of his service and the upholding of his interests.

(*To M. de Creil, Intendant of Rouen, Saint-Germain, 3 February 1673.*) I have seen and examined the memorandum which you sent me concerning all those matters of which you have taken cognizance and upon which the *Cour des Aides* has based its complaints. You ought not hastily to reject the advice which His Majesty has ordered me to give you on the conduct of your affairs, since the King acts with a profound and thorough understanding [of these things] which cannot be forestalled by mis-statement of facts. . . .

For my own part, I must again tell you that it is difficult, not to say impossible, to mislead me on this subject. I believe that I have already advised you that you must take care to deal only with those matters which are within your own purview, and, as long as you obey this injunction, you need never worry about all the true or false complaints which may be made to me. However, on this last occasion, it was your own memorandum which did you the bad turn of which you complain, because it made it quite clear that you had been administering all those matters concerning *tailles* [property taxes] which are within the jurisdiction of the magistrates and the *Cour des Aides* [financial courts]. Once and for all, be careful to restrain yourself within those powers given you by the orders of the Council,

and, concerning taxes, by the regulations registered in the *Cour des Aides*. If the magistrates and the *Cour des Aides* misinterpret these, advise me and await the necessary powers to remedy their decisions.

I assure you that I did not know that there had been from twenty to twenty-four tax collectors in each parish, since the number who should be chosen each year, in each of the three *élections* [districts], is contained in the regulations, and it did not seem likely that these regulations would be so easily avoided. Tell me all you have to say on this subject, so that I can render an account of it to the King.

Of all the abuses which come before us from the *généralités,* there is none at present which seems more important to the Council than that [practised] by the assistants to the Receivers of the *Tailles,* who, under the name of the Receivers, make assessments, in conjunction with the magistrates, to defray the court costs and fees and which they apply to their own profit. As was provided by the order of the Council of 4 July, 1664, concerning the regulation of this disorder, pray inform me if it is known or practised in the *généralité* of Rouen, and particularly apply yourself to finding out if any of the Receivers of *Tailles* or Commissioners of Revenue are guilty of this, in order that you may either apply the necessary remedy through your authority or advise me about it.

(*To M. Bidé de la Grandville, Intendant of Limoges, Saint-Germain, 14 April 1673.*) I feel that I ought to inform you that a writ of cease-and-desist which you have issued against the ladies of Fontaine-Chalandray because of certain *corvées* [labor services] in their lands, seems quite extraordinary to us, the intention of the King having never been that the powers which he conferred upon you could or ought to be widened to include the ordinary rights and usages running with land or to summon the *seigneurs* before you to contest these rights, and, least of all, to give cease-and-desist orders to persons of quality: but only that, in case of a great and manifest grievance, you could, in making examples before the whole province of two or three of the gentry most noted for the abuses committed on their estates, reconcile the others to their duty through this means. But you could not have issued the writ against these ladies of quality without being accused of extending the powers which the King gave you beyond his intentions.

I cannot forbear advising you that you must set this affair to rights, and take care in the future to act with more circumspection in similar matters. I shall not tell you what the occasion requires, deeming it necessary to leave you free to do as you think best, and, furthermore, no one will ever know that I have written you my feelings on this subject.

(*To M. de Bezons, Intendant of Limoges, 16 November 1680.*) The King having been advised by M. de Marillac, intendant in the *généralité* de Poitiers, that a man named Baudoin has been guilty of a great many frauds in several parishes of the province of Saintonge, under the pretext of collecting for the *corvées* to repair roads, and on the strength of a commission of the tribunal of the King's lands at Paris giving him permission, His Majesty gave *Sieur* de Marillac verbal powers to institute proceedings against Baudoin; and, this having been done, he has been condemned to the galleys for life and forced to make restitution to those whom he had swindled.

As *Sieur* de Marillac has informed me that in the process of trying Baudoin, he learned that, in the *élection* de Saint-Jean-d'Angely, in the *généralité* of Limoges, there are several other people who have similar commissions and who, under the same pretext, are plaguing the people, I feel free to request that you hunt them down, not only in that *élection*, but throughout the entirety of the *généralité* of Limoges, in order to halt their depredations. If you have the facilities there to try them and to make examples of them, the King will, upon your request, send you the authority to try them and to impose the maximum penalties. . . .

(*To M. d'Herbigny, Intendant of Grenoble, Versailles, 16 November, 1680.*) I was surprised to learn, by your letter of the 28th last, that you had levied on the *élection* of Vienne an assessment of 4,700 livres, for the construction, subject to my approval, of a bridge to facilitate the transportation of the harvest to Grenoble.

You know as well as I that it is not permissible to make such an assessment on the people without a writ of the King affixed with the Great Seal, and you must take care to do nothing contrary to that general usage of the realm, and never to give so bad an example to the authorities of that province, who are only too much inclined to go beyond the bounds, and to those who will succeed to your position.

(*To M. Morant, Intendant of Aix, Sceaux, 1 July, 1682.*) On the subject of the ordinance which you have drawn up concerning the waters of Aubagne, I am obliged to point out that if one acknowledges the principles which you advance—of the public welfare—it would be a simple matter to overturn all the established regulations of the realm. To which I must add that the King alone can make such resolutions, and that it distinctly is not our place to decide in these particulars what is the greatest good to the public since we do not have the power.

I believe I am obliged to give you this advice, because I have always deemed it necessary, for the good of the King's service and of the public welfare, that the superior courts should not seem to reverse the ordinances of the intendants and commissioners in the provinces. Since there were no difficulties in revoking this ordinance and since the Council was agreed, you should take care never again to act in like fashion, because, having admonished you once, I shall not hesitate to see to it that justice be done, and that the Council reverse your order.

I shall report at the next meeting of the Council on the suggestions which you have sent concerning the public works and the tolls; I am certain that His Majesty will agree with them. You ought afterwards to apply yourself to repairing the roads and to forcing the *seigneurs* to repair and maintain those roads on which they levy the tolls.

As you fully appreciate the importance of these public works to the good of the province, I am sure that you will give them your complete attention. . . .

4. *The Parlements.* The *Parlement* of Paris was primarily a law court which exercised jurisdiction, both primary and appelate, over more than two-thirds of France. The magistrates who composed it—some two or three hundred—had either inherited or purchased their offices. Since the *Paulette* (1604) they had been irremovable. In the *Pays d'États* there were nine other *Parlements*. Much of the Paris *Parlement*'s political power derived from the fact that no edict, decree, or ordinance, could be enforced by a court until it had been registered by *Parlement*. The possibility of their vetoing the royal will, particularly when the latter took the form of creating new offices, is obvious. In the selection below (an edict of Louis XIII), Richelieu, in 1641, expresses the Crown's reaction to the *Parlement*'s pretensions. After his accession Louis XIV reaffirmed Richelieu's position at repeated intervals, saying for instance in 1667 that "our courts of *Parlement* shall be held to proceed forthwith with the publication of ordinances, edicts, declarations, and other documents as soon as they have been registered, without causing any delay thereto, and in precedence of any other matters." [13]

There is nothing which serves more to conserve and strengthen empires than general recognition by his subjects of the sovereign's power; this serves to rally and unite happily all the parties in the state. From this union comes a force which assures its greatness and its felicity. It seems that, since monarchies are based on the rule of one person, this rule is like the soul which animates them and which provides life and vigor in proportion to its own perfection. But just as this absolute authority elevates states to the high point of their glory, so when it has been weakened, one sees the states consequently decline in position. No need to leave France for evidence here; the reigns of our predecessors furnish plenty of examples . . .

[Then follows the story of the monarchy's low point during the Wars of Religion in the sixteenth century and the threats to royal power during the minority of Louis XIII]. Our *Parlement* of Paris, although well-intentioned, attempted by a policy (which has no precedent and which seriously damaged the fundamental laws of this monarchy) to control the government of our kingdom and our person. The circumstances at the time prevented any remedy being taken against so great an evil. . . .

[It is necessary] to show *Parlement* the legitimate use of that authority which our predecessors and ourselves have vested in them; our purpose here is to ensure that something established for the good of the people does not produce the opposite effect, as would happen if the officials, instead of being content with that power which makes them judges over man's life and the fortunes of our subjects, tried to undertake the government of the state which belongs only to the prince.

As a result, on the advice of our council and out of our own certain knowledge, full power, and royal authority, we have said and declared and do say and declare that our said court of *Parlement* of Paris and all our other courts have only been established to give justice to our subjects; we expressly prohibit and forbid them, in the future, to take cognizance of any kind of affairs similar to those they have previously asserted, or generally of all activities which might concern the state, the administration, government of all which we reserve for ourselves and our royal successors, unless we give them the power and special command by our letters patent, reserving for ourselves the right to ask the advice of our said Court of *Parlement* on public affairs, when we consider it desirable for the good of our service.

We desire and intend that our edicts and declarations which have been verified in this form (in our presence and seated in our bed of justice) shall be fully carried out according to their form and tenor, hereby forbidding to our said court of *Parlement* of Paris and all others to oppose our acts in any fashion, except that our officials may make such remonstrances as they consider to be for the best interests of our service; after which remonstrances, we wish and desire that they obey our desires and execute the edicts according to the verification which will have been done on our authority. . . .

As to the edicts and declarations which will have been sent them concerning the government and administration of the state, we command and order them to publish them and register them without taking any cognizance of them or holding any deliberations over them; and as for the edicts and declarations concerning our finances, we wish and desire that when such edicts are sent them, if they find some difficulty in the verification, that they retire towards us for us to represent them, in order that we can provide and judge suitably, without their being able on their own authority to make any changes and modifications or to use these words, "we ought not or could not," which are injurious to the authority of the prince.

B.   CHURCH AND STATE

As a source of authority the French monarchy had as rivals the religious bodies in France, the Roman Catholic Church and the Huguenots, as the Protestants were called. In 1598, to end the Religious Wars which had disrupted the kingdom in the sixteenth century, Henry IV issued the Edict of Nantes, an edict which granted French Protestants not only freedom of worship but also certain extra-legal military and political rights to guarantee this freedom. Richelieu had, by armed force, destroyed the military and political privileges of the Huguenots, but he left them their civil and religious rights. The following documents indicate the nature of Louis' religious policy not only as it affected the Protestant minority among his subjects, but in relation to the Papacy.

1. *The Declaration of the Gallican Church, 1682.* The following declaration, drafted by Bossuet, was approved by an assembly of leading French churchmen in March, 1682, and confirmed by a royal edict.[14]

Many people are striving to overthrow the decrees of the Gallican Church . . . and to destroy the foundations of its liberties, which are based on the sacred canons and on the tradition of the Fathers; others, under the pretext of defending them, have the audacity to attack the supremacy of St. Peter and his successors, the Popes of Rome. . . . The heretics, for their part, are doing their utmost to make this power, which keeps the peace of the Church, intolerable to kings and peoples.

Wishing to remedy these inconveniences, we,

the archbishops and bishops assembled at Paris by order of the King, with other ecclesiastical deputies who represent the Gallican Church, have judged it necessary to make the regulations and the declaration which follows:

1. That St. Peter and his successors, Vicars of Jesus Christ, and the whole Church herself, have received power of God only in things spiritual, and pertaining to eternal salvation, not in things civil or temporal, the Lord Himself having said, "My kingdom is not of this world," and also "Render unto Caesar the things that be Caesar's, and unto God the things that are God's"; as also firmly declareth the Apostle, "Let every soul be subject unto the higher powers: for there is no power but of God; the powers that be are ordained of God; whosoever therefore resisteth the power, resisteth the ordinance of God."

Therefore kings and princes are in no wise subjected by God's appointment to any ecclesiastical power in temporal things; neither can the authority of the Keys of the Church directly or indirectly depose them, or their subjects be dispensed from the obedience and fidelity of their oaths to the same; and this doctrine we affirm to be necessary for the maintenance of public peace, no less profitable to the Church than to the State, and to be everywhere and every way observed as agreeable to the Word of God, to the tradition of the Fathers and the example of the Saints.

2. That the full powers held by the Holy Apostolic See and the successors of St. Peter, as Vicars of Christ, in spiritual things, are the same as the decrees of the holy Oecumenical Council of Constance in [1415], put forth in its fourth and fifth sessions, which were approved by the Holy Apostolic See, confirmed by the practice of all the Church and of the Roman Pontiffs, and religiously observed at all times by the Gallican Church; that they abide in full force, and that the Gallican Church does not uphold those who would impugn their authority, or say that they were adopted by the Council only at a time of schism. . . .

4. And that although the Pope has a chief voice in matters of faith, and that his decrees concern all Churches, nevertheless his judgment is not unalterable, except with the consent of the Church. . . .

2. *The Revocation of the Edict of Nantes, 1685.*[15]

Louis, by the grace of God king of France and Navarre, to all present and to come, greeting: King Henry the Great, our grandfather of glorious memory, being desirous that the peace . . . should not be troubled on account of the R.P.R. [Religion prétendue réformée, "the Religion called the Reformed"] . . . by his edict granted at Nantes in the month of April, 1598, regulated the procedure to be adopted with regard to those of the said religion . . . so as to put himself in a better position to labor, as he had resolved to do, for the reunion to the Church of those who had so lightly withdrawn from it. . . .

The King, our late lord and father, in the exercise of his usual clemency, granted them yet another edict at Nîmes, in July 1629, by means of which, tranquillity being established anew, the said late king, animated by the same spirit and the same zeal for religion as the king, our said grandfather, had resolved to take advantage of this repose to attempt to put his said pious design into execution. But foreign wars having supervened soon after, so that the kingdom was seldom tranquil from 1635 to the truce concluded in 1684 with the powers of Europe, nothing more could be done for the advantage of religion beyond diminishing the number of places for the public exercise of the R.P.R., interdicting such places as were found established to the prejudice of the dispositions made by the edicts, and suppressing the bi-partisan courts, these having been appointed provisionally only.

God having at last permitted that our people should enjoy perfect peace, we, no longer absorbed in protecting them from our enemies, are able to profit by this truce (which we have ourselves facilitated) , and devote our whole attention to the means of accomplishing the designs of our said grandfather and father, which we have consistently kept before us since our succession to the crown.

And now we perceive, with thankful acknowledgment of God's aid, that our endeavors have attained their proposed end, inasmuch as the better and the greater part of our subjects of the said R.P.R. have embraced the Catholic faith. And since by this fact the execution of the Edict of Nantes and of all that has ever been ordained in favor of the said R.P.R. has been rendered nugatory, we have determined that we can do nothing better, in order wholly to obliterate the memory of the troubles, the confusion, and the evils which the progress of this false religion has caused in this kingdom, and which furnished occasion for the said edict and for so many previous and subsequent edicts and declarations, than entirely to revoke the said Edict of Nantes, with the special articles granted as a sequel to it, as well as all that has since been done in favor of the said religion.

1. Be it known that for these causes and others us hereunto moving, and of our certain knowledge, full power, and royal authority, we have, by this present perpetual and irrevocable edict, suppressed and revoked, and do suppress and revoke, the edict of our said grandfather, given at Nantes

in April 1598, in its whole extent, together with the particular articles agreed upon in the month of May following, and the letters patent issued upon the same date; and also the edict given at Nîmes in July 1629; we declare them null and void, . . . we desire, and it is our pleasure, that all the temples of those of the said R.P.R. situate in our kingdom, countries, territories, and the lordships under our crown, shall be demolished without delay.

2. We forbid our subjects of the R.P.R. to meet any more for the exercise of the said religion in any place or private house, under any pretext whatever. . . .

3. We likewise forbid all noblemen, of what condition soever, to hold such religious exercises in their houses or fiefs, under penalty to be inflicted upon all our said subjects who shall engage in the said exercises, of imprisonment and confiscation.

4. We enjoin all ministers of the said R.P.R., who do not choose to become converts and to embrace the Catholic, apostolic, and Roman religion, to leave our kingdom and the territories subject to us within a fortnight of the publication of our present edict, without leave to reside therein beyond that period, or, during the said fortnight, to engage in any preaching, exhortation, or any other function, on pain of being sent to the galleys. . . .

7. We forbid private schools for the instruction of children of the said R.P.R., and in general all things whatever which can be regarded as a concession of any kind in favor of the said religion.

8. As for children who may be born of persons of the said R.P.R., we desire that from henceforth they be baptized by the parish priests. We enjoin parents to send them to the churches for that purpose, under penalty of five hundred livres fine, to be increased as circumstances may demand, and thereafter the children shall be brought up in the Catholic, apostolic, and Roman religion, which we expressly enjoin the local magistrates to see done.

9. And in the exercise of our clemency towards our subjects of the said R.P.R. who have emigrated from our kingdom, lands, and territories subject to us, previous to the publication of our present edict, it is our will and pleasure that in case of their returning within the period of four months from the day of the said publication, they may, and it shall be lawful for them to, again take possession of their property, and to enjoy the same as if they had all along remained there: on the contrary, the property abandoned by those who, during the specified period of four months, shall not have returned into our kingdom, lands, and territories subject to us, shall remain and be confiscated in consequence of our declaration of the 20th of August last.

10. We repeat our most express prohibition to all our subjects of the said R.P.R., together with their wives and children, against leaving our kingdom, lands, and territories subject to us, or transporting their goods and effects therefrom under penalty, as respects the men, of being sent to the galleys, and as respects the women, of imprisonment and confiscation.

11. It is our will and intention that the declarations rendered against the relapsed shall be executed according to their form and tenor.

12. As for the rest, liberty is granted to the said persons of the R.P.R., pending the time when it shall please God to enlighten them as well as others, to remain in the cities and places of our kingdom, lands, and territories subject to us, and there to continue their commerce, and to enjoy their possessions, without being subjected to molestation or hindrance on account of the said R.P.R., on condition of not engaging in the exercise of the said religion, or of meeting under pretext of prayers or religious services, of whatever nature these may be, under the penalties above mentioned of imprisonment and confiscation. This we do give in charge to our trusty and well-beloved counselors, etc.

Given at Fontainebleau in the month of October, in the year of grace 1685, and of our reign the forty-third.

C.   THE STATE AND ECONOMIC LIFE

Colbert, already encountered by the student, was particularly interested in the economic reorganization of France. His economic policies and practices, while not altogether peculiar to him, were so pronounced that they have been called "Colbertism" by historians. The documents which follow have been selected to illustrate his ideas and methods—first his intentions, second his achievements.

1. *Colbertism: Theory.*

(A letter to the merchants of Marseilles, 1664.) [16]
Very dear and well beloved:

Considering how advantageous it would be to this realm to reestablish its foreign and domestic commerce . . . we have resolved to establish a council particularly devoted to commerce, to be held every fortnight in our presence, in which all the interests of merchants and the means conducive to the revival of commerce shall be considered and determined upon, as well as all that which concerns manufactures.

We also inform you that we are setting apart, in the expenses of our state, a million livres each year for the encouragement of manufactures and the increase of navigation, to say nothing of the considerable sums which we cause to be raised to supply the companies of the East and West Indies;

That we are working constantly to abolish all the tolls which are collected on the navigable rivers;

That there has already been expended more than a million livres for the repair of the public highways, to which we shall also devote our constant attention;

That we will assist by money from our royal treasury all those who wish to reestablish old manufactures or to undertake new ones;

That we are giving orders to all our ambassadors or residents at the courts of the princes, our allies, to make, in our name, all proper efforts to cause justice to be rendered in all cases involving our merchants, and to assure for them entire commercial freedom.

That we will comfortably lodge at our court each and every merchant who has business during all the time that he shall be obliged to remain there, having given orders to the grand marshal of our palace to indicate a proper place for that purpose, which shall be called the House of Commerce. . . .

That all the merchants and traders by sea who purchase vessels, or who build new ones, for traffic or commerce shall receive from us subsidies for each ton of merchandise which they export or import on the said voyages.

We desire, in this present letter, not only to inform you concerning all these things, but to require you, as soon as you have received it, to cause to be assembled all the merchants and traders of your town of Marseilles, and explain to them very particularly our intentions in all matters mentioned above, in order that, being informed of the favorable treatment which we desire to give them, they may be the more desirous of applying themselves to commerce. Let them understand that for everything that concerns the welfare and advantage of the same they are to address themselves to Sieur Colbert. . . .

(*A Memorandum, 1666.*) [17] It is necessary to observe carefully, on all purchases, that they must always be made in France rather than in foreign countries, even if the goods should be a little inferior in quality and a little more expensive, because when money does not go out of the kingdom the advantage to the state is double, in that

since the money stays in it, it does not grow poor, and the subjects of the king earn their living and use their energy.

For example, the three thousand musket barrels, $3\frac{1}{2}$ feet long and of the caliber of 16 to the pound, ordered in Biscaye, could easily be ordered either in Forez or Nivervais; and it would be a fine thing to begin to establish the manufacture of them in Angoumois, or in Guienne, or in Brittany.

(*A Memorandum, 1669.*) The commerce of all Europe is carried on by ships of every size to the number of 20,000, and it is perfectly clear that this number cannot be increased, since the number of people in all the states remains the same and consumption likewise remains the same; and that of this number of 20,000 ships the Dutch have 15,000 to 16,000, the English about 3,000 to 4,000 and the French 500 to 600. . . .

It must be added that commerce causes a perpetual combat in peace and war among the nations of Europe, as to who shall win the most of it. . . .

Commerce is a perpetual and peaceable war of wit and energy among all nations. It is carried on by 20,000 vessels and this number cannot be increased. Each nation works incessantly to have its legitimate share of commerce or to gain an advantage over another nation. The Dutch fight at present, in this war, with 15,000 to 16,000 ships, a government of merchants, all of whose maxims and power are directed solely toward the preservation and increase of their commerce, and much more care, energy, and thrift than any other nation.

The English with 3,000 to 4,000 ships, less energy and care, and more expenditures than the Dutch.

The French with 500 to 600.

Those two last cannot improve their commerce save by increasing the number of their vessels, and cannot increase this number save from the 20,000 which carry all the commerce and consequently by making inroads on the 15,000 to 16,000 of the Dutch.

(*A Memorandum, 1670.*) Your Majesty has undertaken a war of money against all the states of Europe. Your Majesty has already conquered Spain, Italy, Germany, England, and some others, in which he has caused great misery and want, and by despoiling them he has enriched himself. Only Holland is left, and it fights with great resources: its commerce with the North, which brings it so many advantages and such a great reputation for its sea forces and its navigation; that of the East Indies, which brings it every year 12,000,000 in cash; its commerce with Cadiz and that with Guinea and an infinity of others in which its strength consists and resides. Your Majesty has formed companies which, like armies, attack them everywhere. . . .

Many other new establishments that your Majesty is making are so many reserve corps that your Majesty creates and brings out of nothingness to perform their duty in this war, in which your Majesty sees clearly that he is winning every year some considerable advantage of such a sort that even the vanquished cannot conceal their losses and make them known by the continual complaints that they utter, through the mouths of their merchants, as to the decrease of their commerce.

This war, which consists only in wit and energy, and of which the spoil is the most powerful republic since that of the Romans must be the prize of victory, cannot soon be finished. Or to put it better, it should be one of the chief objects of the application of your Majesty during his whole life.

(*A Memorandum, 1672.*) If the King conquers all the provinces subject to and forming part of the States of the United Provinces of the Netherlands, their commerce becoming commerce of the subjects of the King, there would be nothing more to desire; and if afterwards His Majesty, examining what would be most advantageous to do for the commerce of his old and new subjects, thought it for the good of his service to divide the advantages of this commerce by cutting down a part of that of the Dutch so as to transfer it into the hands of the French, it would be easy to find the necessary expedients to which the new subjects would be obliged to submit.

2. *Colbertism: Practice.* Since Colbertism, by definition, affected all parts of the French economy, it is manifestly impossible to print enough documents to illustrate completely the practice of Colbertism. The document which follows has been selected to demonstrate certain aspects of the subject.[18]

(*An Edict for the Establishment of the Royal Tapestry Factory, November 1667.*) The manufacture of tapestries has always appeared to be so customary and so useful a practice that prosperous countries have established such industries and, by special inducements, have attracted the ablest workers into their territories. In fact, our grandfather, King Henry [IV] the Great, finding his country at peace, thought there was no better way for his people to enjoy the fruits of peace than by restoring the trade and the manufacture that foreign and civil wars had almost destroyed in the kingdom. To carry out his plans he would have established by a decree of January 1607 the manufacture of all kinds of tapestry, in Paris as well as in other appropriate cities. . . . [Reasons are here given why nothing came of these early plans.]

Our desire to make commerce and industry flourish in our kingdom has led us to reestablish [the production of tapestries] and to make such establishments in definite places; to give them a fixed place we have purchased the mansion of the Gobelins and several houses nearby, have summoned painters of the highest reputation, tapestry workers, sculptors, gold and silver-smiths, cabinet-makers and other outstanding workers, from various arts and crafts, to be housed there. We have given each of them apartments and special privileges so that the number of workers will increase daily, that the outstanding workers in all kinds of manufacturing will come on our invitation to give us the skills that they have so that the work done here will clearly surpass in art and beauty the best made by foreign countries. We have thought it necessary, in order to strengthen these establishments, to give them a permanent form and to provide them with regulations suitable to this end. [Some of the regulations follow:]

1. It is to be made public that the manufacture of tapestries and other works will remain established in the mansion of the Gobelins, the houses, land, and outer buildings belonging to us. On the main entrance of the mansion a marble tablet shall be placed containing our arms and the inscription: ROYAL MANUFACTURE OF FUR–NISHINGS FOR THE CROWN.

2. The factories and the buildings will be administered by the orders of our beloved loyal councilor, M. Colbert, superintendent of our buildings, arts, and manufactures in France and of his successors in the same office.

3. Direct control of the manufacturing belongs to M. Le Brun, our leading painter, under title of director.

4. The superintendent of our buildings and the director under him will keep the factories supplied with good painters, master-workers in tapestry, jewelers, foundry workers, engravers, stone workers, cabinet-makers in wood and ebony, dyers, and other good workers in all kinds of arts and crafts that are established there or that the superintendent of our buildings may regard it as necessary to establish. . . .

11. The workers employed in these manufacturing plants will live in the houses nearest the mansion of the Gobelins. That they and their families may live in complete liberty, we desire that 12 of the houses in which they live will be exempt from quartering of officers and soldiers or of any other military people. To give effect to this it is our desire that safeguards be provided by the secretary of those in charge of the department of war on the basis of certification coming from the said superintendent of buildings.

[Articles 12, 13, and 14 confer on foreign workers the rights of naturalized French citizens and exempt them from many of the obligations normally required of citizens of France.]

15. The director of the factory will have the right to establish breweries in proper places to make beer for the workers without being interfered with by brewers of beer or without having to pay taxes on the beer. . . .

17. And we expressly prohibit any merchant or other person, of what ever quality or condition he may be, from buying or importing any foreign tapestries and from selling any foreign tapestries or any other than those which are at present in our kingdom, on penalty of confiscation of the goods, and a fine of half their value. . . .

3. Colbert's Opinion of the French Businessman.

What Colbert thought of the businessmen with whom he had to deal is displayed in the following passages garnered from his letters and miscellaneous papers written during his years as minister.[19]

For a long time I have been convinced that you only have to let the merchants know that you want to do something to help them, to have them dislike it. . . .

They [the directors of the West India Company] think only of their own interests and not of the general welfare of the state and of the islands. But for you [M. de Baas, Lieutenant-General of the West Indies] and for me, who should raise ourselves above private interests to seek the general good, with which, in a brief time, that of the company will coincide, we should always support complete liberty of commerce. . . .

Especially, I beg you to be on guard against the advice you will get from merchants because you well know that they always consult only their individual interests without examining what would be for the public good and the advantage of commerce in general. . . .

Merchants . . . nearly always understand merely their own little commerce and not the great forces which make commerce go. . . .

The merchants of Marseilles . . . are folk who live only from day to day and see only the small profit that they can make immediately. . . .

There are no greater enemies of general commerce and of the order which should be established than the merchants of Marseilles. . . . The little merchants of Marseilles, not believing that there is any commerce other than that which passes through their shops, would willingly overturn all general commerce in the hope of a little immediate profit, which would ruin them in the end. . . .

It will be necessary for you to act with care because all merchants as a rule wish to have complete liberty in all that has to do with their trade, and particularly in manufactures of which they wish always to change and reduce the lengths, widths, and qualities for considerations of some small profit that they make, and which tends to the ruin of manufactures, of which the principle consists, in a state as flourishing and as great as this, in making them always equal in length, width, and goodness. To attain this degree of fidelity, it is necessary to go entirely beyond the motives of little individual interests, which do not deserve consideration in connection with the general motives of the good of the state.

XIV

The Palace of Versailles: A Visual Approach to History

ITALY must now yield to France the prize and garland which it has borne away hitherto from all the nations of the earth, in what regards the excellency of architecture, the beauty of carving, the magnificence of painting, and the invention of aqueducts. . . . Versailles alone suffices to secure forever to France the glory it has at present, in surpassing all other kingdoms in the science of building: and it is beholding for this high esteem to the grandeur and magnificence of Louis the Great.

Sieur Combes

CONTENTS

(The pictorial materials necessary for the study of this Problem may be obtained from the publisher.)

QUESTIONS FOR STUDY

PART I

1. What successive steps were taken to transform the hunting lodge of Louis XIII into the palace of Louis XIV?

2. Compare the east and west façades. What changes took place in the transformation of a small private hunting lodge into a great palace?

3. In what respects does the relation of the palace to the town of Versailles differ from that of the Louvre to the city of Paris?

4. To what extent were the interiors related to the ceremonial splendor of contemporary dress and manners?

5. To what does the term *piano mobile* refer? What is its relation to the rest of the palace? How does it reflect the daily life of the court?

6. In what respects has the character of the chapel as a church been altered to accommodate the religion of Louis XIV?

7. What specific indications are there that this is a religious structure?

PART II

8. What is Félibien's opinion of the position of a great artist in relation to his own country? How do we feel about this today?

9. How do Félibien's and Poussin's concepts of a landscape painting differ from a photograph of a landscape?

10. What does Félibien mean by "nature" and "reality"? Is it the same as our understanding of them?

11. List the several qualities, the absence of which, in Félibien's opinion, would destroy the value of a painting. Are they the qualities you expect to find in a work of art?

12. Can you discover any of these qualities in the architecture and surroundings of the palace itself?

INTRODUCTION TO THE PROBLEM

With the exception of Problem VI, previous problems have considered the evidence of texts alone. At this point we deal again with other historical materials, and it seems advisable to restate the proper approach to them. The written word is not the only key to the past. The historian must be prepared to analyze and evaluate the physical remnants of society. Often these remnants are considered by succeeding generations as art. Sometimes the vestiges themselves are merely stones or nondescript fragments. The archaeologist can recreate the original objects or monuments from these fragments: the historian of art interprets the remains or the restorations, and by a critical analysis, he sheds new light on the written accounts of the time.

As you have learned, volumes of texts are available for the study of the seventeenth century. Without studying the palace of Versailles, however, it is difficult to achieve any understanding of the physical appearance of the surroundings created for the absolute monarchy in France. The meaning of the "grand style," of the formal gardens, and of the vast chambers of Versailles must be comprehended if we are to have any sense of the physical realities of seventeenth-century culture.

In order to understand these realities, the historian must learn to use such materials as buildings, sculpture, painting, furniture, and all the objects of use and pleasure. This he can do through plans, engravings, and photographs. He will need to know some of the terms used by architects, artists, and historians of art.

Like any historical event, the work of art is a fact in time. But unlike many historical events, the work of art is also an object in space. It is the visible, tangible expression of the thoughts and the feelings of powerful, orderly, and creative minds. We must learn to detect, observe, and describe the ways in which the work of art exists in time and space.

A special approach is therefore necessary. Among the visual documents assembled for your study are architects' plans and elevations, as well as airplane views and photographs of exteriors, interiors, and details. Contemporary paintings of people and events, as well as a few objects of the period, are provided. A few texts relating to the historical interpretation of this material are supplied in the following pages. Remember, however, that visual materials are *primary historical sources* in and of themselves.

The questions accompanying each section are a guide to the problems involved. Every question can be answered on the basis of the evidence presented. Study the pictures carefully, and answer the questions to the best of your ability. These questions are designed to accompany the various groups of pictures.

In conclusion, a word on the history of Versailles. Between 1627 and 1631 Louis XII employed the architect Le Roy to build a hunting lodge at Versailles, which he called the Château Chétif or Château des Cartes. No further construction was undertaken until in 1661 Louis XIV initiated his building program under the direction of the architect Le Vau, the painter Le Brun, and the gardener Le Nôtre. By 1668 two shifts of laborers were working constantly. Ten years later the king placed the famous Jules Hardouin Mansard in charge of construction, and by 1682 enough of the building had been completed so that Louis moved his court to Versailles.

Construction nevertheless continued until near the end of the reign of Louis XIV, though there were periods when the program was pushed more rapidly than at others. In 1684 the workmen at Versailles numbered 22,000; the next year 36,000 workmen were employed. The buildings were completed at intervals. The Hall of Mirrors was done in 1679 and the service quarters or *Grand Commun* in

1682. The great south and north wings, the latter including quarters for the courtiers whom Louis wished to have constantly about his person, were finished between 1679 and 1689. The royal stables and orangerie were completed in the same period. The last building constructed in Louis XIV's reign was the royal chapel, commenced in 1700 and finished in 1710, five years before his death.

Thus, from 1682 to 1710, the Grand Monarch lived always amid the construction of the grand palace which he was erecting as a monument to himself and his glory. When building ceased during Louis' last and most exhausting war, the complete palace and gardens had cost the French nation nearly sixty-six million *livres*.

Part I.   VERSAILLES AS A WORK OF ART

LOUIS XIV LEAVES PARIS

The following explanation for Louis' withdrawal from Paris to Versailles is taken from the *Memoirs* of the Duc de Saint-Simon (1675–1755). Saint-Simon, a soldier, diplomat, and courtier, was himself born at Versailles. He was by no means an admirer of Louis XIV, but his *Memoirs,* though prejudiced, are full of information.[1] The opening paragraphs, though quoted in the previous Problem, are particularly apt at this point.

He early showed a disinclination for Paris. The troubles that had taken place there during the minority made him regard the place as dangerous; he wished, too, to render himself venerable by hiding himself from the eyes of the multitude: all these considerations fixed him at St. Germains soon after the death of the Queen, his mother. It was to that place he began to attract the world by fêtes and gallantries, and by making it felt that he wished to be often seen.

His love for Madame de la Vallière, which was at first kept secret, occasioned frequent excursions to Versailles, then a little card castle, which had been built by Louis XIII—annoyed, and his suite still more so, at being frequently obliged to sleep in a wretched inn there, after he had been out hunting in the forest of Saint Léger. That monarch rarely slept at Versailles more than one night, and then from necessity; the King, his son slept there, so that he might be more in private with his mistress; pleasures unknown to the hero and just man, worthy son of Saint Louis, who built the little château.

These excursions of Louis XIV by degrees gave birth to those immense buildings he erected at Versailles; and their convenience for a numerous court, so different from the apartments at St. Germains, led him to take up his abode there entirely shortly after the death of the Queen. He built an infinite number of apartments, which were asked for by those who wished to pay their court to him; whereas at St. Germains nearly everybody was obliged to lodge in the town, and the few who found accommodation at the château were strangely inconvenienced.

The frequent fêtes, the private promenades at Versailles, the journeys, were means on which the King seized in order to distinguish or mortify the courtiers, and thus render them more assiduous in pleasing him. He felt that of real favors he had not enough to bestow; in order to keep up the spirit of devotion, he therefore unceasingly invented all sorts of ideal ones, little preferences and petty distinctions, which answered his purpose as well. . . .

As for the King himself, nobody ever approached his magnificence. His buildings, who could number them? At the same time, who was there who did not deplore the pride, the caprice, the bad taste seen in them? He built nothing useful or ornamental in Paris, except the Pont Royal, and that simply by necessity; so that despite its incomparable extent, Paris is inferior to many cities in Europe. St. Germains, a lovely spot, with a marvellous view, rich forest, terraces, gardens, and water he abandoned for Versailles; the dullest and most ungrateful of all places, without prospect, without wood, without water, without soil; for the ground is all shifting sand or swamp, the air accordingly bad.

But he liked to subjugate nature by art and treasure. He built at Versailles, on, on, without any general design, the beautiful and the ugly, the vast and the mean, all jumbled together. His own apartments and those of the Queen are inconvenient to the last degree, dull, close, stinking. The gardens astonish by their magnificence, but cause regret by their bad taste. You are introduced to the freshness of the shade only by a vast torrid zone, at the end of which there is nothing for you but to dismount or descend; and with the hill, which is very short, terminate the gardens. The violence everywhere done to nature repels and wearies us despite ourselves. The abundance of water, forced up and gathered together from all parts, is rendered green, thick, muddy; it disseminates humidity, unhealthy and evident; and an odor still more so. I might never finish upon the monstrous defects of a palace so immense and so immensely dear, with its accompaniments, which are still more so.

But the supply of water for the fountains was all defective at all moments, in spite of those seas of reservoirs which had cost so many millions to establish and to form upon the shifting sand and marsh. Who could have believed it? This defect became the ruin of the infantry which was turned out to do the work. Madame de Maintenon reigned. M. de Louvois was well with her, then. We were at peace. He conceived the idea of turning the river Eure between Chartres and Maintenon, and of making it come to Versailles. Who can say what gold and men this obstinate attempt cost during several years, until it was prohibited by the heaviest penalties, in the camp established there, and for a long time kept up; not to speak of the sick—above all, of the dead—that the hard labor and still more the much disturbed earth, caused? How many men were years in recovering from the effects of the contagion! How many never regained their health at all! And not only the sub-officers, but the colonels, the brigadiers and general officers, were compelled to be upon the spot, and were not at liberty to absent themselves for a quarter of an hour from the works. The war [Louis' invasion of the Palatinate] at last interrupted them in 1688, and they have never since been undertaken; only unfinished portions of them exist which will immortalize this cruel folly. . . .

Part II.   THE GRAND STYLE AND ITS CREATORS

In order that the palace of Versailles might properly represent in its interior embellishment the visual splendor of the absolute monarchy a new type of painting was required which should express the autocratic ideal in the clearest, most uncomplicated way, but which should yet appeal to the fastidious taste of the monarch and his courtiers. The creation of this style of painting for interior decoration was the work of Charles Le Brun (1619–1690).

Le Brun's talents were more those of a superior executive than of an original artist. Talent he had, but his real accomplishment consisted in his ability to determine the direction the new style was to take, and to reduce its principles to a series of concepts which could be taught in the royal schools and academies of painting, sculpture, and the minor arts.

Le Brun and his associates took as their point of departure for the formulation of the new style the works of Nicolas Poussin (1594–1665), the foremost French painter of the early seventeenth century. Although Poussin, who was born in Normandy and educated in Paris, spent most of his life in Rome, where he could work undisturbed by the intrigue which plagued an artist who remained near the court in Paris, his works were regularly shipped back to France and earned him an immense fame during his lifetime. The student's analysis of the Grand Style in seventeenth century painting is to be based on the examination of the works of Poussin in the light of the type of art criticism which was practiced in France two decades after his death and in which the principles animating the Grand Style can be discovered.

A Conversation between Two Artists

The following text consists of the concluding paragraphs of Poussin's life and works, published in 1688 by André Félibien (1619–1695) in his *Entrétiens sur les Vies et sur les Ouvrages des plus excellens Peintres Anciens et Modernes*. In these *entrétiens* or conversations, Félibien discusses with his imaginary friend, Pymander, the character of the work of the most famous artists of antiquity and modern times. Félibien, who was a practicing architect and historiographer, represents the point of view of the official, governmental art, but his accurate observations show that he possessed a sensitive, inquiring mind.[2]

The student should read the following paragraphs while observing the panels of photographs of Poussin's work. Each figure within brackets refers to numbered photographs on one of the panels and to the accompanying question. The question should be answered on the basis of the student's application of Félibien's remarks to the particular paintings illustrated. When the student has answered the questions to his own satisfaction, he should re-read the entire passage and answer the questions for study.

"I don't ask," said Pymander, "that you try to remember any more paintings; you have named quite enough. But continue, if you don't mind, with your analysis of the great qualities of this illustrious painter. For although I believe that I am well acquainted with him from what I have seen of his work and from what I have just heard you say, I confess that I had not suspected that he held such a considerable place among the most celebrated painters; and I am delighted that France has produced a man so distinguished that the Italians themselves, as you said so often, have recognized him as the Raphael of France."

"It is true," I replied, "that France and Italy have never had more expert painters. They greatly resemble each other in the grandeur of their conceptions, in their choice of noble and lofty subjects, in the good taste of their drawing, the beautiful and natural disposition of their figures, in their strong and vivid expression of all the feelings of the soul [1]. Both are more interested in form than in color, and have preferred that which interests and satisfies the reason and the spirit to that which satisfies only the eyes [2]. Also, the more one considers their work, the more one loves and admires them.

"Please do not imagine that the comparison I make between these two men is a means I use to praise Poussin all the more. I do not intend to establish his worth by comparing his works to those of great painters, either those of the past, those of his own period, or those who have worked since, no matter in what country. Each one has had particular talents; and if some of them have possessed great talent, I do not believe that for such a reason one should lessen the esteem in which Poussin is held. I have at other times talked to you of the different qualities which gave Titian and Correggio their reputations: the excellence and singular beauty of their work did not prevent people from considering Raphael as their master since he possessed qualities so great that they made him unequalled.

"But if one wished to make some distinction between Raphael and Poussin one could say that Raphael received from Heaven his knowledge and the skill of his brush, whereas Poussin's wonderful understanding and everything that was marvellous in his art derived from the force of his genius and from the extent of his studies.

"In order to evaluate correctly our foremost French painter, it is necessary to consider him alone, without comparing him to others; and taking into account his particular talents, one would have difficulty finding among those I have mentioned any who could be compared to him.

"It seems to me that I have acquainted you adequately with the force of his inventive genius and his good taste in choosing only great and illustrious subjects [3]. The paintings which I have described to you must have convinced you of his knowledge of composition. You have been able to see the science behind the art of drawing figures, giving the proper proportions to people according to sex, age, and different conditions [4]. It was he who first made apparent the admirable art of handling subjects in the most noble way, and who, like a torch, shed light on what others had done only in disorder and confusion.

"He studied continuously everything pertaining to his profession and never started a picture without first having thought over carefully the positions of the figures, all of which he drew with great care. One could even tell from his first ideas and simple sketches that he made of them that his work would be as good as could be expected of him [5]. He put out on the table little models which he covered with clothes to judge the effect and the arrangement of all the figures together; and tried so hard to make things true to life that I have seen him considering stones, lumps of earth, and even pieces of wood, in order to secure a better imitation of terraces and tree trunks [6]. He painted carefully and in a very special manner. The colors arranged on his palette were always the right ones so that he never made an unnecessary stroke of the brush and never mixed his colors [7]. It is true that his hand shook so that he could not work as easily as other painters, but the force of his genius and his good judgment made up for the weakness of his hand.

"No matter what he was working on, he never acted with undue energy. He took things easily, never seeming more tired at the end of his work than at the beginning because the fire that warmed his imagination was always of the same strength. The light which illuminated his thoughts was of uniform quality, always pure and unclouded [8]. Even though he was forced to show vehemence and sometimes anger and indignation in his pictures, even though he was obliged to depict sorrow, he never got too upset, but always acted with the same prudence and wisdom. When he wanted poetic subjects he painted them in a flowery and elegant manner; and if, in the Bacchanals, he had to please and amuse the humorous actions and ways in which one sees them, he nevertheless has done so with more gravity and modesty than many other painters who have taken too many liberties [9].

"It is true that one can see in his work, as if it were a special skill, the care which he has taken to paint with love and charm this kind of subject, embellishing them more than the historical subjects he painted, in which are found pure and well adorned but unlabored truths, and in which he often dispensed with some of the opulence the subjects should have had, the lack being compensated for by the beauty of the figures [10].

"One never sees depicted in his paintings any motions which do not seem suitable to the people who make them. That disagreeable foreshortening, that unreality of uneasy and often ridiculous poses and action, for which certain painters seek, and for which they have such a strong preference because they say this gives more life to their figures, are never found in Poussin's pictures [11]. Everything in his work seems natural, easy, suitable and agreeable; each person does gracefully and well what he should be doing.

"He succeeded just as well in expressing all the passions of the soul. I have pointed out to you that no matter what sort they are, he never exaggerates them; he knows exactly to what degree they should be recorded [12]. And what is more, he knows perfectly how to discern the people capable of strong emotions, and in what manner to depict them.

"One can find nothing too studied, nor too carelessly treated, in his pictures. The buildings, the clothes, and all the arrangements generally, are suitable to his subject [13]. Light and shadow are diffused as nature shows them. He does not try to make his figures seem nobler nor to make them seem stronger or weaker than they should be. He understands perfectly the relationship between colors, and even though he uses clear and bright colors equally in the foreground and background, he disperses them, weakens them, and arranges them so that none of them nullifies another. And they always give a good effect. I have talked so often to you of his skill in painting all sorts of landscapes and making them pleasing and natural, that one can say that excepting Titian, one cannot find a painter who has done any comparable to his. He painted all kinds of trees perfectly, expressing their differences and their motion. He arranged terraces in a natural but well chosen way, made water look clear, embellishing it with reflections of adjacent objects, decorated the fields and hills with cities and well constructed buildings, making the farthest objects look smaller with wonderful skill; and, which gives his work that special quality, depicting the atmosphere of different days by arrangements of clouds and vapors rising in the air, knowing exactly the difference between those of morning and evening [14]. . . .

"That is the way in which he painted perfectly all kinds of subjects, even the most extraordinary aspects of Nature, no matter how difficult they might be to represent, adding to his landscapes [15] suitable stories or actions.

"Should not all these things which I have been telling you be considered favorable to Poussin without our being also obliged to wait for the judgment of some acknowledged authority?"

"Indeed," said Pymander, "I believe that what is approved by the public should also be approved by the more erudite men. The great esteem in which everyone holds Poussin's paintings constitutes a kind of popular judgment in which I see no difference of opinion between the ignorant and the more educated."

Finally we talked of several skilled painters who have worked for a long time, and who with the help of study and long practice have become able to express their thoughts nobly. But after having considered their best works and even after having examined the frescoes of the old school (antiquity), particularly the Aldobrandini Marriage, whose simplicity and nobility impressed upon Poussin the genius of those men, one must admit that this painter, without adhering to one particular style, had become master of himself and author of all the beauty which fills his paintings, and that he learned nothing from contemporary painters except to avoid their faults; that we are indebted to him for what knowledge we may have of perfection in art. And one can say that he has rendered a great service to his country in giving to it the learned creations of his spirit which raised considerably the honor and glory of French painters and which will serve in the future as models to those who would excel in their profession.

Pymander wished to speak to me, but we were interrupted by the arrival of several people, which obliged us to bring our conversation to a close and to put off until another time that which we still wished to say.

XV

The "Glorious" Revolution of 1688

A PEOPLE may let a king fall, yet still remain a people; but if a king let his people slip from him, he is no longer a king.

George Savile, first Marquis of Halifax

CONTENTS

QUESTIONS FOR STUDY

PART I

1. Evaluate the importance of the personalities of Charles and James in the fall of the House of Stuart.

2. How would Machiavelli have appraised Charles and James as princes?

3. What were Louis XIV's interests in England?

4. Who stood to gain more by the Treaty of Dover, Louis or Charles?

5. How well do the terms of the Declaration of Indulgence of 1673 indicate that Charles understood the prejudices of his subjects?

6. What was the principal objection of the Commons to Charles' Declaration?

7. "James II, in his Declaration of Indulgence (1687), tried to play both ends against the middle." Explain.

8. "James II behaved as if the civil wars had never been fought." Explain.

9. What rights did James infringe on, in his dealings with the Universities?

10. "James might have had his army if it had not been for his religion." Explain.

11. After 1688 the Whigs claimed all the credit for effecting the Glorious Revolution. How far do they rightfully deserve that credit?

12. "Nobody loves a failure." How far do you think this is responsible for posterity's judgment of the Stuarts?

PART II

13. What clues do you find as to why the revolution of 1688 has been called "glorious"?

14. What is the constitutional importance of the first act of the Convention Parliament?

15. What major points of conflict between crown and parliament during the previous ninety years were settled in 1688–1690?

16. What is the importance of the Act of Settlement of 1701?

17. Compare the interpretations of Macaulay and Petrie. Which do you think is closer to the truth as you understand it? How do you account for the differences in their positions?

18. What facts does Petrie ignore? What facts, particularly of an economic nature, does Macaulay ignore?

19. Why is it difficult for an Englishman to write a history of the revolution of 1688?

INTRODUCTION TO THE PROBLEM

The Restoration of Charles II in 1660 seemed to many Englishmen little short of a miracle: "This day," wrote John Evelyn in his diary, "His Majesty Charles the Second came to London after a sad and long exile and calamitous suffering both of the king and the Church. . . . This was also his birthday, and with a triumph of above 20,000 horse and foot, brandishing their swords and shouting with inexpressible joy; the ways strewed with flowers, the bells ringing, the streets hung with tapestries, fountains running with wine; trumpets, music, and myriads of people flocking. . . . I stood in the Strand and beheld it, and blessed God. And all this was done without one drop of blood shed, and by that very army which rebelled against him; but it was the Lord's doing, for such a restoration was never mentioned in any history, ancient or modern, since the return of the Jews from the Babylonian captivity; nor so joyful a day and so bright ever seen in this nation, this happening when to expect or effect it was past all human policy." [1]

The "inexpressible joy" with which most Englishmen greeted the Restoration did not endure. The return of Charles II solved the immediate problem of re-establishing a stable government, but the terms upon which Charles II ascended the throne left open numerous vital issues which had brought on the Civil Wars. Many of the religious and financial questions of the earlier reigns remained unsettled, and the king accepted few formal limitations upon his powers with regard to the law and to the "rights and privileges" of the parliament.

Moreover, a new element of conflict was added in the form of Catholicism in the royal family. The queen was a Catholic. "The king never committed himself until he lay on his death-bed, but his sympathies were not concealed." The king's brother, who ascended the throne as James II in 1685, was an avowed Catholic who converted his first wife and married a Catholic as his second. A Catholic royal family as head of a Protestant Church and an overwhelmingly Protestant state was an anomalous situation inevitably fraught with friction and irritation.

The Restoration did not, therefore, allay domestic strife. Old issues and new produced a continuation of internal quarrels, which were, to a great extent, canalized into a new form of conflict, the rivalry of political parties. The politically potent subjects of the crown were not all agreed, but tended rather to align themselves on either side of questions of great importance. Thus there came into existence the two historic factions of Whigs and Tories, which, though agreed on numerous fundamental points, fought on opposite sides on many of the major issues of the day and struggled for power and influence in the state.

To the domestic issues and party struggles were added the problems of foreign policy. Across the Channel, France and Holland were continually at swords' points. England was drawn to Holland by the religious tie of Protestantism, but repelled from her by a bitter commercial rivalry. France was not yet a serious business competitor, but she was a Catholic state with grandiose ambitions on the continent which might threaten England's security. Thus England had points of enmity and friendship with both countries, and Englishmen were continually torn between a desire to destroy their commercial rival and a growing dread of extending the power of the ambitious Louis XIV. The policy of the state alternated between war with the Dutch and alliance with the Dutch against France, and the natural dilemma as to which cause was to the true interest of England became involved with the political, religious and financial issues at home.

The period of the Restoration was thus an era in which were prolonged the struggles of earlier reigns, complicated and intensified by new questions. So explosive were the issues that they eventually burst forth in a new political over-turn, the "Glorious" Revolution of 1688.

While the whole period may be regarded as critical, two specific crises have been selected to introduce the student to the major issues and partisans involved. The documents illustrating these crises make up Part I of this Problem; those in Part II indicate the nature of the Revolutionary Settlement and the interpretations put on it by later historians.

Part **I.**   THE COMING OF REVOLUTION

A.   THE ROYAL BROTHERS

The seventeenth century in England is famous for the character study. Bishop Burnet, in intimate contact with the affairs of his time, began his *History of His Own Time* in 1683 and in it included character sketches.

1. *Charles II, by Burnet.*[1]

The king was then thirty years of age, and, as might have been supposed, past the levities of youth and the extravagance of pleasure. He had a very good understanding. He knew well the state of affairs both at home and abroad. He had a softness of temper that charmed all who came near him, till they found how little they could depend on good looks, kind words, and fair promises; in which he was liberal to excess, because he intended nothing by them, but to get rid of importunities, and to silence all further pressing upon him. He seemed to have no sense of religion: Both at prayers and sacrament he, as it were, took care to satisfy people, that he was in no sort concerned in that about which he was employed. So that he was very far from being an hypocrite, unless his assisting at those performances was a sort of hypocrisy (as no doubt it was).

But he was sure not to increase that by any the least appearance of religion. He said once to myself, he was no atheist, but he could not think God would make a man miserable only for taking a little pleasure out of the way. He disguised his Popery to the last. But when he talked freely, he could not help letting himself out against the liberty that under the Reformation all men took of inquiring into matters of religion: For from their inquiring into matters of religion they carried the humor farther, to inquire into matters of state. He said often, he thought government was a much safer and easier thing where the authority was believed infallible, and the faith and submission of the people was implicit: About which I had once much discourse with him.

He was affable and easy, and loved to be made so by all about him. The great art of keeping him long was, the being easy, and the making everything easy to him. He had made such observation on the French Government, that he thought a king who might be checked, or have his ministers called to an account by a parliament, was but a king in name. He had a great compass of knowledge, tho' he was never capable of much application or study. He understood the Mechanics and Physic; and was a good chemist, and much set on several preparations of mercury, chiefly the fixing it. He understood navigation well: But above all he knew the architecture of ships so perfectly, that in that respect he was exact rather more than became a prince. His apprehension was quick, and his memory good.

He was an everlasting talker. He told his stories with a good grace: But they came in his way too often. He had a very ill opinion of men and women; and did not think that there was either sincerity or chastity in the world out of principle, but that some had either the one or the other out of humor or vanity. He thought that nobody did serve him out of love: And so he was quits with all the world, and loved others as little as he thought they loved him. He hated business, and could not be easily brought to mind any: But when it was necessary, and he was set to it, he would stay as long as his ministers had work for him. The ruin of his reign, and of all his affairs, was occasioned chiefly by his delivering up at his first coming over to a mad range of pleasure. . . .

And, in the state his affairs were then in [when he was in exile] he accustomed himself to say to every person, and upon all occasions, that which he thought would please most: So that words or promises went very easily from him. And he had so ill an opinion of mankind, that he thought the great art of living and governing was, to manage all things and all persons with a depth of craft and dissimulation. And in that few men in the world could put on the appearance of sincerity better than he could: Under which so much artifice was usually hid, that in conclusion he could deceive none, for all were become mistrustful of him. He had great vices, but scarce any virtues to correct them: He had in him some vices that were less hurtful, which corrected his more hurtful ones.

He was during the active part of life given up to sloth and lewdness to such a degree, that he hated business, and could not bear the engaging in any thing that gave him much trouble, or put him under any constraint. And, tho' he desired to become absolute, and to overturn both our religion and our laws, yet he would neither run the risk, nor give himself the trouble, which so great a design required. He had an appearance of gentleness in his outward department: But he seemed to have no bowels nor tenderness in his nature: And in the end of his life he became cruel. He was apt to forgive all crimes, even blood itself: Yet he never forgave any thing that was done against himself, after his first and general act of indemnity, which was to be reckoned as done rather upon maxims of state than inclinations of mercy.

2. James II, by Burnet.[2]

I will digress a little to give an account of the Duke's character, whom I knew for some years so particularly, that I can say much upon my own knowledge. He was very brave in his youth, and so much magnified by Monsieur Turenne, that, till his marriage lessened him he really clouded the King, and pass'd for the superior genius. He was naturally candid and sincere, and a firm friend, till affairs and his religion wore out all his first principles and inclinations. He had a great desire to understand affairs: And in order to that he kept a constant journal of all that pass'd of which he showed me a great deal.

The Duke of Buckingham gave me once a short but severe character [sketch] of the two brothers. It was the more severe, because it was true: The King (he said) could see things if he would, and the Duke would see things if he could. He had no true judgment, and was soon determined by those whom he trusted: But he was obstinate against all other advices. He was bred with high notions of kingly authority, and laid it down for a maxim, that all who opposed the King were rebels in their hearts. He was perpetually in one amour or other, without being very nice in his choice: Upon which the King said once, he believed his brother had his mistresses given him by his priests for penance. . . .

B. THE CRISIS OF 1670–74

After the Restoration the management of affairs of state was largely in the hands of the Lord Chancellor, Edward Hyde, Earl of Clarendon. It was he who engineered much of the Restoration Settlement, part of which—the Clarendon Code—bears his name. His power and his personality bred opposition, however, and in 1667 he fell from power. The immediate cause of his downfall was the war with the Dutch. This war, ended by the Peace of Breda in 1667, while it brought to England, New York and New Jersey, had been by no means a completely successful venture for England, and Clarendon was chosen as a scapegoat. The banishment of Clarendon marked a turning point both in domestic and foreign policy. Charles II gave to no single minister as much power as the Chancellor had possessed; after 1667 he chose five advisers ("the cabal"), an arrangement which allowed him to pursue his own policies with considerable freedom.

[handwritten margin note: But Clarendon opposed the Code.]

1. *The Secret Treaty of Dover, 22 May 1670.* In 1668 England turned to her old enemies the Dutch, and with them and with Sweden formed the Triple Alliance, a league designed primarily to check French ambitions in the Low Countries. But the king of England had other policies and other motives. Alliance with the Dutch was distasteful to him. As republicans, and as commercial and naval rivals, they seemed to threaten his policies and his kingdom, and the Triple Alliance was scarcely concluded before Charles embarked on another course. The negotiations which led up to the Treaty of Dover were extraordinarily secret, and only a very few of Charles' ministers were admitted to his confidence. The text of the treaty was not published until 1830.[3]

For the perpetual union and friendship between the two kings and their states, articles so secret and advantageous to both monarchs have been agreed upon that a treaty of similar importance can hardly be found in any period of history.

The King of England, being convinced of the truth of the Roman Catholic religion is resolved to declare it, and to reconcile himself with the Church of Rome as soon as the state of his country's affairs permit. He has such confidence in the fidelity and affection of his subjects that none of them, not even those who (as yet) have been denied a full outpouring of divine grace, will fail in their due obedience to their sovereign. But as there are always unquiet spirits who mask their designs under the guise of religion, the King of England, for the peace of his kingdom, will avail himself of the assistance of the King of France, who, on his part, as he is anxious to contribute to a design glorious not only for the King of England but for the whole of Catholic Christendom, promises to pay to the King of England, the sum of two million livres tournois, the first half payable three months after ratification of the present

[handwritten margin note: One could not depend on them.]

treaty, the other half three months later. In addition, the King of France undertakes to provide, at his own expense, 6,000 troops for the execution of this design, if they should be required. The time for the declaration of Catholicism is left entirely to the discretion of the King of England.

The King of France will never violate the peace which he has concluded with Spain, nor will he do anything inconsistent with the terms of the treaty of Aix-la-Chapelle; so that it will be possible for the King of England to act in conformity with the conditions of the Triple Alliance.

If the King of France should acquire any fresh claims or rights on the Spanish dominions, the King of England will assist him by land and sea to enforce these rights.

Each of the contracting sovereigns has a sufficiently large population to justify their joint resolution to humble the pride of the States General [of Holland], and to destroy the power of a people which has not only shown ingratitude to those who have helped it to create its republic, but has had the insolence to set itself up as a sovereign arbiter among other states. Accordingly both sovereigns will jointly declare war on the States General, and neither will engage in a treaty or truce without the other. . . .

In the joint hostilities agreed upon the King of France will defray all the expenses of the campaign by land, the King of England agreeing to supply at his charge 6,000 foot.

For the war by sea the King of England will arm at least 60 men-of-war and 10 fireships, to be joined by a French auxiliary fleet of at least 30 good ships, the whole to be under the command of the Duke of York. To assist the King of England to defray the costs of the campaign, the King of France undertakes to pay him each year the sum of three million livres tournois, for so long as the war may last. The English share of the conquests from the Dutch shall be Walcheren, Sluys and Cadsand. . . .

After the King of England has made the declaration specified in article 2, it will be free for the King of France to decide the time for the joint declaration of war.

Should there be found in any treaty of either crown with another state any clause inconsistent with the terms of this treaty, such clause shall be null and void. . . .

2. *The Declaration of Indulgence.* The first indication of Charles' new policy can be seen in the following declaration issued on March 15, 1672. At the time Parliament was not in session.[4]

Charles Rex.

Our care and endeavors for the preservation of the rights and interests of the Church, have been sufficiently manifested to the world, by the whole course of our government since our happy restoration, and by the many and frequent ways of coercion that we have used for reducing all erring or dissenting persons, and for composing the unhappy differences in matters of religion, which we found among our subjects upon our return; but it being evident by the sad experience of twelve years, that there is very little fruit of all these forcible courses, we think ourselves obliged to make use of that supreme power in ecclesiastical matters, which is not only inherent in us, but hath been declared and recognized to be so, by several statutes and acts of Parliament; and therefore we do now accordingly issue this our declaration, as well for the quieting of our good subjects in these points, as for inviting strangers in this conjecture to come and live under us; and for the better encouragement of all to a cheerful following of their trades and callings, from whence we hope, by the blessing of God, to have many good and happy advantages to our government; as also for preventing for the future the danger that might otherwise arise from private meetings and seditious conventicles.

And in the first place, we declare our express resolution, meaning and intention to be, that the Church of England be preserved, and remain entire in its doctrine, discipline and government, as now it stands established by law; and that this be taken to be, as it is, the basis, rule, and standard of the general and public worship of God, and that the orthodox conformable clergy do receive and enjoy the revenues belonging thereunto, and that no person, though of a different opinion and persuasion, shall be exempt from paying his tithes or dues whatsoever. And further we declare, that no person shall be capable of holding any benefice, living, or ecclesiastical dignity or preferment of any kind, in this our kingdom of England, who is not exactly conformable.

We do in the next place declare our will and pleasure to be, that the execution of all, and all manner of penal laws in matters ecclesiastical, against whatsoever sort of nonconformists or recusants, be immediately suspended, and they are hereby suspended; and all judges, judges of assize and jail delivery, sheriffs, justices of peace, mayors, bailiffs and other officers whatsoever, whether ecclesiastical or civil, are to take notice of it, and pay due obedience thereto.

And that there may be no pretense for any of our subjects to continue their illegal meetings and conventicles, we do declare, that we shall from time to time allow a sufficient number of places as they shall be desired, in all parts of this our kingdom, for the use of such as do not conform to the Church of England, to meet and assemble in order to their public worship and devotion, which places shall be open and free to all persons.

But to prevent such disorders and inconveniences as may happen by this our indulgence, if not duly regulated; and that they may be the better protected by the civil magistrate; our express will and pleasure is, that none of our subjects do presume to meet in any place, until such places be allowed, and the teacher of that congregation be approved by us.

And lest any should apprehend that this restriction should make our said allowance and approbation difficult to be obtained, we do further declare, that this our indulgence as to the allowance of the public places of worship, and approbation of the preachers, shall extend to all sorts of nonconformists and recusants, except the recusants of the Roman Catholic religion, to whom we shall in no wise allow public places of worship, but only indulge them their share in the common exemption from the penal laws, and the exercise of their worship in their private houses only.

And if after this our clemency and indulgence any of our subjects shall pretend to abuse this liberty, and shall preach seditiously, or to the derogation of the doctrine, discipline or government of the established church, or shall meet in places not allowed by us, we do hereby give them warning, and declare we will proceed against them with all imaginable severity. And we will let them see, we can be as severe to punish such offenders when so justly provoked, as we are indulgent to truly tender consciences.

Given at our court at Whitehall this 15th day of March, in the four and twentieth year of our reign.

3. *Declaration of War on the Dutch.* On March 17, 1672, two days after the issuance of the Declaration of Indulgence, Charles declared war on the Dutch. "Incidents" had already occurred; in the summer of 1671, an English yacht had fired on Dutch ships in the Channel for failing to salute the English flag, and early in March, 1672 a small English force had attacked a large Dutch convoy off the Isle of Wight.[5]

We have been always so zealous for the quiet of Christendom and so careful not to invade any Kingdom or State, that we hope you will do us the justice to believe, that it is nothing but inevitable necessity which forces us to the Resolution of taking up arms.

[Account here follows of the causes of the First Dutch War, 1665–7, and the subsequent violation of the Treaty of Breda by the Dutch in Surinam.]

But it is no wonder that they venture these outrages upon our subjects in remote parts when they dare be so bold with Our Royal Person and the honor of this nation so near us as in their own country, there being scarce a town within their territories, that is not filled with abusive pictures and false historical medals and pillars. . . .

The right of the flag is so ancient . . . it was never questioned and it was expressly acknowledged in the Treaty of Breda, and yet this last summer it was not only violated by their commanders at sea, and that violation afterwards justified at the Hague, but it was also represented by them in most Courts of Christendom as ridiculous for us to demand. . . . An ungrateful insolence. . . .

We have therefore thought fit to declare and do hereby declare, that we will prosecute war both by sea and land against the States General of the United Provinces and all their subjects and inhabitants, . . . willing and requiring all our subjects to take notice of the same.

4. *The Commons and the Declaration of Indulgence.* When Parliament convened in February, 1673, the provisions of the Declaration of Indulgence had been in effect for almost a year. The passages which follow indicate the reaction of the Commons to Charles' religious policy. The first selection, an account of the debates on February 10, 1673, is taken from a diary kept by Sir Edward Dering, M.P. for East Retford and a moderate supporter of the king. The remaining selections are from the *Journals* of the Lords and Commons.[6]

(*Commons' Debates, February 10, 1673.*) This day according to order we were to take into consideration the King's declaration concerning tender consciences, and that clause particularly which did declare all the penal laws in matters of religion to be suspended.

The speaker put them in mind of the debate adjourned to this day, and for long time no man stood up at all to speak.

At last Sir George Reeves stood up, and said he perceived that those gentlemen that were so warm for this debate on Saturday were now grown cool in it, and therefore desired the House would proceed to something else.

Then Sir Thomas Meres stood up, and said though they were willing to proceed very calmly in this business yet they should find they were not cool in it, though there be always too many gentlemen in this House that are but luke-warm in matters of religion, or to that effect; words that from another man would not have passed without some exception taken to them.

But he moved nothing at all, and again a long silence was in the House, till at last Sir Thomas Lee moved for reading the King's declaration, which was to be the subject matter of the debate; which was done and after that a long and unusual silence in the House a third time, till the speaker putting them in mind that time was precious, and it was now half past eleven, my Lord Cavendish then stood up, and desired that the reasons of the House given to his Majesty upon the like occasion in March 1662 might be read, which being seconded by Sir John Mounson, was done, and those reasons read, which were indeed direct to the matter in hand, and full against all indulgence to dissenters in religion; one reason among others being that there were laws of uniformity in force, which could not be dispensed with but by act of parliament, and that his Majesty's declaration from Breda, or any otherwise, could not bind him against the advice of his people tendered in parliament, with other things to this purpose.

Then Mr. Waller stood up and made a long premeditated speech concerning the power of the King in ecclesiastical matters; the usefulness to the people of his power of dispensing, instanced particularly in the dispensing of keeping of Lent, which because it pleased us, we did not complain of.

Then Mr. Powle made a long speech to the contrary, showing that the King could not dispense, much less suspend, the laws in being.

Mr. Seymour, Sir Robert Howard, and Sir George Downing spoke for the declaration. Colonel Strangways, Sergeant Seys, and Mr. Whorwood and Sir Thomas Meres against it.

Mr. Attorney General opened at large the King's power in ecclesiastical matters; that it was the same with what it was in temporal; that his supremacy as head of the church was chiefly negative, and exclusive of all others, particularly of the Pope, and so it was put in the 39 Articles, and so in the oath of supremacy; that the convocation could make no canons without the King's consent, and yet even then they did not bind without authority of parliament; but that in particular cases the King might judge of the expediency of many laws, and dispense with them *pro bono publico;* that he might pardon the penalties of any laws after they were broken was known by all; that in many cases he might dispense with the law before it was broken, as in the act of navigation, when we wanted provisions to set out our fleet, and could not have them but in foreign bottoms, he had done, and with very just reason. . . .

But the debate quickly went off from justifying and maintaining the clause to the manner of laying it asleep; the words of the question moved by many being that we should vote it illegal. Others, thinking that too harsh, would have us proceed by petition to the King that

he would be pleased to consider the consequences of those words; that they gave us some apprehensions of invalidating our laws without the due proceedings which we conceive ought to be by acts of parliament; and that he would please to declare that the laws in matters of religion and uniformity were still in force, notwithstanding the said declaration; and for the wording of it, it might be done with more respect to his Majesty, and with more full security of what we desired by a petition than it could be done by a vote; and therefore moved that a committee might be appointed to draw up such an address to his Majesty. This was moved by Sir Robert Carr, seconded by Mr. Secretary, myself, Mr. Attorney General, and Sir Thomas Osborne; but opposed by Sir Thomas Meres, Sir Thomas Lee, Sergeant Seys, and others.

That which I said was to this purpose: that we were told on all sides that this was a very nice question, and so indeed it was; that many a good man there, and desirous to do his duty to his King and his country, might yet be very doubtful what to advise them to; that I was no advocate for that clause in the declaration which was now under debate because that I did not see any material difference between an universal indefinite, unlimited suspension of laws, as this seemed to be by the declaration, and a total repeal and abrogation, which no man had yet affirmed the King had power to do. But yet I did most willingly join with these gentlemen who had made it their desires that it might be suffered at least *decenter cadere* [to perish decently]; that there might pass no vote upon this occasion which might so much as in appearance lessen the entire happy harmony that was between the King and this House; that if we did look back what our ancestors had done in this place, it might be some directions to us what to do; that I should not look further back than to 3rd *Caroli* [1628], a parliament that was zealous enough for the liberty of those who sent them thither, and which had been already often cited in the debates of this day.

They had then many reasons to complain of the violation of their laws, and in matters of supreme importance. . . . That yet all this produced but a petition and address commonly known by the name of the Petition of Right; and that secured them. That thanks be to God the case was now very different, no man could yet say that anyone's liberty or property had been invaded in the least, or that suffered to the value of a hair of his head. That what we complained of was rather what we feared than what we felt; that I would not deny but these fears were worthy of our consideration by men in the trust under which we were, but I would not have any jealousy from a doubtful word or unweighed expression put us upon anything that might be inconvenient or so much as ungrateful to his Majesty. That we all agreed in the end, and I, as much as any man, aimed at the security of our laws, only debated about the means of coming to it. That it was yet but 4 days since Mr. Speaker had, in the name of the House, desired leave of his Majesty to address ourselves to him in all cases of difficulty and importance; that I did not know any case more important likely to happen than this, and therefore thought it proper to make use of that liberty we had asked and his Majesty had granted; that from so gracious a King to so dutiful and loyal a parliament we could no ways doubt of a satisfactory answer; and therefore humbly moved them to name a committee to draw up an address to his Majesty upon the subject matter of this debate.

At last, the question being stated and called for, it was moved that the previous question should be put; *viz.*, whether the question should be put or not. And the House being divided, the yeas that stayed in were 168, the noes that went out were 116.

After this the main question was put in these words, "whether the penal statutes of this kingdom in matters ecclesiastical can be suspended otherwise than by act of parliament," and carried full in the negative without dividing the House. Then they ordered a committee to draw up an address to the King upon this vote and the debate of the House. And Tuesday being Shrove Tuesday and Wednesday Ash Wednesday, the House adjourned to Thursday.

(*14 February.*) . . . Mr. Powle reports from the committee appointed to prepare and draw up a petition and address to his majesty the said petition and address; which he read in his place and, after, delivered the same in at the clerk's table. And the same, being again twice read, is as followeth, *viz.:*—

Most gracious sovereign: We, your majesty's most loyal and faithful subjects, the commons assembled in parliament, do in the first place, as in all duty bound, return your majesty our most humble and hearty thanks for the many gracious promises and assurances, which your majesty hath several times during this present parliament given to us, that your majesty would secure and maintain unto us the true reformed Protestant religion, our liberties, and properties; which most gracious assurances your majesty hath out of your great goodness been pleased to renew unto us more particularly at the opening of this present session of parliament.

And further we crave leave humbly to represent that we have with all duty and expedition taken into our consideration several parts of your maj-

esty's last speech to us, and withal the declaration therein mentioned for indulgence to dissenters, dated the 15th of March last. And we find ourselves bound in duty to inform your majesty that penal statutes in matter ecclesiastical cannot be suspended but by act of parliament. We therefore, . . . do most humbly beseech your majesty that the said laws may have their free course until it shall be otherwise provided for by act of parliament; and that your majesty would graciously be pleased to give such directions herein, that no apprehensions or jealousies may remain in the hearts of your majesty's good and faithful subjects.

Resolved, etc., that this house doth agree with the committee in the petition and address by them drawn up to be presented to his majesty. . . .

(*24 February.*) . . . Mr. Secretary Coventry reports and presents in writing from his majesty his answer to the humble petition and address of this house, which . . . is as followeth, *viz.:*—

Charles R. His majesty hath received an address from you, and he hath seriously considered of it, and returneth you this answer: that he is very much troubled that that declaration which he put out for ends so necessary to the quiet of his kingdom, and especially in that conjuncture, should have proved the cause of disquiet in this house of commons and give occasion to the questioning of his power in ecclesiastics; which he finds not done in the reigns of any of his ancestors. He is sure he never had thoughts of using it otherwise than as it hath been entrusted in him—to the peace and establishment of the Church of England and the ease of all his subjects in general.

Neither doth he pretend to the right of suspending any laws where in the properties, rights, or liberties of any of his subjects are concerned, nor to alter anything in the established doctrine or discipline of the Church of England; but his only design in this was to take off the penalties the statutes inflict upon the dissenters, and which he believes, when well considered of, you yourselves would not wish executed according to the rigor and letter of the law. Neither hath he done this with any thought of avoiding or precluding the advice of his parliament; and, if any bill shall be offered him which shall appear more proper to attain the aforesaid ends and secure the peace of the church and kingdom, when tendered in due manner to him, he will show how readily he will concur in all ways that shall appear good for the kingdom. . . .

(*26 February.*) . . . Mr. Powle reports . . . an answer agreed by the committee . . . , which . . . is as followeth, *viz.:*—

Most gracious sovereign: We, your majesty's

most humble and loyal subjects, the knights, citizens, and burgesses in this present parliament assembled, do render to your sacred majesty our most dutiful thanks for that, to our unspeakable comfort, your majesty hath been pleased so often to reiterate unto us those gracious promises and assurances of maintaining the religion now established and the liberties and properties of your people. And we do not in the least measure doubt but that your majesty had the same gracious intentions in giving satisfaction to your subjects by your answer to our last petition and address.

Yet, upon a serious consideration thereof, we find that the said answer is not sufficient to clear the apprehensions that may justly remain in the minds of your people by your majesty's having claimed a power to suspend penal statutes in matters ecclesiastical, and which your majesty does still seem to assert . . . to be entrusted in the crown and never questioned in the reigns of any of your ancestors—wherein we humbly conceive your majesty hath been very much misinformed; since no such power was ever claimed or exercised by any of your majesty's predecessors, and, if it should be admitted, might tend to the interrupting of the free course of the laws and altering the legislative power, which hath always been acknowledged to reside in your majesty and your two houses of parliament.

We do therefore, with an unanimous consent, become again most humble suitors unto your sacred majesty that you would be pleased to give us a full and satisfactory answer to our said petition and address, and that your majesty would take such effectual order that the proceedings in this matter may not for the future be drawn into consequence or example.

. . . Resolved, etc., that the whole address be agreed to as it was brought in by the committee. . . .

(*8 March.*) . . . His majesty sitting in his royal throne, adorned with his crown and regal ornaments, commanded the gentleman usher of the black rod to give notice to the house of commons that they attend his majesty presently. The commons being come with their speaker, his majesty made this short speech following: "My lords and gentlemen: . . . If there be any scruple remain with you concerning the suspension of penal laws, I here faithfully promise you that what hath been done in that particular shall not for the future be drawn either into consequence or example. . . ."

Next the lord chancellor reported . . . that his majesty had the last night, in pursuance of what he then intended and declared this morning concerning the suspension of penal laws not being for the future drawn either into consequence or example, caused the original declaration under the great seal to be cancelled in his presence;

whereof himself and several other lords of the council were witnesses. . . .

5. *The Religious Policy of the Commons.* The withdrawal of the Declaration of Indulgence was not enough to satisfy the Commons. In the previous session there had been introduced a bill to prevent the growth of popery. This bill, later to be known as the "Test Act," received the royal assent on March 29, 1673.[7]

An act for preventing dangers which may happen from popish recusants. For preventing dangers which may happen from popish recusants and quieting the minds of his majesty's good subjects: be it enacted . . . that all and every person or persons, as well peers as commoners, that shall bear any office or offices civil or military; or shall receive any pay, salary, fee, or wages by reason of any grant from his majesty; or shall have command or place of trust from or under his majesty or from any of his majesty's predecessors . . . within the realm of England, . . . or in his Majesty's navy, . . . or shall be of the household or in the service or employment of his majesty or of his royal highness the duke of York, who shall inhabit, reside, or be within the city of London or Westminster or within thirty miles distant from the same . . . ; the said person and persons shall personally appear . . . in his majesty's high court of chancery or in his majesty's court of king's bench, and there in public . . . take the several oaths of supremacy and allegiance. . . . And the said respective officers aforesaid shall also receive the sacrament of the Lord's Supper according to the usage of the Church of England . . . in some parish church upon some . . . Sunday immediately after divine service and sermon. . . .

[The next article provides similar tests to be taken by every new appointee to such office within stated times after his appointment.]

And be it further enacted . . . that all . . . that do . . . refuse to take the said oaths and sacrament in the said courts and places . . . shall be *ipso facto* adjudged incapable and disabled in law . . . to have . . . the said office or offices. . . . And be it further enacted that all . . . that shall . . . refuse to take the said oaths or the sacrament as aforesaid . . . , and yet after such neglect and refusal shall execute any of the said offices or employments after the said times expired . . . , and being thereupon lawfully convicted . . . , shall be disabled from thenceforth to sue or use any action, bill, plaint, or information in course of law, or to prosecute any suit in any court of equity or to be guardian of any child or executor or administrator of any person or capable of any legacy or deed or gift, or to bear any office within this realm of England, . . . ; and shall forfeit the sum of £500, to be recovered by him that shall sue for the same. . . .

And be it further enacted that, if any person or persons, not bred up by his or their parent or parents from their infancy in the popish religion and professing themselves to be popish recusants, shall breed up, instruct, or educate his or their child or children, or suffer them to be instructed or educated, in the popish religion, every such person, being thereof convicted, shall be thenceforth disabled of bearing any office or place of trust or profit in church or state. . . .

And be it further enacted . . . that at the same time when the persons concerned in this act shall take the aforesaid oaths of supremacy and allegiance, they shall likewise make and subscribe this declaration following, under the same penalties and forfeitures as by this act is appointed: "I, A.B., do declare that I do believe that there is not any transubstantiation in the sacrament of the Lord's Supper, or in the elements of bread and wine, at or after the consecration thereof by any person whatsoever."

6. *The Commons and the Dutch War.* On October 27, 1673 Charles asked Parliament for additional funds with which to carry on the war. In the selections which follow, the reaction of the Commons is demonstrated. The first selection is taken from an account of proceedings in the House of Commons written by Anchitel Grey, M.P. for Derby; the others are from the *Journals* of the Commons.[8]

Mr. Russell. The business of this day is "Money." . . . Would not vote things hand over head; let us consider what we give this money for, and consider what we give as destructive to the nation (by maintaining this war) and the Protestant religion. The French king calls this war a "Catholic war" and seeing we are upon so wrong a bottom, and if betrayed by those about the king let us tell him plainly of it. Former Parliaments have done it; and moves to pass a negative vote upon "Money."

Mr. Secretary Coventry. Knows not that ever the House of Austria had the name of Huguenot among them, though Holland joined with them. We can have war with Holland without religion in the case, they once had with the French as we have now. . . . Consider they [the Dutch] have provided a great fleet against the summer, and you will give no money, and so have no fleet; which way will you secure the plantations [colonies] and Tangier?

Mr. Sacheverell. Is one of those that think "giving of money" one of the greatest grievances. It seems to him that those villainous counsellors, that persuaded the king to make this war, have deceived him in this speech; do not they know of the unpaid taxes granted this last session with the prizes and the customs? . . . It was said before . . . "Give money and grievances shall be redressed." . . . The army is so insolent that they may turn you out of doors. . . . If redress of grievances be an argument for "Money" you will never want grievances. Will you not heighten France by giving more money, . . . that he may have dominion at sea which we now contend for? And by this negative we may deliver ourselves both from France and Rome.

Mr. Attorney Finch. This is an English and no other war. . . . The king may engage in a war; but when his people shall storm him out of it, the hour will come that his enemies wish for, for the Dutch will now be upon greater terms, having ever desired such a storm as the king could not allay.

Mr. Powle. Shall never think that privilege of Parliament is not violated so long as a Privy Councilor sits in the Chair. He that was contriver of the Declaration [of Indulgence] made Lord Privy Seal and another as much concerned made chief governor of Scotland. This is to bring in popery in triumph.

Sir William Coventry. Thinks it better we had no fleet; thinks not so highly of the Dutch nor meanly of ourselves but that we may do well without the King of France. . . . The French interest is to keep us from being masters of the sea; the French have pursued that interest well; moves to insert in the question, "unless it shall appear that the obstinacy of the Dutch shall make a supply necessary."

[The Commons then refuse a supply.]

(*January 24, 1674.*) A message from His Majesty by Sir Edward Carteret, Usher of the Black Rod.

Mr. Speaker, His Majesty commands this honorable House to attend him immediately in the House of Peers.

And accordingly Mr. Speaker, with the House went up to attend His Majesty.

Mr. Speaker reports that, because he would not trust his memory, His Majesty had been pleased to deliver to him his speech in writing: which he read to the House; which is as follows, *viz.:*—

My Lords and Gentlemen,

At the beginning of this session I told you (as I thought I had reason to do), that the States General had not yet made me any proposals which could be imagined with intent to conclude, but only to amuse.

To avoid this imputation they have now sent me a letter by the Spanish ambassador, offering me some terms of peace, upon conditions formerly drawn up, and in a more decent style than before.

It is upon this that I desire your speedy advice: For, if you shall find the terms such as may be embraced, your advice will have great weight with me: And if you find them defective, I hope you will give me your advice and assistance how to get better terms.

Upon the whole matter I doubt not but you will have a care of my honor, and the honor and safety of the nation, which are now so deeply concerned.

(*January 27, 1674.*) The House then resolved into a Committee of the whole House to proceed in the consideration of His Majesty's last speech.

Mr. Speaker left the Chair.

Sir Charles Harbord took the Chair of the Committee.

Mr. Speaker resumed the Chair.

Sir Charles Harbord reports from the Committee of the whole House a vote and resolve of the Committee to be presented to the House: which was delivered in at the clerk's table; and is as follows; *viz.:*—

That, upon consideration of His Majesty's gracious speech, and the proposals from the States General of the United Provinces, this committee is of opinion that His Majesty be humbly advised to proceed in a treaty with the said States, in order to a speedy peace.

7. *The Treaty of Westminster, February 9, 1674.*[9]

It is concluded and agreed that from this day there shall be a firm and inviolable peace, union and friendship betwixt His Majesty the King of Great Britain and the High and Mighty Lords the States General of the United Provinces, and betwixt all their subjects whether within Europe or without, in all regions and places whatsoever. . . .

IV. That the aforesaid States General of the United Provinces in due acknowledgment on their part of the King of Great Britain's right to have his flag respected in the seas hereafter mentioned, shall and do declare and agree, that whatsoever ships or vessels belonging to the United Provinces whether vessels of war or others or whether single or in fleets, shall meet in any of the seas from Cape Finisterre to the middle point of the land Van Staten in Norway, with any ships or vessels belonging to his Majesty of Great Britain, whether those ships be single or in greater number, if they carry His Majesty of Great Britain's flag or jack, the aforesaid Dutch vessels or ships shall strike their flag and lower their top sail, in the same manner and with as much respect as hath at any time or in any place been formerly practised towards any ships of His Majesty of Great Britain or his predecessors, by any ships of the States General or their predecessors.

C. THE CRISIS OF 1685–88

In 1685, Charles II, having fulfilled his primary policy of "never going again on his travels," died in his bed at Whitehall. The last years of his reign had not been peaceful. In 1678 England had been convulsed with the hysteria of the Popish Plot, the principal results of which had been a violent increase of anti-Catholic feeling, and a serious attempt to exclude Charles' brother James, an avowed Catholic, from the succession. The attempt at exclusion failed and Charles, favored by a popular revulsion against the violent measures of the Exclusionists, or "Whigs," built up a strong party of Anglican Tories around the monarchy. Thus he passed to James a reasonably stable throne.

1. *Catholics in the Army: the King and the Parliament.* In the spring of 1685 James II had to face rebellion. The Duke of Monmouth, an illegitimate son of Charles II, was put forward by the Whig extremists as the rightful heir to the throne and the protector of the Protestant interest. Monmouth attracted relatively few adherents, and the militia, stiffened by the tiny regular army, put down the rebellion with little trouble. Parliament, summoned before the rebellion, had given James agreeable evidence of its loyalty by voting funds; in their second session, James went before them confidently

with a request for more money. The selections which follow are taken from Anchitel Grey's *Debates*.[10]

(*The king's speech, November 9, 1685.*) My Lords and Gentlemen,

After the storm that seemed to be coming upon us when we parted last, I am glad to meet you all again in so great peace and quietness; God Almighty be praised, by whose blessing that Rebellion was suppressed! But when we reflect what an inconsiderable number of men began it, and how long they carried it on without any opposition, I hope everybody will be convinced that the militia, which hath hitherto been so much depended on, is not sufficient for such occasions; and that there is nothing but a good force of well-disciplined troops in constant pay that can defend us from such as, either at home or abroad, are disposed to disturb us: And, in truth, my concern for the peace and quiet of my subjects, as well as for the safety of the Government, made me think it necessary to increase the number to the proportion I have done: That I owed as well to the honor as the security of the nation; whose reputation was so infinitely exposed to all our neighbors, by having so evidently lain open to this late wretched attempt, that it is not to be repaired without keeping such a body of men on foot that none may ever have the thought of finding us again so miserably unprovided.

It is for the support of this great charge, which is now more than double to what it was, that I ask your assistance in giving me a supply answerable to the expenses it brings along with it: and I cannot doubt, but what I have begun, so much for the honor and defense of the Government, will be continued by you with all the cheerfulness and readiness that is requisite for a work of so great importance.

Let no man take exception that there are some officers in the army not qualified, according to the late tests, for their employments: The gentlemen, I must tell you, are most of them well-known to me: And, having formerly served with me on several occasions and always approved the loyalty of their principles by their practice, I think them now fit to be employed under me. And I will deal plainly with you, that, after having had the benefit of their service in such a time of need and danger, I will neither expose them to disgrace, nor myself to the want of them, if there should be another rebellion to make them necessary to me.

(*The Commons debate, November 12.*) Sir Winston Churchill. Some other than the militia is necessary to be found: I move a supply for the army.

Lord Preston. We have lately had an unfortunate proof, how little we are to depend upon the militia, and therefore we must all approve of His Majesty's increasing the forces to what they are. France is formidable, now Holland's forces are greatly increased, and we must be strong in proportion, for preservation of ourselves and Flanders and toward that, the good harmony betwixt the King and this House hath greatly contributed. It has had two other great effects abroad. 1. The French King's army last spring was marching towards Germany; Crequi was far advanced; but when the King of France heard the kindness of this House to the King, and the defeat of Mon-mouth, he recalled them. 2. The French and Spaniards had also a difference about Haye and Fonterabia: The French advanced their troops and recalled them on this news. This is the noble effect of the harmony between the King and this House who have (I hope) brought the same Heart and Loyalty they had the last time here. Hence we may conclude, these levies made by the King are just, reasonable, and necessary. And so let us vote a supply to answer His Majesty's present occasions.

Earl of Ranelagh. The question is, whether a supply or not? I do not intend to arraign the militia, but seeing a soldier is a trade and must (as all other trades are) be learned, I will show you where the militia has failed; *viz.*, at Chatham; and in June last, when the late Duke of Monmouth landed and had but eighty-three men, and £300 in money, who, in spite of the militia, nay in spite of such other force as the King could spare hence, brought it so far as he did. If the King of France had landed then, what would have become of us? I say, the militia is not insignificant, but an additional force is necessary and so a supply that is answerable to it. . . .

Sir Thomas Clarges. If it shall appear to you that the King's revenue that he hath already be sufficient to supply all the occasions what then need we give him more? It is moved that we should proceed by paragraphs. To come first to the militia, who (let me tell you) did considerable service in the late Rebellion, and if a great nobleman of this Kingdom had been supplied and assisted, it had soon been quelled. A confidence betwixt the King and his people is absolutely needful, let it come whence it will; our happiness consists in it. His Majesty, on his first entrance on the Crown, told us, "he had been misrepresented, and that he would preserve the Government in Church and State now established by law, and would maintain us in all our just rights and privileges."

Over-joyed at this, we ran hastily in to him; we gave four millions (reckoning what we added to him for life was worth) at once. The present revenue is £1,900,000, or two millions, yearly; the charge of the Government (admitting this army kept up) is but £1,300,000 yearly: And pray let us not forget that there was a Bill of Exclusion debated in this House; I was here, and showed myself against it; the arguments for it were, "That we should, in case of a Popish successor, have a Popish army." You see the Act of the Test already broken, but pray remember what the late Lord Chancellor told you, when the late King (of blessed memory) passed that Act: The words were to this effect; "By this Act you are provided against Popery, that no Papist can possibly creep into any employment."

I am afflicted greatly at this breach of our liberties, and seeing so great difference betwixt this speech and those heretofore made, cannot but believe this was by some other advice. This, struck at here, is our all, and I wonder there have been any men so desperate as to take any employment not qualified for it; and I would therefore have the question, "That a standing army is destructive to the country.". . .

Sir William Trumbull. The Kingdom is guarded by law; we are now in perfect peace; the King is both feared and loved; an army little needed; men justly afraid: That which made the last rebellion as it was, the man that headed it was a favorite of the faction, and though he had got such a number, he was beaten by 1800 men only. I am against an army.

Mr. Seymour. This last rebellion has contributed to our future peace and those engaged in it have sung their penitential psalm and their punishment rejoiced at by all good persons. I do not commend the militia, yet it is not to be rejected, but to be new modeled; and for my part, I had rather pay double to these, [meaning for keeping up the militia] from whom I fear nothing, than half so much to those, of whom I must ever be afraid; and, say what you will, it is a standing army. The last force preserved the peace and was sufficient to do it, in the late King's time, and is now; all the profit and security of this nation is in our ships; and had there been the least ship in the Channel, it would have disappointed him.

Supporting an army is maintaining so many idle persons to lord it over the rest of the subjects. The King declared, "That no soldiers should quarter in private houses"; but that they did: "That they should pay for all things they took"; but they paid nothing for almost all they took. And for officers to be employed not taking the tests, it is dispensing with all the laws at once; and if these men be good and kind, we know not whether it proceeds from their generosity or principles: For we must remember, it is treason for any man to be reconciled to the Church of Rome; for the Pope, by law, is declared an enemy to this Kingdom.

A supply given, as moved for, is a kind of an establishing an army by Act of Parliament; and when they have got the power into their hands, we are then to derive it from their courtesy; and therefore I would have the question be, "That the safety of the Kingdom doth not consist with a standing force": And this, it may be, well disappoint these persons that make it their business this way, to make themselves useful. . . .

Sir Richard Temple. I must concur with the King that the militia is not sufficient: I am for mending the militia, and to make it such as the King and Kingdom may confide in it; to trust to mercenary force alone is to give up all our liberties at once. If you provide a constant supply to support them by setting up an army, Sir Thomas Meres has turned it into a supply for the navy. There is no country in the world that has a law to set up an army. We have already made an ample supply for the Government. It is for kings to come to the House, from time to time, on extraordinary occasions; and if this army be provided for by law, they will never more come to this House.

I am for giving for the extraordinary charge past. Armies are useful when occasion is for them; but if you establish them, you can disband them no more. I am for a supply, but not on this score of the militia: There was not a company formed till 1588; and as soon as Queen Elizabeth had done with her army, she disbanded it. Armies have been fatal often to princes. The Army, in the late King's time, often turned out their leaders. I am for going to the House for leave for a bill to mend the militia.

Sir Winston Churchill. The Beef-Eaters [Tower of London guards], at this rate, may be called an army.

Sir Thomas Hussey. The colonel may say what he will of the Beef-Eaters, as he nick-names them; but they are established by Act of Parliament. . . .

The question being put, that a supply be given to His Majesty,

Sir Thomas Clarges moved, that the words, "towards the support of the additional forces," may be added: which was carried in the negative, 225 to 156; and then these votes passed:

Resolved, *Nemine contradicente,* That a supply be given to His Majesty; and that the House be moved to give leave to bring in a bill to render the militia useful.

Which were agreed to by the House.

(*The Commons' address, November 16.*) We your Majesty's most loyal and faithful subjects, the Commons in Parliament assembled, do in the first place (as in duty bound) return your Majesty our most humble and hearty thanks for your great care and conduct in supporting the late Rebellion, which threatened the overthrow of this Government both in Church and State, and the utter extirpation of our religion as by law established, which is most dear unto us, and which your Majesty hath been pleased to give us repeated assurances you will always defend and support; which with all grateful hearts we shall ever acknowledge.

We farther crave leave to acquaint your Majesty that we have, with all duty and readiness, taken into our consideration your Majesty's gracious speech to us: And as to that part of it, relating to the officers in the army, not qualified for their employments, according to an Act of Parliament made in the 25th year of the reign of your Majesty's Royal Brother, entitled, An Act for preventing Dangers which may happen from Popish Recusants, we do, out of our bounden duty, humbly represent unto your Majesty, that those officers cannot by law be capable of their employments; and that the incapacities they bring upon themselves thereby, can no way be taken off but by an Act of Parliament.

Therefore, out of that great deference and duty we owe unto your Majesty, who have been graciously pleased to take notice of their services to you, we are preparing a bill to pass both Houses for your royal assent, to indemnify them from the penalties they have now incurred: and because the continuing of them in their employments may be taken to be a dispensing with that law without Act of Parliament (the consequence of which is of the greatest concern to the rights of all your Majesty's subjects, and to all the laws made for security of their religion) we therefore, the knights, citizens, and burgesses of your Majesty's House of Commons, do most humbly beseech your Majesty that you would be graciously pleased to give such directions therein that no apprehensions or jealousies may remain in the hearts of your Majesty's good and faithful subjects.

2. *Catholics in the Army: the King and Courts.* After his failure in Parliament, James turned to the law courts. In 1686 a test case was arranged in which Sir Edward Hales, a Catholic holding a colonel's commission, was sued by his coachman Godden according to the provisions of the Test Act. In defense Hales pleaded that he had received the King's letters patent dispensing with the oaths in his case. The speech of the Lord Chief Justice follows.[11]

. . . In the case of Godden and Hales, wherein the defendant pleads a dispensation from the king, it is doubted whether or no the king had such a prerogative. Truly, upon the argument before us, it appeared as clear a case as ever came before this court; but, because men fancy I know not what difficulty when really there is none, we were willing to give so much countenance to the question in the case as to take the advice of all the judges of England.

They were all assembled at Serjeants' Inn, and this case was put to them. . . . And I must tell you that there were ten upon the place that clearly delivered their opinions. . . . My brother Powell said he was inclined to be of the same opinion, but he would rather have some more time to consider of it. But, he has since sent by my brother Holloway to let us know that he does concur with us. To these eleven judges there is one dissenter, brother Street, who yet continues his opinion that the king cannot dispense in this case. But that's the opinion of one single judge against the opinion of eleven.

We were satisfied in our judgments before and, having the concurrence of eleven out of twelve, we think we may very well declare the opinion of the court to be that the king may dispense in this case. And the judges go upon these grounds: —(1) that the kings of England are sovereign princes; (2) that the laws of England are the king's laws; (3) that therefore 'tis an inseparable prerogative in the kings of England to dispense with penal laws in particular cases and upon particular necessary reasons; (4) that of those reasons and those necessities, the king himself is sole judge; and then, which is consequent upon all; (5) that this is not a trust invested in, or granted to, the king by the people, but the ancient remains of the sovereign power and prerogative of the kings of England; which never yet was taken from them, nor can be. And therefore, such a dispensation appearing upon records to come [in] time enough to save him from the forfeiture, judgment ought to be given for the defendant.

3. *Catholics in the Universities.* James hoped to introduce his co-religionists not only into the army but also into the universities and even into the Church of England. The following account of these activities is taken from Bishop Burnet's *History of His Own Times.* Burnet was a firm Protestant, but while his writings against popery incurred the enmity of the court party, his deprecation of the persecution of papists gained him the hatred of the extreme anti-Catholic faction. He held various ecclesiastical offices, but in 1684 thought it advisable to go into voluntary exile on the continent. In 1689 William made him Bishop of Salisbury.[12]

Jefferies [the Lord Chief Justice] was much sunk at court and Herbert was the most in favor. But now [1686] Jefferies, to recommend himself, offered a bold and illegal advice, for setting up an ecclesiastical commission, without calling it the high commission, pretending it was only a standing court of delegates. The act that put down the high commission in the year 1640, had provided by a clause, as full as could be conceived, that no court should be ever set up for those matters, besides the ordinary ecclesiastical courts. Yet, in contempt of that, a court was erected, with full power to proceed in a summary and arbitrary way in all ecclesiastical matters, without limitations to any rule of law in their proceedings. This stretch of the supremacy, so contrary to law, was assumed by a king, whose religion made him condemn all that supremacy that the law had vested in the crown. . . .

The deanery of Christ's Church [College], the most important post in the university [of Oxford], was given to Massey, one of the new converts [to Catholicism], though he had neither the gravity, the learning, nor the age that was suitable to such a dignity. But all was supplied by his early conversion: and it was set up for a maxim, to encourage all converts. He at first went to prayers in the chapel. But soon after, he declared himself more openly. Not long after this, the president of Magdalen college died. That is esteemed the richest foundation in England, perhaps in Europe; for though their certain rents are but about £4 or £5000 yet it is thought that the improved value of the estate belonging to it is about £40,000. So it was no wonder that the priests studied to get this endowment into their hands.

They had endeavored to break in upon the university of Cambridge in a matter of less importance, but without success: and now they resolved to attack Oxford by a strange fatality in their counsels. In all nations the privileges of colleges and universities are esteemed such sacred things, that few will venture to dispute these, much less to disturb them, when their title is good, and their possession is of a long continuance: for in these, not only the present body espouses the matter, but all who have been of it, even those that have only followed their study in it, think themselves bound in honor and gratitude to assist and support them. . . .

They began with Cambridge upon a softer point, which yet would have made way for all the rest. The king sent his letter, or *mandamus,* to order F. Francis, an ignorant Benedictine monk, to be received a master of arts; once to open the way for letting them into the degrees of the university.

The truth is, the king's letters were scarce ever refused in conferring degrees: and when ambassadors or foreign princes came to those places, they usually gave such degrees to those who belonged to them as were desired. The Morocco ambassador's secretary, that was a Mahometan, had that degree given him; but a great distinction was made between honorary degrees given to strangers, who intended not to live among them, and those given to such as intended to settle among them: for every master of arts having a vote in the convocation, they reckoned that, if they gave this degree, they must give all that should be pretended to on the like authority: and they knew all the king's priests would be let in upon them, which might occasion in present great distraction and contentions among them;

and in time they might grow to be a majority in the convocation, which is their parliament.

They refused the *mandamus* with great unanimity, and with a firmness that the court had not expected from them. New and repeated orders, full of severe threatenings in case of disobedience, were sent to them: and this piece of raillery was everywhere set up, that a papist was reckoned worse than a Mahometan, and that the king's letters were less considered than the ambassador from Morocco had been.

Some feeble or false men of the university tried to compound the matter, by granting this degree to F. Francis, but enacting at the same time, that it should not be a precedent for the future for any other of the like nature. This was not given way to: for it was said, that in all such cases the obedience that was once paid would be a much stronger argument for continuing to do it, as oft as it should be desired, than any such proviso could be against it.

Upon this the vice-chancellor was summoned before the ecclesiastical commission to answer this contempt. He was a very honest, but a very weak man. He made a poor defense. . . . But he having acted only as the chief person of that body, all that was thought fit to be done against him was to turn him out of his office. . . . The university chose another vice-chancellor, who was a man of much spirit: and in his speech, which in course he made upon his being chosen, he promised that, during his magistracy, neither religion nor the rights of the body should suffer by his means. . . .

And now all people began to see that they had taken wrong measures of the king, when they thought that it would be easy to engage him into bold things, before he could see into the ill consequences that might attend them, but that being once engaged he would resolve to go through with them at all adventures. When I knew him, he seemed to have set up that for a maxim, that a king when he made a step was never to go back, nor to encourage faction and disobedience by yielding to it.

After this unsuccessful attempt upon Cambridge, another was made upon Oxford, that lasted longer and had greater effects; which I shall set all down together, though the conclusion of this affair ran far into the year after this that I now write of. The presidentship of Magdalen was given by the election of the fellows. So the king sent a *mandamus* requiring them to choose one Farmer, an ignorant and vicious person, who had not one qualification that could recommend him to so high a post besides that of changing his religion. *Mandamus* letters had no legal authority in them: but all the great preferments of the church being in the king's disposal, those who did pretend to favor were not apt to refuse his recommendation, lest that should be afterwards remembered to their prejudice.

But now, since it was visible in what channel favor was like to run, less regard was had to such a letter. The fellows of that house did upon this choose Dr. Hough, one of their body, who, as he was in all respects a statutable man, so he was a worthy and a firm man, not apt to be threatened out of his right. They carried their election, according to their statutes, to the bishop of Winchester, their visitor: and he confirmed it. So that matter was legally settled. This was highly resented at court. . . .

The cause was brought before the ecclesiastical commission. The fellows were first asked why they had not chosen Farmer in obedience to the king's letter? And to that they answered by offering a list of many just exceptions against him. The subject was fruitful, and the scandals he had given were very public. The court was ashamed of him and insisted no more on him: but they said that the house ought to have shown more respect to the king's letter than to have proceeded to an election in contempt of it.

The ecclesiastical commission took upon them to declare Hough's election null, and to put the house under suspension. And, that the design of the court in this matter might be carried on without the load of recommending a papist, Parker, bishop of Oxford, was now recommended: and the fellows were commanded to proceed to a new election in his favor.

They excused themselves, since they were bound by their oaths to maintain their statutes: and by these, an election being once made and confirmed, they could not proceed to a new choice, till the former was annulled in some court of law: church benefices and college preferments were freeholds, and could only be judged in a court of record: and since the king was now talking so much of liberty of conscience, it was said, that the forcing men to act against their oaths seemed not to agree with those professions. In opposition to this it was said that the statutes of colleges had been always considered as things that depended entirely on the king's good pleasure; so that no oaths to observe them could bind them, when it was in opposition to the king's command.

This did not satisfy the fellows: and, though the king, as he went through Oxford in his progress in the year 1687, sent for them and ordered them to go presently and choose Parker for their president, in a strain of language ill suited to the majesty of a crowned head (for he treated them with foul language pronounced in a very angry tone), yet it had no effect on them. They insisted still on their oaths, though with a humility and submission that they hoped would have mollified him. They continued thus firm. A subaltern commission was sent from the ecclesiastical commission to finish the matter. Bishop Cartwright was the head of this commission, as Sir Charles Hedges was the king's advocate to manage the matter. . . .

The new president was turned out. And, because he would not deliver the keys of his house, the doors were broken open: and Parker was put in possession. The fellows were required to make their submission, to ask pardon for what was past, and to accept of the bishop for their president. They still pleaded their oath: and were all turned out, except two that submitted. So that it was expected to see that house soon stocked with papists. The nation, as well as the university, looked on all this proceeding with a just indignation. It was thought an open piece of robbery and burglary, when men, authorized by no legal commission, came and forcibly turned men out of their possession and freehold.

4. *King James' Declaration of Indulgence, 1687.* A further twist in James' religious policy can be seen in the Declaration of Indulgence issued on April 4, 1687, selections from which follow.[13]

His Majesty's gracious Declaration to all his loving subjects for liberty of conscience.

. . . We cannot but heartily wish, as it will easily be believed, that all the people of our dominions were members of the Catholic Church, and yet we humbly thank Almighty God, it is and has of long time been our constant sense and opinion, . . . that conscience ought not to be constrained nor people forced in matters of mere religion. . . .

[Opening clause of Declaration promises to protect the clergy of the Church of England in the free exercise of their religion and in the enjoyment of their possessions.] . . . We do likewise declare that it is our royal will and pleasure that . . . the execution of all . . . penal laws . . . be immediately suspended.

And . . . we straightly charge and command all our loving subjects, that—like as we do freely give them leave to meet and serve God after their own way . . . be it in private houses or places publicly hired or built for that use— we . . . do hereby command that no disturbance of any kind be made or given unto them under pain of our displeasure. . . .

We do hereby further declare that . . . the oaths commonly called "the oaths of supremacy and allegiance," and also the several tests and declarations mentioned in the Acts of Parliament made in the five and twentieth and thirtieth years of the reign of our late royal brother, King Charles II, shall not . . . hereafter be required to be taken, declared or subscribed by any person . . . whatsoever, who is or shall be employed in any office or place of trust, either civil or military, under us or in our Government . . . and . . . we do hereby give our free and ample pardon unto all nonconformists, recusants and other our loving subjects for all crimes and things . . . done contrary to the penal laws. . . .

5. *The King and a Future Parliament.* King James was well aware that he could not govern indefinitely without calling a Parliament, and he was also aware that the members of the last House of Commons were not in sympathy with his current activities. He sought, therefore, to find means of providing himself with a sympathetic House. The following account of his method of proceeding is taken from the diary of Sir John Reresby, an M.P. and Governor of York.[14]

The king caused the lord lieutenants of most if not all counties of England to call together all their deputy lieutenants and the justices of the peace, and to ask them these three questions:

1. In case the King should call a Parliament and they should be chosen of it, would they give their votes to take away the test and the penal laws?

2. Would they give their votes for the choosing of such members as they believed would be for the taking them away?

3. Would they live peaceably with such as dissented from them in religion, as good Christians ought to do?

Several lord lieutenants that refused to execute this order were turned out, and papists put in their places; and the deputy lieutenants and justices of the peace that did not give a satisfactory answer were generally displaced. This was indeed putting the thing too far, and the wonder of all men to what purpose it was done. For what answer could a man give that was to be a member of Parliament till he heard the reasons and debates of the House? And who could tell the temper of intention of him that was voted for till he came into the House? And if men had a mind to deceive the king, how easy (nay, how likely) was it for them to pretend to be of one judgment now and of another when they were of the House?

Besides, it struck at the very foundation of Parliaments to pre-engage men before they came there, where they were to be allowed the freedom both of their speech and judgments. The most general answer that was given by Protestants of the Church of England was this, that they would give their votes so, if of the House, as the reasons of the debate directed them; that they would vote for such as they thought would do so; and that they would live quietly with all men as good Christians and loyal subjects.

There was about this time great removes of officers, military and civil, and most corporations were purged of their Church of England aldermen, and papists or dissenters put in their places.

6. *The King and the Seven Bishops.* In May, 1688, James issued a second Declaration of Indulgence, repeating the substance of the first and adding a promise that a Parliament should meet before fall. He also issued an order in council to the bishops, instructing them to have the Declaration read in all parish churches throughout the kingdom. The results of these acts are described by John Evelyn, the celebrated diarist.[15]

May 18th. The king, enjoining the ministers to read his Declaration for giving liberty of conscience (as it was styled) in all the churches of England, this evening, 6 bishops, Bath and Wells, Peterborough, Ely, Chichester, St. Asaph, and Bristol, in the name of all the rest of the bishops, came to his majesty to petition him that he would not impose the reading of it to the several congregations within their dioceses; not that they were averse to the publishing it for want of due tenderness towards dissenters, in relations to whom they should be willing to come to such a temper as should be thought fit, when that matter might be considered and settled in parliament and convocation; but that, the Declaration being founded on such a dispensing power as might at pleasure set aside all laws ecclesiastical and civil, it appeared to them illegal, as it had done to the Parliament in 1661 and 1672, and that it was a point of such consequences, that they could not so far make themselves parties to it as the reading of it in church in time of divine service amounted to.

The king was so far incensed at this address that he with threatening expressions commanded them to obey him in reading it at their perils, and so dismissed them.

20th. I went to Whitehall Chapel, where, after the morning lessons, the Declaration was read by one of the choir who used to read the chapters. I hear it was in the Abbey Church, Westminster, but almost universally forborn throughout all London: the consequence of which a little time will show.

25th. All the discourse now was about the bishops refusing to read the injunctions for the abolition of the Test, etc. It seems the injunctions came so crudely from the secretary's office that it was neither sealed nor signed in form, nor had any lawyer been consulted, so as the bishops who took all imaginable advice, put the Court to great difficulties how to proceed against them. Great were the consults, and a proclamation expected all this day, but nothing was done. The action of the bishops was universally applauded and reconciled many adverse parties, papists only excepted, who were now exceedingly perplexed, and violent courses were every moment expected. Report was that the Protestant secular lords and nobility would abet the clergy. . . .

June 8th. This day the Archbishop of Canterbury, with the bishops of Ely, Chichester, St. Asaph, Bristol, Peterborough, and Bath and Wells, were sent from the Privy Council prisoners to the Tower, for refusing to give bail for their appearance, on their not reading the declaration for liberty of conscience; they refused to give bail, as it would have prejudiced their peerage. The concern of the people for them was wonderful, infinite crowds on their knees begging their blessing, and praying for them as they passed out of the barge along the Tower wharf.

10th. A young prince born, which will cause disputes.

About 2 o'clock we heard the Tower ordnance discharged, and the bells ringing for the birth of a Prince of Wales. This was very surprising, it having been universally given out that her majesty did not look till the next month.

13th. I went to the Tower to see the bishops, visited the Abp. and Bps. of Ely, St. Asaph, and Bath and Wells.

14th. Dined with my Lord Chancellor.

15th. Being the first day of term, the bishops were brought to Westminster on habeas corpus, when the indictment was read, and they were called on to plead; their counsel objected that the warrant was illegal, but after long debate it was over-ruled, and they pleaded. The court then offered to take bail for their appearance, but this they refused, and at last were dismissed on their own recognizances to appear that day fortnight; the Abp. in £200, the bishops £100 each.

29th. They appeared; the trial lasted from 9 in the morning to past 6 in the evening, when the jury retired to consider of their verdict, and the courts adjourned to 9 the next morning. The jury were locked up till that time, 11 of them being for an acquittal, but one (Arnold a brewer) would not consent. At length he agreed with the others. The Chief Justice Wright behaved with great moderation and civility to the bishops. Alibone, a papist, was strongly against them; but Holloway and Powell, being of opinion in their favor, they were acquitted. When this was heard, there was great rejoicing; and there was a lane of people from the King's Bench to the water side, on their knees, as the bishops passed and repassed, to beg their blessing. Bonfires were made that night, and bells rung, which was taken very ill at Court, and an appearance of near 60 earls and lords, &c. on the bench, did not a little comfort them, but indeed they were all along full of comfort and cheerful.

Note, they denied to pay the Lieut. of the Tower (Hales, who used them very surlily) any fees, alleging that none were due.

17th. Was a day of thanksgiving in London and 10 miles about for the young prince's birth; and a form of prayer made for the purpose by the Bp. of Rochester.

The night was solemnized with bonfires and other fire-works, &c.

July 2nd. The two judges, Holloway and Powell, were displaced.

7. *The Invitation to William of Orange, 30 June 1688*. On the night of the acquittal of the seven bishops the following letter was sent to William of Orange.[16]

We have great satisfaction to find by 35 [Russell] . . . that your Highness is so ready and willing to give us such assistances as . . . [he has] related to us. We have great reason to believe, we shall be every day in a worse condition than we are and less able to defend ourselves. . . . The people are so generally dissatisfied with the present conduct of the government in relation to their religion, liberties, and properties (all of which have been greatly invaded) . . . that your Highness may be assured, there are nineteen parts out of twenty of the people . . . who would contribute to it, if, they had such protection to countenance their rising as would secure them from being destroyed before they could get to be in a position able to defend themselves. . . .

Much the greatest part of the . . . gentry are as much dissatisfied . . . many of the officers [are] so discontented that they continue in their service only for a subsistence . . . and very many of the common soldiers do daily show such an aversion to the Popish religion, that there is the greatest probability imaginable of great numbers of deserters which would come from them, should there be such an occasion; and amongst the seamen, it is almost certain, there is not one in ten who would do them any service in such a war. . . . If upon a due consideration of all these circumstances, Your Highness shall think fit to adventure upon the attempt . . . there must be no time lost, in letting us know your resolution concerning it, and in what time we may depend that all the preparations will be ready.

(signed)

Shrewsbury	[Protestant convert from Catholicism]
Devonshire	[Whig]
Danby	[Tory]
Lumley	[Protestant convert from Catholicism]
Bishop of London	[Tory]
Russell	[Whig]
Sydney	[Whig]

Part II.   THE REVOLUTIONARY SETTLEMENT

The invitation to William of Orange in June was followed by William's invasion of England in November, 1688. But no battle took place. James wavered and procrastinated, as his adherents gradually deserted him, until he finally took refuge in flight. After one unsuccessful attempt to flee, James finally made his way into France without having struck a blow in his own defense, and William was left master of the kingdom. By a series of legislative acts, Parliament then endeavored to eradicate the sources of domestic conflict. The Bill of Rights, passed immediately after the Revolution, was succeeded by further enactments in the next fifteen years, by which Parliament circumscribed the power of the Crown and did much to establish the supremacy of Parliament in English government. The following documents illustrate the means taken by Parliament to secure the "rights and privileges" for which they had fought so long. In the final selections in the Problem the student is introduced to the final objective of the historian's task—the interpretation of a complex historical event.

A.   THE REVOLUTIONARY SETTLEMENT, 1689–1701

William of Orange, who had been invited on June 30, 1688, landed on November 5; on December 10 James first tried to leave the country. Meanwhile, the peers, under Halifax, had set up a provisional government. On December 23 William was authorized by a group of peers and commons to hold elections for a Convention Parliament, to meet on January 22, 1689.

1. *The First Act of the Convention Parliament, 1689*. The following document was the first act of the Convention Parliament and appears in the statute book as 1 Will. and Mary, cap. 1, 1689.[17]

An Act for removing and preventing All Questions and Disputes concerning the Assembling and Sitting of the Present Parliament.

For preventing all doubts and scruples which may in any wise arise concerning the meeting, sitting and proceeding of this present Parliament, be it declared and enacted . . .

II. That the Lords Spiritual and Temporal and Commons convened at Westminster, the two and twentieth day of January in the year of Our Lord one thousand six hundred eighty eight, and there sitting on the thirteenth day of February following, are the two Houses of Parliament, and so shall be and are hereby declared, enacted and adjudged to be to all intents, constructions, and purposes whatsoever, notwithstanding any want of writ or writs of summons or any other defect of form or default whatsoever, as if they had been summoned according to the usual form, and that this Present Act and all other Acts, to which the royal assent shall at any time be given before the next prorogation after the said thirteenth of February, shall be understood, taken and adjudged in law to begin and commence upon the said thirteenth of February on which day their said Majesties at the request and by the advice of the Lords and Commons did accept the crown and royal dignity of King and Queen of England, France and Ireland, and the dominions and territories thereunto belonging. . . .

2. *The Bill of Rights, 1689*. Like most pieces of legislation, the Bill of Rights, which follows, is as much a résumé of the past as it is a prophecy for the future.[18]

Whereas the said late King James II having abdicated the government, and the throne being thereby vacant, his Highness the prince of Orange (whom it hath pleased Almighty God to make the glorious instrument of delivering this kingdom from popery and arbitrary power) did (by the advice of the lords spiritual and temporal, and diverse principal persons of the Commons) cause letters to be written to the lords spiritual and temporal, being Protestants, and other letters to the several counties, cities, universities, boroughs, and Cinque Ports, for the choosing of such persons to represent them, as were of right to be sent to parliament, to meet and sit at Westminster upon the two and twentieth day of January, in this year 1689, in order to such an establishment as that their religion, laws, and liberties might not again be in danger of being subverted; upon which letters elections have been accordingly made.

And thereupon the said lords spiritual and temporal and Commons, pursuant to their respective letters and elections, being now assembled in a full and free representation of this nation, taking into their most serious consideration the best means for attaining the ends aforesaid, do in the first place (as their ancestors in like case have usually done), for the vindication and assertion of their ancient rights and liberties, declare:

1. That the pretended power of suspending laws, or the execution of laws, by regal authority, without consent of parliament is illegal.

2. That the pretended power of dispensing with the laws, or the execution of law by regal authority, as it hath been assumed and exercised of late, is illegal.

3. That the commission for erecting the late court of commissioners for ecclesiastical causes, and all other commissions and courts of like nature, are illegal and pernicious.

4. That levying money for or to the use of the crown by pretense of prerogative, without grant of parliament, for longer time or in other manner than the same is or shall be granted, is illegal.

5. That it is the right of the subjects to petition the king, and all commitments and prosecutions for such petitioning are illegal.

6. That the raising or keeping a standing army within the kingdom in time of peace, unless it be with consent of parliament, is against law.

7. That the subjects which are Protestants may have arms for their defense suitable to their conditions, and as allowed by law.

8. That election of members of parliament ought to be free.

9. That the freedom of speech, and debates or proceedings in parliament, ought not to be impeached or questioned in any court or place out of parliament.

10. That excessive bail ought not to be required, nor excessive fines imposed, nor cruel and unusual punishments inflicted.

11. That jurors ought to be duly impaneled and returned, and jurors which pass upon men in trials for high treason ought to be freeholders.

12. That all grants and promises of fines and forfeitures of particular persons before conviction are illegal and void.

13. And that for redress of all grievances, and for the amending, strengthening, and preserving of the laws, parliament ought to be held frequently.

And they do claim, demand, and insist upon all and singular the premises, as their undoubted rights and liberties; and that no declarations, judgments, doings, or proceedings, to the prejudice of the people in any of the said premises, ought in any wise to be drawn hereafter into consequence or example.

To which demand of their rights they are particularly encouraged by the declaration of his Highness the prince of Orange, as being the only means for obtaining a full redress and remedy therein.

Having therefore an entire confidence that his said Highness the prince of Orange will perfect the deliverance so far advanced by him, and will still preserve them from the violation of their rights, which they have here asserted, and from all other attempt upon their religion, rights, and liberties:

The said lords spiritual and temporal, and commons, assembled at Westminster, do resolve that William and Mary, prince and princess of Orange, be, and be declared, king and queen of England, France, and Ireland, the dominions thereunto belonging, to hold the crown and royal dignity of the said kingdoms and dominions to them the said prince and princess during their lives, and the life of the survivor of them; and that the sole and full exercise of the regal power be only in, and executed by, the said prince of Orange, in the names of the said prince and princess, during their joint lives; and after their deceases, the said crown and royal dignity of the said kingdoms and dominions to be to the heirs of the body of the said princess; and for default of such issue to the princess Anne of Denmark, and the heirs of her body; and for default of such issue to the heirs of the body of the said prince of Orange. And the lords spiritual and temporal, and commons, do pray the said prince and princess to accept the same accordingly. . . .

Upon which their said Majesties did accept the crown and royal dignity of the kingdoms of England, France, and Ireland, and the dominions thereunto belonging, according to the resolution and desire of the said lords and commons contained in the said declaration.

3. *The Mutiny Act, 1689.* To all students of English and continental history in the seventeenth century, the position of the Mutiny Act in the settlement of 1689 is clearly central. The pertinent sections are quoted below.[19]

Whereas the raising or keeping a standing army within this kingdom in time of peace, unless it be with consent of parliament, is against law; and whereas it is judged necessary by their Majesties and this present parliament that during this time of danger several of the forces which are now on foot should be continued, and others raised, for the safety of the kingdom, for the common defense of the Protestant religion, and for the reducing of Ireland.

And whereas no man may be forejudged of life or limb, or subjected to any kind of punishment, by martial law or in any other manner than by the judgment of his peers and according to the known and established laws of this realm, yet nevertheless it being requisite for retaining such forces as are or shall be raised during this exigence of affairs in their duty, an exact discipline be observed, and that soldiers who shall mutiny or stir up sedition or shall desert their Majesties' service be brought to more exemplary and speedy punishment than the usual forms of law will allow. . . .

II. Be it therefore enacted by the king's and queen's most excellent Majesties, by and with the advice and consent of the lords spiritual and temporal and commons in this parliament assembled, and by authority of the same, that, from and after the twelfth of April in the year of our Lord one thousand six hundred eighty-nine, every person being in their majesties' service in the army and being mustered and in pay as an officer or soldier, who shall at any time before the tenth day of November in the year of our Lord one thousand six hundred eighty-nine excite, cause, or join in any mutiny or sedition in the army, or shall desert their majesties' service in the army, shall suffer death or such other punishment as by a court marshal shall be inflicted. . . .

VII. Provided always, that this act or anything therein contained shall not extend or be anywise construed to extend to or concern any the militia forces of this kingdom.

VIII. Provided always, that this act shall continue and be in force until the said tenth of November in the said year of our Lord one thousand six hundred eighty-nine, and no longer. . . .

X. And no sentence of death shall be given against any offender in such case by any court unless nine of thirteen officers present shall concur therein, and if there be a greater number of officers present, then the judgment shall pass by the concurrence of the greater part of them so sworn, and not otherwise, and no proceedings, trial, or sentence of death shall be had or given against any offender but between the hours of eight in the morning and one in the afternoon.

4. *The Toleration Act, 1689.* Although it bears comparison with such contemporary events as the Revocation of the Edict of Nantes (1685), the Toleration Act of 1689 must be studied primarily as a solution to the question of freedom of worship as it had developed in England during the preceding century and a half. In this connection it is important for what it leaves unsettled as well as for its more permanent accomplishments.[20]

An Act for exempting their Majesties' Protestant Subjects, differing from the Church of England, from the Penalties of certain Laws.

Forasmuch as some ease to scrupulous consciences in the exercise of religion may be an effectual means to unite their Majesties' protestant subjects in interest and affections: . . .

II. Be it enacted . . . That neither the statute made in the three and twentieth year of the reign of the late Queen Elizabeth, intituled An act to retain the Queen's Majesty's subjects in their due obedience; nor the statute made in the twenty-ninth year of the said Queen intituled An act for the more speedy and due execution of certain branches of the statute made in the three and twentieth year of the Queen's Majesty's reign, *viz.* the aforesaid act; nor that branch or clause of a statute made in the first year of the reign of the said Queen intituled, An act for the uniformity of common prayer and service in the church . . . by all person, having no lawful or reasonable excuse to be absent, are required to resort to their parish church or chapel, or some usual place where the common prayer shall be used, upon pain of punishment by the censures of the church, and also upon pain that every person so offending shall forfeit for every such offense twelve pence; nor the statute made in the third year of the reign of the late King James the first, intituled, An act for the better discovering and repressing popish recusants; nor that other statute made in the same year, intituled An act to prevent and avoid dangers which may grow by popish recusants; nor any other law or statute of this realm made against papists or popish recusants; except . . . the statute made in the thirtieth year of . . . King Charles the second, intituled an act for the more effectual preserving the King's person and government by disabling papists from sitting in either house of parliament; shall be construed to extend to any person or persons dissenting from the Church of England, that shall take the oaths mentioned in a statute made by this present parliament . . . and that shall make and subscribe the declaration mentioned in a statute made in the thirtieth year of the reign of King Charles the second . . . which oaths and declaration the justices of peace at the general sessions of the peace . . . are hereby required to tender and administer to such persons as shall offer themselves to take, make, and subscribe the same, and thereof to keep a register; and likewise none of the persons aforesaid shall give or pay, as any fee or reward, to any officer or officers belonging to the court aforesaid, above the sum of sixpence, nor that more than once, for his or their entry of his taking the said oaths, and making and subscribing the said declaration; nor above the further sum of sixpence for any certificate of the same, to be made out and signed by the officer or officers of the said court.

III. And be it further enacted . . . That all . . . persons already convicted or prosecuted in order to conviction of recusancy . . . grounded upon the aforesaid statutes, or any of them, that shall take the said oaths mentioned in the said statute in this present parliament, and make and subscribe the declaration aforesaid . . . and to be thence respectively certified into the Exchequer, shall be thenceforth exempted and discharged from all the penalties, seizures, forfeitures, judgments, and executions, incurred by force of any of the aforesaid statutes, without any composition, fee, or further charge whatsoever.

IV. And be it further enacted . . . That all . . . persons that shall take the said oaths, and make and subscribe the declaration aforesaid, shall not be liable to any pains, penalties, or forfeitures, mentioned in an act made in the five and thirtieth year of the reign of the late Queen Elizabeth . . . nor an act made in the two and twentieth year of the reign of the late King Charles the second . . . nor shall any of the said persons be prosecuted in any ecclesiastical court, for or by reason of their nonconforming to the Church of England.

V. Provided always . . . That if any assembly of persons dissenting from the Church of England shall be had in any place for religious worship with the doors locked, barred, or bolted, during any time of such meeting . . . , shall not receive any benefit from this law, but be liable to all the pain and penalties of all the aforesaid laws recited in this act, for such their meeting, notwithstanding his taking the oaths, and making and subscribing the declaration aforesaid.

VI. Provided always, That nothing herein contained shall . . . exempt any of the persons aforesaid from paying of tithes or other parochial duties, or any other duties to the church or minister, nor from any prosecution in any ecclesiastical court, or elsewhere for the same. . . .

XVII. Provided always . . . That neither this act, nor any clause, article, or thing herein contained, shall . . . extend to give any ease, benefit, or advantage to any papist or popish recusant whatsoever, or any person that shall deny in his preaching or writing the doctrine of the Blessed Trinity, as it is declared in the aforesaid articles of religion.

5. *The Act of Settlement, 1701.* Although it occurs over ten years later the Act of Settlement may well be taken as the essence of the Revolutionary Settlement.[21]

An Act for the further Limitation of the Crown and better securing the Rights and Liberties of the Subject.

I. Whereas in the First Year of the Reign of Your Majesty and of our late most gracious Sovereign Lady Queen Mary (of blessed Memory) An Act of Parliament was made intituled An Act for declaring the Rights and Liberties of the Subject and for settling the Succession of the Crown wherein it was (amongst other things) enacted, established, and declared, That the Crown and Regal Government of the Kingdoms of England, France, and Ireland, and the Dominions thereunto belonging should be and continue to Your Majesty and the said late Queen during the joint lives of Your Majesty and the said Queen and to the Survivor.

And that after the Decease of Your Majesty and of the said Queen the said Crown and Regal Government should be and remain to the Heirs of the Body of the said late Queen, and for Default of such Issue to her Royal Highness the Princess Ann of Denmark and the Heirs of her Body, and for Default of such Issue to the Heirs of the Body of Your Majesty and it was thereby further enacted that all and every Person and Persons that then were or afterwards should be reconciled to or shall hold Communion with the See or Church of Rome or should profess the Popish Religion or marry a Papist should be excluded and are by that Act made forever incapable to inherit, possess, or enjoy the Crown and Government of this Realm and Ireland and the Dominions thereunto belonging, or any part of the same, or to have, use, or exercise any regal Power, Authority, or Jurisdiction within the same.

And in all and every such Case or Cases the People of these Realms shall be and are thereby absolved of their allegiance. And that the said Crown and Government shall from time to time descend to and be enjoyed by such Person or Persons being Protestants as should have inherited and enjoyed the same in case the said Person or Persons so reconciled, holding Communion, professing, or marrying, as aforesaid, were naturally dead. . . . And your Majesty's said Subjects having Daily Experience of Your Royal Care and Concern for the present and future welfare of these Kingdoms and particularly recommending from your Throne a further provision to be made for the Succession of the Crown in the Protestant Line for the Happiness of the Nation and the Security of our Religion.

And it being absolutely necessary for the Safety, Peace, and Quiet of this Realm to obviate all Doubts and Contentions in the same by reason of any pretended Titles to the Crown, and to maintain a Certainty in the succession thereof to which your Subjects may safely have Recourse for their Protection in case the Limitations in the said recited Act should determine. Therefore for a further Provision of the Succession to the Crown in the Protestant Line We, Your Majesty's most dutiful and Loyal Subjects, the Lords Spiritual and Temporal and Commons in this present Parliament assembled, do beseech Your Majesty that it may be enacted and declared, and be it enacted and declared by the King's most Excellent Majesty by and with the Advice and Consent of the

Lords Spiritual and Temporal and Commons in this Present Parliament assembled, and by the authority of the same, that the most Excellent Princess Sophia, Electress and Duchess Dowager of Hanover, Daughter of the most Excellent Princess Elizabeth, late Queen of Bohemia, Daughter of our late Sovereign Lord King James the First of happy Memory, be and is hereby declared to be the next in Succession in the Protestant Line to the Imperial Crown and Dignity to the said Realms of England, France, and Ireland, and of the Dominions thereunto belonging, after His Majesty and the Princess Ann of Denmark, and in Default of Issue of the said Princess Ann and of His Majesty respectively, and that from and after the Deceases of His said Majesty our now Sovereign Lord, and of Her Royal Highness the Princess Ann of Denmark, and for Default of Issue of the said Princess Ann and of His Majesty respectively, the Crown and Regal Government of the said Kingdoms of England, France, and Ireland, and of the Dominions thereunto belonging, with the Royal State and Dignity of the said Realms, and all the Honors, Styles, Titles, Regalities, Prerogatives, Powers, Jurisdictions, and Authorities to the same belonging and appertaining, shall be, remain, and continue to the said most Excellent Princess Sophia and the Heirs of her Body being Protestants.

And thereunto the said Lords Spiritual and Temporal and Commons shall and will in the Name of all the People of this Realm . . . do faithfully promise That after the Deceases of His Majesty and Her Royal Highness and the failure of the Heirs of their respective Bodies, to stand, to maintain and defend the said Princess Sophia and the Heirs of her Body being Protestants according to the Limitation and Succession of the Crown in this Act specified and contained, to the utmost of their Powers, with their Lives and Estates, against all Persons whatsoever that shall attempt anything to the contrary. . . .

III. And Whereas it is requisite and necessary that some further Provision be made for securing our Religion, Laws, and Liberties from and after the Death of His Majesty and the Princess Ann of Denmark, and in Default of Issue of the Body of the said Princess and of his Majesty respectively, Be it enacted by the King's most excellent Majesty by and with the Advice and Consent of the Lords Spiritual and Temporal and Commons in Parliament assembled, and by the Authority of the same.

That whosoever shall hereafter come to the Possession of this Crown shall join in Communion with the Church of England as by Law established.

That in case the Crown and Imperial Dignity of this Realm shall hereafter come to any Person not being a Native of this Kingdom of England, this Nation be not obliged to engage in any War for the Defense of any Dominions or Territories which do not belong to the Crown of England, without the consent of Parliament.

That no Person who shall hereafter come to the possession of the Crown shall go out of the Dominions of England, Scotland, and Ireland, without the consent of Parliament.

That from and after the Time that the further Limitation by this Act all Matters and Things relating to the well governing of this Kingdom which are properly cognizable in the Privy Council by the Laws and Customs of this Realm shall be transacted there and all Resolutions taken thereupon shall be signed by each of the Privy Council as shall advise and consent to the same.

That after the said Limitation shall take Effect as aforesaid, no Person born out of the Kingdoms of England, Scotland, or Ireland, or the Dominions thereunto belonging (although he be naturalized and made a Denizen) (except such as are born of English parents) shall be capable to be of the Privy Council, or a Member of either House of Parliament, or to enjoy any Office or Place of Trust, either Civil or Military, or to have any Grant of Lands, Tenements, or Hereditaments, from the Crown to himself or to any other or others in trust for Him.

That no Person who has an Office or Place of Profit under the King, or receives a Pension from the Crown, shall be capable of serving as a Member of the House of Commons.

That after the said Limitation shall take Effect as aforesaid, Judges Commissions be made *Quam diu se bene Gesserint,* and their Salaries ascertained and established, but upon the Address of both Houses of Parliament it may be lawful to remove them.

That no pardon under the Great Seal of England be pleadable to an Impeachment by the Commons in Parliament.

IV. And whereas the laws of England are the birthright of the people thereof and all the Kings and Queens who shall ascend the throne of this realm ought to administer the Government of the same according to the said laws and all their officers and ministers ought to serve them respectively according to the same the said Lords Spiritual and Temporal and Commons do therefore humbly pray that all the laws and statutes of this realm for securing the established religion and rights and liberties of the people thereof and all other laws and statutes of the same now in force may be ratified and confirmed. And the same are by his Majesty by and with the advice and consent of the said Lords Spiritual and Temporal and Commons and by authority of the same ratified and confirmed accordingly.

B.   THE HISTORIANS INTERPRET THE REVOLUTION

As a great climax in the constitutional history of England and the freedom of the individual before the state, the Revolution of 1688 has naturally been of interest to historians. So controversial an event cannot help but have produced a variety of interpretations. Two of them follow, and the student is asked to criticize and appraise them in the light of his own understanding and knowledge of the Revolution. The first selection, by Thomas Babington Macaulay (1800–1859) is part of a vast *History of England,* originally planned to cover from 1685 to 1820, though in fact it never got beyond 1702. Macaulay was writing the section quoted below in 1848, a year which saw most of continental Europe convulsed by wide-spread revolution for the fourth time in less than sixty years. Sir Charles Petrie (1895–   ), a Scotsman, has written several books on the Stuart kings and their cause. The second selection is from his *The Stuart Pretenders* (1933).[22]

1. *Macaulay on the Revolution.*

Thus was consummated the English Revolution. When we compare it with those revolutions which have, during the last sixty years, overthrown so many ancient governments, we cannot but be struck by its peculiar character. Why that character was so peculiar is sufficiently obvious, and yet seems not to have been always understood either by eulogists or by censors.

The Continental revolutions of the eighteenth and nineteenth centuries took place in countries where all trace of the limited monarchy of the Middle Ages had long been effaced. The right of the prince to make laws and to levy money had, during many generations, been undisputed. His throne was guarded by a regular army. His administration could not, without extreme peril, be blamed even in the mildest terms. His subjects held their personal liberty by no other tenure than his pleasure. Not a single institution was left which had, within the memory of the oldest man, afforded efficient protection to the subject against the utmost excess of tyranny. Those great councils which had once curbed the regal power had sunk into oblivion. Their composition and their privileges were known only to antiquaries.

We cannot wonder, therefore, that, when men who had been thus ruled succeeded in wresting supreme power from a government which they had long in secret hated, they should have been impatient to demolish and unable to construct, that they should have been fascinated by every specious novelty, that they should have proscribed every title, ceremony, and phrase associated with the old system, and that, turning away with disgust from their own national precedents and traditions, they should have sought for principles of government in the writings of theorists, or aped, with ignorant and ungraceful affectation, the patriots of Athens and Rome. As little can we wonder that the violent action of the revolutionary spirit should have been followed by reaction

equally violent, and that confusion should speedily have engendered despotism sterner than that from which it had sprung.

Had we been in the same situation; had Strafford succeeded in his favorite scheme of Thorough; had he formed an army as numerous and as well disciplined as that which, a few years later, was formed by Cromwell; had a series of judicial decisions, similar to that which was pronounced by the Exchequer Chamber in the case of ship-money, transferred to the crown the right of taxing the people; had the Star Chamber and the High Commission continued to fine, mutilate, and imprison every man who dared to raise his voice against the government; had the press been as completely enslaved here as at Vienna or at Naples; had our Kings gradually drawn to themselves the whole legislative power; had six generations of Englishmen passed away without a single session of Parliament; and had we then at length risen up in some moment of wild excitement against our masters, what an outbreak would that have been!

With what a crash, heard and felt to the farthest ends of the world, would the whole vast fabric of society have fallen! How many thousands of exiles, once the most prosperous and the most refined members of this great community, would have begged their bread in foreign cities, or have sheltered their heads under huts of bark in the uncleared forests of America! How often should we have seen the pavement of London piled up in barricades, the houses dinted with bullets, the gutters foaming with blood! How many times should we have rushed wildly from extreme to extreme, sought refuge from anarchy in despotism, and been again driven by despotism into anarchy! How many years of blood and confusion would it have cost us to learn the very rudiments of political science! How many childish theories would have duped us! How many rude and ill-poised constitutions should we have set up, only to see them tumble down! Happy would it have been for us if a sharp discipline of half a century had sufficed to educate us into a capacity of enjoying true freedom.

These calamities our Revolution averted. It was a revolution strictly defensive, and had prescription and legitimacy on its side. Here, and here only, a limited monarchy of the thirteenth century had come down unimpaired to the seventeenth century. Our parliamentary institutions were in full vigor. The main principles of our government were excellent. They were not, indeed, formally and exactly set forth in a single written instrument; but they were to be found scattered over our ancient and noble statutes; and what was of far greater moment, they had been engraven on the hearts of Englishmen during four hundred years. That, without the consent of the representatives of the nation, no statute could be enacted, no tax imposed, no regular soldiery kept up; that no man could be imprisoned, even for a day, by the arbitrary will of the sovereign; that no tool of power could plead the royal command as a justification for violating any legal right of the humblest subject, were held, both by Whigs and Tories, to be fundamental laws of the realm. A realm of which these were the fundamental laws stood in no need of a new constitution.

But, though a new constitution was not needed, it was plain that changes were required. The misgovernment of the Stuarts, and the troubles which that misgovernment had produced, sufficiently proved that there was somewhere a defect in our polity; and that defect it was the duty of the Convention to discover and to amend.

Some questions of great moment were still open to dispute. Our constitution had begun to exist in times when statesmen were not much accustomed to frame exact definitions. Anomalies, therefore, inconsistent with its principles and dangerous to its very existence, had sprung up almost imperceptibly, and not having, during many years, caused any serious inconvenience, had gradually acquired the force of prescription. The remedy for these evils was to assert the rights of the people in such language as should terminate all controversy, and to declare that no precedent could justify any violation of those rights. . . .

And yet this revolution, of all revolutions the least violent, had been of all revolutions the most beneficent. It finally decided the great question whether the popular element which had ever since the age of Fitzwalter and De Montfort, been found in the English polity, should be destroyed by the monarchical element, or should be suffered to develop itself freely, and to become dominant. The strife between the two principles had been long, fierce, and doubtful. It had lasted through four reigns. It had produced seditions, impeachments, rebellions, battles, sieges, proscriptions, judicial massacres. Sometimes liberty, sometimes royalty, had seemed to be on the point of perishing.

During many years one half of the energy of England had been employed in counteracting the other half. The executive power and the legislative power had so effectively impeded each other that the state had been of no account in Europe. The King-at-Arms, who proclaimed William and Mary before Whitehall Gate, did in truth announce that this great struggle was over; that England, long dependent and degraded, was again a power of the first rank; that there was entire union between the throne and the Parliament; that the ancient laws by which the prerogative was bounded would thenceforth be held as sacred as the prerogative itself, and would be followed out to all their consequences; that the executive administration would be conducted in conformity with the sense of the representatives of the nation; and that no reform, which the two Houses should, after mature deliberation, propose, would be obstinately withstood by the sovereign.

The Declaration of Right, though it made nothing law which had not been law before, contained the germ of the law which gave religious freedom to the Dissenter, of the law which secured the independence of the Judges, of the law which limited the duration of Parliament, of the law which placed the liberty of the press under the protection of juries, of the law which prohibited the slave-trade, of the law which abolished the sacramental test, of the law which relieved the Roman Catholics from civil disabilities, of the law which reformed the representative system, of every good law which has been passed during a hundred and sixty years, of every good law which may hereafter, in the course of ages, be found necessary to promote the public weal, and to satisfy the demands of public opinion.

The highest eulogy which can be pronounced on the Revolution of 1688 is this, that it was our last revolution. Several generations have now passed away since any wise and patriotic Englishman has meditated resistance to the established government. In all honest and reflecting minds there is a conviction, daily strengthened by experience, that the means of effecting every improvement which the constitution requires may be found within the constitution itself.

Now, if ever, we ought to be able to appreciate the whole importance of the stand which was made by our forefathers against the House of Stuart. All around us the world is convulsed by the agonies of great nations. Governments which lately seemed likely to stand during ages have been on a sudden shaken and overthrown. The proudest capitals of Western Europe have streamed with civil blood. All evil passions, the thirst of gain and the thirst of vengeance, the antipathy of class to class, the antipathy of race to race, have broken loose from the control of divine and human laws. Fear and anxiety have clouded the faces and depressed the hearts of millions. Trade has been suspended, and industry paralyzed. The rich have become poor, and the poor have become poorer. Doctrines hostile to all sciences, to all arts, to all industry, to all domestic charities, doctrines which, if carried into effect, would, in thirty years, undo all that thirty centuries have done for mankind, and would make the fairest provinces of France and Germany as savage as Congo or Patagonia, have been avowed from the tribune and defended by the sword. Europe has been threatened with subjugation by barbarians, compared with whom the barbarians who marched under Attila and Alboin were enlightened and humane. The truest friends of the people have with deep sorrow owned that interests more precious than any political privileges were in jeopardy, and that it might be necessary to sacrifice even liberty in order to save civilization.

Meanwhile, in our island the regular course of government has never been for a day interrupted. The few bad men who longed for license and plunder have not had the courage to confront for one moment the strength of a loyal nation, rallied in firm array round a parental throne. And if it be asked what has made us to differ from others, the answer is that we never lost what others are wildly and blindly seeking to regain. It is because we had a preserving revolution in the seventeenth century that we have not had a destroying revolution in the nineteenth. It is because we had freedom in the midst of servitude that we have order in the midst of anarchy. For the authority of law, for the security of property, for the peace of our streets, for the happiness of our homes, our gratitude is due, under Him who raises and pulls down nations at his pleasure, to the Long Parliament, to the Convention, and to William of Orange.

2. *Petrie on the Revolution.*

After the birth of the Prince of Wales on June 10th, 1688, events began to move rapidly. The famous warming-pan myth was an afterthought, for William sent a special envoy to London to congratulate the King, and it was not until the ambassador arrived that his master realized how strong was the opposition to James. Few men have been born under a more unhappy star than the infant who was to be known in later days as "Old Mr. Misfortunate." Within a month of his birth the Seven Bishops were acquitted for their refusal to allow the Declaration of Indulgence to be read in their respective dioceses, and on the

same day the Whig leaders invited William to come over.

While Mary was the heir to the throne those who were dissatisfied with James felt that they could afford to wait for a few years to undo what he had done; after all, the King was in his fifty-fifth year, and as Charles II had died at that age, his expectation of life was not great. Now, however, there was a Prince of Wales, the situation was completely changed, and the perpetuation of a Catholic dynasty was assured. William, who probably did not care whether the King of England were a Catholic or a Protestant, provided that the kingdom itself was numbered among the enemies of France, foresaw a long period of English neutrality, and so resolved that the time had come to strike. For him it was now or never. . . .

The England that James left was in a more disordered condition than at any date since the Interregnum. The progress of events during the last weeks of 1688 had been so rapid as to leave the country breathless, and it was not for some time that the various schools of thought became crystallized into parties. The landing of William and his swift advance on London, combined with the irresolution and flight of James, had undoubtedly taken the nation by surprise, and before it had fully recovered a new régime had been established. In these circumstances, it is in no way surprising that the hardest part of William's task was not to win the throne, but to retain it.

The Revolution was the work of a minority, and of a comparatively small minority at that. It was not the result of a national rising against a hated and tyrannical monarch, for, as has been said, had James kept his head he might have kept his crown as well. It was rather due to a discontented faction, more powerful than numerous, which found an energetic and capable leader, and achieved its purpose by the rapidity of its movements. The Whigs, in short, were efficient, and the Jacobites were not, and this fact explains the victory of the one and the defeat of the other.

How small the minority was it is not easy to say, for as late as 1742 Pulteney told George II that two-thirds of the nation was Tory, and, as we shall see, Jacobitism retained a strong hold upon the country until a good many years later than that. On the other hand, it is quite clear that the prevalent feeling in 1688 was apathy, for James did not arouse the same enthusiasm that his father and brother had done. Indeed, it would almost appear that the battle over the Exclusion Bill had exhausted the political energy of the English people, for the dynastic struggle which began with the Revolution left the mass of the population curiously indifferent, which would certainly not have been the case had the fall of the Stuarts been the result of a popular movement.

At the same time, William was favored by an amount of luck that in retrospect seems almost uncanny. Shrewd judge of character that he was, he had probably gauged the weakness of his father-in-law, and had calculated that he would leave the kingdom, though the pusillanimity of James in the hour of crisis clearly took most of his contemporaries by surprise. William had also, it is more than probable, realized that once his rival had crossed the Channel, Parliament, however reluctant it might be to take the step, would have no other course open to it but to declare the throne vacant, and then ask him to occupy it. Many another man in a similar position would have been content to rely upon the gratitude of the British nation, or rather upon that of the Whigs who had invited him over from Holland, but he made no such mistake.

In reality, he had every whit as much need of the Whigs as they had of him, but he played his cards so skilfully that it appeared that they were completely in his hands. In this he displayed an ability far above that of his Hanoverian successors, for the first two Georges were always quite obviously the tools of a faction. William used all men, and trusted none, unless it were the faithful Bentinck, so that, although the Whigs were chagrined to find that they had saddled themselves with a master instead of having engaged a servant, they were never able to reverse the respective positions. William was not an amiable character, but not even his worst enemy could deny that he was a statesman of the very first order.

Even so, James committed blunders that no man, including his own astute son-in-law, could have foreseen. The flight to France might possibly have been prophesied by one who knew him as well as William did, but that he would be able to get the Prince of Wales away too was surely contrary to expectation, and yet if the child had been left behind Parliament would certainly never have passed him over to make a foreigner King of England. In effect, James burnt his boats so completely that William appeared to have gained the crown with consummate ease, though the situation required more careful handling than was evident on the surface. Closely related as he was to the House of Stuart, he was a foreign prince, and of a country that had been at war with England three times within the last forty years. Moreover, the dynasty which he was dis-

placing was in its third generation in two of the British kingdoms, while in the other it had been reigning since the fourteenth century.

In these circumstances, it was clear that, although an initial success might prove to be half the battle, it was certainly not all of it, and William was under no illusions on that score. The idea, too prevalent in many of the older histories, that he was carried from Torbay to Westminster on a wave of popular enthusiasm, and that once the crown had been placed upon his head he was secure, had no foundation whatever in fact. . . .

Enough has been said of James II to give the clue to his character. None of the more serious charges that were once brought against him can be proved, and his blunders were very clearly due to the limitations of his intellect. Although he was, of all men, the most loyal to his friends, he lacked those qualities that induce the public to forgive their possessor a multitude of sins, and he was not, as the Spaniards say, *simpatico.* Yet his aim, religious toleration, was a noble one, and in pursuing it he was in advance of his age. Unfortunately, he committed so many mistakes in the way in which he attempted to accomplish it, that he raised widespread suspicion as to his motives. In later life his nerve gave way at the critical moment, and he became one of those timid, but obstinate, men who are the despair of their friends. Withal, however, he never ceased to be a patriotic Englishman, and though he was always quite willing to avail himself of foreign support in his efforts to regain his throne, he never proposed to sacrifice any material English interest in return.

The final verdict would appear likely that he was right in his object, but wrong in the means he employed to achieve it. The consequences of his blunders were felt not only by his own dynasty, but by the peoples of the three kingdoms which he lost. Upon England and Scotland they brought the curse of civil war and a threat of upheaval that did not pass away for more than half a century, while in Ireland, in addition to these evils, they produced a division among the population that is as marked today as ever it was, for the partition of that country between an Irish Free State and a Government of Northern Ireland is directly due to James and Tyrconnel [a prominent Irish Jacobite]. In fine, James reigned too late to restore Catholic supremacy in the British Isles, and too early to establish religious toleration without the greatest difficulty, and, given his character, his ultimate failure as a monarch was thus inevitable.

NOTES

NOTES TO PROBLEM I

The quotation on the title page of this Problem is taken from *1066 and All That* by W. C. Sellar and R. J. Yeatman, published by E. P. Dutton & Co., Inc., New York, publisher and copyright holder, 1931, pp. 17–18, 29–30.

[1] G. B. Adams, *Civilization during the Middle Ages* (N. Y., 1922), p. 190. Reprinted by permission of Charles Scribner's Sons.

[2] *Monumenta Germaniae Historica, Scriptores* (Hanover, 1829), II, 217–55; *Annales Xantenses et Annales Vedastini*, ed. B. von Simson (Hanover and Leipzig, 1909), pp. 12–18. Another translation of many of the same passages in J. H. Robinson, *Readings in European History* (N. Y., 1904), I, 158–62.

[3] Jules Lair, ed., "Dudonis Sancti Quintini De Moribus et Actis Primorum Normanniae Ducum," *Mémoires de la Société des Antiquaires de Normandie* (Caen, 1865), 3rd S., III, 166–71. An account of the same incident, drawn from other chroniclers, is translated in R. G. D. Laffan, *Select Documents of European History* (N. Y., 1930), pp. 14–15.

[4] This passage is translated from the 13th and 14th chapters of the *Germania,* which are to be found on pp. 289–91 of R. P. Robinson's recent critical edition (Middletown, Conn., 1935). Of the numerous translations of Tacitus probably the most readily available is the Modern Library Edition (1942) of the Church and Brodribb translation.

[5] E. de Rozière, *Recueil Générale des Formules usitées dans l'Empire des Francs du Ve au Xe Siècle* (Paris, 1859–71), I, 8–9, 69. Another translation in University of Pennsylvania, *Translations and Reprints* (Philadelphia, University of Pennsylvania Press), IV (1897), no. 3, pp. 3–4.

[6] Rozière, *Recueil Générale des Formules*, I, 433–36. Another translation in U. of Pa. *Tr. & Repr.*, IV (1897), no. 3, pp. 6–8.

[7] *Monumenta Germaniae Historica, Legum*, Sectio II (Hanover, 1883), I, 26–28. Another translation in Thatcher & McNeal, *Source Book*, p. 357.

[8] *Monumenta Germaniae Historica, Legum*, Sectio II (Hanover, 1897), II, 68–69. Another translation in Thatcher & McNeal, *Source Book*, pp. 360–61.

[9] *Monumenta Germaniae Historica, Legum*, Sectio V (Hanover, 1886), I, 43–44. Other translations in Thatcher & McNeal, *Source Book*, p. 352; Ogg, *Source Book*, pp. 211–12.

[10] W. Altmann and E. Bernheim, *Ausgewaehlte Urkunden* (Berlin, 1895), pp. 262–63. Another translation in Thatcher & McNeal, *Source Book*, p. 353.

[11] *Monumenta Germaniae Historica, Legum*, Sectio II (Hanover, 1897), II, 361–63. Another translation in U. of Pa. *Tr. & Repr.*, IV (1897), no. 3, p. 14.

[12] W. L. Gruchy, ed., *L'Ancienne Coutume de Normandie* (Jersey, 1881), p. 93. Another translation in Ogg, *Source Book*, p. 217.

[13] The translation is that of Sir Edward Coke in *The First Part of the Institutes of the Laws of England or A Commentary on Littleton* (London, 1738), Bk. II, ch. II, sections 91–92, pp. 67–68. It is also to be found in a more recent edition, E. Wambaugh, *Littleton's Tenures in English* (Washington, 1903), p. 43.

[14] H. Pirenne, ed., *Histoire du Meurtre de Charles le Bon, comte de Flandre, par Galbert de Bruges* (Paris, 1891), p. 89. Another translation in U. of Pa. *Tr. & Repr.*, IV (1897), no. 3, p. 18.

[15] A. Longnon, ed., *Documents Rélatifs au Comté de Champagne et de Brie* (Paris, 1901–14), I, 469–70. Another translation in Thatcher & McNeal, *Source Book*, pp. 369–70.

[16] DuCange, *Glossarium Mediae et Infimae Latinitatis*, ed. L. Favre (Niort, 1883–87), V, 105. Another translation in Thatcher & McNeal, *Source Book*, pp. 364–65.

[17] N. Brussel, *Nouvel Examen de l'Usage Générale des Fiefs en France pendant le XI, le XII, le XIII, et le XIV Siècles* (Paris, 1750), I, 3, note a. Translation in U. of Pa. *Tr. & Repr.*, IV (1897), no. 3, pp. 15–16.

[18] M. Bouquet, *Recueil des Historiens des Gaules et de la France*, ed. L. DeLisle (Paris, 1760), X, 463. Another translation in U. of Pa. *Tr. & Repr.*, IV (1897), no. 3, pp. 23–24.

[19] P. Viollet, ed., *Les Établissements de Saint Louis* (Paris, 1881–86), II, 95–96. Another translation in U. of Pa. *Tr. & Repr.*, IV (1897), no. 3, p. 30.

[20] Bouquet, *Recueil des Historiens des Gaules*, XXIII, 752–83. Another translation in U. of Pa. *Tr. & Repr.*, IV (1897), no. 3, pp. 31–32.

[21] Latin text and translation, F. M. Stenton, *The First Century of English Feudalism* (Oxford, 1932), pp. 206, 281–82. Reprinted by permission of The Clarendon Press.

[22] F. Liebermann, *Die Gesetze der Angelsachsen* (Halle, 1903–16), I, 575. Another translation in U. of Pa. *Tr. & Repr.*, IV (1897), no. 3, pp. 32–36.

[23] Gruchy, *L'Ancienne Coutume de Normandie*, pp. 108–09. Another translation in Ogg, *Source Book*, pp. 222–23.

[24] Gruchy, *L'Ancienne Coutume de Normandie*, pp. 99–104. Another translation in Ogg, *Source Book*, pp. 224–25.

[25] Liebermann, *Gesetze der Angelsachsen*, I, 507. Other translations in E. P. Cheyney, *Readings in English History* (Boston, 1922), pp. 131–32; A. J. Robertson, *The Laws of the Kings of England from Edmund to Henry I* (Cambridge, 1925), p. 263.

[26] Thomas Madox, *History and Antiquities of*

the Exchequer of the Kings of England (London, 1769), I, 315 ff. Another translation in Ogg, *Source Book,* p. 226.

[27] This passage is from the *Dialogue of the Exchequer* and may be found either in Madox, *History and Antiquities of the Exchequer,* II, 425; or in W. Stubbs, *Select Charters* (9th ed.; Oxford, 1913), p. 230. Another translation in E. F. Henderson, *Select Historical Documents of the Middle Ages* (London, 1907), pp. 102–03.

[28] A. Teulet, *Layettes du Trésor des Chartes* (Paris, 1863–1902), III, 70. Another translation in U. of Pa. *Tr. & Repr.,* IV (1897), no. 3, pp. 33–34.

[29] *Rotuli Hundredorum* (London, 1818), II, 783. Another translation in Cheyney, *Readings,* p. 136.

[30] Stubbs, *Select Charters* (1870 ed.), pp. 96–98. Another translation in U. of Pa. *Tr. & Repr.,* (1894), I, no. 1, pp. 3–5.

[31] Suger, *Vie de Louis VI le Gros,* ed. H. Waquet (Paris, 1929), pp. 14–20, 34–38. Another translation in Robinson, *Readings,* I, 199–201.

[32] Bouquet, *Recueil des Historiens des Gaules,* XI, 510–11. Another translation in Ogg, *Source Book,* pp. 230–32.

[33] J. H. Round, *Geoffrey de Mandeville* (London, 1892), pp. 381–83.

NOTES TO PROBLEM II

The quotation on the title page of this Problem is taken from G. Santayana, *Reason in Religion* (New York, 1945), pp. 94–96. Reprinted by permission of Charles Scribner's Sons.

[1] S. Baldwin, *The Organization of Medieval Christianity* (N. Y., 1929), p. 1.

[2] Cyprian, *De Unitate Ecclesiae, the Latin Text translated with an Introduction and Brief Notes,* ed. E. H. Blakeney (London, 1928), pp. 13, 15, 16, 17, 27, 33, 35. Reprinted by permission of Society for Promoting Christian Knowledge.

[3] *Codex Theodosianus,* ed. G. F. Haenel (Bonn, 1829), II, 1476, 1496. Translation in J. H. Robinson, *Readings in European History* (N. Y., 1904), I, 23–24. Reprinted by permission of Ginn and Company. A translation of the complete *Codex* by Prof. Clyde Pharr of Vanderbilt University will be published shortly.

[4] *Monumenta Germaniae Historica, Legum,* Sectio II (Hanover, 1882), I, 68–70. Translation in University of Pennsylvania, *Translations and Reprints* (Philadelphia: University of Pennsylvania Press), VI (1899), no. 5, pp. 2–3.

[5] H. Denzinger, *Enchiridion Symbolorum et Definitionum* (Wurzburg, 1895), pp. 201 ff. Translation in Robinson, *Readings,* I, 348–54. Reprinted by permission of Ginn and Company.

[6] S. Baluzus, *Capitularia Regum Francorum* (Paris, 1687), II, 679–80. Translation in H. C. Lea, *Studies in Church History* (Philadelphia, 1883), pp. 345–46.

[7] "Of Plaintiffs" and "Of Contracts" in *The Mirror of Justices,* ed. E. G. Whittaker (London: Selden Society, 1895), pp. 45, 73. "Of Exceptions" in *Britton,* ed. F. M. Nichols (Oxford, 1865), I, 322.

[8] D. Martène, *Thesaurus Novus Anecdotorum* (Paris, 1717), IV, 147. Translation in U. of Pa. *Tr. & Repr.,* IV (1897), no. 4, pp. 29–30. Another translation in R. D. G. Laffan, *Select Documents of European History,* pp. 101–03.

[9] Latin text with French translation in Bernard Gui, *Manuel de l'Inquisiteur,* ed. G. Mollat (Paris, 1922–27), I, 22–26. English translation in U. of Pa. *Tr. & Repr.,* III (1896), no. 6, pp. 7–8. Another translation in Robinson, *Readings,* I, 381–83.

[10] M. de La Bigne, *Maxima Bibliotheca Veterum Patrum* (Lyons, 1677), XXV, 247. Translation in U. of Pa. *Tr. & Repr.,* III (1896), no. 6, pp. 6–7. Also in Robinson, *Readings,* pp. 364–65.

[11] *The Summa Theologica of St. Thomas Aquinas literally translated by Fathers of the English Dominican Province* (London, 1911–35), Part II (Second Part), First number, pp. 153–58.

[12] *Historia Diplomatica Frederici Secundi,* ed. J. L. Huiliard-Bréholles (Paris, 1859), IV, Pt. 1, pp. 5–7. Translation in U. of Pa. *Tr. & Repr.,* III, no. 6, pp. 10–12. Another translation in Robinson, *Readings,* I, 384–87.

[13] *Liber Exemplorum,* ed. A. G. Little (Aberdeen, 1908), p. 3. Translation in G. G. Coulton, *Life in the Middle Ages* (Cambridge, 1928–30), I, 152. Reprinted by permission of University Press, Cambridge.

[14] *Caesari Heisterbachensis Monachi Ordinis Cesterciensis Dialogus Miraculorum,* ed. J. Strange (Cologne, 1851), II, 129–34. Translation in Coulton, *Life in the Middle Ages,* I, 69. Another in *The Dialogue on Miracles, Caesarius of Heisterbach,* trans. H. von E. Scott and C. C. Swinton Bland (London, 1929), II, 58–64.

[15] *Chronicon de Lanercost,* ed. J. Stevenson (Edinburgh, 1839), pp. 183–84. Translation in Coulton, *Life in the Middle Ages,* IV, 211. Another translation in *The Chronicle of Lanercost,* ed. Sir H. Maxwell (Glasgow, 1913), pp. 151–54.

[16] *Mémoires de la Société des Antiquaires de la Morinie,* VI (1841–43), Pt. II, pp. xl–xli. Translation in Coulton, *Life in the Middle Ages,* I, 168–69.

[17] *Acta Sanctorum,* ed. J. Bolland (Paris, 1863ff.), I, 633. Translation in Coulton, *Life in the Middle Ages,* I, 32–33.

[18] *Patrologiae Cursus Completus, Series Latina,* ed. J. P. Migne (Paris, 1844–66), vol. 145, columns 294, 307–08. From translation in H. O. Taylor, *The Medieval Mind* (London, 1930), I, 385–86. By permission of The Macmillan Company, publishers.

[19] Migne, *Patrologiae Latina,* vol. 66, cols. 215–932. Translation in E. F. Henderson, *Select Historical Documents of the Middle Ages* (London, 1896), pp. 274–300. Reprinted by permission of G. Bell & Sons, Ltd. Another translation in *The Rule of St. Benedict,* ed. F. A. Gasquet (London, 1909).

[20] *Recueil des Chartes de l'Abbaye de Cluny,* ed. A. Bruel (Paris, 1876), I, 124–28. Translation in Henderson, *Select Documents,* pp. 329–33. Another translation in F. A. Ogg, *A Source Book of Medieval History* (N. Y., 1907), pp. 247–49.

[21] The first three paragraphs and the last three in Migne, *Patrologia Latina,* vol. 185, cols. 225–49. The remainder in *Acta Sanctorum,* XXXVIII, 101–369. Translation in Ogg, *Source Book,* pp. 251–60. Reprinted by permission of the American Book Company.

[22] *Bullarium Romanum* (Turin, 1857–94), III, 394. Translation in Henderson, *Select Documents,* pp. 344–46. Reprinted by permission of G. Bell & Sons, Ltd. Other translations in Ogg, *Source Book,* pp. 375–76, and P. Robinson, *The Writings of St. Francis of Assisi* (Philadelphia, 1906), pp. 64–74.

[23] L. Amoni, *Legenda S. Francisci Assisiensis* (Rome, 1880), app., p. 110. Translation in Ogg, *Source Book,* pp. 376–78. Reprinted by permission of American Book Company.

NOTES TO PROBLEM III

The quotation on the title page of this Problem is from Arnold J. Toynbee, *A Study of History, Abridgement of Volumes I–VI by D. C. Somervell* (Oxford, 1947), pp. 352–53. Reprinted by permission of Oxford University Press, New York.

[1] J. M. Thompson and E. N. Johnson, *An Introduction to Medieval Europe* (New York: Norton, 1937), p. 373.

[2] C. Mirbt, *Quellen zur Geschichte des Papsttums* (Tubingen, 1911), p. 107. Translation in R. G. D. Laffan, *Select Documents of European History* (New York, 1930), pp. 21–22. Reprinted by permission of Methuen & Co., Ltd.

[3] E. Bernheim, *Quellen zur Geschichte des Investiturstreits* (Leipzig, 1907), I, 12–14 and 14–17. Translation in Laffan, *Select Docs.,* pp. 23–24, and E. F. Henderson, *Select Historical Documents of the Middle Ages* (London, 1896), p. 364. Reprinted by permission of G. Bell & Sons, Ltd.

[4] From B. J. Kidd, *Documents Illustrative of the History of the Early Church* (London, 1941), III, 123–24. By permission of The Macmillan Company, publishers.

[5] Migne, Patrologia; *Cursus completus patrologia latina* (Paris, 1852), vol. 148, cols. 289f. Translation in Thatcher and McNeal, *Source Book,* pp. 142–43. Reprinted by permission of Charles Scribner's Sons.

[6] E. Caspar, *Das Register Gregors VII* in *Monumenta Germaniae Historica . . . Epistalae selectae* (Balm, 1920–23), p. 188. Translation in Kidd, *Documents,* p. 126. By permission of The Macmillan Company, publishers.

[7] Reprinted from *The Correspondence of Pope Gregory VII,* translated with an introduction by Ephraim Emerton. No. XIV of the series Records of Civilization: Sources and Studies. Copyright 1932 by Columbia University Press, pp. 11–12.

[8] *Ibid.,* pp. 46–48.

[9] Bernheim, *Quellen,* I, 40–43. Translations in Thatcher and McNeal, *Source Book,* pp. 134–35 (reprinted by permission of Charles Scribner's Sons) and Laffan, *Select Docs.,* p. 26. Reprinted by permission of Methuen & Co., Ltd.

[10] Ekkehard, *Chronicon universale,* ad. an. 105–07 et seq. in H. Pertz, ed. *Monumenta Germaniae Historica,* VI, 198 et seq. Translation in J. H. Robinson, *Readings in European History* (New York, 1904), I, 266–71. Reprinted by permission of Ginn & Company.

[11] Emerton, *Correspondence,* pp. 81–83. Reprinted by permission of Columbia University Press.

[12] *Ibid.,* pp. 18–19.

[13] *Ibid.,* pp. 8 and 15–16.

[14] *Ibid.,* pp. 80–81 and 86–90.

[15] Bernheim, *Quellen,* I, 70–71. Translation in Thatcher and McNeal, *Source Book,* pp. 151–52. Reprinted by permission of Charles Scribner's Sons.

[16] Emerton, *Correspondence,* pp. 90–91. Reprinted by permission of Columbia University Press.

[17] Bernheim, *Quellen,* I, pp. 73–77. Translation in Laffan, *Select Docs.,* pp. 30–33. Reprinted by permission of Methuen & Co., Ltd.

[18] Bernheim, *Quellen,* I, 78–80. Translation in Henderson, *Select Hist. Docs.,* pp. 377–79. Reprinted by permission of G. Bell & Sons, Ltd.

[19] Bernheim, *Quellen,* I, 68, translation in Laffan, *Select Docs.,* pp. 26–29 (reprinted by permission of Methuen & Co., Ltd.) and Thatcher and McNeal, *Source Book,* p. 155. Reprinted by permission of Charles Scribner's Sons.

[20] Emerton, *Correspondence,* pp. 102–05. Reprinted by permission of Columbia University Press.

[21] *Ibid.,* pp. 105–107.

[22] The various translations of the chroniclers concerning Canossa are reprinted from F. Duncalf and A. C. Krey, *Parallel Source Problems in Medieval History* (New York: Harper, 1912), pp. 56–59 and 75–77. Reprinted by permission of Harper & Brothers.

[23] Bernheim, *Quellen,* I, 86–87. Translation in Henderson, *Select Hist. Docs.,* pp. 384–85. Reprinted by permission of G. Bell & Sons., Ltd.

[24–30] As in note 22 above the translations of the chroniclers are reprinted from Duncalf and Krey, *Parallel Source Problems,* pp. 40–56, 59–71, 77–87.

[31] Emerton, *Correspondence,* pp. 111–13. Reprinted by permission of Columbia University Press.

NOTES TO PROBLEM IV

The quotation on the title page of this Problem is from G. N. Clark, *The Wealth of England from 1496 to 1760* (Oxford, 1946), p. 1. By permission of Oxford University Press, New York.

[1] University of Pennsylvania, *Translations and Reprints* (Philadelphia, University of Pennsylvania Press), III (1896), no. 5, p. 1.

[2] Record Commission, *Rotuli Hundredorum* (London, 1812–18), II, 658–59. Translation in U. of Pa., *Tr. and Repr.*, III (1896), no. 5, pp. 4–7.

[3] *Publications of the Surtees Society*, LXXXII, 16–179. Translation in U. of Pa. *Tr. and Repr.*, III (1896), no. 5, pp. 24–27.

[4] Translation in A. E. Bland, P. A. Brown, and R. H. Tawney, *English Economic History, Select Documents* (London, 1914), p. 84. Reprinted by permission of G. Bell & Sons, Ltd.

[5] G. Espinas and H. Pirenne, eds., *Recueil de Documents Relatifs à l'Histoire de l'Industrie Drapière en Flandre* (Brussels, 1906), I, 219–23. Translation in R. C. Cave and H. H. Coulson, *A Source Book for Medieval History* (Milwaukee, 1936), pp. 250–52. Reprinted by permission of The Bruce Publishing Company.

[6] A. Doren, *Entwicklung und Organisation der Florentines Zünfte im 13. und 14. Jahrhundert* (Leipzig, 1897). Translation in Cave and Coulson, *Med. Ec. Hist.*, pp. 258–59.

[7] Translation in H. T. Riley, *Memorials of London and London Life* (London, 1868), pp. 542–44.

[8] G. Espinas and H. Pirenne, *Rec. de Doc. Rel. à l'Hist. de l'Ind. Drap. en Flan.*, II, 22. Translation in Cave and Coulson, *Med. Ec. Hist.*, pp. 253–56. Reprinted by permission of The Bruce Publishing Company.

[9] M. Hull, H. Krieger, R. Reynolds, "Notai Liguri del Sec. XII, Guglielmo Cassinese, 1190–1192," *Documenti e Studi per La Storia del diritto commerciale Italiano*, XIII (1938), 165.

[10] M. Chiandano, ed., *Notai Liguri del Sec. XII, Oberto, Scriba de Mercato* (1186) (Genoa, 1940), p. 1.

[11] Hull, Krieger, and Reynolds, "Not. Lig. del Sec. XII, Gug. Cass., 1190–1192," *Doc. e Stud.* (Turin, 1938), XIII, 45.

[12] Abbott Payson Usher, *The Early History of Deposit Banking in Mediterranean Europe* (Cambridge, 1943), vol. I, 251–53. Reprinted by permission of Harvard University Press.

[13] R. Doehaerd, *Les Relations commerciales entre Gênes, La Belgique, et l'outremont* (Brussels, 1941), II, doc. 684.

[14] G. Fagniez, *Documents relatifs à l'Histoire de l'Industrie et du Commerce en France* (Paris, 1898), II, 22–25.

[15] Riley, *Memorials*, pp. 250–51.

[16] *Ibid.*, pp. 162–65.

[17] Translation in Bland, Brown, and Tawney, *Engl. Econ. Hist. Sel. Docs.*, pp. 164–68. Reprinted by permission of G. Bell & Sons, Ltd.

[18] Arthur Eli Monroe, *Early Economic Thought* (Cambridge, 1924), pp. 53, 55, 63, 66, 67, 71, 77. Reprinted by permission of Harvard University Press. For the selections from St. Thomas, B. Jarrett, *Social Theories of the Middle Ages, 1200–1500* (London, 1926), p. 156. Reprinted by permission of Ernest Benn, Limited.

NOTES TO PROBLEM V

The quotation on the title page of this Problem is taken from William Stubbs, *The Constitutional History of England* (Oxford, 1875), II, 101–02.

[1] Record Commission, *Rotuli Hundredorum* (London, 1812–18), I, 13–14. Latin text and translation in H. M. Cam, *The Hundred and the Hundred Rolls* (London, 1930), pp. 248–57. Reprinted by permission of Methuen & Co., Ltd.

[2] Translation (from the original manuscript) in *Collections for a History of Staffordshire* (London, 1884), Part I, Vol. V, 117–21.

[3] Record Commission, *Statutes of the Realm* (London, 1810–28), I, 26–39.

[4] *Ibid.*, I, 45–61.

[5] Walter of Hemingburgh, *Chronicon*, ed. H. C. Hamilton (London, 1848–49), II, 5–7. Translation in H. Johnstone, *A Hundred Years of History* (London, 1912), pp. 152–53. Reprinted by permission of Longmans, Green & Co., Inc.

[6] Record Commission, *Placita de Quo Waranto* (London, 1818), pp. 750–51. The translation is free, and has somewhat condensed the original, but, it is hoped, without violating the sense.

[7] *Ibid.*, pp. 337–38.

[8] These writs of summons, in the order printed, are taken from F. Palgrave, ed., *Parliamentary Writs* (London: Record Commission, 1827), I, 30, no. 5; I, 31, no. 6; I, 83, no. 2; I, 88, no. 2; I, 29, no. 4; I, 56, no. 12; I, 49, no. 41. The first, second, and fifth writs are translated in University of Pennsylvania, *Translations and Reprints* (Philadelphia: University of Pennsylvania Press), I (1894), no. 6, pp. 29–31.

[9] These royal orders and proclamations, in the order printed, are taken from the following sources: *Parliamentary Writs*, I, 407, no. 59; *ibid.*, I, 113, no. 8; F. W. Maitland, ed., *Memoranda de Parliamento* (London, 1893), pp. lvi–lvii; *ibid.*, pp. 3–4.

[10] C. D. Yonge, ed., *The Flowers of History, . . . collected by Matthew of Westminster* (London, 1853), II, 501, 504–05, 509–10, 513, 519, 522–23, 527–28, 533, 536, 547, 557–59, 561–62, 593–94.

[11] These petitions, in the order printed, are taken from the following sources: *Parliamentary Writs*, I, 104, no. 45; *Memoranda de Parliamento*, p. 305, no. 472; *Rotuli Parliamentorum*, I, 52, no. 83; *ibid.*, I, 61, no. 191; *ibid.*, I, 164, no. 44; *ibid.*, I, 165, no. 55; *ibid.*, I, 61, no. 195; *ibid.*, I, 169, no. 90; *ibid.*, I, 85, no. 26; *ibid.*, I, 58, no. 156; *ibid.*, I, 143; *ibid.*, I, 154, no. 1.

[12] *Memoranda de Parliamento*, pp. 4–5.

[13] *Parliamentary Writs*, I, 157, no. 48.

[14] *Ibid.*, I, 85, no. 10.

[15] *Ibid.*, I, 51, no. 1.

NOTES TO PROBLEM VI

The quotation on the title page of this Problem is from Herbert Read, *Art and Society*

(N. Y.: Macmillan, 1937), p. 1. By permission of The Macmillan Company, publishers.

[1] E. Viollet-le-Duc, *Dictionnaire de l'Architecture Française* (Paris, 1854), I, 345–49. Quoted from *Bibliothèque de l'École de Chartres*, VII, 371–75.

[2] Taken from *Religious Art in France, XIII Century*, by E. Mâle (Engl. Trans., N. Y., 1913), pp. 23–26. Published by E. P. Dutton & Co., Inc., New York.

NOTES TO PROBLEM VII

The quotation on the title page of this Problem is taken from St. Anselm's *Proslogion*, printed in J. P. Migne, *Patrologiae Cursus Completus*, CLVIII (Paris, 1853), p. 227.

[1] Reprinted from *The Two Cities, by Otto, Bishop of Freising*, translated with introduction and notes by Charles Christopher Mierow. No. IX of the series Records of Civilization: Sources and Studies. Copyright 1928 by Columbia University Press, pp. 93–97. Mierow's translation is based on the text by Hofmeister in *Scriptores Rerum Germanicarum in Usum Scholarum* (Hanover and Leipzig, 1912).

[2] *Chronicles of the Crusades* (London, 1870), pp. 74–76, 98–101. In this translation the chronicle of de Templo is incorrectly attributed to Geoffrey de Vinsauf: see the definitive edition of the Latin text by W. Stubbs, *Chronicles and Memorials of the Reign of Richard I* (London, 1864).

[3] J. A. Giles, ed., *Roger of Wendover's Flowers of History* (London, 1849), I, 1–2. Giles' translation is based on the text edited by H. O. Coxe (London, 1841–44).

[4] J. Dickinson, ed., *The Statesman's Book of John of Salisbury* (N. Y.: F. S. Crofts & Co., 1927), pp. 3–11, 64–65, 258–61, 335–36, 372–73, 375. Dickinson's translation is based on the text of the *Policraticus* edited by C. C. J. Webb (Oxford, 1909).

[5] From F. W. Coker, ed., *Readings in Political Philosophy* (N. Y., 1938), pp. 216–21. Reprinted by permission of The Macmillan Company, publishers. Coker's translation is based on the Paris edition (1871–80) of Aquinas' *Opera Omnia*, of which *De Regimine Principum* is in vol. XXVII.

[6] C. L. Kingsford, ed., *The Song of Lewes* (Oxford, 1890), pp. 43–53. Kingsford's edition contains both text and translation. An earlier redaction and translation is in T. Wright, ed., *The Political Songs of England from the Reign of John to that of Edward II* (London, 1839), pp. 72–121.

[7] Taken from *Arthurian Romances by Chrétien de Troyes* by W. W. Comfort, ed. (N. Y.: Everyman's Library, 1928), pp. 2, 56–59, 210–13, 221–22. Published by E. P. Dutton & Co., Inc., New York. Definitive collected edition of texts is *Christian von Troyes, Sämtliche Werke*, ed. Foerster (Halle, 1884–99).

[8] F. W. Bourdillon, ed., *Aucassin and Nicolette, A Love Story: edited in Old French and rendered in modern English* (London, 1887), pp. 93–101.

[9] J. Hutton, ed., *Saint Louis, King of France, by the Sire de Joinville* (London, 1868), pp. 40–42, 56–58, 146–48, 163–64. Hutton's translation is based on the text published in vol. XX of *Recueil des Historiens des Gaules et de la France*, ed. Daunou and Naudet (Paris, n.d.). Other English translations have been made by Thomas Johnes (Hafod, 1807), Ethel Wedgwood (London, 1906), Sir Frank Marzials (N. Y.: Everyman's Library, 1915), and Joan Evans (Oxford, 1938).

[10] *The "Summa Theologica" of St. Thomas Aquinas literally translated by the Fathers of the English Dominican Province* (London, 1911–35), I, 1–17.

[11] H. A. Bellows, ed., *Historia Calamitatum* (St. Paul, 1922), pp. 36–46. The Latin text is in Migne, *Patrologiae Cursus Completus*, CLXXVIII, 113–82.

[12] *St. Louis, King of France*, ed. Hutton, pp. 8–10.

[13] R. Steele, ed., *Mediaeval Lore from Bartholomew Anglicus* (London, 1905), pp. 23, 39, 42, 75–76, 78–79, 84–87, 88–90, 149–51. Reprinted by permission of John W. Luce & Company. Steele's translation is based on the sixteenth-century English translation of *De Proprietatibus Rerum* published by Thomas Berthelet in 1535.

NOTES TO PROBLEM VIII

The quotation on the title page of this Problem is from Mark Twain, *Tom Sawyer Abroad* (New York, 1929), p. 16. Reprinted by permission of Harper and Brothers.

[1] St. Augustine, *The City of God* (London, 1890), II, 97–98.

[2] E. Brehaut, *An Encyclopedist of the Dark Ages: Isidore of Seville* (Volume XLVIII in the Columbia University Studies in History, Economics and Public Law) (New York, 1912), pp. 143–47, 239–40, 244–49. Reprinted by permission of Longmans, Green & Co., Inc.

[3] C. Babington, ed., *Polychronicon Ranulph Higden Monachi Cestrensis* (London, 1865), I, 43ff.

[4] From *The Travels of Sir John Mandeville* (London, 1923), pp. 129, 160–62. Reprinted by permission of The Macmillan Company, publishers.

[5] H. Yule, *Cathay and the Way Thither* (London, 1866), II, 287–95.

[6] V. de Castro E Almieda, *Conquests and Discoveries of Henry the Navigator* (London, 1936), pp. 130–37, 152–53. Reprinted by permission of Allen & Unwin, Ltd.

[7] R. Barlow, *A Brief Summe of Geographie*, (Vol. LXIX, 2nd Series, Works issued by the Hakluyt Society) (London, 1932), pp. 180–82. Reprinted by permission of Hakluyt Society.

[8] A. Galvano, *The Discoveries of the World,* Bethune ed. (London, 1862), pp. 241–42.

[9] Taken from *The Principal Navigations, Voyages, Traffiques and Discoveries of the English Nation,* by R. Hakluyt, J. Masefield, ed. Published by E. P. Dutton & Co., Inc. (London, 1907), pp. 20–23, 35–36.

NOTES TO PROBLEM IX

The quotation on the title page of this Problem is taken from J. H. Robinson and H. W. Rolfe, *Petrarch, The First Modern Scholar and Man of Letters* (N. Y., 1914), p. 452. Translation is based on the 1496 edition of Petrarch's *Secretum.* Reprinted by permission of G. P. Putnam's Sons.

[1] W. K. Ferguson, *The Renaissance* (N. Y., 1940), p. 2. Reprinted by permission of Henry Holt & Co., Inc., publishers.

[2] Ferdinand Schevill, *The First Century of Italian Humanism* (N. Y.: F. S. Crofts & Co., 1928), pp. 51–53. Translation based on *Der Briefwechsel des E. S. Piccolomini, herausgegeben von R. Wolkan. Fontes Rerum Austricarum,* II Abtheilung, LXI, 7.

[3] M. Whitcomb, *A Literary Source-Book of the Renaissance* (Philadelphia, 1900), pp. 13–15. Reprinted by permission of University of Pennsylvania Press. Translation based on text of Petrarch's *Epistolae de Rebus Familiaribus et Variae,* ed. G. Fracasetti (Florence, 1859–63).

[4] J. H. Robinson and H. W. Rolfe, *Petrarch, The First Modern Scholar and Man of Letters* (N. Y., 1914), pp. 275–78. Reprinted by permission of G. P. Putnam's Sons. Translation based on text in Fracasetti's edition of *Epistolae de Rebus Familiaribus et Variae.*

[5] Robinson and Rolfe, *Petrarch,* 245.

[6] Ephraim Emerton, *Humanism and Tyranny* (Cambridge, 1925), pp. 312, 320. Reprinted by permission of Harvard University Press. Text in F. Novati, *Epistolario di Coluccio Salutati* (Rome, 1891–1911), IV, 170.

[7] Ferdinand Schevill, *First Century of Italian Humanism* (N. Y.: F. S. Crofts & Co., 1928), pp. 44–45. Translation based on text in *Rerum Italicarium Scriptores,* ed. Muratori (Milan, 1731), XIX, 920.

[8] W. G. and E. Waters, *The Vespasiano Memoirs* (London, 1926), pp. 102–05. Reprinted by permission of George Routledge & Sons, Ltd. Text of *Vite di Uomini Illustri del Secolo XV* edited by L. Frati (Bologna, 1892–93).

[9] W. H. Woodward, *Vittorino da Feltre and Other Humanist Educators* (Cambridge, 1905), pp. 161–78. Reprinted by permission of University Press, Cambridge.

[10] R. H. H. Cust, *The Life of Benvenuto Cellini* (London, 1910), I, 93–96; II, 296–303. Reprinted by permission of G. Bell & Sons, Ltd. Cust's translation is based on the Italian text edited by O. Bacci (Florence, 1901).

[11] J. H. Robinson, *Readings in European History* (Boston, 1904), I, 532–34. Reprinted by permission of Ginn and Company. Text in the edition of O. Bacci (Florence, 1901).

[12] From *The Man of the Renaissance* by Ralph Roeder, copyright 1933 by Ralph Roeder. By permission of The Viking Press, Inc., New York, N. Y., pp. 503–05, 505–06. Text in F. Nicolini's edition of Aretino's *Lettere* (Bari, 1913–16).

[13] Cust, *Life of Cellini,* I, 1–7. Reprinted by permission of G. Bell & Sons, Ltd.

[14] Giorgio Vasari, *Lives of Seventy of the Most Eminent Painters, Sculptors, and Architects,* ed. E. H. and E. W. Blashfield and A. A. Hopkins (N. Y., 1896), II, 49–61. Reprinted by permission of Charles Scribner's Sons. Text of Vasari's works edited by G. Masselli (Florence, 1832–38).

[15] Waters, eds., *Vespasiano Memoirs,* pp. 181–83. Reprinted by permission of George Routledge & Sons, Ltd.

[16] L. E. Opdycke, *The Book of the Courtier by Count Baldesar Castiglione* (N. Y., 1903), pp. 19, 22–24, 25–32, 59, 62–63, 65–66. Reprinted by permission of Charles Scribner's Sons. Translation based on V. Cian's edition of the text (Florence, 1894).

NOTES TO PROBLEM X

The quotation on the title page of this Problem is taken from Lord Acton, *Lectures on Modern History* (London, 1906), pp. 101, 105. By permission of The Macmillan Company, publishers.

[1] H. von der Hardt, *Magnum Oecumenicum Constantiense Concilium* (Frankfurt, 1700), I, 104–05. Translation in University of Pennsylvania, *Translations and Reprints* (1896), III, no. 6, p. 28.

[2] O. Rinaldi, *Annales Ecclesiastici* (Paris, 1864–83), XXIX, 230–31. Translation based on F. Gregorovius, *Lucretia Borgia* (New York, 1903), pp. 7–8. For an account of the authenticity of the letter and a slight revision of Rinaldi's text see *Revue des Questions Historiques* (Paris, 1881), XXIX, 367–69.

[3] Translation in Leonard F. Dean, *The Praise of Folly* (Chicago, 1946), pp. 79–82, 95–96, 101–03. The text used by Mr. Dean was Erasmus, *Omnia Opera* (Leyden, 1703).

[4] *Corpus Juris Canonici* (Friedburg, 1881), II, 1304. Translation in H. Bettenson, *Documents of the Christian Church* (Oxford, 1903), pp. 256–57.

[5] Friedrick Myconius, *Historia Reformationis,* ed. E. S. Cyprian (Leipzig, 1718), II, 14–15. Translation in J. C. L. Gieseler, *A Compendium of Ecclesiastical History* (Edinburgh, 1865), V, 362. Also in B. J. Kidd, *Documents Illustrative of the Continental Reformation* (Oxford, 1911), pp. 19–20.

[6] Translation in H. Wace and C. A. Buckheim, *First Principles of the Reformation* (Philadelphia, 1885), pp. 6–14. The translators

used as their text the Erlangen edition (1828–70).

[7] Translation in Wace and Buckheim, *First Principles,* pp. 104–25.

[8] Translation in Wace and Buckheim, *First Principles,* pp. 147, 243–44.

[9] Martin Luther, *Opera Latina* (Frankfurt, 1865–73), VI, 8–14. Translation in H. C. Bettenson, *Documents,* pp. 280–83.

[10] *Institutes of the Christian Religion by John Calvin. Translated from the Latin and Collated with the Author's Last Edition in French,* ed. John Allen (Philadelphia, 7th American edition, 1936), I, 274–75, 336–37; II, 175–76, 555, 651.

[11] J. Calvin, *Opera,* ed. G. Baum (Brunswick, 1863–1900), X, 51. Translation in U. of Pa. *Tr. & Repr.,* III (1896), no. 3, pp. 10–11.

[12] Translation in Wace and Buckheim, *First Principles,* pp. 18–19, 20–21, 86, 87.

[13] Translation in Martin Luther, *Works* (Philadelphia, 1915ff.), III, 236, 237–38, 239–40, 251. Reprinted by permission of Muhlenberg Press, Philadelphia, Pa.

[14] J. Dumont, *Corps Universel Diplomatique du Droit des Gens* (Amsterdam, 1726–31), Vol. IV, Pt. 4, pp. 88ff. Translation in J. H. Robinson, *Readings in European History* (N. Y., 1934), II, 113–16. Reprinted by permission of Ginn & Company.

[15] *Institutes,* II, 770, 772–73, 791, 802–03, 804–05.

[16] John Knox, *The History of the Reformation in Scotland,* ed. W. M'Gavin (Glasgow, 1832), pp. 250, 252, 253.

[17] *Institutes,* I, 785, 786, 787, 789–91.

[18] Richard Baxter, *A Christian Directory* (London, 1678), pp. 108, 111, 336, 378, 381.

NOTES TO PROBLEM XI

The quotation on the title page of this Problem is from Lord Acton, *Lectures on Modern History* (London, 1906), pp. 50–51. By permission of The Macmillan Company, publishers.

[1] Taken from *The Prince,* by N. Machiavelli, translated by W. K. Marriott (London, 1908). Published by E. P. Dutton & Co., Inc., New York, pp. 53–63, 91, 121–23, 127–29, 133–36, 141–45, 149–54, 163, 177–93, 203–07.

[2] F. W. Coker, *Readings in Political Philosophy* (New York: Macmillan, 1938), pp. 374–80. The translation is by Professor Coker.

[3] E. Lamond, ed., *A Discourse of the Common Weal of this Realm of England* (Cambridge, 1929), pp. 15–18. Reprinted by permission of University Press, Cambridge.

[4] S. D'Ewes, *The Journals of all the Parliaments during the Reign of Queen Elizabeth* (London, 1682), pp. 551–52, 674.

[5] R. H. Tawney and E. Power, *Tudor Economic Documents* (London, 1924), I, 325–30. Reprinted by permission of Longmans, Green & Co., Inc.

[6] A. E. Bland, P. A. Brown, and R. H. Tawney, *English Economic History, Select Documents* (London, 1914), pp. 387–90. Reprinted by permission of G. Bell & Sons, Ltd.

[7] Tawney and Power, *Tudor Economic Documents,* I, 214–16. Reprinted by permission of Longmans, Green & Co., Inc.

[8] Taken from *The Principal Navigations, Voyages, Traffiques and Discoveries of the English Nation,* by R. Hakluyt, J. Masefield, ed. Published by E. P. Dutton & Co., Inc. (London, 1907), III, 370–71, 372–73, 377.

[9] Horatio F. Brown, ed., *Calendar of State Papers . . . Relating to . . . Venice* (London, 1897), IX (1592–1603), pp. 371, 557; Victor Von Klarwill, ed., *The Fugger News-Letters* (London, 1924), pp. 250–51. Reprinted by permission of John Lane, The Bodley Head, Ltd.

[10] Tawney and Power, *Tudor Economic Documents,* III, 265–70. Reprinted by permission of Longmans, Green & Co., Inc.

[11] T. Mun, *England's Treasure By Forraign Trade* (Oxford, 1933), pp. 5–13, 71–73. Reprinted by permission of Basil Blackwell & Mott, Ltd.

NOTES TO PROBLEM XII

The quotation on the title page of this Problem is taken from *King Charles, His Speech Made upon the Scaffold at Whitehall-Gate* (London, 1649), reprinted in J. G. Muddiman, *Trial of King Charles the First* (London, 1928), p. 262.

[1] Petyt, *Jus Parliamentarium* (London, 1739), pp. 227–43. Also available in J. R. Tanner, *Constitutional Documents of the Reign of James I* (Cambridge, 1930), pp. 217–30.

[2] Charles Howard McIlwain, ed., *The Political Works of James I* (Cambridge, 1918), pp. 307–10. Reprinted by permission of Harvard University Press. Also available in Tanner, *Constitutional Documents,* pp. 15–17, 245–47, 153–55.

[3] *Journals of the House of Commons,* I, 431–32. Also available in Tanner, *Constitutional Documents,* pp. 245–47.

[4] Petyt, *Jus Parliamentarium,* pp. 326–28. Also available in Tanner, *Constitutional Documents,* pp. 153–55.

[5] John Rushworth, *Historical Collections of Private Passages of State, Weighty Matters of Law, Remarkable Proceedings in Five Parliaments* (London, 1721), I, 40–41. Also available in G. W. Prothero, *Select Statutes and Other Constitutional Documents Illustrative of the Reigns of Elizabeth and James I* (4th Ed.: London, 1913), pp. 307–10.

[6] Rushworth, *Historical Collections,* I, 43–44. Also available in Prothero, *Select Statutes,* pp. 310–11.

[7] Rushworth, *Historical Collections,* I, 44–46. Also available in Prothero, *Select Statutes,* pp. 311–12.

[8] Rushworth, *Historical Collections,* I, 46. Also available in Prothero, *Select Statutes,* pp. 312–13.

[9] Rushworth, *Historical Collections,* I, 53. Also available in Prothero, *Select Statutes,* pp. 313–14.

[10] Rushworth, *Historical Collections*, I, 53–54.

[11] W. Notestein and F. H. Relf, eds., *Commons Debates for 1629* (Minneapolis, 1921), pp. 103–06. Reprinted by permission of University of Minnesota, University Press.

[12] The text is Daniel, II, 1–5, 13–19, 24–28, 31–35. The interpretation is from M. James and M. Weinstock, eds., *England During the Interregnum* (London, 1935), p. 171. Reprinted by permission of Longmans, Green & Co., Inc. The protest is from T. Birch, ed., *A Collection of the State Papers of John Thurloe, Esq.* (London, 1742), IV, 381–83.

[13] The first, second, third, and fifth selections are adapted from C. H. Firth, ed., *The Clarke Papers* (Westminster: Camden Society, 1894), II, 209–12, 218–21. The fourth selection is from W. H. Dunham and S. Pargellis, eds., *Complaint and Reform in England, 1436–1714* (N. Y., 1938), pp. 669–70, 675. Reprinted by permission of Oxford University Press.

[14] Dunham and Pargellis, *Complaint and Reform*, pp. 680–87, 690–91.

[15] James and Weinstock, eds., *England During the Interregnum*, pp. 137–39. Reprinted by permission of Longmans, Green & Co., Inc.

[16] Adapted from A. S. P. Woodhouse, *Puritanism and Liberty* (London, 1938), pp. 52 ff. Reprinted by permission of J. M. Dent & Sons, Ltd.

NOTES TO PROBLEM XIII

The quotation on the title page of this Problem is used on the title page of Sir Charles Petrie, *Louis XIV* (London, 1938).

[1] Jacques-Bénigne Bossuet, *Œuvres Complètes*, ed. F. Lachat (Paris, 1862–66), XXIII, 533 ff., 558 ff., 642 ff. Translation in J. H. Robinson, *Readings in European History* (N. Y., 1934), II, 273–77. Reprinted by permission of Ginn and Company.

[2] The first four paragraphs in *Ecrits Inédits de Saint-Simon*, ed. P. Faugère (Paris, 1880–93), I, 85; translation in Robinson, *Readings*, II, 285–86. The remainder in *The Memoirs of the Duke of Saint-Simon on the Reign of Louis XIV and the Regency*, translated by Bayle St. John (London, 1926), II, 357, 358, 359, 364–65.

[3] *Ibid.*, III, 21, 23.

[4] *Ibid.*, III, 23.

[5] *Ibid.*, III, 26–27.

[6] *Ibid.*, II, 363–64.

[7] [Laurent Morellet], *An Historical Explanation of What there is most Remarkable in that Wonder of the World the French King's House at Versailles* (London, 1684) (first 3 pages, unnumbered, in "Instructions to the Reader"); pp. 1–7, 11–12, 14, 15–16, 17, 41–42.

[8] *Mémoires Inédits de Louis-Henri de Loménie, Comte de Brienne*, ed. F. Barrière (Paris, 1828), II, 154–58.

[9] The first two paragraphs in Saint-Simon, *Memoirs*, III, 22–23. The remainder in P. Faugère, *Ecrits Inédits*, I, 216, 231.

[10] E. Lavisse, *Histoire de France* (Paris, 1900–11). Vol. II, Pt. II, p. 410.

[11] P. Clément, *Lettres, Instructions, et Memoirs de Colbert* (Paris, 1867), IV, 27–43.

[12] *Ibid.*, IV, 68, 69; II, Pt. i, 266, 270–71, 282–83; IV, 513, 512–13, 517.

[13] F. A. Isambert, *Recueil Général des Anciennes Lois Françaises* (Paris, 1821–23), XVI, 529–35.

[14] *Ibid.*, XIX, 384–85.

[15] *Ibid.*, XIX, 530–34. Translation in Robinson, *Readings*, II, 287–91. Reprinted by permission of Ginn & Company.

[16] Clément, *Lettres*, II, Pt. ii, pp. 426–27. Translation in Robinson, *Readings*, II, 279–80.

[17] Clément, *Lettres*, VI, 260–70. Reprinted from Charles W. Cole, *Colbert and a Century of French Mercantilism*. Copyright 1939 by Columbia University Press. I, 343. Clément, *Lettres*, VII, 250–51. Translation in Cole, *Colbert*, I, 343–44. Clément, *Lettres*, Vol. II, Pt. ii, pp. 658–60. Translation in Cole, *Colbert*, I, 446. Clément, *Lettres*, III, Pt. i, pp. 76–79. Translation in Cole, *Colbert*, II, 333.

[18] P. Boissonnade, *Colbert*, 305–07.

[19] Cole, *Colbert*, I, 334–35.

The maps in this Problem have been adapted from those given in W. R. Shepherd, *Historical Atlas*, 9th ed. (N. Y.: Henry Holt & Co.), 146, 147, and from Vidal-Lablache, *Atlas général*. Shepherd and Vidal-Lablache maps were based primarily on Boileau, *Etat de la France en 1789* and thus represent the country in the latter years of the eighteenth century. The material for the reconstruction of France in 1700 would be very difficult to assemble. Although minor changes in the administrative arrangements occurred all through the eighteenth century, it is safe to argue that the essential divisions remained the same during the period.

NOTES TO PROBLEM XIV

The quotation on the title page of this Problem is taken from the opening pages, which are unnumbered, of Sieur Combes (Laurent Morellet), *An Historical Explanation of What there is most Remarkable in that Wonder of the World, the French King's House at Versailles* (London, 1684).

[1] *The Memoirs of the Duke of Saint-Simon on the Reign of Louis XIV and The Regency*, tr. Bayle St. John (London, 1888), II, 363–64, 369–70.

[2] André Félibien, *Entretiens sur les Vies et sur les Ouvrages des plus excellens Peintres Anciens et Modernes* (Paris, 1685–88), II, 434–42.

NOTES TO PROBLEM XV

The quotation on the title page of this Problem is from *The Complete Works of G. Savile*,

First Marquess of Halifax, ed. Sir Walter Raleigh (Oxford: Clarendon Press, 1912) , p. 183.

[1] G. Burnet, *Bishop Burnet's History of His Own Time* (London, 1724–34) , I, 611–13. Reprinted in D. N. Smith, *Characters from the Histories and Memoirs of the Seventeenth Century* (Oxford, 1918) , pp. 218–20.

[2] Burnet, *History*, I, 168–70. Reprinted in Smith, *Characters*, pp. 253–56.

[3] F. A. M. Mignet, *Négociations Relatives à la Succession d'Espagne sous Louis XIV* (Paris, 1835–42) , III, 187–97. Translation in D. Ogg, *England in the Reign of Charles II* (Oxford, 1934) , I, 344–46. Reprinted by permission of The Clarendon Press.

[4] F. Bate, *The Declaration of Indulgence* (London, 1908) , pp. 76–78. Reprinted by permission of University Press of Liverpool.

[5] *Privy Council Register* (Ms) , LXIII, 195; printed in T. G. Stone, *England under the Restoration* (London, 1923) , pp. 34–35. Reprinted by permission of Longmans, Green & Co., Inc.

[6] *The Parliamentary Diary of Sir Edward Dering 1670–1673*, ed. B. D. Henning (New Haven, 1940) , pp. 114–18. Reprinted by permission of Yale University Press; *Journals of the House of Commons* (London, 1803–63) , IX, 252, 256, 257; *Journals of the House of Lords* (London, ?–1887) , XII, 549. The selections from the *Journals* are reprinted in C. Stephenson and F. G. Marcham, *Sources of English Constitutional History* (N. Y., 1937) , pp. 567–69.

[7] *Statutes of the Realm* (London, 1810–18) , V, 782–83. Reprinted in Stephenson and Marcham, *Sources*, pp. 555–56.

[8] Anchitel Grey, *Debates of the House of Commons from the Year 1667 to the Year 1694* (London, 1769) , II, 197–209. Reprinted in Stone, *England*, 36–38; *Commons Journals*, IX, 298, 299.

[9] G. Chalmers, *A Collection of Treaties between Great Britain and Other Powers* (London, 1790) , I, 172. Reprinted in Stone, *England*, pp. 39–40.

[10] Grey, *Debates*, VIII, 353–62.

[11] T. B. Howell, *A Complete Collection of State Trials to 1783* (London, 1816–26) , XI, 1197–98. Reprinted in Stephenson and Marcham, *Sources*, pp. 582–83.

[12] Burnet, *History* (second edition, 1833) , III, 108–09, 146–58.

[13] *Privy Council Register* (Ms) , LXXXII, 1. Printed in Stone, *England*, pp. 122–23. Reprinted by permission of Longmans, Green & Co., Inc.

[14] *Memoirs of Sir John Reresby*, ed. A. Browning (Glasgow, 1936) , pp. 478–79. Reprinted by permission of Jackson, Son & Co.

[15] *Diary of John Evelyn*, ed. H. B. Wheatley (London, 1906) , III, 46–50.

[16] Sir J. Dalrymple, *Memoirs of Great Britain and Ireland* (London, 1771–73) , I, app., pp. 228–31. Reprinted in Stone, *England*, pp. 80–81.

[17] *Statutes of the Realm*, VI, 23. Also reprinted in C. G. Robertson, *Select Statutes, Cases and Documents to Illustrate English Constitutional History* (London, 1935) , pp. 105–06.

[18] A. P. Cheyney, *Readings in English History* (N. Y., 1922) , pp. 545–47. Reprinted by permission of Ginn and Company.

[19] *Ibid.*, pp. 549–50.

[20] *Statutes of the Realm*, VI, 74–76. Also reprinted in Robertson, *Select Stat.*, pp. 124–26, 128.

[21] *Statutes of the Realm*, VII, 636–38. Also reprinted in Robertson, *Select Stat.*, pp. 152–56.

[22] From T. B. Macaulay, *The History of England from the Accession of James the Second* (London, 1914) , III, 1304–08, 1310–12. Reprinted by permission of The Macmillan Company, publishers. C. Petrie, *The Stuart Pretenders* (Boston, 1933) , pp. 63–64, 67–69, 102–23. Reprinted by permission of Curtis Brown, Ltd.